INTRODUCTION TO NONPROFIT MANAGEMENT

THE IVEY CASEBOOK SERIES

A SAGE Publications Series

Series Editor

Paul W. Beamish
Richard Ivey School of Business
The University of Western Ontario

Books in This Series

CASES IN ALLIANCE MANAGEMENT
Building Successful Alliances
Edited by Jean-Louis Schaan and Micheál J. Kelly

CASES IN BUSINESS ETHICS
Edited by David J. Sharp

CASES IN ENTREPRENEURSHIP
The Venture Creation Process
Edited by Eric A.Morse and Ronald K.Mitchell

CASES IN GENDER AND DIVERSITY IN ORGANIZATIONS
Edited by Alison M. Konrad

CASES IN OPERATIONS MANAGEMENT
Building Customer Value Through World-Class Operations
Edited by Robert D. Klassen and Larry J.Menor

CASES IN ORGANIZATIONAL BEHAVIOR
Edited by Gerard H. Seijts

CASES IN THE ENVIRONMENT OF BUSINESS
International Perspectives
Edited by David W. Conklin

MERGERS AND ACQUISITIONS
Text and Cases
Edited by Kevin K. Boeh and Paul W. Beamish

CASES IN LEADERSHIP
Edited by W. Glenn Rowe

INTRODUCTION TO NONPROFIT MANAGEMENT

Text and Cases

EDITED BY

W. GLENN ROWE
The University of Western Ontario

MARY CONWAY DATO-ON
Rollins College

Los Angeles | London | New Delhi
Singapore | Washington DC

Los Angeles | London | New Delhi
Singapore | Washington DC

FOR INFORMATION:

SAGE Publications, Inc.
2455 Teller Road
Thousand Oaks, California 91320
E-mail: order@sagepub.com

SAGE Publications Ltd.
1 Oliver's Yard
55 City Road
London EC1Y 1SP
United Kingdom

SAGE Publications India Pvt. Ltd.
B 1/I 1 Mohan Cooperative Industrial Area
Mathura Road, New Delhi 110 044
India

SAGE Publications Asia-Pacific Pte. Ltd.
33 Pekin Street #02-01
Far East Square
Singapore 048763

Acquisitions Editor: Patricia Quinlin
Editorial Assistant: Katie Guarino
Production Editor: Karen Wiley
Permission Editor: Adele Hutchinson
Copy Editor: Sarah J. Duffy
Typesetter: C&M Digitals (P) Ltd.
Proofreader: Laura Webb
Cover Designer: Candice Harman
Marketing Manager: Kelley McAllister

Printed in the United States of America

Library of Congress Cataloging-in-Publication Data

Rowe, W. Glenn.
Introduction to nonprofit management: text and cases/
W. Glenn Rowe, Mary Conway Dato-on.

p. cm.
Includes bibliographical references

ISBN 978-1-4129-9923-6 (pbk.)

1. Nonprofit organizations—Management. 2. Nonprofit organizations—Management—Case studies. I. Dato-on, Mary Conway. II. Title.

HD62.6.R69 2013
658′.048—dc23   2011049047

This book is printed on acid-free paper.

11 12 13 14 15 10 9 8 7 6 5 4 3 2 1

CONTENTS

INTRODUCTION TO THE IVEY CASEBOOK SERIES

As the title of this series suggests, these books are all drawn from the Ivey Business School's case collection. Ivey has long had the world's second-largest collection of decision-oriented, field-based business cases. More than a million copies of Ivey cases are studied each year. There are more than 2,000 cases in Ivey's current collection, with more than 6,000 in the total collection. Each year approximately 200 new cases are registered at Ivey Publishing (www .ivey.uwo.ca/cases) and a similar number are retired. Nearly all Ivey cases have teaching notes available to qualified instructors. The cases included in this volume are all from the current collection.

The vision for the series was a result of conversations I had with Sage's Senior Editor, the late Al Bruckner, starting in September 2002. Over the next few months, we were able to shape a model for the books in the series that we felt would meet a market need. I am appreciative that Lisa Cuevas Shaw continues to support the series.

Each volume in the series contains text and cases. Some text was deemed essential in order to provide a basic overview of the particular field and to place selected cases in an appropriate context. We made a conscious decision to not include hundreds of pages of text material in recognition of the fact that many professors prefer to supplement basic text material with readings and/or lectures customized to their interests and the interests of their students.

The editors of the books in this series are all highly qualified in their respective fields. I was delighted when each agreed to prepare a volume. We very much welcome your comments on this casebook.

Paul W. Beamish
Series Editor

PREFACE

The purpose of this nonprofit organizations (NPOs) casebook is to help MBA students, senior undergraduate business students, and students interested in NPOs to better understand the nuances of NPO leadership and management. Our expectation is that this understanding will make them more effective NPO leaders and managers and will enable them to more effectively lead their NPOs as they face a myriad of opportunities and challenges throughout their careers. It is also expected that the cases and accompanying text will be useful to volunteers who serve on NPO boards of directors and/or work within NPOs in an unpaid capacity. This casebook may be used alone or serve as a supplement to a nonprofit organization textbook such as Worth's (2012) *Nonprofit Management: Principles and Practice* (2nd ed.).

The 28 cases selected for this casebook describe complex issues related to NPOs that require the attention of the decision maker in the case. The idea is to put each student in the place of the decision maker and to see the different ideas that each student decision maker espouses in class. The cases are written to generate discussion in the classroom as students grapple with difficult decisions that have grabbed the attention of real-world NPO leaders and managers already.

Each chapter begins with a quote that has been selected to introduce the concepts and theories in that chapter. In addition, we have placed a list of key topics covered in each chapter immediately after the opening quote. For each chapter, we briefly summarize concepts related to NPO leadership and management and describe the relevance of the issues and problems in the cases associated with each chapter. As a whole, the cases provide students with the opportunity to practice and hone several skills, including the ability to analyze, to make decisions, to apply lessons learned, and to plan and engage in oral communication.

This casebook is designed to help professors facilitate discussion on NPO concepts and theories among students interested in NPOs and a career in the sector as well as to engage students in that discussion. The cases are selected for their integrative issues such as NPO leadership, NPO financial management, advocacy and lobbying, international perspective, and so on. These issues will surface in several cases and are not emphasized in only one case. There is much opportunity for professors to refer to previous cases, to foreshadow future cases, and to integrate learning from one case to another. The cases describe NPOs in the United States (50%), Canada (25%), and other countries (25%).

ACKNOWLEDGMENTS

We want to acknowledge and thank all of those involved in the writing of this book. First, we want to thank the staff at Ivey Publishing and the case writers who so generously spent much time and effort in writing these NPO cases. Second, we owe a huge debt of gratitude to Karin Schnarr, who gave so much of her time to help with case selection and so much else. Third, this project would not have happened without the initiative, support, and encouragement of Lisa Cuevas Shaw and Paul Beamish. Fourth, we want to thank Ronald F. Piccolo and J. B. Adams (authors of Chapter 4) and Eileen Weisenbach Keller (author of Chapter 6). Fifth, we would also like to thank the following reviewers for their helpful comments: Salley Wertheim, John Carroll University; Jama Rand, Seattle Pacific University; Nathan Pelsma, Boston College; Young-Joo Lee, University of Texas, Dallas; Sylvia Benatti, University of District of Columbia; Donna McGinnis, University of Washington, St. Louis; Raine Dozier, Western Washington University; Laurie Paarlberg, University of North Carolina-Wilmington; Thomas Klein, University of Toledo; Pier Rogers, North Park University; and Roland Kushner, Muhlenberg College. Finally, Sarah Duffy did a wonderful job as our copy editor—thank you.

To Fay, Gillian, and Ryan—what can I say, I love you so much.

—Glenn Rowe

To Airam and Mom—my hope and my foundation, maraming salamat.

—Mary Conway Dato-on

1

THE NONPROFIT ORGANIZATION IN SOCIETY

Strategic planning is likely to become part of the repertoire of public and non-profit planners.

—Bryson (1988)

Key Topics: economics of the nonprofit sector, purpose of the nonprofit sector in society, defining the nonprofit sector on the national and global levels, analyzing the nonprofit environment, future of the nonprofit sector

THE NONPROFIT SECTOR ECONOMIC IMPACT

What's in a name? The nonprofit sector, interchangeably known as the voluntary, social economy, civil society, third, NGO, or charitable sector, influences national and global economies regardless of its title. In fact, the sector is much larger than previously believed. A recent study indicated that, globally, the sector represents US$2.2 trillion in operating expenditures—larger than the gross domestic product (GDP) of all but six of the 40 countries studied (Salamon, 2010).

According to the same study, there are nearly 56 million full-time equivalent workers in the international nonprofit sector, representing 5.6% of the economically active population of the countries investigated. Interestingly, throughout the recent recession the sector boosted its employment faster than business or government did (Salamon, 2010). In a pilot study of eight countries (Australia, Belgium, Canada, the Czech Republic, France, Japan, New Zealand, and the United States), the nonprofit sector's weight was equal to or exceeded GDP contributions of major industry sectors such as utilities, construction, finance, and banking (Salamon, 2010). If the civil sector were a national economy, it would be the world's seventh largest, just ahead of Brazil, Italy, and Spain. Despite this large base, the trend is toward even further growth (Salamon, Haddock, Sokolowski, & Tice, 2007).

The expansion and transformation in the sector are, in fact, so great that it has been described as

> a veritable "global associational revolution" . . . [with] a massive upsurge of organized private, voluntary activity in virtually every region of the world—in the developed countries of North America, Western Europe, and Asia; throughout Central and Eastern Europe; and in much of the developing world. (Salamon et al., 2007, pp. 1–2)

Significant sector growth is also evident in the United States. Nonprofit institutions in the United States

> blend private structure with public purpose and perform various services in American society. Included within this sector are more than half of the Nation's general hospitals; nearly half of its higher education institutions; most of its family service agencies; almost all of its symphonies; substantial proportions of its nursing homes; and most of its homeless shelters, soup kitchens, community development agencies, and hospices. (Salamon & Sokolowski, 2005, p. 19)

In Canada, virtually all hospitals and universities are nonprofit organizations (NPOs). Nonprofits, in other words, permeate all areas of society in the United States and Canada.

The figures on the economic impact of the nonprofit sector are also quite impressive. Taken together, approximately 1.4 million NPOs registered with the U.S. Internal Revenue Service in 2005—a 27.3% growth rate over 10 years. In 2006, total private giving reached $295 billion, more than doubling over the same 10-year period. In 2006, 26.7% of adults in the United States said they volunteered through an organization, spending a total of 12.9 billion hours volunteering. While the national GDP grew by about 35% from 1995 to 2005, after adjusting for inflation (Bureau of Economic Analysis, 2007), revenues

and assets for reporting nonprofits grew by at least 54% (Blackwood, Wing, & Pollak, 2008).

In Canada the nonprofit sector has reached $100 billion Canadian in total revenues and was 7% of the overall economy in 2009. This makes the nonprofit sector 10 times bigger than the automotive manufacturing sector and larger than the oil/gas/mining extraction sector or the retail trade. In 2007 paid work accounted for $86.9 billion Canadian in the nonprofit sector, and the revenue in this sector (excluding universities and hospitals) was split 50/50 between earned and unearned revenue. Government grants (one source of unearned revenue) accounted for only 20% of revenue (Shapcott, 2009).

Coupled with this remarkable global growth is a blend of excitement and anxiety among NPO leaders, managers, and researchers. These reactions stem from large-scale opportunities created for NPOs due to three key globalization trends: (1) global poverty and inequalities in income distribution, (2) changing political landscape in a post–Cold War environment, and (3) redefinition of international intervention priorities, that is, movement away from foreign aid toward individual and organizational development philanthropy (Edwards, Hulme, & Wallace, 1999). In response to the sector's development, pressure on NPO managers mounts as they adapt to the shifting global environment and decreases in government, and sometimes private, funding in most major markets (Griffiths, 2005; Ritchie, Swami, & Weinberg, 1999).

All this growth, excitement, and anxiety can be boiled down to three main challenges in the NPO's competitive environment: (1) achieving goals and managing activities with undersized staffs and budgets; (2) competing for scarce resources with increasing numbers of new NPOs; and (3) the growing use of the Internet for communications and donations, which simultaneously offers possibilities while opening the sector to scams (Chiagouris, 2005). Such challenges have forced NPO leaders to become much savvier in entrepreneurial and managerial skills.

Altogether the sector's rapid growth, economic impact, environmental pressures, and current challenges require reexamination of previously used constructs, methods, and theories. At the same time fundamental change in the sector's operating environment seems to require significant adjustments in organizational structure and strategy. This combination of internal and external tension provides a perfect opportunity for NPO managers (and students of NPO management) to adapt and apply new learning.

NONPROFIT SECTOR'S REASON FOR BEING

Why does the nonprofit sector exist? There are three theoretical approaches that answer this question very differently. First, failure theories suggest that NPOs survive in the space where government and free markets fail (Weisbrod, 1988). Under this philosophy, NPOs provide goods and services necessary to society that are not profitable for businesses to provide and are underfunded by government agencies due to political realities. A second approach views NPOs from an entrepreneurial perspective and concludes that these organizations exist because someone had a vision and acted upon it. Combining these two schools of thought results in a third, potentially more comprehensive theory: Lohmann's (1992) theory of the commons. Lohmann argues that NPOs provide common goods that combine the interests of certain individuals (i.e., NPO service recipients) without benefiting all society (as in public goods). Within this third approach rests the idea that NPOs do more than fill gaps between for-profit and government services and often generate their own income through sales of tickets and services— what is becoming known as *social enterprise.*

While there are differences of opinion about the motivation for the existence of NPOs, few argue about the need for the services provided. The global economic downturn has increased the demand for nonprofit services as more citizens find themselves in need of assistance (Venture Philanthropy Partners, 2003). In response to this economic squeeze, NPOs often are called upon to fill societies' needs. Now more than ever before, NPOs must think strategically about their "business" and seriously consider the environment in which they operate. They need to understand that sound organizational principles, heretofore known as sound business principles, apply to nonprofit as well as to for-profit organizations.

NONPROFIT SECTOR DEVELOPMENT AND DEFINITION

What organizations should be included in the nonprofit sector? Issues of diverse and inconsistent data, documentation, and resources keep researchers, managers, and policymakers from understanding the global nonprofit sector in general and the organizational level in particular. To overcome these limitations several associations conduct ongoing, comprehensive research projects. Significant advancements achieved by the Johns Hopkins Center for Civil Society are noteworthy. The Center's Comparative Nonprofit Sector Project (CNP) research uses common definitions, categorization, and methodologies to facilitate comparison between countries in order to "move beyond description to explanation, to determine why the nonprofit sector takes the form it does in different places" (Perez-Aleman & Sandilands, 2008, p. 24).

Salamon and colleagues (2010) note that differing development of the nonprofit sector (and correspondingly, organizations) within nations depends on power struggles among four important drivers: socioeconomic classes, sociodemographic groups (e.g., ethnic, religious, geographic, tribal), state and church, and "core" versus "periphery" countries. From these tensions one of five types of NPO sectors develop: liberal, welfare partnership, social democratic, statist, and traditional.

A liberal prototype might be found in the United States, where the nonprofit sector features a professional nonprofit workforce, extensive volunteerism, and relatively limited reliance on government support. Conversely, a welfare partnership consists of a large paid workforce, a relatively small volunteer workforce, and high government support of the sector (Salamon et al., 2010).

Five factors are considered important to understanding the size and capacity of the nonprofit sector in any given country: (1) population heterogeneity (the more diverse the population the larger the sector), (2) the scope of the welfare system (the sector tends to fill social service gaps left by the state) (3) level of development (nations lacking an economic middle class tend to have a smaller nonprofit sector; as economies grow from developing to developed, the number of nonprofits likely increases), (4) the legal system (common law correlates more highly with prevalence of NPOs—versus civil law), and (5) history and tradition (which lead to distinct, culturally based societal support systems; Salamon & Anheiner, 1992).

Acknowledging the sector's differential development facilitates understanding of how an NPO might interact with different institutions within the nation (e.g., government, for-profit sector) and be influenced by the traditional political, economic, social, and technological environmental factors studied in international business. Studying the sector's development may also help uncover the willingness of NPOs to absorb new ideas. This is particularly important because several authors suggest that NPO managers and governments that oversee them are very conservative in adopting new managerial tactics (Matzkin, 2008; Palotta, 2010) or what we referred to earlier as sound organizational principles. NPO managers who understand these interactions are better able to manage societal factors that influence the success of their organization's efforts.

Along with the unique ways in which the nonprofit sector develops within national borders, countries often define the sector differently. Culture, law, and economy (i.e., tax systems) all influence the definition of the sector as distinct from for-profit and government sectors. In addition to these influencing factors, the diversity of organizations within the sector complicates a single definition. In the end, however, several cross-border commonalities exist from which boundaries can be set for the sector. Salamon

(2010, pp. 177–178) notes five such characteristics, concluding that the nonprofit sector consists of entities that are

1. Organizations,

2. Private (e.g., not state-based, as are government agencies),

3. Not profit distributing,

4. Self-governing, and

5. Noncompulsory.

As such, one can conclude that the sector includes both formal and informal organizations serving and/or advocating for members (e.g., unions, religious groups), the public, or both. The definition is thus broader than the traditional nongovernmental organization (NGO) term common in developing markets and the NPO classification used in the United States. However, the definition is not as broad in scope as either civil society or civil economy (see Figure 1.1).

STUDYING THE ENVIRONMENT OF NPOS

How can NPO managers grasp the growing, rapidly changing environment in which their organizations operate? Managing within the social service, nonprofit sector has become much more complex, forcing NPO managers to adapt for-profit strategy concepts (Kong, 2008). One key strategy tool is to investigate an organization internally and externally. In other words, to understand the success and failure of NPOs and improve an organization's operations, nonprofit leaders must use tools to analyze the environment in which their organizations exist and methods to understand how environmental changes affect organizational goals and viability—it is important that an NPO's strategy be aligned with its environment. Below are several strategic approaches that guide such analyses.

Political, Economic, Social, and Technological (PEST): The PEST analysis (also referred to as PESTLE when Legal and Environmental factors

Figure 1.1   Social Economy and the Nonprofit Sector: An Alternative Conception

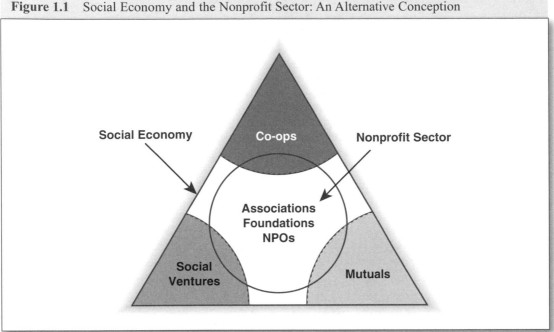

Source: Salamon, 2010, p. 183. Reprinted with permission.

are included in the analysis) classifies external environmental issues that influence an organization. The PEST is a generic orientation tool, used to see where an organization or product/service lies in the context of what is happening outside that will, at some point, influence what is happening inside an organization. From this classification of factors, NPO leaders can more easily anticipate how the issues identified in each category shape attitudes and actions of various stakeholders associated with their organization (e.g., service recipients, funders, volunteers). Conducting a PEST analysis also enables managers to anticipate changes across different factors and plan accordingly. While a PEST is relatively easy to construct, the development of strategies from an understanding of environmental circumstances is challenging for most managers but critical to the success of utilizing this management tool.

Strengths, Weaknesses, Opportunities, and Threats (SWOT): The SWOT is often used in conjunction with the PEST. The combination refines some of the generic/macro nature of the PEST by classifying the external issues as either opportunities to be exploited or threats to be managed or minimized based on the internal strengths and weaknesses of the organization or its service offering. To make the lists of SWOT elements more useful and informative, categorize or cluster the ideas around major points. This requires a higher level of analysis than simply listing the items; it involves more decision making as factors are compared and prioritized. Another important aspect of good SWOT analysis specifically is to qualify statements with supporting data. Some of the supporting data is "fact," while other data relies on judgment. Both are necessary in this type of analysis.

Resource-Based View of the Firm (RBV): This approach to developing strategy for organizations combines the external focus of the PEST analysis with some of the internal components of a SWOT analysis. RBV offers clarity by linking an organization's internal capabilities (what it does well) with its micro-level environment (what the market demands and what competitors offer). The key to using RBV comes in correctly—and objectively—recognizing the organization's resources (Collis & Montgomery, 2008).

A nonprofit's resources may be physical (e.g., buildings, equipment) or intangible (e.g., brand names, routines, processes, culture). Using these resources in unique, unmatched ways can lead to capabilities that result in long-term success. For a resource to serve as a bedrock of strategy it must meet five basic criteria (Collis & Montgomery, 2008):

1. Durable value—This is a risky proposition even where protection by patent, copyright, or trademark are evident.

2. Hard to copy—The resource must be imbedded in processes that make the resource in isolation less valuable.

3. Tied to the organization—Human resources, for example, are movable.

4. Lack substitutes—What is the basic resource that enables the delivery of a nonprofit good or service? Can it be replaced by a higher-value option?

5. Competitively superior—What, specifically, about the resource enables competitive distinction?

With RBV, nonprofit managers are forced to look simultaneously inside and outside the organization to determine future direction. Identified resources can then be linked to organizational functions and processes that distinguish the NPO's position from others. For long-term success, continuous identification and investment in resources is necessary.

Sector or Industry Analysis (5-Factor Analysis and Strategic Profile): Michael Porter (1979) provided a framework that depicts an industry as being influenced by five forces: threat of rivalry, power of buyers, power of suppliers, threat of new entrants (includes an analysis of barriers to entry and exit), and threat of substitutes. Organizational leaders seeking to develop an edge over competitors can use this model to grasp the context in which the organization operates. By understanding the concentration of rival service providers in the sector, an NPO manager can predict how changes in one organization's position may affect other players in the sector. For example, when trouble erupted in the Central Florida Blood Bank in 2010 (Tracy, 2010), which enjoyed a near monopolistic competitive position in the NPO sector, there were few alternatives for blood donors or users. It wasn't until the South Florida Blood Bank entered the geographic market, thus increasing the competitive structure of the sector, that donors and recipients had an alternative source. The resulting increase in competitive ratio affected the collection, price, and delivery of blood in the Central Florida region. The astute NPO leader will not include every NPO in its area in this analysis, but only those that would be considered "closest competitors" for the resources needed by the NPO.

Recently, the authors of *Blue Ocean Strategy,* Kim and Mauborgne (2005), developed an alternative to the ever-popular 5-factor model of analyzing the competitive landscape. Their tool, the strategic profile, provides a graphic depiction of an organization's strategy versus its competitors or major competitive blocks (e.g., high versus low priced). The graph, known as the value curve, succinctly captures an organization's relative performance across key competitive factors of an industry or service area in the nonprofit sector. The purpose of the value curve is twofold. First, it captures the current conditions in the known market. This allows an NPO leader to understand where the competition is currently investing and the factors on which the sector competes. Second, it provides a focal point for action by reorienting from *competitors* to *alternatives* and from *customers* to *noncustomers*. More information on the blue ocean strategy concepts can be found at www.blueoceanstrategy.com.

The cases that follow are selected to emphasize the role of nonprofit organizations in society and provide opportunities to apply some of the various analytical models discussed in the chapter.

FUTURE OF THE NONPROFIT SECTOR

This chapter has highlighted the development of the nonprofit sector while providing tools for analyzing its environment to enable assessment of the external environments in which nonprofits operate. It seems appropriate to close with a view to the future. What challenges will the leaders in the sector face, and what philosophies, skills, and resources will be needed to address these challenges? The W. K. Kellogg Foundation, in cooperation with the Monitor Institute, produced a comprehensive study exploring these questions (Fulton, Kasper, & Kibbe, 2010). The report highlights the changing context in which nonprofits and their stakeholders operate and identifies 10 trends that can help funders and NPOs amplify results over the next decade. Figure 1.2 encapsulates the report, but it is definitely worth reading in its entirety (http://www.wkkf.org/knowledge-center/resources/2010/07/Next-for-Philanthropy.aspx). The framework provided

Figure 1.2 What's Next? Acting Bigger and Adapting Better

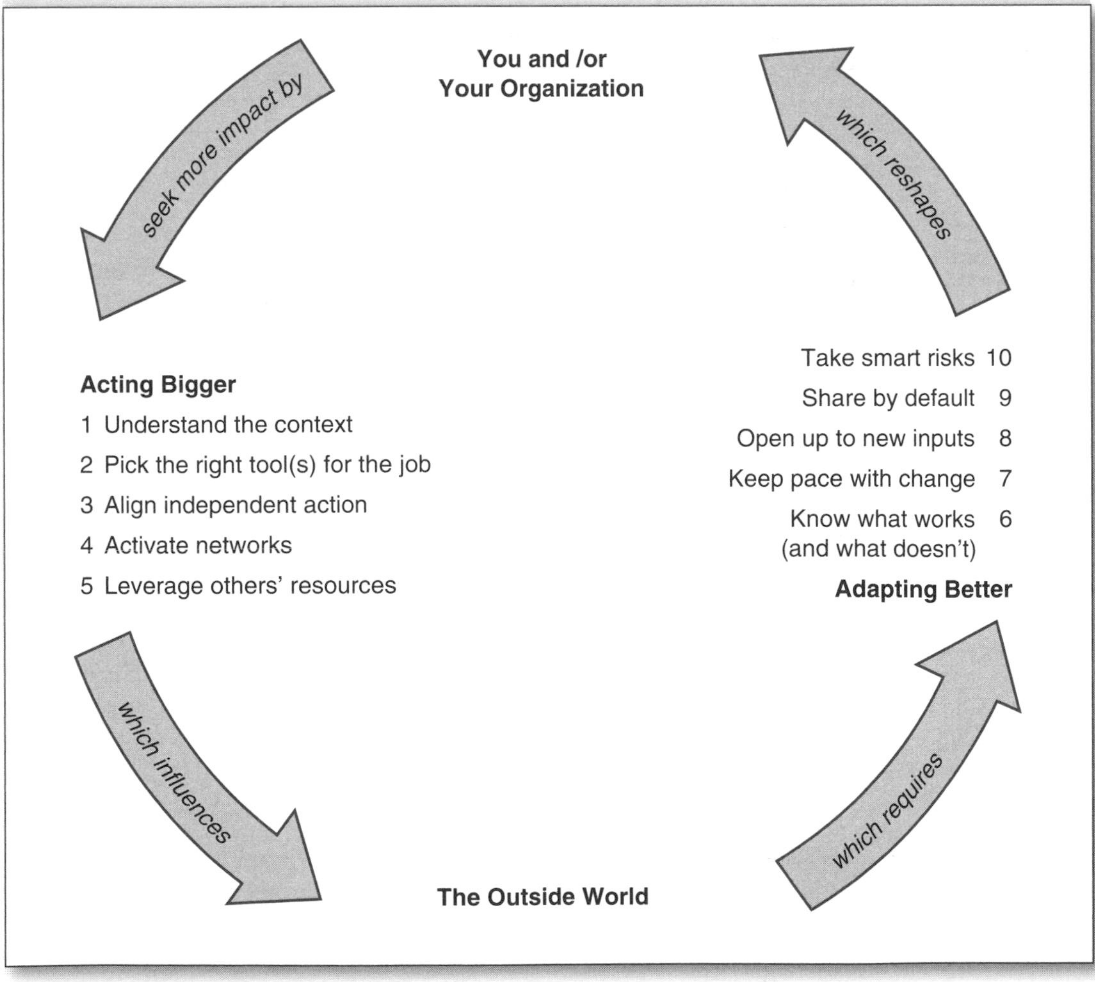

You and /or Your Organization

seek more impact by

which reshapes

Acting Bigger

1 Understand the context
2 Pick the right tool(s) for the job
3 Align independent action
4 Activate networks
5 Leverage others' resources

Take smart risks 10
Share by default 9
Open up to new inputs 8
Keep pace with change 7
Know what works 6
(and what doesn't)

Adapting Better

which influences

which requires

The Outside World

Source: Fulton et al., 2010. Reprinted with permission.

also serves as a template from which to consider the content of this book. The details on meaning and implementation techniques for the 10 steps offered in the model can be found across the chapters of this text. The cases provided in each chapter illustrate how various actors and organizations faced challenges and developed strategies to overcome them.

CASES

Mote Aquaculture Park: Sturgeon Project (United States): The project manager is faced with evaluating a number of issues such as political-legal forces, local and international economics, production technologies, and sociocultural forces. Further, industry factors also play a key role. As he considers Mote Aquaculture Park's current situation, the project manager knows that a thorough review of these environmental factors is necessary.

Elephant Walk Thru (International): The Sri Lanka Wildlife Conservation Society's management team knew that they had conceived a unique project, Elephant Walk Thru. Their primary task in the ensuing months would be to identify salient external opportunities and threats posed by stakeholder groups. Equally important would be to evaluate the continually changing political-legal and economic environments prior to constructing the facilities.

REFERENCES

Blackwood, A., Wing, K. T., & Pollak, T. (2008). *The nonprofit sector in brief: Facts and figures from the Nonprofit Almanac 2008.* Washington, DC: Urban Institute Center for Nonprofits and Philanthropy.

Bryson, J. M. (1988). A strategic planning process for profit and non-profit organizations. *Long Range Planning, 21*(1), 73–81.

Bureau of Economic Analysis. (2007). *National economic accounts—Gross domestic product percent change from preceding period.* Retrieved from http://www.bea.gov/national/xls/gdpchg.xls

Chiagouris, L. (2005). Nonprofit brands come of age: Commercial sector practices shed light on nonprofit branding success. *Marketing Management, 14*(5), 30.

Collis, D. J., & Montgomery, C. A. (2008). Competing on resources. *Harvard Business Review, 86*(7,8), 140–150.

Edwards, M., Hulme, D., & Wallace, T. (1999). NGOs in a global future: Marrying local eelivery to worldwide leverage. *Public Administration & Development, 19*(2), 117–136.

Fulton, K., Kasper, G., & Kibbe, B. (2010). What's next for philanthropy: Acting bigger and adapting better in a networked world. Cambridge, MA: Monitor Institute.

Griffiths, M. (2005). Building and rebuilding charity brands: The role of creative agencies. *International Journal of Nonprofit and Voluntary Sector Marketing, 10*(2), 121.

Kim, W. C., & Mauborgne, R. (2005). *Blue ocean strategy: How to create uncontested market space and make the competition irrelevant.* Cambridge, MA: Harvard Business School Press.

Kong, E. (2008). The development of strategic management in the non-profit context: Intellectual capital in social service non-profit organizations. *International Journal of Management Reviews, 10*, 281–299.

Lohmann, R. A. (1992). *The commons.* San Francisco, CA: Jossey-Bass.

Matzkin, D. S. (2008). Knowledge managment in the Peruvian non-profit sector. *Journal of Knowledge Management, 12*(4), 147–159.

Palotta, D. (2010). *Uncharitable: How restraints on nonprofits undermine their potential.* Medford, MA: Tufts University Press.

Perez-Aleman, P., & Sandilands, M. (2008). Building value at the top and the bottom of the global supply chain: MNC-NGO partnerships. *California Management Review, 51*(1), 24–33.

Porter, M. E. (1979, March-April). How competitive forces shape strategy. *Harvard Business Review*, 137–145.

Ritchie, R. J. B., Swami, S., & Weinberg, C. B. (1999). A brand new world for nonprofits. *International Journal of Nonprofit & Voluntary Sector Marketing, 4*(1), 26–42.

Salamon, L. M. (2010). Putting the civil society sector on the economic map of the world. *Annals of Public and Cooperative Economics, 81*(2), 167–210.

Salamon, L. M., & Anheiner, H. K. (1992). In search of the non-profit sector II: The problem of classification. *Working Papers of the Johns Hopkins Comparative Non-Profit Sector Project,* No. 3. Baltimore, MD: Johns Hopkins Institute for Policy Studies.

Salamon, L. M., Anheiner, H. K., List, R., Toepler, S., Sokolowski, S. W., & Associates. (2010). *Global civil society: Dimensions of the nonprofit sector.* Greenwich, CT: Kumarian Press.

Salamon, L. M., Haddock, M. A., Sokolowski, S. W., & Tice, H. S. (2007). *Measuring civil society and volunteering: Initial findings from implementation of the UN Handbook on Nonprofit Institutions.* Baltimore, MD: Johns Hopkins Center for Civil Society Studies.

Salamon, L. M., & Sokolowski, S. W. (2005, September). Nonprofit organizations: New insights from QCEW data. *Monthly Labor Review,* 19–26.

Shapcott, M. (2009). *Canada's non-profit sector: Big, growing, important.* Retrieved from http://www.wellesleyinstitute.com/blog/canadas-non-profit-sector-big-growing-important

Tracy, D. (2010, March 10). Blood-bank chief Anne Chinoda resigns. *Orlando Sentinel.* Retrieved from http://www.orlandosentinel.com

Venture Philanthropy Partners. (2003). *The changing nonprofit funding environment: Implications and opportunities.* Washington, DC: Author.

Weisbrod, B. A. (1988). *The nonprofit economy.* Cambridge, MA: Harvard University Press.

MOTE AQUACULTURE PARK: STURGEON PROJECT

INTRODUCTION

Jim Michaels, the sturgeon project manager for Mote Aquaculture Park (MAP), took a brief reprieve from his review of caviar production statistics and peered out his office window to observe the new construction of the only commercial demonstration sturgeon project in the United States. He was in the midst of preparing a briefing for a 2005 board meeting with Mote Marine Laboratory Directors, the primary funding organization for MAP. As he pored over industry statistics, he reflected on the highly complex nature of the aquaculture industry. With his extensive experience in this industry, he knew that the future success of this project required continual evaluation of a number of market forces and that many environmental factors had recently changed. Michaels knew that political-legal forces played a significant role, but that local and international economics, production technologies, as well as sociocultural forces would have a significant influence on the project's level of success. Further, industry factors also played a key role. As he contemplated MAP's current situation, he knew that a thorough review of these environmental factors was necessary. He would have to determine what forces posed critical threats to MAP as well as potential opportunities for future growth. However, since sturgeon farming and caviar production in the United States was a new industry, he knew that the application of traditional models of evaluation may not universally apply in the case of MAP.

MOTE AQUACULTURE PARK—HISTORY

Situated on 200 acres in west-central Florida, MAP developed the sturgeon project in 1998, in an effort to grow and sell commercially viable Siberian sturgeon meat and caviar in U.S. and European markets. Funded for construction with venture capital from Mote Marine Laboratory, Inc. (see Exhibit 1 for selected financials), the park utilized innovative, state-of-the-art recirculating technologies that would eventually hold and grow almost 200 metric tons of fish on a

Exhibit 1 Mote Marine Laboratory Selected Financials, 2004

Revenues	
Protect Our Reefs	2.04%
Restricted Contribution	6.43%
Education & Distance Learning	4.03%
Other Programs	1.19%
Unrestricted Contributions	3.35%
Mote Foundation Grants & Investment	1.54%
Memberships	3.24%
Aquarium	16.83%
Research	61.34%
Total Revenues	**$21,475,632****
Expenses & Net Assets	
Increase in Net Assets*	7.58%
Fund-raising	4.08%
Protect Our Reefs	1.29%
Other Programs	2.29%
Operations/G&A	9.88%
Education & Distance Learning	4.59%
Aquarium	15.05%
Research-Direct & Indirect	55.24%
Total Expenses and Net Assets	**$21,475,632****

Source: www.mote.org.

*Includes construction, property, and equipment.

**Does not include change in Net Assets of Mote Marine Foundation.

minimal water supply of 100 gallons per minute. By 2009, this system was expected to produce 77 metric tons of fish and 4.2 metric tons of caviar each year. In pursuit of these outcomes, MAP had adopted the following goals:

1. To develop, test and demonstrate the commercial applicability of innovative aquaculture technologies and to protect fishery resources.

2. To develop innovative husbandry and sturgeon caviar processing techniques that will help Florida become one of the world centers of sturgeon and caviar production.

3. To help promote the development of a commercial aquaculture industry in the state of Florida.

4. To produce and market sturgeon products that will demonstrate the economic feasibility of production technologies, support research and demonstration project costs, and to support Mote's aquaculture research efforts.

5. To disseminate new technologies through pilot-scale and commercial demonstration.

SEAFOOD PRODUCTION AND CAVIAR DEMAND

As the fastest-growing source of food in the world, seafood had acquired a demand that continued to outstrip global supplies. While about 135 million metric tons of seafood was consumed worldwide, the United States consumed about 4.6 million metric tons of seafood in 2000. American consumers spent about $54.4 billion[1] on the consumption of about 16.3 pounds (7.4 kg) of fish and shellfish per person, every year. This figure was more than double the per capita consumption 50 years ago. By comparison, in 2000, Americans consumed about 62 pounds of beef per capita. To meet this demand for seafood, more than $10.1 billion of seafood was imported each year. By contrast, U.S. seafood exports, in

the amount of $3 billion, had resulted in a seafood trade deficit worth more than $7 billion, second only to the oil trade deficit. The majority of imported seafood products included 5.7 million pounds of shrimp, salmon and shellfish. Of this amount, about $45.8 million worth of caviar was imported while less than $4 million worth was produced in the United States each year.

Up until the early part of the 20th century, sturgeon were one of the most common fishes in North America, enabling American caviar to account for 90 per cent of the world's supply. By the early 1900s, however, lake and river sturgeon were nearly extinct, and production shifted to the Caspian Sea, where approximately 2,500 metric tons of caviar was produced in the early 1980s. Throughout the latter part of the 20th century, this region of the world accounted for 90 per cent of the world's sturgeon caviar production; however, with the dissolution of the Soviet Union, the greatest portion of this supply had disappeared, dwindling production levels to several hundred tons by 2000. As the wild sturgeon populations continued to decline, some experts estimated that caviar exports from Eastern Europe would eventually be eliminated. This grim prediction was of particular concern to Americans, who consumed 80 per cent of the commercially produced caviar.

THE AQUACULTURE INDUSTRY

Because oceans had reached their maximum sustainable yields, increased demand for seafood could only be met through the agriculture of the oceans, known as aquaculture. With total production at more than 45 million metric tons in 2000, the farming of fish and shellfish was the fastest-growing food sector, valued at more than $56 billion annually. Aquaculture, the organized cultivation of aquatic animals, was the only sustainable means of meeting the

---

[1]All currency is in U.S. dollars unless noted otherwise.

increasing demand. Aquaculture-derived caviar production, at less than 50 tons annually, comprised only a small portion of worldwide aquaculture. In fact, in light of historical demand for caviar, it was unlikely that worldwide production (both from natural stocks and from aquaculture) would reach the production levels of the 1980s (see Exhibit 2).

Since the majority of aquaculture projects involved the harvest of seafood from net pens in coastal marine environments and man-made ponds, sustainability—an industry's ability to have minimal impact on the environment—of the aquatic environment was a key concern. In aquaculture, sustainability was an important concept due to the interdependence between the cultivation of aquatic organisms and the natural resources afforded by the environment. In some countries, aquaculture projects were undertaken in conjunction with the natural environment. For example, shrimp farms have been constructed on the fringes of natural mangrove tidal zones. While this was a very convenient method for establishing farms, the long-term sustainability

of these projects required close monitoring to ensure that the natural habitats were not stressed by the high concentration of farmed species. Overuse of natural habitats could have a devastating impact on a given aquaculture project. For example, the white shrimp industry in China collapsed as a result of both poor aquaculture farming techniques and the resultant depletion of natural resources necessary to sustain shrimp populations.

In contrast to aquaculture systems that utilized a combination of natural habitat and planned production, MAP utilized self-contained, recirculating systems, with minimal impact on the environment. Environmentalists and an increasingly aware general populace desired aquaculture production that minimized discharge of waste products and water consumption. To this end, the MAP facility was designed to have zero wastewater discharge, with an infiltration pond that served as the repository for any aquaculture waste. This system was designed to allow discharge from the production process to percolate back into the ground. As a recirculating

Exhibit 2 Wild and Farm-Raised Sturgeon Harvests Worldwide

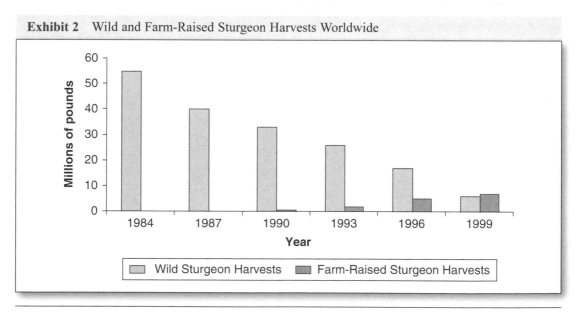

Source: Mote Aquaculture Park Annual Report, 2004.

project, MAP not only offered a suitable alternative for over-harvested sturgeon for caviar, but also had a minimal ecological footprint.

THE MAP DECISION TO GROW STURGEON

With a cartilaginous skeleton and bony plates instead of scales, members of the sturgeon family are among the oldest species of fish on earth. There are more than two dozen species of sturgeon in the northern hemisphere, living in both salt and fresh water habitats, many of which are listed as threatened or endangered under the Endangered Species Act. The sturgeon's shovel-like nose, which acts like a siphon, gives the fish a distinct look when compared with traditional fish.

MAP originally intended to grow species of sturgeon that were native to Florida and the southeastern United States. The plan was to gather eggs and sperm from the wild domestic population, returning donor sturgeon to their native habitat, and to cultivate the fertilized eggs at MAP. But federal authorities prohibited the cultivation of indigenous species that were listed as either threatened or endangered under the Endangered Species Act. As a result, MAP directed its focus toward non-indigenous sturgeon species from Eastern Europe; the current inventory of sturgeon included three different imported Russian species. Each year's sturgeon population was referred to as a "class." The classes of 1998, 1999 and 2000 were Bester Hybrids, a breed that combined two Russian sturgeon species (scientific name: *Huso huso* and *Acipenser ruthenus*). The 2001 class consisted of the Russian sturgeon, *Acipenser gueldenstaedti*, as well as Siberian sturgeon, *Acipenser baeri*. MAP's research had shown that, of these three species, the Siberian sturgeon was best suited for aquaculture production. Therefore, MAP would focus on importing Siberian sturgeon for all additional sturgeon stocks until MAP's own stock of fertilized sturgeon eggs was available in

2006. Ultimately, MAP's plan for the future was to produce enough Siberian sturgeon eggs and fingerlings to supply other aquaculture farms.

MAP Operations

In total, MAP housed five different aquaculture projects: sturgeon, pompano, shrimp, conch and snook. The production of sturgeon meat and eggs accounted for the largest resource commitment by MAP. Sturgeon production followed a three-phase process spanning about seven years. In the first phase (approximately 2.5 years), sturgeon were grown from eggs to approximately four kilograms in weight. At this target weight, harvestable sturgeon would produce four (8- to 10-ounce) fillets, the average fillet size for most restaurants. At the completion of the first phase, sturgeon would undergo a biopsy to determine their sex. The male sturgeon would be harvested for fillets, while the females would be retained for the second phase of the production process and would continue growing in the aquaculture system until they reached egg-producing size. In the second phase, the female sturgeon were grown until they ranged from five to seven years of age. A biopsy during the second phase would determine the level of caviar development. Fish that were ready to produce caviar in their fifth and/or sixth year would be segregated from the rest of the population. This sub-population would be subjected to subsequent biopsies to determine exactly when the eggs would be ready for harvest. Follow-up biopsies were conducted routinely to identify additional sturgeon that were ready to produce caviar. This process was repeated until all the sturgeon in the second phase had produced caviar. In the third phase of the sturgeon's growth process, caviar was harvested and the fish was processed for preparation of fillets.

Revenue Generation

There were three potential sources of income associated with the MAP sturgeon project. First, since a portion of each class of sturgeon would be harvested and slaughtered for meat, the project would derive about 18 per cent of its revenue from the sale of sturgeon meat. Second, caviar would be harvested from the mature five- and six-year-old female sturgeon. Caviar, accounting for about 80 per cent of MAP's future revenue stream, would be sold to wholesalers and distributors for market consumption. Third, MAP planned to over-produce fingerlings for sale to tropical fish wholesalers in the ornamental fish trade, accounting for the remaining two per cent of MAP's revenues.

Facilities

MAP administrative and production facilities were located on a single 200-acre site in Sarasota, Florida. In order to support the sturgeon's growth process, MAP utilized a state-of-the-art hatchery and uniquely designed "Grow Out" facilities. The sturgeon were housed in each of these facilities during various stages of their growth cycle. The hatchery currently held approximately 9,500 fingerlings, which constituted the "Class of 2003." This building was equipped with the most advanced filtration systems on the market, including ultraviolet and biofilter technologies. Grow Out-1 (GO-1), an 8,600-square-foot greenhouse-style building, went into operation in May 2002. This facility was stocked with approximately 31 tons of fish, ranging in size from one-half kilogram (one pound) to six kilograms, contained in 12 tanks, each holding 8,200 gallons of water. Grow Out-2 (GO-2), a 26,400-square-foot facility, was nearing completion and represented a significant expansion to MAP's production capabilities. This facility would utilize cutting-edge technology to ensure the most efficient, cost-effective operating system. This building would house 16 tanks, each with an 18,700-gallon capacity, as well as sludge-collection tanks, oxygen gas distribution systems and electrical generation capabilities for other expansion grow-out facilities in the future. These tanks would contain sturgeon ranging from three

to 10 kilograms in weight. Currently, four of the tanks in GO-2 were stocked with sturgeon that had been transferred from GO-1.

Four additional tanks were in the process of preparation for the transfer of GO-1 sturgeon. The remaining eight tanks were being equipped with a "drop filter" system, considered to be one of the most technologically advanced systems of its kind. The custom-designed filters offered operational simplicity, energy efficiency and frugal water requirements for sludge discharge, as compared with traditional "drum" filters. Overall, these new filters would enable MAP to maintain a minimal environment imprint in the long run. Groundbreaking for Grow Out-3 occurred in May 2004. With 26,400 square feet and a similar design to GO-2, this facility would also be equipped with 16 tanks and the same basic design as GO-2. Grow Out-3 was scheduled to be online by the end of 2005. Sturgeon meat and caviar would be processed in a 1,675-square-foot facility, also currently under construction. The top management expected that locating the processing facility on-site would enhance overall shelf life of the meat and caviar, as well as provide economies of scale in the production process.

CAVIAR AND STURGEON DEMAND

Global demand for caviar was on the increase, with the majority being consumed in the former Soviet republics, Europe and Japan. As mentioned earlier, 80 per cent of commercially produced caviar was consumed by Americans; however, overall demand fluctuated with economic growth and was correlated with consumers with high disposable incomes. In general, many caviar consumers also valued sustainability of natural resources and were sensitized to the fact that critical sturgeon habitats (such as the Caspian Sea) had been depleted.

There were three broad classes of caviar on the market. The variety of caviar depended upon the sturgeon species from which they originated.

Flavor, egg size, color, texture and shelf life also varied among caviar species. The largest sturgeon, beluga (scientific name: *Huso huso*), produced the highest-quality, elite caviar. This caviar had a mild taste. Consumers described it as delicate and sweet with a light nutty flavor. Retail prices in 2004 for this variety ranged from more than $100 for a one-ounce serving (28.5 grams) to more than $3,500 for 35 ounces (1 kilogram), which provided about 20 individual servings. Osetra (scientific name: *Acipenser gueldenstaedti*) was the medium-grade caviar. Osetra had a light golden color that consumers also described as having a sweet, nutty flavor. Retail prices for this variety ranged from $61 for a one-ounce serving to more than $2,000 for 35 ounces. Sevruga (scientific name: *Acipenser stellatus*) was the lowest-quality caviar. This variety was light gray in color and had a savory taste. Retail prices for this variety ranged from $49 per ounce to more than $1,400 for a 35-ounce tin.

THE ROLE OF TECHNOLOGY IN CAVIAR PRODUCTION

Technology played an important role in the production of caviar. There were two layers of technology that existed in this market: husbandry (i.e. breeding) and filtration/production. With regard to husbandry (breeding), new technologies were continually emerging. For example, Mote Marine Laboratory, part of the family of research facilities in the Mote Marine system, had been developing and utilizing cutting-edge fish-breeding technologies for more than three decades.

With regard to filtration and production technologies, there were three broad types of aquaculture systems in use: recycling systems (or recirculating), irrigation ditch (or pond systems) and cage systems. Recycling systems, the most efficient for water usage, typically utilized large plastic or fiberglass fish tanks housed inside or outside, depending on the farm. These systems were self-contained environments since fish feeding, water purification and waste discharge were closely monitored and controlled. While a wide array of filtration technologies abounded, common methods included natural water purification via filter media with ultraviolet or ozone disinfectant systems. When properly balanced, these recycling systems could produce the highest yield of edible protein per acre than any other system.

In contrast, pond systems were developed by constructing a pond and stocking it with desired fish species and plants to balance the pond's water chemistry. Although the least expensive of the aquaculture methods, pond systems were criticized for having a larger impact on the surrounding environment due to wastewater runoff and chemical leeching into the surrounding soil. These systems had the potential to utilize as much as one cubic meter of water per square meter of pond per year.

As the name implied, cage systems utilized existing water resources and a very porous composite or synthetic structure to contain the fish. Since these systems utilized existing water resources (e.g. lakes, rivers), a variety of fish species could be raised, but similar to the pond systems, with their high densities of fish per cubic meter, cage systems could have an adverse impact on local ecosystems.

POLITICAL-LEGAL ISSUES

Nationally, there were a number of countervailing forces impacting sturgeon production and demand via aquaculture. For example, scientists were reporting lower levels of indigenous species of sturgeon in the Missouri and Mississippi Rivers, and commercial fishing was blamed for the decreases in populations. The channelization of rivers had also impacted the population statistics via the disruption of natural sturgeon spawning sites. Further, the growth in demand for the North American sturgeon eggs for caviar had significantly deteriorated the natural sustainability of the species. As a result, there were an array of activist groups and legislative organizations seeking further restrictions in sturgeon harvests, as well as limits to habitat depletion. For example, conservation groups, such as the Waterkeepers Northern California, petitioned the National Marine Fisheries Service in 2001 to protect indigenous green sturgeon, native to the rivers of Oregon and California. The Waterkeepers Northern California had sought Endangered Species Act status for the green sturgeon, on claims that populations were decreasing due to pollution, over-fishing and various alterations to waterways. Conservation issues relating to sturgeon were not limited to the Pacific Northwest or the Deep South. Amidst dwindling numbers of lake sturgeon in the Great Lakes, conservation groups were also lobbying to protect over-fishing from commercial ventures.

With regard to beluga sturgeon, a species that was not indigenous to the United States, U.S. Fish and Wildlife Service desired to place restrictions on commercial production and imports. Conservation groups, such as SeaWeb, Caviar Emptor and National Resources Defense Council, argued that cultivation of the Eastern European species of sturgeon could harm sturgeon populations native to the United States. Further, groups argued that production would hinder existing Endangered Species Act protection of domestic sturgeon. Although they came dangerously close to facing an outright ban on beluga sturgeon, the aquaculture industry breathed a sigh of relief when, effective March 4, 2005, the U.S. Fish and Wildlife service issued a special rule (Section 4(d) of the Endangered Species Act of 1973) to allow trade and domestic cultivation of the threatened beluga sturgeon. This recent agreement and other global pacts, such as the Convention on International Trade in Endangered Species (CITES), have had a direct influence on the production and import/export of sturgeon.

While commercial aquaculture projects offered suitable alternatives to the problems of habitat and species depletion, there were many legislative acts afoot that could constrain aquaculture projects. For example, under the Clean Water Act, the United States Environmental Protection Agency recently finalized legislation aimed at reducing the solid-waste discharge in wastewater. This single piece of legislation would impact more than 245 farm-raised fish facilities that dump farm wastewater into U.S. waters.

Internationally, there were also a variety of factors lending to the highly complex nature of sturgeon demand. For example, over the past 10 years, the Caspian Sea sturgeon production has dwindled, resulting in greater demand for North American caviar. According to outdoorcentral.com news network, consumers were seeking alternatives to Russian beluga caviar. The North American shovelnose caviar from Missouri commanded a market price of $275 to $300 per 14-ounce tin, whereas beluga caviar from Russia commanded prices of $2,400 per pound.

INTERNATIONAL AQUACULTURE

The demand for seafood, the fastest-growing source of food in the world, continued to outstrip global supplies. About 135 million metric tons of fish were produced worldwide. Asia was the largest producer of aquaculture products, with a total of almost 42 million metric tons harvested. China was the largest Asian producer, with 32 million metric tons, followed by India and Japan, with two million and 1.3 million metric tons respectively. Aquaculture from China provided an important export for this nation, as U.S. imports of Chinese aquaculture products had more than doubled since 1998. Norway, Spain and France produced the majority of Europe's two million metric tons of aquaculture products annually.

With this backdrop of international aquaculture production, Canada was the leading supplier of U.S. seafood. Canada's primary aquaculture product was Atlantic salmon, with 68,000 metric tons produced in 2000. Overall, this sector in Canada's economy was expected to show continual growth in light of the government's financial and political commitment to the industry. In the United States, about 430,000 metric tons (valued at $1 billion) of seafood was produced via aquaculture in 2000, ranking the U.S. eighth globally in aquaculture production. Almost 94 per cent of the pink salmon harvested from Prince William Sound in Alaska was the result of artificial means of salmon breeding.

In the international arena, annual increases in production worldwide were estimated to be less than 50 tons; however, current production numbers may not be a good indicator of future sturgeon caviar supplies. The international wild card was China. Currently, large numbers of fertilized sturgeon eggs were being imported and utilized in grow-out facilities for the consumption of sturgeon meat. If their strategies shifted toward egg production, China could have a significant impact on world caviar prices over the course of the next decade.

THE U.S. STURGEON AQUACULTURE INDUSTRY

Currently estimated at $1 billion annually, the U.S. commercial production of caviar began in the 1990s. Many sources suggested that the U.S. aquaculture industry was experiencing growing pains. In contrast with wholesale buyers of seafood who were very well organized, aquaculture producers were largely fragmented and disorganized. The majority of domestic caviar production was located in California, where white sturgeon was the primary species. While MAP was the only commercial demonstration sturgeon project in the United States, there were a growing number of sturgeon production facilities located in Florida. For example, with 17 acres in Homestead, Florida, Rokaviar Sturgeon Farm was a recirculating facility capable of sturgeon spawning, grow-out and processing. Sturgeon Aquafarms, LLC (SAF) (www.sturgeonaquafarms.com), also located in Florida, imported live Caspian Sea sturgeon to their facility in June 2003, to begin grow-out. Currently, this farm supported more than 1,000 sevruga sturgeon, as well as 70 adult beluga sturgeon, one of the highest-quality caviar species.

SUPPLIERS-TECHNOLOGY AND STURGEON EGGS

There were a number of factors influencing the availability of necessary supplies for aquaculture-derived products. For a firm engaged in international sources of supply, such as sturgeon eggs, the strength of the dollar against other currencies had a direct impact on production costs. Grain, fish meal and fish oil prices also played key roles in the costs of production since a large portion of farm-raised species' diets were derived from a combination of these products. For example, corn and soybean meal, primary ingredients in catfish aquaculture feeds, exhibited substantial price increases in 2003 due to inflationary pressures. These trends were expected to continue in the future.

BUYERS

In order to meet the increasing U.S. demand for seafood over the next 25 years, industry experts estimated that there would need to be a six-fold increase in either domestic aquaculture production or equivalent imports. Two-thirds of the $54.4 billion U.S. consumers spent on seafood was at restaurants and other food-service establishments. Retail seafood sales comprised the remaining demand. The bulk of retail seafood sales was facilitated through various supermarkets. Since the majority of supermarket seafood demand was derived from consumers desiring price and convenience, the origin of the seafood was not a key factor. As a result, the majority of seafood at larger retail outlets had a variety of origins, ranging from international sources to domestic, including both naturally sourced and aquaculture-derived. Further, there had been a great deal of consolidation in the industry, resulting in fewer larger buyers that had driven down wholesale prices.

As wild stocks of sturgeon continued to decline, and more species were protected under the Endangered Species Act, competition for aquaculture-derived caviar would be limited. Domestically, California was the leader in aquaculture-derived caviar. Currently, California produced approximately six to seven metric tons of white sturgeon caviar each year. This level of production was expected to more than double over the course of the next decade.

THE MAP MANAGEMENT TEAM

MAP was managed by a team of individuals with aquaculture business, production and research expertise. Dr. Kevan Main, center director, provided administrative management, technical oversight and assisted the project manager in pursuing supplemental grant funding for the project. Dr. Main had more than 18 years of experience in the culture of tropical and subtropical fishes and invertebrates from Asia, the Pacific Islands and the mainland United States. Jim Michaels, the sturgeon project manager and staff scientist, oversaw the sturgeon production and research staff at MAP. He was responsible

for managing the sturgeon production and research efforts, facility design and construction, and assisting with pursuing grant funding for the project. Michaels had more than 17 years of experience in commercial sturgeon farming and had worked with tilapia and sturgeon in recirculating culture systems. Heather Hamlin, senior biologist and production manager, was responsible for the day-to-day production logistics and the research and development program. Hamlin had expertise in recirculating systems, larval rearing of marine and freshwater species and brood stock maintenance. Constance Beaulaton, the staff biologist, had expertise in larval rearing, water chemistry and recirculating systems. She was responsible for the care of the larval and fingerling stocks, water chemistry and the computerized inventory management program.

In view of the myriad of countervailing forces that would impact MAP operations and its future success, Michaels knew that, with this team of aquaculture experts and state-of-the-art recirculating aquaculture facilities, MAP was poised for success in the future.

ELEPHANT WALK THRU

An ecotourism project, integrating wildlife conservation, economic development and human development to ensure the continuity of community-based wildlife conservation efforts in Sri Lanka.

The Sri Lanka Wildlife Conservation Society's (SLWCS) management team knew they had

conceived a very unique project in Elephant Walk Thru (EWT), but the success of this innovative ecotourism project would hinge on the society's ability to balance the needs of a diverse group of stakeholders as well as various economic and political-legal forces faced by the

William J. Ritchie, Matthew S. Shell, Ravi Corea and Chandeep Corea prepared this case solely to provide material for class discussion. The authors do not intend to illustrate either effective or ineffective handling of a managerial situation. The authors may have disguised certain names and other identifying information to protect confidentiality.

organization. SLWCS's primary task in the ensuing months would be to identify salient external opportunities and threats posed by stakeholder groups. Equally important would be to evaluate the continually changing political-legal and economic environments prior to constructing the EWT facilities.

BACKGROUND

Founded in 1995, the Sri Lanka Wildlife Conservation Society (SLWCS), (registered in the United States as a 501(c) non-profit, tax-exempt organization) had been working exclusively in Sri Lanka to protect native species while aiding the social development of the Sri Lankan people. Headed by Ravi Corea, president, and Chandeep Corea, projects director (see Exhibit 1), the SLWCS began its first major project in 1998—an innovative electric fence designed to resolve conflicts between the native villagers and the elephants in Sri Lanka

and protect the surrounding forests (see Exhibit 2). During the administration of the fence project, three key issues emerged that prompted a move to acquire forestland from the Forest Department for the development of Elephant Walk Thru.

According to Ravi,

> Although the immediate human/elephant conflicts were resolved, surrounding forests were still being damaged by local villagers, highlighting the need for economic incentives for rural residents to save their environment. Second, there needed to be a sustainable means of using forest resources, protecting key buffer areas.

Finally, Ravi was busily pursuing grants and other sources of external funding for subsequent conservation projects, redirecting his talents toward fund-raising and away from the core conservation tasks he had originally sought to undertake. Ravi realized that something had to be done to address these issues. In 2000, he applied to the Sri Lanka Board of Investments for forestland for

---

Exhibit 1   The Management Team

Chief Executive Officer—Ravi Corea

SUMMARY BIO: Ravi Corea has been involved in wildlife conservation in Sri Lanka for more than two and a half decades. Ever since his childhood, Ravi has shown a keen interest in natural history, and today Ravi is a student on a scholarship at the prestigious Columbia University's Center for Environmental Research & Conservation in New York, finishing a degree in Environmental Biology. Ravi has worked for the National Zoological Gardens (Dehiwala Zoo) as a Student Guide Lecturer and has conducted research on reptiles, fishes, birds and elephants of Sri Lanka. In 1995, Ravi initiated the establishment of the Sri Lanka Wildlife Conservation Society, a non-profit, fully incorporated, tax-exempt organization based in the United States. Ravi presently functions as its founding president. Ravi has also established the project Saving Elephants by Helping People—the first community-integrated effort in Sri Lanka to help resolve human-elephant conflict at Gamburu-Oya/Pussellayaya, Wasgomuwa. The Wildlife Trust, the Disney Wildlife Conservation Fund, Computer Associates International Inc. and the U.S. Fish & Wildlife Service have provided funds for this ongoing project. Columbia University, the Wildlife Conservation Society (New York) and the National Office of the American Society for the Prevention of Cruelty to Animals (ASPCA) funded Ravi's earlier research efforts. Ravi has also obtained the financial support of the Abercrombie & Kent Global Foundation and the International Elephant Foundation, United States, for the conservation efforts of the Sri Lanka Wildlife Conservation Society in Sri Lanka. Ravi Corea presently resides in the State of New Jersey in the United States.

(Continued)

Exhibit 1 (Continued)

Director—Chandeep Corea

SUMMARY BIO: BSc, Marine Biology. Final year MSc in Forestry and Environmental Management. Founding partner of a successful Web-design company, ENIGMA (Pvt.) Ltd. Projects director of the Sri Lanka Wildlife Conservation Society, United States. Chandeep has extensive fieldwork experience working in Sri Lanka on wildlife conservation projects. He has worked with Dr. Wolfgang Dittus on the Smithsonian Institution–funded Torque Macaque Study in Polonnaruwa. A team member of Dr. Prithiviraj Fernando's Southern Area Elephant Radio Collaring Program funded by Global Environmental Facility, Chandeep participated in the Zoological Survey of Sri Lanka co-ordinated by Lyn De Alwis (President's Counsel for WildLife Conservation). Additionally, he is working with villagers to establish small eco-lodges for local visitors to experience nature with minimal impact on the environment.

Director—Jayantha Jayawardene

SUMMARY BIO: Wildlife Consultant. Formerly ADB Wildlife Project Director. Formerly senior manager at Finlay's Plantations. Member of Presidential Task Force on Wildlife Conservation, Southern Development Authority, Mahaweli Ministry. Publisher/Editor of Sri Lanka Nature. Member of Asian Elephant Specialist Group. Author of book on Sri Lanka Elephant. Founder/member of Biodiversity and Elephant Conservation Trust.

Chief Architect—Sanjeeva Guneratne

SUMMARY BIO: Faculty Member, Department of Architecture, University of Sri Lanka, Katubedda. He is presently working on his PhD in Architecture at the University of Milwaukee, Wisconsin, United States.

Source: Company files.

Exhibit 2 Fighting to Survive in Sri Lanka

Fighting to Survive in Sri Lanka

The elephants of Sri Lanka, once 20,000 strong, face an uncertain future. Their habitat is being destroyed, and local villagers and ivory poachers threaten their very existence. Today, fewer than 4,000 wild elephants live in this agricultural island country. With an annual birthrate of four per cent and a death rate of six per cent, that's not good news. And since 70 per cent of the elephant population lives outside of the country's national parks and sanctuaries, the death toll will likely only grow. In fact, some regional elephant populations already border on extinction.

For six decades now, the Sri Lankan government has been clearing vast expanses of jungle to make room for human settlements. Most of the land has been cleared without consideration for ecological issues, such as how the wild animals would be affected. Not surprisingly, the elephants have reacted by invading nearby villages.

Push Comes to Shove

Although elephants in Sri Lanka have been raiding farmers' crops since time immemorial, these were rare intrusions, and most Sri Lankans maintained a certain reverence for elephants. In recent times, however, the conflict has intensified. Unprecedented human encroachment on the elephants' habitat has isolated many elephant populations, leaving the animals with no choice but to raid farmers' crops in order to survive. As a result, an estimated 100 to 150 elephants are harassed, shot, poisoned and electrocuted each year as farmers retaliate. Socio-economic surveys conducted in villages with intense conflict show that the average village incurs about $28,500 worth of property and crop damage annually from these elephant raids.

But crops and wallets aren't the only casualties. Each year, elephants kill approximately 60 villagers. Thanks to years of harassment by humans, the elephants are very aggressive and will kill a person on sight. No villager will venture out of his home or hut after six o'clock in the evening, and on some days, children cannot go to school because elephants are obstructing the roads. There's also an emotional cost to this human–elephant conflict. The elephant's royal status is deeply ingrained in the local culture, religion and folklore. So Sri Lankans are faced with a difficult moral dilemma: They revere the elephant, but at the same time they persecute it. This internal conflict takes a toll on the community. When an elephant is killed or dies of injuries caused by people, the whole village gathers to pay solemn respect to the dead animal.

Killing an elephant in Sri Lanka is not just a cultural taboo, it's also illegal. In fact, the killing of all wildlife is prohibited, yet poaching incidences in the country are on the rise. The Sri Lanka Department of Wildlife Conservation (DWLC) does its best to catch the murderers, but it's a difficult task.

Don't Fence Me In

To combat these problems, the DWLC developed a program to fence the elephants into the country's national parks, thereby creating sanctuaries for them. But the attempts to contain the elephants have met with varying degrees of success. Because they're built along human-made boundaries, the fences mean nothing to the elephants, who have their own cultural and ecological boundaries. The fences are also costly to build and require a great deal of expensive manpower to maintain. More important, they have done little to protect the majority of elephants, who roam outside the boundaries of the national parks. Without the safety of these parks, the roaming elephants are more prone to violent poacher attacks.

In 1997, the Sri Lanka Wildlife Conservation Society proposed a more effective solution. The idea was to fence off elephant-restricted areas, such as villages and large agricultural fields, with solar-powered electric fences, leaving vast expanses of land outside the fenced areas for the elephants to range. Launched in 1998, the pilot project, called Saving Elephants by Helping People (SEHP), is managed and operated by the society. The village of Gamburu-Oya/Pussellayaya, situated in the central province of Sri Lanka, was completely encircled by a 10-kilometre fence using funds provided by the Wildlife Trust (www.wildlifetrust.org), the Disney Wildlife Conservation Fund (www.disney.com) and Computer Associates International (www.cai.com). The SEHP project provided all of the equipment needed to build the fence, while the Gamburu-Oya/Pussellayaya villagers provided the labor. Any items or materials that could be bought from the village were contracted locally, thereby channeling some of the project money into the village's economy.

From the start, the fencing was very effective in deterring the elephants. In 1997, 12 elephants were killed in Gamburu-Oya/Pussellayaya, compared with eight elephants in 1998 and only one in 1999. According to the regional office of the DWLC, there have been no reports of crop raiding, property damage, or human or elephant deaths since then.

With the threat of the elephants removed, the villagers were able to turn their attention to helping the government catch local poachers. Now that the villagers support elephant conservation, they're more willing to give information about known poachers to help the DWLC apprehend them.

Source: Ravi Corea. Reprinted with permission.

the eventual development of EWT. Two years later, with national and local governmental approval for the release of the land, Ravi and his management team awaited final approvals for the release of the land from the Land Commissioner, but many questions regarding the implementation of the project remained unanswered.

Both Ravi and Chandeep knew that their plan was ambitious, as this ecotourism product would push the traditional boundaries of eco-based tourism. They knew that the success of EWT would hinge on their ability to design the project so that it might be suitable for five very diverse stakeholder groups:

1. SLWCS and related constituencies,

2. the villagers,

3. the indigenous animal species and surrounding forests,

4. other nature-based initiatives in Asia, and

5. tourists.

The months during 2002 proved to be a significant period for EWT, as members of the management team introduced the EWT concept to the international community through a variety of conferences. Ravi and Chandeep attended the Eco-Tourism Summit in Quebec, Canada (sponsored by the World Tourism Organization in May 2002), and the International Elephant Symposium in Orlando, Florida (sponsored by the International Elephant Foundation in November 2002). Members of the EWT management team were also participants in a delegation with the Sri Lankan Prime Minister, Ranil Wickremasinghe, to the United States in 2002. These events helped the team to further develop EWT's organizational goals and assess its internal strengths and weaknesses. The concept of EWT was clearly emerging as an innovative venture that could be a model for low-impact, maximum benefit, nature-based tourism in Asia.

Equipped with a solid understanding of the mission and objectives of EWT, Ravi and Chandeep were keenly aware of the operational resources that would secure the success of the organization for years to come. But given their own international experiences and information gathered during eco-related conferences, they knew that there was a vast number of factors, external to the project and beyond their control, that would significantly influence the success of the Elephant Walk Thru. Meetings were scheduled in an effort to foster further analysis.

During gatherings with his management team, Ravi expressed particular concern with EWT's ability to balance the variety of expectations held by stakeholders, many of which posed potential threats to EWT. At the same time, he knew that there were multiple opportunities for EWT that had not yet been identified. Ravi felt that the political-legal and economic factors would be particularly important and that the organization would need a comprehensive list of external opportunities and threats affecting the eco-tourism project before it could undertake the major task of raising funds and constructing the facilities.

ORGANIZATIONAL BACKGROUND

Sri Lanka has been called the "biodiversity hotspot" of the world. SLWCS believes that if wildlife conservation projects involving local communities are to survive, in the long term, they need an economic base. Additionally, rural communities must see direct positive benefit from the conservation work performed in their communities as well as some level of social improvements from the funds that are generated from activities.

NATIONAL BACKGROUND

The political environment of Sri Lanka has been both unstable and ineffective over the last 20 years. Internal fighting between the violent Liberation Tigers of Tamil Eelam (LTTE) and the national government has stifled economic growth and created a sense of fear among the citizens of the country. However, things have started to change. The LTTE and the government reached a ceasefire agreement on February 21, 2002, an event that signalled the start of a new era in Sri Lanka. In June 2003, the international aid community (including the United States) pledged a massive aid/grant package of $4.5 billion for the development of Sri Lanka, an amount equal to the aid package pledged to Afghanistan after the fall of the Taliban. The new government that was subsequently established in Sri Lanka was very business-friendly. Its leader, Prime Minister Ranil Wickremasinghe, was one of the most experienced political leaders in Asia. Under his leadership, the country worked hard to encourage foreign investment and backed up this mandate by opening up for competition industries that had been state-run.

The economy in Sri Lanka had long depended on agriculture as a major source of income. However, agriculture was the least dynamic sector of the economy, accounting for only 19.4 per cent of gross domestic product (GDP) in 2001. Agriculture had done little to elevate rural incomes, even though almost one-third of the working population still worked in this industry. The textile industry, another major industry in the country, was facing falling prices, cheaper sources and high investment costs to stay competitive. Of the major industries in Sri Lanka, the service sector was by far the most dynamic, and the potential for growth in this industry far exceeded any other. One of the industries that had not been utilized much was the tourism industry. According to the U.S. Embassy, "The outlook for tourism is encouraging, due to the cease-fire." The telecommunications industry represented another bright spot in the Sri Lankan economy, fuelling the growth of information technology as well as the development of the Internet and e-commerce in Sri Lanka. Because of its modern telecommunications industry, Sri Lanka had a direct connection to many of its international trading partners.

The nation's infrastructure represented one of its most significant opportunities. The involvement of the government in the management of transportation, roads and power generation had left it behind the times. The main system of roads had not been significantly improved since the nation's independence more than 50 years previously. But the new government was in the process of widening smaller trunk roads and developing several new highways that connected the capital city of Colombo with key cities. Power shortages had plagued the country since 1994, making it difficult for businesses, especially those in manufacturing, to survive. One of the strengths in the nation's infrastructure was the Bandaranaike International Airport, which was fairly modern and could handle approximately three million people per year. A major expansion of the airport, which was located on the outskirts of Colombo, was planned for 2004. The expansion would increase passenger handling capacity by two million per year and would improve the airport's air navigation systems.

ORGANIZATIONAL GOALS

The long-term goals of the SLWCS and the proposed Elephant Walk Thru were:

1. To contribute to the long-term protection and conservation of the elephant, including the resolution of human-elephant conflict.

2. To use suitably trained local people with the guidance of scientists and conservationists to gather data on the local elephant population.

3. To conduct surveys of the plant and animal species in the central province and ascertain their conservation status.

4. To increase the awareness, knowledge, skills and economic well-being of the local people. The project sought to develop economic incentives for wildlife conservation and create opportunities for villagers to participate in field and eco-tourism projects. Through such efforts, SLWCS hoped to change the attitude of villagers toward wildlife conservation and protection and encourage them to take the message of wildlife conservation to other communities.

5. To form partnerships that would help in the long-term conservation of Sri Lanka's natural resources, while allowing for sustainable development.

Since 1997, the SLWCS has been working in Sri Lanka to resolve human-elephant conflict, making use of community participation. The top management of Elephant Walk Thru believed that revenues from business operations, as well as a mix of foreign aid and grants, were important to develop an economic base for the project's long-term survival.

PROJECT

In an effort to ensure the long-term survival of the project and with the co-operation of the Board of Investment of Sri Lanka, Elephant Walk Thru would lease 25 acres near a forest that extended all the way from the dry zone through the intermediate zone to the wet zone of Sri Lanka. Although the country had seen some terrible fighting in the past, the project area had never been one of conflict. This particular forest, which had a high diversity of habitats, had equally diverse fauna and flora. A field scouts program to monitor, observe and record elephants in this forest was also a part of this project. These scouts would be recruited from the local villages, trained and educated in the wildlife of the area. Eventually, they would function as field guides to visiting guests, earning a reasonably high wage from an alternate, environment-friendly, sustainable source that would supplement the meagre living they made from agriculture. The guides would also conduct environmental awareness programs for other communities, schools, etc. in this area.

OPERATIONS

Elephant Walk Thru would provide guests with an up-close and personal jungle experience. Amenities such as four-wheel-drive (4WD) vehicles, experienced field guides and trackers, hot and cold water facilities, quality food and beverage services, etc. would be provided to guests.

FORMAT OF VISIT

Upon arrival in Sri Lanka, visitors would spend one to two nights in Colombo at a boutique hotel or rented villa home to acclimatize and relax in a relatively homey environment. Following this brief period, visitors would be taken by luxury 4WD vehicles to the project site (about five hours from Colombo). During this five-hour journey to the eco-lodge, there would be several stops to visit places of interest (e.g. Pinnawella, Dalada Maligawa, Dambulla cave drawings).

Visitors would spend four to seven nights at the eco-lodge. The eco-lodge was only a 15- to 45-minute drive away from the large game reserves of Wasgamuwa N.P. and Maduruoya N.P. Additionally, the vast Knuckles Mountains and Forests were within a one-hour drive of the eco-lodge. The members who ran the tours would organize day trips to all of these locations on an individual basis at charges of approximately US$150 per head per day. Although the main part of the trip would be spent away from civilization, visitors could still visit the major cities where they could shop.

ACCOMMODATIONS

Central Lodge and Research Station

There would be a central lodge with overnight accommodations, such as cabanas and tented semi-luxury camps, and other hospitality services for guests. There would also be a research station and a nature centre, which would, with time, include a library and a natural history collection, documenting the biodiversity of the region. The main administrative and management hub of the conservation projects would also be situated here.

Village Hospitality Centres

Participating village households would have some basic infrastructure such as plumbing and kitchen facilities developed for them to host overnight guests. This would give the guest a chance to experience a day in the life of a rural farmer, a fisherman, "a toddy tapper," a wild honey collector, "a chena cultivator," etc.

Overnight Camps

There would be elephant and horseback treks into the neighboring forest with an overnight camping stop at a choice of several pre-selected areas to observe the local wildlife, bird watch, absorb the beauty of the forest and to give the guest an opportunity to commune with nature. The site would be a lakefront (tank/reservoir) where elephants came to drink, bathe and socialize, especially during the night. On moonlit nights, guests would have the opportunity to ride in inflatable boats to observe the elephants from the water. This would be the best way to observe elephants, without causing undue alarm. Refreshments would be provided as guests silently moved along, watching the elephants go about their way of life. Alternatively, guests would be able to observe these elephants from a comfortable viewing hut built on a nearby tree. While observing the elephants and other wildlife, guests could enjoy an aperitif or hot or cold drinks. This forest area was classified as Divisional Secretariat forest and was not part of either the Forest Department or the WildLife Department.

Ancient Villages

There were many ancient villages in the area, including one that was over 300 years old. The villages were human habitations caught in a time warp. Two villages, which were about 15 minutes' drive from the project site, were supplied by two perennial springs and completely surrounded by the jungle, cut off from the rest of the world. The native people there still worshiped at shrines built under huge ancient, spreading banyan trees and fig trees. Guests would be taken in the afternoon to see these villages. Since the route followed the thick canopy jungle, guests

would get an opportunity to feel the primordial quality of the jungle on the return trip in the late evening. If they were lucky, they would also encounter elephants, leopards and bears along the route. This could be a walking safari or an expedition in Land Rovers, depending on the needs and sense of adventure of the guests.

ELEPHANT WALK THRU INFRASTRUCTURE

Eco Tree Lodges

After the initial use of village hospitality centres, the project would progress towards canopy-level tree lodges. The basic concept was to have eight to 10 habitat-immersed, canopy-level tree lodges integrated into the existing forest structure. None of the structures, except for the supporting beams and columns, would be built on the ground in order to minimize the ecologically detrimental edge effects that can be caused by ground construction. The height of all these well-camouflaged structures would be at a level where they could provide unimpeded access to the forest floor, from elephants to shrews. The construction engineering would be integrated in such a manner that existing large trees would support luxury tree huts. Each hut would have a bedroom and living room with efficiencies, modern bathroom, intercom and telephone, and wrap-around balcony. All the support structures would be well camouflaged to blend with the forest environment.

Next, the tree huts would be connected to an elevated central lodge by canopy walkways. Infrastructure facilities would include offices, kitchen, restaurant and dining room, game room, library, video parlor and a lecture hall. The swimming pool would be a natural-looking rock pool fed by natural spring water. All facilities would be connected to each other by elevated walkways. This resort would be a unique feature in Sri Lanka and would be one of the first entirely elevated nature tourism resorts in the world. It would also ensure maximum safety to the visitors and allow for the forest and the forest floor to remain totally untouched with the minimal disturbance to the animals at all times.

VEHICLES

- Three Land Rover Td5 Defender County station wagons
- One 4WD commuter van with air conditioning to transport guests back and forth and to be used as the general purpose vehicle for the lodge
- Two Zodiac Grand Raid Mark III inflatable boats with Honda 50HP outboard engines

FINANCES

With an estimated 10 guests paying US$400 per night, the jungle tree house accommodations would generate up to US$4,000 in gross revenues each day. Since the daily costs per guest, including staff, fuel and food is estimated at US$50, the estimated profit at full occupancy is US$3,500 per day. Most of this income would be reinvested in the village and in other wildlife projects. This type of operation allows for maximum benefit to be generated for the country at minimum costs.

TOURISM IN SRI LANKA

In 1966, the government established the Ceylon Tourist Board, which has worked hard to expand the industry in Sri Lanka. The country's main attractions included the beach resorts on the southwestern coastal region, although many tourists also visited the ancient cities of the dry zone. The tourism industry had suffered severely when the fighting between the national government and the Liberation Tigers erupted in 1983. The February 2002 ceasefire allowed the tourism industry to once again regain its marketability and its quest for European and American visitors. At that point, the Sri Lanka Tourist Board

moved away from its traditional "Sun, Sea and Sand" promotion to a more modern theme, which called Sri Lanka "A Land Like No Other."

PROMOTION WITH INTERNATIONAL PARTNERS

The SLWCS began working with Abercrombie & Kent of the United States on its conservation projects. Abercrombie & Kent was one of the world's largest high-end tourism companies. The use of multinational corporations to raise funds served as one of the biggest opportunities for Elephant Walk Thru. The companies built goodwill with consumers through environmentally friendly practices, and EWT gained funds besides revenues from tourists. As such, EWT decided to aim for high-end customers, going for quality rather than quantity. The anticipated rate for visitors was US$300 to US$500 per night per person. There was a 20-guest limit at the lodge at any one time.

LONG-TERM PROSPECTS

This nature tourism resort was targeted for high-end, up-market clients. Most of the world's tourism services, especially those in Sri Lanka, were targeted to attract package tourists. There was a large group of affluent tourists who were willing to pay premium prices for novel, unusual and high-quality services and opportunities to experience nature. This market segment had mostly eluded Sri Lankan tour operators because there were no true eco-tour services on the ground to attract this particular group of tourists. More recently, nature tourism had begun to be extensively promoted—such as in Sri Lanka Tourist Board's new slogan: "A Land Like No Other"—but was still in its infancy.

There were large, untapped, high-end eco-tourist markets in the United States, Canada, Europe, Australia, the Middle East, Japan, China and New Zealand. By developing partnerships with international eco-tour operators such as Abercrombie & Kent and Discovery Tours, EWT hoped to tap into these markets. Internationally, the international tourism industry had suffered some serious setbacks over the years with the increase of terrorism. American travellers, one of the targeted ecotourist groups, were reluctant to travel internationally after the World Trade Center tragedy in 2001 and during the 2003 war with Iraq. However, the long-term prospects of attracting upper-class eco-tourists from the United States and Europe remained bright. In fact, some Americans have been joining the eco-tourism bandwagon within the United States. There are various tree house resorts scattered throughout the United States and internationally, and they offer a concept very similar to that of EWT, minus the amazing experience of observing elephants (see Exhibit 3 for selected World Wide Web links).

Since Elephant Walk Thru would be the only operation in Sri Lanka providing such an unusual nature experience, initially the SLWCS would have full market share, playing a leadership role in introducing some very novel concepts in design, service

Exhibit 3	Related Tree House World Wide Web Links

- http://treehouses.com
- http://www.treehousesofhawaii.com
- http://www.tourindiakerala.com/treehouse.htm
- http://eureka-net.com/treehouse

and quality. The players would be the affluent international nature tourists who were willing to pay a premium for the best possible nature experiences and hospitality services. It was highly unlikely that the market would shift away from ecotourism since this type of tourism had become the most economically and biologically sustainable way of using the world's depleting biodiversity resources. The cost and prices would be set according to international standards to match or compete with what else was being offered in the market. As competition increased, with other operators emulating the same concepts, it would be a challenge for EWT to be more innovative while remaining environmentally friendly.

2

STARTING THE NONPROFIT ORGANIZATION

To develop business leaders who think globally, act strategically and contribute to the societies in which they operate.[1]

Key Topics: steps for starting a nonprofit organization, mission, vision, and values for nonprofits, legal implications for nonprofits, strategic planning, organizational structure

Who starts a nonprofit organization (NPO) and why? While many concerned citizens start an informal nonprofit to meet a short-term and local need (e.g., to clean up the neighborhood, to raise funds for a small local event), such activities don't usually need ongoing resources. Starting a formal nonprofit to inspire a long-term change in one's community, however, is a more complex affair. In the latter case, the creator wants to ensure that the organization is an enduring entity apart from its members (e.g., can have its own bank account and enter into contracts). Establishing such a sustainable NPO is a daunting process for even the most dedicated change agent. Table 1 lists the basic steps to follow.

At a deeper level, start-up issues that must be resolved cover legal, financial, and managerial matters. Specifics to be addressed in this chapter range from defining the purpose to structuring the organization to developing a strategic plan, while also briefly referring to recruiting, training, and retaining a board of directors, paid staff, and volunteers. Once the basic structure is set, the real fun begins with the day-to-day management of all the puzzle pieces. The following sections examine the beginning steps of this complex process. The remainder of the text discusses the details of components needed to build and manage a sustainable nonprofit once the organization launches.

With such an overwhelming list of things to accomplish, where does one begin? For a

---

[1]The Richard Ivey School of Business (The University of Western Ontario) Mission Statement.

Table 2.1 Basic Steps to Starting an NPO

Activity	Comment
Name the organization and register a domain name for a website.	Consider uniqueness and descriptive elements of the name as well as availability of domain names.
Draft mission and vision statements with supporting values.	
Recruit board members.	
Retain professional legal, tax, and insurance agent/assistance.	
Draft articles of incorporation with government agencies.	Secure board approval before sending to appropriate government agency.
File for tax-exempt status as appropriate.	
Secure other government certifications.	These include but are not limited to solicitation license to petition donations, mail permit for bulk mailing, federal employer number and unemployment insurance (as employees are hired).
Write the business plan.	Use the plan to organize efforts and seek support (financial and other) from interested stakeholders.
Develop the organization structure to achieve the goals established in the business plan.	Determine the balance of paid and volunteer human resources needed to achieve goals and outline how they will be coordinated.

Source: McNamara, 2008. Reprinted with permission.

change agent to influence society she must first understand—and very explicitly state—what she wishes to change and have a vision for how the change will occur. This is generally accomplished through identification of core values that will drive the organization to achieve its mission and a clearly articulated vision of what the future will be once the change occurs.

Defining the Purpose

Values

Core values for an organization are a set of beliefs that are paramount; they are identified internally and need no validation from the external environment. An organization should be careful not to *create* core values; rather the process of organizational self-examination should *identify* core values. In other words, core values are something an NPO or its leader already has. The point of identifying these values is to inspire and motivate constituencies as well as to align strategies with internal and external communication of the organization's mission and vision.

Identifying values at the outset of an organization's life enables the founder (and any subsequent leaders) to guide strategy, structure, control, and reward systems. Thus in the initial stages of organizational development, the process of self-examination may be more of a public commitment to or formalized articulation of values already existing in the founders. Many nonprofits refer to their core values as their "founding stories," upon which they build meaningful experiences (Crutchfield & McLeod Grant, 2008).

Once core values have been identified, they can drive strategy and be connected to an organizational or brand personality (see Chapter 9). Most organizations will have three to five core values. If more than that are identified, leaders may be confusing these values with operating practices, business strategies, or cultural norms.

Mission

Fundamentally, a mission statement *communicates the purpose* of an organization. This purpose should be based on the defined core values while also being unique, setting the organization apart from similar ones in the community (what we referred to as *closest competitors* in Chapter 1). A well-crafted mission also defines the scope of an organization's operations and services (Marshall & Johnston, 2010). Thus when faced with environmental pressures to expand services beyond organizational capacity (a reality for many NPOs), leaders can turn to the mission and ask, "Does this activity serve our mission?" If not, the organization and its constituents would be better served by the NPO *not* offering assistance but referring the matter to another organization that provides the needed service within the scope of its mission. Such referrals build a vital network (discussed in Chapter 7), which has been found to be one of the most important factors for NPO effectiveness (Bernstein, 1997).

Having a strong mission statement can enable more efficient strategic effort based on greater focus and standardization, thus maximizing expenditure effectiveness. Jim Collins (2001) crystalized this idea in what he calls the Hedgehog Concept: "to attain piercing clarity about how to produce the best results, and then exercising the relentless discipline to say, 'No thank you' to opportunities that fail the hedgehog test" (para. 12).

These decisions also help an NPO manager avoid goal displacement, which can result when a nonprofit is overly dependent on external contributors for resources (Pfeffer & Salancik, 1978; Worth, 2012). By adhering to a well-defined mission, visions become reality. The focus should be on *the doing*—what the NPO does to create the better world its vision describes.

When undertaking the task of creating a mission statement, there is always the question of who should be involved in the process. It is extremely important to the success of a mission that it be supported at all levels of the organization. As such, NPO leaders should engage the board, employees, and key volunteers in (re)constructing a mission statement. If the leadership decides the current mission statement successfully encapsulates the values (discussed above) and the purpose of being (*raison d'être*), inculcating all employees and volunteers into the organization's culture through mission training is critical to successfully connecting the mission with strategy execution.

Below is a sample of well-constructed mission statements:

- "Harbor House seeks to eliminate domestic violence by providing safety, shelter, counseling, education, advocacy and justice." Harbor House of Central Florida (www.harborhousefl.com/about-harbor-house/a-place-to-heal)
- "New Art, New Ideas." The New Museum (www.newmuseum.org/about/mission_statement)
- "To strengthen the impact, effectiveness and leadership of nonprofit and philanthropic organizations through education and management assistance." Rollins College Philanthropy & Nonprofit Leadership Center (www.rollins.edu/pnlc/aboutus/index.html)

Vision

Visions are big ideas. Vision statements are big ideas written down so they can be shared. Clarity of vision, more than any specific strategy, keeps NPOs on course—particularly during periods of growth. A vision is the future an organization wants to create for the community it wishes to impact. An effective vision statement will therefore tell the world what change the NPO wishes to create for the future of its community. If there is nothing to change, there is no vision. If there is no vision for an improved situation, there is no need for the organization.

Vision statements evolve from the values and mission of the organization. The values represent the NPO's core ideology. This core serves as the yin to the yang of the envisioned future. The envisioned future consists of a 10- to 30-year goal and a vivid description of what accomplishing that goal would look like. A true 10- to 30-year goal will motivate employees and focus efforts. This goal should be at the highest level, a goal with which all members of an organization can identify. The vivid description of this goal will aid in motivating employees and volunteers by recognizing exactly what achieving this goal will look like (J. C. Collins & Porras, 1996).

The following are a few examples of vision statements:

- "No child in our city will go to bed hungry in the evening." (a soup kitchen)
- "In two decades our services will no longer be needed." (a literacy program)
- "We will be recognized as the best symphony orchestra in America." (symphony orchestra)
- "We envision a vibrant nonprofit sector that is valued by the community for its innovation, leadership, and integral role in determining quality of life." Rollins College Philanthropy & Nonprofit Leadership Center (http://www.rollins.edu/pnlc/aboutus/index.html)
- "We are Canada's leadership school. We develop leaders." (Richard Ivey School of Business 2010 Annual Report, p. 16.)

Combining Elements to Achieve the Purpose

For successful attainment of purpose, the values, mission, and vision must combine with the NPO's efforts and resources to provide intense clarity, known as the Hedgehog Concept (J. Collins, 2001). It is only through this clarity of purpose that a newly formed organization can build and maintain a sustainable future. The unwavering "hedgehog" single-mindedness results when three areas overlap

into one focal point. These areas and the corresponding questions that guide the NPO to concentrate on the intersection include:

- Values, mission, and vision—what is the organization passionate about?
- Programs and services—what can the organization do better than anyone else in the world?
- Resources—what drives the organization's engine, economically and sustainably?

NONPROFIT AS A LEGAL ENTITY

Once the values, mission, and vision that will drive the NPO have been clearly articulated, the leader must begin the process of incorporating the nonprofit as a recognized entity in the community in which it plans to operate. As discussed in Chapter 1, many types or entities exist under the nonprofit umbrella. In the United States an organization with a mission to serve the public interest must file incorporation papers with the state to receive exemptions from state and federal taxes (in Canada, status can be granted provincially or federally).

The U.S. Internal Revenue Service categorizes nonprofits into 30 classifications based on their tax-exempt status. Inclusion in the different classes determines many operating policies and legal restrictions on organizational activities. The tax codes and corresponding consequences are very complicated. Consultation with accountants, lawyers, and other professionals specializing in the nonprofit sector is recommended when starting a nonprofit and developing the mission precision to ensure proper classification (e.g., charitable nonprofit versus advocacy organization).

While many suggest that philanthropy remains predominantly an American cultural phenomenon (Worth, 2012), the globalization of philanthropy and the civil sector necessitates the investigation of the legal ramifications of establishing an NPO in different countries. National and local governments across the globe naturally employ varying attitudes and laws regarding the establishment and operation of nonprofit or non-governmental organizations. Presently, few national tax systems provide the level of tax advantage for individual or corporate philanthropy found in the United States, but a trend in that direction is evident among some European nations (Worth, 2012).

A deeper discussion of international and global nongovernmental organizations is found in Chapter 13. From its inception, however, a nonprofit should contemplate its long-term scope and decide whether legal considerations outside its home nation will influence initial incorporation.

THE ORGANIZATIONAL PLAN

Once the founders decide what an organization stands for (i.e., its values), its purpose (i.e., mission), and what it hopes to achieve (i.e., its vision), it is now time to plan how to achieve the vision. This process usually begins with a business plan. While writing a business plan is essential because it formalizes intentions, it is useless without implementation.

Kawasaki (2004) outlines 10 important steps to developing a for-profit business plan. Adapting this to the nonprofit setting results in seven basic components.

1. The problem: What do you envision improving in society?

2. The solution: How will you uniquely solve the problem?

3. The business model: What approach (e.g., tactics, strategy, structure) will you use to deliver the solution?

4. The competition: Who else in the community offers services that address the problem, and why is your solution better? Alternatively, why has no one addressed this problem before?

5. The team: Who will you bring together to solve the problem (e.g., board, volunteers, paid staff)? How will you attract them to the cause and keep them in the organization?

6. The support you need: What financial backing is necessary to achieve the organization's purpose or to enable the solution to the identified community issue? What sources of finance will you use (e.g., grants, self-generated income)?

7. The results: What accomplishments do you hope for, when, and how will you know you've achieved results (i.e., measurement)?

A business plan, by nature, focuses on the future—which is essentially unpredictable. This does not excuse one from writing the plan. Potential funders or investors want to feel confident that the change agent has at least thought through the process of providing solutions and has anticipated some of the challenges that may arise as the vision is pursued. Kawasaki (2004), like many other authors and strategists, emphasizes that the plan, while written deliberately, is emergent in nature. This means that the plan is a starting point that becomes a living document once the organization begins operating. This is where the business plan morphs into the strategic planning process (see Chapter 6).

THE TEAM: ORGANIZATIONAL STRUCTURE

Having a strong mission statement and a business plan can help a change agent understand the manner in which to organize activities for solving the problem—but structuring the team is also necessary. Historically, two factors influence the organizational structure of an NPO. First, the nonprofit organizational team (versus for-profit and governmental agencies) intertwines an interdependence of highly qualified paid staff with able volunteers. Although individual NPOs may design different roles for volunteers and paid staff, each must balance the planning, leading, organizing, and controlling (PLOC) of the two constituencies in a manner that recognizes their unique motivations and capabilities while also enabling mission accomplishment.

Many nonprofits initially begin as voluntary efforts with one person (often the founder) serving as the central decision maker. As the organization grows, the original centralized structure may constrain the breadth and depth of the NPO's potential and positive impact on the community. At this point the founder should refer to the mission and vision of the organization to determine if expansion—and the corresponding loss of centralized control—best accomplishes the desired results. This is often easier said than done, with many organizations experiencing Founders Syndrome. This condition occurs when an organization operates consistent with the personality of someone in the organization (usually the founder) rather than according to its mission (McNamara, 2008). Chapter 8 and its corresponding cases investigate the intricacies of structure and human resources (e.g., professional staff, board of directors, volunteer workers) more deeply.

The second aspect that is particularly relevant to how a founder structures an NPO is the degree of resource dependency. Although organizations are not powerless captives of their funding sources, their structure is sometimes determined more by what grantors deem important than by what service recipients may need. This common "chasing of the grant" can cause mission creep and alter hiring and retention patterns. For example, the director of a homeless shelter may determine the need for drug-dependency counseling but finds only grant opportunities for welfare-to-work classes. Rather than offer no services, the director may find herself serving a less-crucial need. Few grants are available to support basic organizational or administrative needs, and this may force NPO structures to be built around programs rather than organizational functions (e.g., marketing, finance, office operations).

Similarly, organizations that are dependent on a few large sources of sponsorship may centralize operations to achieve consistent communication and ensure compliance with the funder. Healthcare organizations that become heavily dependent on government insurance plans such as Medicaid, for example, design their service delivery to comply with these mandates. With a wider range of public and private funding, an organization may become more decentralized because it can rely on monetary and volunteer support from various stakeholders with differing interests. The flexibility provided by multiple funders enables decisions to be made closer to constituents, thus responding to their needs rather than the needs of the supporter. It is important to access funding with no strings attached. The CEOs of Teen Challenge in London, Ontario, Canada, and Compassion Canada, for example, have committed to not accepting any funding (i.e., government funding) if it comes with strings attached.

To overcome resource dependency, many nonprofits seek alternative funding through earned income strategies, social entrepreneurship, and fee-for-service initiatives (Worth, 2012). Chapters 10 and 11 discuss issues related to financial resources such as fundraising, earned income, and financial management. Chapter 14 investigates opportunities presented by social entrepreneurship.

Another factor influencing organizational structure—task environment—is not unique to the nonprofit sector. All establishments striving to achieve a goal must consider the complexity and repetitiveness of their processes when developing structure. Generally speaking, more flexibility is needed when tasks are complex, unique, and unpredictable—think emergency response teams. A decentralized structure is needed to respond to such environments. When operations are sequential, unambiguous, and cyclical, however, operations can be managed from a central office with greater ease.

The cases that follow highlight issues that arise when a dedicated change agent seeks to formalize efforts through the development of a formal organization.

CASES

The Launch of Durra: Women in Islamic Banking (United States): This case focuses on the vice president and regional head of corporate banking for Noor Islamic Bank in Dubai as she arrives in the United States to promote the first global network for women in Islamic banking and finance, known as Durra. The case introduces students to the concepts behind Islamic banking and the reasons why certain types of risky financial products are not permitted under Islamic law. Islamic banks have been growing at a rate of 15% per year and have assets approaching $1 trillion, despite the recent banking crisis. Islamic banks also have a hard time filling the 30,000 new jobs created each year because of the specialized training required. One of the purposes of Durra is to help more women fill critical positions in Islamic banking and to help them manage their careers in order to assume leadership positions. The case also raises questions about how best to build a nonprofit organization. Issues include how to attract new members and financial backers and how to build a useful and robust website that fulfills the needs of the organization.

MIA, Philippines (International): The newly appointed country director of MIA Philippines, a nonprofit organization with a mandate to alleviate poverty in developing countries, is faced with the challenge of designing and managing a development assistance project that would establish a go-to-market supply chain for a remote Filipino fishing village. The country director has to enter a new country, launch the project, deal with the constraints of a foreign culture, manage the expectations of major stakeholders while trying to manage a multicultural team, and conclude the project on

time. The value of the case lies in the realistic assessment of stakeholders' motivation, their capabilities and assets, and project constraints during the design and implementation stages. Value chain analysis, value added analysis, and stakeholder analysis are used to assess the applicability of project design, impact, and long-term success.

REFERENCES

Bernstein, P. (1997). *Best practices of effective nonprofit organizations.* New York, NY: Foundation Center.

Collins, J. (2001). *Good to great and the social sectors.* Retrieved from http://www.jimcollins.com/books/g2g-ss.html

Collins, J. C., & Porras, J. (1996). Building your company's vision. *Harvard Business Review, 74*(5), 65–77.

Crutchfield, L. R., & McLeod Grant, H. (2008). *Forces for good: The six practices of high-impact nonprofits.* San Francisco, CA: Jossey-Bass.

Kawasaki, G. (2004). *The art of the start.* New York, NY: Penquin.

Marshall, G. W., & Johnston, M. W. (2010). *Marketing management.* New York, NY: McGraw-Hill.

McNamara, C. (2008). *Field guide to developing, operating and restoring your nonprofit board.* Minneapolis, MN: Authenticity Consulting.

Pfeffer, J., & Salancik, G. R. (1978). *The external control of organizations: A resouce dependence perspective.* New York: Harper & Row.

Worth, M. J. (2012). *Nonprofit management: Principles and practice* (2nd ed.). Thousand Oaks, CA: Sage.

THE LAUNCH OF DURRA: WOMEN IN ISLAMIC BANKING

Fauzia Vohra, vice president and regional head of Corporate Banking for Noor Islamic Bank PJSC in Dubai, arrived in the United States to promote the launch of Durra, the first global organization for women in Islamic banking and finance. Durra (Arabic for "pearl") was created

in 2007, under the patronage of Her Highness Sheikha Jawaher Bint Mohammed Al Qassimi, chairperson of the Supreme Council for Family Affairs and wife of the Ruler of Sharjah, one of the seven emirates that made up the United Arab Emirates (UAE).

In the wake of the 2008 financial crisis, Islamic banking was one of the few sectors in the banking industry that continued to thrive. The types of risky derivatives and loans that were behind the steep losses experienced by many institutions were not permitted under Islamic law; as such, Islamic banks had been less affected by the crisis. In 2009, most banks had cut jobs in an effort to trim costs. In the United States alone, the banking industry shed an average of 46,000 jobs per month. Two of the largest banks, Citigroup and Bank of America, had announced cuts of 63,000 and 35,000 positions respectively.[2]

Islamic banks, on the other hand, were growing at a rate of 15 per cent per year, and their assets were approaching $1 trillion.[3] Even as the ranks of unemployed bankers continued to grow, Islamic banks faced a challenge filling the 30,000 new jobs created each year because of the specialized training required. Vohra hoped that Durra could help more women fill these critical positions. In addition, Durra would provide ongoing training and support to women who were already working in the industry, thereby helping them to assume leadership positions.

BACKGROUND

Islamic Banking

Islamic banking and finance (IBF) was first conceptualized at the Third Islamic Conference in 1972. At the conference, finance ministers from predominantly Muslim countries had discussed the importance of replacing western banking and its emphasis on interest with banking that conformed to Islamic teachings. As a result of these discussions, 47 member states agreed to create the Islamic Development Bank to provide development assistance, offer interest-free loans and participate in approved equity markets.[4] The IBF model soon expanded to private institutions that sought to offer investment products grounded in *Shari'a* (Islamic law).

In general, Islamic law was based on three sources: the Koran, tradition and consensus. The Koran, which dated from the seventh century, was the central religious text of Islam and, by far, the most authoritative document on which all decisions were based. Tradition, also known as *hadith,* was the work of Islamic jurists in the eighth and ninth centuries, and was based on the sayings and practices of the prophet Muhammad. The jurists' task was to provide guidance on specific issues that were not well defined in the Koran. Much of the legal and economic foundation of Islam dated from this period. When neither the Koran nor *hadith* could resolve a specific issue, it was debated among Islamic scholars. Consensus, or *ijma,* was reached when the majority held the same opinion.

Over the centuries, Islamic scholars developed a large corpus of legal rules and precedents concerning financial contracts. Nevertheless, traditional sources provided limited guidance to modern banking and finance, especially in matters involving complex transactions that had no

[2]Chavon Sutton, "U.S. Bank Job Cuts Slow, But Bloodshed Not Over Yet," Reuters, June 9, 2009, reuters.com/ article/2009/06/09/us-jobs-wallstreet-analysis-idUSTRE55860N20090609, accessed June 10, 2009.

[3]All funds in U.S. dollar, unless specified otherwise.

[4]Elias G. Kazarian, *Islamic Versus Traditional Banking: Financial Innovations in Egypt,* Westview Press, Boulder, CO, 1993, pp. 2–3.

medieval equivalents. Instead, Islamic banks often relied on guidance through *ijma*.[5] Although *ijma* relied on interpretation, wherever possible, logical analogies to *hadiths* were used to provide justification for modern *fatwas*. A *fatwa* was a legal opinion given by one or more qualified Islamic scholars on a subject that was not clearly defined in Islamic law and tradition. Although *fatwas* were not always legally binding, they were often used as precedents for subsequent legal decisions.

Islamic banks differed from western banks in several important ways. By being grounded in *Shari'a*, their business practices had to conform to Islamic principles. Foremost among these was *lariba*, or the avoidance of interest. Interest in any form was often interpreted as a form of usury (*riba*) and therefore prohibited under Islamic law. Financial speculation, considered by many Islamic scholars to be a form of gambling, was usually proscribed, although futures that decreased risk by ensuring a stable price for goods over an extended period could be deemed lawful. According to one prominent Islamic scholar:

> It is important to distinguish between gambling (which must be avoided) and other kinds of risk-taking. In the words of Irving Fisher, a gambler seeks and takes unnecessary risks. . . . A farmer sells future grain contracts in order to protect himself from a fall in prices, whereas a food processor buys future grain contracts in order to protect himself from a rise in prices. Both parties benefit, for even though each one is taking some risk, the total risk is less, and they can proceed with their production plans on the basis of agreed prices.
>
> Another example is oil futures sold by oil companies and purchased by airlines. Without these contracts, the fluctuations in oil prices would expose future planning in both industries to almost impossible risks. Since direct deals between farmers and food processors or between oil companies and airlines would be costly and cumbersome, it is efficient to have middlemen or intermediaries. Some sort of clearing arrangements soon follow. In short, we have a new market for commodity futures. . . . Future markets have a decisive impact on spot markets, making them more stable.[6]

Finally, Islamic banks could not participate in or support the production and distribution of proscribed goods and services and were expected to engage in charity and economic development.

Shari'a Councils

In order to attract Muslim clients, banks sought specific *fatwas* for their products. These were issued by *Shari'a* councils of qualified scholars who had been trained in finance and economics. Once a *fatwa* was given, a devout Muslim could participate in a given financial product. Any layperson who, in good faith, followed the *fatwa* of a qualified scholar was considered blameless in the eyes of God, even if the *fatwa* had been given in error.[7]

Shari'a council members were usually unwilling to deviate from or criticize traditional decisions and rulings. Whenever possible, councils tried to adapt existing law to new financial products. As a result, new rules were formulated only when technological and economic advances were without precedents, however vague. In disputed or difficult cases, scholars sought advice beyond the immediate councils they belonged to. Occasionally, conferences were organized to discuss important issues and to make rulings.[8]

Despite the apparent desire for consensus and uniformity, differences of opinion were not uncommon. *Fatwas* issued by one council could

---

[5]Ibid., pp. 71–76.

[6]Mohammad Nejatullah Siddiqi, "Islamic Banking and Finance: A Series of Three Lectures Delivered at UCLA in a Fall 2001 Seminar for the Business Community," http://www.international.ucla.edu/article.asp?parentid=15056, accessed February 1, 2007.

[7]Frank Vogel and Samuel Hayes, *Islamic Law and Finance,* Kluwer Law International, The Hague, 1998, p. 23.

[8]Ibid., pp. 35–36.

contradict *fatwas* issued by another council. Rulings that were based on circumstances unique to a certain time or place could be overturned when new circumstances arose.[9]

Shari'a scholars were in high demand as a result of the recent rapid growth in Islamic finance. At the same time, Islamic products were also becoming more complex. Therefore, at a time when demand was rising, fewer jurists had the requisite knowledge to understand complex financial instruments. Vohra explained:

> It is no longer just plain vanilla products like home loans and car loans that are in high demand, but also high-end products like the Islamic bond. In Islamic banking there are 14 types of Islamic bonds, and a lot of work goes into structuring those bonds, providing documentation, and so on. They are often listed on foreign exchanges. The technical knowledge required to understand these transactions is very high.

Investment and Borrowing Alternatives

Banks devised profit-sharing schemes to provide a return on deposited funds and to lend capital to entrepreneurs. Profit-sharing distributions were usually paid on invested capital, such as small business loans. The *mudaraba* contract was the most common method for providing such loans. Under the terms of the contract, the bank provided funds to entrepreneurs who had no collateral. Instead of paying interest on the loan, the entrepreneur paid a share of earnings, usually one-third, to the bank.

Since most of the risk was borne by the bank, entrepreneurs without collateral usually benefited more from *mudaraba* contracts than from traditional loans. Moreover, borrowers who did not normally qualify for a loan were occasionally able to access funds through *mudaraba* contracts. Critics observed that entrepreneurs could minimize the bank's return by incurring unnecessary business expenses, such as acquiring luxury vehicles or unnecessary technology. Although advocates countered that Islamic ethics would encourage entrepreneurs to deal honestly with banks, studies have shown that ethical motives have not always been effective, particularly "when a society expands and becomes heterogeneous."[10] Because lenders in *mudaraba* contracts lacked a high level of trust, they depended on monitoring to ensure that funds were properly utilized for their intended purpose. The use of monitoring, however, introduced additional agency costs that did not exist in traditional debt financing arrangements.[11]

Muslims could also invest in traditional dividend-bearing notes, which, in practice, were very similar to *mudaraba* contracts. Of particular importance was that payments were based on profit-sharing as opposed to a guaranteed return over a specific period of time.[12] Similarly, investment in common shares could be justified because any capital gains resulted from actual or potential earnings, while stockholders assumed business risks along with entrepreneurs and other shareholders.

In countries with historically high inflation, the value of non-interest-bearing deposits decreased over time. As a result, potential customers were reluctant to deposit funds when other instruments, such as purchasing gold or silver, offered greater security. Profit-sharing arrangements had the potential to mitigate the problem of inflation, but also resulted in losses during periods of negative earnings. Many depositors were unwilling to accept such risk and would either deposit funds in traditional banks or invest in less risky products.

---

[9]Ibid., pp. 43–44.

[10]Elias G. Kazarian, *Islamic Versus Traditional Banking: Financial Innovations in Egypt,* Westview Press, Boulder, CO, 1993, pp. 115–116.

[11]Paul S Mills and John R. Presley, *Islamic Finance: Theory and Practice,* Macmillan, London, 1999, p. 35.

[12]Ibid., pp. 15–16.

To meet the needs of risk-averse clients, most Islamic banks offered products that were nearly identical to those offered by non-Islamic banks. The most common financial instrument, accounting for up to 90 per cent of IBF activities, was *murabaha,* commonly translated as "markup."[13] Under *murabaha,* the bank purchased an asset and then sold it back to a client after adding a predetermined markup, usually equivalent to value of interest over the life of a loan. The purchaser would then proceed to pay for the asset in installments, while the asset itself was held as collateral.

By earning a predetermined fixed rate of return, *murabaha* was essentially equivalent to interest-based lending. As a result, some *Shari'a* scholars accused Islamic banks of using semantic devices to conceal *riba.* They also questioned the objectivity of *Shari'a* councils who were paid by the banks to issue *fatwas* in favor of questionable financial instruments, such as *murabaha,* which found little support in Islamic scripture and tradition.[14] In some places, opponents of the *murabaha* called for markup payments to be banned for being un-Islamic. The government of Sudan, for example, promised to ban markup accounts for Islamic banks operating within its territory. Experts warned that such actions would "cripple" local businesses that relied on "the high-liquidity and low-risk profile" offered by *murabaha* accounts.[15]

Another controversial investment alternative was Islamic bonds, known as *sukuk. Sukuk* were asset-backed Islamic financial certificates that provided fixed or floating rates of return. Although often described as the Islamic equivalent to bonds, *sukuk* differed from traditional bonds in several important ways. For example, *sukuk* could be used only to raise funds for the construction of specific and identifiable assets, and those assets were required to be utilized in some way by the *sukuk* holder (i.e. rented). In addition, *sukuk* could not be traded on the open market.[16] Yet, because *sukuk* offered investors a fixed rate of return without the inherent risks associated with a particular venture, some conservative scholars criticized *sukuk* certificates as a bold-faced attempt to evade the prohibition of *riba.*[17]

Not all Muslims adhered to IBF *fatwas.* Many, in fact, continued to prefer traditional western banking services over Islamic alternatives. In most Muslim countries, traditional banking prospered side by side with Islamic banking. In addition, a considerable number of wealthy Middle Eastern investors participated in offshore banking, particularly with Swiss banks, which were safe havens of choice during political and economic crises.[18] Among those who deposited savings in traditional interest-bearing bank accounts, a significant number refused to accept interest, providing a windfall of additional earnings for western-style banks.[19]

---

[13]Elias G. Kazarian, *Islamic Versus Traditional Banking: Financial Innovations in Egypt,* Westview Press, Boulder, CO, 1993, p. 227.

[14]Bill Maurer, *Mutual Life, Limited: Islamic Banking, Alternative Currencies, Lateral Reason,* Princeton University Press, Princeton, NJ, 2005, pp. 73–74.

[15]Frank Vogel and Samuel Hayes, *Islamic Law and Finance,* Kluwer Law International, The Hague, 1998, p. 9.

[16]A. Tariq, *Managing Financial Risks of Sukuk Structures,* unpublished Master's Thesis, Loughborough University, Leicester, U.K., 2004, pp. 20–23.

[17]"What Is Sukuk?," *Islamic Economics & Finance,* March 23, 2007, islamicbanking.worldmuslimmedia.com/what-is-sukuk/, accessed September 4, 2007.

[18]Frank Vogel and Samuel Hayes, *Islamic Law and Finance,* Kluwer Law International, The Hague, 1998 p. 6.

[19]Ibid., p. 25.

Modern Islamic Finance

The need for Islamic banking and finance grew out of the abundance of oil wealth generated in the Middle East beginning in the 1970s. Recent estimates placed the value of IBF investments at between $50 billion and $100 billion, and growing at an average annual rate of approximately 15 per cent.[20] Mirroring western finance, IBF centers included London and New York, but also several major cities in the Middle East and Asia, namely Dubai, Hong Kong and Singapore.

Local banks that offered Islamic financial products often lacked the sophistication and resources of large western banks. For example, the largest Islamic bank, Al Rajhi Bank of Saudi Arabia, at $21 billion in assets, ranked 286th among the world's largest publicly traded financial institutions.[21] By comparison, each of the top 10 banks had assets in excess of $1 trillion.

Muslims could also invest in non-Islamic products, provided the products did not violate Islamic law. A significant amount of wealth in the Middle East was already being invested in conventional products, but in an Islamic way. In such cases, the individual investor had the responsibility to determine whether a particular product was *Shari'a*. Islamic banking simplified this process by ensuring all products were approved through properly issued *fatwas*. For example, Dow Jones created an Islamic Market (DJIM) Index in 1999, which tracked the performance of stocks approved for Islamic investors worldwide.

Dow Jones ensured the reliability of the DJIM index by consulting a *Shari'a* board of Islamic scholars who had sufficient religious and financial training to make informed judgments. To be included in the index, a company did not have to be Islamic *per se,* as long as the principles of the company adhered to Islamic teachings, even if such adherence was unintentional.[22] Inversely, any company that may have produced or distributed banned products, such as alcohol, pork or pornography, was automatically excluded. Hotels, grocers and meat plants were automatically excluded because of the probability that these companies were engaged in prohibited activities. Companies that had a debt-to-equity ratio greater than 33 per cent were also excluded because of the prohibition of interest.

Dow Jones & Company was one of numerous western companies to cater to the needs of Muslims. In the 1990s, a growing cadre of American and European banks began to recognize the potential value in attracting Muslim clients, not only from the Middle East but from Europe, North America and Southeast Asia. Chase Manhattan Bank, Citibank and HSBC were among the better known brokers to set up Islamic desks. Many Muslims viewed western banks as more professional and more economically secure than their Middle Eastern counterparts and therefore welcomed their entry into the IBF market. As one analyst explained:

> Notable scandals and failures and the political impact of the Gulf War have cast a cloud over some domestic institutions. By comparison, western operators enjoy an aura of deep pockets, geographic diversification, and reputations for sophisticated, reliable and innovative banking.[23]

However, in the wake of the 2008 financial crisis, that perception had begun to change. Suddenly, Islamic banks were viewed as being safer than western banks. As banks across Europe and North America shed jobs and closed operations, Islamic banks experienced accelerated growth. For the first time, non-Muslim investors began to take a significant interest in Islamic investments.

---

[20]Ibid., p. 5.

[21]"The Forbes Global 2000," Forbes.com, March 29, 2007, accessed April 25, 2007.

[22]Bill Maurer, *Mutual Life, Limited: Islamic Banking, Alternative Currencies, Lateral Reason,* Princeton University Press, Princeton, NJ, 2005, pp. 105–106.

[23]Frank Vogel and Samuel Hayes, Islamic Law and Finance, Kluwer Law International, The Hague, 1998, p. 7.

The Role of Women
in Islamic Banking

Muslim women have always played an important role in business and finance. In the sixth century A.D., Khadījah bint Khuwaylid, the first wife of Prophet Muhammad (PBUH), was already a successful merchant and trader when she met her future husband. Later, she became the first convert to Islam and provided support to her husband in his effort to spread the faith.

In recent times, women have continued to play important roles in business and finance. In the UAE alone, banks employed 12,000 women (approximately 40 per cent of the workforce). However, most women were employed in lower level positions, and they often faced barriers to advancement, mostly because of career developmental needs and some cultural hindrances. Of the 536 branch managers in the UAE, 117 were women, and for many, branch manager was the highest level they could achieve within a bank.

Vohra recalled the first time she was interviewed for a position at an Islamic bank. She had worked for several years in commercial finance at a conventional financial institution where she had structured corporate credit to Fortune 500 clients.

> I came from an international finance background, and the first time I came to the UAE, I had an interview with an Islamic bank. They told me that I couldn't have the job because I was a woman and they did not employ women in front-end commercial roles. This is not something the religion lays down. . . . Muslim women have been involved in commerce or in business from the time of the religion's inception. Shortly thereafter I was employed by an Islamic Bank in Sharjah, which provided tremendous career support to women.

Vohra explained that other women faced similar issues:

> In Saudi Arabia, women still cannot assume the role of CEO [chief executive officer], and have moved outside the country to assume such roles in other commercial banks. There is no dearth of talent in this region. The greater issue in the Middle East lies with training and development of the larger masses of women in the commercial banking space, especially Islamic banking.

At the same time, banks increasingly saw women as an important market. A Saudi law that required a male member of the family to represent female members in investment decisions was lifted in 2004, giving women control over their assets for the first time. Nearly one-third of Saudi women had brokerage accounts, and 40 per cent of family run businesses were headed by women. Within the Gulf Cooperation Council (GCC), which included Saudi Arabia, the UAE, Bahrain, Oman, Kuwait and Qatar, women held approximately $40 billion in liquid assets. Vohra explained:

> Many studies have indicated that women are efficient at saving money and in Islamic countries, they feel a spiritual obligation to invest according to Islamic principles and therefore look to transacting with Islamic banks in the region within the ladies' section of these banks.

She also noted that "significant growth in female entrepreneurs and mature female investors has led to the need of more sophisticated Islamic products and services." These initiatives included "ladies' sections" in Islamic banks, and even the establishment of "ladies' banks" that catered exclusively to women.

Outside of the GCC, the situation was different. Malaysia had always been progressive in promoting the advancement of women into leadership roles through various programs. For example, Zeti Akhtar Aziz, governor of the Central Bank of Malaysia, has held senior level positions in finance since 1985. In 2004, she helped create the Institute of Islamic Banking and Finance, which offered doctoral degrees and post-graduate certificates in Islamic finance to both men and women.

Other prominent women in Islamic finance included Jamelah Jamaluddin, CEO of RHB Islamic Bank, Fozia Amanulla, CEO of EONCAP Islamic Bank, and Shamshad Akhtar, governor of the State Bank of Pakistan. Even *Shari'a* councils began to admit female Islamic scholars, beginning with Engku Rabiah Adawiah Engku Ali, a professor of Islamic law at Malaysia's International Islamic University.

THE FOUNDING OF DURRA

Durra began as an informal group of eight female Islamic bankers who wanted to expand the role of women bankers within the GCC, explained Vohra, who was one of the founding members. "We then went to Her Royal Highness of Sharjah and said 'We want to create a knowledge bank for women in banking.'" At the time, leaders in the GCC were already taking steps to promote the role of women in society. Vohra further noted that "The royalty in the UAE very strongly promote education and very strongly promote the role of women in economic development."

Her Royal Highness agreed to provide full support, not only for a knowledge bank but also for a global organization that, according to its mission statement, "[empowered] women to enhance their contribution to global economic development through a focused approach which optimizes their potential in the Islamic Banking industry."

To achieve that vision, it sought to do the following:

- Provide seminars, workshops and conferences internationally to raise awareness, impart knowledge and share best practices in Islamic finance.
- Launch certificate and degree programs specializing in Islamic finance in partnership with established educational institutions.
- Provide coaching and mentoring programs to develop "best in class" expertise.
- Participate in career fairs to attract a larger female participation in the Islamic banking industry globally.
- Partner with business women['s] associations to synergize and further leverage growth opportunities.
- Reward and recognize the contribution of women in the Islamic banking sector.

Vohra felt the best way to encourage women to study Islamic finance was to create separate courses.

> If we want more women to participate in Islamic banking, we have to have a system that makes them comfortable and [is] aligned to cultural sensitivities, so that they are willing to come and learn.

The biggest hurdle facing Durra was finding sponsors for the organization to have a significant impact on the industry. One solution was to create awareness about the organization at public forums. In her effort to spread awareness, Vohra traveled extensively to universities and banks around the world.

The next step was to create a website where members could exchange ideas and learn about career opportunities. Vohra also wanted the website to include registration tools and the ability to collect member fees. It also needed a way to verify the identity and qualifications of applicants. Other proposed features included the following:

- Discussion boards—a moderated social networking application similar to LinkedIn and other professional networking sites.
- News—up-to-date news feeds of stories on Islamic finance pulled from other websites and news services.
- Feature articles—reports written by members and professionally reviewed and edited.
- Job board—listings of available positions in Islamic finance and related fields.
- Career advice and mentoring.
- Educational opportunities—listings of available courses and certificate programs in Islamic finance at recognized colleges and universities, and offerings of online continuing education courses.
- Events—listings of international seminars, chapter gatherings and informal gatherings.

The website could be used to capture data on the number of women working in management positions in Islamic banking, their positions and their level of education and training. This data would help Durra to identify gaps, so that programs could be modified to meet the specific needs of the community. Finally, the site needed to be in both English and Arabic to ensure the broadest reach.

As Vohra neared the end of her U.S. visit, where she had spoken to potential academic partners, banks and public officials, she wondered what further actions she should take to promote Durra.

Clearly, a professional website was a priority. Yet several unanswered questions remained, such as how to evaluate the ability of web developers to provide a quality site, how much the development costs would be, and who should be responsible for ongoing service and maintenance? She also began to consider additional steps she might need to take to promote the launch of Durra in Europe, Australia and other areas of the world.

MIA, PHILIPPINES

Steve McKenzie was feeling queasy as the 4x4 SUV hit another pothole. The village of San Hagon was still a three-hour drive away and he had no idea what awaited them there once they arrived. McKenzie, a management consultant from New Jersey, was part of a team that was working on a pilot project instigated by a Danish non-governmental organization (NGO) to alleviate poverty in a remote fishing village in the Philippines. He thought to himself, "Is it going to be possible to re-establish the distribution channel they had worked so hard to setup over the last 16 months?" Fish deliveries from San Hagon had abruptly stopped more than a month ago. McKenzie had been temporarily hired by the NGO's outgoing country director on short notice to head the fact-finding mission.

THE PHILIPPINES

The Philippines was first put on the map by Portuguese adventurer Magellan, working for the Spanish throne, on March 16, 1521. The Philippines had become a Spanish colony and was the first country to be named after a sovereign, Phillip II of Spain.[1] Spanish rule had continued until 1898 when the Philippines had become an American colony following the Spanish-American War for the stately sum of $20 million. In 1942 during WWII, the Philippines had fallen under Japanese occupation and was liberated by American and Filipino forces under the leadership of General Douglas MacArthur in a fiercely contested battle that raged on between 1944 and 1945. The Philippines attained its independence on July 4, 1946, and had a

[1]www.ualberta.ca/~vmitchel/fw2.html, accessed September 7, 2008.

functioning democratic system.[2] The Philippines Archipelago consists of 7,100 islands, covering an area of 299,735 square kilometers, and is slightly larger than Arizona. The capital city of Manila is situated on the largest Philippine island of Luzon. The Philippines has a gross domestic product (GDP) per capita of $3,400.[3] The percentage of the population of the Philippines living below US$2 a day was 45.2 per cent in 2006.[4]

PHILIPPINE BUSINESS ENVIRONMENT

Research conducted in 2009 showed that the Philippines was ranked 140th for ease of doing business and 155th for starting a business, out of a total of 178 countries. It took an average 15 procedures and a total of 52 days to complete business startup procedures in the Philippines, compared to six procedures and 44.2 days and 5.8 procedures and 13.4 days for the same process in Asia and Organisation for Economic Co-operation and Development (OECD) countries, respectively.[5] The Philippines had the second lowest savings and investment as share of GDP ratio in Asia[6] (see Exhibit 1).

PHILIPPINE FISHING INDUSTRY

The Philippines has total territorial waters of 2.2 million square kilometers, of which coastal waters comprise 266,000 square kilometers and coastal reef area (10 to 20 fathoms deep, where reef fishing takes place) comprise 27,000 square kilometers.[7]

Exhibit 1 Philippine Savings and Investment as Share of GDP 1996–2001 Average (%)

	Savings/ GDP	Investment/ GDP
China, People's Republic of	40.1	37.8
Korea	33.5	31.8
Malaysia	45.2	33.4
India	22.9	24
Taiwan	26.1	23.7
Bangladesh	19.7	21.5
Thailand	32.5	28
Philippines	18.9	20.4
Indonesia	26.9	23.2
Pakistan	12.5	17.1

Source: www.adb.org/Documents/Books/ADO/2002/Update/ad02002update.pdf, accessed November 18, 2008.

In 2003, the Philippines ranked eighth among the top fish-producing countries in the world with its total production of 3.62 million metric tons of fish, crustaceans, mollusks and aquatic plants (including seaweed). The production constituted 2.5 per cent of the total world production of 146.27 million metric tons.[8]

The fishing industry's contribution to the country's GDP was 2.3 per cent and 4.2 per cent, at current and constant prices, respectively. The industry employed a total of 1,614,368 fishing

---

[2]https://www.cia.gov/library/publications/the-world-factbook/geos/rp.html, accessed September 7, 2008.

[3]Ibid.

[4]www.adb.org/Documents/Books/Key_Indicators/2008/Country.asp, accessed December 25, 2008.

[5]www.doingbusiness.org/ExploreEconomies/?economyid=153, accessed November 15, 2008.

[6]www.adb.org/Documents/Books/ADO/2002/Update/ad02002update.pdf, accessed December 18, 2008.

[7]www.scribd.com/doc/354869/2005-Fisheries-Profile, accessed December 5, 2008.

[8]www.scribd.com/doc/354869/2005-Fisheries-Profile, accessed November 15, 2008.

operators nationwide,[9] of which the artisanal fisheries sector accounted for 1,371,676.[10]

Artisanal fishing operations were typically family-based and used smaller craft. There were a total of 469,807 fishing boats in the Philippines, of which 292,180 were non-motorized and 177,627 were motorized.[11] Fish was not only an important source of nutrition, but as fishing did not require landownership or special permits it was an employment of last resort for people who had no other means of subsistence.

MIA, DENMARK

MIA was established in Denmark in 1975 by wealthy businessman Hagen Nordstrom, who dedicated the NGO to his wife Mia and made fighting poverty his life's work. (MIA stood for "beloved" in Danish.) MIA had initially focused solely on poverty-alleviating projects in Africa and had expanded its operations to Latin America and the Caribbean only in the early 1990s.

The grandson of Nordstrom, Gillis Nordstrom, had taken over as MIA chairman in 2004 on the eve of the Bander Aceh Tsunami of December 26, 2004, which devastated Southeast Asia and killed as many as 130,000 people.[12] Nordstrom had taken initiative and redirected MIA to focus on disaster recovery and poverty alleviation projects in Southeast Asia.

MIA had established an office in Manila in January 2006, and the young Danish development economist Borje Petersen was hired to manage the MIA Philippines office. Petersen was paid a starting salary of $75,000 a year plus housing, slightly below average for a comparable development economist position.

Petersen knew that MIA's attention was focused on Indonesia and Malaysia, which had been the hardest hit by the tsunami, and was anxious to carve out a position for MIA Philippines by designing an exceptional project. As the expansion into Asia was the pet project of MIA's chairman, Petersen felt assured that funding would be easily appropriated and even expedited.

Petersen knew that the average overseas posting for a development economist for MIA was two years and had quickly established contact with local and international stakeholders and set up numerous meetings with large development project counterparts such as the Asian Development Bank, the World Bank and the German development aid organization GFZ to get an expedited understanding of the Philippines and its unique needs.

Based on the initial research, Petersen had decided that, whereas an agricultural project would be feasible, it would take a long time to realize and the outcome could be complicated given the Philippines' proneness to be hit by typhoons. Petersen's research had revealed that small-scale aquaculture projects had been successfully implemented in the Philippines in the past. However, there were hardly any projects to speak of directed at artisanal fishing, and picking up on the vested opportunity and his desire to deliver fast results and prove himself worthy of the task that MIA and its chairman demanded, he had chosen to design a project helping artisanal fishermen.

Petersen had researched the possibility of helping a fishing village close to Manila and the search for the ideal village had come to a successful ending when MIA's driver, Vicente Tubo, had mentioned how some of his distant cousins fished for a living in a fishing village seven to nine hours by car from Manila. A fact-finding mission to the village Barangay San Hagon was undertaken and the village was thus chosen as the beneficiary of MIA's pilot project in the Philippines.

[9]NSO 2002 Census for Fisheries.

[10]www.scribd.com/doc/354869/2005-Fisheries-Profile, accessed November 15, 2008.

[11]www.scribd.com/doc/354869/2005-Fisheries-Profile, accessed December 5, 2008.

[12]www.cityu.edu.hk/searc/tsunami/index.html, accessed November 18, 2008.

BARANGAY SAN HAGON

Barangay San Hagon boasted 125 households and had a resident population of 625. San Hagon lay on the south coast of Luzon, the largest island of the Philippines.

The Barangay was the smallest administrative division in the Philippines and stemmed from the Spanish "Barrio."[13] Barangay San Hagon was administered by a local government unit (LGU) and consisted of seven Barangay council members and a chairman. The chairman of Barangay San Hagon was Rafael Buenaventura, age 59, who had held office for more than a decade.

Fishing villages in the Philippines were very vulnerable to external risk, especially natural calamities such as typhoons, flooding and fish kills, which severely affected their financial situation.

BARANGAY SAN HAGON'S ECONOMY

Fishing was the main occupation of the village. Secondary occupations included rice farming, fruit and vegetable growing and livestock raising. The service sector consisted of boat builders, mechanics, barbers, tailors, drivers and Sari-Sari store operators (mom and pop–type convenience stores). Fishing was undertaken exclusively by men, whereas most of the other occupations and post-fishing activities were undertaken by the women of the village.

The village boasted 12 overseas workers employed as unqualified laborers in different parts of the Arabian Peninsula who sent back remittance payments. It was believed that more than 10 million Filipinos worked overseas and supported their families with remittance payments. The daily income for the San Hagon fisherman was approximately $1 per day.

The fishermen of San Hagon used "banka boats," the traditional outrigger type of boat used in Southeast Asia. Whereas some fishermen had utilized traditional means of fishing with hook and line, gill nets and bamboo fish traps, the majority chose to use blast and cyanide fishing.

Blast fishing consisted of throwing an explosive charge or a stick of dynamite into the sea. The explosion instantly killed every living organism within its range including coral reef. A number of the fish would float and the fishermen would scoop them up. Quite a large number of the dead fish, however, would stay submerged. Homemade explosives from readily available materials such as powdered potassium nitrate or an ammonium nitrate and kerosene mixture packed in glass bottles were often used. These mixtures were often unstable and exploded prematurely, maiming or killing fishermen. Each village had a number of limbless fishermen and a story of how an explosive device had killed a fellow fisherman.[14]

Cyanide fishing consisted of squirting cyanide into the caves/dwellings of the fish in the coral reef. Fishermen used makeshift pumps, which pumped oxygen down a plastic tube, to dive into the sea. The method was dangerous and most fishermen had experienced some form of bends while diving. The cyanide killed up to 75 per cent of the fish on contact. Cyanide also killed the coral reef.[15] Once the coral reef died, fish were displaced as a result of the break in the food chain and lack of protection.

Blast and cyanide fishing did not need any real skill and fishing knowledge and even though

[13]www.i-site.ph/Factfinder/barangay.html, accessed December 23, 2008.

[14]www.panda.org/about_wwf/what_we_do/marine/problems/problems_fishing/destructive_fishing, accessed December 24, 2008.

[15]www.panda.org/about_wwf/what_we_do/species/news/stories/index.cfm?uNewsID=5563, accessed December 23, 2008.

both methods were illegal and there were numerous laws in place, it was impossible to effectively enforce these laws.

SAN HAGON'S CAPITAL ASSETS

The village of San Hagon had basic capital assets on which it based its competitive position. Most fishing villages in the region had similar capital resources.

Human Capital

Education: Most of the villagers had some high school education.

Skills: Fishing and farming skills were learnt from an informal network of fellow villagers, friends, etc.

Employment: Most villagers had multiple occupations in order to generate enough income to make a living.

Social Capital

Access to governmental and non-governmental information sources: The village had limited access to governmental and non-governmental organizations for the dissemination of knowledge. Information was disseminated from an informal network of fellow fishermen, friends and relatives.

Role of women: The women of the village were active in the work force as a source of free labor but had little decision-making power.

Natural Capital

Access to natural resources: The villagers had free access to the ocean, land and water.

Resource ownership: Nearly all villagers owned their small plots of land where they farmed or raised livestock.

Financial Capital

Access to financing: The village had limited access to public or private financing.

Savings potential: The villagers had limited savings potential due to their limited income.

Income generation: The subsistence fishing, farming and livestock raising activities of the village coupled with services provided by the villagers allowed for subsistence living conditions.

Remittances: The village had 12 overseas workers who regularly sent remittances to support their families.

Physical Capital

Access to electricity: The village owned an old diesel generator that provided electricity. The generator required frequent maintenance work and was out of commission frequently when there was no money to purchase diesel fuel. This occurred due to lack of income as a result of poor fishing results, increased expenditures during the months when school-aged children needed supplies and in times when collecting past dues owed by households became a problem.

Access to modes of communication: Due to its remote location and small population, the village did not have access to phone lines or wireless phone service. The nearest phone line was located in San Jose, a larger settlement that was three hours away by car.

Access to transportation: San Hagon only had internal dirt roads and road access was a problem, especially in the rainy season. Roads connecting San Hagon to the outer world were mostly unpaved and it was difficult to navigate the roads at night or during the rainy season, which was five to six months of the year. Manila, the capital of the Philippines, was located seven to nine hours away by car.

Whereas most people in the village walked, the bicycle/tricycle was the preferred mode of transport. The better-off households boasted small motorcycles, of which there were more than a dozen.

Transport to and from the village was provided by a Jeepney (an extended U.S. military jeep left over from WWII), the traditional form of public transport in the Philippines operated by one of the villagers that usually left for San Jose early in the morning and returned in the afternoon. Jeepneys transported people, fruits and vegetables, livestock, etc.[16]

Access to safe water supply: The village did not have running water and depended on numerous deep fresh water wells for its fresh water supply.

Home ownership: More than 95 per cent of households owned their own dwellings. The better-off households had cement walls and galvanized iron sheet roofing.

Boat ownership: Banka boat ownership was close to 100 per cent. Approximately one third of these bankas were motorized.

Other: Most households owned modest household appliances and facilities, such as televisions, radios and electric fans.

Existing Modus Operandi

Under the prevailing conditions, fishermen would put aside enough to feed their families and sell the rest of the catch at the village square or exchange it against fruits, vegetables, rice and other staple goods. The price of fish was not fixed and would fluctuate when there was an oversupply and the barter equivalent of other products would go up in price. Prices of fish and other goods were also affected by delays in the arrival of supply Jeepneys, which supplied the village's three Sari-Sari stores.

Commerce with other villages was limited, as these villages had a similar economic setup. Few buyers ever came to San Hagon due to the remoteness of the village and the poor road conditions. The few that came were treated suspiciously, as there had been numerous occasions when smaller buyers had taken the fish on consignment but had not paid for them. The larger traders avoided San Hagon completely and opted to do business with villages that were more accessible.

Fish was an easily perishable commodity and transporting fish for more than a couple of hours without refrigeration or cold storage was not possible due to the prevailing heat. There was no access to ice in the region and the cost of a refrigerated vehicle was beyond the village's means. Some fishermen chose to dry excess fish and sell it locally, even though dried fish made less profit than fresh fish, or consume it themselves when fresh fish supplies were low.

Even though the villagers complained at times, they had accepted the lifestyle they led, as they did not have the financial means or knowledge to alter their situation. The only other alternative was to leave the village, migrate to larger cities and look for jobs, of which there were only low-paying, menial ones. The mantra, "Give a man a fish; you have fed him for a day. Teach a man to fish; and you have fed him for a lifetime," had become a reality when MIA had chosen to help the village of San Hagon.

The village inhabitants had seen the effects of NGO assistance and how it had transformed the livelihood of other fishing villages. The appearance of a European NGO was a blessing and meant an influx of much-needed money.

Diving Villages and Environmental Protection

A number of fishing villages in the region had made the transition from fishing village to diving village with the help of foreign NGOs. Diving villages were villages that catered to the scuba diving expat community and wealthy Filipinos who could afford the sport. Fishermen in these villages had been transformed into tour guides and diving instructors. The transformed villages earned up to 10 times more income and helped to protect the environment.

---

[16]www.philippines.hvu.nl/jeepneys1.htm, accessed December 24, 2008.

Project San Hagon: "Hitting Many Birds With One Stone"

After initial assessment and consideration of its own capabilities, MIA had considered converting San Hagon into a diving village. Petersen, however, had later shied away from a tourism-related project for three reasons:

1. Competition: There were already two villages in the region that had already achieved name recognition and were much easier to access than San Hagon.

2. Damaged product: A significant portion of San Hagon's coral reef had been damaged.

3. Time factor: It would take a long time to transform San Hagon to a diving village.

Instead, MIA had designed a project that would entail the livelihood improvement of the village, empower women and encourage environmental protectionism. Petersen had remembered the old Danish saying "hit many birds with one stone" as he designed the project.

Project Identification

MIA had proposed that in return for stopping blast and cyanide fishing and reverting back to traditional means of fishing, the village would receive a grant to establish a fishing cooperative, construct a fish processing/cooperative building with all office furnishings and receive a new diesel generator, fish processing equipment, packaging equipment and training on how to process and package fish. In addition, MIA would copyright a brand name for the village, have all marketing communication materials prepared and arrange shelf space as the exclusive supplier of malls and supermarkets in Metro Manila.

It was foreseen that reverting back to traditional methods of fishing would decrease the amount of fish that were caught, but establishing San Hagon as a direct supplier to large buyers

would garner top prices and substantially increase income and offset any losses.

MIA's project intended to emphasize the importance of fish as a healthy food, and highlight fishing as a generator of employment and income and as a means to protect the environment (see Exhibit 2).

Exhibit 2 Project San Hagon Fact Sheet

Objectives	
1) Increase $1/day income to $4	
2) Integrate more women into the workforce	
3) Promote environment conservation	
Project Cost Forecast	$
Procurement	18,000
Construction	5,000
Training	1,500
Salaries	
MIA local consultants/month	1,500
SHFC management salaries/month	230
Operational Cost	
Truck rental/month	850
Truck driver salary/month	375
SHFC workers' salaries/month	1,000
Fuel/month	3,500
Packaging material/month	250
Additional Costs	
Procurement	4,000
Additional driver salary/month	375
Additional fuel/month	1,250
Execution	
Mr. Petersen, MIA director, The Philippines	
Mr. Perez, project manager, San Hagon	

PROJECT IMPACT ASSESSMENT

Economic impact: The business model would allow households to increase their income from $1 to $4 per day. Fish that was not in demand by the cooperative could be used for household consumption or sold/bartered/dried.

Social impact: Women would become a part of the workforce and earn salaries for the first time in their lives and have disposable income. The extra income would also help women become more independent.

Environmental impact: The destructive blast and cyanide fishing methods would cease. This would halt the destruction of the coral reef and help increase fish stocks. Fishermen would become environmental conservationists and promote the concept of sustainability.

PROJECT PREPARATION

A knowledgeable and experienced team was assembled to manage project San Hagon. Ricardo Perez, age 65, was hired to head the local team, help with local authorities and overcome language barriers. Perez had worked as a marketing director for the San Miguel Company, a large Philippine conglomerate with a focus on the food and beverage industry, who were the makers of the famous "San Mig"

beer. Perez had been consulting with small- to mid-sized Filipino companies ever since he retired at age 60.

MIA also planned to rely on its extensive database and intranet to share knowledge and achieve maximum participation in the project. Any MIA employee, regardless of rank, experience and location, could comment on projects online. Petersen posted a Gantt chart and encouraged questions and guidance from his peers (see Exhibit 3). The only restriction placed on the project by MIA was that MIA could not engage in direct or indirect payments according to its by-laws.

Three-year financial projections for the San Hagon Fishing Cooperative (SHFC) had shown that the project would make a small profit in year one and then realize its full potential in year two and year three once the learning curve constraints had been overcome (see Exhibit 4).

PROJECT APPROVAL

MIA Philippines had completed project preparations and gotten project approval and funding from MIA headquarters. The project was a first for MIA, as the NGO usually focused more on gender and education projects.

Perez and his team had prepared the application for local approval and had submitted the

---

Exhibit 3 Project San Hagon Gantt Chart

ID	Task Name	Start	Finish	Duration	Apr 2007				May 2007				Jun 2007				Jul 2007				Aug 2007				Sep 2007		
					1/4	8/4	15/4	22/4	29/4	6/5	13/5	20/5	27/5	3/6	10/6	17/6	24/6	1/7	8/7	15/7	22/7	29/7	5/8	12/8	19/8	26/8	2/9	9/9	16/9	23/9
1	Permits	4/2/2007	5/25/2007	8w																									
2	Formation of SHFC	4/2/2007	6/22/2007	12w																									
3	Procurement	6/11/2007	7/6/2007	4w																									
4	Construction	6/11/2007	7/6/2007	4w																									
5	Training	7/26/2007	8/1/2007	1w																									
6	Test packaging	7/31/2007	8/6/2007	1w																									

Exhibit 4 Project San Hagon Three-Year Financial Projections

	Year 1	Year 2	Year 3
REVENUE	255,200	382,800	382,800
Cost of goods sold	236,880	236,880	236,880
Fixed cost	12,600	12,600	12,600
TOTAL COST	249,480	249,480	249,480
INCOME BEFORE TAXES	5,720	133,320	133,320

Note: All amounts in US$ at $1 = 56 Filipino pesos

Fiscal year ends December 31

application to the local Fisheries and Aquatic Resources Management Council (FARMC) in San Jose for approval. The FARMC was the policymaking body for the fisheries and aquatic resources of the Philippines. The vetting process by the local FARMC had been completed after two months, after numerous on-site meetings and presentations. Petersen had been frustrated at the speed of the approval process and had directed Perez to intercede frequently. Petersen had thought to himself, "We are extending a grant and transferring knowledge and still there is all this slow-moving bureaucracy to deal with."

Research

Concurrently with the project permit applications, MIA had conducted one month of catch research in San Hagon to determine the quantity of fish caught by the fishermen. The survey had revealed that it would be possible to catch on average 1,250 kilograms per day (2,750 pounds per day) of prime quality fish for processing.

PROJECT SAN HAGON VALUE CHAIN

MIA had undertaken a value chain analysis of the project process and assessed how the analysis could be used to improve the project performance (see Exhibit 5). Breaking down the cost

structure had further revealed that the cost structure was typically top-loaded by ingoing logistics and that the major expenditure was fuel (see Exhibit 6).

PROJECT START-UP

Petersen had felt that the slow application process had cost MIA too much time and he had decided to do things the "Danish way" at the project implementation phase, instilling tight controls, frequent meetings and time management to speed up the project.

MIA had concluded that the key success factors were to:

1. Provide grants to acquire new assets.

2. Transfer knowledge and train stakeholders in acquiring and maintaining new capabilities.

3. Increase the value chain contribution of San Hagon villagers.

4. Package and transport a differentiated product to urban centers where there would be demand for the product.

Two teams were formed and the work was divided up as follows:

Team One: Product development and packaging

Team Two: Transportation, distribution, and advertising and promotion

Exhibit 5 Value Chain Analysis

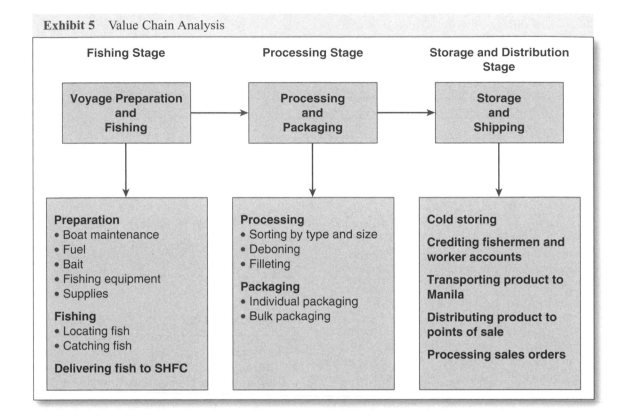

Product Development and Packaging

Tuna, prawns, lobsters, groupers and crabs were chosen as the product types that would be most in demand in Manila. Focus was to be placed on tuna and grouper fish, the two favorite types of fish in the Philippines.

Research had determined that the demand in Manila for chilled, packaged fish fillets was similar to demand in American/European urban centers. The product appealed to the "A" income level: upwardly mobile, health-conscious customers that had time constraints.

Concurrently the team had researched basic packaging machinery that could be operated and maintained under adverse climatic conditions with ease by the fishermen. The packaging

machinery, along with stainless steel fish processing work stations and other equipment, was purchased by MIA, transported and set up in San Hagon.

Transportation, Distribution, and Advertising and Promotion

A small refrigerated truck was leased for a year along with a driver to transport the catch from San Hagon to Metro Manila. It was planned that the cooperative would generate enough cash to purchase the truck in due time and that a San Hagon villager would be employed to replace the hired driver in the near future.

The team had come up with the brand name "ISSAGA," which in the local Tagalog dialect

Exhibit 6 Value Chain Cost Structure

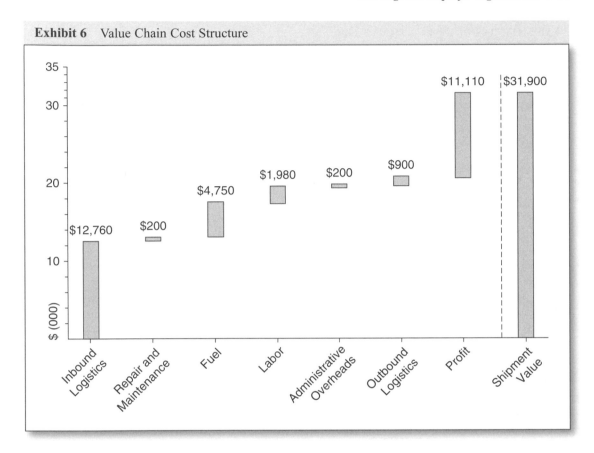

was short for "Isda Sakdal Gawad" or most-prized fish. "ISSAGA" had been registered as a brand name, art work had been designed and packaging materials and labels were printed.

Petersen had personally helped with the marketing arrangements, and the venerated HUI malls and supermarkets in Manila had agreed to support the project and provide free shelf space. Petersen had met William Hui, a leading businessman of Chinese decent, at a social function at the Danish embassy. Getting shelf space in a Manila supermarket was in itself a great feat, as acquiring retail space in Philippine supermarkets was difficult, time consuming and expensive.

HUI malls had also agreed to promote ISSAGA-branded fish products at points of sale. Hui, Perez and countless others had called in favors, and Manila TV stations, newspapers and magazines had agreed to support the project and showcase their corporate social citizenship by providing free public relations.

The project would streamline the distribution cycle and increase profit margins for both supplier and buyer (see Exhibit 7).

With most of the work at the lower end of the distribution chain completed, the focus had been shifted to the top end and MIA had directed the fishermen of San Hagon to form a fishing cooperative. MIA and other stakeholders needed a formal counterpart they could address and it was hoped that being part of a formal organization would instill a sense of ownership and result in commitment and responsibility on the part of the villagers.

Exhibit 7 Distribution Cycle Analysis

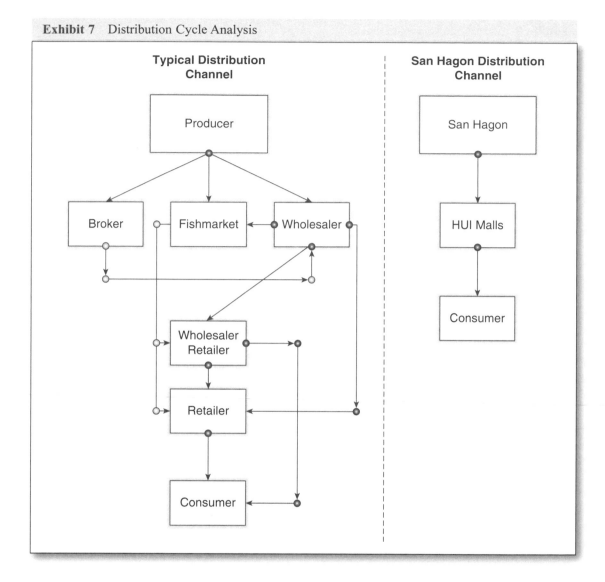

SAN HAGON FISHING COOPERATIVE

Chairman Buenaventura was chosen as the president of the newly formed SHFC. His two sons-in-law were appointed as manager and as treasurer of the cooperative, respectively. A basic contract was signed between MIA and the SHFC depicting the scope of the project, registration of fixed assets and depreciation scheduling.

MIA insisted from the onset that all fishermen join the fishing cooperative. One hundred per cent membership to the fishing cooperative was important because:

1. It was necessary to aggregate the catch of the village to make it feasible for the catch to be sold to the buyer HUI malls.

2. MIA wanted all stakeholders in San Hagon to benefit from the poverty-alleviation project.

STAKEHOLDER CONFLICT

MIA had initially donated $5,000 to the cooperative, and a basic building large enough to house the fish processing and packaging line, with cement walls and a corrugated steel roof, was quickly constructed. The building work was done by the villagers, who received a wage in return for their labor.

The first disagreement had occurred when Buenaventura had insisted that he receive $150 and the other cooperative employees receive monthly salaries of $100 as remuneration for the work that they would provide. MIA had initially balked at the salary demand and had threatened to call off the project. Buenaventura had, however, remained persistent and Petersen, after two weeks of deliberations and absolute inertia on the part of the villagers, had directed Perez to negotiate the demand in an attempt to rescue the project. An agreement for $100 a month for Buenaventura and $65 for his sons-in-law had been thus reached to be paid for the duration of a year.

The next conflict had arisen when Buenaventura did not want to fully disclose how much it had cost to build the cooperative building. MIA had later learnt that Buenaventura had thrown a "fiesta," a Philippine celebration that included free drinks and "lechon" pork roast on charcoal, to celebrate the new building.

At this stage, Petersen had started to wonder if he had made a serious mistake in choosing San Hagon as the pilot project and Perez as project manager. Afraid of the consequences to his career if he terminated the project, he had decided to push on even if it meant accepting additional demands.

Demands for help were frequent. Villages neighboring San Hagon had heard about the project and the MIA office received numerous phone calls daily asking MIA to extend its help to other villages. MIA had been busy turning down the inquiries, citing limited resources.

Time was a resource of which Petersen did not have plenty. He was often frustrated at the speed at which things happened in the Philippines. Project manager Perez seemed competent enough

and had vast amounts of experience and was technically adapt. He couldn't decide whether the slow progress was a result of Perez's speed or the inability or unwillingness of the San Hagon cooperative council to hurry things along. His frustration increased, as with each passing month he was not able to report progress to MIA headquarters.

Mindful of his standing at MIA Denmark and in his quest to speed up the project, Petersen had started to adopt a more confrontational approach, especially at the weekly project coordination meetings with Perez and the rest of the team. Perez always reported how much progress they were making. Perez and the rest of the team continuously assured Petersen that this was how business was conducted in the Philippines. Petersen was tired of hearing this. The other nerve-wracking problem was that the word "no" did not exist in the Philippine language. It was considered rude to say "no" and hence every question and every inquiry got a positive answer. There were, however, different shades of "yes," with some meaning "no," some meaning "maybe" and some which really meant "yes." It had taken Petersen more than six months to figure this out. He instructed all his employees not to feel embarrassed to say "no" to him. But that had only resulted in further embarrassing his employees. He sometimes felt that he was getting nowhere. With only the one active project to show for, Petersen needed to quickly complete this project and start new projects if he was to stand a chance of getting promoted and assuming greater responsibilities in a bigger MIA office.

Working at MIA had begun to feel like a tug-of-war between himself and the Filipino staff, with Petersen trying to quicken the pace and the staff slowing him down at every turn. Petersen wished that Perez would take more initiative and use his decision-making power rather than run even the smallest decisions by him first. At times he had begun to suspect that Perez was slowing down the project intentionally to keep receiving his salary longer. Salaries in the Philippines were low compared to those in Europe or America, especially in retirement, and after making $1,000 to $1,500 as a marketing director in San Miguel, Perez was only making $300 in retirement. The $700 salary MIA was paying him was quite a boost to his income.

RICARDO PEREZ

Perez had felt that he urgently needed to complete the project. He had chosen to continue working well into retirement, as his pension payment was not sufficient enough to maintain his lifestyle and put his youngest daughter through college.

Perez had completed his bachelor of arts degree at the University of the Philippines, and had obtained a prestigious certificate for food service management at Cornell University, New York, United States. He had interviewed with MIA and accepted its job offer, because foreign NGOs usually paid better than their Filipino counterparts and, more importantly, on time.

Before retirement, Perez had managed more than 175 employees. Even though the San Hagon project was basic compared to what he was accustomed to managing and even though the MIA country manager was young enough to be his son, the pay was generous. Perez had seen himself as advisor and mentor to the young Petersen and had tried to show him the way business was done in the Philippines. He had interceded frequently to expedite the permission process and facilitated MIA's dealings with the San Hagon fishing cooperative. True to Philippine culture, Perez had always shown the utmost respect for Petersen, especially in public, and portrayed him as the all-powerful leader of MIA. Having young Petersen make all decisions had been a part of his show of respect and deference to Petersen's authority.

Young Petersen had, however, been difficult to deal with. The whole project had taken an unpleasant turn, as Petersen had gotten extremely confrontational at meetings. Perez had heard about the difficulties of working with Americans and Europeans. Filipinos did not like confrontation.

"Pakikisama" (group loyalty) and the importance of maintaining social harmony were a part of his management style and disagreement or interpersonal tension of any sort at the workplace was extremely distasteful for Perez. Petersen had caused him "hiya" (embarrassment) in front of the rest of the team. His team, while staying silent during meetings, had approached him afterwards and empathized with him.

Perez had felt elated when the planning stage was over and the project had entered the implementation stage, which was more in his comfort zone. Perez had designed the new product-to-market process and ensured that he would spend most of his time out of the office and avoiding Petersen.

NEW PRODUCT-TO-MARKET PROCESS

Deboning, Filleting and Packaging

In order to add value to the product and to offset the cost of cleaning and filleting the fish at a higher cost by HUI employees, it was planned that the deboning, filleting and packaging would be done in San Hagon. The cooperative had called upon the women of the village who were experienced in preparing fish to help with processing the catch. It was planned that women in the village interested in the opportunity would be paid in return for the quantity of fish they processed. If demand for the work outweighed supply, there would be a waiting list and all interested women would get their chance to earn extra income when their turn came. Once deboned and filleted, the fish would be individually packaged in sealed cellophane packets and packed in 40-kilogram containers.

The SHFC encouraged all fishermen to bring in their catch to the cooperative early in the morning, where the catch was assessed and weighed according to the product needs of HUI malls for the week. Each fisherman had an account at the SHFC and his account was credited according to the daily catch brought in. The fishermen were free to do whatever they wanted with the catch not purchased by HUI malls. HUI malls were only interested in selling the finest quality fish in two of their exclusive high-end malls. Second- and third-tier fish were delivered to the remaining five mid-market HUI malls in Metro Manila.

As a differentiating factor, the project called for the product to be sold chilled. Upscale customers in Manila preferred chilled and filleted fish because they felt it was safer than fresh fish and easier to prepare.

Storage and Transport

Taking into account the problematic supply of electricity and high cost of establishing a cold chain, which would have required a substantial cold storage facility investment in the village, and in line with providing sustainable low-technology solutions, it was planned that the fish would be stored in a refrigerated truck which operated its cooling unit 24 hours per day and would be used as both a transport and storage facility. The refrigerated truck would make daily trips to Manila and distribute the product.

Sales and Distribution

HUI malls had insisted that the allocated shelves be stocked by the San Hagon cooperative. The driver would make deliveries and stock the shelves of seven different HUI malls in Manila. Fish deliveries would be made on a consignment basis and payments based on real sales were to be made to San Hagon on a weekly basis. The model had some problems, as payment by HUI malls was delayed.

HUI MALLS

William Hui had been one of the facilitators of the project. By providing free shelf space for San Hagon, he had received free public relations and showcased the corporate social responsibility of

his company. HUI malls had financially benefited as well, receiving good-quality filleted fish at bargain prices without having to invest in setting up or managing procurement and processing operations. Hui's business savvy had become even more apparent when he was approached by a reputable Japanese buyer who had recently purchased ISSAGA fish at one of his malls and had inquired about selling the product in Japan.

IMPLEMENTATION PROBLEMS

Under the careful guidance of Perez, the fishermen had conducted the first limited packaging test runs. The process was fraught with problems at first. Deboning and filleting fish commercially was very different from filleting for self-consumption. At first the SHFC had wanted to package all kinds of fish, regardless of size and quality. HUI malls had rejected at least 25 per cent of the initial shipments before the SHFC had bowed to the quality standards set forth by HUI malls. Spillage and spoilage was another problem. Nearly 15 per cent of produce was lost in this way. This had been due to refrigeration problems and the freshness of the fish.

Fish was a sensitive product and had a very short shelf life unless stored properly and it had become clear that not all fishermen brought in their catch in the morning. Sometimes the truck was late in picking up the day's catch, which led to late deliveries.

Aggregating enough supply to make the business run profitably was an issue at first. Even though all fishermen had joined the cooperative, supply problems due to adverse weather conditions and sometimes due to the complacency of the fishermen had resulted in the shipment truck making a loss nearly 50 per cent of the time.

Once the product was on the supermarket shelf however, it sold well. "But the process of getting the product on the shelf is inefficient to such a degree that the cooperative is making a loss," Petersen had thought when conducting an interim project evaluation.

INTERIM PROJECT EVALUATION

Perez had put his vast experience to good use and had intervened to iron out the problems. The logistic problem was solved by hiring two new drivers from the village to man the truck. The initial driver's contract was terminated. MIA purchased and donated a second-hand refrigerated truck body with a powerful diesel-operated air conditioner, which was used to store the daily catch if the truck was not available to pick up or deliver the product. Perez's interventions had worked and the profits had started to seep in.

PROJECT COMPLETION REPORT

After a full year of careful scrutiny to make sure the project did not suffer from continuity problems, Petersen had sent in his project evaluation report to MIA Denmark and had lauded the project as a great success.

The results of the project had started to show in San Hagon, as most villagers had upgraded their huts to cement-walled, galvanized, iron sheet–roofed buildings. Most homes had upgraded their TVs and purchased karaoke players to supplement their home entertainment. The most visible improvement was the number of banka boats that were now outfitted with engines.

FISH DELIVERIES CEASE

MIA's country director, Petersen, was preparing to transfer to MIA Africa when the phone call from HUI malls had come in informing MIA of the abrupt halt in fish deliveries more than a month ago and asking MIA for its help. HUI malls had inferred that they were ready to negotiate with the SHFC to improve business terms if need be.

Petersen had unwillingly agreed to send a fact-finding mission to understand what had gone wrong and hired McKenzie to head the fact-finding team, as the initial San Hagon project team had already been disbanded.

3

NONPROFIT ORGANIZATION GOVERNANCE AND STRUCTURE

"When my mom applied to college, she put being popular as her main extracurricular activity."—Quinn. Too often, nonprofits recruit board members because of their social status or popularity. They justify this because of the funds and connections they may bring with them. We criticize colleges for accepting students for the same reasons. Shouldn't nonprofits also recruit and elect board members for their abilities and desire to govern the organization?[1]

Key Topics: stakeholder analysis, board selection, board governance, role of volunteers, partnerships with other organizations, structure-strategy alignment

Thus far in this book we've discussed the importance of the nonprofit sector to society and how concern for issues in society transforms into a sustainable nonprofit organization (NPO). Once the organization is established, the focus shifts to understanding the connections the new nonprofit has to other actors in society. In other words, one might ask: What should a nonprofit "look like" as an organization and who should "run the show"?

This stakeholder analysis should underscore the interdependencies a nonprofit has with community constituents. The NPO governing board serves to bring the community into the organization and keep it connected to the society it serves. It must be remembered that no organization in the nonprofit sector operates as an island, thus building partnerships with other NPOs, government agencies, and for-profit entities can improve service provision and enhance the sustainability of the organization.

---

[1]http://www.nonprofitlawblog.com/home/2011/05/quotes-from-glee-and-nonprofit-governance.html.

STAKEHOLDER ANALYSIS

Before analyzing stakeholders one should understand what a stakeholder is as well as how stakeholders influence, and are influenced by, an organization. Wymer, Knowles, and Gomes (2006) define stakeholders as "groups that have a meaningful interest in the nonprofit organization. Generally, these include the organization's clients, board members, employees, volunteers, donors, granting organizations, government, other nonprofits, and the communities served by the NPO" (p. 19). Once the stakeholders are known, one can ask why they are important. This is where stakeholder analysis comes in.

The process of stakeholder analysis begins with the identification of "the characteristics, values, perceptions, expectations and concerns of stakeholders, including clients or customers, donors, and relevant government officials" (Worth, 2012, p. 175). Clearly this practice can quickly result in an overwhelming list of personalities and entities with which the NPO must communicate and maintain relationships. Thus, the identification should quickly be followed by a prioritization of the stakeholders.

Critical stakeholders are those who most influence the creation and destruction of organization value (Jones, 2005). NPO managers need to weigh conflicting demands among stakeholders against some preexisting criteria to decide which action to take or which interested party to listen to when faced with limited resources and time.

Consider four factors when prioritizing stakeholders (Jones, 2005) and ask: What is the degree of

1. resource dependency,
2. strategic significance,
3. relationship interconnectivity, and/or
4. attractiveness or image benefits associated with being in the relationship?

Stakeholders who rank high on all four factors should take the highest priority. When importance weight is different across the four factors, the NPO manager must decide which factors are most important to the accomplishment of the organization's mission. While this may sound easy, it is in fact extremely difficult in practice. Having an a priori list of factors and a strong mission with guiding values (see Chapter 2) can keep NPO leaders from making crucial mistakes because they are listening to the wrong stakeholders.

While an a priori list of factors (or questions to ask regarding factor importance) will vary by organization, the list may include the following (Conway Dato-on, Weisenbah Keller, & Shaw, 2009):

1. Which clients and benefactors does the organization depend on most heavily for sustainability?

2. Which individuals or groups are most closely aligned with the NPO's competencies?

3. How does the NPO measure relationship "health" to ascertain imbalance or undue influence in a relationship? (Unhealthy or imbalanced relationships may indicate possible conflict of interest.)

4. Does a relationship provide positive status with a key donor or client group?

The main stakeholders in a nonprofit are the board of directors, the paid management (usually referred to as the CEO and his or her management team), and the volunteers. The next sections briefly describe the roles and relationships as applied to the operational control and structure of a nonprofit.

BOARD SELECTION

Nonprofit governing boards have the ultimate responsibility for mission accomplishment and organizational sustainability (Worth, 2012). This requires the skill of looking outward while keeping the focus inward. Such duality makes the role of a board member truly a boundary-spanning one; each member becomes a critical link between the organization and the community. Thus, getting "the right people on the bus" (Collins, 2001) is critical to success.

How board members are selected may influence how the organization operates and what priorities are set (Worth, 2012). Boards can be composed of elected members or be self-perpetuating through selection of new members by existing members—or some hybrid thereof. The original charter of the organization must establish founding members of the board as well as the method for selection of future members. According to Worth, there are advantages and disadvantages to elected, selected, and hybrid boards (Table 3.1).

In addition to these governing boards, an NPO may decide to have advisory boards for the purpose of harnessing different skill sets. Such advisory boards are common when constituencies served have multiple, possibly conflicting needs (e.g., for universities—faculty, students, parents, donors, and hiring managers in the community; for hospitals—doctors, patients, and administrators). Such boards offer advice to the governing board and paid managers (i.e., CEO) but do not have legal responsibility for the organization's actions. When managed correctly, advisory boards can strengthen the connection between the organization and various external stakeholders.

BOARD GOVERNANCE

Once board members are set, clarity of role and accountability empowers organizational success. Legal precedence exists that substantiates a board's duties of *care, loyalty,* and *obedience* (Worth, 2012). These minimum obligations can be summarized as exercising due diligence, avoiding conflict of interest, and maintaining legal compliance (e.g., tax requirement, human resource management, Sarbanes-Oxley Act, Canada Revenue Act). To ensure adherence to responsibilities, board member agreements

Table 3.1 Types of Governing Boards

Type of Board	Advantages	Disadvantages
Elected	May keep organization, board, and CEO more responsive to stakeholders' (e.g., members, clients) needs.	Politicization of election process may create discord and uneven skill base among members. Turnover due to election cycle limits long-term focus.
Self-perpetuating	Helps facilitate stability in organizational culture and goals. Enables balance of board skills and talents (e.g., financial management, fundraising, marketing, legal, human resources).	Board may become overly focused on status quo, resulting in missed opportunities. Connection to community or constituency may weaken over time. Passive deference to CEO may result.
Hybrid (combination of elected and self-perpetuating)	Provides possibility to balance stability with accountability.	Faction among elected vs. appointed members may create discord or variability in commitment to organization.

Source: Worth, 2012. Reprinted with permission.

should substantiate sanctions for noncompliance and enumerate guidelines for remaining true to any established by-laws.

Since the Sarbanes-Oxley Act of 2002 substantially changed the way many for-profit entities remain in compliance, it is worth clarifying how the Act applies to NPOs. Two provisions of the Sarbanes-Oxley Act apply to nonprofit organizations operating in the United States. To be in compliance with the Act, nonprofits must adhere to regulations regarding maintaining (and destroying) records and protecting whistleblowers (BoardSource & Independent Sector, 2006). It is worth noting that in the wake of the corporate scandals that lead to the development of the Act, many states also passed legislation with similar intent. Due diligence of applicable federal, state, and local laws at start-up and during establishment of governance structures and covenants is warranted.

Perhaps more important than the legal implications of the Sarbanes-Oxley Act is the change in sentiment resulting from ethical breaches in nonprofit management as well as the establishment of the law. For example, from 2005 to 2007 the Panel on Nonprofit Sector issued several principles and ethical guidelines for governing boards in particular and nonprofit operations in general (Independent Sector, 2007; Panel on Nonprofit Sector, 2005). While these overarching principles of responsibility are helpful, more specificity may assist nonprofits in developing and managing a successful board. Some consensus exists in the literature on five primary functional responsibilities of NPO boards (Axelrod, 1994; Ingram, 2003; Nason, 1993):

1. Appoint, support, and evaluate the CEO.

2. Establish what the organization stands for (i.e., its values), its purpose (i.e., mission), and what it hopes to achieve (i.e., its vision).

3. Approve programmatic initiatives (recommended by the CEO) that support the mission and monitor the execution of these initiatives by the CEO.

4. Safeguard financial stability and management.

5. Design metrics for measuring organizational performance to establish accountability.

CEO

The relationship between the governing board and the CEO receives extensive coverage in the popular press and academic literature. There is no one-size-fits-all description or prescription for successfully managing the roles; however, the relationship is crucial to leading and controlling all efforts in pursuit of the mission.

Carver (2006) strongly posits that a nonprofit CEO is a full-time professional who implements policies established by the governing board. Keeping operations separate from policy decisions, according to Carver, is beautiful in its simplicity while also minimizing conflict and maintaining focus. Research conducted by Chait, Ryan, and Taylor (2005) and disseminated by BoardSource, an organization that "strives to support and promote excellence in board service" (www.boardsource.org), claims that Carver's view is overly simplistic. Chait et al. suggest that the board and the CEO must share interwoven responsibilities across three important areas: finances, strategy, and vision for the future.

Perhaps the three constant consensus points in the literature regarding the board–CEO relationship are (1) the need for nonprofit organizations to be transparent in setting expectations of performance and duties for both the CEO and the governing board, (2) the usefulness of explicitly stating the role of the CEO on the board (e.g., ex-officio board member without voting rights), and (3) the importance of keeping communication open between these two critical entities and the community that the organizations serve. These elements combined, and legitimately adhered to, can keep the focus on what is important—organizational effectiveness. Consultation of documents and policy recommendations such as those found in *Primer for Directors of Not-for-Profit Corporations: Rights, Duties and*

Practices (Broder & McClintock, 2002) for Canada and *Strengthening Transparency Governance Accountability of Charitable Organizations* (Panel on Nonprofit Sector, 2005) for the United States is recommended for further discussion of the topic.

Volunteers

The nature of nonprofit organizations necessitates dependency on volunteerism. While the subject of volunteer management is discussed in length later in Chapter 8, it is appropriate here to consider volunteers as stakeholders in order to examine their influence on resource dependency, relationship interconnectivity with the CEO and board, and sway on organizational image.

Contingent on the size, financial strength, and work of the NPO, the level of volunteer dependency varies. When the ratio of volunteers to paid staff is high, the CEO may become more involved with volunteer and relationship governance. The character of the volunteer work also changes the relationship to the CEO. When volunteers are primarily transitory (e.g., a beach clean-up), low relationship interconnectivity is evident, meaning more time is spent recruiting than managing volunteers. When enduring, high-interactivity (e.g., Big Brothers, Big Sisters) relationships exist, CEOs must commit a great deal of time to building governance mechanisms and fostering relations. Finally, high visibility of volunteers to clients and the community can influence an NPO's image. This high image dependency dictates increased training, thus more direction by the CEO. In summary, in terms of governance, the type, number, and visibility of volunteers mandate different control mechanisms (i.e., recruiting, training, certifying) by the CEO and the board.

Similarly, the structure of the organization is influenced by the role and relationship length of volunteers. In many small nonprofits, volunteers serve important, organizational sustaining roles (i.e., church deacons, Meals on Wheels food delivery). While the roles volunteers play vary across different organizations, the need to produce desired results crosses all organizations and influences the positions volunteers may hold.

NPO Networks

While Chapter 7 delves into the topic of nonprofit networks in greater detail, here we consider how other nonprofits within the same community may influence the governance and structure of a focal NPO.

History is full of stories in which parties come together to accomplish goals previously considered too big to conceive of achieving. These stories speak to the power of NPO networks. Networks, whether formal or informal, enhance the external impact of an organization.

Wasserman (2005) describes formal networks in which combinations of shared resources enabled health and dental care delivery to continue despite facility closures. When this type of collaboration is evident, it is often facilitated through an advisory board of representatives from participating organizations, with roles and responsibilities established in written agreements. Such arrangements generally require that each participating organization have clear governance policies to assist board members in serving the greater good of the community (e.g., quality delivery of health and dental care) without loss of responsibility of *care, loyalty,* or *obedience* to the governing board.

With ever-increasing competition for funds from dwindling resources of government agencies, individuals, and (in some cases) corporations, a network of like-minded nonprofits can cooperate to increase combined visibility. Such a pooling of resources can decrease each individual organization's fundraising costs while potentially increasing funds raised to accomplish the NPO's mission. Organizational structure may also be impacted if fundraising and/or lobbying professionals are shared across organizations.

Governing board members, as boundary-spanning agents, can keep the NPO informed of such opportunities for collaboration across different organizations. If roles and responsibilities are not clearly established for the governing board, networking prospects can be missed or mismanaged. The latter was evident in the 2009–2010 board scandal resulting in the forced resignation of the board chair at the Central Florida Blood Center (Tracy, 2010). Investigative journalism revealed that networking efforts among board members had not been properly vetted. The entire community lost faith in the organization as evidence of lack of due diligence, failure to avoid conflict of interest, and possible lapses in legal compliance emerged. Such incidences highlight the need for formalized governance structure within and between nonprofit boards.

EFFECTIVENESS

Having taken time to investigate the interplay of various stakeholders that guide governing boards, we are still left with the question: What leads to a governing board's effectiveness? Certainly, understanding the roles described here is necessary, but it doesn't seem sufficient. We are not alone in this conclusion. In fact, a great deal of research has been undertaken to identify practices and policies that precipitate board effectiveness.

BoardSource (2005) compiled the following list of "twelve principles of governance that power exceptional boards," representing the consensus of experts:

1. Constructive partnerships—positive, interdependent relationships between CEO and board members

2. Mission drive—development and maintenance of mission, vision, and guiding values

3. Strategic thinking—focus on key success factors that guide the organization's direction

4. Cultures of inquiry—sound policies derived from constructive debate based on mutual respect

5. Independent-mindedness—the interest of the organization takes precedent above all else (of course, this assumes that these issues are legal, moral and ethical)

6. Transparency—all stakeholders have access to appropriate, accurate information regarding operations, finances, and results

7. Integrity—strong, articulated ethics supported by oversight mechanisms and sanctions

8. Results-based focus—measurement of milestones to ascertain mission accomplishment across all programs and services

9. Sustaining resources—link vision to plans with adequate resources, both financial and human

10. Intentional board practices—governing board policies and procedures that support organizational priorities

11. Continuous learning—ongoing assessment of performance of board members and organizational value

12. Revitalization—planned transition based on strategic recruitment and diversity

Knowing what characteristics are linked to effectiveness is useful for NPO leaders and board members. Developing those characteristics, however, is difficult. Success is the combined result of leadership (Chapter 4), management (Chapters 8, 11), and momentum (Chapter 10). Having the right board member on the bus with a governing map in hand can improve the likelihood of success in the organization's trip toward mission accomplishment.

Strategy–Structure Alignment

Thus far, our focus has been on board members, their relationship with other stakeholders, and board characteristics that can enable success of organizational initiatives. A more comprehensive way to investigate board effectiveness is to check whether all elements of the organization are aligned around shared values. Many tools are available to conduct such an alignment check. One popular tool from the business literature is the McKinsey 7-S Model. Developed in the early 1980s by Tom Peters and Robert Waterman (1982), the model provides a framework with which to understand how organizational elements are interrelated. The model suggests that, for an organization to perform well, seven vital elements should be aligned and be mutually reinforcing. The elements (Figure 3.1) are organized into two categories, hard and soft.

Hard Elements

- **Strategy**—plan devised to achieve organizational goals and differentiate one organization from another in the community served
- **Structure**—the way the organization and board assigns responsibilities, who reports to whom
- **Systems**—daily activities and processes that staff/volunteers/board members/CEO follow to accomplish tasks and goals

Soft Elements

- **Shared Values**—core values that permeate the organization's culture, and the general work ethic (see Chapter 2)
- **Style**—style of leadership adopted (see Chapter 4)
- **Staff**—staff/volunteers/board members/CEO and their general competences or expertise (including numbers, length of service, etc.)
- **Skills**—tangible skills of staff/volunteers/ board members/CEO (e.g., education level, certifications)

NPO leaders can use the model to identify what element(s) needs to be realigned or changed to improve performance. Peters and Waterman (1982) suggest that whatever type of organizational change is proposed or needed (restructuring, new processes, organizational merger, new systems, change of leadership, etc.), the model can be used to ascertain how organizational elements are interrelated, thus anticipating that the

Figure 3.1 McKinsey's 7-S Model

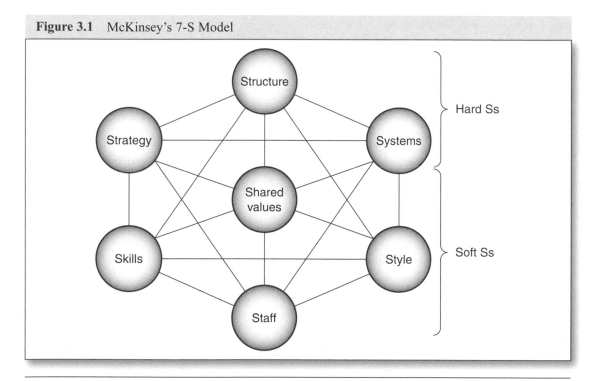

Source: Adapted from Robert H. Waterman, Jr. and Tom Peters.

wider consequences of any change made to one element is taken into consideration.

In this chapter we began by considering the relationships a nonprofit has within itself and with other actors in society. In doing so we've contemplated the important role of the governing board in relation to the CEO, volunteers, and overall nonprofit organizational effectiveness. The discussion concluded with a list of characteristics of an exceptional board and a model to consider how organizational elements come together to enable success. The two cases that follow bring to life the theoretical discussion presented throughout the chapter.

CASES

OHNo Swim Club: Organizational Governance and Mission (United States): The OHNo Swim Club is a small nonprofit organization whose board of directors is swayed from its mission by one of its wealthy members. In the process, the club loses control of its mission, makes a decision that comes close to financially bankrupting the organization, and eventually loses several members before it rebuilds itself with a stronger dedication to its mission. Through the rebuilding process, it learns the importance of choosing board members with financial sophistication, the difficulties of a start-up enterprise and the importance of maintaining a mission and communicating that mission to members.

YMCA of London, Ontario (Canada): The CEO of a multisite and multibusiness YMCA must determine how to more than double participation levels in the next 5 years. The case describes how the London YMCA has grown in both participation and size. However, the corporate-level strategy has become complicated and the board of directors, CEO, and senior management team need to consider a new M-form structure. This has many implications for the CEO, the senior managers, and the future growth of the London YMCA.

REFERENCES

Axelrod, N. R. (1994). Board leadership and board development. In D. O. Renz & Associates (Eds.), *The Jossey-Bass handbook of nonprofit leadership and management.* (119–136). San Francisco, CA: Jossey-Bass.

BoardSource. (2005). *The source: Twelve principles of governance that power exceptional boards.* Washington, DC: Author.

BoardSource & Independent Sector. (2006). *The Sarbanes-Oxley Act and implications for nonprofit organizations.* Retrieved from http://www.boardsource.org/dl.asp?document_id=558

Broder, P., & McClintock, N. (Eds.). (2002). *Primer for directors of not-for-profit corporations: Rights, duties and practices.* Ottowa, Ontario, Canada: Industry Canada.

Carver, J. (2006). *Boards that make a difference: A new design for leadership in nonprofit and public organizations.* San Francisco, CA: Jossey-Bass.

Chait, R. P., Ryan, W. P., & Taylor, B. E. (2005). *Governance as leadership: Reframing the work of nonprofit boards.* Hoboken, NJ: BoardSource/Wiley.

Collins, J. (2001). *Good to great: Why some companies make the leap . . . and others don't.* New York, NY: HarperCollins.

Conway Dato-on, M., Weisenbach Keller, E., & Shaw, D. (2009). Adapting for-profit branding models to small nonprofit organizations: A theoretical discussion and model proposition. In *Proceedings of the 2009 World Marketing Congress.* Ruston, LA: Academy of Marketing Science.

Independent Sector. (2007). *Principles for good governance and ethical practice: A guide for charities and foundations.* Washington, DC: Author.

Ingram, R. T. (2003). *Ten basic responsibilities of nonprofit boards.* Washington, DC: National Center for Nonprofit Boards.

Jones, R. (2005). Finding sources of brand value: Developing a stakeholder model of brand equity. *Brand Management, 13*(1), 10–32.

Nason, J. W. (1993). Responsibilities of the governing board. In R. T. Ingram & Associates (Eds.), *Governing independent colleges and universities* (pp. 97–113). San Francisco, CA: Jossey-Bass.

Panel on Nonprofit Sector. (2005). *Strengthening transparency governance accountability of charitable organizations: Final report to Congress and the nonprofit sector.* Washington, DC: Independent Sector.

Peters, T. J., & Waterman, R. H. (1982). *In search of excellence.* New York, NY: Harper & Row.

Tracy, D. (2010, March 10). Blood-bank chief Anne Chinoda resigns. *Orlando Sentinel.* Retrieved from http://www.orlandosentinel.com/

Wasserman, L. (2005). *Nonprofit collaboration and mergers: Finding the right fit. A resource guide*

for nonprofits. Milwaukee, WI: United Way of Greater Milwaukee.

Worth, M. J. (2012). *Nonprofit management: Principles and practice* (2nd ed.). Thousand Oaks, CA: Sage.

Wymer, W., Knowles, P., & Gomes, R. (2006). *Nonprofit marketing: Marketing management for charitable and nongovernmental organizations:* Thousand Oaks, CA: Sage.

OHNO SWIM CLUB: ORGANIZATIONAL GOVERNANCE AND MISSION

Brian Welliver had mixed feelings as he drove to the board meeting with his wife, Linda. He was about to submit his resignation from the position of head coach of the swim club, OHNo. He was sad about not being with the children, who ranged from age six to 18, but he was somewhat happy about no longer having to deal with certain parents. As he drove, his mind wandered over the past three years and, most especially, the events of the past three months.

THREE YEARS AGO

OHNo was first created in conjunction with some parents who wished to be more involved in competitive swimming. OHNo was the initials of the three suburbs that this club was meant to service. This collection of suburbs made up a school district with several elementary and middle schools and two high schools. Welliver was self-employed, but also served part time as the

head swim coach for one of those high schools. He saw a shortage of quality swimmers who tried out for his high school team, not for lack of enthusiasm, but because the students had little preparation. Other sports, such as basketball and baseball, did not have such a problem because of a very rich system of community-based programs, starting with very young children. For swimming, not much existed to prepare the participants for the level of physical conditioning and competition that they would face.

OHNo was created with the goal of introducing children in the three suburbs to competitive swimming before they reached the junior and senior high level. It was relatively low cost to avoid discouraging parents who might balk at paying fees for yet another organized children's sport. It also provided an off-season training opportunity for high-school swimmers. In addition, the spirit of the club was rather low key and encouraged individual accomplishments and improvement, rather than a focus on swim meet results. The club's goals were to introduce children to competitive swimming, develop their stamina, improve their techniques, while at the same time not "burn out" the children on the sport before they were old enough to compete at the junior and high school level. Welliver considered the burn-out factor to be very important because swimming is a sport that could be run all year round, unlike other sports such as baseball or soccer, where the weather and facilities automatically forced students to take a break.

In the greater metro area there were at least a dozen other swim clubs, many of whom had aggressive competitive missions, more stringent participation requirements and higher fees. OHNo was going after a market niche that these other clubs did not consider important and that was in a school district that could use the support.

The workouts were conducted in the district at various elementary and middle schools that had swimming pools. The children were divided into three groups, based on age and ability, and each group had at least one part-time coach. The school district was very generous in not demanding payment for pool rental until the club was mature enough to cover costs. This favor came from the fact that the club had a mission: in the long run, it would support the swimming programs at the two high schools. For the first three years, the club survived by the efforts of a dedicated group of parents, the deferment of pool fees and Welliver's sacrifices. Besides coaching, Welliver would do many of the backroom chores such as registration, scheduling competitive meets, negotiating fees and hiring young, certified coaches. In theory, he was to be paid a salary of $20,000 per year, but Welliver would frequently forgo pay so that there would be sufficient cash to pay the other coaches.

After three years in operation, OHNo had approximately 90 regular swimmers and an annual revenue of about $50,000. It owed the district approximately $6,000 in back pool fees and owed Welliver about $2,000 in back pay. Financially, the club was becoming more stable and was starting to chip away at its back debts. A volunteer with a good heart, but no accounting background, took over the treasury function to lessen the time demands on Welliver. Unfortunately, this caused the books to get temporarily out of balance by almost $20,000.

THREE MONTHS AGO

At this point, several events were set into motion. Welliver knew he would need to replace the current coach for the beginning swimmers group in five months because the current coach was going to college. He was immediately informed that a member of the board might have found a replacement named Sveltlana. Sveltlana happened to be a woman who was a two-time member of the national Olympic team for an Eastern European country. A condition was made that she had to be hired almost immediately. Welliver had a hard time understanding why such a person would want to coach six-year-olds at a newly started, small swim club for $12 per hour. The board member who recommended her happened to be the president of a multimillion-dollar firm. His wife was a very active volunteer, and he had two young daughters in the program. When Welliver asked for details, he learned that Sveltlana needed to have an employment sponsor for visa purposes. She had some experience coaching high school kids, but not young children. The board member was willing to pay for the legal costs of getting the visa. He was also willing to donate $6,000 to subsidize her pay temporarily so she could be paid an extra $8 per hour above the club's regular pay of $12 per hour, for a total of $20 per hour. The donation was conditional upon the hiring of this specific coach, with no promise that additional donations would be made once the $6,000 was used up. It was strongly implied by the benefactor that, somehow, this coach should be used for the group in which his two daughters swam. In addition, if this coach was no longer employed by OHNo, then the balance of this donation was to be returned to the benefactor.

In a nutshell, Welliver was very concerned. First, it appeared that there could be potential legal liability with respect to hiring someone who was not a U.S. citizen. Second, this coach had to be hired immediately, rather than in five months. This would temporarily increase operating expenses, without causing an increase in revenue, at a time when the financial books were currently out of balance. Third, this coach was obviously not meant for the beginners. Therefore, a beginner's coach would have to be hired in five months anyway. Fourth, this coach would be paid more than all the other coaches, resulting in potential morale problems. Fifth, there was no guaranteed financing source that would exist after the $6,000 was used up. Sixth, it appeared that this kind of hiring would start moving the club away from its original mission. Last, it felt uncomfortable for such a young, small club to be financially beholden to one family. He had to admit his irritation that coaching decisions no longer appeared to be his sole domain.

In the course of two board meetings, Sveltlana was hired. Welliver realized that the majority of the board was made up of parents who lived outside the school district that this club was intended to serve. They were very active volunteers to be sure, but in retrospect it seemed odd that they had not joined any of the other swim clubs that served the metro area. They were very enthusiastic about "taking the club to the next level." The board temporarily made the benefactor the president of the board and approved the hiring of Sveltlana. Making the benefactor the president was done to expedite the legal paper work of hiring a non-U.S. citizen. This group of board members was very interested in increasing the competitive nature of the club. They wanted more intense workouts and more focus on producing potential national- and Olympic-quality swimmers and were not as concerned about the burn-out factor.

Welliver did his best under the circumstances. It just so happened that his intermediate coach wanted to start a special group for the children who were too fast for the intermediate group, but not mature enough for the senior group. By letting Sveltlana take over the intermediate group, this new group could be formed. It would also allow Sveltlana to get more experience coaching

younger children. Also, some good news occurred when the books were finally balanced. The club still owed the school district for pool fees and Welliver for back pay, but the $20,000 error was a simple bookkeeping issue and not additional debt.

A substantial number of the parents whose children were coached by Sveltlana seemed to be pleased with the rigor of the workouts. Welliver had to admit that he also had learned some new drills. However, Sveltlana really seemed to have only one coaching style. He felt that with some experience, she could be quite valuable to the entire club once she learned that children of different age groups needed different motivations and coaching styles. He felt she would be ready for that role in a couple of months.

Unfortunately, the board could not wait. The next couple of board meetings were very uncomfortable. Various board members felt that Sveltlana should be used immediately as a floating coach for all the sessions and not be used to staff a particular group—especially one in which their children did not swim. Some parents started switching their kids back from the "super intermediate" group to the intermediate group, just to be with Sveltlana. Board members interrupted Welliver's own coaching sessions to air their complaints. At one point, a board member told Welliver that he should step aside and let Sveltlana become the head coach and threatened that if Welliver didn't agree, then maybe the board should replace him.

This was the last straw, and Welliver decided to resign. Out of solidarity, Tim, the club's intermediate coach, decided to resign as well. Tim was a young college student who had been hired two years earlier. He turned out to be a diamond in the rough in the sense that the school district eventually recognized his skill and hired him to work part time as the swim coach for the other high school in the district. Welliver and Tim turned in their resignations with the agreement that they would stay for two months to end the current swimming cycle. Welliver suggested that his back pay could be paid off by letting his high-school-aged daughter swim in lieu of fees. The benefactor immediately proclaimed that such a small swim club could not afford to pay such a large severance package to a resigning coach. Before Welliver could speak, Sam, a board member who did live in the school district and who had always been supportive of Welliver, reminded the board that this was back pay officially owed to Welliver, not a "severance package." Sam then resigned from the board that very night, in disgust.

PRESENT EVENTS

The next two months turned out to be even more chaotic. The school district announced that because of a failed school bond initiative, they would be demanding immediate payment of back pool fees and that the rates would go up. The club's board members soon discovered that there had been a lot of economic value in Welliver's leadership. For instance, it was discovered that Welliver's board membership with the state sanctioning body was instrumental in achieving the club's charter and aided its participation in and hosting of sanctioned swim meets. Also, the two resigning coaches were high school coaches within the school district and, thus, had building keys. Now the club would have the additional expense of hiring a district employee to unlock the pool area, stay for the workout and lock the building afterward. Also, if the replacement coaches were not certified lifeguards, as the original coaches were, then lifeguards would have to be hired as well. In the process of juggling all these complications, no recruitment effort took place to get new beginning swimmers into the pipeline, while the senior swimmers started to graduate and leave the club. All in all, the financial outlook for the club began to look very bleak. In reaction to the resignations, a large number of parents, who previously were either apathetic or uninformed about governance issues, started to question the board in person and by petitions. Some parents even withdrew their children from the club.

Eventually, the majority of the board members, including the benefactor, announced that they were going to resign from the board, quit OHNo and start their own swim club with a more intense, Olympic-style goal. They then proceeded to recruit members from OHNo by "cherry picking" almost 20 of the fastest swimmers in the club, and by taking Sveltlana with them. The balance of the donation was now returned to the benefactor. At this point, Welliver and the former intermediate coach agreed to come back, and the club started the process of rebuilding its membership. Though there was a huge drop in enrolled swimmers, the return of the coaching staff and Sveltlana's resignation resulted in savings that gave the club a reasonable financial outlook for the future.

YMCA OF LONDON, ONTARIO

As Shaun Elliott, chief executive officer, prepared for the last senior management planning session in 2005, he reflected on what the YMCA of London (the London Y, or the association) had achieved in the last four years. Since joining in 2001, Elliott had led the organization from a deficit of $230,000[2] to a projected surplus of almost $1 million by the end of this fiscal year. This turnaround had been accomplished through a careful balance of internal cost cutting and

Pat MacDonald prepared this case under the supervision of W. Glenn Rowe solely to provide material for class discussion. The authors do not intend to illustrate either effective or ineffective handling of a managerial situation. The authors may have disguised certain names and other identifying information to protect confidentiality.

[2]All funds in Canadian dollars unless specified otherwise.

growth through partnering and program expansion. Innovative partnerships with other organizations had allowed the London Y to expand its programs and facilities with minimal capital investment. In addition to its now solid financial performance, the London Y was on track to exceed its targeted participation level of 46,500 individuals by the end of 2005. It was now time for Elliott to turn his attention to achieving the next level of growth: participation levels of 102,000 individuals by 2010. He knew that to achieve an increase of this magnitude, senior management would need to increase their focus and its capacity and that he would need to spend more time on longer-term strategic initiatives and community relations. He wondered if this was possible given the current situation.

THE YMCA

The Young Men's Christian Association (YMCA) was an international federation of autonomous not-for-profit community service organizations dedicated to meeting the health and human service needs of men, women and children in their communities. The YMCA was founded in London, England, in 1844, in response to the unhealthy social conditions resulting from the industrial revolution. Its founder, George Williams, hoped to substitute Bible study and prayer for life on the streets for the many rural young men who had moved to the cities for jobs. By 1851, there were 24 YMCAs in Great Britain and the first YMCA in North America had opened in Montreal. Three years later, in 1854, there were 397 separate YMCAs in seven nations, with a total of 30,400 members.[3]

From its start, the YMCA was unusual in that it crossed the rigid lines that separated the different churches and social classes in England at the time. This openness was a trait that would lead eventually to YMCAs including all men, women and children regardless of race, religion or nationality. In 2005, the YMCA was in more than 120 countries around the world and each association was independent and reflected its own unique social, political, economic and cultural situation. YMCAs worldwide shared a commitment to growth in spirit, mind and body, as well as a focus on community service, social change, leadership development and a passion for youth.[4]

A similar, although separate organization, the Young Women's Christian Association (YWCA) was founded in 1855 in England.[5] It remained a separate organization; however, some YMCAs and YWCAs chose to affiliate in order to best serve the needs in their communities.

THE YMCA IN CANADA

The London Y was a member of YMCA Canada, the national body of the 61 Canadian member associations. YMCA Canada's role was to foster and stimulate the development of strong member associations and advocate on their behalf regionally, nationally and internationally. YMCA Canada was a federation governed by a national

[3]http://www.ymca.net/about_the_ymca/history_of_the_ymca.html. Accessed February 23, 2006.

[4]http://www.ymca.ca/eng_worldys.htm. Accessed Feb. 23, 2006.

[5]http://www.ywca.org/site/pp.asp?c=djISI6PIKpG&b=281379. Accessed February 23, 2006.

voluntary board of directors which oversaw national plans and priorities. Volunteer board members were nominated by the member associations. YMCA Canada's President and CEO were accountable to the board for national operations. The national office had only 20 employees in 2005, reflecting the relative autonomy of the member associations.

As in the rest of the world, YMCAs in Canada served people of all ages, backgrounds and abilities and through all stages of life. They were dedicated to helping people attain a healthy lifestyle and encouraging them to get involved in making their community a better place. As charities, the YMCA member associations relied on the support of their communities, the private sector, governments and other agencies. YMCA fundraising campaigns helped to provide better programs and facilities, as well as greater accessibility and financial assistance to include as many people as possible.[6]

Earlier in 2005, YMCA Canada, in conjunction with its member associations, had developed a strong association profile, which comprised a wide range of performance measures similar to a balanced scorecard. Implementation of this measurement tool was voluntary, although YMCA Canada encouraged individual associations to use it to assess their performance and to compare their performance with other associations. According to the YMCA Canada strong association profile, a strong YMCA position profile is as follows:

- demonstrates that it is having an impact on individuals' spirits, minds and bodies, while building strong kids, strong families and strong communities;
- assists people to participate in the YMCA who otherwise could not afford to be involved;
- is seen as a valued contributor to the community;
- has the capacity to influence the community relative to its strategic priorities;
- has quality programs that help members meet their personal goals;

- demonstrates growth in participation over time;
- offers a variety of programs that are accessible to the community;
- has a culture of involving their members continually by encouraging them to give their time, talent and treasure to the YMCA;
- has identified key audiences and has a communications plan that addresses each audience.

The London Y had piloted an earlier version of the strong association profile and had already set annual targets for 2005 through to 2010 (see Exhibit 1). The London Y planned to implement these targets and measures as part of its 2005 strategic planning cycle.

THE YMCA OF LONDON

Founded in 1856, the YMCA of London was a multi-service charity that described its mission as providing "opportunities for personal growth in spirit, mind and body for people of all backgrounds, beliefs and abilities."[7] Its articulated values and the principles by which it operates were:

- **Honesty:** to tell the truth, to act in such a way that you are worthy of trust, to have integrity, making sure your actions match your words.
- **Caring:** to accept others, to be sensitive to the well-being of others, to help others.
- **Respect:** to treat others as you would have them treat you, to value the worth of every person, including yourself.
- **Responsibility:** to do what is right, what you ought to do, to be accountable for your behaviour and obligations.

The association served almost 28,000 children annually through childcare and camping at 16 childcare locations, two residential camps, one outdoor education centre and numerous summer day camps and after school program locations. In 2004, the London Y had

---

[6]http://www.ymca.ca/eng_abouty.htm. Accessed February 23, 2006.

[7]http://www.londony.ca/. Accessed February 24, 2006.

Exhibit 1 The YMCA of London Participation Targets

	2005	2006	2007	2008	2009	2010	5-yr inc	avg inc
Childcare								
Infant	70	70	70	70	70	70	0%	0%
Toddler	140	140	140	140	140	140	0%	0%
Preschool	608	672	736	832	928	1,024	68%	14%
School Age	316	316	316	316	316	316	0%	0%
Childcare Total	**1,134**	**1,198**	**1,262**	**1,358**	**1,454**	**1,550**	**37%**	**7%**
Camping and Educational Services								
CQE	1,815	2,215	2,215	2,439	2,471	2,471	36%	7%
Day Camp	5,350	5,457	5,566	5,677	5,791	5,907	10%	2%
Outdoor Education	5,800	6,960	9,048	9,953	10,948	12,043	108%	22%
Children's Safety Village	12,000	13,500	14,000	14,000	14,000	14,000	17%	3%
Community School Program	1,630	1,880	2,130	2,380	2,630	2,880	77%	15%
Camping Total	**26,595**	**30,012**	**32,959**	**34,449**	**35,840**	**37,301**	**40%**	**8%**
Health Fitness and Recreation								
CBY full fee	5,450	5,580	5,750	5,825	6,000	6,200	14%	3%
CBY assisted	2,210	2,330	2,450	2,500	2,525	2,650	20%	4%
CBY programs	4200	4,580	4,975	5,750	6,875	8,050	92%	18%
BHY full fee	1,500	1,525	1,900	2,100	2,400	2,700	80%	16%
BHY assisted	300	305	380	420	480	540	80%	16%
BHY programs	1,600	7,565	9,100	10,195	11,480	13,125	720%	144%
ELY full fee		1,025	1,050	1,050	1,075	1,200		
ELY assisted		205	210	210	215	240		

(Continued)

Exhibit 1 (Continued)

	2005	2006	2007	2008	2009	2010	5-yr inc	avg inc
ELY programs		4,085	5,010	5,280	5,755	6,225		
SCY full fee	481	865	1,155	1,155	1,155	1,155	140%	28%
SCY assisted	26	74	100	110	110	110	323%	65%
SCY programs	773	826	865	905	925	945	22%	4%
WDY full fee	1,822	1,844	1,879	1,913	2,400	3,040	67%	13%
WDY assisted	373	405	426	449	600	760	104%	21%
WDY programs	4,900	5,680	6,480	6,935	8,140	9,375	91%	18%
New location full fee	n/a	n/a	n/a	5,000	7,000	7,000		
New location assisted	n/a	n/a	n/a	1,250	1,750	1,750		
HFR Total	**18,735**	**31,214**	**35,250**	**49,797**	**57,135**	**63,315**	**238%**	**48%**
Grand Total of Participants	**46,464**	**62,424**	**69,471**	**85,604**	**94,429**	**102,166**	**120%**	**24%**
Volunteers								
Childcare								
Camping								
CBY								
BHY		55	60	65	70	75		
ELY		15	20	25	30	35		
SCY	20	23	27	30	35	40	100%	20%
WDY	35	38	42	45	60	80		
Total	**55**	**131**	**149**	**165**	**195**	**230**		

Source: YMCA of London, 2005 Strategic Planning Documents.

provided 13,025 health, fitness and recreation (HFR) memberships for children and adults at five branches: three in London, one in Strathroy and one in Woodstock. In addition, the St. Thomas YMCA was operated by London Y senior management under contract. To ensure that no one was turned away because of an inability to pay, in 2004, the association provided 2,994 assisted HFR memberships, 1,100 assisted "camperships" and assistance to 310 children in child care. The association had a very positive brand position in the community and its internal research had shown that referrals were the number one source of new members and participants.

The last four years had been a time of renewal and change for the London Y (see Exhibit 2). Revenue had increased by 50 per cent and the association had transformed an operating deficit of $230,000 in 2001 to an expected $1 million operating surplus by the end of 2005 (see Exhibit 3). In 2004, childcare contributed 38 per cent of total revenue, HFR

Exhibit 2 The YMCA of London Growth, 2001 to 2005

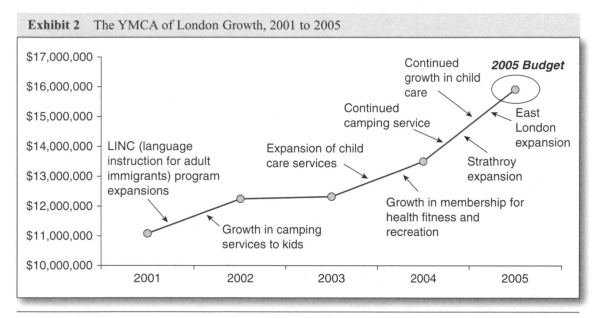

Source: Company files.

Exhibit 3 The YMCA of London Schedule of Operations

	2005 Projected	Year ended Dec. 31 2004	Year ended Dec.31, 2003	Year ended Dec. 31, 2002	Year ended Dec. 31, 2001
REVENUE					
Memberships	3,647,014	3,560,527	3,364,190	3,139,980	3,183,699
Child Care	6,811,401	4,958,138	4,037,612	4,516,214	4,576,632
Camp Fees	2,192,237	2,121,787	2,023,885	2,020,531	1,978,414
Community Programs	260,676	442,927	532,606	863,573	414,659
Program Service Fees	328,495	228,500	342,727	302,069	299,177
United Way	205,999	185,250	169,989	164,619	178,818
Ancillary Revenue	544,748	519,225	458,768	633,102	252,935

(Continued)

Exhibit 3 (Continued)

	2005 Projected	Year ended Dec. 31 2004	Year ended Dec.31, 2003	Year ended Dec. 31, 2002	Year ended Dec. 31, 2001
Donations and Fundraising	341,701	297,917	371,996	416,779	128,190
Employment Initiatives	989,141	891,815	792,983		
International Contributions and Grants					
Total Revenue	15,321,412	13,206,086	12,094,756	12,098,106	11,058,547
EXPENSES					
Salaries and Benefits	9,550,594	8,525,862	7,663,975	7,718,093	7,288,194
Program Costs	973,935	1,357,277	1,237,143	946,329	1,013,640
Facilities	2,060,400	1,830,450	1,746,122	1,918,676	1,878,400
Promotion	165,180	178,053	140,143	183,441	164,600
Association Dues	163,543	157,570	137,985	136,795	132,777
Travel and Development	214,130	222,013	238,060		
Office Expenses	285,302	276,835	284,382		
Professional and Other Fees	247,592	247,430	302,695		
Miscellaneous	149,741	168,117	128,503		
Administration				840,048	763,095
International Development				41,239	46,023
Total Expenses	14,399,676	12,963,607	11,879,008	11,784,621	11,286,729
EXCESS (DEFICIENCY) OF REVENUE OVER EXPENSES	921,736	242,279	215,748	313,485	–228,182

Source: The London YMCA Annual Reports, 2004, 2003, 2002, 2001.

contributed 27 per cent and 16 per cent of revenue came from camping (see Exhibit 4 for the YMCA of London revenue). The remaining revenue sources included government programs and contracts, community programs, donations and the United Way. Almost 90 per cent of the London Y's revenue was self-generated through program and participation fees.

The responsibility for all development and fundraising activity was in the process of being moved into the YMCA of London Foundation, an affiliated but separate organization which had a strong record of investing and securing grants. In its newly expanded role, the foundation was expected to support capital campaigns, conduct annual campaigns and enhance planned giving.

Exhibit 4   The YMCA of London Revenue, 2004

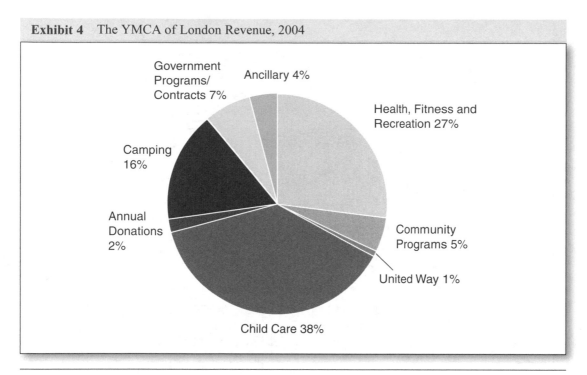

Government
Programs/
Contracts 7%

Ancillary 4%

Health, Fitness and
Recreation 27%

Camping
16%

Annual
Donations
2%

Community
Programs 5%

United Way 1%

Child Care 38%

Source: The YMCA of London Annual Report, 2004.

The London Y's structure included the CEO, who was accountable to a volunteer board of directors (the board). Seven general managers and one manager reported to the CEO along with three senior directors and one director. The general managers and manager were responsible for service areas or locations, including camping and outdoor education, childcare, community services, London HFR, the Woodstock District YMCA, the St. Thomas Elgin Family YMCA, the Strathroy-Caradoc Family YMCA, overall facilities and employment initiatives. The senior directors and director were responsible for finance, development, human resources and communications, respectively (see Exhibit 5). The number of senior managers had not increased in the last four years.

With the introduction of the strong association profile framework for performance measurement, all senior managers would have performance agreements and work-plans that they had planned together. Measures of participation, program quality and financial performance would be tracked and accountability would be to the group. Once the measures and targets were well established, it was expected that compensation decisions would be based on each senior manager's performance against their plans.

In 2005, the association had over 500 permanent staff with an additional 200 seasonal staff. Full-time employees made up 35 to 40 per cent of the total and the remaining 60 to 65 per cent were part-time employees. Annual staff satisfaction surveys consistently showed high levels of both satisfaction and commitment to the association. However, wages were a persistent issue with staff in the child care centres and finding suitable HFR staff had been particularly challenging.

Exhibit 5 The YMCA of London Organization Chart

YMCA of London
Organization Chart
September 2005

Shaun Elliott
C.E.O.

- **Susan McGugan** Senior Director of Finance
  - Stella Perry Accountant
  - Colleen Reiners Accountant
  - Mary Kilbourn-John Accounts Payable Administrator
  - Eric Krueger Manager Information and Technology
  - Dan Bridge Computer Technician
  - Marilyn Himbury Information Analyst
  - Kadhim Hassan Manager Employment Initiatives
    - Nancy Pollard – LINC
    - Arden DeMarsh – FPSYIP
    - Krista Gillespie – Youth Gambling Project

- **Vacant** Senior Director of Development
  - Vacant Development and Executive Administrator

- **Elaine Woods** GM Strathroy Caradoc Branch
  - Heather Aldred-Trepanier Director of Member Relations
    - Angela Rita Aquatics Supervisor
    - Vacant Group Fitness and Recreation Supervisor
    - Vacant Family and Youth Supervisor
    - Bob Nichols Facility Supervisor
  - Michelle Lalich-VanVliet Director Child and Youth Programs Strathroy
  - Eric Symons Program Director Strathroy Branch
  - Jan Dawes Director Recreational Programs

- **Ron Luckman** GM Woodstock Y

- **Anne Baxter** Director Communications
  - Kelly Smith Director High/Scope
  - Teresa Sulowski Director Blessed Kateri and St. Catherine of Siena
  - Suzie Walton Director St. Theresa
  - Kelly Heddle High/Scope Trainer
  - Dawn Blake Director Kids and Company
  - Kathy Destun Director University CC
    - Nancy Nowicki Director, Bob Hayward
    - Tammy-Lyn Hudson Director Cornerview

- **Anne Rae** GM ChildCare
  - Katnie Tait-Raynor High/Scope Trainer
  - Chris Moss ChildCare Administrator
  - Pam Patterson Director St. Marguerite d'Youville
  - Robin Legault-Harris Director Windy Woods
  - Nancy Nurse Director River Valley
  - Jodie Nieuwenhuizen Director St. Vincent de Paul
  - Jennifer Gilbert Director Kidworks
  - Bonnie Bohner Director Woodstock
  - Erin Daley Director Lorne Ave

- **Andrew Lockie** GM of Camping and Outdoor Education
  - Brian Shelley Director CQE
  - Vacant Assistant Director CQE
  - Vacant Director OE and Day Camp
  - Erika Andersen Assistant Director CQE Outpost
  - Vacant Supervisor Camp Facilities
  - Gina Casavecchia Administrator
  - Kelly Hunt Program Director Community Schools
  - Kenley Cooke Director Northeast Project
  - Trish Edwards Director School Programs St. Francis and St. Pius
  - Rebecca Webster Director School Programs

- **Wayne Stinchcombe** Senior Director HR Development
  - Nancy Wilson Payroll Administrator
  - Darlene Teather Program Director CBY
    - Caribel Medina Rec. and Instructional Supervisor CBY
    - Shannon Fuller Conditioning Supervisor CBY
    - Timarra Milmine Aquatics Supervisor CBY
    - Patti Asselstine Director CBY Member Involvement
    - Lisa Jakob Sales and Service CBY Supervisor
    - Vacant Sales and Service CBY Supervisor
    - Christina Harley Sales and Service CBY Supervisor

- **Vacant** GM London HFR

- **Richard Awad** GM Facilities
  - Bill Kearns Housekeeping CBY Supervisor
  - Vinda Holtby Site Director BHY
    - Bryan Awad Supervisor Facilities
    - Ricardo Mathison Supervisor Land Programs
    - Becky Finch Aquatics Supervisor BHY

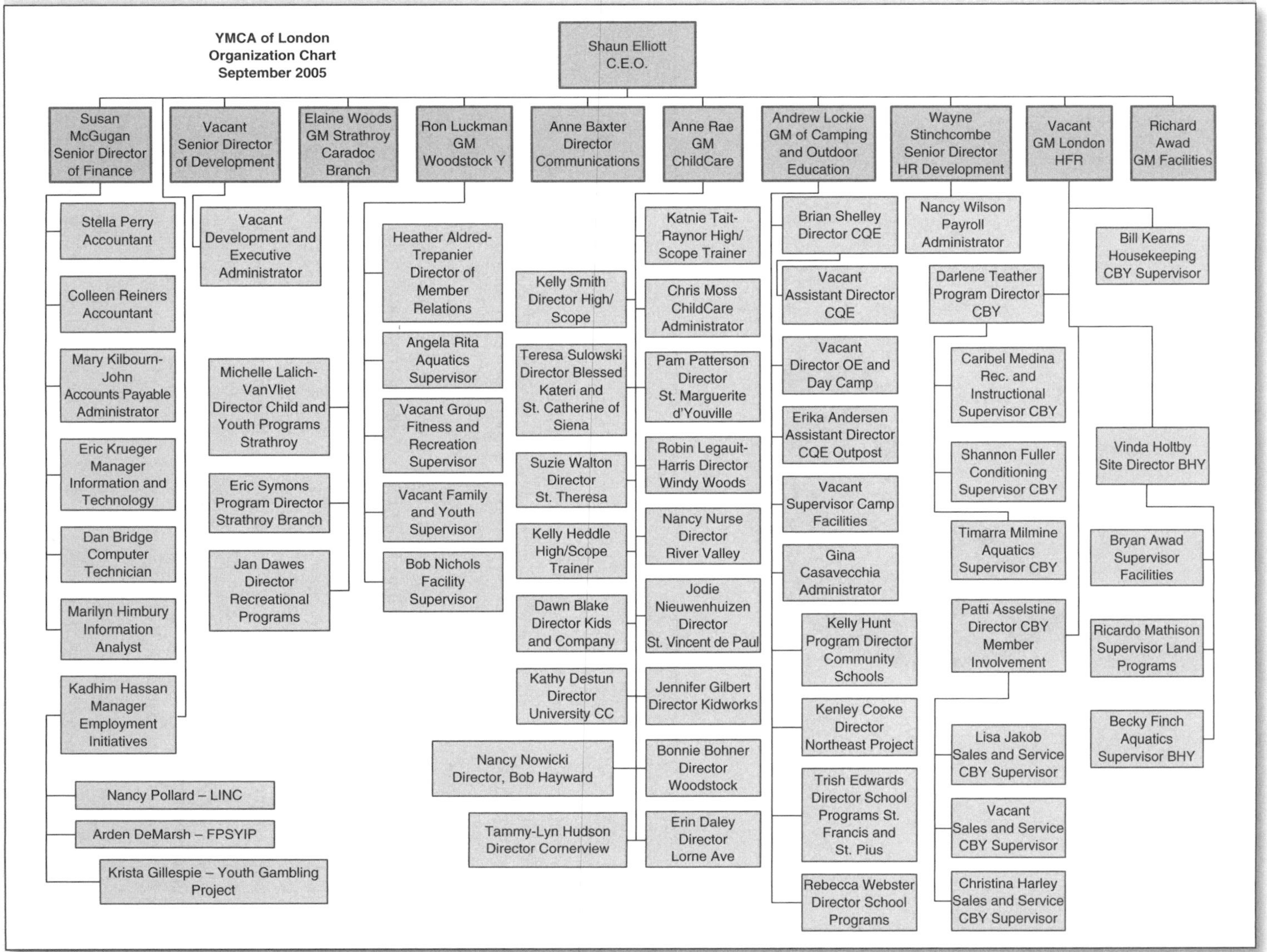

During the last four years, the board and senior management of the London Y had identified partnering as a key strategy to achieve the association's long-term strategic objectives in its three core service areas: HFR, childcare, and camping and outdoor education. Senior management moved quickly to seize opportunities for a number of new partnerships.[8] A new HFR facility in East London was developed in partnership with the London Public Library. Partnerships were established with Kellogg Canada Inc. and John Labatt Ltd. for the London Y to operate their on-site HFR facilities. Childcare services had grown more than 50 per cent, primarily as a result of a partnership with the University of Western Ontario.

Some partnerships were opportunistic or tactical but were nonetheless guided by their fit with the long-term goals and values of the London Y. For example, a partnership with the Children's Safety Village made resources available to pursue a new full-service HFR location in an underserved area of the city, thus expanding service and programs. In the absence of a significant capital infusion, senior management believed that new partnerships were critical to the London Y achieving its participation target of 102,000 individuals by 2010.

CORE SERVICE AREAS

Health, Fitness and Recreation

One of the longest-standing services that the London Y provided was HFR. These services were offered through five branches, each led by a general manager. These included: the London Centre YMCA (CBY), the Bob Hayward (BHY) and East London (ELY) all located in London; the Strathroy-Caradoc Family YMCA (SCY) located 40 kilometres west of London; and the YMCA of Woodstock and District (WDY)

located 50 kilometres east of London. By 2005, the London Y had served more than 18,700 individuals through its HFR programs, and by 2010, the association had a target of serving more than 63,000 in six locations, an increase of 238 per cent. The St. Thomas Y was located 35 kilometres south of London.

The branches were membership-based and offered health and fitness programs for children, families and adults. Twenty-five per cent of the London Y's members received an assisted membership and paid one-third of the cost on average. Programs for children and youth were estimated to cost more than four times the association's programs for adults, yet generated lower fees. Children's programs and services often ran at a loss. The London Y depended on full fee–paying adult HFR members to cross-subsidize assisted memberships and children's programs.

The largest challenge to the London Y attracting full-fee adult members was the proliferation of fitness facilities for adults. Market-research commissioned by the London Y in 2002 indicated that approximately 30 per cent of the 193,845 adults in London would join a fitness facility and that 25.5 per cent of adults were already members of a fitness club. The potential for market growth was assessed as limited. The research also showed significant penetration of the market by private sector providers with the primary competition in London coming from the Good Life Clubs with 37 per cent market share and the Athletic Club with 22 per cent of the market. The London Y was third in the London market, with a share of 12 per cent. The competition had increased recently with the entrance of the Premier/Mademoiselle chain of fitness clubs into the City of London.

The private clubs operated under a very different economic model than the London Y, typically leasing equipment and facilities. They targeted the adult market only and they did not offer pools or as wide a range of programming as the London Y.

---

[8]All of the London Y's partnering relationships have approximately the same legal structure which involves a facilities lease and an operating or service provision agreement. There are no fees paid to the partners as all services are provided on a fee-for-service basis and the London Y covers the operating costs of the facility.

In contrast to the private operators, the London Y owned relatively large facilities with pools. Only the two newest branches in London and Strathroy (ELY and SCY) did not have pools, although interest in adding a pool to the SCY had already been raised in the community.

A number of the London Y facilities were aging and required significant capital reinvestment or replacement. The CBY was 25 years old and required ongoing maintenance and refurbishment. The BHY in East London and the WDY were each 50 years old and were not wheelchair accessible. Both buildings required significant capital investment to meet and maintain modern standards. Unfortunately, the BHY was not ideally located so the potential for new members would be limited. More positively, the City of Woodstock had expressed an interest in partnering with the association to develop a new community facility as part of the city's master recreational plan. Replacing the WDY building was considered to be an imperative and partnering with the city was the association's preferred strategy.

Senior management of the London Y believed that to remain relevant in the HFR market as well as meet its targets, the association must develop new facilities in London's north and west ends. The City of London's master recreational plan supported partnership in the delivery of recreational programs and the association had begun discussions with the city regarding development of a new HFR facility in the north end. The city's plan also identified the southwest of the city as a priority site for an HFR facility.

Retention was a key part of membership growth as research showed that two-thirds of new members leave within the first year. Currently, the London Y had relatively high retention rates for members that lasted beyond one year at CBY (76 per cent), WDY (80 per cent) and BHY (75 per cent). ELY and SCY had been in operation less than two years, and retention rates, while high, were expected to decrease. The association had targeted overall HFR retention rates of 55 per cent at BHY, ELY and SCY next year, increasing to more than 70 per cent by 2010. While the association planned to continue its focus on families and to differentiate itself as a values-based organization, it also planned to offer specialized programs targeted at specific groups such as cardiac rehabilitation, weight loss, osteoporosis treatment, etc. to enhance both member retention and new member attraction. This would require increased staff with increased qualifications, resulting in increased costs. To offset these expected cost increases HFR management would need to determine ways to increase revenues or fees.

Although the CEO managed most of the HFR facilities, each facility was run as a separate unit by its general manager. Each branch did its own hiring, staff training, uniform purchasing, program development, and sales and promotion materials. This had resulted in inconsistencies in program quality, program delivery, member service, staff management, facility maintenance and house-keeping between branches. There were significant economic and operational inefficiencies as well. Senior management believed that increased consistency would contribute to increased efficiency, allowing the association to serve more members and to retain more of the existing members. However, there were no coordinating mechanisms for HFR other than the CEO. With financial stability and revenue growth as his priorities, he had not had sufficient time to work with each of the HFR general managers. Also, the CEO was not himself an experienced HFR manager, having spent his career in financial services prior to joining the association.

HFR staff tended to be young and at the beginning of their careers. Finding and retaining appropriate HFR staff had been challenging for the London Y. Work had begun on developing relationships with the local Community College and University to establish a placement/apprentice program to identify strong candidates. Also a skill/aptitude profile of HFR staff was in development based on YMCA Canada's standards and training for HFR staff.

The senior management team had developed a number of strategic initiatives for HFR for the coming year. In summary they were:

- develop a new facility in London in partnership with the city of London
- develop a new facility in Woodstock
- manage and promote the Bob Hayward and East London facilities as one branch
- initiate discussions with the town of Strathroy for the development of a pool
- focus on program development and quality, and develop a new revenue structure to support increased quality of service

Childcare Services

Childcare services were the London Y's largest source of revenue. These services were offered through 16 childcare centres located in London (12 locations), Strathroy (two locations), St. Thomas and Woodstock (one location each). The centres were mostly located in leased premises, with only the Woodstock centre operating in a facility owned by the association. In 2004, the London Y had served 1,139 children in three categories: infant, toddler and preschooler. By 2010, the association planned to serve an additional 415 preschoolers, for a total of 1,554 children. The London Y childcare centres were similar to other providers in offering full-time, part-time and flexible care options and its fees were set between the midpoint and the high end of fees charged in London. Infants are considerably more expensive to serve due to the higher staff-to-child ratios required.

Childcare is highly regulated through Ontario's Day Nursery Act (DNA). The DNA prescribes staff-to-children ratios by age, as well as physical space design, procedures, food preparation and all other aspects of operations. Wage enhancement subsidies were established by the provincial government 10 years ago, as private centres were made public and regulations were established. The subsidies were considered to be necessary for the financial feasibility of centres; however, they had remained at the same levels since their introduction in the early 1990s. Many levels of government were involved with the regulation and funding of childcare, including the Province of Ontario, the Ministry of Community and Social Services, the Ministry of

Health, cities and counties, and in some instances, boards of education. It was expected that the landscape of childcare would undergo significant change in 2006 and beyond based on provincial initiatives and programs resulting from proposed increases in federal funding.

Subsidies for childcare fees are available to low-income families through the cities and counties. These subsidies did not typically cover all of the fees and the London Y absorbed the shortfall as part of its support to the community.

There were two other large childcare providers in London: London Children's Connection with 13 centres and London Bridge with 11 centres. Unlike these service providers, the London Y offered unique programming through its use of the High Scope curriculum and its values-based programming. In fact, the London Y's curriculum and values focus were key reasons that The University of Western Ontario decided to partner with the association. In addition to the High Scope curriculum, the London Y also offered HFR memberships to each full-time child, discounts for HFR family memberships, summer day camp discounts for customers, swimming as part of their programs and family input through parent advisory committees.

The number of children aged zero to four was expected to decline until the year 2012 in the communities the association currently served. However, senior management believed that opportunities for expansion existed in some of the rural communities and counties that were near existing locations. To continue to maintain full enrollment, the association would need to closely monitor local demographics, competitors' expansion and new subdivision development.

The London Y employed a large number of early childhood educators. Wage scales in the industry were lower than in many other industries. While the London Y had made every effort to provide reasonable compensation and reward good performance, staff satisfaction surveys consistently identified wages as an issue. It was now suspected that the London Y was paying slightly below the average childcare wages in the City of London. Management realized that they must carefully balance wage increases and additional managers against their goal of maintaining a surplus.

Communication and consistency among the centres seemed to require constant attention. Some operational processes had been centralized, such as subsidies and collections, while most processes remained with each centre, including the purchasing of supplies and food preparation. Procedures had been standardized with a common operation manual, although there were still many opportunities for greater consistency and standardization.

With more than 50 per cent growth in childcare since 2001, the general manager's scope of authority had become very large. By 2005, she had 18 people reporting directly to her, including all 16 centre directors. This created significant barriers to relationship-building, both internally with staff and externally with parents, potential partners, funding organizations and regulators. It was also a challenge during budget review when the general manager of childcare had to review 16 centre budgets and the overall childcare budget in the same time frame as, for example, a general manager in HFR whose one budget might be smaller than one of the larger childcare centres.

While the nature and the extent of the changes in programs and program funding were unclear, senior management believed that the complex regulatory environment gave a distinct advantage to an experienced and competent childcare provider. The London Y was confident that it had good working relationships with the cities of London, Woodstock, Strathroy and St. Thomas, the counties in which it operated, and with both the Public and the Roman Catholic School Boards.

Partially in response to the changes expected in the childcare environment, the London Y had begun to explore partnership or merger opportunities with other service providers. In addition to operating advantages, management believed a partnership might also enhance their ability to influence government funding.

The senior management team had developed a number of strategic initiatives for childcare services in the coming year. In summary they were:

- explore partnerships or mergers with other providers
- identify and initiate opportunities in rural areas
- enhance wage structure in balance with budget limitations
- monitor changes in government policy, acquire the best and earliest information and develop appropriate contingency plans.

Camping and Outdoor Education

The London Y expected to serve more than 26,500 participants through camping and education programs in 2005. Residential camping programs were delivered in July and August to almost 2,000 children aged six to 17 at two sites in Northern Ontario, Camp Queen Elizabeth and Camp Queen Elizabeth (CQE) Outpost. Summer day camps served more than 5,000 children aged three to 15 with a variety of programs, running from traditional day camps to sports camps and other specialty camps. During the school year more than 1,500 children were served through community school programs delivered in cooperation with school boards. Another 12,000 children were served annually through programs given by police and firefighters at the Children's Safety Village located in the Upper Thames Conservation Authority area near the city of London. Finally, almost 6,000 children and adults participated in outdoor education programs, including leadership and team-building programs offered at various locations.

Camp Queen Elizabeth had been in operation for 50 years and had an excellent reputation. Each year the Camp was booked to capacity and each year those bookings occurred earlier. Similar to other residential camps, much of the activity was outdoors and programming included water sports, crafts and climbing. Fees were amongst the highest in YMCA camping and the return rate of campers was the highest of all YMCA camps in Ontario. Campers tended to be more homogeneous and from higher-income families; however, assisted spots were made available for those unable to afford the fees.

Camp Queen Elizabeth was located on land leased from Parks Canada, a federal department. The current lease was due to expire in 2007 and the London Y had postponed capital investment in the facilities pending renewal of the lease. The association had now received assurance from Parks Canada that the lease would be renewed, so a long-overdue refurbishment of the camp's infrastructure could be planned.

The CQE Outpost property had been purchased as a hedge against renewal of the Camp Queen Elizabeth lease as well as for additional capacity to serve older youth with adventure and canoe trips. Service to older youth had not increased as planned and there appeared to be little demand for this type of service. Management was now exploring the possibility of selling the property and using the proceeds towards the renovation of Camp Queen Elizabeth.

The London Y offered a wide variety of day camp and outdoor education programs during all weeks of the summer and, to a limited extent, in the shoulder seasons of spring and fall. During the summer, the association ran a bussing network throughout the City of London to collect and return participants to designated drop-off points. Programming was value-based and emphasized character development more than skill development. Other summer day camp providers included the local University, the City of London, a variety of private businesses and not-for-profit organizations, and churches. The London Y day camps offered the same size groups and staff ratios as other day camp providers and in some cases the offerings were quite undifferentiated. The service needs and selection processes for families and children were not clearly understood by the London Y, although it appeared to management that there were a number of different segments

such as skills-based camps, traditional camps and camps that were more like a childcare service.

The association had recently invested some capital dollars in its outdoor education program and developed two new sites in partnership with Spencer Hall, run by the Richard Ivey School of Business, and Spencer Lodge, run by the Boy Scouts of Canada. With these new partners and facilities the association hoped to increase the number of its outdoor education program participants by more than 100 per cent by 2010.

The community school program, funded by the United Way and the London Y, was an after school program aimed at improving the academic performance and the social skills of children in higher-risk neighbourhoods. The focus was on literacy, social skills and recreation, and the programs were delivered in a number of designated schools. London Y staff worked closely with teachers to identify children who would benefit from participation in the program. This program continued to expand as much as funding and staffing would allow.

Each school year the Children's Safety Village targeted students in grades one to four with its programs on broad safety topics, including pedestrian safety, bike safety, fire safety, electrical safety and other household hazards.[9] As a result of their partnership agreement, the London Y's Camping and Outdoor Education operations moved from their dilapidated offices at the association's outdoor education centre to the Children's Safety Village site and the London Y took over management of the site. While the London Y was responsible for the physical operation, the Children's Safety Village Board continued to govern the organization, resulting in some overlapping responsibilities.

Camping and outdoor education offered a wide variety of programs in a large number of locations under a number of different names. Each program produced its own sales and promotion materials and parent communications. A number of programs and facilities were not

---

[9]http://www.safetyvillage.ca/about.htm. Accessed February 28, 2006.

clearly identified as part of the YMCA, such as Camp Queen Elizabeth or the Children's Safety Village. Management believed that there were a number of opportunities to send a more consistent message to the community and to strengthen the London Y's brand.

The senior management team had developed a number of strategic initiatives for camping and outdoor education in the coming year. In summary they were:

- identify day camp market segments and deliver programs to meet identified needs
- sell the CQE Outpost site and use the proceeds to improve Camp Queen Elizabeth, ensuring that current and expected demand can be accommodated
- negotiate a new governance model and transfer governance of the YMCA Children's Safety Village to the YMCA of London
- ensure that all facilities and programs are clearly identified as part of the London YMCA
- leverage opportunities to serve more individuals in outdoor education programs

ELLIOTT'S CONSIDERATION OF THE SITUATION

Elliott realized that each of the association's three main service areas had very different business models and dynamics and that this created challenges for organizational focus and expertise, resource allocation and communication. He also knew that while the challenges coming from this multi-service approach were abundant and the synergies limited, neither the board of the London Y nor the senior management wished to reduce the range of services that the association provided to the community. Elliott's challenge was how to best manage the association as a whole while appropriately nurturing each of the core service areas. He had a number of concerns.

The recent growth had put significant strain on both the capacity and capabilities of the senior managers. Elliott was concerned that there were simply not enough managers to deliver the targeted growth and, particularly, the new partnership relationships that would need to be established.

Over the last few years Elliott felt that he was the "chief business development officer," searching out partnering opportunities with external organizations and developing both the opportunity and the relationship through to the final agreement. The service area leaders had been focusing on operations and did not have the time, or perhaps the inclination, to think about innovative ways for their areas to serve more people. He believed that it was now time for the service area leaders to take on the development role and to identify and create their own growth opportunities.

In addition to greater capacity, Elliott believed that the senior management team needed to increase its focus on higher-level strategic issues affecting the whole association. With 12 people at the table, senior management team meetings were not as effective as they might have been and in fact some members only contributed when the discussion was about their specific location. Also, the meetings tended to over-emphasize day-to-day HFR operations simply because there were so many HFR general managers at the table. This meant that they were perhaps under-emphasizing the association's other key service areas of childcare and camping.

Along with decreasing senior management's focus on HFR, Elliott knew that he too needed to spend less time on day-to-day HFR operations and more time on strategic initiatives and community relations. However, with four HFR general managers reporting to him and with HFR representing the biggest operational challenges and the largest growth target, he knew that HFR needed the undivided attention of a capable senior manager. Also, he did not know how the HFR general managers would respond to any changes that might be perceived as a loss of status or position.

Elliott had real fears about creating a potentially unnecessary layer of management or, even worse, an elite group that became out of touch with the staff and the various locations. He worried about becoming out of touch with the operations himself. One of the first things that Elliott had done when he joined the association in 2001 was to eliminate most of the so called "head office" positions, including the chief operating officer, the head of HFR and the head of development. He did not think that the association could afford those roles at that time and he still believed in carefully balancing expenses and overhead with the need for resources to support expansion. Elliott also had concerns about how the community would perceive a charitable organization that significantly increased its senior management personnel. Finally, he worried about moving too quickly.

CONCLUSION

Elliott recognized that in trying to determine what was best for the London Y, he must consider the business model and strategy of each of the core service areas while taking into account the overall mission and values of the association. He needed to be confident that any changes would increase the management capacity and focus within each area as well as free him up to focus on longer-term strategic initiatives. Elliott was concerned about introducing more overhead expense just when the association's financial performance was stable. He did not have much time left to ponder as he wanted the senior management team to consider any potential organizational changes in the last planning session, which was scheduled for next week.

4

LEADERSHIP IN NONPROFIT ORGANIZATIONS

RONALD F. PICCOLO AND J. B. ADAMS

Woodrow Wilson called for leaders *who, by boldly interpreting the nation's conscience, could lift a people out of their everyday selves. That people can be lifted* into *their better selves is the secret of* transforming *leadership.*

—James Macgregor Burns (1978, p. 462)

Key Topics: leadership versus management, transformational leadership, leading change, special considerations of leadership applied to nonprofit setting

In 2006, Richard Moyers described 10 basic responsibilities for executive-level leaders in the nonprofit sector. While many of these responsibilities generally apply to the for-profit sector, several emerge as particularly relevant for CEOs in nonprofit organizations. For example, nonprofit CEOs must (a) express a deep commitment to the organization's mission, (b) share responsibility for resource development and control with a volunteer board of directors, and (c) build external relationships that support the development and execution of organizational strategy. As such, while effective leadership in a nonprofit organization can be informed by the most popular models of business management, nonprofit organizations place unique demands on those at the executive level.

Differences between the for-profit and nonprofit sectors are revealed in the types of activity commonly seen from top leaders, especially CEOs. These differences are often fostered by the conditions that characterize the environment in which CEOs operate. For example, nonprofit CEOs rely heavily on a network of volunteers (e.g., board of directors) who share responsibility for and control of important organizational functions. This is not the case in the for-profit sector. As a consequence, the most effective CEOs in the nonprofit sector tend to be externally focused in pursuit of support from stakeholders who have little (or no) direct involvement with the organization.

Further, nonprofit CEOs rely more heavily on the nature and utility of the organization's mission. Given that many of its supporters are external to the organization (and thus outside of the CEO's direct supervision and span of formal authority), nonprofit organizations need to be guided by a CEO who has a deep and faithful commitment to the mission, and the ability to communicate that mission in a compelling way for a diverse set of stakeholders. As described by Worth (2012), effective leaders in nonprofit organizations focus on mission, external relationships, and shared power with a wide range of stakeholders.

There exists a number of other notable differences between for-profit and nonprofit organizations, including the compensation and reward systems for employees, the methods for measuring and reporting on organizational performance and program impact, and the reality that demand and/or need for service often dramatically exceeds an organization's ability to satisfy that need. These differences are reflected in the activity of nonprofit CEOs and revealed in the cultures that emerge in for-profit and nonprofit organizations (see Chapter 3). Two important realities characterize the unique responsibilities of nonprofit CEOs: shared responsibility with a volunteer board for operations (e.g., strategic planning, resource development, control) that are central to organizational functioning, and the need to effectively exhibit behaviors that involve both management and leadership (Rowe, 2001; Worth, 2012).

Given this context, the purpose of this chapter is to (a) provide a brief overview of management and leadership models in general and (b) introduce transformational leadership theory, a concept that is especially relevant for executive management in the nonprofit sector.

MANAGEMENT AND LEADERSHIP

Although the terms are often used interchangeably, management and leadership tend to characterize psychological, emotional, cognitive, and behavioral patterns that are quite different. Managers are typically described as those who are focused on the effective operation of a particular organizational unit. Managers tend to emphasize planning and budgeting, policies, rules and normative procedures, control of resources, problem solving, and the use of tangible rewards to direct employee behavior. Leaders, on the other hand, are described as those who are more visionary about the organization's future, emphasizing direction (instead of planning), organizational change (instead of custom), inspiration, and risk taking (instead of careful and prudent adherence to normative routines). In that vein, leadership is more reliant on purpose, vision, and mission, while management relies on short-term objectives, efficiency, and control.

Throughout the early part of the 20th century, most of the examinations and characterizations of leaders (and leadership) emphasized the identification of individual differences that distinguished leaders from non-leaders. In 1950, Ralph Stogdill published an important study that found significant differences in intelligence, self-confidence, persistence, and orientation toward achievement between leaders and non-leaders. Consistent with the "Great Man" theory of leadership (Carlyle, 1840/2008), these and similar studies (e.g., Kirkpatrick & Locke, 1991) relied on the identification and examination of individuals who achieved exceptional success. An implication of this research was that leaders are born (not made) to the extent that they are graced in birth with traits associated with leadership (e.g., extraversion, charisma). The earliest conceptions of leadership, therefore, focused on individual differences revealed famously by Thomas Carlyle (1840/2008), who argued, "For, as I take it, Universal History, the history of what man has accomplished in this world, is at bottom the History of the Great Men who have worked here" (p. 1). Kirkpatrick and Locke (1991) echoed Carlyle's remarks, noting, "It is unequivocally clear that leaders are not like other people" (p. 58).

During the second half of the 20th century, the leadership literature expanded beyond traits to include observable patterns that could be learned, trained, and developed over time (i.e., leaders are made). Most influential in this "behavioral" movement was a series of studies conducted in the 1940s at Ohio State University. After examining hundreds of discrete behaviors by managers and leaders across organizations, industries, and functions, the Ohio State studies identified two broad clusters of leader behaviors that were related to leader effectiveness: consideration and initiating structure. *Consideration* is the degree to which a leader shows concern and respect for followers, looks out for their welfare, and expresses appreciation and support. A considerate leader is oriented toward developing relationships and mutual trust with followers and makes special efforts to have followers feel comfortable with the leader and confident in their own abilities to complete assignments.

Initiating structure, on the other hand, is the degree to which a leader defines and organizes his or her role and those of his or her followers. Leaders who initiate structure are oriented toward task and goal attainment and seek to establish specific patterns of communication with followers. In addition, these leaders make special efforts to maintain standards for the manner in which work is to be accomplished.

The behavioral approach to understanding leadership remained popular for several decades, and both consideration and initiating structure generated considerable empirical study. Whereas the two behaviors seem to be fulfilled through different mechanisms, both are associated with follower attitudes and work-related behaviors. A recent meta-analysis provided estimates for the impact of consideration and initiating structure across six criteria: follower job satisfaction, follower satisfaction with the leader, follower motivation, leader job performance, group/organization performance, and leader effectiveness (Judge, Piccolo, & Ilies, 2004). According to Judge et al., consideration is strongly related to outcomes that indicate follower satisfaction, while initiating structure is strongly related to outcomes that indicate performance (e.g., leader job performance). The best leaders, therefore, are those who are able to exhibit both sets of behaviors.

In the past three decades, the leadership concept and much of the scholarly research on leader effectiveness have evolved beyond the simple examination of individual traits or behaviors. Modern approaches to understanding excellent leadership recognize that leadership is an influence process (Rowe, 2001) not limited to positions of formal authority within an organizational structure. Instead of defining leadership as a set of outstanding individual qualities or a specific set of motivating behaviors, those in academia and in the popular press regard leadership as a process by which one individual develops and exercises influence over others (e.g., Maxwell, 1993). Thus, modern conceptions of leadership regard it as an interactive process that fosters relationships between leaders and those who are led. Indeed, effective leadership, especially in nonprofit organizations, is not assigned exclusively to those who occupy positions of formal authority, nor is leadership limited to the interactions between two specific parties (leader and follower). Rather, successful leaders in an organization are those who build social capital with coworkers and develop effective relationships with stakeholders both internal and external to the organization. The central model of this modern leadership approach was introduced in the late 1970s by Bernie Bass. He described it as *transformational leadership.*

The following section summarizes the major tenets of transformational leadership theory. In doing so, the terms *charismatic* and *transformational* are used interchangeably. Although some scholars have pursued obscure distinctions in the way these two concepts are measured and expressed, the leadership behaviors that characterize both approaches are functionally and practically identical. Several of the reasons why transformational leaders are particularly effective are also introduced, highlighting how the theory can be applied in nonprofit organizations.

TRANSFORMATIONAL LEADERSHIP

Based in part on James McGregor Burns's (1978) book *Leadership*, Bernie Bass (1990) introduced transformational leadership theory to capture the extraordinary impact of exceptional leaders on followers and their organizations. This theory asserts that certain leader behaviors not only influence followers' attitudes and behaviors, but also inspire them to move beyond their own self-interest in pursuit of collective, altruistic, and organization-level objectives. In contrast to exchange-oriented models of management, where motivation and control depend on the contingent exchange of tangible rewards for specific behavioral patterns or performance outcomes, transformational leadership theory describes the process by which leaders enhance the commitment of followers to a well-articulated vision and arouse followers and stakeholders to develop new ways of thinking about an organization's mission and its problems. These leaders create strong, emotional connections with followers, attend to their individual needs, and help them reach their potential. Given that nonprofit CEOs are especially dependent on the commitment of stakeholders to a compelling mission and vision, the transformational leadership model is especially relevant for leading a nonprofit organization.

Transformational leadership theory is a broad, process-based approach to leadership that was developed, in part, from research on prominent political leaders. The theory suggests that certain leaders, through their charisma, vision, and intellect, can elevate followers' frames of reference, ideological values, and attitudes toward self, peers, and the nature of their interactions with an organization. In contrast to economic models, which imply that followers tend to act to satisfy their own self-interests, transformational leadership theory asserts that followers are inspired by leaders who articulate a compelling vision, who help followers identify a higher purpose in their work, and who recognize contributions to organizational objectives.

Since its original introduction by Burns (1978) and Bass (1990), transformational leadership theory has evolved to describe four dimensions of transformational behavior: idealized influence, inspirational motivation, intellectual stimulation, and individualized consideration. *Idealized influence* is the degree to which leaders behave in admirable or positive charismatic ways that cause followers to identify with them. *Inspirational motivation* is the degree to which leaders articulate a vision that is appealing and inspiring to followers. *Intellectual stimulation* concerns how and whether leaders challenge assumptions, take risks, and solicit followers' ideas. *Individualized consideration* measures a leader's proclivity to attend to followers' needs, act as a mentor or coach, and listen to followers' concerns and desires.

The effectiveness of a nonprofit CEO depends in large part on his or her ability to foster an emotional connection among stakeholders with the organization's mission. Nonprofits depend on the generous goodwill of volunteers and donors, who rarely see any direct tangible return for their investments of time or money. In addition, for the altruistic pursuit of a valuable mission, employees within nonprofit organizations often forgo careers in the for-profit sector that could be more lucrative in terms of compensation and benefits. Indeed, the rewards for those working in the nonprofit sector are usually less direct or tangible than for those in the business community (Pallotta, 2008). Thus, nonprofit CEOs must not only effectively manage limited resources in service of broad missions; they must also inspire emotional support across a range of stakeholders (e.g., employee, community partners, donors, clients). As such, effective leadership in a nonprofit organization is often directly related to the tenets and practices of transformational leadership theory.

THE TRANSFORMATIONAL LEADERSHIP PROCESS IN NONPROFIT ORGANIZATIONS

In the past two decades, transformational leadership theory has been the most widely researched concept in the leadership literature. A search of recent publications in the *PsycINFO* database reveals more studies on transformational leadership since 1990 than all other modern theories of leadership. Hundreds of studies have revealed the concept's utility in business, military, political, educational, and social service organizations, as well as across multiple organizational levels and diverse cultural contexts. In sum, the theory has enjoyed broad empirical support and its tenets are widely generalizable.

Among the varied reasons why transformational leaders are effective, perhaps the most relevant for nonprofit organizations is the leader's ability to convince followers—both formally and informally—to see their own goals as consistent with those of the organization. That is, those influenced by transformational leaders are more likely to forgo their own short-term self-interests for the sake of the broader interests of the organization and to identify the organization's goals as their own. This is most often accomplished by encouraging followers to connect their own self-identities with the organization. Through storytelling and the use of rituals that emphasize shared values among the organization and its individual members, these especially effective leaders transform the frames of reference for followers such that they personally identify with the mission, values, objectives, and outcomes of the organization. This is particularly valuable for nonprofits operating in today's competitive environment.

Fostering Emotional Connections

So why would transformational leaders inspire emotional connections among stakeholders? Although a great deal of the research and popular prescriptions of effective leadership rely on rational and cognitive reactions by followers, a number of recent studies provide evidence that leadership depends a great deal on one's ability to foster an emotional connection among followers with the leader's vision and an organization's mission. Indeed, leadership is inherently an emotional process, and specific aspects of the transformational approach align with emotional development in followers.

Leaders who exhibit *individual consideration* provide feedback for stakeholders and indicate the group's progress toward stated goals. This behavior gives followers information about their progress and is likely to elicit general feelings of consideration and happiness.

Intellectual stimulation, when demonstrated by a leader, encourages creative thinking about common problems in ways that stimulate followers to increase their level of cognitive and emotional engagement.

A leader who articulates clear and compelling visions of the future, which encourages feelings of hope and optimism, practices *idealized influence.*

The most effective transformational leaders combine these three emotional processes to develop followers while also achieving the organization's mission. These leaders use imagery and conceptual language, much of which carries emotional valence, the kind of imagery that could inspire a deep connection to the organization's mission. Further, these leaders are themselves emotionally expressive, regularly using affect-laden words that are meant to capture an audience and raise the influence of their discussions. Thus, by means of emotional contagion, followers of transformational leaders may naturally assume the leader's mood and emotion level.

Leading Transformational Change

Given the description of transformational and charismatic leaders, it would seem as if these leaders had the magical ability to charm any group of willing followers to sacrifice their own immediate short-term interests in pursuit of some lofty, idealistic vision for which there exists no direct, tangible benefit. On the contrary, the method by which transformational leaders initiate and execute change is very systematic, capable of being described as a process that evolves in three distinct stages. An important illustration of the leadership process was presented by Conger and Kanungo (1998) in *Charismatic Leadership in Organizations.*

In Stage 1, transformational leaders recognize shortcomings of the existing status quo and effectively articulate the need for serious organizational change. In doing so, these leaders clarify the organization's identity in a way that is appealing to a broad set of potential supporters. Ronald Reagan, for example, in his early speeches as the newly elected U.S. president, described the dangerous and constrictive nature of the American economy in an attempt to highlight the need for change in policy and organizational structure, a common attribute of charismatic leadership. Similar ideas about the status quo were expressed by then Governor Bill Clinton during his announcement for a U.S. presidential run in October 1991, and again by then Senator Barack Obama, whose primary slogan during his 2008 presidential campaign was "hope and change." Beyond their extraordinary individual qualities and personal charm, Reagan, Clinton, and Obama each attempted to recognize and persuasively articulate shortcomings in the existing status quo, then describe the need for change in a compelling and convincing manner.

In Stage 2, transformational leaders identify opportunities in the environment and communicate a vision for a vastly improved future state. Perhaps the most profound example of this is Martin Luther King Jr.'s "I Have a Dream" speech, in which he identified an idealized future, shifted the attention of followers beyond their own self-interests to lofty, higher order ideals, and used powerful images of attractive future possibilities. During this stage, transformational leaders often draw on the history, traditions, and originating values of an organization in an attempt to connect future progress to the core ideals on which the organization was founded. Dr. King, for example, referred directly to America's core principles (freedom, liberty, equality) as stated in the country's founding documents. Another example of persuasive language used to describe a compelling future state can be found in the computer business, where Apple's Steve Jobs saw computers as a way to "unleash human creativity and enjoyment" and introduced new products designed to "revolutionize higher education."

Finally, in Stage 3, transformational leaders arouse commitment to expressed goals and inspire confidence among followers in their own abilities to carry out the leader's vision. Stage 3 is characterized by the leader's expression of self-efficacy, personal risk taking, and selfless leadership, all in an attempt to empower followers to participate fully in the accomplishment of organizational objectives. In that vein, a research study conducted by Shamir, House, and Arthur (1993) examined follower reactions to charismatic (transformational) leadership and argued that leaders achieve their desired results by enhancing the confidence and self-efficacy of followers. Evidence of Stage 3 transformational change can be found in interviews with GE's Jack Welch, who regularly suggested that his vision for GE would be realized when employees were excited about their work and felt empowered to create and to grow. Welch not only recognized opportunities for GE's global development, but created a sense among employees that they each had the ability, resources, and support to achieve the CEO's grand vision. As Kouzes and Posner (1995) noted, "leaders make it easy for people to take risks: by taking whatever actions are required in order to make people feel safe and secure" (p. 80).

SUMMARY

Leadership in nonprofit organizations is different from analogous positions in business or the public sector. This difference is shaped in large part by a couple of distinct characteristics of organizations in the nonprofit sector: shared responsibility for and control of resources with volunteers and heavy reliance on the efficacy of mission to engage a diverse set of stakeholders for whom there is no direct or tangible benefit. As such, the most successful leaders in the nonprofit sector will connect emotionally with supporters, convince followers to forsake their own personal self-interests for altruistic motives, and inspire confidence in pursuit of significant organizational change (more on managing change is found in Chapter 6). Nonprofit CEOs must also exhibit the best traits of prudent resource management as well as lofty, inspired leadership.

CASES

Good Intentions Gone Awry at the National Kidney Foundation (International): T. T. Durai spent 37 years of his life volunteering and working with the National Kidney Foundation Singapore (NKF), eventually becoming its CEO. During his tenure, NKF grew from a small foundation to Singapore's largest charity, bringing in $166 million in revenue and operating 21 dialysis centers. But in 2007, Durai's leadership was questioned when he was charged with corruption. The subsequent court case revealed a long list of dubious business practices, including conflicts of interest, misrepresentations of organizational performance, and wasteful spending. Durai was convicted and sentenced to 3 months in jail. The case invites you to consider the ethical issues associated with leading a large-scale nonprofit organization, how NKF might have avoided Durai's scandal, and recommendations for rebuilding the charity's reputation.

Dickinson College: Inspiration for a Leadership Story (United States): In 1999, William Durden was named president of Dickinson College, a small liberal arts college and his undergraduate alma mater. When initially contacted about the position, he was uninterested; as an alumnus he had become frustrated by the college's weak reputation. But after discussions with Dickinson stakeholders, he decided to accept an offer from the college's Board of Trustees, convinced there was a genuine desire for change. Soon after starting, he determined that one of the college's primary problems was that it had failed to establish a strong and clear identity for itself— an organizational purpose that could serve as a source of pride. His efforts led him to a greater awareness and appreciation of the writings of Dr. Benjamin Rush, one of America's founding

fathers and the man who secured the charter for the college in 1783. The case invites you to consider the purpose of an identity story as a tool for providing direction, the challenges inherent in crafting an effective organizational identity story, tactical decisions involved in delivering the identity story to various stakeholder audiences, and the role a leader can play in the process.

REFERENCES

Bass, B. M. (1990). From transactional to transformational leadership: Learning to share the vision. *Organizational Dynamics, 18,* 19–32.

Burns, J. M. (1978). *Leadership.* New York, NY: Harper & Row.

Carlyle, T. (2008). *On heroes, hero-worship, and the heroic in history.* (Original work published 1840) Retrieved from http://www.gutenberg.org

Conger, J. A., & Kanungo, R. N. (1998). *Charismatic leadership in organizations.* Thousand Oaks, CA: Sage.

Judge, T. A., Piccolo, R. F., & Ilies, R. (2004). The forgotten ones? The validity of consideration and initiating structure in leadership research. *Journal of Applied Psychology, 89,* 36–51.

Kirkpatrick, S. A., & Locke, E. A. (1991). Leadership: Do traits matter? *Academy of Management Executive, 5*(2), 48–60.

Kouzes, J. M., & Posner, B. Z. (1995). *The leadership challenge.* San Francisco, CA: Jossey-Bass.

Maxwell, J. C. (1993). *Developing the leader within you.* Nashville, TN: Thomas Nelson.

Moyers, R. L. (2006). The nonprofit chief executive's ten basic responsibilities. Washington, DC: BoardSource.

Pallotta, D. (2008). *Uncharitable: How restraints on nonprofits undermine their potential.* Lebanon, NH: University Press of New England.

Rowe, W. G. (2001). Creating wealth in organizations: The role of strategic leadership. *Academy of Management Executive, 15,* 80–93.

Shamir, B., House, R. J., & Arthur, M. B. (1993). The motivational effects of charismatic leadership: A self-concept based theory. *Organization Science, 4,* 577–594.

Stogdill, R. M. (1950). Leadership, membership and organization. *Psychological Bulletin, 47,* 1–14.

Worth, M. J. (2012). *Nonprofit management: Principles and practice* (2nd ed.). Thousand Oaks, CA: Sage.

GOOD INTENTIONS GONE AWRY
AT THE NATIONAL KIDNEY FOUNDATION[1]

In June 2007, the former chief executive officer of the National Kidney Foundation Singapore (NKF), Thambirajah Tharmadurai (T. T.) Durai was charged with corruption and sentenced to three months in jail. Just less than two years earlier, he was the prolific CEO who transformed the NKF from a small foundation into Singapore's largest charity with twenty-one dialysis centres. Under T. T. Durai's control, revenue grew from $17 million to $116 million.[2] T.T. Durai spent 37 years of his life volunteering and working with the NKF. What happened to this man, who over all these years had been respected for his dedication to charity work and leading the NKF?

NKF: THE BEGINNING

The National Kidney Foundation (NKF) was first established as a dialysis unit at the Singapore General Hospital (SGH) in 1969. The unit was located in the attic of the hospital and consisted of only two beds and one metal tray. From 1970 to the 1980s, the NKF made several accomplishments. These included completing the first renal transplant operation in Singapore in 1970, and organizing the first overseas transplant in 1983, where a kidney was flown from the United States for a kidney patient. The first kidney dialysis centre was also opened in September 1982 at the Kwong Wai Shiu hospital, with 10 dialysis machines.[3]

The philosophy of the NKF to maintain "healthy reserves that can withstand even the direst economic times"[4] was formed during the early years of its establishment. At Kwong Wai Shiu hospital, free treatment was offered to patients without any thought about costs. As a result, NKF funds dried up in 1986. Board members then had to make the painful decision of selecting which of their 32 patients would have to leave the hospital, which basically meant sending them home to their deaths.[5]

Besides trying its best to give all kidney patients a chance to receive treatment for their illnesses, the NKF took into consideration their

---

Hwee Sing Khoo, Audrey Chia, and Vivien K. G. Lim wrote this case solely to provide material for class discussion. The authors do not intend to illustrate either effective or ineffective handling of a managerial situation. The authors may have disguised certain names and other identifying information to protect confidentiality.

Ivey Management Services prohibits any form of reproduction, storage or transmittal without its written permission. Reproduction of this material is not covered under authorization by any reproduction rights organization. To order copies or request permission to reproduce materials, contact Ivey Publishing, Ivey Management Services, c/o Richard Ivey School of Business, The University of Western Ontario, London, Ontario, Canada, N6A 3K7; phone (519) 661-3208; fax (519) 661-3882; e-mail cases@ivey.uwo.ca. Copyright © 2010, Ivey Management Services Version: (A) 2010-04-19.

[1]This case has been written on the basis of published sources only. Consequently, the interpretation and perspectives presented in this case are not necessarily those of the National Kidney Foundation or any of its employees.

[2]All funds are in Singapore dollars unless otherwise noted. US$1 = S$1.5 on April 19, 2009.

[3]National Kidney Foundation, "History of NKF," National Kidney Foundation website, www.nkfs.org/index .php?option=com_content&task=view&id=86&Itemid=83&limit=1&limitstart=2, accessed March 2, 2009.

[4]S. Long, "The NKF: Controversially ahead of its time?" *The Straits Times,* April 19, 2004, quoting Richard Yong, accessed March 2, 2009, from Factiva database.

[5]S. Long, "The NKF: Controversially ahead of its time?," *The Straits Times*, April 19, 2004, accessed March 2, 2009, from Factiva database.

psychological needs as well. From as early as 1989, the charity's dialysis centres were designed with the comfort of the patient in mind. Careful thought was put into creating a warm and cheery environment through creative design themes for the patient during dialysis.[6]

DURAI'S EARLY YEARS AND THE RISE OF A NEW CHIEF EXECUTIVE OFFICER

In his university days, T.T. Durai was already an active volunteer with the NKF. His name, Thambirajah Tharmadurai, meant "a charitable man" in Tamil. Dynamic in his university years, he was vice-president of the then-University of Singapore Students' Union in the late 1960s. Even back then, Durai was described as well dressed, ambitious and surrounded by many friends. He was also a grassroots leader, and an appointed member of the Pasir Panjang Community Centre management committee.

Durai won the Outstanding Young Person Award in 1972, an award recognizing not just outstanding individual achievement in an individual's own field, but also someone with an outstanding track record of service to the community. Other recipients of the award include the then-Brigadier General (NS) Lee Hsien Loong in 1975, now the current prime minister of Singapore. Durai graduated from the University of Singapore with a law degree, and worked for the government legal service for six years until 1977. In that period of time, he also attained a master's of law in London. Upon leaving the government legal service, Durai joined the law firm Rodyk and Davidson in 1979 and worked there for four years[7] before starting his own firm Saddiqe, Durai & Partners in 1983. He later became the honorary secretary of the NKF, and then officially CEO in June 1992, after 21 years as a volunteer at the charity.

T. T. Durai was known to be a refined and articulate man who kept a low profile. The CEO recognized each NKF patient by name, and was known to care deeply for them. Durai was viewed as a far-sighted and hardworking CEO who kept 12- to 14-hour workdays and worked seven days a week. He also ate and showered in his office. The man was described as a "hands-on" boss who often scheduled presentations on Sundays, and conducted weekly training sessions called "CEO speak" with staff at the Kim Keat headquarters auditorium. These sessions lasted almost two hours at times. Similarly, he was a firm CEO who ensured that NKF employees always kept in mind that their salaries were drawn from donor funds. This prudent mentality was reinforced by the implementation of fines ranging from $5 for arriving late for work to $30 for failing to turn off the lights. However, in an interview in 2004, NKF directors emphasized that senior executives and above travelled by business class, while remaining employees flew economy class. The charity went to great lengths to protect its reputation, as seen by the legal suits against some members of the public for wrongful allegations, which Durai felt might tarnish the charity's name.

Archie Ong, an ex-volunteer of the NKF, was sued in 1997 by Durai and five other members of the NKF's executive committee for defamation. Ong commented to another NKF volunteer that NKF funds were misspent, and that Durai flew first class for his business trips. The case was settled out of court, with Ong publishing a public apology in the two major local newspapers declaring that the statements made were "totally baseless and untrue." Ong also paid for legal costs and damages, which were in turn donated to the NKF. Durai explained his reason for the suit: "Reputation is something which is sacrosanct to any institution of public character and it's so with the NKF. And we have to preserve it so that it's not hurt by gross untruths."[8]

---

[6]"Shophouse-style complex designed to reflect country's heritage and exude warmth," *The Straits Times,* September 9, 1989, accessed March 2, 2009, from Factiva database.

[7]K. Wong, "Confident, cocky, combative and . . ." *The New Paper,* July 14, 2005, accessed March 2, 2009, from Factiva database.

[8]S. Vasoo, "NKF chief, 5 members suing ex-volunteer for slander," *The Straits Times,* August 19, 1997, accessed March 2, 2009, from Factiva database.

In 1998, aero-modelling instructor Piragasam Singaravelu was similarly sued for alleging that Durai flew first class. This case was also settled out of court, with Singaravelu paying legal costs, damages and publishing a public apology as in the earlier legal suit involving Archie Ong.[9] In 1999, Tan Kiat Noi made a public apology and paid $50,000 in damages for sending out a defamatory email message about the NKF paying outlandishly high bonuses to its employees. The email was estimated to be received by about 100,000 people.

Similarly, Durai would send out meticulously worded replies to the media to refute any allegations made by members of the public and other organizations against the NKF. Durai defended the NKF on several occasions in letters to the media on issues ranging from the charity's recruitment practices to the socio-economic groups subsidized by the NKF as compared to another non-profit organization, the KDF (Kidney Dialysis Foundation). Launched in 1996, the KDF aimed to help the poorest kidney patients in Singapore. The KDF saw itself as filling a gap by assisting the poorest, while the NKF believed it was already doing that, and that the KDF represented competition.[10]

A NEW DIRECTION FOR THE NKF

"Please call 10 times because it's the 10th anniversary of the show. You might not win a prize, but we can guarantee you a place in heaven." —T. T. Durai[11]

With Durai at the NKF's helm, the charity grew to become Singapore's largest charity. It improved its accessibility to kidney patients by establishing a total of 21 dialysis centres by 2005. Singapore had a high occurrence of kidney failure, where approximately 750 people were diagnosed with kidney failure every year.[12] Approximately 8.2 per cent of Singaporeans suffered from diabetes, and 20.1 per cent from hypertension. The charity aimed to prevent kidney-related diseases and ensure that kidney patients received affordable healthcare. This was done primarily through efforts at educating the public. The NKF also provided subsidized health-screening programs, dialysis care, renal transplants and rehabilitation programs for kidney patients. The charity was made up of more than 40 departments, which reported directly to Durai (see Exhibit 1).

Durai also believed in research to develop kidney disease prevention programs, and led the NKF's foray into pre-dialysis care. In 1997, the NKF teamed up with the renal division of Brigham and Women's Hospital (BWH), Harvard Medical School's teaching hospital in Boston, United States. Through this partnership, the NKF would be able to enlist the help of BWH and draw on its expertise in developing a complete renal program involving prevention, early detection and intervention.[13]

Durai strongly believed that every patient should be responsible and contribute to their dialysis treatment: "We expunged the notion of welfarism from the programme as we knew it was a sure way to go into bankruptcy." He stood firmly by the "patient-also-pays" policy he implemented in 1988, where patients had to pay subsidized dialysis fees promptly or risk being fined $25. The NKF assessed the patient's overall

[9]*The Straits Times,* "NKF chief gets public apology," December 11, 1998, accessed March 2, 2009, from Factiva database.

[10]*The Straits Times,* "NKF war of words—the nub of the issue," May 11, 1997, accessed March 2, 2009, from Factiva database.

[11]*The Straits Times,* "10th year, so call 10 times," March 28, 2003, accessed March 2, 2009, from Factiva database.

[12]National Kidney Foundation, "Understanding End-Stage Renal Disease (ESRD)," National Kidney Foundation website.

[13]*The Straits Times,* "NKF teams up with American hospital," March 14, 1997, accessed March 2, 2009, from Factiva database.

Exhibit 1 NKF Organizational Chart Under T.T. Durai's Leadership

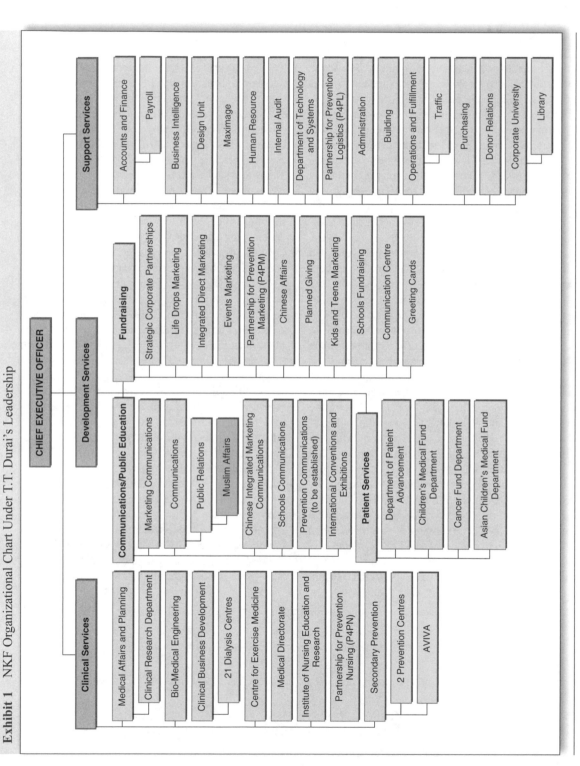

Source: KPMG, "A Report on the National Kidney Foundation," 2005.

financial situation, namely, income, number of dependants, family support and medical record, to determine to what extent the patient should be subsidized. Patients were also expected to continue working and adhering to their stipulated diets as the conditions for dialysis fees subsidies. Incentives were offered to encourage the patient's family to be engaged in the treatment process. For example, the charity would lower treatment fees if the patient's children did well in school or attained a place in university. The success of this tough stance silenced critics, with 97 per cent of the patients going back into the workforce as compared to 30 per cent of patients in the West. Mortality rates at below five per cent were also lower than nine per cent in Japan and 20 per cent in the United States in 1994. In line with the NKF's view of having sufficient resources to cushion patients in bad times, Durai stated in 1994 that the next aim for the charity was to raise $100 million over the next decade. He explained: "The NKF has to be around for our children and our children's children. And for that we need money."[14]

Other countries such as Bangladesh, China, India, Malaysia and Pakistan also sought the expertise of the NKF for their own dialysis programs. The NKF's biggest consultancy role was in 2004, when the Samoan government approached the NKF to help establish and operate a dialysis program in Samoa, based on the Singapore model. Durai said, "This is a testimony to the faith of Singapore's people who've helped us to build this institution—now, we can help other people in the world."[15]

This focused attitude also saw Durai continue with a decade-long campaign to help the Muslim community understand kidney donation. Muslims were previously exempted from the Human Organ Transplant Act (HOTA) due to religious reasons. As a result, Muslims were accorded lower priority if they needed a kidney transplant unless they had pledged to be a donor previously. The easing of a fatwa (religious edict) by the Islamic Religious Council of Singapore (Muis) allowed Muslims to pledge their organs without having to secure signed consent from their waris (close male family member). With the easing of the fatwa, the NKF contributed $250,000 to the drive to educate the Muslim community on organ-pledging.[16]

The first member of the public to bequeath a legacy to the NKF was Lucky Tan in 1994. Tan was afflicted by colorectal cancer and renal failure but unfortunately died before the official dissolution of his joint tenancy of a residential property worth $2.5 million (US$1.66 million) with his first wife. The NKF initially decided not to contest the will as lawyers advised that they did not have a strong case. Durai felt the NKF should not "take a gamble on public funds in taking the case to court although the stakes were high." The charity later decided to pursue the case, and an agreement was reached almost seven years later in 2001 where it was decided that 30 per cent of the property's valuation would be given to the NKF if Tan's widow sold the house or died, whichever happened first. According to Durai, this was a matter of honouring a dying man's wish. Other members of the public who bequeathed wealth to the NKF in their wills include Rosslyn Mak, a childcare teacher who left the NKF a flat[17] worth $700,000 in 1997, and Chia Foong Ying, who left $3.4 million to the charity in 2000.[18]

---

[14]M. Nirmala, "NKF's patients-also-pay policy works, says Durai," *The Straits Times,* May 10, 1994, accessed March 2, 2009, from Factiva database.

[15]"NKF to help Samoa set up dialysis scheme," *The Straits Times,* July 13, 2004, accessed March 2, 2009, from Factiva database.

[16]R. Basu, "Muslim group's drive for organ donation," *The Straits Times,* September 2, 2004, accessed March 2, 2009, from Factiva database.

[17]An apartment flat built and developed by the Housing and Development Board (HDB). The board managed public housing in Singapore, where about 85 per cent of the population was housed in flats, a solution for land constraints.

[18]W. Tan, "She leaves," *The Straits Times,* January 23, 2003, accessed March 2, 2009, from Factiva database.

MARKETING STRATEGIES

"Relentless innovation over the years has brought new ways of fund-raising: greeting cards, live charity shows, donations via SMS, consultancy services, even selling its spare telemarketing capacity to private companies. In the social service sector, the NKF is the unparalleled paragon of the art of 'heartsell.'"[19]

Dialysis subsidies for patients came from funds obtained from public donations. The NKF raised funds through several innovative methods, ranging from traditional fundraising methods, such as donation cards or the sale of festive greeting cards, to televised charity shows appealing for call-in donations. Through the introduction of its novel fundraising method using telephone polling back in 1994, the NKF's fundraising efforts generated record-breaking donations on their annual NKF television charity shows, which featured performances by local and international artists. The first charity show raised $4.5 million and offered attractive prizes in a lucky draw for caller donors, such as a condominium unit worth $750,000 (US$500,000) as the top prize.

Instead of depending solely on generous, one-time donations from affluent individuals or companies, the NKF tapped small monthly donations ranging from $3 to $5 from the average Singaporean. These contributions from about one million Singaporeans were deducted automatically every month through Giro transfer,[20] and added up to form a substantial stream of funds to the charity's reserves. These small monthly donations were garnered from the public through free on-site health screenings, which the NKF personnel and nurses conducted every day at companies' buildings, churches, condominiums and even army camps. Upon each individual's completion of the health screening, which included blood, body fat and urine tests, the NKF staff would make a heartfelt plea for a monthly contribution to the charity. The LifeDrops Program was also set up in 1987 to help sustain the healthcare programs that the NKF launched to care for kidney failure patients. The minimum donation amount was $5 per month ($60 per year), and donors had the choice of donating through Giro or credit card.

In another unique move, the NKF joined forces with insurance giant Aviva to increase its revenues by referring potential clients to Aviva from its vast donor database of around one million individuals who had donated to the NKF over the past decade. These included individuals who had used the health-screening service, as well as the NKF's own employees. The Aviva-NKF Life & Health Hub was opened on April 7, 2005, in the central business district of Singapore, the third in the NKF's innovative network of prevention centres. The alliance would allow the NKF to receive at least $1 million yearly in referral fees from Aviva. Reactions from the public varied; some donors felt it constituted an invasion of donor privacy if they were subjected to promotional materials from a commercial firm (Aviva), while others lauded it as an innovative method of fundraising for a righteous cause.[21]

DIVERSIFICATION

The NKF branched out to support children and youths afflicted by other severe illnesses that needed expensive medication and broad medical attention by establishing the NKF Children's Medical Fund (NKF-CMF) on Children's Day, October 1, 2001. The fund assisted more than

---

[19]S. Long, "The NKF: Controversially ahead of its time?," *The Straits Times*, April 19, 2004, accessed March 2, 2009, from Factiva database.

[20]Direct transfer of funds from one bank account to another.

[21]L. Tan, "Creative move or invasion of privacy?" *The Straits Times,* April 3, 2004, accessed March 2, 2009, from Factiva database.

2,500 chronically ill children by subsidizing costly treatments and rehabilitative care. In addition, the fund contributed to the annual operating expenses for the Shaw-NKF Children's Kidney Centre (CKC), which was a one-stop centre with medical facilities for kidney failure and transplants, and related issues.

Under Durai's direction, the NKF took up the fight against cancer as well, establishing the NKF Cancer Fund in November 2004. The NKF Cancer Fund would cover the costs of research, screening programs and public education in the hope of curbing the increasing rate of cancer. The fund was also aimed at alleviating the financial burden on cancer patients and their families through subsidies and emotional support.[22]

The Golden Tap

On April 19, 2004, an article on the NKF by journalist Susan Long was published in the *Straits Times.* The article featured an interview with a contractor who was enraged with the charitable foundation that hired him to install pricey bathroom fittings, including a gold-plated tap, in its CEO's personal office bathroom. Issues such as the impressive $189 million in reserves accumulated by the NKF over the years, and the lack of transparency regarding salaries and benefits of its executives, were also included in the article.

On April 23, 2004, Durai and the NKF sued the Singapore Press Holdings (SPH) and senior writer Susan Long for defamation. Durai and the NKF argued that the article severely damaged their integrity and reputation as it could be construed that the NKF and Durai mishandled the public donations made to the NKF by splurging money on Durai's bathroom fittings.

Revelations in Court

The trial between Durai and the SPH was instructive in that it revealed surprising information about Durai's high remuneration package and travel perks. Durai received a total of $1.8 million in pay and performance bonuses for his past three years of service. It turned out that NKF funds were used for retrofitting the bathroom in his office with a golden tap and other expensive materials. When asked in court if the cost of the tap was excessive, Durai replied, "We do not consider it expensive. It is not a tap. It is a mixer together with a shower."[23] The lack of transparency in the NKF's dealings with the public, media and even in court, was an issue highlighted by the defence counsel. On his reluctance to disclose his salary despite repeated requests from the defence, Durai explained that it was "a personal matter," that he was a private person, and that it was up to the board to decide. The defence counsel pointed out that there was a responsibility for Durai to provide this information to the people, as his salary was funded by public donations.[24]

Most notably, Durai did travel first class on his overseas trips. He explained in court that this was allowed by the NKF board as long as the cost of the first-class tickets did not exceed the Singapore Airlines business-class rate. When asked about the previous cases of individuals sued by the NKF for alleging that he flew first class, Durai stood by his claim that he did not fly first class then, and that even when he did, he topped up the difference himself. News of Durai's extravagance was particularly difficult for the public to accept, as Singapore workers faced tough times after the Asian financial crisis in 1997. Despite the difficult economic times, two out of three Singaporeans

---

[22]R. Basu, "NKF lends a hand to fight cancer," *The Straits Times,* November 25, 2004, accessed March 2, 2009, from Factiva database.

[23]W. K. Wong and M. Quah, "NKF CEO retracts claim of SPH 'agenda,'" *The Straits Times,* July 12, 2005, accessed March 2, 2009, from Factiva database.

[24]"A private man's $600,000 pay—is it of public interest?" *The Straits Times,* July 12, 2005, accessed March 2, 2009, from Factiva database.

donated a percentage of their annual income to the NKF. The public felt betrayed upon learning that their hard-earned money was channeled toward Durai's personal expenses and remuneration, with only 10 cents of every dollar donated going to the intended beneficiaries, i.e., the kidney patients.

Durai withdrew his allegation against the SPH after two days of intense grilling on the witness stand, where he conceded that the article did not defame him and the NKF. Despite retracting the suit, Durai still maintained his stand that "he did nothing wrong" and saw no reason to step down. He also told reporters after dropping his defamation suit that he "did not think the case would have much impact on the public."[25]

Unbeknownst to him, a public backlash was already brewing, and spiking after each day's legal proceedings were publicized in the media. About 6,800 NKF donors withdrew their support for the NKF and 40,000 individuals even went online to petition for Durai's dismissal. Members of the public inundated the media with angry letters. One individual summed up the feelings of the majority in his letter:

> My initial reaction was, "Who have I been donating to all these years? The NKF patients or its CEO?" Is this the kind of . . . society that we should be proud of and proclaim to the world? That CEOs and chairmen of non-profit charitable organizations which accept donations from the public need to be rewarded such obscene amounts in order to do their jobs? And even have the audacity to sue others for defamation and damages when they are discovered?—Ricky Lee [26]

Others vandalized and wrote graffiti on the walls of the NKF headquarters to express their disapproval. Soon after, Durai and the entire NKF board made the decision to step down on July 14, 2005.

The trial between the SPH and Durai also revealed other issues and inconsistencies. Under Durai and his team, the NKF had evolved into a "perpetual money-making machine," preoccupied with fundraising at the expense of patients' welfare. Besides adopting highly commercialized fundraising strategies on television, Durai's team even created a slush fund from discounts received from medical drug suppliers. This was officially termed "sponsorship liability account," a discretionary fund at Durai's disposal and use when the NKF's fundraising cost exceeded the Ministry of Health's rule that fundraising costs should not exceed 30 per cent of the amount raised. Approximately 10 cents out of every charity dollar were used to subsidize direct treatment costs. Durai was also alleged to have inflated patient numbers to attract more donations—this he claimed to be a miscommunication of numbers from his department heads to him.

It was also revealed during court proceedings that Durai failed to disclose several business relationships he had with the companies to which the NKF awarded IT and call centre contracts. Durai and former NKF employee Matilda Chua were joint investors in Global Net, a company set up for call centre work and which operated from the same premises as Proton Web, the company to which the NKF call centre contract was awarded. Matilda Chua was also the Singapore representative of Proton Web.[27]

The charity also informed the *Straits Times* during an interview that it needed $62.4 million per year to support its patients. However, the 2003 audited statement showed that only $31.6 million was spent on dialysis and transplantation. The NKF's assertion that its reserves

---

[25]"T. T. Durai: I have done nothing wrong," *The Straits Times,* July 13, 2005, accessed March 2, 2009, from Factiva database.

[26] M. Quah, "NKF faces public backlash," *Business Times Singapore,* July 14, 2005, accessed March 2, 2009, from Factiva database.

[27] W. K. Wong, "Business relationship with ex-NKF staff not disclosed," *Business Times Singapore,* July 13, 2005, accessed March 2, 2009, from Factiva database.

of $262 million would last only three years was thus deemed inaccurate in court.[28]

The reaction of the public contrasted with the support Durai's staff showed him after the revelations in court. Durai received a standing ovation from a full auditorium at NKF headquarters after he encouraged his staff to carry on striving for the patients, and not let his court case affect their morale. According to his deputy director of communications, Durai had not taken a holiday besides one day of compassionate leave since 1992, and worked relentlessly for the patients. Another manager of the NKF's patient advancement department undergoing subsidized dialysis said he owed T. T. Durai his life. To him, Durai always exhibited integrity, and insisted that food hampers received by the NKF during the New Year were given to needy patients. This positive view was echoed by other patients, who felt that Durai deserved his pay, as the bottom line was the number of patients he saved.[29] Staff reacted with emotional outbursts and tears upon Durai's announcement of his resignation. As described by a new employee of the NKF, "In a normal organization, when you have been there only for a month, you don't feel much about it. But Durai trains us personally and we feel close to him, and we feel sad that he has to leave." Another assistant manager described Durai as a guiding light to the staff, "but I think we will be okay as he has trained us so well."[30]

At the press conference where he announced his resignation, Durai shared his thoughts about stepping down. "I have been running NKF for 37 years and I think it's time that a new leadership takes over because I strongly believe in change . . . a new style."[31]

STEPPING DOWN

Following the departure of Durai and his team, the new board of directors at the NKF commissioned KPMG to write a report in July 2005. This report noted that most of the management problems at the NKF during Durai's reign stemmed from the fact that all responsibilities in the organization were entrusted to Durai alone. The investigation also revealed that under Durai, the NKF inflated the number of patients who were actually receiving subsidies, i.e., the NKF was subsidizing fewer patients and at a lower cost than it reported.[32]

In addition to using unorthodox accounting methods, Durai received an annual salary (including bonuses) amounting to about $600,000. As well, Durai had access to a fleet of eight chauffeur-driven cars. The NKF was also responsible for paying the road tax, repair and maintenance bills of a Mercedes-Benz 200 that Durai personally owned. Over a period of 7.5 years, Durai charged more than $2 million to the charity's American Express corporate credit card for his overseas travel. Of this amount, $1 million was spent on hotel bills alone, approved by Durai himself. He stayed in top-of-the-line establishments like the Ritz-Carlton, Sheraton, Westin and Hyatt and flew first class on business trips.

It was also revealed in court that Durai and his team went on a study trip to Las Vegas, which

[28]S. Loh, "Enough for just 3 years? More like 30 to 40 years," *The Straits Times,* July 13, 2005, accessed March 2, 2009, from Factiva database.

[29]J. Teo, "Staff give T. T. Durai standing ovation," *The Straits Times,* July 14, 2005, accessed March 2, 2009, from Factiva database.

[30]T. Sua, "Tears and gestures of support as CEO announces resignations," *The Straits Times,* July 15, 2005, accessed March 2, 2009, from Factiva database.

[31]T. Tan, "It's time for leadership change: Durai," *The Straits Times,* July 15, 2005, accessed March 2, 2009, from Factiva database.

[32]KPMG, "A Report on the National Kidney Foundation," 2005, www.nkfs.org/download/nkf_report_161205.pdf, accessed July 1, 2007.

cost $70,000. Regarding this trip, Durai stated that it was suggested by media company MediaCorp: "MediaCorp suggested a study trip to the entertainment capital of America two years ago to get fresh ideas for the NKF's televised fund raisers." He also justified the trip, saying that new ideas were gleaned from this study trip. In addition, the Vegas trip was "not the first overseas outing for NKF and MediaCorp staff."[33] Study trips had been organized to Hong Kong and Japan for staff of both companies to generate ideas for the fundraiser shows. Such information unraveled by the court proceedings disappointed the public and led to much cynicism with regard to charitable organizations. The public questioned how much of its donation actually benefited its intended beneficiaries.

In February 2007, the new National Kidney Foundation sued former chief executive officer T. T. Durai and three other former NKF directors—Richard Yong (ex-NKF chairman), Loo Say San (ex-NKF treasurer), and Matilda Chua (ex-NKF director)—for breach of duty. In a surprising turn of events on January 10, 2007, which was the third day of the trial, Durai accepted liability for all claims brought against him by the new NKF management and agreed to the terms spelled out.

CORPORATE GOVERNANCE AND ORGANIZATIONAL STRUCTURE

"The board has come out too strongly to back the CEO for my liking," said a corporate governance expert. "It looks like the board was thinking only of his performance in raising funds. But it also needs to think ethically. Clearly, he wasn't completely ethical. The board has to set the tone for the kind of values in an organization."[34]

A not-for-profit organization does not operate with a profit-seeking motive, and adopts a different kind of mission as compared to a for-profit

business venture. Instead of shareholders with the goal of profit maximization, altruism is the main driving force for the organization. The board of directors, which Durai repeatedly referred to as those who granted him his entitlements, were all volunteers of the charity, and the board operated parallel to an executive committee. The executive committee was described by Durai as the "overall supreme decision maker of the NKF."

The executive committee was set up during an annual general meeting (AGM) in 2002 with "total powers to manage the affairs of the National Kidney Foundation," and appeared to challenge the influence and power of the former board. Durai was an active participant of the executive committee, but was officially a member of neither the board nor the committee. This was his rationalization on the witness stand for not being required to reveal his salary—he was not a director.

Other than the executive committee, the NKF also set up an audit committee and prided itself on being the first charity to voluntarily establish an audit committee to improve its internal system. The committee, however, did not appear to be able to put across its recommendations and was described as having only "served cosmetic purposes" without posing a real challenge to the NKF management. Other committees included the finance committee and the remuneration subcommittee, established in 1997 and 2004, respectively. Similarly, the work of these committees was poorly documented; the meeting minutes of the finance committee were reported to be destroyed in a "computer crash," while the remuneration sub-committee only conducted a round of performance appraisals in 2004. Not required to account for its performance, the board of directors was comfortable with the executive committee assuming its powers. The executive committee approved all proposals by the management team.

[33]"$70,000 Vegas trip 'useful,'" *The Straits Times,* June 9, 2006, accessed March 2, 2009, from Factiva database.

[34]W. K. Wong, "Public's attention turns to NKF Board," *Business Times Singapore,* July 14, 2005, accessed March 2, 2009, from Factiva database.

Durai held the core power as the CEO, and his approval was required for all NKF activities. It was significant that the executive committee had the authority to assign "those powers they see fit" to the chief executive. The establishment of the executive committee thus ensured a concentration of power in Durai's hands. Because of the loyalty and respect commanded by Durai from fundraising achievements, the board supported his decisions. As a result, the internal controls of the NKF did not operate according to the requirements befitting an outfit of the NKF's size. Rather, it was run in an *ad hoc* manner and not with established procedures. Executive powers were bestowed upon associates trusted by Durai, even though they were volunteers and not officially employees of the charity. Pay adjustments were carried out several times in a year and occasionally backdated; contracts made with companies related to NKF directors and volunteers were approved. There were forty-eight heads of departments in the NKF; all reported directly to T. T. Durai. Durai's financial rewards were based on the success of the NKF's fundraising.[35]

It appeared that the charity did not have a firm human resource structure in place. Heads of departments were not required to submit annual capital budgets, and approval of study or conference leave requested by staff was based on the discretion of senior management. There were also no clear guidelines on the funding amount or days of leave to which staff were entitled. Employees allocated company mobile phones were not specifically given usage caps, and some bills added up to almost $800 monthly.[36] Besides annual and event-specific bonuses, employees were given up to 10 months' salary of *ex gratia* exit payments when they resigned from the NKF. Exclusive matrimonial, bereavement and one-off bonuses were also given to certain staff members (see Exhibit 2).

GOVERNMENTAL REGULATION FOR CHARITIES

All charities in Singapore were under the Charities Act, which supported the improvement of administration by monitoring charities for any abuse of funds, and providing them with any useful information. The Act upheld the efficient use of charitable resources through this framework. Charities that obtained IPC (Institution of Public Character) status were required to submit audited accounts and present financial information online under the Income Tax Act. The Ministry of Finance then evaluated the eligibility of IPCs for tax-deductible donations. Since 1999, the NKF's accounts were audited by Pricewaterhouse Coopers (PwC). Between the end of 1999 and 2001, officers from the National Council of Social Service (NCSS) had reduced the validity period of the NKF's IPC status from five years to two to three months at a time. The NCSS executed the above decision as it disapproved of certain NKF practices, such as the inflation of patient subsidies and cost of dialysis, the rise in staff cost, and more money being diverted to fundraising than the development of patient welfare programs. Correspondence records showed that the NCSS conveyed only concerns regarding regulatory issues related to the NKF to the Commissioner of Charities, and not its disapproval of the above NKF issues. In 2004, the government formed a committee to investigate how charities that were declared IPCs were run to improve transparency and accountability.

The focus of regulators appeared to be mainly on possible exploitation of tax-exempt receipts by charities, instead of governance issues. Without working governance mechanisms in place, the NKF management team, under the charismatic and influential chief executive, redefined its mission as amassing the greatest amount

---

[35]KPMG, "A Report on the National Kidney Foundation," 2005, www.nkfs.org/download/nkf_report_161205.pdf, accessed July 1, 2007.

[36]G. Ee, "NKF clarifies human-resource issues," *The Straits Times,* ST Forum, December 8, 2005, accessed May 2, 2009, from Factiva database.

Exhibit 2 Exclusive Bonuses and Payments for Certain Employees

Employee	Amount or number of months of salary	Nature of payment	Employee	Amount or number of months of salary	Nature of payment
Q	$5,000	Bereavement	J	1 month	Special bonus
R	0.5 month	Matrimonial bonus	AF	0.5 month	Special bonus
S	0.5 month	Matrimonial bonus	I	1 month	Special bonus
T	1 month	Matrimonial bonus	AG	1 month	Special bonus
U	$3,500	One-time bonus	AH	2 months	Special bonus
V	0.5 month	Payment bonus	AI	1 month	Special bonus
W	0.5 month	Payment bonus	AJ	1 month	Special bonus
D	0.5 month	Payment bonus	AK	5 months	Ex gratia
X	1 month	Special bonus	AL	5 months	Ex gratia
Y	10 months	Ex gratia	AM	5 months	Ex gratia
Z	10 months	Ex gratia	AN	3 months	Ex gratia

Employee	Amount or number of months of salary	Nature of payment	Employee	Amount or number of months of salary	Nature of payment
AA	6 months	Ex gratia	AO	$20,000	Ex gratia
AB	2 months	Ex gratia	AP	$20,000	Ex gratia
AC	1 month	Ex gratia	AQ	$12,000	Ex gratia
AD	1 month	Ex gratia	AR	$5,000	Ex gratia
AE	1 month	Ex gratia			

Source: KPMG, "A Report on the National Kidney Foundation," 2005.

Notes: Names of employees have been redacted to protect the privacy of the individuals. Ex gratia: A voluntary payment given to the employee by the company out of kindness without any legal obligation.

of funds as soon as possible.[37] The charity under Durai soon went on to raise funds for non-kidney-related causes, establishing a reputation as "a very efficient fund-raising outfit" which was able to "raise funds a lot more effectively using non-traditional methods."[38]

DURAI'S CONVICTION

On June 22, 2007, Durai, 59, was criminally prosecuted and sentenced to three months' imprisonment for using a false invoice to mislead the NKF into releasing $20,000 to his friend, interior designer David Tan Kee Kan, in 2004. When Durai's defence was called, he chose to remain silent. The $20,000 was paid to Tan's consultancy company, DTC Pte Ltd, for services that were never carried out. Instead, the payment was a personal reward for Tan for assistance he had given Durai. Durai also reached a $4 million settlement with the new NKF and

agreed to repay the new NKF in installments over the next four years. With the settlement, the new NKF board would not further engage in legal proceedings to declare him bankrupt (see Exhibit 3).

Why did Durai and the NKF take the SPH to court without an evident strategy? Was Durai too confident after winning his previous lawsuits? Where does one draw the line between full transparency and salary/benefits disclosure? What should the key performance indicators (KPIs) of leaders in voluntary welfare organizations be, and how should top executives in these organizations be compensated? Was Durai a good leader? If so, was he an ethical leader? If not, where did he go wrong? These were just some of the many questions that ran through everyone's mind during the court proceedings. As CEO of a charitable organization using public funds, moral accountability appeared to be lacking in this case. How would Durai's actions be viewed if he were CEO of a private organization instead?

Exhibit 3 Timeline of Events

July 2005: T. T. Durai sues Singapore Press Holdings (SPH) for defamation. Details about Durai's pay package, questionable commercial links and mismanagement of funds emerge in court, and Durai drops the suit against SPH.

Durai and his entire team step down after a strong public backlash. Gerard Ee is appointed interim chairman and the Inland Revenue Authority of Singapore (IRAS) begins its audit.

August 2005: The Commercial Affairs Department is called in to assess unusual transactions.

November 2005: Independent auditor KPMG releases a negative report on the NKF.

December 2005: The Singapore government accepts partial blame for the NKF fiasco and begins announcing changes in order to better regulate the charity sector.

April 2006: Durai is arrested and charged with submitting false payment claims. Matilda Chua is charged with falsifying accounts at a company where both she and Durai were directors. Richard Yong and Loo Say San are charged for their role in the deal between the NKF and Pharis Aboobacker's company. The NKF also launches a civil lawsuit to recover about $12 million from Durai, his business associate Aboobacker and ex-NKF board members Chua, Yong, and Loo.

---

[37]"Govt will act if review uncovers wrongdoings," *The Straits Times,* July 15, 2005, accessed May 2, 2009, from Factiva database.

[38]A. Chang, "Despite furor, S'pore needs more fund-raising units like NKF: Khaw," *The Straits Times,* July 15, 2005, accessed May 2, 2009, from Factiva database.

June 2006: Durai, Yong, Chua and Loo file their defence against the civil lawsuit. They name other board members as third parties. The suit is later widened to involve the entire charity's board.

August 2006: Four other board members dragged into the civil suit deny any wrongdoing on their part.

September 2006: A full-time Commissioner of Charities is appointed.

November 2006: The Inland Revenue Authority reports tax irregularities in the old NKF.

January 2007: The civil suit goes to court. Durai concedes judgment on the third day of trial.

February 2007: The ex-directors of the NKF lose their civil suit and drop third-party claims against the other board members. Separately, Yong and Loo are called up to testify against Durai in a criminal trial.

March 2007: Yong and Loo plead not guilty in their own criminal trials on charges that they did not exercise due diligence, allowing Aboobacker's firm to claim money for work not done. Durai's interior designer friend David Tan provides damaging testimony in his trial that he was given $20,000 by Durai as a "token of appreciation."

April 2007: The NKF issues statutory demands, a prelude to bankruptcy proceedings, on Yong, Loo and Chua to foot legal bills and damages.

May 2007: Yong and Loo are convicted on criminal charges. Both are fined the maximum $5,000 for failing in their charity duties, but avoid jail terms. It is found that Yong and Loo have been disposing their assets since February. Both are declared bankrupt. Yong flees the country.

June 2007: Durai is convicted. Separately, he reaches a $4 million settlement payment with the NKF. A warrant of arrest is issued for Yong.

July 2007: Yong and his wife are arrested in Hong Kong.

August 2007: Richard Yong is extradited to Singapore from Hong Kong.

September 2007: Richard Yong is sentenced to 15 months in jail for illegally transferring nearly $4 million into his wife's overseas account, and for breaking the Bankruptcy Act. Yong appeals against his jail sentence.

December 2007: Matilda Chua is fined $10,000 for falsifying accounts in her company (Global Net Relations).

June 2008: Durai begins a three-month jail term.

Source: Compiled by authors.

DICKINSON COLLEGE: INSPIRATION FOR A LEADERSHIP STORY (IN THE VISION OF A FOUNDING FATHER)

On a mid-October morning in 1999, William G. (Bill) Durden got up from his desk and looked out his window onto the main green of the campus. Many thoughts filled his mind. The prior January, the board of trustees had named him the 27th president of his alma mater, Dickinson College. In a few weeks, on October 30, during the autumn board meeting,

Associate Professor Michael J. Fratantuono wrote this case solely to provide material for class discussion. The author does not intend to illustrate either effective or ineffective handling of a managerial situation. The author may have disguised certain names and other identifying information to protect confidentiality.

he would be officially instated and deliver his inaugural address.

In both personal and professional terms, the appointment represented a dramatic turn of events. When contacted by the Dickinson search committee in late autumn of 1998, Durden was not initially interested in the position. Yes, he had graduated from Dickinson in 1971, was certainly grateful for the education he had received and was mindful of the opportunities that had flowed from that experience.[1] However, he was serving as the president of a division of the Sylvan Learning Systems, Inc. and the vice-president of academic affairs for the Caliber Learning Network, positions that he found challenging and rewarding. Furthermore, as an alumnus, he had become increasingly angry and frustrated that over the past few decades, the school had not realized its potential; sometimes he had even been embarrassed that the name Dickinson did not command more respect in academic and professional circles. He only agreed to take the job after talks with trustees, alumni, faculty and students convinced him there was a genuine, broad-based desire for fundamental change at the college.[2]

Once he decided to accept and was named by the board, Durden began the process of transition. In the spring, he had visited the college several times. On July 1, at the start of the academic year, he had moved into the president's office in West College, Dickinson's most historically significant building. In the final days of August, as the semester started, he had mingled with students and their families, and prepared his convocation speech. Over the past nine months, Durden had uncovered what he regarded as two shortcomings at the college. The first quickly surfaced. For its entire 216-year history, the college had never had a fully articulated strategy. That realization had informed Durden's first major goal: the college would have a strategic plan by the spring of 2000. Towards that end, in the spring of 1999 he had asked the dean and other administrators to invite respected members of the college to serve on a special committee. During the summer, he and the group read more than 1,200 pages of white papers, reports, self-studies, and other documents that had been written in recent years about Dickinson. Informed by that background material, with the start of the semester, the committee began to meet each week to start the process of writing a first draft of a high-level strategic plan, one that would identify a vision and mission, defining attributes, and priorities for the college. Their objective was to complete a first draft by late autumn, so that the document could be vetted by faculty, students, administrators and trustees; redrafted over the winter; recirculated; and then released in final form to the community by the end of

---

---

[1]For example, Durden won a Fulbright Scholarship, studied in Switzerland and Germany, and earned a Ph.D. in German language and literature from Johns Hopkins University. He had stayed on at Johns Hopkins, taught in the German department for 16 years, and had become the executive director of the well-known Center for Talented Youth (CTY). He had acted as a consultant and advisor to numerous government agencies, non-profit organizations, and foundations in the field of education. "President William G. Durden, Biography," Dickinson College web site, http://www.dickinson.edu/about/president, accessed July 28, 2007.

[2]Bill Durden, "Comments as Guest Lecturer for the Dickinson College course, Financial Transformation of Dickinson College, February 6, 2007," Dickinson College, Carlisle, PA.

the academic year. Later that day, he would be attending another such meeting, participating not as a convener or facilitator, but as a contributor to the conversation. While the work was tough going, the attitude among committee members was upbeat and they had started to make some good progress.

The second shortcoming, more subtle and deeply embedded, involved the culture of the college. For much of the 20th century, the Dickinson community had lacked the sense of organizational pride and purpose one typically encountered at a college with a national reputation for excellence. Previous leaders had been comfortable with the status quo and had not conveyed a sense of urgency with respect to the internal and external challenges that confronted the school. Dickinson had remained relatively anonymous in the field of higher education, had failed to establish a strong and clear identity—the type of identity that could help distinguish the college from rivals and contribute to the experience of students, the sense of purpose of the faculty, and the affinity of alumni. That insight had come to Durden some two months earlier. During orientation week, he had gone on a day-hike with a group of students, and engaged in a lengthy conversation with a rising senior who had earned good grades and been deeply involved in campus life before spending time abroad during her junior year. The same evening, she sent him an e-mail and confessed that despite all that she had accomplished and experienced, she still did not have a clear sense of what it meant to be a Dickinsonian. That troubled Durden: if such an accomplished student could not explain what a Dickinson education stood for, then who could?[3]

The disturbing, albeit important, exchange with the young lady gave Durden a new purpose. That is, while Durden had—in addition to reading college documents for the special committee—also spent time throughout the summer studying the history of the college, the exchange had prompted him to revisit the circumstances associated with the college being granted a charter from the Assembly of Pennsylvania in 1783. Durden had become particularly intrigued by the life and writings of Dr. Benjamin Rush, the man responsible for founding the college. During a period of American history characterized by dramatic change in political, social, and economic affairs, Rush had articulated a clear and compelling vision for Dickinson. Unfortunately, in rather short order, those managing college affairs chose to disregard Rush and dismiss some of the central elements of his plan. Soon thereafter, Rush and his vision faded as guiding lights: by the 1900s, new generations of Dickinson faculty and students—including Durden when he was an undergraduate—never heard much at all from old hands about the man, his efforts, or his ideas.

Through his various life experiences, Durden had developed a somewhat non-traditional view about leadership. First, while he was a voracious reader, he did not spend much time with popular books about business management. Instead, he far preferred to read works of literature and visit museums for insights about human nature and group dynamics. Second, he had come to appreciate the power of a leadership story for motivating and channeling the energies of members of an organization. In his various posts, he always asked himself and those around him, "What is our story?" and given the story, "How are we doing?"[4] Durden now wondered, could Rush's vision and the history surrounding the college's origin be translated into a leadership story that informed the strategic plan and helped establish a strong sense of identity among members of the Dickinson community?

[3]Bill Durden, "Leadership, Language Study, and Global Sensibility," keynote address delivered at the East Asia Regional Council of Overseas Schools (EARCOS), Ho Chi Minh City, Vietnam, November 2, 2004, http://www.dickinson.edu/about/president/earcos.html.

[4]Bill Durden, comments as guest lecturer, February 6, 2007.

TURBULENT EVENTS, CLEAR VISION (1681–1783)

Early History of Pennsylvania and of Carlisle[5]

William Penn was born in London in 1644 to a family of wealth and status—his father was Admiral Sir William Penn. He gradually gravitated to the beliefs of the Society of Friends, or Quakers, then a persecuted sect. Despite his conversion, he retained the trust of the Duke of York (later King James II) and thus good social standing at the King's Court. Given his beliefs, Penn petitioned the Crown for land in the Americas that might serve as a haven for those of all religious persuasions. Ultimately—and at least in part due to an outstanding debt of £16,000 owed to the estate of the admiral, who had passed away in 1670—King Charles II signed the Charter of Pennsylvania, named in honor of the elder Penn, in March of 1681. Later that year, Penn visited the colony and summoned a general assembly. Under the charter, while officials bearing the title lieutenant-governor would represent the interests of the Penn family, the assembly would concentrate on matters of concern to residents.

During the 1700s, immigrants to the colony tended to cluster according to their heritage. English Quakers and Anglicans gathered in the southeast, in and around Philadelphia, which became a vibrant center for commercial, political, and intellectual life. Germans, many among them followers of the Lutheran faith, tended to move to the central part of the colony and take up farming. Scottish and Irish settled further west and were primarily frontiersmen and practitioners of Presbyterianism.

To help shape development, in 1750 the Assembly established Cumberland County, which included all of Pennsylvania west of the Susquehanna River. In 1751, Carlisle, a community of between 500 and 1,000 people, who were mostly of Scottish-Irish descent, was designated as the county seat.[6]

In the 1750s, hostilities broke out between settlers and Indian tribes, and then between the British and the French over lands in the Allegheny Mountains and the Ohio River Valley. Carlisle served as an outpost for royal and provincial militias heading west, a place "where the wagon roads ended and the pack horse trails began."[7] By 1756, when the French and Indian War was officially declared, defenses in Carlisle had been fortified. By 1758, Carlisle was a boom town, with some speculating it might grow into a metropolis.[8]

In the 1750s and 1760s, Carlisle was also witness to a power struggle between two factions of Presbyterians, one that was being waged on a larger scale in congregations, grammar schools, and colleges throughout the colonies. Generally speaking, the Old Side (conservatives) displayed the two defining characteristics of the religion: they organized themselves into a traditional governance structure, under which congregations belonged to presbyteries, and presbyteries to synods; and they accepted traditional Calvinist theology, which asserted that God had to intervene in order for an individual to achieve salvation—essentially, a form of predestination that dismissed the relevance of human volition and self-reliance in shaping one's spiritual destiny. The New Side (progressives) had no quarrel with governance structure, but influenced by the Enlightenment, they saw a greater role for the

---

[5]Most of this section is based on information found at the website of the Pennsylvania Historical and Museum Commission: http://www.phmc.state.pa.us/bah/pahist/quaker.asp, accessed July 2, 2007.

[6]Charles Coleman Sellers provides a nice sketch of the history of Carlisle and the town's most prominent citizens in *Dickinson College: A History,* Wesleyan University Press, Middletown, CT, 1973, chapter 2. A digital version of the book is available at http://chronicles.dickinson.edu/histories/sellers/toc_frame.html.

[7]Ibid, p. 22.

[8]Ibid, p. 22 and p. 31.

individual: a person could evaluate scripture, attempt moral self-improvement, and in a moment of transformation be touched by God's grace and experience a personal "revival."[9] In Carlisle, while members of the Old Side maintained a dominant position in the local congregation, advocates of New Side principles established a foothold.

By the late 1760s, a Carlisle minister had begun to offer lessons to the boys living in the town. In 1772, construction of a church, under the leadership of an Old Side clergyman, was completed, and it afforded space for regular school lessons. In keeping with the practices found in grammar schools of the day, boys 10 years of age and older studied moral philosophy ("the application of sound doctrine to right living"), Latin, Greek, and other topics. Schools such as this were only a step below and in some cases were an adjunct to the handful of colleges that had been established in the colonies.[10] In 1773, the Assembly granted a deed to a plot of land for a grammar school in Carlisle. Nine of Carlisle's most prominent residents, men who had achieved their status through their military, church, or commercial activities, were named to the school board.[11] While the school was immediately successful, the outbreak of the American Revolutionary War distracted all parties from the task of constructing a schoolhouse. Lessons continued to be held in the Presbyterian Church.

In 1781, the trustees were finally able to initiate construction of a new building. They also were intent on requesting a formal charter from the assembly, a document that would give the school status as a permanent corporation. In 1782, Colonel John Montgomery, one of the trustees, shared news of those developments with Dr. Benjamin Rush. Rush, who believed that an educated citizenry was the key to preserving liberties that had been earned during the American War for Independence, became intrigued—and a bit obsessed—by the prospect of establishing a college in Carlisle.[12] Within a year Rush, in consultation with Montgomery and in conjunction with his compatriot and friend John Dickinson, would see his vision become a reality.

John Dickinson and Benjamin Rush: Founding Fathers of a New Country[13]

John Dickinson was born in 1732 and was raised as a Quaker on his family's Maryland wheat and tobacco plantation. He received his higher education in London. Upon his return to the colonies, he settled in Philadelphia, began the practice of law, and was elected to the Pennsylvania Assembly. Dickinson became more deeply involved in public affairs when parliament levied the Stamp Act of 1765. Under the pen name A Farmer, he wrote

---

[9]D. G. Hart and John R. Muether, "Turning Points in American Presbyterian History Part 3: Old Side versus New Side, 1741–1758," New Horizons, web site of the Orthodox Presbyterian Church, http://www.opc.org/nh .html?article_id=46, and The American Presbyterian Church, History of American Presbyterianism, http://www .americanpresbyterianchurch.org/.

[10]Charles Coleman Sellers, *Dickinson College: A History,* Wesleyan University Press, Middletown, CT, 1973, p. 3.

[11]James Henry Morgan, *Dickinson College: The History of One Hundred and Fifty Years 1783–1933, Mount Pleasant Press, Carlisle, PA, 1933,* chapter 1. The book is also available in digital form at http://chronicles.dickinson. edu/histories/morgan/chapter_1.html.

[12]Charles Coleman Sellers, *Dickinson College: A History,* Wesleyan University Press, Middletown, CT, 1973, chapter 3 provides a history of the grammar school.

[13]This section is based on a range of sources, including the respective entries for Benjamin Rush and John Dickinson found in the Chronicles of Dickinson College, Encyclopedia Dickinsonia, http://chronicles.dickinson.edu/ encyclo/r/ed_rushB.html and http://chronicles.dickinson.edu/encyclo/d/ed_dickinsonJ.htm, as well as a variety of other websites dealing with John Dickinson, Richard Henry Lee and the Second Continental Congress.

12 powerful essays that were published in newspapers throughout the colonies. Therein, he criticized the act on the grounds that it contradicted traditional English liberties, citing legal authorities and the works of antiquity to buttress his arguments. He was elected to the First Continental Congress of 1774 and made a significant contribution by drafting declarations in the name of that body. He was also elected to the Second Continental Congress.

On June 7, 1776, Richard Henry Lee of Virginia introduced a resolution in the Second Congress declaring the union with Great Britain dissolved, proposing the formation of foreign alliances, and suggesting the drafting of a plan of confederation to be submitted to the respective states. Dickinson stood in opposition, believing the colonies should first form a confederation before declaring independence from Great Britain. One month later, on July 4, 1776, Dickinson held to his principles and in an act of moral courage, did not sign the Declaration of Independence. Given Dickinson's opposition to the declaration, he was assigned to a committee to draw up Articles of Confederation. The Congress was unable to reach agreement on the articles until November 17, 1777, at which time the articles were forwarded to each of the thirteen states. The articles were finally approved by a sufficient number to become operative on July 9, 1778.

At the conclusion of the Congress, Dickinson took a position as a colonel in the Continental Army. However, he eventually resigned his commission, due to what he interpreted as a series of insults stemming from the public stance he had taken. While there is a mixed record, some accounts suggest he subsequently served as a private soldier at the Battle of Brandywine. Following that service, he remained centrally involved in political affairs. In 1782, Dickinson was elected president of the Supreme Executive Council of Pennsylvania, a post equivalent to a modern-day governor. In 1786 he participated in and was elected president of a convention at Annapolis to revise the Articles of Confederation.

The brief session was soon adjourned, in favor of a constitutional convention held in Philadelphia from May to September, 1787. In the latter gathering, Dickinson drafted passages that dealt with the election of and powers for the President of the United States. The constitution was completed in 1787. To promote ratification, Dickinson wrote nine widely read essays under the pen name Fabius. The constitution was adopted in 1788 and took effect in 1789, thereby replacing the Articles of Confederation. While amended over time, it is the oldest, operative, written constitution in the world. Given his patriotic efforts, Dickinson earned a spot in U.S. history as the "Penman of the Revolution."

Benjamin Rush was born in 1745 on a farm near Philadelphia. He was raised in the Calvinist tradition. He earned his bachelor's degree in 1760 from the University of New Jersey (subsequently renamed Princeton), returned to Philadelphia and studied medicine from 1761 until 1766, and then moved abroad and earned a degree in medicine from the University of Edinburgh (Scotland) in June 1768. He returned once again to Philadelphia in 1769 and started a private practice while also serving as the professor of chemistry at the College of Philadelphia. He wrote essays on a range of subjects. His commentary about the emerging crisis between the colonies and Britain brought him into association with men such as John Adams and Thomas Jefferson. When the American Revolutionary War broke out in 1775, Rush joined the Continental Army as a surgeon and physician. In June 1776, he was appointed to the Second Continental Congress. Unlike Dickinson, when the time came, he chose to sign the declaration.

In April 1777, Rush was appointed surgeon-general of the Continental Army. However, he soon became embroiled in a dispute with Dr. William Shippen Jr., director of hospitals for the Continental Army, about medical conditions for the troops. He wrote letters about his concerns to key persons, including Commander in Chief George Washington.[14] When he received

---

[14]*Letters of Benjamin Rush,* Princeton University Press, Princeton, NJ, 1951, Volume 1, pp. 180–182.

no answers, Rush wrote a letter to Patrick Henry: therein, he repeated his concerns and expressed doubts about Washington's leadership.[15] After Henry disclosed the contents of the letter to Washington, Rush was asked to appear before a congressional committee. The committee sided with Shippen, prompting Rush to resign his commission. Nonetheless, Rush would not let the matter drop. He continued to write letters to Washington and other leaders, claiming that Shippen was guilty not only of mismanagement, but also of selling supplies intended for patients for his own profit. In one such letter to Nathaniel Greene, he unleashed his scathing wit.

I find from examining Dr. Shippen's return of the numbers who die in the hospitals that I was mistaken in the accounts I gave of that matter in my letters to you. . . . All I can say in apology for this mistake is that I was deceived by counting the number of coffins that were daily put under ground. From their weight and smell I am persuaded they contained hospital patients in them, and if they were not dead I hope some steps will be taken for the future to prevent and punish the crime of burying Continental soldiers alive.[16]

In January of 1780, Shippen was arrested. In what was regarded as an "irregular trial," which included Shippen wining and dining members of the hearing board, he was acquitted by one vote.[17] Rush eventually repaired his private relationship with Washington; but given that Washington had already started his rise to god-like status at the time of Rush's letter to Patrick Henry, the incident undermined Rush's public reputation for a number of years to come.

Rush returned to his practice in Philadelphia in 1778. In 1780, he began to lecture at the new University of the State of Pennsylvania. In 1783, Rush joined the staff of the Pennsylvania Hospital. He was relentless in his efforts to help battle the yellow fever epidemics which repeatedly surfaced in Philadelphia between 1793 and 1800; however, he was excoriated by some contemporaries for his aggressive advocacy and use of purging (bleeding) as proper treatment for the disease. Ultimately, he gained the reputation as a pioneer, credited with writing the first textbook published in the United States in the field of chemistry and the first major treatise on psychiatry. At the time of his death in 1813, he was regarded as the preeminent physician in the United States.

In 1787, Rush briefly reentered politics: he actively advocated ratification of the constitution and was appointed to the ratifying convention for the state. Of greater significance, Rush was an ardent social activist—he helped found the Pennsylvania Society for Promoting the Abolition of Slavery—and a prolific writer, advocating prison reform, abolition of capital punishment, temperance, better treatment of mental illness, universal health care, and a robust system of education. In 1797, he was appointed by President John Adams to be treasurer of the United States Mint, a post he occupied until he passed away.

Rush's Values and World View

Rush was a complex character. He accumulated an enormous breadth of formal knowledge, was a keen observer of everyday events, and was able to engage in either detailed analysis or sweeping generalization. He was a man of principle who would not back down in the face of pressure. At times, he was charming and persuasive, at others, nasty and domineering. While he could be a loyal, devoted, and caring friend, he sometimes abruptly turned on those who did not share his sentiments or opinions, and only later sought reconciliation.

[15]Ibid, pp. 182–183.

[16]Ibid, p. 195.

[17]"William Shippen, Jr.," University of Pennsylvania Archives, http://www.archives.upenn.edu/people/1700s/shippen_wm_jr.html, accessed September 23, 2007.

All of Rush's efforts to institute social reforms and promote the cause of education in the new country were informed by his assertion that the struggle for independence was a never ending process, illustrated for example by a public statement he made in 1787.

> There is nothing more common than to confound the terms of American Revolution with those of the late American war. The American war is over; but this is far from being the case with the American Revolution. On the contrary, nothing but the first act of the great drama is closed.[18]

Rush was the type of man who, as the years passed by, could be found arguing positions he had previously rejected—at times he even appeared to be self-contradictory.[19] Despite that tendency, at the most fundamental level he was concerned with two sets of relations: the configuration of social institutions such as family, church, school, and state; and the role of the individual within the context of those institutions.

Rush was informed by and contributed to three major intellectual movements of his time. First was the Scottish Enlightenment.[20] The University of Edinburgh, where Rush received his medical training, was an important center of the movement. Like their French counterparts, Scotsmen wrote about the power of the human mind to uncover the logic of natural laws, and celebrated the scientific achievements of the 17th century. However, they had an additional point of emphasis: they were concerned that Scotland, which in 1707 had been unified with an economically superior England, risked becoming a poverty-stricken backwater. Thus, men such as David Hume and Adam Smith investigated moral philosophy, history, and political economy in order to better understand the process of economic growth and development, in hope of applying insights and keeping Scotland economically vibrant.

Second, Rush was raised as a Calvinist. He gradually became sympathetic to the teachings of the New Side Presbyterians. The College of New Jersey was decidedly Presbyterian in its affiliation. While at Edinburgh, Rush, acting at the behest of some of the College of New Jersey Trustees, wrote to and visited with the progressive Scottish clergyman John Witherspoon, and convinced Witherspoon and his wife that Witherspoon should accept the presidency of the college. That was a maneuver important in the ongoing struggle being waged at the school between Old Side and New Side factions. Nonetheless, in later years, Rush became frustrated with Presbyterian elders and began to attend services of various Christian faiths. Even later in life, he withdrew to his own private reflections on religious matters.

Third, in terms of political philosophy, Rush's position also changed. In the years preceding the American Revolution, he was radical in his beliefs, calling for an overthrow of existing authority. As the prospect of independence became more certain, Rush became more conservative. For example, in the early 1780s, he asserted that democracy "meant rule by an elite drawn from the whole," with the elite reflecting the influence of God's grace.[21] A few years later, in the debate regarding the need for a bill of rights in the U.S. Constitution, Rush was sympathetic to the conservative views associated with the Federalist Party of John Adams, and stood in opposition to the Democrat-Republicans and Thomas Jefferson, who favored a more egalitarian concept of democracy.

> There can be only two securities for liberty in any government . . . representation and checks. By the first the rights of the people, and by the second the

[18]*Letters of Benjamin Rush,* Princeton University Press, Princeton, NJ, 1951, Volume 1, p. lxviii.

[19]Ibid, introduction.

[20]Department of Economics, New School for Social Research, "Scottish Enlightenment," The History of Economic Thought http://cepa.newschool.edu/het/schools/scottish.htm.

[21]Charles Coleman Sellers, *Dickinson College: A History,* Wesleyan University Press, Middletown, CT, 1973, p. 53.

rights of representation, are effectively secured. Every part of a free constitution hangs upon these two points; and these form the two capital features of the proposed Constitution of the United States. Without them, a volume of rights would avail nothing; and with them, a declaration of rights is absurd and unnecessary.[22]

In the presidential election of 1796, however, he favored Jefferson, who was defeated by Adams. In the early 1800s, he maintained a steady correspondence with Jefferson, who by that time had been elected president, as well as with Adams.

In 1797, when Rush was seeking the position at the U.S. Mint, Judge Richard Peters, a longtime Philadelphia Federalist, was asked by Secretary of State Pickering to provide a written evaluation of Rush. Peters suggested that Rush had made a series of bad political choices over time—he had, after all, gravitated to the Democrat-Republicans—and had suffered from the Shippen affair. But he went on to say the following:

> I lament his Want of Stability, for he certainly has great Merit, unshaken Integrity & eminent Talents. . . . I admire his Abilities, lament his Foibles, & with them all sincerely love him, therefore I cannot but wish him gratified.[23]

Securing a College Charter[24]

Rush imagined that the college in Carlisle would be part of a larger system that also included a handful of colleges located throughout the state and a university in Philadelphia. At the outset, it would be located at the site of the grammar school. He initially asserted that it should be affiliated with one religion—in this case the Presbyterian Church—and that a symbiotic relationship existed between religion and learning.

Religion is best supported under the patronage of particular societies. Instead of encouraging bigotry, I believe it prevents it by removing young men from those opportunities of controversy which a variety of sects mixed together are apt to create and which are the certain fuel of bigotry. Religion is necessary to correct the effects of learning. Without religion I believe learning does real mischief to the morals and principles of mankind; a mode of worship is necessary to support religion; and education is the surest way of producing a preference and constant attachment to a mode of worship.[25]

Rush soon realized that in order to achieve his objective of founding a college, he would have to win the support of three groups of constituents. First were the leaders of Carlisle, for although Montgomery endorsed the idea, others who were on the board of the grammar school were resistant. Second was the Donegal Presbytery, composed of elders from congregations located in communities throughout the region. Third was the Assembly of Pennsylvania. The need to win over the last group led him to retreat from the notion of an exclusive affiliation with the Presbyterian Church, and to consider a nonsectarian school, one that could be endorsed by clergymen of other Christian faiths, including the Lutherans, and could eventually win financial support from the assembly.

Thus, during the first eight months of 1783, Rush adapted four sets of tactics. First, he contacted influential and wealthy friends from Philadelphia to elicit political support and financial commitments for the college. Among those he visited was John Dickinson, who was by that time the president of the Supreme Executive Council of Pennsylvania. Dickinson rejected Rush's first proposal to name the school John and Mary's College after Dickinson and his wife, on grounds that it sounded too much like the

---

[22]*Letters of Benjamin Rush,* Princeton University Press, Princeton, NJ, 1951, Volume 1, p. 453.

[23]Ibid, p. 1210.

[24]The following paragraph is based on James Henry Morgan, *Dickinson College: The History of One Hundred and Fifty Years 1783–1933,* Mount Pleasant Press, Carlisle, PA, 1933, chapter 2.

[25]*Letters of Benjamin Rush,* Princeton University Press, Princeton, NJ, 1951, Volume 1, pp. 294–295.

College of William and Mary, which had been named for British royalty; however, he gradually warmed to the idea of a college that would bear his family name.[26] Second, Rush wrote letters to those he knew objected to the plan, and made his case for a school: it would obviate the need for young men from the Carlisle region to travel to Philadelphia or New Jersey for an education; and it would contribute to the emergence of a new commercial center in Carlisle, thereby raising land prices and creating better economic balance with Philadelphia, which dominated the eastern part of the state.[27] Third, in light of the heavy Scottish-Irish presence in the region, Rush argued that the college would provide a sound educational foundation to young men who aspired to be ministers in the Presbyterian Church. Fourth, he told those he contacted about the pledges of money and support he had already earned from others, and held out the promise of positions on the board of trustees of the college to people representing different professions, religions, and parts of Pennsylvania. As Rush acknowledged, the going was not easy.

[One group of opponents] accuse us of an attempt to divide the Presbyterians. . . . [To some groups] they say our college is to be a nursery . . . of the Old Lights [Old Side]—with the Old Lights they accuse us of a design to spread the enthusiasm of the New Lights [New Side] through the state. . . . In some of their letters and conversations I am considered as a fool and a madman. In others I am considered as a sly, persevering, and dangerous kind of fellow. Almost every epithet of ridicule and resentment in our language has been exhausted upon me in public newspapers and in private cabals since the humble part I have acted in endeavoring to found a college at Carlisle.[28]

Nonetheless, his methods worked. He successfully neutralized critics in Carlisle. In spring of 1783, the Donegal Presbytery endorsed the idea of a college. And, on September 9, 1783, by a margin of only four votes, the General Assembly of Pennsylvania approved the Dickinson College charter, entitled "An act for the establishment of a college at the borough of Carlisle, in the county of Cumberland, in the state of Pennsylvania."[29]

The date of the charter fell only six days after the September 3, 1783, signing of the Treaty of Paris, an event that formally ended the American Revolutionary War and included recognition by the United Kingdom and by France of the thirteen colonies as independent states.

Rush's Vision for the New College

Rush's philosophical leanings informed his vision of a Dickinson education. At the third Carlisle meeting of August 1785, Rush shared his "Plan of Education for Dickinson College." The original document, which survived, is filled with notations, suggesting Rush's plan was modified during conversations with other board members. The initial curriculum actually approved by the board included instruction in six major areas of study: (1) philosophy of the mind, moral philosophy and belles lettres (the translation from French is "fine letters" or "fine literature"), economics, and sociology; (2) Greek and Latin; (3) history and chronology; (4) mathematics; (5) English; and (6) natural philosophy (science).

As far as Rush was concerned, the curriculum was not ideal. For example, in his plan, Rush had placed chemistry in the same cluster of courses as mathematics and natural philosophy; but it was

---

[26]Charles Coleman Sellers, *Dickinson College: A History,* Wesleyan University Press, Middletown, CT, 1973, p. 55.

[27]*Letters of Benjamin Rush,* Princeton University Press, Princeton, NJ, 1951, Volume 1, pp. 294–296.

[28]Ibid, pp. 299–300.

[29]A digital copy of the original charter is available at the Chronicles of Dickinson College, http://chronicles.dickinson.edu/archives/charter_orig/. A digital copy of the original plus subsequent amendments through 1966 are available at http://chronicles.dickinson.edu/archives/charter_1966/charter.html#amendments.

lined through. Given that Rush was one of the leading experts in the field in the United States, and that he believed that chemistry was fundamental to other sciences and could be applied to fields of practical importance in the new nation, such as agriculture and manufacturing, the omission of chemistry as a stand-alone topic in the initial Dickinson curriculum had to be a source of frustration to him: indeed, the first professor in that field did not arrive at Dickinson until 1810.[30] Furthermore, while Rush believed that history and government were critical courses, he downplayed the significance of moral philosophy. Finally, despite his low opinion regarding the study of Greek and Latin, he had made a strong concession: in light of the central place those languages held in the education of the times, they should be included in Dickinson's program. But he did expect that modern languages such as French and German should also be taught.[31] However, as was the case with chemistry, the first faculty member who was expert in Spanish, Italian and French did not arrive on the scene until 25 years had passed. It took even longer for a professor of German to come to Dickinson.

Rush's disappointment with the shape of the initial Dickinson curriculum did not stop him from speaking out and staying involved in educational reforms. In 1786, Rush wrote the first version of an essay entitled, "Upon the spirit of education proper for the College in a Republican State," in which he more clearly and fully articulated his view of the purpose, principles, and content of the education that should be provided at Dickinson College (see Exhibit 1). He asserted that a liberal education should be informed by the core values associated with religious doctrine—especially that of the New Testament—in order to cultivate virtue; in turn, virtue was essential to liberty, and liberty to a republican form of government. An education should promote a sense of homogeneity, civic duty, and patriotism among young men and women who had a critical role to play in shaping the new nation. With respect to the residential experience, students should live with host families rather than in dormitories, in order to learn civility and to develop an appreciation of family values. In terms of lifestyle, students should have a balanced diet, avoid consuming liquor, and be exposed to rigorous physical activity and manual labor, all for the purpose of learning discipline and achieving balance in the conduct of life and affairs. A college should be located in a county seat, so that students could leave the classroom, visit the courthouse and witness government in action. The curriculum should not be preoccupied with the classics, but instead should include subjects—from history, to contemporary foreign languages such as French and German, to mathematics and chemistry—that were useful, that would help strengthen the intellectual, economic, political, and technical foundations of the new republic.

In "Thoughts on Female Education," written in 1787, he argued that in America, which had fewer class distinctions and a lower prevalence of servants than did England, a woman needed an education so she could be a partner to her husband in managing household property and affairs.[32] In "Observations on the Study of Greek and Latin," written in 1791, Rush posited that because useful knowledge was disseminated in contemporary languages, time spent studying

---

[30]Charles Coleman Sellers, *Dickinson College: A History,* Wesleyan University Press, Middletown, CT, 1973, Appendix A, pp. 507–508.

[31]Ibid, pp. 81–82.

[32]Benjamin Rush, "Thoughts Upon Female Education, Accommodated to the Present State of Society, Manners, and Government in the United States of America—July 28, 1787," *Essays Literary, Moral, and Philosophical,* Thomas & Samuel F. Bradford, Philadelphia, 1798, available in digital form at http://deila.dickinson.edu/cdm4/document.php?CISOROOT=/ownwords&CISOPTR=19843.

Exhibit 1   Selected Passages From Benjamin Rush, "Of the Mode of Education Proper in a Republic"

The business of education has acquired a new complexion by the independence of our country. . . .

An education in our own, is to be preferred to an education in a foreign country. The principle of patriotism stands in need of the reinforcement of prejudice . . . formed in the first one and twenty years of our lives.

Our schools of learning, by producing one general, and uniform system of education, will render the mass of the people more homogenous, and thereby fit them more easily for uniform and peaceable government.

The only foundation for a useful education in a republic is to be laid in Religion. Without this there can be no virtue, and without virtue there can be no liberty, and liberty is the object and life of all republican governments. . . .

Next to the duty which young men owe to their Creator, I wish to see a regard to their country, inculcated upon them. [Our student] . . . must love private life, but he must decline no station . . . when called to it by the suffrages of his fellow citizens. . . . He must avoid neutrality in all questions that divide the state, but he must shun the rage, and acrimony of party spirit.

[To improve students' ability to absorb their lessons] it will be necessary to subject their bodies to physical discipline. . . . [T]hey should live upon a temperate diet . . . should avoid tasting Spirituous liquors. They should also be accustomed occasionally to work with their hands. . . . [They should receive guidance on] those great principles in human conduct—sensibility, habit, imitations and association.

[Students should not be crowded] together under one roof for the purpose of education. The practice is . . . unfavorable to the improvements of the mind in useful learning. . . . [If we require them to separately live in private households] we improve their manners, by subjecting them to those restraints which the difference of age and sex, naturally produce in private families.

A knowledge of [the American language is essential] . . . to young men intended for the professions of law, physic, or divinity . . . [and] in a state which boasts of the first commercial city in America.

The French and German languages should . . . be . . . taught in all our Colleges. They abound with useful books upon all subjects.

Eloquence . . . is the first accomplishment in a republic. . . . We do not extol it too highly when we attribute as much to the power of eloquence as to the sword, in bringing about the American Revolution.

History and Chronology [are important because the] . . . science of government, whether . . . related to constitutions or laws, can only be advanced by a careful selection of facts, [especially those related to the] . . . history of the ancient republics, and the progress of liberty and tyranny in the different states of Europe.

Commerce . . . [is] . . . the best security against the influence of hereditary monopolies of land, and, therefore, the surest protection against aristocracy. I consider its effects as next to those of religion in humanizing mankind, and lastly, I view it as the means of uniting the different nations of the world together by the ties of mutual wants and obligations.

Chemistry by unfolding to us the effects of heat and mixture, enlarges our acquaintance with the wonders of nature and the mysteries of art . . . [and is particularly important] [i]n a young country, where improvements in agriculture and manufactures are so much to be desired.

[T]he general principles of legislation, whether they relate to revenue, or to the preservation of liberty or property . . . [should be examined, and towards this end, a student should] be directed frequently to attend the courts of justice . . . [and for this reason] colleges [should be] established only in county towns.

[T]he prerogatives of the national government . . . [should be studied, including] those laws and forms, which unite the sovereigns of the earth, or separate them from each other.

[W]omen in a republic . . . should be taught the principles of liberty and government; and the obligations of patriotism should be inculcated upon them.

Source: Selected by the case author from Benjamin Rush, "Of the Mode of Education Proper in a Republic," *Essays, Literary, Moral & Philosophical,* Printed by Thomas and Samuel F. Bradford, Philadelphia, 1798. (Available in digital form at http://deila.dickinson.edu/theirownwords/title/0021.htm; accessed July 23, 2007.)

Greek and Latin crowded out topics more relevant to a republic.[33] He also pointed to the instrumental and intrinsic nature of a liberal education.

> The great design of a liberal education is to prepare youth for usefulness here, and happiness hereafter.[34]

Citing rationales similar to those he cited when founding Dickinson, Rush continued to endorse other educational initiatives. For example—and perhaps a reflection of his disappointment about the absence of German language at Dickinson[35]— he helped found in 1787, in Lancaster, Pennsylvania—located only 55 miles from Carlisle—the German College, which was subsequently named Franklin College and even later Franklin and Marshall College. Since instruction would be in English, he believed the school would help German-speaking citizens in that part of the state be more quickly assimilated and eliminate barriers between them and English-speaking inhabitants. Meanwhile, he felt that capability in German could be preserved, and employed to understand books and articles from the sciences and other fields written in that language. He also believed the school would help unite the Calvinists and Lutherans among the German population.[36]

As another illustration of his thinking, in 1788, Rush publicly advocated a federal university to help prepare youth for civil and professional life, one which students would attend after completing a college education in their respective home states.[37] A promising handful should be deployed to Europe, and others selected to travel the United States, to collect insights on the latest innovations in agriculture, manufacturing, commerce, the art of war, and practical government, in order to report these to their faculty. The purpose of the curriculum for the University was much like that he had proposed for Dickinson College: it should be forward looking and practical in its orientation.

> While the business of doing education in Europe consists in lectures upon the ruins of Palmyra and the antiquities of Herculaneum, or in disputes about Hebrew points, Greek particles, or the accent and quantity of the Roman language, the youth of America will be employed in acquiring those branches of knowledge which increase the conveniences of life, lessen human misery, improve our country, promote population, exalt the human understanding, and establish domestic social, and political happiness.[38]

Rush and Nisbet[39]

On the important question of who should serve as the first headmaster, Rush strongly endorsed well-renowned scholar Dr. Charles Nisbet of Montrose, Scotland, who had completed his studies at Edinburgh in 1754—twelve years prior to the time when Rush started his studies— and was also deeply influenced by the Scottish

---

[33]Benjamin Rush, "Observations on the Study of Latin and Greek Languages, As a Branch of Liberal Education, With Hints of a Plan of Liberal Instruction, Without Them, Accommodated to the Present State of Society, Manners, and Government in the United States—August 24, 1791," *Essays Literary, Moral, and Philosophical,* Thomas & Samuel F. Bradford, Philadelphia, 1798, p. 21, available in digital form at http://deila.dickinson.edu/cdm4/document.php?CISOROOT=/ownwords&CISOPTR=19843.

[34]Ibid, p. 27.

[35]This possibility was suggested by Bill Durden, interview with the case author, October 23, 2007.

[36]*Letters of Benjamin Rush,* Princeton University Press, Princeton, NJ, 1951, Volume 1, pp. 420–429.

[37]Ibid, p. 491–495.

[38]Ibid, p. 494.

[39]This section is primarily based on James Henry Morgan, *Dickinson College: The History of One Hundred and Fifty Years 1783–1933,* Mount Pleasant Press, Carlisle, PA, 1933, chapter 4.

Enlightenment. Rush had first heard of Nisbet when John Witherspoon, who had initially declined the invitation to become president of the College of New Jersey, had suggested Nisbet as a worthy candidate. At their April 1784 meeting, the board unanimously elected Nisbet the first principal of the college. Following that meeting, John Dickinson, as chairman of the board of trustees, wrote to Nisbet, informing him about the position. Nisbet was not initially eager for the job. Thus, from December 1783 to June 1784, Rush took it upon himself to write letters to Nisbet, describing in enthusiastic if not hyperbolic terms the prospects for the college.

> The trustees of Dickinson College are to meet at Carlisle on the 6th of next April to choose a principal for the College. I have taken great pains to direct their attention and votes to you. From the situation and other advantages of that College, it must soon be the first in America. It is the key to our western world.[40]
>
> [T]he public is more filled than ever with expectations from your character. They destine our College to be THE FIRST IN AMERICA under your direction and government. [Rush provided the emphasis in his original letter].[41]
>
> Our prospects . . . brighten daily. . . . Indeed, Sir, every finger of the hand of Heaven has been visible in our behalf. . . . Dickinson College, with Dr. Nisbet at its head, bids fair for being the first literary institution in America.[42]

Rush's repetition of the phrase "first in America" in his series of letters was provocative, for it had two possible meanings: Dickinson would become the foremost college in the new country, in terms of quality; and, in light of the date September 9,

1783, coming as it did only six days after the signing of the Treaty of Paris, Dickinson had been the first college to receive a charter in the newly recognized country.

Nisbet ultimately succumbed to Rush's persuasiveness and accepted the post. His first months in America were filled with highs and lows. He arrived with his family in Philadelphia, on June 9, 1785. They stayed with Rush for three weeks before departing for Carlisle on June 30. Rush wrote to a friend, "The more I see of him, the more I love and admire him."[43] Nisbet reached Carlisle on July 4, 1785, took the oath of office the next day, and got to work. Ten days later, July 15, he wrote his first letter to Rush, and was somewhat critical of conditions in Carlisle—for example, he pointed to the need for a new building, describing the grammar school as shabby, dirty, and too small to accommodate all the students. Soon thereafter, he and his entire family contracted malaria. He became demoralized, and in August informed Rush that he had experienced a change of heart, would relinquish the position of principal and return to Scotland as soon as feasible.

Perhaps Rush, like an overly protective parent, was offended by Nisbet's early criticism of the college. Perhaps he was disappointed with Nisbet's lack of resolve. Perhaps he was beginning to get a different read on the man. For whatever reason, by the time of the August 9, 1785, board meeting in Carlisle, Rush had soured on Charles Nisbet. He ignored a note delivered to him on Nisbet's behalf, and did not visit the Nisbet family, who were still convalescing. Nisbet, at first perplexed, grew angry. In the ensuing years, the relationship between the two men remained strained.

[40]*Letters of Benjamin Rush,* Princeton University Press, Princeton, NJ, 1951, Volume 1, p. 316.

[41]Ibid, p. 334.

[42]James Henry Morgan, *Dickinson College: The History of One Hundred and Fifty Years 1783–1933,* Mount Pleasant Press, Carlisle, PA, 1933, chapter 1, p. 31–32.

[43]James Henry Morgan, *Dickinson College: The History of One Hundred and Fifty Years 1783–1933,* Mount Pleasant Press, Carlisle, PA, 1933, p. 34.

GLORIOUS INTENTIONS, DISAPPOINTING OUTCOME (1785–1816)

In summer 1785, the board accepted Nisbet's resignation and appointed faculty member Robert Davidson as acting principal for the first year of classes. At the outset, the attributes of the school bore little resemblance to a modern liberal arts college. The school was in session year round, except for one-month breaks in October and May, with commencement occurring on the last Wednesday of September. Fees ranged from $15 to $25 per year. The campus consisted of one building, the original Carlisle Grammar School, which had been ceded to the college in 1783. In 1786, the building was enlarged from its original two-story, two-room dimensions. The original faculty consisted of only four professors, including the head of the Grammar School. Enrollment in the classes of 1787 to 1816 fluctuated between zero and 60. Students found it relatively hard to earn an undergraduate degree, as the average number who actually received a diploma during that period was often less than 75 per cent of each class.[44] In terms of scale, Dickinson was typical of the times: for example, in the 1780s, while Columbia College had two professors and some two dozen students, the College of New Jersey had two professors, a provost, and roughly 60 students.[45]

Meanwhile, Nisbet decided he and his family would wait until spring of 1786 to return to Scotland. Over the winter months, the weather cooled, Nisbet and family recovered their health, and he had a change of heart. By February of 1786, he expressed in writing his desire to be reinstated. While Rush was opposed, the Carlisle-based members of the board rallied to the idea, and in May of 1786 reelected him as first principal of Dickinson College. His performance as principal was influenced by a range of factors, including his own character traits, the structure in place for governing the college, financial pressures, and efforts to construct the first major building on the college campus.[46]

Nisbet was a relentless worker and generally regarded as a brilliant scholar, a man who possessed deep knowledge about an extraordinary range of subjects. In addition to serving as principal, Nisbet carried a full-time teaching load, responsible for lectures in philosophy of the mind, moral philosophy and belles lettres, economics, and sociology. His lectures—which the students wrote verbatim in their notebooks—were remarkable for their breadth and insights. Nisbet was extremely well liked and admired by his students. Although Nisbet tended to place a higher value on the classics than did Rush, intellectually speaking the two men appeared to be in fundamental agreement about the purpose of a liberal education.[47] Unlike Rush, however, Nisbet remained politically conservative throughout his life. Ultimately, he was not able to sympathize with the dominant values and

[44]Author's computations, based on information found in "Alumni 1787–1900," Encyclopedia Dickinsonia, Dickinson Chronicles, http://chronicles.dickinson.edu/encyclo/a/alumni/.

[45]Charles F. Himes, *A Sketch of Dickinson College,* Lane S. Hart, Harrisburg, 1879, Chapter 1, page 3. A digital version of this book is available at the Chronicles of Dickinson College, http://chronicles.dickinson.edu/histories/himes, accessed July 23, 2007.

[46]This section is based on James Henry Morgan, *Dickinson College: The History of One Hundred and Fifty Years 1783–1933,* Mount Pleasant Press, Carlisle, PA, 1933, chapters 5–10, and Charles Coleman Sellers, *Dickinson College: A History,* Wesleyan University Press, Middletown, CT, 1973, chapters 5 and 6.

[47]Dickinson College History Professor John Osborne, interview, September 6, 2007, and Dickinson College Archivist Jim Gerencser, interview, September 7, 2007, each suggested that Rush and Nisbet were actually closer in their way of thinking than one might expect, given the tension in their personal relationship.

institutions of the new country and he regarded himself an outsider in his community.[48]

Throughout his administration, Nisbet—who was quite good at being critical of events but quite ineffective at being persuasive[49]—was constrained by his formal relationship with the board of trustees. Under the original charter, neither the principal nor any faculty member could serve on the board, and by 1786, the board had adopted an even more stringent policy—the principal and faculty were prohibited from attending board meetings.

When the charter for Dickinson was being drafted, Rush had endorsed the idea that the president of the college should be subservient to the board of trustees. He based his opinion on what he had observed at the College of Philadelphia: he believed that a controlling and rigid-minded president had dominated the board to the detriment of the school.[50] Nevertheless, Rush objected to this new development at Dickinson on both philosophical and practical grounds. In a letter written to the trustees in October of 1786, Rush wondered why his plan, which had been agreed [to] by the board in August of 1785, had not been adopted. He was particularly concerned that the behavior of the boys was "irregular" and that the faculty was not imposing discipline.

> . . . I beg leave to recommend that the trustees would exercise a watchful eye over their own authority, and that they would divide the government of the College among every branch of the faculty agreeably to the spirit and letter of our charter. Unless this be the case, the dignity and usefulness of our teachers will be lessened and destroyed, and the republican constitution of the College will

be reduced to the despotism of a private school. When our professors cease to be qualified to share in the power of the College, it will be proper to dismiss them, for government and instruction are inseparably connected.[51]

However, the situation did not change. Given that making the journey to Carlisle from any of the cities to the east was a difficult undertaking; that seven of the nine Carlisle men who had been on the board of the grammar school were also members of the board of the college; and that only nine people were needed for a quorum, the Carlisle contingent of the board were in a position to dominate college governance and micromanage daily affairs.

In its early history, the endowment of the college never exceeded $20,200, an amount achieved in 1784. Thus, the endowment did not generate large annual returns. Furthermore, the small number of students paying tuition caused the college to experience budget deficits. Given those difficulties, the trustees repeatedly appealed to the Assembly for assistance; in turn, the Assembly responded with modest annual grants that averaged about $550 per year. However, budget pressures continued, the college took out loans, and overall debts began to rise.

Furthermore, the college had some difficulties in raising contributions. Rush assigned some of the blame to Nisbet. He believed that when Nisbet announced his decision to retire that first year, and when he continued to publicly complain about the treatment he had received at the hands of Rush and more generally about the state of affairs in America, he did harm to the reputation of the college.[52] By 1799, Rush—who had become a supporter of Jefferson—was even

[48]James Henry Morgan, *Dickinson College: The History of One Hundred and Fifty Years 1783–1933,* Mount Pleasant Press, Carlisle, PA, 1933, p. 66.

[49]Charles Coleman Sellers, *Dickinson College: A History,* Wesleyan University Press, Middletown, CT, 1973, p. 79.

[50]Ibid, pp. 139–140.

[51]*Letters of Benjamin Rush,* Princeton University Press, Princeton, NJ, 1951, Volume 1, p. 397.

[52]*Letters of Benjamin Rush,* Princeton University Press, Princeton, NJ, 1951, Volume 1, p. 537.

more distressed that Nisbet was expressing pro-Federalist sentiments in his classroom, thus undermining the college's ability to raise contributions from Democratic-Republicans.[53]

In 1800, the board voted to reduce Nisbet's salary from $1,200 to $800 per year, to reduce those of the other faculty as well, and to borrow $2,000. In 1801, the board sold stock worth another $2,000. In spring 1802, the board stopped making full payment of faculty salaries. Those developments impacted the morale of Nisbet and his faculty.

Meanwhile, in 1799 the college purchased a seven-acre parcel of land on the then-existing western boundary of Carlisle, for $151. The board began to solicit contributions, and on June 20, the cornerstone for a building called New College was set in place. The board hoped construction would be finished by winter, but progress was slow. That fact, along with the college's mounting financial difficulties, fueled speculation that Dickinson would have to close its doors. Finally, in the winter of 1802–1803, New College was receiving final touches: sadly, on February 3, 1803, the building burned to the ground.

In the aftermath of the disaster, the trustees demonstrated their determination. They appealed to the presbytery for financial assistance. They visited Philadelphia, Baltimore, New York and Norfolk to raise funds, and met with success. In Washington D.C., they won a personal contribution of $100 from President Thomas Jefferson, as well as contributions from other important political figures. Buoyed by the inflow of funds, the board solicited help from one of the foremost architects and engineers of the time, Benjamin Latrobe, who graciously agreed to contribute a design for a replacement building larger than the first. The new building—which became known in later decades, when other buildings were added to the campus, as West College—would be constructed of limestone with brown sandstone accents, and would be multipurpose in nature, providing dormitory, dining hall, chapel, and classroom space for the students and living quarters for the faculty. Once again, Rush had to accept a compromise, as the plan to house students in the building, rather than to have them board with local families, ran counter to his philosophy of education. The cornerstone of the building was laid on August 8, 1803. It was first used for academic purposes in November of 1805.

Charles Nisbet died from complications associated with pneumonia on January 18, 1804. While they had been at odds for the better part of 20 years, at the last it appears that Rush and Nisbet managed to find some common ground, judging by a letter Rush wrote to Montgomery when Nisbet died.

> He has carried out of our world an uncommon stock of every kind of knowledge. Few such men have lived and died in any country. I shall long, long remember with pleasure his last visit to Philadelphia, at which time he dined with me in the company [of two friends]. His conversation was unusually instructing and brilliant, and his anecdotes full of original humor and satire.[54]

Following Nisbet's death, the board once again turned to Robert Davidson[55] to serve as acting principal, a position he held for the next five years. While never formally elected as such, he came to be recognized as the second principal of Dickinson College. Financial pressures were a reality throughout Davidson's tenure. Although Davidson was an outstanding churchman, he was not a successful college president. Of note, John Dickinson, still serving as a trustee of the college, died on February 14, 1808.

---

[53]Ibid, p. 812.

[54]Ibid, p. 878.

[55]This section is based on James Henry Morgan, *Dickinson College: The History of One Hundred and Fifty Years 1783–1933*, Mount Pleasant Press, Carlisle, PA, 1933, chapter 14.

Davidson was succeeded by Jeremiah Atwater,[56] a Presbyterian who was serving as the first president of Middlebury College when informed of the post at Dickinson. A devout, conservative Presbyterian, he hoped to create a culture at Dickinson based on religious principles, and in this sense was in step with Rush. However, upon his arrival, he was aghast at the state of affairs in Carlisle, complaining in correspondence to Rush that the boys were prone to "drunkenness, swearing, lewdness, & dueling" and the faculty did not take responsibility for imposing discipline.[57] Atwater quickly took steps to introduce the type of discipline typical of that found in the colleges of New England.

During Atwater's tenure, financial pressures continued to plague the college, especially given efforts to add dining rooms and other features to the interior of the college building. Given the small scale of the college and the relatively low standard of living at the time, the ongoing construction drained resources, consumed the entire endowment, and forced the college into debt. In light of developments, Rush wrote in 1810 about raising tuition, which he understood would limit access to a liberal education.

I wish very much the price of tuition be raised in our College. Let a **learned** education become a luxury in our country. The great increase of wealth among all classes of our citizens will enable them to pay for it with more ease than in former years when wealth was confined chiefly to cities and to the learned professions. Besides, it will check the increasing disproportion of learning to labor in our country. This suggestion is not intended to lessen the diffusion of knowledge by means of reading, writing, and arithmetic. Let those be as common and as cheap as air. In a republic no man should be a voter or juror without a knowledge of them. They should be a kind of sixth or civil sense. Not so with **learning**. Should it become **universal**, it would be as destructive to civilization as universal barbarism. (Emphasis provided by Rush.)[58]

During the first three years of Atwater's term, the number of students at the college nearly tripled. But the War of 1812 had a negative impact on student attendance and graduation rates. As time passed, Atwater became increasingly discouraged by the unyielding financial difficulties, and by internal dissention among his faculty. On April 19, 1813, Atwater lost a sympathizer when Benjamin Rush died rather suddenly at his home.

In early 1815, the trustees ordered Atwater and each professor to submit a weekly written report to the secretary of the board that identified all student absences or transgressions. In a corrosive environment of friction among the faculty and hostility between the faculty and the board, that proved to be the last straw. Within the year, Atwater retired from the college, as did the other faculty. The college was in shambles.

In November of 1815 the board elected John McKnight,[59] a professor and member of the board of trustees at Columbia University and influential Presbyterian, to serve as fourth principal of Dickinson. In December 1815, a Dickinson student was killed in a duel. The incident further undermined the college's reputation. In 1816, the board of trustees closed down the college.

Dickinson remained closed for five years, resumed operations in 1822, and then closed its doors again in 1832.

Despite the enormous strains of the first 50 years and the sad circumstances associated with

---

[56]This section is based on James Henry Morgan, *Dickinson College: The History of One Hundred and Fifty Years 1783–1933,* Mount Pleasant Press, Carlisle, PA, 1933, chapter 15, and Charles Coleman Sellers, *Dickinson College: A History,* Wesleyan University Press, Middletown, CT, 1973, chapter 7.

[57]James Henry Morgan, *Dickinson College: The History of One Hundred and Fifty Years 1783–1933,* Mount Pleasant Press, Carlisle, PA, 1933, p. 183.

[58]*Letters of Benjamin Rush,* Princeton University Press, Princeton, NJ, 1951, Volume 1, p. 1053.

[59]This section and the next are based on James Henry Morgan, *Dickinson College: The History of One Hundred and Fifty Years 1783–1933,* Mount Pleasant Press, Carlisle, PA, 1933, chapter 16.

the closing of the college, many of the young men who attended Dickinson during the era 1785 to 1832 went on to highly successful careers. Their number included ministers, college professors and presidents, secondary school teachers and principals, representatives and senators at the state and national levels of government, a U.S. president and members of the executive branches of various administrations, military officers, lawyers and judges, physicians, civil servants, and businessmen.[60]

In order to reopen the college yet again, the board of trustees realized they had to end their loose affiliation with the Presbyterian Church and accept the invitation of the Methodist Episcopal Church to establish an alliance. In 1834, the college was reopened. Over the next 130 years, Dickinson experienced eras of growth and decline. The college's fortunes were influenced by external events, such as wars, economic fluctuations, and shifts in social norms. They were also influenced by internal factors, including the governance structure, the culture and the financial health of the college. Finally, they were influenced by the leadership and management abilities of individual presidents and the relationships each man had been able to forge with various constituents. Throughout that period, Dickinson remained a school with a relatively conservative and parochial culture.

In the 1960s, the college began the lengthy process of separation from the Methodist Church. By the 1970s, the college was characterized by a culture based on cooperation and collegiality. In that environment, the faculty greatly enhanced the curriculum, as reflected in more breadth in the foreign languages and opportunities for international education, innovative teaching methods in the sciences, interdisciplinary programs of study, and more faculty-student interaction. Dickinson had an enrollment of approximately 1,600 students. By the mid-1990s, the relationship between the Methodist Church and Dickinson was cordial—the church continued to hold approximately $2 million in trust on behalf of the college and conducted its own decennial review of the college's performance. However, the church had no substantive influence on matters related to college policy or strategy.

MOUNTING FRUSTRATIONS

In the early 1980s, the external environment confronting colleges became more challenging: costs of providing an education continued to rise, families were becoming less willing and able to pay higher tuition fees, and the public increasingly questioned the relevance of a liberal arts education. In that competitive environment, Dickinson made two strategic choices. First, given the dominant, egalitarian culture of the 1960s and 1970s, the college did not celebrate the accomplishments of any single department over others and continued to describe itself as a pure liberal arts college. Second, the college opted to award aid to incoming students on a loan-first rather than grant-first basis, and to award less overall aid than other colleges—to illustrate, through the mid-1990s, Dickinson had an average discount rate[61] of 24 per cent, compared to a discount rate of 33 per cent of most rivals.[62] Between 1988 and 1996, applications

---

[60]A matrix that describes professions pursued by alumni graduating during the administrations of various presidents is provided in James Henry Morgan, *Dickinson College: The History of One Hundred and Fifty Years 1783–1933,* Mount Pleasant Press, Carlisle, PA, 1933, pp. 396–397.

[61]The discount rate states, in percentage terms, the reduction from the full tuition price paid by the average student. To say this in another way, a 24 per cent discount rate implied that Dickinson realized $.76 for each $1.00 of the posted tuition price.

[62]The data included in this paragraph and the next is based on the PowerPoint presentation, "Dickinson College: A Case Study in Financial Transformation," created by Annette S. Parker (Class of 1973), vice-president and treasurer of the college, spring 2007.

for first-year admissions dropped from 4,438 to 2,829, the acceptance rate rose from 40 per cent to 84 per cent, enrollment dropped from 2,079 to 1,824, and average SAT scores for admitted students dropped from 1,216 to 1,150.

To combat that trend, in the mid-1990s, the college moved to a grant-first aid approach, and aggressively elevated average aid awards. At one level, the tactic worked. From 1996 to 1999, applications rose from 2,829 to 3,434; the acceptance rate fell from 84 per cent to 64 per cent; and average SAT scores rose from 1,150 to 1,193. At another level, it was a serious mistake. By 1999, the discount rate had risen to 52 per cent, and the college was experiencing an operational deficit of roughly $5 million with an even larger deficit forecasted for the following year. Those deficits could only be covered in the short term by drawing down the endowment, and were clearly unsustainable in the long run.

More broadly, there was gnawing concern among various members of the college community that successive administrations had been ineffective relative to those at rival schools in terms of managing admissions and raising funds. For example, while there were certainly many highly motivated and talented students entering the college, Dickinson remained a school with regional appeal that primarily received applications from students living in the Mid-Atlantic states. By the early 1990s, some among that group regarded Dickinson as a "safety" school rather than as a first choice. Furthermore, while Dickinson prided itself on admitting students who were first in their family to receive a college education, and while it had good socio-economic diversity, it had very low representation from students of color or from international students. With respect to financial profile,

although Dickinson's endowment was experiencing relatively high returns, by the end of 1998, it stood at only $143 million, an amount that did not measure up well to the endowments of other colleges.

Those circumstances prompted Dickinson's Committee on Planning and Budget to release a white paper in the spring of 1996 to the entire faculty. The paper asserted that Dickinson had to develop a "grounding vision."

> Dickinson must be able to show ... that a liberal education is simultaneously the most humanly fulfilling and ennobling **and** the most practical education. And it must be able to show that the liberal arts education offered **by this College** is superior to one offered elsewhere. (Emphasis included in original.)[63]

In response, college President A. Lee Fritschler formed a task force on the future of the college, consisting of a student and six senior faculty and administrators, to convene in early summer of 1997, for the purpose of identifying problems and proposing general solutions. Their report was released to the faculty, under the cover letter and signature of President Fritschler, on June 18. The telling language contained in the preface echoed the themes of the white paper.

> We want Dickinson to be generally recognized as one of the twenty-five most prestigious liberal arts colleges in the United States within the next ten years. . . . [We envision] Dickinson as a living and learning community that embraces change, that regards diversity as an essential feature of an educational community, and that declares liberal education to be the most humanly liberating and practical preparation for citizenship in an interdependent, competitive, culturally-complex world.[64]

---

[63]Planning and Budget Committee, April 29, 1996, "A White Paper," Dickinson College internal document, p. 2.

[64]"Report for the President's Task Force on the Future of the College," June 18, 1997, Dickinson College internal document, pp. 1–2.

The report offered the following diagnosis: "The College's greatest external challenge is visibility, the greatest internal challenge is communication." To address the former, the college had to stop describing itself as a "pure liberal arts college" with "balance across all departments" and start celebrating core competencies, such as "excellence in international education." To address the latter—which involved concerns that in light of growing difficulties, the administration was becoming insular and less than transparent—steps had to be taken to reopen communication channels among administration, faculty, students and trustees.

In late 1997, President Fritschler indicated to the community he would resign his position in June of 1999. In January of 1998, a search committee was named to find a new president.

THE CHALLENGE OF CREATING AN IDENTITY STORY

When Bill Durden agreed to be president of Dickinson College, he was aware that the board of trustees wanted to improve the reputation and the financial foundation of the college, but did not have a detailed blueprint on how to proceed; instead, they hoped they could establish high expectations and grant a new president a broad mandate to engineer a transformation. He was aware that the program of study was first-rate and the internal governance system was sound.

Durden also knew that there was an intense desire for change and progress among the faculty and some members of the administration: he had come to appreciate that desire via conversations during the spring and from his extensive review of previously written white papers and self-studies during the summer months.

Of all the documents he had read, a passage included in the 1997 Report of the President's Task Force—"We want Dickinson to be generally recognized as one of the 25 most prestigious liberal arts colleges in the United States within the next ten years"—was most provocative. While he would certainly give it more thought, his initial reaction was that such an externally focused objective—based on rankings produced by for-profit organizations such as *U.S. News and World Report*—might be a distraction from what he saw as the appropriate areas of concentration: the organizational culture and capabilities and the financial foundation of the college. Furthermore, he believed those rankings were based on a set of flawed metrics that did not properly capture the relative strengths of various institutions, including Dickinson. Finally, he was also troubled by what he saw as an emerging tendency in America to regard higher education as a standardized commodity: he believed that the increased attention being paid by the public to the rankings was a manifestation of that tendency.

Via his various experiences, Durden had come to believe in the power of a leadership story. He acknowledged that he had been influenced by the work of psychologist and leadership theorist Howard Gardner (see Exhibit 2).[65] Given his general assessment of the situation at Dickinson and prompted by his conversation with the rising senior who had expressed her concerns about what it meant to be a Dickinsonian, Durden had over the past several weeks started to imagine a story based on Rush and the founding of the college that he believed would help create a unique Dickinson identify. But several issues and questions remained unresolved. Durden knew that he had to achieve greater clarity regarding the story's purpose and target audience and its structure and content. He also had to think more about the tactics and timing he would employ in introducing the story to the Dickinson community.

---

[65]Bill Durden, interview with case author, August 31, 2007, Dickinson College, Carlisle, PA.

Exhibit 2   Role of a Leader and the Relevance of an Identity Story

Leaders are "persons who, by word and/or personal example, markedly influence the behaviors, thoughts, and/or feelings of a significant number of their fellow human beings."

Leaders influence other people either *directly,* through the stories they communicate to others; or *indirectly,* through the ideas they create. Examples of these two types include Winston Churchill, a direct leader who sits at one end of a spectrum, and Albert Einstein, an indirect leader who sits at the other. Other leaders would fall somewhere between those two, with most corporate and political leaders closer to the spot occupied by Churchill, and most artists and researchers closer to the spot occupied by Einstein.

Direct leaders achieve their effectiveness in one of two ways: they *relate* stories to others, and they *embody* those stories, thereby serving as an example which inspires others. The ability to embody stories is much more relevant to direct leaders than indirect leaders.

While it may be hard to draw precise lines between categories, leaders can be ranked as *ordinary, innovative,* or *visionary.* An "ordinary leader . . . simply relates the traditional story of his or her group as effectively as possible. . . . The innovative leader takes a story that has been latent in the population, or among the members of his or her chosen domain, and brings new attention or a fresh twist to that story. . . . [T]he visionary leader . . . [is not] content to relate a current story or to reactivate a story drawn from a remote or recent past . . . [and therefore] actually creates a new story."

"The ultimate impact of the leader depends most significantly on the particular story that he or she relates or embodies, and the receptions to that story on the part of audiences. . . . [A]udience members come equipped with many stories that have already been told and retold. . . . The stories of the leader . . . must compete with many other extant stories; and if the new stories are to succeed, they must transplant, suppress, complement, or in some measure outweigh the earlier stories, as well as contemporary counterstories."

"[L]eaders present a *dynamic* perspective to their followers: not just a headline or snapshot, but a drama that unfolds over time, in which they—the leader and followers—are the principal characters or heroes. Together, they have embarked on a journey in pursuit of certain goals, and along the way and into the future, they can expect to encounter certain obstacles or resistances that must be overcome. Leaders and audiences traffic in many stories, but the most basic story has to do with issues of *identity.* And so it is the leader who succeeds in conveying a new version of a given group's story who is likely to be effective. Effectiveness here involves fit—the story needs to make sense to audience members at this particular historical moment, in terms of where they have been and where they would like to go."

Source: Howard Gardner, in collaboration with Emma Laskin, *Leading Minds: An Anatomy of Leadership,* Basic Books, a Division of HarperCollins Publishers, New York, NY, 1995.

5

PERFORMANCE MEASUREMENT

Nonprofit organizations need to view revenue as a resource needed to achieve their missions. Obviously, revenues must exceed expenses over the long-term or an NPO will not survive.

—Glenn Rowe

Key Topics: balanced score card, customer feedback, competitive comparison, strategic objectives, blue ocean strategy

What makes an organization "good" at what it does? Or, as Jim Collins (2001) would ask, "What makes an organization great?" Most would acknowledge that accountability, effectiveness, and achievement of desired performance outcomes are minimal requirements for any organization's success. These requirements demand a measurement system relative to an organization's mission, vision, values, and strategic plan. This chapter discusses methods for establishing such systems. In doing so, we echo Worth's (2012) concern that "nonprofit managers must be committed to performance measurement but should not become overly focused on it to the detriment of delivering their mission's programs" (p. 157).

PERFORMANCE MEASUREMENT PROCESS

Before engaging in performance measurement, it is vital to understand the level and scope of the process. Measurement can be conducted for *effectiveness* or *performance* at the program/project or organizational level. Effectiveness relates to achieving the mission, while performance is a broader concept that considers financial results and other variables related to the overall organization.

Once the scope and level of analysis are determined, several questions should be answered about the evaluation process:

1. WHAT is to be evaluated—or assessed for effectiveness?

2. HOW should it be assessed?

3. WHO is responsible for conducting the assessment?

4. TO WHOM should the results be reported?

Budgets and other resource constraints may influence the answers to these questions, but rest assured that both internal and external nonprofit organization (NPO) stakeholders want ongoing evaluation and continuous improvement. For example, many donors and foundations require performance measurements at various stages of funding. This fact—along with increased calls for nonprofit accountability from monitoring organizations such as Wise Giving Alliance (www.bbb.org/us/wise-giving), Charity Navigator (www.charitynavigator.org), the Better Business Bureau, (www.bbb.org), and Guidestar (www2.guidestar.org) as well as the government (e.g., IRS form 990) and the general public (via blogs and other social media)—translates into a need for performance measurement and transparency across the nonprofit sector.

In Canada, in addition to reporting to the Canada Revenue Agency (www.cra-arc.gc.ca), NPOs can belong to organizations on a voluntary basis that encourage transparency and performance measurement. Compassion Canada (www.compassion.ca) states on its website that NPOs have come under greater scrutiny by "watchdog agencies." In addition, donors are now researching institutions they support in much more depth. Consequently, accountability standards are much more stringent. Compassion Canada is a member of Imagine Canada (www.imaginecanada.ca) and the Canadian Council of Christian Charities (www.cccc.org). Both of these organizations are NPOs themselves, and their goal is to strengthen standards of accountability for NPOs in Canada.

Imagine Canada states that it has more than 350 NPOs involved in its Ethical Code Program (www.imaginecanada.ca/ethicalcode), which is designed to raise awareness regarding accountability and ethics on the part of charities in Canada. These charities generate more than $2 billion Canadian in fundraising revenue.

Table 5.1 outlines different types of evaluative processes that may be used within organizations. Using a compilation of evaluation methods enables nonprofit leaders to keep stakeholders and the various monitoring agencies mentioned here abreast of their organizational goals and progress toward mission fulfillment.

PERFORMANCE MEASUREMENT TOOLS

Tools for gauging results of organizational efforts and resource expenditures relative to the NPO's plan come in many shapes and sizes. The strategic triangle of 3Cs by Kenichi Ohmae (2005) serves as a guide to organize the multitude of tools available. Ohmae suggests that, to develop sustained competitive advantage, strategists should focus on three main players: the corporation (i.e., the nonprofit organization), the customer (i.e., the stakeholder), and the competitor (i.e., other organizations that provide similar services to target clients or in the targeted service area). If the NPO manager fills her toolbox with the proper instruments to measure each of these elements or perspectives, she will be able to assess—and hopefully improve—the performance of her organization.

In assessing the NPO (*corporation* in Ohmae's parlance), the key is to understand the competitive advantage that enables an NPO to sustain exceptional service. (More on identifying and exploiting core competencies and competitive advantage is found in Chapter 6.) A tool used to convert intangible assets that usually form a competitive advantage to tangible outcomes is the balanced score card (BSC). This tool also incorporates the customer's perspective into its performance measurement.

Balanced Score Card

Recalling that all performance measures must relate directly to an organization's mission, vision, and strategy, Kaplan and Norton (1992) developed the concept of the BSC, encouraging

Table 5.1 Types of Evaluation

Type	Description and Purpose
Rolling	Appropriate for smaller nonprofits. Leaders select one or two focal projects, programs, or operational areas per year to evaluate and construct learning growth on a year-over-year basis.
External	Contractor or other external party (e.g., student group) conducts program-specific or organization-wide evaluation over a specified period.
Internal	Internal staff or contractor with a deep, long-term objective conducts program-specific or organization-wide evaluation over a specified period.
Summative	Seeks information about activity after (or toward end) of program or project.
Formative	Internal investigation of a program while it is in progress.
Process	Answers the question of "what to do." Focuses on how to improve project, strategy, or specific operational efforts. Assesses the quality of activities. For example, measures whether training sessions are at full capacity, breaking even (revenue versus expense), and/or whether participants rate the experience well.
Outcome or Impact	Gauges program or project completion of specified objectives. Measures whether desired goals are achieved. Focuses on the results, versus the process, organizations or programs undertake to enact change. For example, training outcome evaluation would ask if participants function differently post-workshop.
Participatory	Includes feedback from clients or beneficiaries in the evaluation. May include qualitative interviews, focus groups, or quantitative surveys of current or past service recipients.

Source: Festen & Philbin, 2007. Reprinted with permission.

organizations to move beyond an overreliance on financial metrics in their strategy evaluation. The tool also helps organizational leaders convert intangible assets into tangible outcomes (Kaplan & Norton, 2000). In applying the BSC to the nonprofit sector, Kaplan (2001) claims that it bridges the gaps among mission, strategy, and daily operations by emphasizing the process with which to achieve strategic focus. The traditional for-profit BSC includes metrics related to financial performance, customer satisfaction, internal business processes, learning, and growth.

Some NPOs and governmental agencies have adopted the BSC as an essential strategic tool (Bryson, 2005; Wall, Kirk, & Martin, 2004), demonstrating that it is scalable and capable of providing alignment and focus to various organizations. The application of the BSC to the nonprofit sector is not without its detractors (Kong, 2008), but it can provide focus for nonprofits seeking to consider the pull from various stakeholders and limited resources while focusing on mission accomplishment.

Kaplan (2001) suggests several tweaks to the BSC in its application to NPOs (Table 5.2). First, the traditional BSC should be redrawn to place the mission at the focal point (vs. financial success in the for-profit sector). The measures in the four other perspectives demonstrate short-term (e.g., quarterly, annual) targets and feedback that enable year-over-year control and accountability to the mission.

Table 5.2 Balanced Score Card (BSC) Adapted to Nonprofit Organizations

BSC Perspectives for Nonprofit Organization	Sample Activities, Goals, Stakeholder Involvement to Chart Progress and Measure Achievement
Social impact perspective	Articulate the organization's mission and vision.
Constituent perspective	Articulate specific stakeholders (e.g., employee, client, volunteer) and the impact each has on mission accomplishment.
Internal operations/key levers perspective	List specific goals internal to the organization that will lead to mission accomplishment (e.g., grow size and caliber of staff applicant pool, select high-quality staff to fill vacant positions, increase effectiveness of staff training, build database of stakeholders to improve community network).
Financial perspective	Record financial needs to achieve objectives and overall mission (e.g., grow and diversify revenue base, improve financial management skills of key staff, increase grant application effectiveness through training of development staff).
Learning growth perspective	List specific goals (e.g., technology purchase, training, brand development) that will build and/or sustain organizational success.

Source: Kaplan, 2001.

To measure performance relative to the NPO "customer," one must first acknowledge the complexity in defining such a customer. Because nonprofits have both clients and donors, whom they serve is not always clear. Following the stakeholder analysis discussed in Chapter 3, NPO managers may find listing several key stakeholders (i.e., clients and key donors) in parallel to be most effective.

Once leaders determine two or three high-level strategic themes (see Chapter 6 for discussion of strategic planning), explicit strategies, objectives, activities, and targets can be established to measure achievement. Table 5.3 illustrates a generic BSC for a nonprofit whose high-level theme is to improve brand equity.

Some nonprofit managers find the BSC too cumbersome to manage. Paton (2003) offers a more simplistic approach to multipoint performance evaluation in his *dashboard* model. The dashboard analyzes organizations from five perspectives across short-, medium-, and long-term horizons:

1. Current Results—monthly comparisons to established objectives (e.g., financial reporting)

2. Underlying Performance—annual reviews of programs and support functions

3. Risks—formal monitoring process to assess risks (financial, legal, reputational, and environmental)

4. Assets and Capabilities—annual assessment of physical and intangible assets that build capacity for future performance (e.g., financial investments, organizational reputation, expertise)

5. Change Projects—regular initiative to enable continuous improvements in programs and assets.

Ultimately, Paton's (2003) dashboard seeks to answer two fundamental questions: Does it work? ("Do the different activities, services, and programs achieve intended results?" pp. 139–140) Is the organization well run?

Table 5.3 Connecting a Balanced Score Card to a Nonprofit's Strategic Objectives

Strategic Initiative: Improve NPO Brand Equity	Objective	Activity	Measure	Target	Time Mo./ Qtr./Yr.	Ownership
Financial			**Income Growth**	**2012 20%**		**Board of Directors**
Develop brand	Increase brand awareness	Organize community leader breakfast	# attendees	120		Board Members 1, 2
	Improve brand image	Develop direct mail campaign to support reputation value	# of inquiries # of new volunteers # of new sponsorships	250 15 5		Board Member 3, 4
Stakeholder Focus			**Grow Donor Base**	**2012 15%**		**Executive Director**
Event attendees (*Incidental donors*)	Experience the brand	Annual Gala	# attendees Post-event surveys	400 80% satisfaction		Board Member 5, 6 Volunteer 1, 2
Occasional donors	Establish brand loyalty	Telethon	# converted to committed donors	≥ 25%		Volunteer Coordinator
Committed donors	Enhance brand position	Face-to-face solicitation	Amount of increased giving 5 exceptional gifts	avg. ≥ 20% per donor $2,500/ea.		Director of Development
Internal Processes			**Improve Tracking System**	**100% donor info. accurately maintained, secured and accessible 24/7**		**Director of Development**
Donor database	Collect data to profile current prospective donors	Brand surveys	Response rate	≥ 50% per segment		
Learning and Growth			**Recruit/Train Volunteers**			**Staff Member**
Sell the brand	Develop staff skills	Fundraising training	Funds raised	$250,000		

Source: Adapted from Conway Dato-on, Weisenbach Keller, & Shaw, 2009.

Customer Feedback

The increasingly competitive environment nonprofits face due to reduced government funding, increased outsourcing of government social services through voucher-type systems, and decreased private giving (Hall, 2011) has transformed the client–NPO relationship. In addition to these environmental changes, a new cadre of wealthy entrepreneurs who view philanthropy as financial investments in transformation of systemic problems pressures nonprofits to become even more responsive to newly empowered customers and investors. Such responsiveness requires an efficient method of measuring customer/client experiences and a *needs-centered orientation* (Wymer, Knowles, & Gomes 2006).

Marketing researchers provide guidance on appropriate quantitative and qualitative methods for gathering, analyzing, and disseminating information gathered from organizational stakeholders (Wymer et al., 2006). Qualitative surveys of key stakeholders and potential donors helped Lake Eola Charter School (LECS; see the first case at the end of this chapter) understand the strength of its brand. LECS leaders also used qualitative focus groups to gather data about how parents and students visualized and described the brand while learning what characteristics the school should emphasize more. Effectiveness and simplicity are key when applying this process to nonprofits that may face financial constraints. Festen and Philbin (2007) suggest several ways to keep ongoing evaluation processes from overtaking delivery of critical services.

Often nonprofits may find strategic partnerships helpful in gathering customer feedback. Many universities offer low-cost or no-cost marketing research assistance to nonprofits in the community (Conway Dato-on & Gassenheimer, 2010) or house centers for nonprofit research (e.g., Rollins College Philanthropy and Nonprofit Leadership Center, www.rollins.edu/pnlc; the Center for Philanthropy at Indiana University, www.philanthropy.iupui.edu). Ronnie DeNoia at LECS found both these resources valuable in assessing her organization's performance. The Center for What Works (http://whatworks .org) also offers tools and tips on performance measurement.

Competitive Analysis

While the BSC helps nonprofit leaders assess performance from various perspectives, and customer feedback aids in evaluating various program/organizational processes and outcomes, Ohmae (2005) reminds us that no performance assessment would be complete without understanding alternatives available to donors and clients with whom the NPO seeks to build relationships. In other words, performance must be compared to the competition.

A common method of assessing the competition is *competitive benchmarking*. "Through this approach, organizations try to identify the best practices of other organizations they consider to be similar to them, and thus learn ways to improve their own operations" (Worth, 2012, p. 63). Again, such performance measurement may happen at the program or organizational level.

Detractors of benchmarking in the nonprofit sector point out several potential pitfalls to this approach:

1. Benchmarking may eventually result in different organizations within the same field doing things in much the same way. This generally happens when NPO leaders lose mission focus or when one's own competitive advantage is not understood fully.

2. It can be difficult to isolate indicators that lead to program or organizational effectiveness.

3. Identifying which organizations are comparable takes time and effort and may result in false comparisons and conclusions. For example, nonprofits in different locales may face very dissimilar funding environments, more or less favorable volunteer prospects, and unique staff situations.

Benchmarking is a useful tool, but perhaps more for learning than assessing overall organizational performance. When applied effectively, however, benchmarking can be valuable for examining specific program or administrative functions and learning best practices that can be altered for adoption within another NPO.

Whether an organization uses benchmarking, NPO leaders should be aware of what alternatives to their organization's goods and services are available for the target customer or client. Two methods for comparing alternatives—one visual and one numerical—are the perceptual map and the competitive analysis matrix.

The *perceptual map* is a visual representation of the importance of different dimensions and the perceptions of alternatives along those dimensions for one or more target populations. The map depends on the positioning an organization (and/or its service offerings) has in the mind of the target audience, be that clients or funders.

To build a map, market research must be available to uncover the dimensions that the NPO's target audience uses to evaluate alternatives and an understanding of the level of importance that different dimensions hold.

Figure 5.1 shows the perceptual map a children's museum might construct when viewing its attraction versus alternative activities available to children (Garibay, 2011). Once the museum understands how children perceive its facilities versus other alternatives, it can develop programs that either fill a gap in the knowledge or activity level or seek to market itself in such a way that repositions the opinion children hold of the museum. For example, a museum's marketing might emphasize that prior knowledge is not necessary to have fun at the museum.

A *competitive analysis matrix* focuses on key factors that distinguish competitive services and

Figure 5.1 Perceptual Map: Museum Versus Alternative Activities for Children

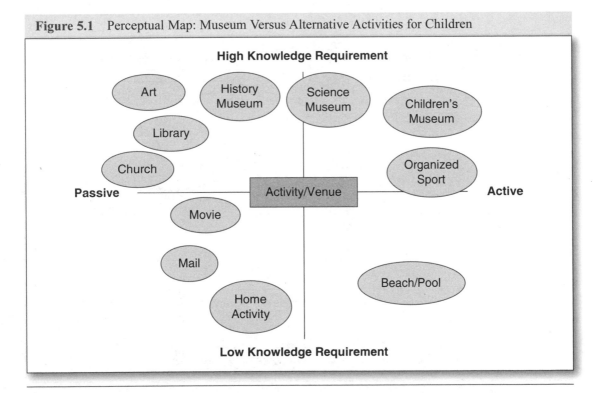

Source: Adapted from Garibay, 2011.

are of value to current and/or potential clients. The method for developing the matrix is similar to that outlined by Kim and Mauborgne (2005) in their development of a "blue ocean" strategy. (See Chapter 1 for additional discussion of this strategy.) Table 5.4 and Figure 5.2 display a comparison among different service providers in children's athletic services.

Table 5.4   Competitive Analysis Matrix for Children's Athletic Services

Factor	Kid City	Gymboree	My Gym
Number of services provided	4	1	1
Location convenience	4	5	.5
Price	4	5	4
Amenities	4.5	4	4
Safety	5	4.5	4.5
Qualified teachers	5	5	4
Teacher-to-kid ratio	5	4.5	4
OVERALL RATING	31.5	29	22

Scale = 1 (*not desirable*) to 5 (*desirable*).

Figure 5.2   Visual Representation of Competitive Analysis Matrix for Children's Athletic Services

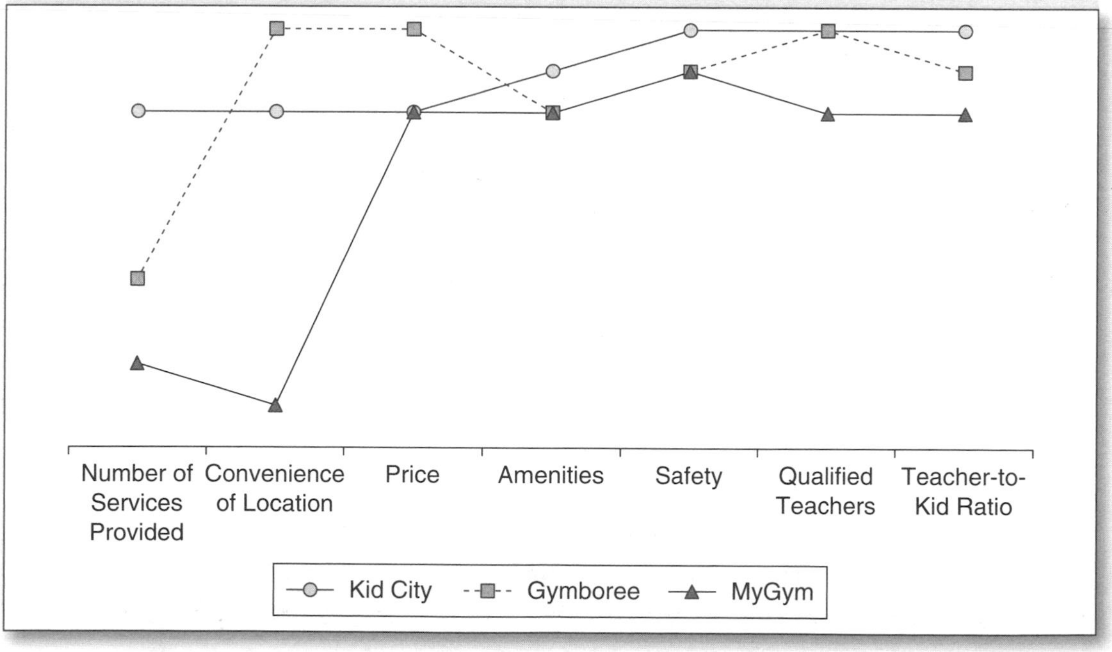

Source: Created by authors using blue ocean strategy template (Kim & Mauborgne, 2005).

Keep in mind that the purpose of the competitive analysis, in any form, is to examine organizational or programmatic advantages and disadvantages versus those offered by other service providers in the area. What the NPO manager does with the performance measurement information is equally important to conducting the evaluation. Results should be fed into a cycle of planning and strategy development. More on this will be found in succeeding chapters.

CASES

Lake Eola Charter School (United States): In late 2009, Ronnie DeNoia, principal of Lake Eola Charter School, in downtown Orlando, Florida, completed a course on nonprofit branding at the Philanthropy and Nonprofit Leadership Center at a local college. She was energized and ready to apply the new learning to evaluate the school's competitive position and to determine its level of mission fulfillment and progress toward goals. Well suited for running a school, with a doctorate in education administration, DeNoia had taken the class to shore up her understanding of planning for and managing an NPO. In her mind, the key lesson was the need for an environmental analysis to better understand the school's internal environment and external competitors in order to improve the position of the school vis-à-vis the community's educational needs. She employed an MBA intern to help her develop tools for an internal and external environmental scan. The intern just wrapped up the data collection and analysis. DeNoia was ready to use the summer "down time" to make changes for the 2010 academic year, if only she knew how to proceed.

Otago Museum (International): In existence since 1868, the nonprofit Otago Museum, in New Zealand, had undergone several changes and expansions during its history and was regarded as curator of a broad-based collection of Maori and South Pacific artifacts. In January 2010, the Otago Museum's CFO was instructed by the museum's CEO to create a BSC for the museum. The current CEO had brought a sense of customer orientation and financial acumen to the general running of the museum, evidenced by examination of customer satisfaction via surveys and focus groups and various efforts to diversify income streams. The development of a BSC was seen as a practical way to reinforce and further motivate employee behavior congruent with the focus on customer service and financial acumen. The resulting BSC needed to articulate clearly the museum's objectives and the cause-and-effect relationships linking BSC dimensions with the museum's strategic vision and mission.

REFERENCES

Bryson, J. M. (2005). The strategy change cycle: An effective strategic planning approach for non-profit organizations. In R. D. Herman (Ed.), *The Jossey-Bass handbook of non-profit leadership and management* (pp. 171–203). San Francisco, CA: Jossey-Bass.

Collins, J. (2001). *Good to great: Why some companies make the leap . . . and others don't.* New York, NY: HarperCollins.

Conway Dato-on, M., & Gassenheimer, J. (2010, May). *Service learning through NPOs: The new service-dominant logic in education?* Paper presented at the annual conference of the Academy of Marketing Science, Portland, OR.

Conway Dato-on, M., Weisenbach Keller, E., & Shaw, D. (2009). Adapting for-profit branding models to small nonprofit organizations: A theoretical discussion and model proposition. In *Proceedings of the 2009 World Marketing Congress.* Ruston, LA: Academy of Marketing Science.

Festen, M., & Philbin, M. (2007). *Level best: How small and grassroots nonprofits can tackle evaluation and talk results.* San Francisco, CA: Jossey-Bass.

Garibay, C. (2011, January/February). Responsive and accessible: How museums are using research to better engage diverse cultural communities. *Dimensions.* Retrieved from http://www.astc.org/blog/category/astc-dimensions/

Hall, H. (2011, April 22). Americans gave a lot less in the recession than experts predicted. *The Chronicle of Philanthropy.*

Kaplan, R. S. (2001). Strategic performance measurement and management in non-profit organizations. *Non-Profit Management and Leadership, 11*, 353–370.

Kaplan, R. S., & Norton, D. P. (1992). The balanced scorecard—Measures that drive performance. *Harvard Business Review, 70*, 71–79.

Kaplan, R. S., & Norton, D. P. (2000). Having trouble with your strategy? Then map it. *Harvard Business Review, 78*, 167–175.

Kim, W. C., & Mauborgne, R. (2005). *Blue ocean strategy: How to create uncontested market space and make the competition irrelevant.* Cambridge, MA: Harvard Business School.

Kong, E. (2008). The development of strategic management in the non-profit context: Intellectual capital in social service non-profit organizations.

International Journal of Management Reviews, 10, 281–299.

Ohmae, K. (2005). *The next global stage: The challenges and opportunities in our borderless world.* Upper Saddle River, NJ: Pearson Prentice Hall.

Paton, R. (2003). *Managing and measuring social enterprises.* Thousand Oaks, CA: Sage.

Wall, A., Kirk, R., & Martin, G. (2004). *Intellectual capital: Measuring the immeasurable?* Amsterdam, Netherlands: CIMA.

Worth, M. J. (2012). *Nonprofit management: Principles and practice* (2nd ed.). Thousand Oaks, CA: Sage.

Wymer, W., Knowles, P., & Gomes, R. (2006). *Nonprofit marketing: Marketing management for charitable and nongovernmental organizations.* Thousand Oaks, CA: Sage.

LAKE EOLA CHARTER SCHOOL: SECURING THE BRAND THROUGH ENVIRONMENTAL ANALYSIS

In late 2009, Ronnie DeNoia, principal of the Lake Eola Charter School (LECS) in downtown Orlando, Florida, completed a course on non-profit branding at the Philanthropy & Nonprofit Leadership Center at a local college. She was energized and ready to apply the new learning to evaluate the school's competitive position and to determine its level of mission fulfillment and progress toward goals. Well suited for running a school, with a doctorate in education administration, DeNoia had taken the class at the Philanthropy & Nonprofit Leadership Center to shore up her understanding of planning and managing a nonprofit organization (NPO). In her mind, the key lesson was the need for an environmental analysis to better understand the school's internal environment and external competitors in order to improve the position of the school vis-à-vis the community's educational needs. She employed an MBA intern to help her develop tools for an internal and external environmental scan. The intern had just wrapped up the data collection and analysis. DeNoia was ready to use the summer "down time" to make changes for the 2010 academic year, if only she knew how to proceed.

CHARTER SCHOOLS
IN THE UNITED STATES

Few doubt that today's public schools in America are troubled. One solution to what many classified as failing public education was the creation of charter schools. Such schools secured a "charter" or operating contract from the state and/or local government delineating enrollment and educational guidelines. As of mid-2010 there were an estimated 4,638 charter schools in 39 states and Washington, D.C., which served less than three per cent of the U.S. school-age population, or slightly more than 1.4 million students.[1] Charters received government funds, but operated independently as nonprofit organizations. As such, charters had to employ marketing strategies to persuade parents to select them instead of neighborhood public or local private schools. The strategies seemed to be working; in March 2010, there were 350,000 families on charter school waiting lists, enough to fill more than 1,000 additional charter schools.[2] Charters held lotteries when applications exceeded available seats.

Education Next and Harvard's Program on Education Policy and Governance (PEPG) combined resources to answer the question, "What do Americans think about their schools?" The surveys were conducted in 2007, 2008 and 2009.[3] The 2009 survey results suggested that the general public approved of charters, with supporters outnumbering opponents two to one. Among African Americans, the approval ratio was four to one. Even among public-school teachers, 37 per cent favored charters, while 31 per cent opposed them. Most charters were located in urban areas, with more than half of all their students coming from minority groups such as African Americans or Hispanics. Data gathered for the survey indicated that more than a third of charter school students were eligible for the federal free or reduced lunch program. Numerous studies emphasized the success of charter schools in terms of graduation rates and test scores.[4] Despite the generally favorable public opinion, charters were not without detractors. Charter critics relied on two often-cited, well-circulated reports: the 2004 study by the American Federation of Teachers (AFT) and a report based on ongoing research by Stanford's Center for Research on Education Outcomes (CREDO), which found more weak charter schools than strong ones.

Despite the mixed data on charter school effectiveness, the Obama administration seemed in favor of such schools and developed incentives to encourage more. To qualify for the U.S. Education Department's 2009 Race to the Top funding campaign, many states lifted restrictions on charter school numbers and enrollment requirements. Tennessee, an ultimate winner in the competition, for example, raised the state's limit on charter schools from 50 to 90. Illinois doubled the allowable number to 120 charters in the state, while Louisiana removed all numerical restrictions.[5] Given the Obama administration's emphasis on improving education through creative solutions, the competitive landscape for

---

[1]"One study of 29 countries found that the level of competition among schools was directly tied to higher test scores in reading and math." Paul E. Peterson, "Charter Schools and Student Performance," *Wall Street Journal* (Online), New York, March 16, 2010.

[2]Ibid.

[3]William Howell, Martin West and Paul E. Peterson, "The Persuadable Public," *Education Next,* 9:4, Fall 2009, http://educationnext.org/persuadable-public, accessed July 13, 2010.

[4]Paul E. Peterson, "Charter Schools and Student Performance," *Wall Street Journal* (Online), New York, March 16, 2010.

[5]Anne Marie Chaker, "Expanding the Charter Option," *Wall Street Journal,* August 13, 2009, pp. D1-D2.

charter schools in the country would become more crowded in the near future. Todd Ziebarth, a vice-president for policy at the National Alliance for Public Charter Schools in Washington, D.C., supported the expansion of charter schools across the country but cautioned that, along with the high-quality charter schools, some "bad schools—those with poorly defined missions" might arise.[6]

CHARTER SCHOOLS IN CENTRAL FLORIDA

In Florida, the charter school law was enacted in 1996. By 2009, there were 356 charter schools enrolling more than 104,000 students.[7] In a letter to the *Wall Street Journal,* Florida's Governor Crist wrote that in 2009 the state ranked "third nationally in the number of charter schools and fourth in the number of charter-schooled students." He quoted the "2009 Quality Counts: Portrait of a Population" report released in January 2009, noting that "Florida's education ranking jumped from 14th to 10th in the nation, and its overall grade improved from a C+ to a B-."[8]

The state of Florida placed no restriction on the number of charter schools and mandated that all charters be approved and financial records be reviewed by the local school board. According to the charter school law, students enrolled in a charter school were funded as if they were in a basic or special program as appropriate, and were funded the same as students enrolled in other public schools in the school district. According to state mandate, teachers in charter schools needed to be certified, could collectively

bargain, were not required to join local teachers' unions and would not be eligible for state retirement as were public school teachers. The State Department of Education was required to prepare an annual report comparing test scores of charter school students with test scores of comparable public school students in their school district.[9]

Florida joined the Race to the Top campaign and attempted to receive funding for both public and charter school initiatives. The state finished fourth in the first round of competition—just missing funding opportunities—and applied for the second round in early June 2010. Throughout the state, tempers flared regarding the role of teachers' unions and merit pay.[10] Some stated that this discord was the primary reason for the state missing funding in the first round and hoped the shortcoming would be overcome in round two.

Within Central Florida (including the Orange County School District where LECS resided), support for charter schools was fierce among parents but missing in the press. Reviews of local press coverage showed articles about the poor performance and inadequate services of charter schools, outnumbering positive articles. For example, articles dating back to 2007 gave abundant detail of under-representation of certain student groups, citing facts such as 60 per cent of charters served a smaller portion of students who qualified for free and reduced-price meals than their typical district school and trailed the districts by three per cent in service to disabled students. Carlo Rodriguez, who oversaw charters for the state, attributed the enrollment differences to parent preferences. Articles also

---

[6]William Howell, Martin West and Paul E. Peterson, "The Persuadable Public," *Education Next,* 9:4, Fall 2009, http://educationnext.org/persuadable-public, accessed July 13, 2010.

[7]www.publiccharters.org/states, accessed June 3, 2010.

[8]*Wall Street Journal* (Eastern Edition), New York, January 10, 2009, p. A10.

[9]http://mb2.ecs.org/reports/Report.aspx?id=65, accessed June 3, 2010.

[10]Chris Williams, "Walking away from millions: 9 states pass on 'Race to the Top' education grant program," June 1, 2010, http://education.gaeatimes.com/2010/05/31/walking-away-from-millions-9-states-pass-on-race-to-the-top-education-grant-program-4055, accessed June 3, 2010.

complained about the requirement of parent volunteering in charter schools (typically 40 hours annually)[11] without discussing the advantages of parental involvement in their children's education. The local papers also overemphasized the financial trouble of poor-performing schools while barely mentioning the numerous charter schools run as financially viable organizations (e.g. "Charter School in Orange Must Shape Up or Shut Down—Audit finds lavish spending by administrators despite heavy debt";[12] "District probe closes Orange charter school—The facility was mismanaged and lacked financial accountability, officials say"[13]). Below these headlines that highlighted the closing of one school each year, the content briefly mentioned that there were 19 other charter schools in the district without such financial difficulties. Notwithstanding this bad press, Florida earned a "B" for its charter school law in a study by the Center for Education Reform in 2009 ("A"-rated states were California, Minnesota and Washington, D.C., with a majority of states receiving a grade of "C"),[14] suggesting Florida's oversight of charter schools was adequate.

This press coverage left a bad taste in the mouths of many in Orlando and the Central Florida community. Although Lake Eola Charter School was often cited as the exception to the rule, the overall bad impression of charter schools resulted in a public relations nightmare and marketing challenge for DeNoia and her school board. DeNoia mentioned that "every year after the annual charter school bashing by the *Sentinel*" she would have to "get on the phone and call students' families and LECS supporters to point out that their school was financially sound and highly ranked in comparison to both other charter schools and local public schools." DeNoia also used the school's website to emphasize this point: "We are proud to report that we are in our Magnolia Avenue facility for the eleventh year and have achieved fiscal stability (and a surplus), a remodeled school, and a curriculum that resulted in Lake Eola Charter School receiving another 'A' as part of the Governor's Award Program" (nine years running).[15]

LAKE EOLA CHARTER SCHOOL: FROM YESTERDAY TO TODAY

DeNoia was in the unique position of running both a school and a nonprofit organization. She felt confident in her ability to design a curriculum, assess student performance, and manage teachers. She was less confident in her ability regarding the management of a nonprofit. Despite this reservation, she was proud of LECS and was eager to discuss its origins and its future. DeNoia recalled the history of the school where she had dedicated what seemed like "every waking moment" over the past decade with energy and enthusiasm. Although she had a board of directors upon which she could rely for advice, she felt responsible for the integrity and destiny of the school.

We conceived Lake Eola Charter School as a K–8 center of educational excellence fourteen years ago [1996], and received charter approval in 1998. The first year presented challenges of the actual physical location. We acquired and converted an old parking garage on a major road in downtown Orlando. The concept was to build a school that utilized all the downtown public facilities, rather than building an isolated school that needed to create all its own resources—where education was separated from

[11]Vicki McClure and Mary Shanklin, "Charters serve fewer poor, disabled," *Orlando Sentinel,* March 25, 2007.

[12]*Orlando Sentinel,* April 8, 2008.

[13]*Orlando Sentinel,* July 4, 2007.

[14]"Charter Laws Across the States," www.edreform.com/About_CER/Charter_School_Laws_Across_the_States/?Charter_School_Laws_Across_the_States, accessed June 4, 2010.

[15]www.lecs.org, accessed June 4, 2010.

daily life. We envisioned [and have been successful in] using the Lake Eola park for physical education, the public library for research/reading, and downtown architecture for history and geometry lessons. The second year brought challenges of fiscal stability. During this time, the board actively secured public and private funding and developed the concept for the LECS Foundation [ultimately established in 2004] as an ongoing supporting body for the school. Beginning in the third year, we fine-tuned a first-class, non-textbook curriculum utilizing resources from primary source materials such as websites and practical application exercises. We continued to strengthen the curriculum and the teaching staff every year. Moving forward, we'd like to find a new facility and expand our charter to include high school. Our waiting list is too long and has been for years. A new facility would enable us to better meet the educational needs of our community. After all, that's what this is all about—right?

Unlike many public schools, Lake Eola Charter School employed a cluster system for students after grade three. This system placed students in the fourth and fifth grades in mixed-grade classes. Similarly, middle schoolers (sixth, seventh, and eighth grades) were assigned to mixed-grade classes. This flexibility encouraged communication among students of various ages and created a more family-like atmosphere. Teachers facilitated active learning rather than "pouring it in"—thus developing ownership of one's education on the part of students. Educational research suggested that such approaches improved critical thinking skills. All lessons were differentiated to meet each student where he or she was rather than where their ages dictated they should be.

Another aspect that contributed to the family-like culture was parental involvement. There was no tuition fee at LECS but parents were required to volunteer twenty-five hours per school year for families with one child enrolled at LECS and thirty hours per school year for families with two or more children enrolled at LECS. Alternatively,

parents could "purchase" their required volunteer hours, if absolutely necessary, at the rate of $10.00 per hour. Most parents exceeded the minimum requirement of volunteer hours. Parents were committed to their children's education and routinely demonstrated that commitment through active involvement.

To ensure continued educational success among students and help teachers develop themselves professionally, DeNoia invested LECS time and money into ongoing professional training for teachers. She was particularly proud of the reading curriculum at the school, which encouraged self-paced reading among students. Rather than focusing on having students read required texts, critical reading skills were applied to all reading via extensive reading logs, based on Nancie Atwell's research. Students select among three challenge levels: choice in challenge, just right, and holiday reading. This choice is what promotes the competitive spirit; students average 20–25 books per year. The teacher responsible for designing the reading curriculum often presented at professional conferences where she also made sure she was current in educational methodology. In-house seminars encouraged teachers to share what they had learned at such professional conferences with others on staff.

LECS and its students received much acknowledgment for academic accomplishments, including the Governor's Recognition Program. Students achieved success at the local, state and national levels in a variety of competitions, such as the National Geographic Geography Bee, the Modern Woodsmen Oration Contest, the Dr. Nelson Ying Science Fair, the Florida Science and Engineering Fair, Odyssey of the Mind, No Boundaries, and the Radiant Peace program. Further, LECS eighth-grade students received high admission rates to International Baccalaureate Diploma Programs, magnet schools[16] and advanced placement programs in

---

[16]A magnet school is one that exists within the public school system yet exists outside of zoned school boundaries. The purpose of a magnet school is that it usually has something special (e.g. academic or creative emphasis) to offer over a traditional public school, which makes attending them an attractive choice to many students. Most magnet schools require students to apply and be accepted based on demonstration of proficiency in the area of the school's emphasis. Source: www.publicschoolreview.com/articles/2, accessed August 13, 2010.

private and public high schools throughout Florida. Communication with LECS alumni indicated satisfaction with academic preparedness and high success in post-LECS academic endeavors.

Focus group and survey data collected from LECS students, employees and parents by the intern DeNoia employed showed high satisfaction with the school. Selected survey results are included in Exhibit 1.

Exhibit 1   Survey Data Collected From LECS Donors, Students, Employees and Parents

Donor Responses

How well does Lake Eola Charter School satisfy your needs?

Answer Options	Response Percent	Response Count
Very Poorly	0.0%	0
Poorly	0.0%	0
Somewhat Poorly	0.0%	0
Somewhat Well	0.0%	0
Well	15.4%	2
Very Well	76.9%	10
Unable to Answer	7.7%	1
answered question		13
skipped question		4

How much do you like Lake Eola Charter School?

Answer Options	Response Percent	Response Count
Strongly Dislike	0.0%	0
Dislike	0.0%	0
Somewhat Dislike	0.0%	0
Somewhat Like	0.0%	0
Like	23.1%	3
Strongly Like	76.9%	10
Unable to Answer	0.0%	0
answered question		13
skipped question		4

How trustworthy is Lake Eola Charter School?

Answer Options	Response Percent	Response Count
Not at all Trustworthy	0.0%	0
Less Trustworthy	0.0%	0
Somewhat Less Trustworthy	0.0%	0
Somewhat Trustworthy	0.0%	0
Trustworthy	23.1%	3
Very Trustworthy	76.9%	10
Unable to Answer	0.0%	0
answered question		13
skipped question		4

(Continued)

Exhibit 1 (Continued)

How favorable is your overall attitude toward Lake Eola Charter School?

Answer Options	Response Percent	Response Count
Very Unfavorable	7.7%	1
Unfavorable	0.0%	0
Somewhat Unfavorable	0.0%	0
Somewhat Favorable	0.0%	0
Favorable	15.4%	2
Very Favorable	76.9%	10
Unable to Answer	0.0%	0
answered question		13
skipped question		4

How would you assess the educational value of Lake Eola Charter School?

Answer Options	Response Percent	Response Count
Very Poor	0.0%	0
Poor	0.0%	0
Somewhat Poor	0.0%	0
Somewhat Good	0.0%	0
Good	7.7%	1
Very Good	92.3%	12
Unable to Answer	0.0%	0
answered question		13
skipped question		4

Lake Eola Charter School is an educational leader among schools in the Orlando area.

Answer Options	Response Percent	Response Count
Strongly Disagree	0.0%	0
Disagree	0.0%	0
Somewhat Disagree	0.0%	0
Somewhat Agree	7.7%	1
Agree	38.5%	5
Strongly Agree	53.8%	7
Unable to Answer	0.0%	0
answered question		13
skipped question		4

The level of donor satisfaction with the overall service Lake Eola Charter School provides has _____.

Answer Options	Response Percent	Response Count
Declined Significantly	0.0%	0
Declined Somewhat	7.7%	1
Been Stable	30.8%	4
Increased Somewhat	7.7%	1
Increased Significantly	0.0%	0
Unable to Answer	53.8%	7
answered question		13
skipped question		4

Parent Responses

How well does Lake Eola Charter School satisfy your needs?		
Answer Options	Response Percent	Response Count
Very Poorly	0.0%	0
Poorly	0.0%	0
Somewhat Poorly	2.1%	2
Somewhat Well	7.2%	7
Well	25.8%	25
Very Well	63.9%	62
Unable to Answer	1.0%	1
answered question		97
skipped question		10

How much do you like Lake Eola Charter School?		
Answer Options	Response Percent	Response Count
Strongly Dislike	0.0%	0
Dislike	1.0%	1
Somewhat Dislike	2.1%	2
Somewhat Like	3.1%	3
Like	14.4%	14
Strongly Like	78.4%	76
Unable to Answer	1.0%	1
answered question		97
skipped question		10

How trustworthy is Lake Eola Charter School?		
Answer Options	Response Percent	Response Count
Not at all Trustworthy	1.0%	1
Less Trustworthy	1.0%	1
Somewhat Less Trustworthy	2.1%	2
Somewhat Trustworthy	4.1%	4
Trustworthy	18.6%	18
Very Trustworthy	71.1%	69
Unable to Answer	2.1%	2
answered question		97
skipped question		10

(Continued)

Exhibit 1 (Continued)

How favorable is your overall attitude toward Lake Eola Charter School?

Answer Options	Response Percent	Response Count
Very Unfavorable	0.0%	0
Unfavorable	1.0%	1
Somewhat Unfavorable	3.1%	3
Somewhat Favorable	5.2%	5
Favorable	30.9%	30
Very Favorable	58.8%	57
Unable to Answer	1.0%	1
answered question		97
skipped question		10

How would you assess the educational value of Lake Eola Charter School?

Answer Options	Response Percent	Response Count
Very Poor	0.0%	0
Poor	0.0%	0
Somewhat Poor	0.0%	0
Somewhat Good	4.1%	4
Good	9.3%	9
Very Good	86.6%	84
Unable to Answer	0.0%	0
answered question		97
skipped question		10

Lake Eola Charter School is an educational leader among schools in the Orlando area.

Answer Options	Response Percent	Response Count
Strongly Disagree	0.0%	0
Disagree	2.1%	2
Somewhat Disagree	2.1%	2
Somewhat Agree	4.1%	4
Agree	13.4%	13
Strongly Agree	77.3%	75
Unable to Answer	1.0%	1
answered question		97
skipped question		10

The level of parent satisfaction with the overall service Lake Eola Charter School provides has _____.

Answer Options	Response Percent	Response Count
Declined Significantly	1.0%	1
Declined Somewhat	8.2%	8
Been Stable	38.8%	38
Increased Somewhat	24.5%	24
Increased Significantly	13.3%	13
Unable to Answer	14.3%	14
answered question		98
skipped question		9

Source: Compiled by intern for LECS.

DeNoia believed that the success of the school—as revealed by the survey responses—emanated from the strong mission and vision that kept all staff focused on the same goal. In other words, based on the mission statement, parents, staff and potential donors learned why the school existed and were able to give their time and money with confidence. The mission statement and vision were as follows:

Mission: Lake Eola Charter School's mission is to provide differentiated instruction leading to mastery of national standards, and to use best practices to develop comprehension, computation, critical thinking, character and community service in our family of learners in the city of Orlando.

Vision: Lake Eola Charter School's vision is to create a laboratory environment for other urban schools to observe best practices that produce a positive result in math, science, social studies and language arts. This vision not only includes using city resources to build lifelong skills, but also to establish a personal connection to the citizens and cultivate a sense of community service.

After completing the course on nonprofit branding, DeNoia knew it was important to engage in strategic planning for her organization so that over time the school's strengths would continue to build and be leveraged to realize the vision. Such planning, she learned, included gathering data about LECS in three important areas: (1) organizational effectiveness and performance, (2) measuring strengths and weaknesses against peers (benchmarking), and (3) measuring performance against mission. So, DeNoia set the intern to work gathering the information to enable the strategic planning process to begin.

LECS: ORGANIZATIONAL EFFECTIVENESS AND PERFORMANCE

DeNoia felt great about the feedback received from students, staff and parents collected in surveys and focus groups. She knew there was room for improvement, however, and instructed the intern to collect and organize information on LECS. DeNoia could provide her idea of what worked and what did not, but she wanted the intern to synthesize the data collected and combine it with information available from the state and popular press in a usable fashion. The intern suggested using a SWOT format. DeNoia did not really know what that entailed but trusted the intern was learning something about this in his MBA program and told him to proceed.

Looking more closely at LECS, the intern found the following strengths, weaknesses, opportunities and threats from both primary and secondary research.

Strengths: The greatest strength of LECS was the excellent track record of student performance. This conclusion was clearly supported by the average Florida's Comprehensive Assessment Test (FCAT) score students at LECS received. In addition, LECS had been an "A"-rated school for more than nine consecutive years. Another impressive strength of LECS was parent satisfaction with the school. Parents expressed their satisfaction with LECS in focus groups, stating they were extremely happy with their children's performance in the school and the overall structure of the teaching program. A final strength of LECS was the "private school feel the school has with no additional associated costs," as expressed by students and parents. LECS maintained a private school feel because of the culture of the school. The class sizes were relatively small, and there was a close relationship between parents and school administrators/teachers as well as between students and teachers. In addition, the education the students received was perceived to be on par with private schools and was ranked on par based on test scores and student placement.

Weaknesses: The greatest weakness of LECS was the lack of communication from the school to the greater community and parents. Although the school organized charitable events with some regularity (mostly attended by parents and school staff) and although people observed children playing in the park during recess, not many people knew about LECS. This was mainly due to the lack of marketing of the school. The other side of this communication weakness related to the school's communication with parents. During the focus group, parents communicated very strongly about this weakness and many stated this as the number one problem with the school. Parents indicated a very high level of satisfaction with educational excellence in both the quantitative and qualitative research, yet expressed concern with the limited communication about school assignments and activities.

A second weakness of LECS was the limited operating budget of the school. Because the school did not receive as much state funding as public schools, LECS needed donations to make up this difference. This was often difficult, resulting in a school with a smaller budget than its public counterparts.

LECS's third weakness involved searching for donations and the tools necessary to enable this. During research, the intern found several errors/missing data regarding past donors, board of director members, and parents. A flaw in the organization's ability to achieve long-term success was the inability to collect, store and sort relevant data on each stakeholder group. Known in the industry as Constituent Relationship Management (CRM), CRM strategies should (1) enhance the involvement (e.g. volunteer time, donations) of existing stakeholders by motivating them to engage in behaviors that generate higher returns (e.g. more volunteer hours, increased value or frequency of donations), and (2) extend the duration of relationships, thereby maintaining enhanced behavior for a longer period of time. A subset of this weakness was that LECS did not fully leverage the fundraising resources in which the school had invested, i.e., DonorEdge software to help with CRM. Donor contributions made up a significant portion of the school's operating budget, making this weakness very problematic.

DeNoia felt that a fourth weakness, the physical facility of the school, stood in the way of future growth. The facility was outdated, with limited technology. To students and outside observers, the school felt cramped and dark. A new facility with upgraded technology would make the school more attractive to prospective students and donors. A final weakness of LECS was the lack of afterschool programs such as sports and music. Although the school had a very popular Space, Technology and Engineering Program (STEP), for which students expressed passion, the school's lack of other afterschool programs put it at a disadvantage as compared to other public and private schools.

Opportunities: As more parents became dissatisfied with Orange County public schools, there was an opportunity for LECS to attract students from these schools. Since LECS provided an excellent education for no extra cost versus a public school, parents might have been inclined to take their children out of public school and enroll them in charter schools like LECS.

Although LECS was currently at student capacity (with a waiting list each year for more than five years), its excellent educational rating and satisfied parent population provided great leverage points from which to attract public support. Another opportunity for LECS revolved around the state of the economy. When the economy is tight, parents seek more affordable education for their children. Therefore, parents might have been inclined to take their children out of private schools and place them in LECS because of its high academic ratings. This was viewed as an opportunity for LECS to position itself as the solution to the gap between public school service and private school price.

Threats: In contrast to the opportunity a weakened economy provided LECS, it also posed a threat for the school. In a destabilized economy, donors would be less inclined to donate, which negatively affected the operating budget of the school. Another threat came from local newspapers such as the *Orlando Sentinel* that annually published articles disparaging charter schools in Orlando and throughout the state. Although the paper generally gave praise to LECS, the articles overall did not bode well for the school since they gave charter schools a negative connotation. DeNoia was also acutely aware of the threat posed by the high name recognition of the private schools in the area as well as their marketing expertise (on staff and on their boards) and marketing funds. The final threat to LECS was state funding. Despite the recent favorable trend of charter school support among politicians, local teachers' unions and many taxpayers did not support charter schools in theory or in practice. DeNoia noted that, "Lake Eola Charter School operated on less money than the traditional public schools in Orange County. We did not benefit from the half penny sales tax and were required to pay an annual administrative fee to Orange County. This resulted in a drain to our operating budget of more than $50,000 per year." In other words, public schools had more access to state funding than charter schools, and when these charters

were unable to attract donations, this threat presented great problems for these schools.

LECS: BENCHMARKING AGAINST COMPETITORS

At DeNoia's request, the intern compiled a list of private schools located within two miles of LECS. DeNoia considered these to be the potential direct competitors of the school. The resulting list included five schools: The Christ School, Lake Highland Preparatory School, New School Preparatory, St. James Cathedral School and Trinity Lutheran School.[17] The intern decided to use the SWOT analysis and available data to determine what to include in the comparison across schools. The results were compiled in a table (see Exhibit 2).

Exhibit 2   Comparison Information—LECS Versus Private Schools Within Two-Mile Radius

	Orange County Private Schools					
	The Christ School	**Lake Highland Preparatory School**	**New School Preparatory**	**St. James Cathedral School**	**Trinity Lutheran School**	**Lake Eola, Charter School**
Grade Range	K–8	PK–12	PK–8	PK, 3–8	PK–8	K–8
Religious Affiliation	ID	ND	NR	Catholic	Lutheran	ND
Non-Profit?	Yes	Yes	No	Yes	Yes	Yes
Students per Teacher	K-14 P/S-20	12	14	18	12	17
Total Enrollment	350	2035	90	480	230	
Notable Feature	CS, A, D	CS, A, B, D	CS, A, C, D	CS, A, B, C	CS, A, B, C	STEP
2007–2010 Tuition Range	$7,455–$8,225/yr	$9,000–$15,225/yr	$10,400/yr	$5,600–$7,235/yr	$6,500–$6,650/yr	N/A

Source: Orlando Magazine, February 2010.

Note: PK = Prekindergarten; K = Kindergarten; P = Primary; M = Middle; S = Secondary; ID = Interdenominational; ND = Nondenominational Christian; NR = Nonreligious; CS = Competitive Sports; A = Art; B = Band; C = Choir; D = Drama.

[17]Data collected from *Orlando Magazine,* February 2010.

Based on DeNoia's years of experience as a principal and teacher in Orlando, she knew that Lake Highland was the largest and most recognized name in the private school category. Perhaps ironically, it and St. James were the source of most of the students who transferred to LECS from a private school. Lake Highland sat on a beautiful 26-acre site near downtown and provided an enclosed environment for privileged students. DeNoia felt she could not compete with the extensive amenities offered by the school but that LECS offered a more "realistic city feel that prepared students for life." The other private schools were not as big as Lake Highland and focused on their religious affiliations much more. Most, though certainly not all, students in the religiously focused schools came from families that attended corresponding churches.

A second category of competitor schools compared LECS to other charter schools and public schools in the Orlando area.[18] The public schools were chosen because each was an "A" school located within a two-mile radius of LECS. There were 19 charter schools in the Orange County Public School (OCPS) district and four within a close radius of LECS: Nap Ford Community, Hope, Passport and Rio Grande. The four public schools in the same geographic area were Fern Creek, Hillcrest, Princeton and Rock Lake (see Exhibit 3).

Nap Ford Community School, established in 2001, was the newest charter school and stood apart from other charter schools by serving children in one of the most economically depressed areas in Orlando. Its location in Orlando's Parramore neighborhood, a district with a majority of African-American families known for its economic plight and troubled streets, meant a significant percentage of students lived at or below the national poverty level. The school's objective was to target the high-risk neighborhood and provide an educational program that offered children quality education in a positive environment, with a holistic model focused on body, mind and spirit. Hope originally based its charter on offering an inclusion model for autistic children but had since expanded to emphasize an intimate atmosphere that developed children academically and emotionally. Rio Grande, the most similar to LECS in its general education–based charter, had demonstrated inconsistent rankings by the state of Florida in its earlier years but since 2006 reports ranked the schools as either "A" or "B." Finally, Passport School offered an inclusive environment where children with disabilities (approximately 15 per cent of the enrollment) were educated with their non-disabled peers.

Both DeNoia and the intern expressed frustration that the data available on private schools was not the same as that available for public schools. DeNoia noted, however, that private schools were not required by the state of Florida to report the same information that traditional public and charter schools needed to provide. She felt it was unfair and limited parents' ability to compare schools fairly, but it was a reality with which she learned to live.

A third category of potential competitors was homeschooling. When DeNoia arrived at LECS in 2000, "approximately twenty-five per cent of our population was former homeschooled students. While that number has dropped significantly, charter schools traditionally attract homeschoolers and LECS continues to do so." For the 2008–2009 school year, Florida school districts reported home education of 42,431 families or 60,913 students; statewide, the trend had been growing consistently since 1999.[19] This number represented approximately two per cent of the PK–12 enrollment for that year and was the largest year-on-year growth in homeschooling (8.5 per cent) since 2005 (10 per cent). In the Orange County School District (where LECS was located), the most current school year

---

[18]Data in competitive analysis above collected from www.greatschools.com, accessed February 15, 2010.

[19]"Home Education Program," School Choice, Florida Department of Education, October 2009 Newsletter, www.floridaschoolchoice.org, accessed June 25, 2010.

Exhibit 3 Comparison Information—LECS Versus Public and Charter Schools Within Two-Mile Radius

		Criteria					
		Florida School Grade	FCAT Math Grade 3 (%)	FCAT Reading Grade 3 (%)	Students per Teacher	Average Years Teaching	Teachers With Advanced Degree (%)
Charter	Lake Eola Charter School	A	100	94	17	8	31
	Nap Ford Community Charter	N/A	31	31	23	15	14
	Hope Charter School	A	87	81	15	N/A	50
	Passport Charter School	A	50	50	29	28	0
	Rio Grande Charter	B	50	27	12	N/A	29
Public	Fern Creek Elementary	A	75	72	12	14	21
	Hillcrest Elementary	A	78	69	15	15	56
	Princeton Elementary	A	81	81	15	13	38
	Rock Lake Elementary	A	69	57	12	16	22

Source: Compiled by intern for LECS.

showed a decrease of 1.7 per cent of families pursuing the homeschooling option.[20] Neither DeNoia nor the intern was certain how to interpret this contradiction between Orange County and the state of Florida. Since not many homeschooled children had transferred to LECS in recent years, DeNoia told the intern not to worry about this category of competitors unless the data indicated a reason to be concerned.

DeNoia was uncertain if the information compiled by the intern was comprehensive. She thought perhaps she was either missing critical data or that she needed a method of comparison for the information.

[20]Data in competitive analysis above collected from www.greatschools.com, accessed February 15, 2010.

LECS: Moving Forward

DeNoia knew that with the recent political upsurge in support for the concept of charter schools at the federal level and, to a lesser extent, the state level, now was the time to act. It seemed that the last decade of academic success was a strong foundation upon which to build a plan. She had a short-term goal of growing the LECS Foundation to enable completion of the school's two long-term goals: (1) securing a new facility, thus expanding enrollment at the K–8 level, and (2) extending the charter to the high school level. How could she use the data collected to position LECS positively in the community and with various stakeholders (current parents, current and prospective students, possible funders and the board of directors) in order to achieve the objectives? Where should she start?

OTAGO MUSEUM

In January of 2010, Chris Farry, the Otago Museum's chief financial officer, was instructed by the museum's chief executive officer, Shimrath Paul, to design a comprehensive Balanced Score Card (BSC) for the museum. It needed to indicate clearly the museum's strategic objective(s), the strategic business themes that support the objective(s), and the cause-and-effect relationships linking BSC dimensions with strategic themes and objectives.

Museum Background

The Otago Museum in New Zealand began operating on September 15, 1868. At that time, it was located in the post office building in Dunedin's Exchange area, a building in which it shared space with the University of Otago.

As the Otago Museum's collections grew, so too did its need for larger premises. On August 11, 1877, the museum moved into its present site at 419 Great King Street. The cost to construct these purpose-built premises, which at the time featured two main galleries, was £12,500.

In 1877, responsibility for managing the museum became vested with the University of Otago. This arrangement lasted nearly 80 years, and, during this time, the university oversaw two major additions to the museum and helped it to become what in 1929 was described as "the finest teaching museum in the Commonwealth."[1]

In 1955, the museum's ownership transferred to a trust board, which was authorized to attract funding from various local authorities in the Otago region. Generally speaking, the principal funders continued in recent times to be the Dunedin City Council, Clutha District Council, Central Otago District Council, and Waitaki District Council.

Further expansions of the museum occurred in 1963, 1996, and 2002. The latter two expansions

[1] N. Peat, *Otago Museum Collected Stories,* Otago Museum, Dunedin, 2004.

were particularly noteworthy, for they very powerfully showcased the museum's attempt to go beyond its traditional role of displaying static work to creating an environment that was capable of engaging and interacting with visitors. Not coincidentally, the 1996 and 2002 expansions occurred under the leadership of Shimrath Paul. Paul, who became the director in 1995, brought a very fresh approach to the running of the museum. Unlike his predecessors, who were typically biologists or anthropologists, Paul was, among other things, an MBA graduate. As such, he brought a sense of business acumen, including a customer focus, that was less evident in the museum's prior directors. He also diversified the museum's income stream, which at the time of his arrival was about 95 per cent derived from the New Zealand government and the four local authorities noted above. Ever since 2009, only about half of the museum's funding came from these four sources, with the balance being comprised of gift shop sales; the museum café; the hiring of the museum's facility areas for conferences, weddings, seminars, etc.; various special exhibition fees; and the selling of tours to the cruise boat lines as one of the latter's passenger activities.

The museum had about two million items on display or in safekeeping. This number represented about 15 per cent of all museum-held items throughout New Zealand. The museum's collection could best be defined as broad-based. It held a wide array of displays showcasing birds, insects, marine animals, and fossils; owned a variety of significant Maori and Pacific Island artifacts; and boasted a collection of ship builders' models considered to be among the finest in the Southern Hemisphere.

The museum had about 60 full-time equivalent employees. During a typical 12-month period, the museum attracted between 300,000 to 400,000 visitors. With a regional population of about 130,000 people, Otago Museum was the highest-visited museum per capita in Australasia. As Dunedin was not an international gateway, it did not have a large tourist visitation, and maintaining high and increasing visitor numbers relied primarily on encouraging repeat local visitors. Dunedin's relative isolation meant that the museum had to offer an experience that consistently attracted the repeat visitor. In practical terms, this experience translated into the imperative of changing exhibits and offering an excellent whole-visitor experience.

MISSION AND VISION

The Otago Museum was a non-profit organization with the mission of providing "service and development" to its community.[2] The museum prided itself on its ability "to acquire, record, research, conserve, communicate, and exhibit material evidence of people, knowledge and the environment for the education, entertainment and inspiration of local communities and visitors."[3]

The museum's vision statement, as stated in its annual report, was "To be an inspirational museum of which the people of Otago and New Zealand are proud."

The vision statement was supported by a mission statement that, again as stated in the museum's annual report, was "To inspire and enrich our communities, and enhance understanding of the world through our collection, our people and the stories we share."

In striving to accomplish its vision and mission statements, the museum had three primary areas of focus: culture, nature and science. These foci were further enumerated by the following six strategic objectives:

1. To develop our culture and capabilities

2. To continually evolve and grow

3. To increase engagement and quality of experience for our communities through access to and outreach from the museum

4. To actively care for, protect and develop our collections and physical environment

---

[2] Otago Museum Annual Report, 2006–2007.

[3] Ibid.

5. To increase our resources and use them wisely

6. To build and contribute to productive partnerships and strategic alliances

The strategic objectives, and in particular the museum's ability to achieve the objectives, were underpinned by three key results areas:

1. Being seen as a community leader in the offering of knowledge, learning opportunities and experiences that are relevant, contemporary, topical, widely accessible and consistently high in quality.

2. Having staff and the Otago Museum Trust Board work together to demonstrate effective, positive management of collections, resources and skills.

3. Ensuring a culture that is positive and continually developing, where everyone takes responsibility for individual and collective behaviour, demonstrating agreed values and redressing unacceptable ones, as determined collectively and also individually through self and peer assessment.

POSITION AS OF 2010

The museum had achieved large increases in its visitor numbers in recent years. The nearly 20 per cent increase in visitor numbers from 2007 to 2008 was partly attributed to its Discovery World Tropical Forest, which featured more than 1,000 imported tropical butterflies. Of course, other reasons behind its significant rise in patronage included its motivated workforce and its focus on customer satisfaction. As an example of this commitment, the museum had won several tourism and best workplace awards, including in 2006 when it won an Unlimited/JRA Best Places to Work in New Zealand Award under the category "One of the 10 best small workplaces."

Management believed that a major driving force behind the museum's current success was

its organizational culture. This culture was put together by the staff, board and large stakeholders at a strategic planning workshop. Management believed that a healthy culture must be dynamic—owned and implemented by the staff and supported, not driven, solely from the top.

This culture in its strategic plan was:

Through actively, positively and fully sharing our skills and positive attitudes with the team, our individual contributions can become key parts of the Museum's total strengths. Together our collective intelligence and abilities will create a work environment which invigorates, inspires and challenges us—and helps us to achieve our vision and mission for the people of Otago and beyond. Our culture is developed through the agreed behaviours being demonstrated and through the expectation that some behaviours will not be acceptable within our team.[4]

An enumeration of the expected and unacceptable behaviours for working as a team at the museum, which was collated by the whole staff, is presented in Exhibits 1 and 2.

COMPETITIVE ENVIRONMENT

The Otago Early Settlers Museum, the Dunedin Public Art Gallery, and Olveston each embraced a goal that was similar to that of the Otago Museum. Namely, each organization sought to use its collections to enrich its visitors' understanding of the world.

The Otago Settlers Museum was established in 1898 and was commonly heralded as one of New Zealand's finest social history museums. The museum's permanent and temporary exhibitions showcased Otago's rich cultural tapestry and diversity.

The Dunedin Public Art Gallery was established in 1884 and remained in recent times one of New Zealand's most significant art museums. It housed a fine collection of European art, including

[4]Otago Museum Strategic Plan, 2006–2011.

Exhibit 1 Behaviours Expected From Everyone

Passion	Enthusiasm	Fun
Creativity	Imagination	Friendliness
Happy	Positivity	Social
Accountability	Organized	Cooperation
Commitment	Drive	"Can do" attitude
Adaptability	Flexibility	Respect
Curiosity	Proactivity	Openness and honesty
Determination	Loyalty	Dedication
Reliability	Common sense	Professionalism
Hardworking	Helpful	Supportive
Initiative	Inspirational	Self-belief
Know limits	Balance	Sense of purpose
Detail-focused	Self-motivation	Innovative
Continuous learning	Up for a challenge	Strong work ethic
Ethical behaviour	Problem solving	Trust and trustworthiness
Sharing each other's successes	Forthcoming with information	Recognition of our diverse skills
Responsibility	Sharing	Depth
Working to the best of our ability	Recognition of our individuality	Risk aware but not risk adverse
Solution-oriented	Think on our feet	Pride in our work
Asking for help if you need it	Development of self-empowering environment	Understanding our place in the organization
Pulling in the same direction	Appreciation and saying thank you	Listening and understanding
Acknowledging others	Telling it like it is	Giving recognition
Constructive feedback/criticism	Giving help when others need it	Identifying opportunities
Accept when you are wrong, get over it, move on, learn from it	Acceptance of individual's capacity	Meeting both personal and group challenges and objectives
Brainstorming together	Pulling together	Fantastic communication
Value others	Focused on common goals	Adherence to systems
Enjoying ourselves and our teammates	Challenge each other positively	Committed to meeting deadlines
Strength through good group dynamics	Moving outside our comfort zones	Wanting to be part of the team
Focus on the big picture	Giving our personal best	Healthy lifestyles
Working together	Team focus	Community focus

Exhibit 2 Behaviours Not Tolerated

Unconstructive negativity	Insularity
Complacency	Lack of initiative
Narrow-mindedness	Gossiping
Dishonesty	Sulking
Hostility	Not working in the same direction
Bureaucratic restrictions	Exclusion
Bad attitudes	Disinterest
Lack of communication	Not owning the goals
Lack of caring	Backstabbing
Having a narrow focus	Arrogance
Working in silos	Self-importance
Put-downs	Disrespect
Inflexibility	Lack of vision
Wasting resources	Lack of imagination
Wasting opportunity	Unwillingness to help
Blame	Rudeness
Elitism	Ignorance
Whinging/whining/ grizzling	Lack of common sense
Unproductive criticism	Inhospitableness
Discourteousness	Judgmental
Inaccessibility	Laziness

paintings by Monet, Gainsborough, Turner, Rosa, Claude Lorraine, Burne-Jones and Tissot. The collection also featured New Zealand art from 1860 to the present, and had significant holdings of Japanese prints and the decorative arts.

Olveston was the former home of David Theomin and his family. It was designed by London architect Sir Ernest George as an "eloquent expression of one man's dreams." Built in 1906, the 36-room house served as a portal to turn-of-the-19th-century early New Zealand life, albeit a rather privileged life.

The Otago Museum needed to compete in this rather crowded competitive space. To assist with its strategic and operational planning, the museum operated what it called a Resources, Operations and Priorities (ROP) system. Each year the ROP system produced a detailed annual plan as well as a three-year plan and a 15-year development plan. Together these plans formed what the museum referred to as its "Statement of Intent." More specifically, the annual and three-year plans set out the museum's prioritized objectives and the required resources, especially the human and financial resources, needed to achieve these objectives for each of the two specific time periods. Some of the typical intentions showcased in the annual and three-year plans included the range and types of museum exhibits being contemplated, especially any new exhibitions; museum upgrades and renovations; and forecasts of the museum's financial performance.

The three-year plan was less detailed and had a greater strategic focus than the annual plan. In addition, the three-year plan helped provide the context for and parameters around the setting of the annual plan, for it was always the case that the annual plan needed to link with the succeeding three years embodied by the rolling three-year plan.

The adoption of a new annual plan and three-year plan began with senior managers heading off-site for a four- or five-day strategic ROP workshop. This strategic management workshop usually occurred in May. In preparation for the workshop, feedback was solicited from five key stakeholders: the Otago community, the four principal funders (Dunedin City Council, Clutha District Council, Central Otago District Council, and Waitaki District Council), visitors to the museum, staff, and the museum's board.

The strategic workshops were also used as a forum for debating ways to capitalize on the museum's core competencies. Exhibit 3 presents what the museum's management saw as its strengths, weaknesses, opportunities and threats (SWOT).

Exhibit 3 SWOT

Strengths
An Otago-wide organization located in Dunedin
Otago Museum Trust Board Act 1996
Well-developed and proven infrastructure and business practices
Committed, highly skilled team
Community sense of ownership and pride
Ability to "make a difference" in our community
Committed management team focused on developing the organization and the people who are part of it
Location between city centre and university
Well-considered development plan

Weaknesses
Reliance on local authorities with small ratepayer bases for core funding
Resources don't match ambition
Reliance on revenue generation and fundraising
Depreciation largely unfunded
Flat organizational structure limits perception of development opportunities
Visitor parking is limited

Opportunities
Revenue-generation ideas
Harbour development
Settlers Museum redevelopment
Offsite exhibition ideas
Outreach bus
National and international market for exhibits and exhibitions

Threats
Local community spending behaviour
Limited number of quality exhibitions on touring circuit
Skilled/experienced labour shortage in museum sector

FINANCIAL POSITION

According to the chief executive (CE), the museum operated on a very tight budget. Unlike its New Zealand peers, the museum received significantly less funding from the New Zealand government. Te Papa, for example, received about $30 million of national funding during 2009, while the Otago Museum received no national funding and less than $4 million from its four contributing local authorities. Consequently, the museum's senior managers often spoke about a gap between what they perceived as the museum's expected duty and the funding being provided.

The museum attempted to bridge the funding shortage with the introduction of user-pay systems on specific touring exhibitions; profits from its shop and café; and charitable fundraising campaigns. Any remaining funding shortfall required the museum to reschedule or scale back the introduction of its plans, i.e., introduction of new exhibits, hiring of new employees, and museum upgrades and renovations.

The museum's café, gift shop, and tourism and facilities operation were the three main ongoing "business units" expected to make significant contributions to the museum's funding base. The museum's café was operated by an outside contractor, who leased the museum space. The gift shop was directly run by the museum. Gift shop employees were responsible for recommending, sourcing and selling shop items. Discovery World Tropical Forest, an interactive science centre, levied a visitor's admission fee, $9.50 for adults and $4.50 for children, in order to be completely self-funding.

There were a number of other more transitory or minor business units. The former comprised internationally sourced special museum exhibitions, which had a loan fee not able to be covered internally by the museum, where an admission fee was charged to assist with the costs. These admission fees were calculated to encompass all the exhibit's costs, plus a desired profit. Being the first New Zealand museum to source these exhibitions and organizing for the freighting and distribution of the exhibitions to other New Zealand and Australian museums was also used to offset the original exhibition cost and generate a small profit. The profit was intended to be used to support the museum's ongoing activities, including its community programs and any planned gallery redevelopments and structural upgrades. Other business units included the hiring of the museum's facility areas to the public and corporate for special functions, such as office parties, weddings, etc.

Exhibits 4 to 7 present the financial statements for the year ended June 30, 2009.

Exhibit 4 Statement of Financial Performance for the Financial Year Ended June 30, 2009

	2009	Budget	2008
	$	$	$
Income			
Grants—Government and other	248,265	244,321	270,603
New Zealand Lottery Grants Board	–	–	–
Local authorities	3,642,294	3,657,711	3,432,580
Public	1,952,377	1,454,525	2,365,700
Legacies & bequests	5,235	500,000	70,291
Investment income—Dividends	125,206	79,995	165,222
—Interest	607,117	433,293	637,160
Realized net gains/loss on sale of financial instruments			
Instruments	−147,676	–	251,134
Total income	**6,432,818**	**6,369,845**	**7,192,690**
Expenditure			
Employee benefits expense	−2,577,716	−2,577,556	−2,600,211
Depreciation and amortization expense	−1,114,959	−1,293,405	−1,163,797
Other expenses	−2,667,506	−2,636,871	−2,409,319
Total operating expenditure	**−6,360,181**	**−6,507,832**	**−6,173,327**
Surplus for the year	**$72,637**	**($137,989)**	**$1,019,363**

Exhibit 5 Statement of Financial Position as at June 30, 2009

	2009	Budget	2008
	$	$	$
Current assets			
Cash and cash equivalents	6,467,451	220,355	4,367,360
Trade and other receivables	181,081	403,213	224,410
Inventories	153,821	129,757	155,174

	2009	Budget	2008
	$	$	$
Other financial assets	530,673	–	1,974,556
Other current assets	72,295	–	66,315
Total current assets	**7,405,321**	**753,325**	**6,787,815**
Non-current assets			
Other financial assets	3,782,282	7,455,615	4,419,321
Property, plant and equipment	15,765,629	16,733,801	16,723,427
Total non-current assets	**19,547,911**	**24,189,416**	**21,142,748**
Total assets	**26,953,232**	**24,942,741**	**27,930,563**
Current liabilities			
Trade and other payables	468,369	379,563	659,797
Employee entitlements	819,144	–	730,298
Total current liabilities	**1,287,513**	**379,563**	**1,390,725**
Total liabilities	**1,287,513**	**379,563**	**1,390,725**
Net assets	**25,665,719**	**24,563,178**	**26,539,838**
Equity			
Reserves	10,674,458	8,461,525	10,543,847
Capital	14,991,261	16,101,654	15,995,991
	$25,665,719	**$24,563,179**	**$26,539,838**

Exhibit 6 Statement of Recognized Income and Expense for the Financial Year Ended June 30, 2009

	2009	2008
	$	$
Available-for-sale financial assets		
Valuation gain/(loss) taken to equity	–946,756	–799,695
Net income recognized directly in equity	**–946,756**	**–799,695**
Surplus for the year	72,637	1,019,363
Total recognized income & expense for the year	**–874,119**	**219,668**
Statement of changes in equity for the financial year ended June 30, 2009		
Equity at beginning of year	26,539,838	26,320,170
Total recognized income & expense for the year	–874,119	219,668
Equity at end of year	**$25,665,719**	**$26,539,838**

Exhibit 7   Cash Flow Statement for the Financial Year Ended June 30, 2009

	2009	Budget	2008
	$	$	$
Cash flows from operating activities			
Government, local authorities & the public	5,890,126	6,035,942	6,101,572
Dividends	125,206	79,995	165,222
Interest received	603,864	433,293	565,954
Payments to employees	−2,573,082	−2,577,556	−2,500,324
Payments to suppliers	−2,736,138	−2,823,240	−2,146,411
Net cash inflow/(outflow) from operating activities	1,309,976	1,148,434	2,186,013
Cash flows from investing activities			
Proceeds from maturity & sale of other financial assets	1,160,712	–	2,483,441
Proceeds from sale of property, plant & equipment	–	–	–
Purchase of property, plant & equipment	−196,378	-1,104,600	-655,273
Purchase of other financial assets	−174,219	–	-356,987
Net cash inflow/(outflow) from investing activities	790,115	-1,104,600	1,471,181
Cash flows from financing activities			
Repayment of portion of Climate Control Levy	–	–	58,869
Net cash inflow/(outflow) from financing activities	–	–	58,869
Net increase in cash & cash equivalents	**2,100,091**	**43,834**	**3,716,063**
Cash & cash equivalents at the beginning of the financial year	**4,367,360**	**176,520**	**651,297**
Cash & cash equivalents at the end of the financial year	**$6,467,451**	**$220,354**	**$4,367,360**

6

NONPROFIT STRATEGY AND CHANGE

EILEEN WEISENBACH KELLER

There is always a better strategy than the one you have; you just haven't thought of it yet.

—Sir Brian Pitman

Key Topics: applying strategy to the NPO; planning for success; establishing mission, vision, and values; setting effective goals and objectives; situational and external environment analysis; change management

UNDERSTANDING STRATEGY

Were a billboard erected to persuade nonprofit leaders to pursue strategy development, it would probably read STRATEGY: DAUNTING WITH A BIG PAYOFF. Were strategy a brand, its tagline might be *Not for the faint-hearted.* As with most things, the anticipation of tackling the process is generally worse than the actual task. However, to fight the trepidation that this reputation might provoke, nonprofits can use a complex but systematic approach called *strategic management.*

It is easiest to conceptualize strategy by thinking of it as having two fundamental parts: planning and implementing. Planning involves dreaming big, creating a crystal-clear vision of a future place and time, analyzing and understanding the current situation, and estimating and recording the steps needed to traverse from the present to the future envisioned place (see Chapter 2). Implementing requires skilled management guided by impassioned belief in the imagined outcomes, keen understanding of the anticipated strategy, and dogged pursuit of the action plan leading to the envisioned state: strong, strategic leadership (Collins, 2001; Rowe, 2001).

A variety of theoretical approaches to strategy, prescribing different methods and combinations of the planning and implementing stages, have been developed and employed through the years. One theory maintains that strategy is based upon a founder or founding group's passion and vision (Kearns, 2000). Another is built upon an iterative approach responding to emerging issues and trends that impact the organization (Mintzberg, 1994). Finally, a third approach is grounded in an analytical buildup comparing firms' capabilities and weaknesses to the marketplace in which they operate (Barney, 2007; Porter, 1979).

WHY PLAN?

When criticism of strategic planning arises, it usually includes the constraints a plan places upon an organization's ability to respond to unexpected opportunities or developments and/or the fact that planning can be a very time-consuming process with correspondingly high opportunity costs. Strategy is a game plan, specifically a long-term game plan intended to lead to a stronger and more productive future enterprise. Capable leaders and managers realize that even with a well-designed plan, unexpected, uncontrollable circumstances will arise. Anticipating this reality during the preparation of the plan and allowing for flexibility and adaptability in the plan decreases the likelihood that the organization will derail or abandon the plan completely when the unforeseen erupts (Bryson, 2004a).

Why absorb scarce resources such as time and talent in a planning process? Precisely because the typical nonprofit organization's resources are scarce, and planning allows an organization to link resource allocation to a set of goals rather than allocating scant reserves on immediate stimuli that may be costly and fleeting. Organizations that utilize a plan are more able to select how they use scarce resources and base this usage upon a thoughtful long-term

view of the entity and its surroundings. Allison and Kaye (2005) point out that in addition to these benefits, the process of planning creates consensus around decision making, priorities, and the path to success, furthering the likelihood of achievement.

THE PLANNING PROCESS

Although strict agreement on the meaning of strategic terms and process has yet to be found, the relatively generic and straightforward process identified in Figure 6.1 (Worth 2009) is widely accepted as one framing of the fundamentals of strategy and serves as a map for this chapter. Elements of each of the three theories mentioned above are incorporated to complete the explanation of the strategy planning and implementing process.

Planning to plan

Leaders and strategists don't just wake up one day and start formulating strategy. First, it is imperative that they consider who will be involved in the planning, what process they will employ, what information will be needed, and how much time the group will commit to the creation and implementation of a plan. Often this is where nonprofits stop as the magnitude of the demands that strategic planning places on resources crystallizes. The reality of this seems for some organizations too daunting, the pay-off too distant. Many organizations persist despite this menacing fact only to find additional hurdles to overcome as they proceed. The NPO managers who continue despite these hurdles realize the benefits of their resilience and persistence. The plan that results enables them to navigate through future situations that can sometimes be very taxing, and accomplish the organizations' goals.

The constitution of the planning team generally includes a member from each area or function of the NPO. These people, selected for their ability to think conceptually, are visionaries. The

Figure 6.1   Basic Strategic Planning Model

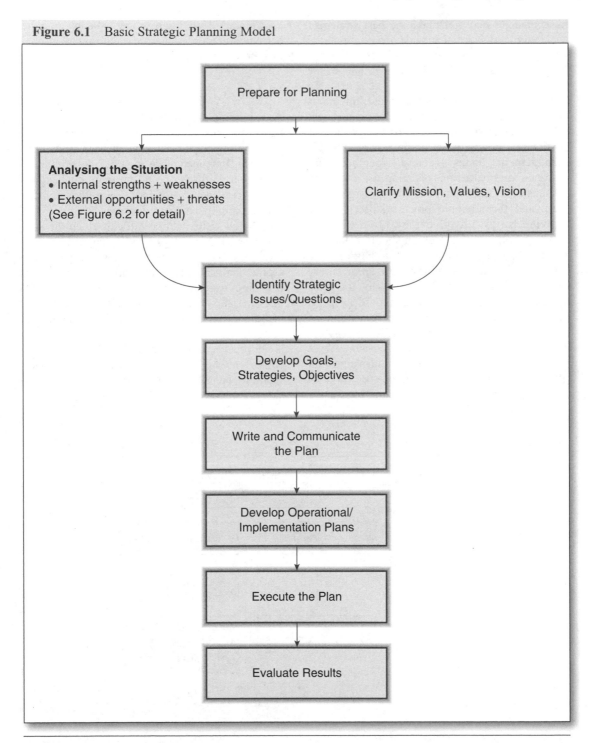

Source: Worth (2009). Reprinted with permission.

best manager may not make the best strategist; the individual's practical side may inhibit the ability to dream about what could be or restrict his or her creativity due to the constraints of the organization's current state (Rowe, 2001). To gain and sustain full commitment, members should be made aware of the time commitment and the nature of the task prior to agreeing to participate. NPOs often struggle with strategic management teams because members are assigned and strategic planning is a tertiary responsibility tacked onto an already large workload, and the strategic process suffers as the individuals rightfully give it low priority.

Once assembled, the group should determine roles and agree upon the process to be followed. As with the formation of any team, an inventory of an individual's skills helps in assigning tasks such as meeting orchestration, record keeping, and internal and external communication of progress and outcomes. In addition, this is the point at which the team must determine what process to employ. Figure 6.1 provides a general guide that can be adjusted to fit the specific character of a strategic planning team. Figure 6.2

adds greater depth to the process of analyzing the current situation. (Chapter 1 offers additional insight to external analysis.)

Vision

As a mission-driven entity, the typical NPO has no trouble imagining how great the world could be if the organization was to succeed in its mission. This imagined place and time in the future is the vision. Perhaps one of the more challenging parts of creating a vision for a nonprofit is limiting it to a simple statement. Consensus around just one shared vision can be difficult given the passion that NPO employees and volunteers bring to their jobs, but converge they must. Vision is the aspirational statement—the harbor toward which the ship must steer. To further the analogy, much like the ship that cannot steer toward different harbors simultaneously, a single NPO cannot concurrently pursue multiple visions. Unity of vision is important, as is clarity, without which the captains of the ship don't know in what direction they should steer. (See Chapter 2 for additional discussion on mission, vision, and values.)

Figure 6.2 Situation Analysis Tools and Outcomes

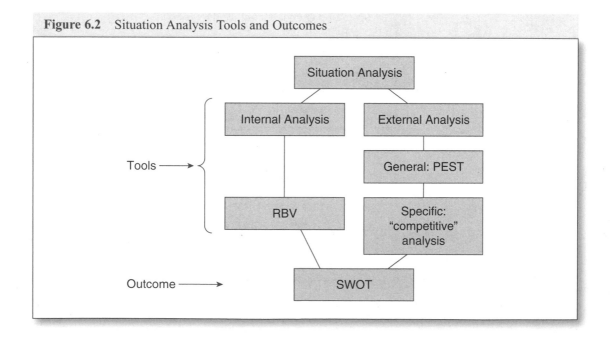

Mission

In the Atlanta Symphony Orchestra case at the end of this chapter, discontent was created for some patrons by a disagreement about the mission of the orchestra. Different expectations regarding the purpose or promise of the organization were at the heart of the conflict. The ability to define concisely the current purpose or raison d'être of the organization is the ability to clarify the mission. In its most stripped-down form, a mission statement includes who will be served, which of their needs will be satisfied, and why the defining organization is uniquely capable of providing for those needs.

The difference between the vision and mission creates the backdrop upon which the strategic plan will be created and executed. The understanding of what is currently lacking, what must be accomplished relative to the vision, is critical. What is needed to achieve the desired state? Of the needed resources and capabilities, what does the organization currently possess? What weaknesses are understood about the enterprise that could hold the group back? Clear, accurate, and thorough understanding of these strengths and weaknesses are the basis of a situation analysis and the common beginning of a Strengths, Weaknesses, Opportunities, and Threats (SWOT) investigation.

Values

Critical to the direction-setting phase of strategy, the articulation of the organization's core values helps clarify and differentiate the identity of the NPO. Values are the principles that the nonprofit considers to be inalienable, those that will guide actions and decisions and persist over long periods of time, perhaps even the life of the organization.

SITUATION ANALYSIS

Clear understanding of the vision, mission, and values is a critical underpinning of strategy. It is not, however, the whole picture. NPOs must carefully consider the marketplace in which they offer their services, understanding with great clarity what is happening within the organization as well as outside of it.

External analyses uncover the nuances of the environment in which the NPO operates. Honest, fair, and thorough internal analysis reveals where the strengths and weaknesses lie within an enterprise; complete external analysis allows for awareness of the marketplace outside the NPO. By combining the outcomes of these analyses, one creates a rendering of the current situation, the summary of which is often captured as a SWOT—a list of the strengths, weaknesses, opportunities, and threats facing an entity at a given time. Strengths and weaknesses are internal issues and are relatively more controllable; opportunities and threats are external and may be difficult or impossible to control, but are necessary to understand. Consider opportunities as those areas that an NPO can take advantage of to increase revenues relative to expenses. On the other hand, threats are those areas that, if not negated or protected from, will increase an NPOs expenses relative to its revenues.

The process of generating the SWOT can be taxing and rather subjective. The tools and methods depicted in Figure 6.2, when applied systematically, reduce the randomness of the situation analysis. When used along with supporting data to substantiate the claims, the SWOT becomes more objective. Systematically utilizing the tools in conjunction with relevant supporting data creates an understanding of the current situation that is thorough, accurate, objective, and quite helpful.

Opportunities and threats are the outcomes of an evaluation of the external landscape in which the enterprise operates. In business, this is referred to as the *competitive environment*. The nonprofit sector does not commonly use this term, but a review of the tools used to analyze competitors reveals many parallels. It is beneficial to think of the external environment as having two levels or layers of significance: general and specific. The broader, more general environment is studied using the acronym PESTLE. Outside of the firm, entities and issues fall into the classifications of Political, Economic, Social, Technical, Legal, and Environmental. The majority of these factors cannot be controlled by the nonprofit, but can have an impact on the enterprise, therefore it is beneficial to consider what to expect from each area. If, for instance, major economic growth is forecasted, a human services NPO might expect a reduction in demand for its offerings as employment increases; the same shift could be very good news for an organization like the Atlanta Symphony Orchestra, as more employment often leads to more patronage.

The second level of the external environment is the more specific one, the one that immediately surrounds the NPO. Conway Dato-on, Weisenbach Keller, and Shaw (2009) recommend a review of the external NPO market based upon three groups, or "competitors": served customers, income/financial entities, and the NPO community, which includes NPO rivals that vie for the same resources (Table 6.1). Using their framework enables a strategist to more thoroughly and accurately assess what is happening in the marketplace and identify where threats and opportunities lie. Detailed identification of each of these segments creates in managers a greater awareness of the needs of those they serve and rely upon as well as the limits or even threats to the resources that are critical to their sustainability.

Although seldom referred to as competitors, these outside forces exist that can pose threats and opportunities to nonprofit organizations. Organizational leaders seeking to develop an edge over competitors can use this model to grasp the context in which the organization operates. Nonprofits, by definition, are mission rather than profit driven, but they must still have a keen understanding of the structure of their segment of the nonprofit sector (see Chapter 1). Within that environment lies competitors vying for many of the same resources, volunteers, employees, grants, and donations, and having the potential to impede the organization's progress.

Internal analysis—the determination of an NPO's strengths and weaknesses—is a critical and difficult process. An organization that understands its missions and the factors that are key to its success will find this procedure easier to navigate. The goal of internal analysis is to understand the organization's proficiencies, what does and does not do particularly well. The strongest abilities, those that the organization relies on most heavily for its performance, should be identified and are referred to as *core competencies*. Per Barney (2007), to qualify fully as a source of sustained competitive advantage (our way of defining a core competency) the activity must meet four criteria:

1. valuable—there is a demand for it

2. rare—unique to the organization (only very few NPOs among a group of NPOs have this core competency)

3. costly to imitate—a barrier exists preventing other organizations from easily performing the same function

4. organized to be exploited

Satisfaction of these four characteristics indicates an ability that could lead to a substantial and sustained competitive advantage over other agencies. These capabilities may be organizational,

Table 6.1 External Environmental Analysis

Served Customer	Income/Financial	NPO Community
• Segmentation • Trends • Unmet needs	• Donor segmentation • Donor motivation • Trends • Expenditures	• Rank, funding • Rank, staff • Priority of service • Trends

such as a strongly positive reputation that enables recruitment of the best employees and volunteers; technical, such as a unique skill provided by the NPO; location, such as the presence in an otherwise unserved market; and/or asset based, such as the possession of a facility with large capacity in an area with high demand.

Internal analysis results in categorizing the NPO's capabilities as either strengths or weaknesses. This means estimating the degree to which an organization does more (a strength) or less (a weakness) in key areas than is fundamentally required to keep the service alive, than what is expected by those served or what is offered by competing agencies. Prioritizing each list from the most important strengths to the least or most troublesome weaknesses to those that are inconsequential is another important step in the situation analysis.

IDENTIFYING STRATEGIC ISSUES

Once the process outlined in Figure 6.2 has been followed, the next stage is Strategic Issue Identification (as in Figure 6.1). The existence of the SWOT list provokes additional scrutiny. Specifically, the NPO must determine which of each strength, weakness, opportunity, and/or threat must be managed or leveraged to reach the group's goals and accomplish the vision.

Kearns's (2000) Strategic Issue Grid is a valuable tool for comparing the internal and external elements of the entity's situation and transforming the list of items into a prioritized understanding of strategic issues. The nexus of the knowledge of the NPO's vision, mission, values, and current situation is the point from which an

action plan is launched. Table 6.2 displays a generic version of the grid and helps the analyst consider how the internal realities will help or hinder the pursuit of available opportunities or deflection/negation of threats.

Key success factors (KSFs) are those fundamental functions that an industry or sector demands an NPO perform if it is to remain viable. Consider the KSFs as a threshold that any organization must cross. If the KSFs are not met, the NPO's existence is threatened. The obvious KSFs that come to mind for nearly all NPOs are sufficient funding and availability of human resources—both voluntary and paid employees. However, while this may be necessary for all or most nonprofits, it is usually not sufficient. For example, a private nonprofit school must certainly educate, and a hospital must heal.

Understanding KSFs allows managers to determine whether their strengths and weaknesses are meaningful. For instance, in the Health Care Center for the Homeless case at the end of this chapter, the organization has a particular strength in supplying outreach healthcare. If it was determined that due to dispersion of the needy population in the county, a key success factor was the ability to mobilize healthcare delivery, this strength becomes more meaningful. On the contrary, a human services provider without this capability would have identified a significant weakness.

The Strategic Issues Grid and the KSF analysis combine to help prioritize and identify those issues that should become central to the strategic plan. If the SWOT analysis and issues analysis are accurate and complete, the organization's needs should become apparent upon their completion. Strengths and weaknesses—the internal capacity of the organization—point to the things the NPO *can* do. Opportunities and threats indicate the available alternatives, or what the organization *might* do. Where these items align indicates what the firm *should* do—it helps separate nonessential issues from those that are strategy critical. The contrast between the internal and external realities force strategists to discern which opportunities to pursue, which threats to guard against, which strengths are critical to

Table 6.2 Strategic Issues Grid

	Opportunities	Threads
Strengths	Strategic Issue	Strategic Issue
Weaknesses	Strategic Issue	Strategic Issue

Source: Worth (2009).

accomplishment of mission and vision, and which weaknesses must be fixed or overcome. The long-term success of the organization is measured by its goal attainment, its mission and vision achievement. Understanding aspects of the environment from the perspective of these established elements allows leaders to formulate strategies despite the presence of threats and weaknesses.

This reminds us that up to this point, no action has been prescribed, no plan put on paper. This is an uncomfortable reality for many a manager or leader who prefers the action of doing rather than the relative inactivity of critically thinking and analyzing. And yet, it is only through analysis and critical thinking that a meaningful and useful action plan can be created. Because NPO resources are often limited and constrained, prioritization of strategic issues is an essential activity. Not every opportunity can be pursued, not every weakness shored up. Bryson (2004b) identified four categories that provide a frame against which strategic initiatives can be judged:

1. Developmental issues that go to the heart of the organization's vision and goals, involving a fundamental change in products or services, customers or clients, service distribution channels, sources of revenue, identity or image, or some other fundamental change.

2. Issues that require no organizational action at present but that must be continuously monitored.

3. Issues that are on the horizon and likely to require some action in the future and perhaps some action now.

4. Issues that require an immediate response and therefore cannot be handled in a routine way (pp. 184–185).

Goals

In strategic terms, goals refer to broad, direction-setting statements of aspiration. They mark a progression toward the vision and are critical to the development of the strategic plan. The by-product of strategic issue generation and prioritization, goals are different from objectives in that they lack the specificity and measurability of objectives. Koteen's (1997) goal typology is used to develop strategic goals:

1. *Programmatic* goals, those that focus on the services offered by the organization.

2. *Institutional* goals, those that address efficiency and other operational issues.

3. *Financial* goals, those that concentrate on resource procurement.

Strategies and Initiatives

Up to this point, the planners have identified mission, vision, issues, and goals based upon the situation at hand, but little has yet been said about how these things will be accomplished. *How* is the essence of strategic planning! All the preceding work has simply been to thoroughly understand with great accuracy the realities of the current situation and the NPO's aspirations. Now, the plan must take shape that identifies what means the organization will use to travel from the current to the future state, and to end up where it intends to be.

Objectives

Objectives are a necessary component of any plan. They are the standard against which progress toward the goals and aspirations (i.e., vision, mission) is measured. The key difference between the goals, discussed previously, and objectives is the specificity of objectives. The acronym SMART is often used to construct the most meaningful and effective objectives. Objectives must be Specific, Measurable, Attainable, Require a reach, and be set on a Timetable. Broadly worded statements of aspiration are needed to set the direction of the organization, but in this stage of strategy development, organizational leaders should articulate specific things that need to happen and how they will be achieved. These should be achievable so that they do not discourage pursuit, but they must also require the organization to reach—to stretch. In other words, the objectives should be achievable, but not easily so. Without reach or stretch, the organization will be unlikely to make progress but rather will maintain status quo. In nearly all cases, status quo is not the goal.

Writing the Plan

The critical next step is to capture the plan in writing, the goal of which is to provide a repository for the strategic thinking, process, and outcomes. The plan authors should summarize the decisions made as succinctly as possible so that the plan is perceived as clear, builds consensus, and motivates associates to read *and use* it. A record of the procedures followed to develop the plan will increase the confidence others have in it and should be included in the document. This record also will be useful to future strategists as a template or guide. Especially important in this written record are the objectives and goals established. A new or updated strategic plan requires an organization to commit to a new course of action, and the plan is the guide for that adjustment. There is no specific, prescribed length for a plan, but the ability to be concise is highly valuable.

STRATEGIC MANAGEMENT AND CHANGE

Strategic management requires that managers, on an ongoing basis, evaluate the organization's progress and monitor changes in the external environment. In addition, a strategy review should be conducted on an annual basis to determine whether changes outside the organization necessitate any shifts in the plan. If the review reaffirms the chosen strategic course, the group continues to implement the existing plan. Often small changes are needed based upon the annual strategic review and occasionally substantial change is warranted.

In the case of substantial change, Kotter (1996) offers a valuable guide to orchestrating change. The eight steps listed next enable

managers to fight the inertia that prevents many organizations from accomplishing needed change.

1. Establish a sense of urgency.
   - An opportunity exists that will not persist and must be capitalized on immediately.
   - A threat exists, and without adjustment, the organization could be endangered.

2. Create a guiding coalition—gather individuals with significant abilities, including personal and/or positional power, to help bring about change.

3. Develop a vision and strategy—as described throughout this chapter.

4. Communicate the change vision—as part of the implementation process described below.

5. Empower broad-based action—ensure that many at different levels in the organization are given the knowledge, understanding, and authority to act on the new direction.

6. Generate short-term wins—identify, pursue, track, report, and celebrate even the smallest gains or progress toward the goal.

7. Consolidate gains and produce more change—keep the momentum going by publicly displaying the progress that is made and the mounting significance of successful change.

8. Anchor new approaches in the culture—find symbols of the old culture and eliminate them; replace them with new cultural icons. For example, if past practice was to reward volunteers and employees with cake and cookies, and the new vision is of a healthy work environment, celebrate employee achievement with a half-hour outdoor break including a brisk walk.

IMPLEMENTATION AND CONCLUSION

In addition to what we recommend above, we suggest the following model for developing an implementation plan. As an analysis is performed, a strategic planning team will develop a list of "what to do." The items on this list will come from all of the in-depth analyses using all of the frameworks described above. For each "what to do" item, we recommend that four questions be asked: (1) Who should be assigned the responsibility for doing this? (2) When should it be done by? (3) How much will it cost? (4) Where will the money come from—donations, fundraising events, government grants, for-profit stores owned by the NPO, debt, and so on. In addition, we suggest a system of monitoring and control to ensure completion of each "what to do." If it needs to be done quickly (e.g., in a month or two), monitoring could consist of verbal and/or written reports on a weekly basis. But if the deadline is much longer in nature (e.g., several years), we suggest quarterly or semiannual reports. Having this information will allow for better control. For example, if we see that a project will come in under budget and well under time, we can shift resources to a project that is over budget and likely to be late.

The direction prescribed by the strategic planning team might be radically new, requiring a change process such as Kotter's (1996), or it might be only slightly different than the past. Regardless, the plan is nothing unless managers and change agents determine how to make stakeholders in the NPO set their sights on new goals and change their attitudes and behaviors. In short, the plan is only as good as its execution. The implementation is a long-term, ongoing process in which all employees and volunteers, at all levels, must be involved. If a particular group or individual is resistant or simply not knowledgeable, then the plan will be slower to succeed and may even falter.

The strategists must be sure to communicate with passion and conviction the elements of the plan and its benefits. Education is key to success. Everyone within the organization must be taught the need for strategy and be held accountable for assisting in the pursuit of the new vision, objectives, and goals. Measures of success (e.g., metrics) and responsibility for recording progress toward milestones must be assigned and monitored. Roadblocks from internal or external sources should be identified and overcome early, if possible. The elements of leadership and management that populate the chapters of this book are the tools that, when developed and consistently employed, enable excellent implementation of a strategic plan for the accomplishment of goals.

CASES

Atlanta Symphony Orchestra (United States): The Atlanta Symphony Orchestra, conducted by its newly appointed music director, performed a rarely heard composition. The musical performance was, by all accounts, superb. While most in the audience cheered the performance, a few audience members stormed out of the concert hall. These people were largely reacting to the high-tech mixed-media show designed by a well-known artist that accompanied the performance. This performance was one of the Atlanta Symphony Orchestra's recent innovative breaks from concert tradition. The vice president and general manager of the Atlanta Symphony Orchestra recognized that, in order to facilitate growth, opportunities existed on stage and off for broadening and enriching the orchestra's services and the concert experiences of its audience.

Health Care Center for the Homeless (United States): Bakari Burns, recent MBA graduate and CEO of the Health Care Center for the Homeless (HCCH) in Orlando, Florida, was eager to implement what he had learned in his MBA classes to build on the strong history and important mission of his nonprofit organization. Burns knew the organization experienced difficulty with recognition and marketplace distinction, primarily due to the public's misperceptions about the relationship between HCCH and the Coalition for the Homeless of Central Florida (currently a separate and independent human services organization located in downtown Orlando). Confusion also existed regarding the relationship between HCCH and its various services, especially the Orange Blossom Family Health Center. Could these issues be affecting donations and the ability to provide quality services? One lesson Burns clearly remembered from school was the importance of asking for help when the path to continued excellence was not clear, so he solicited advice from an external consulting team. The recommendations, delivered to Burns in summer 2010, included significant organizational change accompanied by a suggestion that HCCH rebrand with an amended name and redesign all marketing materials. This advice and the changes in the external environment made it an excellent time to reposition and refocus the organization. Recognizing the need for a new strategy and implementing that strategy are not the same; Burns was not sure how to lead the organization through the change process.

REFERENCES

Allison, M., & Kaye, J. (2005). *Strategic planning for nonprofit organizations*. Hoboken, NJ: John Wiley & Sons.

Barney, J. B. (2007). *Gaining and sustaining competitive advantage* (3rd ed.). Upper Saddle River, NJ: Pearson-Prentice Hall.

Bryson, J. (2004a). *Strategic planning for public and nonprofit organizations* (3rd ed.). San Francisco, CA: John Wiley & Sons.

Bryson, J. M. (2004b). The strategy change cycle. In R. D. Herman & Associates (Eds.), *The Jossey-Bass handbook on nonprofit leadership and management* (2nd ed., pp. 171–203). San Francisco, CA: Jossey-Bass.

Collins, J. (2001). *Good to great: Why some companies make the leap . . . and others don't.* New York, NY: HarperCollins.

Conway Dato-on, M., Weisenbach Keller, E., & Shaw, D. (2009). Adapting for-profit branding models to small nonprofit organizations: A theoretical discussion and model proposition. In *Proceedings of the 2009 World Marketing Congress*. Ruston, LA: Academy of Marketing Science.

Kearns, K. P. (2000). *Private sector strategies for social sector success*. San Francisco, CA: Jossey-Bass.

Koteen, J. (1997). *Strategic management in public and nonprofit organizations*. Westport, CT: Praeger.

Kotter, J. P. (1996). *Leading change.* Boston, MA: Harvard Business School Press.

Mintzberg, H. (1994, January-February). The fall and rise of strategic planning. *Harvard Business Review, 107*–114.

Porter, M. E. (1979, March-April). How competitive forces shape strategy. *Harvard Business Review, 137*–145.

Rowe, W. G. (2001). Creating wealth in organizations: The role of strategic leadership. *Academy of Management Executive, 15,* 80–93.

Worth, M. J. (2009). *Nonprofit management: Principles and practices* (2nd ed.). Thousand Oaks, CA: Sage.

ATLANTA SYMPHONY ORCHESTRA

INTRODUCTION

In November 2001, the Atlanta Symphony Orchestra (ASO), conducted by its newly appointed music director, Robert Spano, performed the rarely heard *A Sea Symphony* by the English composer Ralph Vaughan-Williams. The musical performance of *A Sea Symphony,* with lyrics taken from poems contained in Walt Whitman's *Leaves of Grass,* was by all accounts superb. While most members of the audience cheered the performance, a few stormed out of the concert hall, largely in reaction to the high-tech mixed media show designed by Polish video artist Piotr Szyhalski that accompanied the ASO's performance. Szyhalski's black-and-white video, shown on a single jumbo screen situated behind the orchestra, depicted for some a story all its own. The images of women cutting cloth, banners waving and clocks spinning seemed to be connected only subtly to Whitman's text and Vaughan-Williams' music. This performance of *A Sea Symphony* was one of the ASO's recent occasional and innovative breaks from concert tradition. By adding visual complements to selected concerts and increasing interactions between the musicians on stage and the audience, the ASO was in the midst of broadening its orchestral concert experience. The ASO's performance innovations were the result of a partnership between the artistic stakeholders and the community.

The enhancement of the ASO's concert experience also extended beyond the performance stage. John Sparrow, vice-president and general manager of the ASO since October 2000, was in the midst of reviewing an incentive program intended to encourage the current group of symphony hall ushers to be more service oriented. For example, if an usher overheard an ASO patron talking about finding a place to eat after the concert, Sparrow hoped the usher would be able to approach that patron and say, "I could not help overhearing your need for a place to eat after tonight's performance, so here are a couple of nearby restaurants that we recommend." Sparrow recognized that opportunities existed onstage and offstage for enriching the ASO's services and the concert experiences of its audience.

HISTORY OF THE ATLANTA SYMPHONY ORCHESTRA

The ASO was founded in 1945 as a youth ensemble. The orchestra grew into a semi-professional adult orchestra, then to a professional orchestra in 1947. The orchestra currently employed 95 musicians who were complemented by the ASO Chorus and the Atlanta Symphony Youth Orchestra. The ASO's music directors, conductors who had wide-ranging authority over artistic issues from setting the tempo of a musical performance to the hiring and firing of players (within the contract constraints for unionized orchestras), included Henry Sopkin (1945–1966), Robert Shaw (1967–1987), Yoel Levi (1988–2000) and Robert Spano (2001 to present). ASO musicians were full-time professionals who performed over 200 concerts annually. Many of these musicians, who started with a base salary of $70,000, also engaged in musical instruction as well.[1]

Over the past 30 years, the orchestra had performed at the Woodruff Arts Center's Symphony Hall (WAC), a 1,765-seat concert hall situated in downtown Atlanta. Atlanta, with a population exceeding three million, was the largest metropolitan area in the southeastern United States and represented almost 40 per cent of Georgia's population. The ASO also regularly performed at several local venues, including the Chastain Park Amphitheater, the summer home for the ASO, and other civic and regional venues. While the ASO's music director, like that of other orchestras, oversaw artistic quality and musical performances, there were other individuals involved in the administrative management of the organization (see Exhibit 1).

The ASO, unlike the American "Big Five" orchestras, had toured infrequently.[2] Its first

---

[1] All monetary figures in U.S. dollars.

[2] The "Big Five" traditionally referred to the Boston Symphony Orchestra, Chicago Symphony Orchestra, The Cleveland Orchestra, New York Philharmonic and The Philadelphia Orchestra. These orchestras, widely recognized for their artistic quality, regularly engaged in domestic and international touring and recording with world-renowned conductors. Additionally, these orchestras possessed large annual operating budgets and endowments, the basis for financial stability, which allowed for the offering of a range of musical activities. Generally, the quality and reputation of orchestras was a general indicator of the artistic vitality in the community and a source of civic pride.

Exhibit 1   Atlanta Symphony Orchestra Organizational Structure

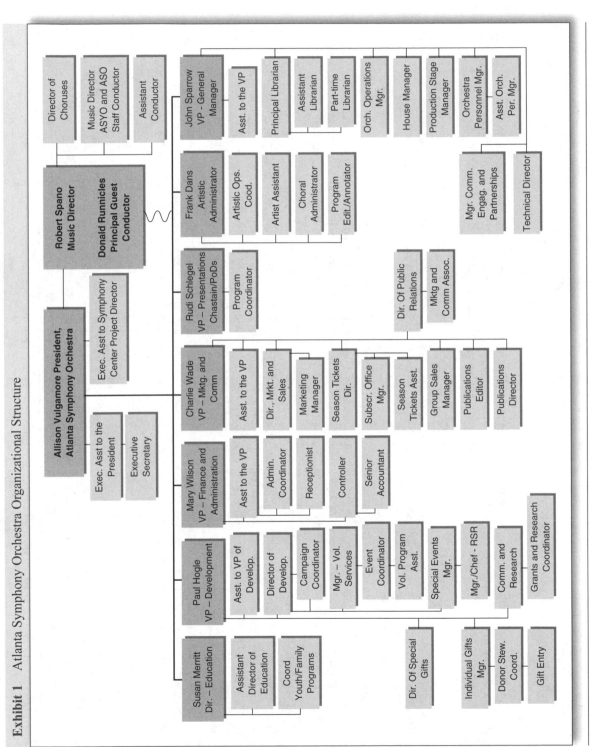

(Continued)

Exhibit 1 (Continued)

Selected Administrative Job Descriptions

President

Responsible for managing the human and financial resources of the orchestra. Also responsible and accountable for all operations aspects of the organization, and implementing the policies set by the board of directors. The president is selected by and reports to the orchestra's board of directors through the board president. His/her artistic counterpart is the music director.

Vice-President—General Manager

Responsible for ensuring that the scheduling and production of all orchestra events (concerts, rehearsals, tours and special events) run smoothly, effectively and in a financially responsible manner. This individual functions as a liaison between the orchestra and the rest of the administrative staff.

Vice-President—Marketing and Communications

Responsible for planning, supervising, administering and evaluating programs that meet/exceed attendance and ticket revenue goals and maximize the visibility of the orchestra. This individual plans and manages public relations (e.g., press, program books), advertising, season subscription and renewal campaigns, audience research, new subscriber activities and merchandising.

Vice-President—Finance and Administration

Responsible for the business and financial operations of the organization (e.g., financial planning, control and reporting). The chief financial officer is also responsible for preparation of the annual operating budget and financial projections, monthly financial statements, banking relations and the administration of payroll, employee benefits and personnel policies.

Vice-President—Development

Responsible for the development, management, implementation and evaluation of fund-raising (e.g., annual campaign, sponsorship, endowment and planned giving programs). This individual is also responsible for making grant applications to federal, state and local government agencies providing arts funding, and researching and applying to private foundations and corporations providing arts grants.

Director—Education

Responsible for designing, developing, administering and evaluating all education and outreach programs (e.g., supervision of all volunteers and staff involved in delivering any aspect of these programs). He/she represents the orchestra to other arts, education and civic institutions to promote constructive working partnerships in the community.

Source: Adapted from American Symphony Orchestra League "Administrative Job Descriptions—The Orchestral Association."

European tour, under the direction of Robert Shaw, took place in 1988. The second European tour, in 1991, under the baton of Yoel Levi, involved presenting concerts in 16 different cities, including London, Paris and Vienna. Subsequent financial challenges led to the decision to defer touring from the mid- to late 1990s in order to facilitate the orchestra's economic growth.

The ASO was the most recognized and active of the orchestras that were based in Georgia (see Exhibit 2). Several of the other Atlanta-based orchestras were non-professional (e.g., Atlanta Community Symphony Orchestra and the Emory Symphony Orchestra) and presented a limited number of performances annually. The ASO's 2001–2002 annual operating budget of $25 million made it the largest performing arts organization in the southeastern United States. However, its endowment, which surpassed $70 million in fiscal year ending (FYE) 2001, generally used to support expenditures with interest and dividend income and to cover budget deficits, was still comparatively small for a major U.S. orchestra. Typically, an orchestra's artistic quality could be quickly assessed based upon the size of that institution's annual operating budget, while its financial soundness was based on the size of its endowment (see Exhibit 3).

The majority of the ASO's concerts, taking place at the WAC, revolved around playing standard classical music compositions performed with world-renowned soloists and, on occasion, under the baton of guest conductors. The scope and quality of the ASO's musical activities and offerings over the past three decades had firmly established the orchestra's reputation, and it enjoyed a strong regional appeal. The ASO was the only North American orchestra to have ever performed at a United States presidential inaugural concert and at Olympic opening and closing ceremonies (see Exhibit 4).

MUSICAL ACTIVITIES AND OFFERINGS

The ASO's performances each year reached nearly half a million people through its various concert series and diverse initiatives in music education and outreach. In addition to its Master Season—Classical Concerts subscription series, the orchestra performed more popular and current music to a variety of audiences through pops and family concerts (see Exhibit 5). Additionally, it offered a full summer schedule, including classical and pop music and free outdoor concerts. Noteworthy musical offerings included:

- Master Season—Classical Concerts: Twenty-four three-performance concerts of traditional and contemporary classical repertoire performed from September through May at the WAC. Performances were given to an estimated audience of 90,000 annually.
- Classic Chastain: Approximately 30 concerts offered through a relationship with the City of Atlanta each June through August. The musical performance featured a mixture of musical styles (e.g., rhythm and blues, country, pop and classical) often accompanied by the ASO. These performances reached an estimated audience of 150,000 annually.
- Holiday Concerts: Approximately 17 concerts centered around the Christmas and New Year season. Holiday standards such as *Messiah* and Strauss family waltzes, polkas and popular Broadway medleys were performed. Attendance for these performances was approximately 22,000 annually.
- Free Outdoor Concerts: The ASO annually performed at various locations in metropolitan Atlanta. Partial funding for these concerts came through grants from the City of Atlanta and Fulton County, with the remainder supplemented from the ASO's operating budget. These performances reached more than 25,000 annually.

In addition, the ASO was actively involved in a number of community-based projects. These included offering annual King Celebration concerts honoring the legacy of Dr. Martin Luther King, Jr., participation in the National Black Arts Festival (joining in 1994 to sponsor a competition for new compositions by African-American composers), and concerts given in collaboration with local churches. In 1995, the ASO embarked on the "Building Bridges to the Community" initiative in metropolitan Atlanta. Programs associated with this initiative included the

Exhibit 2   Symphony Orchestras in Georgia

Orchestra	City	Number of Musicians	Number of Concerts Per Season	Annual Operating Budget Classification	Annual Guest Artist & Guest Conductor Fees Classification
Albany Symphony Orchestra	Albany	80	15	$260,000–$1,050,000	$20,000–$75,000
Atlanta Community Symphony Orchestra	Atlanta	65	5	< $35,000	$1,500–$3,500
Orchestra Atlanta	Roswell	55	6	$100,000–$150,000	$7,000–$20,000
Atlanta Pops Orchestra	Atlanta	55	45–55	$100,000–$150,000	—
Atlanta Symphony Orchestra	Atlanta	95	200+	> $10,000,000	> $1,000,000
Atlanta Symphony Youth Orchestra	Atlanta	120	5	$35,000–$100,000	< $1,500
Augusta Symphony Orchestra	Augusta	80	31	$260,000–$1,050,000	$20,000–$75,000
Coastal Symphony of Georgia	St. Simon's Island	45–50	5	$35,000–$100,000	$1,500–$3,500
Cobb Symphony Orchestra	Marietta	75	7	$150,000–$260,000	$3,500–$7,000
Columbus Symphony Orchestra	Columbus	85	16	$260,000–$1,050,000	$20,000–$75,000
DeKalb Symphony Orchestra	Tucker	88	14	$100,000–$150,000	$7,000–$20,000
Emory Symphony Orchestra	Atlanta	85	4	< $35,000	< $1,500
Gainesville Symphony Orchestra	Gainesville	72	4	$150,000–$260,000	< $1,500
Georgia State University Symphony	Atlanta	80	8	< $35,000	$7,000–$20,000
La Grange Symphony Orchestra	La Grange	42–55	11	$150,000–$260,000	$3,500–$7,000
Macon Symphony Orchestra	Macon	75	26	$260,000–$1,050,000	$7,000–$20,000
Rome Symphony Orchestra	Rome	65	6	$35,000–$100,000	< $1,500
Savannah Symphony Orchestra	Savannah	85	75	$1,050,000–$3,600,000	$75,000–$300,000
Valdosta Symphony Orchestra	Valdosta	75	20	$260,000–$1,050,000	$20,000–$75,000

Source: Musical America Directory.

Exhibit 3 Major and Regional North American Symphony Orchestras

Orchestras With Annual Operating Budgets of $10,000,000 and Above	
• Los Angeles Philharmonic*#	• Buffalo Philharmonic Orchestra
• Pacific Symphony Orchestra (CA)	• New York Philharmonic*
• San Francisco Symphony*	• Cincinnati Symphony Orchestra*
• Colorado Symphony Orchestra	• The Cleveland Orchestra*
• National Symphony Orchestra (DC)	• Columbus Symphony Orchestra (OH)
• Florida Philharmonic Orchestra	• Oregon Symphony
• Atlanta Symphony Orchestra	• The Philadelphia Orchestra*
• Chicago Symphony Orchestra*#	• Pittsburgh Symphony Orchestra*
• Indianapolis Symphony Orchestra	• Dallas Symphony Orchestra
• Baltimore Symphony Orchestra	• Houston Symphony
• Boston Symphony Orchestra*#	• Utah Symphony & Opera
• Detroit Symphony Orchestra	• Seattle Symphony
• Minnesota Orchestra*	• Milwaukee Symphony Orchestra
• The Saint Paul Chamber Orchestra (MN)	• Orchestre Symphonique de Montreal
• Saint Louis Symphony Orchestra	• The Toronto Symphony Orchestra
• New Jersey Symphony Orchestra	

*Among top 10 in annual operating budgets in 2001.

#Annual operating budget exceeding $50 million in 2001.

Orchestras With Annual Operating Budgets of $3,600,000 to $10,000,000	
• Alabama Symphony Orchestra	• Syracuse Symphony Orchestra
• The Phoenix Symphony	• Charlotte Symphony
• Tucson Symphony Orchestra	• North Carolina Symphony
• San Diego Symphony	• Toledo Symphony Orchestra
• The Florida Orchestra	• The Nashville Symphony
• Jacksonville Symphony Orchestra (FL)	• Fort Worth Symphony Orchestra
• Naples Philharmonic Orchestra (FL)	• San Antonio Symphony
• Honolulu Symphony Orchestra	• Richmond Symphony (VA)
• Fort Wayne Philharmonic Orchestra (IN)	• Virginia Symphony Orchestra
• The Louisville Orchestra	• Calgary Philharmonic Orchestra

(Continued)

Exhibit 3 (Continued)

• Louisiana Philharmonic Orchestra	• Edmonton Symphony Orchestra
• Grand Rapids Symphony	• National Arts Centre Orchestra
• Kansas City Symphony	• Orchestre Symphonique de Québec
• Omaha Symphony Orchestra	• Vancouver Symphony
• New Mexico Symphony Orchestra	• Winnipeg Symphony Orchestra
• Rochester Philharmonic Orchestra	

Source: Musical America Directory.

Exhibit 4 ASO Artistic and Musical Event Timeline

Time	Event
September 20, 1945	Corporate charter granted to Atlanta Youth Symphony
January 26, 1947	First performance under the name the Atlanta Symphony Orchestra (ASO)
1950–51	All ASO members are professional musicians
February 2, 1962	First ASO Pops concert
October 19, 1967	Robert Shaw conducts first concert as ASO music director
September 24, 1970	Debut of ASO Chorus
March 4, 1971	First ASO performance in Carnegie Hall
June 1974	ASO begins summer concerts at Chastain Park
1976	ASO wins ASCAP Award, the first of four, for adventuresome programming of American Music
1976	ASO's first commercial recording, "Nativity", released
January 18, 1977	ASO and Chorus perform at Inaugural Concert in Washington for President-elect Jimmy Carter
October 1978	ASO tour of western United States
1979	Release of ASO's first Telarc recording
February 1986	ASO recording of Berlioz's "Requiem" wins four Grammy Awards
March 1988	ASO's first European tour
June 1988	Nationwide syndication of ASO concerts begins on a network of public radio stations
August–September 1988	Robert Shaw steps down as music director and is named music director emeritus; Yoel Levi conducts first concert as ASO music director
February 1991	ASO recording of choral works is the fifth ASO recording in six years to win a Grammy Award
October 1991	ASO's second European tour

July–August 1996	ASO plays in Opening and Closing Ceremonies of the Centennial Olympic Games in Atlanta; ASO and Atlanta Symphony Youth Orchestra perform in eight concerts of the Olympic Arts Festival/Cultural Olympiad
1997	ASO initiates $40 million endowment campaign, the largest ever for a performing arts organization in the Southeast (campaign completed in October 2000)
1999	Arthur Blank Family Foundation commits $15 million gift for new concert hall
February 2000	Appointment of Robert Spano as music director designate and Donald Runnicles as principal guest conductor designate
September 15, 2001	Robert Spano conducts first concert as ASO music director

Source: ASO files.

Exhibit 5 ASO Musical Offerings

Concert Series	Number of Concerts (2001)#	Single/ [Series] Ticket Prices (2001)	Ticket Sale % of Total (2001)	Subscription Sales (% Series Sales)		Average % of Paid House	
				2000	2001	2000	2001
Master Season— Classical Season	72	$19–$57 [$99–$273] *	26.8	71.3	71.4	70.0	71.9
Classic Chastain	30	$33–$73	52.8	54.1	50.4	64.0	69.2
Coffee/New Mornings	4	$16–$32 [$76–$108]	0.6	64.1	64.6	53.1	44.0
Champagne/ SunTrust Pops	12	$21–$57 [$111–$276]	5.5	57.3	58.3	83.1	80.9
Family	8	$15–$20 [$44–$61]	1.6	71.0	76.7	87.0	91.6
Holiday	17	$12–$100	6.3	—	—	77.4	75.1
Special Events	4	$26–$57	2.2	—	—	83.7	74.7
Other**	46	—	4.2	—	—	—	—

Source: ASO files.

Date indicates fiscal year ending.

* Series ticket prices for six concerts.

** These concerts included Saturdays/Casual Classics/ASO to Go, Symphony Street/Young People's Concerts/Atlanta Symphony Youth Orchestra, and Summer concerts.

Atlanta Symphony Youth Orchestra, which was created in 1945, an auditioned and professionally coached organization for high-school age musicians; a Talent Development Program where young minority players were coached and mentored by ASO musicians; and young people's concerts in the Discover, Next Generation, and Symphony Street series.

The ASO launched a number of outreach partnerships through a program titled Partners in Performance (PNP). The program involved taking the orchestra's musicians, individually or in groups, to school children who would not normally meet professional musicians. The program utilized recordings and educational materials along with interactive presentations, master classes and coaching in providing these musical education opportunities. Overall, more than 50,000 youngsters were annually exposed to the ASO. Orchestral players regularly volunteered their time for these activities and joined ASO administrators and community leaders in developing and implementing the mission and activities of the PNP program.

In 2001, the ASO was one of the few remaining North American symphony orchestras actively recording; many of the major classical recording companies found the cost of recording in North America prohibitive. The orchestra began recording for the Cleveland-based Telarc label in 1979, with which it had recorded over 70 records of a wide-ranging repertoire of choral and orchestral works. These recordings garnered the ASO much praise, winning an Audio Excellence Award, Gramophone and Ovation Magazine Awards, and 18 Grammy Awards. The ASO recorded *A Sea Symphony* in conjunction with the November 2001 concerts.

FINANCIAL AND ARTISTIC TROUBLES

From the cutting of staff at Florida's Jacksonville Symphony Orchestra and New York's Rochester Philharmonic Orchestra to the bankruptcy and restructuring of the San Diego Symphony, many regional orchestras were experiencing financial crises by the fall of 2001. Larger, more established major orchestras such as the Pittsburgh Symphony Orchestra, St. Louis Symphony and Toronto Symphony were also on the brink of bankruptcy and asking their musicians to take pay cuts and possibly shorten their performing season. Especially troubling were financial concerns for the Big Five. The Chicago Symphony, long a model of financial solvency, was projecting several years of deficits for the first time in almost two decades. Despite its $59 million budget and $168 million endowment, the Chicago Symphony wound up with a deficit of about $1.3 million in 2001. The Cleveland Orchestra and The Philadelphia Orchestra also faced similar looming deficits.

Several reasons for the financial troubles of many symphony orchestras included:

- Shrinking endowments and funding;
- Competition for the entertainment dollar;
- Declining and aging audiences;
- Decreasing emphasis on musical education;
- Geographic spread away from city and metropolitan centres; and
- Adversarial relations between musicians and management because of conflicting priorities.

Related to these troubles was the artistic concern that symphony orchestras were simply repositories for performing only the core classical repertoire. Orchestras generally were not known for their innovative or novel musical offerings. To some, the symphony orchestra as an art form had become less relevant in society. Relevancy was especially important given that most orchestras faced one further reality beyond their control: society appeared to be moving at an increasingly faster pace and time was a precious commodity. Given that the typical classical orchestral concert lasted two hours, attending a live symphony orchestra concert might become a less prominent activity for present and potential patrons.

The financial troubles facing symphony orchestras—primarily budget deficits and diminishing endowments—and their underlying causes were not new. In 1988, Thomas Morris, managing director of the Cleveland Orchestra, criticized orchestras for their "fundamental lack of leadership, governance, and strategic focus. Better artistic planning, a consistent approach to programming and repertoire, and strong boards are the keys to revitalizing orchestras."[3]

The ASO was not immune to the troubles that many other orchestras faced. Much of the past decade represented a period of turmoil for the ASO. Among the troubles faced were a 10-week musicians' strike in 1996; the death of its long-time music director Robert Shaw, who was a charismatic leader integral to the development of both the orchestra and ASO chorus; strained relations within the orchestra and between its supporters over the departure of Yoel Levi; and a seven-figure budget deficit. All this resulted in morale being at an all-time low by the end of the 1990s. Financially, the orchestra—guided by the need for fiscal discipline—operated at a modest surplus in FYE 2001 with total revenues exceeding $24 million. Total ticket sales for the 2000–2001 season were just under $10 million, with subscription sales accounting for just over 50 per cent of the total ticket sales. While the orchestra offered both fixed and flexible subscription package options, only 10 per cent of subscribers to the Master Season (i.e., the "great patrons") attended 12 or more of the different concert programs offered each season.

The orchestra operated under the financial strategy of balancing its annual operating budget and utilizing what surplus was available. It created a special fund of banked, restricted money that allowed for some artistic freedom to pursue unique musical opportunities as they arose. Overall, the primary financial concern for management was to have an adequate resource foundation for all the ASO's music programming commitments. Toward that end, the orchestra had recently completed a $40 million endowment campaign. Additionally, Atlanta-based businesses such as Delta Airlines and SunTrust Bank sponsored the Master Season and Pops concerts, respectively.

In addition to these financial troubles, one critical challenge the ASO faced was the need to increase its presence within the Atlanta community. According to Robert Spano:

> Here's this great orchestra, here's this very vital, thriving, growing, exciting city, and the two have nothing to do with each other. There's a total disconnect. We're not getting audiences.
>
> That's a challenge that fascinates me. How do you get this credible, viable artistic institution to mean something to the community in which it lives? Because if it doesn't, it's going to die.[4]

As a means to raise awareness, for example, fans attending Atlanta Braves baseball home games were treated to a between-inning video of the ASO and Spano performing the famous conclusion to Giachino Rossini's *William Tell Overture* (i.e., the Lone Ranger theme) while the stadium grounds crew quickly refreshed the baseball infield.

THE LONG-RANGE PLAN AND CREATIVE PARTNERSHIP

In the fall of 1997, ASO musicians, board, staff and volunteers undertook a new initiative to address the turmoil then surrounding the orchestra. Specifically, a planning process was undertaken involving extensive interviews, focus groups and other data-gathering activities with members of the ASO family. The result of the two-year process included a new mission statement, vision and three-year strategy for the ASO.

Emanating from the ASO's Long Range Plan (LRP) (see Exhibit 6) was a revised mission statement that read:

> The Atlanta Symphony Orchestra and its affiliated members are committed to build on our foundation of artistic excellence. We unite in our desire to

---

[3]Thomas Morris, "Is the Orchestra Dead? A Context for Good Health," McBride Lecture, Case Western Reserve University, Cleveland, September 27, 1988.

[4]"The Atlanta Symphony Gets a Jolt of Energy," *New York Times,* December 16, 2001.

serve and to expand our audience through innovative programming, broader venues and increased educational opportunities while balancing artistic growth with financial soundness. We share a heritage of passion for the music. We embrace our responsibility to be a vigorous part of the cultural fabric of our community and to strive to reach national and international audiences.

This vision was intended to provide a snapshot of the organization in the future, and to

---

Exhibit 6 The ASO's Long Range Plan

The objective of the ASO's Long Range Plan was to provide the long-range directions and goals that would guide all proposed actions. Further, it was meant to provide a context for both the orchestra's Three-Year Strategy and for continued artistic and financial planning over the coming years. The plan's directions and goals are detailed below.

1. Invest in the Music
   - Display artistic leadership and creativity.
   - Improve the ASO instrument: hall, musicians, programming.
   - Capitalize on unique assets of ASO chorus and youth orchestra.

2. Engage and Significantly Grow the Audience
   - Engage our audiences and enhance the classical concert experience.
   - Develop and offer a summer classical program to engage current audiences and attract new audiences.
   - Pursue an enhanced role at Chastain and return all parks concerts to Piedmont Park.
   - Significantly increase and strengthen marketing efforts.

3. Serve Our Evolving Community
   - Expand outreach to new audiences; enhance diverse community partnerships.
   - Provide educational programs for ASO audiences, both adults and young people, that enhance their enjoyment, appreciation, and understanding of the musical arts and inspire the community to attend ASO concerts regularly.

4. Engage professional support, build bridges between ASO education offerings, utilize technology and enhance participatory value for attendees, funders and partners.
   - Enhance membership value of the Atlanta Symphony Associates and increase involvement in outreach.

5. Develop and Maintain a Strong Organizational, Technical and Financial Infrastructure
   - Significantly increase and expand development efforts.
   - Leverage technology and staff development for ASO success.
   - Strengthen the ASO's organizational and governance systems, with the goal of clarifying roles and responsibilities and enhancing communication.
     o Strengthen our understanding of roles and responsibilities.
     o Develop evaluation procedures.
   - Build strong communications, well supported by systems and personnel.

Source: ASO files.

articulate the way the organization would look and act in the future to carry out its mission. The vision's main points were to:

- Grow artistic excellence and nurture creativity;
- Serve multi-faceted communities in Atlanta and the southeastern United States;
- Achieve financial strength and soundness; and
- Galvanize the organization and build infrastructure capacity.

A three-year strategy was developed that would be the driving force for the ASO planning process. This strategy focused on putting the organization into the most advantageous position for success and fulfilment of its mission and vision. The three-year strategy revolved around three aims:

- Focus on vision;
- Increase ASO exposure; and
- Increase and leverage revenues.

The LRP was not designed solely to improve the ASO's economic model. Rather, the LRP was initiated to also improve the orchestra's management model.

The 125 participants in the LRP process—individuals representing the community, local businesses, volunteers and the orchestra's board, musicians and staff—were unified by the desire to position the ASO above the orchestral crowd. A critical component in achieving this objective was the creation of a new culture of collaboration. This culture of "creative partnership," which also translated into a sense of ownership and responsibility by the orchestra stakeholders, became the guiding principle at the ASO. The belief was that a creative partnership dictated that collaboration must occur in order to achieve broad institutional ownership of initiatives. Only with the process-focused implementation of these collaborative initiatives would the ASO be successful. The orchestra arranged an annual retreat each September, involving a group of participants similar to that employed in the LRP process, for strategic—financial and artistic—planning and assessment purposes.

A critical component to achieving the objectives of the LRP involved embarking on a campaign of innovation intended to ensure the ASO's highly distinctive artistic identity and musical offerings. Concurrent to this ASO campaign was the selection of a new music director and principal guest conductor, along with the building of a new performance venue.

Search for a New Music Director

By the late 1990s, many of the major North American orchestras, including those in Boston, Cleveland, New York and Philadelphia, were searching for new music directors. The ASO found itself included in this mix as the orchestra's board decided in 1998 not to renew Yoel Levi's contract as music director. Allison Vulgamore, president of the Atlanta Symphony Orchestra since 1993, noted that:

> About 200 people—board, staff, chorus members and musicians—came together in 1998 in order to discuss how to bring the organization back together, post strike, and determine what we were looking for in a music director. Fourteen task forces were created, one of which became the music director search committee.

According to Vulgamore, that search committee's charge was simple. A new music director was needed who would foster creativity in musical programming. Unlike many of the other previously mentioned orchestras who were looking for conductors largely with a European background and/or years of success in leading major orchestras, the ASO chose Robert Spano as its music director. Spano, music director of the Brooklyn Philharmonic, was one of the few American orchestra leaders who had earned an international reputation as an innovative and adventurous programmer and orchestra builder. In describing the ASO's choice, Vulgamore remarked:

> It was clear that we needed to expand our performing repertoire. We desired some experimentation, going so far as not caring just how wild that might be. Thinking wild might result in something interesting.

Proof of this experimentation was found in the ASO's "war room," where much of the important concert programming decisions were made. Programming decisions, normally taking place two to three years in advance and finalized by February of the preceding music season, were perennial problems for most orchestras, since issues such as the marketability of a program were weighed against financial considerations and concerns over artistic integrity (see Exhibit 7). The ASO developed and employed a predictive programming model, premised on considerations of sound budget management and artistic growth, to create its lineup of concerts for the 2001–2002

Master Season. The goal of this programming approach, given the constraints of the operating budget, would be to create a portfolio of concert programs that could be characterized in terms of an A, B, C, or D classification scheme (see Exhibit 8). Given Spano's desire to perform new or seldom-heard classical music in addition to the traditional and oft-performed masterpieces, novel concerts—like the one containing *A Sea Symphony*—had to be balanced with more traditional and recognizable concert programs. This desire to perform classical music that would be novel to both the musicians and audience was offset by the need to figure out what would sell.

Exhibit 7   The Road to Strong Sales and Artistic Adventure

Based on our collective desire to sell more tickets and move forward artistically, we must find ways to bring in audiences with winner programs/artists and very carefully give them something at the same time that they didn't expect but really liked. Here are three points that are critical to moving us toward our goal.

1. Build Trust and Loyalty to New Leadership

   - Approachability both on and off stage
   - Convey excitement and enthusiasm for music
   - Demonstrate a real desire to listen and engage audience
   - Strategic introduction to community at large

2. Programming

   - Scheduling strategically based on what we know and what we will learn
   - Connection between audience and stage is critical
   - Embed new works around more popular pieces or as themes within current subscription packages
   - Still must always give the audience plenty of what they want

3. Concert Format

   - Audience yearns for greater sense of connection to the stage
   - Short enthusiastic comments from stage are well received
   - Video enhancement has great potential
   - Greater use of lighting and other visual enhancements a plus

Connecting to audience + concert enhancement leads to trust, & loyalty leads to bigger audience and opportunity for more adventurous programming.

Source: Charlie Wade, ASO files.

Exhibit 8 ASO's Predictive Programming Model

Inputs to the ASO's predictive programming model included consideration of:

a. composer and piece of music,
b. guest artists,
c. solo instrument type,
d. time of year,
e. performance fees and costs, and
f. what is being performed elsewhere.

Individuals involved in programming included the ASO's music director, principal guest conductor, president, vice-president general manager, vice-president marketing and communications and artistic administrator.

Program Category (attendance in %)	Number of Programs (2001–2002)	Sample Program from Master Season (2001–2002)*
A—90 to 100	3	January 10, 12, 13 (2002) [100%] Beethoven: Two Romances Beethoven: Symphony No. 8 Brahms: Symphony No. 3 Itzhak Perlman, conductor and violin
B—80 to 89	4	November 15, 16, 18 (2001) [83.1%] Rossini/Respighi: La Boutique Fantasque Vivaldi: The Four Seasons Robert Spano, conductor Gil Shaham, violin
C—70 to 79	7	April 25, 26, 27 (2002) [75%] Wagner: Die Walküre—Act III Donald Runnicles, conductor Christine Brewer, soprano James Morris, bass
D—60 to 69	7	November 8, 9, 10 (2001) [68.7%] Debussy: Nocturnes Vaughan-Williams: A Sea Symphony Robert Spano, conductor Christine Goerke, soprano Brett Polegato, baritone ASO Chorus

Source: ASO files.

* Average percentage of paid house per concert in brackets.

ASO musicians were actively involved with the music director selection in an effort to stay true to the organization's commitment towards keeping lines of communication open. Jun-Ching Lin, assistant concert master and one of the five musicians on the 11-member search committee, summarized the process:

> We put together a wish list of the qualities we wanted in a music director, and the word 'collaboration' kept coming up. It was the first time in my 12 years here that I felt the board and management could hear what the musicians were saying. For me, personally, that was worth the entire two and a half years of the search process.[5]

New Performance Venue

The ASO embarked in 1999 on a plan to construct a new performing arts centre. The musicians and management felt the ASO would not be able to achieve its future artistic growth goals at the WAC; as the orchestra's needs grew, the WAC was no longer able to provide the acoustical instrument the orchestra required. The new Symphony Center would be built on three acres at the corner of 14th and Peachtree streets, one block south of the present Woodruff Arts Center campus. The close proximity of the new venue was necessary in order to maintain the ASO's connection with the other residents of the Woodruff Arts Center, such as the Alliance Theatre Company, Atlanta College of Art, High Museum of Art, and the 14th Street Playhouse.

The proposed plan was to build a new home for the orchestra, at an estimated cost of $240 million, by fall 2008. This plan would accomplish many things. Besides offering a 2,000-seat auditorium that would be an acoustically superb home with cutting-edge technology, plans for the multi-purpose arts centre also included educational and administrative facilities, along with restaurants and cafés.

In 2001, the ASO and Houston-based developer Hines announced a six-year development plan to build two residential towers next to the new Symphony Center on 6.2 acres at Peachtree and 14th streets. The first tower, projected to open by 2005 at a cost of between $110 and $125 million, would have 250 to 300 residential units. Retail components would add an additional estimated cost of $5 million. The second tower, expected to be completed in 2007 at a cost of between $120 and $160 million, would include 100 to 125 residential units and 100 to 225 hotel rooms. In order to fund construction of the new hall, the ASO engaged in a massive capital campaign led by Home Depot co-founder Arthur Blank; the early goal was for $200 million to be raised from private individuals, foundations and government.

Estimates prepared by Ernst & Young of the economic impact of the new hall indicated that the proposed Symphony Center project would generate more than $2.1 billion in the state through the year 2017. The ASO contribution alone was estimated at $1.7 billion over the 17-year period from 2000 to 2017.

The ASO worked with the community in planning the new Symphony Center. In describing the project, Vulgamore remarked:

> The 'wow' factor was an important consideration. We want a home that is not only monumentally beautiful, but also welcoming. Of course, the acoustical properties of the new hall are extremely important and should drive most of the architectural and aesthetic decisions. We want the new home of the ASO to be a landmark.

A SEA SYMPHONY

In 2000, a member of the ASO Chorus suggested that the ASO perform Ralph Vaughan-Williams' 1910 composition titled *A Sea Symphony*. Recognizing an opportunity to put the LRP into action, ASO administrators undertook an experiment that would mix the traditional symphony performance with technology. The ASO commissioned, at a

[5]"The Atlanta Symphony Gets a Jolt of Energy," *New York Times,* December 16, 2001.

final cost of $35,000, visual art from Polish video artist Piotr Szyhalski to accompany the performance of the symphony. This rarely performed symphony was composed to evoke the sea as a metaphor for the inexplicable vastness of the cosmos, for mankind's tiny place within it, for the restlessness of life, and for man's ultimate fate—death. Near the end of the 70-minute ASO performance of this symphony, the jumbo screen positioned above the stage displayed a rapid flash of faces augmented by spinning gears and cogs. Above the faces appeared Orwellian double-speak slogans, such as "There is no escape / for you / strong thoughts / fill you / and confidence / you smile!"

The ASO's premier performance on November 8, 2001, immediately drew some heated reaction. One patron, displaying atypical concert hall behavior, shouted "Boo the bastards!" as he left his seat in mid-concert. In all, over a dozen of the audience members expressed opinions about the performance to Michael Granados, ASO season ticket manager. Granados commented:

> We received different reactions. One patron suggested that we should have had medical professionals assess the video to make sure it would not cause epileptic seizures. A different person indicated that the video was fabulous art but a distraction to the music. It appeared that people either hated or loved the video. In the end, the symphony orchestra was not passé that Thursday night. The performance clearly affected concertgoers.

One ASO subscriber e-mailed the local newspaper, *The Atlanta Journal-Constitution* (AJC), the following message:

> I did not go to this performance of such beautiful music to be depressed and upset—an emotional state solely caused by that awful video.

ASO administrators actively observed audience reaction. According to Charlie Wade, the ASO's vice-president, marketing and communications:

> Negative feedback from some of the audience may not be what we want to hear, but at least it provides us with useful information on patron perceptions. The fact that people offered such feedback indicates that they love and care for the ASO's art form. That is a very useful thing.

The AJC newspaper critic who reviewed the performance concluded:

> As a companion to the music, Szyhalski's images seemed banal, dreary once the novelty wore off, and certainly beside the point while the music was playing. . . .
> What was inescapable about Thursday evening was the seismic effect Spano is having on the ASO and its audience. Like it or not, we're on the leading edge of the 21st-century symphony orchestra. It's a rather fun place to be.[6]

The ASO administration viewed the *A Sea Symphony* experiment as an attempt to enhance the concert hall experience in the hope of increasing the orchestra's long-term relevance. Another example of the ASO's innovative efforts was the videotaping of interviews with active American composers whose works were being performed by the orchestra for the first time. One of these interviews was played to the audience prior to the playing of Christopher Theofanidis' composition titled *Rainbow Body*, which proceeded without incident. Another of these interviews was scheduled for display prior to the ASO premier of Jennifer Higdon's work titled *Blue Cathedral* the following May. According to Vulgamore:

> A concern commonly voiced is that orchestras are living in the past and are not connected to the present. The ASO is one orchestra that wants to change that. Doing so may require that we continue to stretch the boundary of performance standards and experiment through calculated risk. Clearly, we have to progress wisely as we go. Perhaps mistakes will be made along the way, but that is a potential outcome that comes with not being afraid to think about trying anything. No other orchestra is doing as much as we are this season to accomplish staying alive and in tune.

---

[6]"Shouting Fan Can't Disrupt ASO Concert," *The Atlanta Journal-Constitution,* November 9, 2001.

Other orchestras had occasionally tinkered with their musical offerings. The New York Philharmonic in the early 1970s offered "rug concerts" in which auditorium seats were removed so that patrons could sit on small carpets and listen to contemporary music. The audience would then debate the music's merits with the musicians. Another one-time trial in combining visuals to music included The Philadelphia Orchestra's 1998 performance of Messiaen's *Turangalila-Symphonie* with color slides of birds and erotic Indian art.

While there was no intention of mixing extra-musical activities into every concert, the ASO administration had already decided on another ASO-commissioned video to accompany a performance of Ravel's *Ma mère l'Oye* (Mother Goose Suite) in the spring of 2003. A subscriber wrote to the ASO after seeing the *A Sea Symphony* performance that:

> We have been subscribers for more than 30 years. We see you offering a variety of novelty items at persons who don't care much for traditional offerings. You may attract some of them but they will never stay. Meanwhile, you are alienating the faithful. If the music can't stand on its own, the gimmicks will never save it. If there is a next time, we will walk out.

DEMYSTIFYING THE CONCERT EXPERIENCE

John Sparrow, along with an increasing number of individuals familiar—or associated—with the orchestra, viewed the ASO as a major U.S. orchestra aspiring towards strengthening its national recognition. As far as Sparrow was concerned, the greatest challenge he faced was not one of justifying the ASO's existence, but demystifying the concertgoers' experience. It was important to get people to experience the ASO in the right way. Given the quality of the orchestra's performances, Sparrow felt the music would stand on its own. Yet, further broadening and enhancing the ASO's services and experiences was an ongoing concern. In addition to deciding how to address the reaction to the *A Sea Symphony* performance, Sparrow noted:

> I would love it if all patrons walked out of an ASO concert with the feeling of having had a great musical experience in which they were comforted, well attended to, and had all their needs met. The ASO should be able to provide a service as seamless as that offered at Nordstrom, and with the consistency found at Wal-Mart.

HEALTH CARE CENTER FOR THE HOMELESS: CHANGING WITH THE TIMES

Bakari Burns, recent MBA graduate and CEO of the Health Care Center for the Homeless (HCCH) in Orlando, Florida, was eager to implement what he had learned in his MBA classes to build on the strong history and important mission of his nonprofit organization. Burns knew the organization experienced difficulty with recognition and marketplace distinction, primarily due to the public's

Mary Conway Dato-on and Eileen Weisenbach Keller wrote this case solely to provide material for class discussion. The authors do not intend to illustrate either effective or ineffective handling of a managerial situation. The authors may have disguised certain names and other identifying information to protect confidentiality.

misperceptions about the relationship between HCCH and the Coalition for the Homeless of Central Florida (currently a separate and independent human services organization located in downtown Orlando). Confusion also existed regarding the relationship between HCCH and its various services, especially the Orange Blossom Family Health Center. Could these issues be affecting donations and the ability to provide quality services? One lesson Burns clearly remembered from school was the importance of asking for help when the path to continued excellence was not clear, and so he solicited advice from an external consulting team. The recommendations, delivered to Burns in summer 2010, included significant organizational change accompanied by a suggestion that HCCH rebrand with an amended name and redesign all marketing materials. This advice and the changes in the external environment made it an excellent time to reposition and refocus the organization. Recognizing the need for a new strategy and implementing that strategy were not the same; Burns was not sure how to lead the organization through the change process.

HCCH

The Health Care Center for the Homeless, Inc. (HCCH), a nonprofit health organization, served the homeless, uninsured and underinsured in Central Florida, including the city of Orlando, and Orange, Osceola and Seminole counties. HCCH was one of several federally and state-funded health centers located in these Florida counties. According to the U.S. Department of Health and Human Services, "Health centers are community-based and patient-directed organizations that serve populations with limited access to health care. These include low income populations, the uninsured, those with limited English proficiency." [1] Health centers are located in most

cities and many rural areas. In 2009, the more than 7,900 health centers around the United States cared for nearly 19 million patients, including 3.4 million who received dental services and 758,000 who received behavioral health care. Thirty-eight per cent of patients served by health centers were uninsured and an estimated 1,018,000 were homeless. Nationally, health centers employed more than 123,000 people in underserved communities and leveraged more than $9 billion in other health resources.[2]

As one of the federally designated health centers, HCCH provided a wide range of health services, including primary care, pediatric care, dentistry, social, mental and behavioral health, vision care and tuberculosis management, at its medical facility, the Orange Blossom Family Health Center. HCCH also staffed a mobile care unit for outreach to those who were unable to travel to the health center independently. In 2010, the organization was in the process of applying for a federal change in scope that would allow it to receive funding for the many uninsured and underinsured clients it served at the Orange Blossom Family Health Center. These funds were part of the Affordable Care Act that provided $11 billion in funding for the operation, expansion and construction of community health centers. This time of significant structural change presented a prime opportunity for HCCH to revitalize. What changes were appropriate could only be determined with a complete understanding of the organization's history and main stakeholders.

History and Services

The Health Care Center for the Homeless[3] was founded in 1993 by Dr. Rick Baxley and a group of concerned physicians. While working with the Coalition for the Homeless of Central Florida,

[1]http://bphc.hrsa.gov, accessed October 20, 2010.

[2]Health Center Program Fact Sheet, www.hrsa.gov/about/organization/bureaus/bphc/bphc.pdf, accessed via http://bphc.hrsa.gov on October 20, 2010.

[3]See http://www.hcch.org.

Dr. Baxley observed a growing problem of illness among homeless individuals around Orlando and knew that they were not receiving adequate medical care. HCCH began as an evening clinic at the Coalition for the Homeless office a few nights a week and eventually spun off as a separate nonprofit organization in 1994. For many years, HCCH operated medical and dental services out of three separate locations. In 2006, the Orange Blossom Family Health Center opened, facilitating delivery of many medical-related services under one roof. With the help of a $1.1 million grant from the Health Resources and Services Administration (HRSA) in 2008, the health center building expanded, providing more medical exam rooms and allowing for further development of the behavioral health team. "The services at HCCH [were] provided in a multi-disciplinary approach combining aggressive street outreach with integrated systems of primary health care, dental, vision, behavioral health, education and patient advocacy."[4]

HCCH was particularly proud of the quality of service offered at the Orange Blossom Family Health Center and its mobile units. Evidence of the professional level of service was seen in the state-of-the-art electronic medical system implemented at the health center in 2006. This Electronic Health Records system created a paperless electronic health record for each patient. The system integrated communication with area health care providers, thus ensuring continuity of care and eliminating duplication of services. The outreach unit, known as the HOPE Team (Homeless Outreach Partnership Effort), sent staff and volunteers to where the homeless lived—on the streets and in the woods (camps). The main goal of the HOPE Team was to connect homeless clients living in the camps with the medical, dental and behavioral health services HCCH provided. Burns noted, "Building trust was often the first step to move homeless individuals toward integrating within society." The HOPE Team provided this link.

HCCH operated an in-house pharmacy at the Orange Blossom Family Health Center that enabled clients to obtain low-cost prescriptions immediately upon receiving medical care. This was very important as many of the homeless or uninsured neglected to fill prescriptions due to monetary and identification issues. A full-time Patient Assistance Program (PAP) Coordinator helped patients obtain free medications through various pharmaceutical companies. According to the 2009 Annual Report, the PAP Program assisted more than 2,000 clients who received more than $2,000,000 in prescription medications. These costs would have been absorbed by HCCH or the client themselves without the joint efforts of the PAP and the companies.

The health center also offered eye exams and distributed eyeglasses free of charge to qualified clients. Through a partnership with Lions Club International and LensCrafters, free screenings and eyeglasses were provided for 30 patients every Thanksgiving. Burns was proud to report, "The HCCH Vision Center is the only source of free optometric services for the homeless in Central Florida." Screening for vision-related issues that could result from diabetes and other chronic illnesses was also available on a scheduled basis at the health center.

To reduce improper use of emergency rooms in local hospitals, HCCH developed a specialized position known as a Health Navigator. The Navigator's job was to reroute homeless individuals from the downtown Orlando Health Emergency Room to the Orange Blossom Family Health Center. At the center, the homeless received consistent medical care with a "medical home" where records were kept and accessed for follow-up care. In 2009, 466 of the patients encountered by the Health Navigator in the Emergency Room became established clients at the health center.[5]

Burns was pleased with the breadth and depth of services and took pride in the numerous accomplishments in the organization's relatively

---

[4]http://www.hcch.org/history.htm, accessed July 9, 2010.

[5]HCCH 2009 Annual Report.

short history. The founding board of directors sought to clarify the organization's purpose through the development of a mission. Burns thought the resulting HCCH mission encapsulated its role in the community and its dedication to quality: "to provide quality health care services that improve the lives of the homeless and medically indigent people of our community." HCCH declared the values with which it pursued this mission in the following values statement: "We are committed and obligated to provide the highest quality of care to all community residents in an atmosphere of dignity and respect. We treat all patients with a truly caring attitude and are aware of the changing needs of the community and strive to be responsive to those needs. We embrace human differences as bonds, not barriers, and believe that quality health care should be universally accessible."

The values statement emphasized the guiding values of dignity, respect, a caring attitude and togetherness. There was no stated vision for HCCH and the board had yet to decide if one was necessary. Some members were not sure why a vision would be needed if the organization already had strong mission and values statements.

Stakeholders

According to the American Marketing Association, organizational stakeholders were "one of a group of publics with which an organization must be concerned. Key stakeholders include consumers, employees, suppliers, and others who have some relationship with the organization."[6] Critical or key stakeholders were those who most influenced the creation and destruction of brand value.[7] Upon reflection, Burns believed that HCCH had five critical stakeholders: patients, donors (corporate and individual), volunteers, staff and the board.

Reviewing the circumstances of each stakeholder group helped Burns understand the environment in which HCCH operated.

Patients: HCCH provided services to the homeless, uninsured and underinsured individuals in the Orlando community. The number of patients served by HCCH spoke volumes about the gravity of the homeless situation in Central Florida. Exhibit 1 shows statistics for patients serviced by HCCH in 2009.

Homelessness continued to be a widespread dilemma throughout the United States, affecting all communities across rural, urban and suburban settings. An estimated two to three million people were homeless during 2009, with approximately 930,589 without shelter on any given night. The Federal Health Care for the Homeless Program was formed to be a leading source of health care for the homeless in the United States, whether patients lived on the street, in shelters, or in transitional housing. Through this program, more than one million

Exhibit 1   HCCH 2009 Patient Statistics

Service Encounter	Number
Primary Medical	17,036
Oral Health	9,620
Behavioral Health/Substance Abuse	2,298
Total Encounters for 2009	28,954
Total Patients Seen at Orange Blossom Family Health Center	8,295
Vision Center Patients Seen*	82
Hope Team Outreach Clients Seen*	809
Hope Team Outreach Encounters*	3,114

Source: HCCH 2009 Annual Report.

* Number not included in total patient figure above.

---

[6]www.marketingpower.com/_layouts/Dictionary.aspx?dLetter=S, accessed August 21, 2010.

[7]Richard Jones, "Finding Sources of Brand Value: Developing a Stakeholder Model of Brand Equity," *Brand Management,* 13:1, 2005, pp. 10–32.

homeless persons were served by health centers funded by the Health Resources and Services Administration (HRSA) in 2009.[8]

Statistics on homeless populations were generally grouped by single men/women, families and veterans. The number of homeless families across the nation had surged by approximately 30 per cent since the recession began in 2007. In Florida, the homeless population for the same period had grown by almost 11 per cent, or about 5,400 people. The number of homeless families in Florida rose 23 per cent from 2008 to 2009, with 7,750 families homeless in 2010 as determined by a mid-year count.[9] In 2008, the total homeless veterans in the Homeless Services Network of Central Florida's one-day count was 1,185. In 2009 the tally jumped to 1,680. Additionally, disheartening results of the 2009 study showed that it took Vietnam veterans an average of six years to plunge into homelessness while post-9/11 veterans only took about 18 months.[10]

Orlando-area homeless advocates tracked the number of homeless school-age children. In Orange, Osceola and Seminole counties, for example, nearly 2,700 homeless children attended public schools in May 2008. A year later, the number grew substantially to 4,200.[11] The fastest-growing population of homeless people was single women with children. Most homeless families were headed by a young mother with two children under the age of six. According to the HCCH 2009 Annual Report's summary of Orlando-area homelessness studies, the chance of someone who was homeless becoming ill could be as much as six times higher than someone who was housed. Homeless individuals were also three times more likely to die from an illness than the general population.

Donors: Burns divided potential individual donor categories demographically. These categories included:

- Baby boomers with high disposable incomes, professionals aged 30–45 and members of community organizations and local churches.
- Seniors and individuals aged 54 or more. Because of their established lifestyles, they were considered good targets for donations, bequests, planned giving and deferred gifts.

When considering donations from corporations, Burns was relentless in pursuing partnerships and donations. The HCCH Development Associate, Terri Betts, was pleased with several notable donations in 2009, including the Walt Disney World Company's $15,000 donation received at the Candlelight Processional held in EPCOT's America Gardens Theatre. Attributed to Burns' and Betts' hard work was the receipt of a $25,000 donation from Florida Hospital in January 2010. HCCH also received a $30,000 grant from the Orlando Magic Youth Fund (OMYF), a fund of the McCormick Foundation, in support of medical services at the Orange Blossom Family Health Center.[12]

Two major fundraising events were held in 2009. Burns recalled the third Annual Central Florida Hospitalist Partners (CFHP) Golf Tournament on October 31, which raised more than $6,700. CFHP was a group of local physicians who had been caring for patients in the largest and most prestigious hospitals and health care systems in Central Florida since 1999. Betts worked hard on the *Femmes de Coeur* Sweetheart Affair in February 2009. That was the last year for the event, which was to be replaced in 2010 by the Heart to Heart Gala. The ongoing support of *Femmes de Coeur* was essential for HCCH,

---

[8]http://bphc.hrsa.gov/about/specialpopulations.htm, accessed October 20, 2010.

[9]Kate Santich, "Report: Homeless families up sharply," *The Orlando Sentinel,* June 17, 2010.

[10]Sepia, "Serving our veterans—Central Florida needs to do more to bring down the increasing numbers of homeless vets," *The Orlando Sentinel,* January 28, 2010.

[11]Kate Santich, "Report: Homeless families up sharply," *The Orlando Sentinel,* June 17, 2010.

[12]HCCH 2009 Annual Report.

and the organization's donations resulted in a dental operatory, decorations for the pediatric waiting area, and funds for the screening mammography program at the Orange Blossom Family Health Center. Since its inception, the *Femmes de Coeur* mammography program for HCCH had provided more than 550 screening mammograms for female clients.[13] Exhibit 2 shows financial activity for HCCH in 2009, including the various sources of support and revenue. Burns noted that the fundraising goal for fiscal year 2010 was $192,390.

Volunteers: Help from volunteers came in the form of medical professionals and medical students donating time with patients as well as

Exhibit 2	HCCH Statement of Activities for the Year Ending September 30, 2009
Support and Revenue	**2009 Totals ($)**
Support:	
Government Grants	2,762,334
Private Support	718,229
In-kind Contributions	990,108
Revenue	898,081
Total Support and Revenue	5,368,752
Expenses and Losses	
Program Services	
Medical Clinic	4,777,113
Tuberculosis Shelter	45,654
Supporting Services	
Management and General	392,072
Fundraising	94,918
Total Expenses and Losses	5,309,757
Increase (Decrease) in Net Assets	58,995

Source: HCCH 2009 Annual Report.

clerical assistance in the record-keeping area. In recruiting volunteers, HCCH emphasized the need to "help at home." This was clearly articulated by HCCH Volunteer Physician of the Year Jaime Torner, MD, who stated, "Charity begins at home. While colleagues go on mission trips to third-world countries I practice my passion daily. Why go around the world when there is work to be done right in your own backyard?"[14]

Partnerships were also an important part of the HCCH volunteer portfolio. Burns repeatedly noted that the quantity and quality of service would not be possible without the support of community partners. These partners included those within the state, such as Florida Hospital, Orlando Health, Heart of Florida, United Way, Walt Disney World, Universal Studios, Bureau of Primary Health Care, Orange County and the City of Orlando, as well as those at the national level, including HUD (Housing and Urban Development). Partnership support included expertise, in-kind and monetary donations. Once the University of Central Florida (UCF) Medical School was opened, Burns looked forward to a strong partnership with its faculty, students and alumni.

Staff and Board of Directors: Fifteen members (including Burns) comprised the board of directors, and most had served with the board more than five years. The medical profession was heavily represented on the board (almost 50 per cent). While the primary role of the board was advisory, several [members] were actively involved in fundraising and guiding the direction of medical services. Professional qualifications of board members included MD (Doctor of Medicine), CPA (Certified Public Accountant), PhD, legal degrees and Fellows of the American College of Healthcare Executives (FACHE). Burns' recently acquired MBA added the business dimension to his Master of Public Heath degree. A relatively recent addition to the board

[13]Ibid.

[14]http://www.hcch.org/volunteer.htm, accessed August 21, 2010.

was Antonio Arias, who brought sales and marketing expertise from his years in medical sales.

HCCH listed 12 permanent staff members, including doctors, nurses, pharmacists, dentists, dental technicians, mental health counselors and office staff. Part-time staff were also employed on an as-needed basis. Five directors were responsible for operating the various service branches of HCCH. All reported directly to Burns. The organizational chart for HCCH is found in Exhibit 3.

Health Care Challenges: 2010 and Beyond

The latest figures from the U.S. Census Bureau showed that the number of uninsured and the percentage of the population without health insurance coverage set record highs, while the percentage covered by employment-based plans had fallen to a record low.[15] In March 2010, Congress passed the $875 billion Affordable Care Act.[16] While there were numerous political and economic motivations for the Act, two undeniable trends acutely showed that the status quo of health care in the United States was unacceptable. First, the percentage of the population covered through employment-based plans had declined each year since 2000. Second, health care costs were skyrocketing for individuals as well as state and federal governments. The Act consisted of many provisions aimed at reducing health care costs, empowering consumers and keeping insurance companies accountable. One provision directly affected HCCH, as it provided new funding to support the construction and expansion of services at community health centers, allowing these centers to serve some 20 million new patients across the country. To take advantage of these funds (and others made available through the economic stimulus bill),

Burns needed to expand the scope of HCCH beyond serving only the homeless to serving anyone in the community who was uninsured or underinsured.

While Burns felt confident about the quality of HCCH's work and the support among donors and volunteers, he also realized that the 2010 census figures were only a small indication of the tremendous changes in the economy and the health care sector. Both Burns and Betts worked tirelessly to finalize the necessary paperwork for the change of scope for HCCH. They knew better than to rely on just one source of funding, however, and as such continued to pursue other sources of support.

With the economic recession that began in 2007 showing limited signs of lifting, Burns realized that donations would be hard to generate, yet that demand for services would increase. The homeless population was already growing in the Orlando area and Burns' experience told him that health care expenditures were often a low priority for the homeless and the hungry.

Fundraising: To understand the economic repercussions of the declining economy, rising unemployment and rising homelessness on HCCH resources, Burns and Betts researched trends in philanthropic giving and nonprofit financial conditions. They felt that knowledge of trends in the nonprofit organization (NPO) sector was critical if the staff and board were to achieve the fundraising goal for fiscal year 2010 ($192,390). According to the Urban Institute, in 2008, total private giving to nonprofit organizations nationwide was $307.7 billion, down two per cent from 2007.[17] The 2008 figures were a continuation of a four-year decline in private giving. More interesting than this aggregate number was the assessment of funding sources for HCCH compared to other nonprofit health care organizations.

[15]Anonymous, "Increase in uninsured shows need for change," *Business Insurance,* 44:37, September 2010, p. 8, accessed October 20, 2010, from ABI/INFORM Global. (Document ID: 2159124001)

[16]The Affordable Care Act details are available at www.healthcare.gov/law/introduction/index.html, accessed October 10, 2010.

[17]"The Nonprofit Sector," The Urban Institute, www.urban.org/publications/412085.html, accessed July 19, 2010.

Exhibit 3 HCCH Organizational Chart

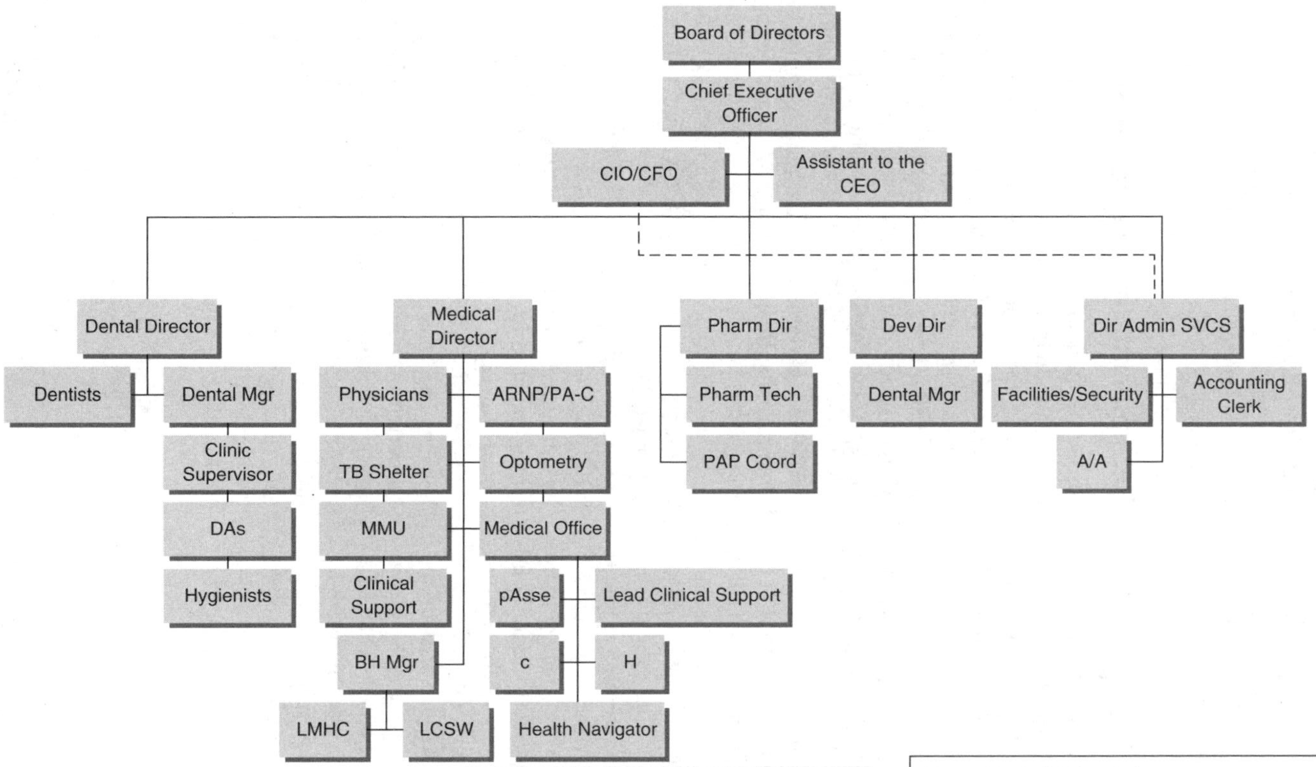

Board of Directors

Chief Executive Officer

Assistant to the CEO

CIO/CFO

Dir Admin SVCS
- Accounting Clerk
- Facilities/Security
  - A/A

Dev Dir
- Dental Mgr

Pharm Dir
- Pharm Tech
- PAP Coord

Medical Director
- ARNP/PA-C
- Optometry
- Medical Office
  - Lead Clinical Support
  - pAsse
  - c
  - H
  - Health Navigator
- Physicians
- TB Shelter
- MMU
- Clinical Support
- BH Mgr
  - LCSW
  - LMHC

Dental Director
- Dental Mgr
  - Clinic Supervisor
  - DAs
  - Hygienists
- Dentists

Key to Medical Abbreviations:
ARNP: Advanced Registered Nurse Practitioner
BH: Behavioral Health
DA: Dental Assistants
LMHC: Licensed Mental Health Counselor
LCSW: Licensed Clinical Social Worker
MA: Medical Assistants
MMU: Mobile Medical Unit
PA-C: Physician Assistant
RN: Registered Nurse

Key to Operations Abbreviations:
Asst: Assistant
CM: Case Manager
Coord: Coordinator
Dir: Director
HOPE: Homeless Outreach Partnership Effort
Mgr: Manager
PAP: Patient Assistance Program
PSR: Patient Services Representative

Key to Administration Abbreviations:
A/A: Administrative Assistant
Admin: Administrative
Dev Assoc: Development Associate
Dev Dir: Development Director
Svs: Services

Source: HCCH files.

The largest source of revenue across public charities was fees from the sale of goods and services, such as patient care (including Medicare and Medicaid). In the human services charities sector, where HCCH was categorized, government provided 48.6 per cent of revenue for human services charities.[18] Based on HCCH's reporting, revenue accounted for only 17 per cent of support and government grants accounted for 52 per cent. The relatively larger dependency on government funding sources made Burns nervous. With the national trend of declining philanthropic donations and pressures to cut government budgets, Burns felt HCCH would have to increase the revenue stream to at least match—but hopefully exceed—the national average.

One way to overcome the perfect storm brewing (i.e. increased homelessness leading to more need and high levels of dependency, all on a base of decreasing financial contributions from private and government sources) was for HCCH to apply for a federal change in scope from a health facility primarily focused on the homeless population to one addressing community-wide needs for quality health care at affordable prices, regardless of housing (e.g. homeless or housed) or insurance status (e.g. uninsured or underinsured). If a change in scope were finalized, the organization would be able to report its full client base to the federal government for funding purposes. Under the current organizational scope, HCCH could only take credit with the government and receive funding (e.g. Medicaid and Medicare support) for its homeless clients.

Furthermore, Burns knew from networking with other social service agencies that if another agency recommended a client seek treatment at HCCH, the client would often respond: "I am not homeless, why would I want to go there?"

Even when Burns and others tried to explain that the Orange Blossom Family Health Center was not only for the homeless, clients (and some agency workers) would insist that they did not want to be seen as homeless and would rather forgo the services offered or go to the hospital emergency room.

Recommendations From Consultants

Burns solicited advice from an external consulting team to help with the kind of misperception voiced in the quote above. The team's recommendations encompassed significant organizational change, including amending the HCCH name and redesigning all marketing materials. All the recommendations were framed around a concept new to Burns: brand orientation. The consulting team explained that brand orientation (BO) was particularly important to nonprofit organizations. Basically, nonprofit brand orientation (NBO) put the image and value of the brand at the core of all activity within the organization in order to effect more positive and effective outcomes.[19]

One consultant explained to Burns that with NBO, the vision for the brand would become the driving force for the organization. Active brand management and NBO could speed up and improve the communication of the brand promise both inside HCCH and to its external stakeholders. The consultants emphasized that donors supported organizations like HCCH because they believed in the cause; in short, they trusted the NPO mission pursuit. Within the framework of NBO, all branding and related marketing activities (e.g. brand name and logo, taglines, communication strategy and tactics including website and promotional materials) would be

[18]Kennard T. Wing, Katie L. Roeger, and Thomas H. Pollak, "The Nonprofit Sector in Brief: Public Charities, Giving, and Volunteering, 2009," www.urban.org/uploadedpdf/412085-nonprofit-sector-brief.pdf, accessed July 19, 2010.

[19]Eileen Weisenbach Keller and Mary Conway Dato-on, "Testing the Premise that Marketing Attitudes and Brand Orientation Correlate with Nonprofit Performance: Connecting Research and Practice," *Proceedings of Academy of Marketing Science Annual Conference,* Dawn R. Deeter-Schmelz, ed., Portland, Oregon, May 26–29, 2010, pp. 86–90.

designed to ensure that the mission was consistently portrayed as HCCH communicated with its diverse stakeholders.

From this general framework, the consulting team made several specific recommendations. In each case, the suggestions were framed by analyzing the current situation and offering a specific action or set of actions. Suggested changes in name, logo, color palette and website are highlighted below.[20]

Organization Name: Current Situation—Historically, the organization operated under two names: Health Care Center for the Homeless, Inc. and the Orange Blossom Family Health Center. The two names were used inconsistently and interchangeably, contributing to confusion and lack of brand identity. The name Health Care Center for the Homeless, Inc. presented several challenges:

1. There was confusion between the Health Care Center for the Homeless and the Coalition for the Homeless based on the historical relationship between the two agencies and the word "homeless" in both organizations' names; and

2. The name was not inclusive of all of the clients the organization served. In addition to serving the homeless, the organization also serviced the uninsured or underinsured. Identifying the services as specifically for the homeless risked alienating some patients from the organization.

The Orange Blossom Family Health Center name also contributed to obstacles:

1. The word "family" could be misperceived by single or childless clients and potential clients. The health center provided a variety of comprehensive health care services, not simply family care or pediatric services; its name should reflect this.

2. The length of the name forced people to shorten it in daily conversation, but the name did not suggest a simple shortened version.

Recommendation: Health Care Center for the Homeless, Inc. doing business as Orange Blossom Health Center—The organization should maintain its incorporated name (Health Care Center for the Homeless, Inc.), but file an Application for the Registration of a Fictitious Name to do business as Orange Blossom Health Center. The incorporated name should be used for behind-the-scenes purposes only, e.g. filing taxes and producing federal reports. Orange Blossom Health Center should be used to refer to the organization in all internal and external communication.

Logo: The logo of an organization was to function in a similar fashion to the name, in that the logo also represented an element of the external and identifiable communication of the organization's brand. The difference was that the logo provided a visual and, in some cases, artistic representation of the brand. This visual cue needed to symbolize the experience promised by the brand.[21] Logos fitted into the communication mix by incorporating an organization's purpose, vision and strategy together in an expressive format that enhanced brand equity.

Current Situation: Since the opening of the health center, HCCH had operated with two logos, which corresponded with its two names. The logos, like the two names, were used inconsistently and interchangeably, creating confusion among target audiences. This confusion manifested when individuals failed to associate the logos with a single brand or organization. Many believed that the logos represented two separate organizations that operated as affiliates, or that the organizations were two entirely isolated entities. (See Exhibit 4 for current logos.)

---

[20]Consulting report submitted to HCCH on February 17, 2010 by Kayla Florio, Skye Guthrie, Sara Miller, Alissa Shortridge, and Luke Taylor.

[21]Stuart Elliot, "A new survey finds that for some brands and companies, logos can be image breakers," *The New York Times,* Financial Desk, November 1, 1994, Late Edition, D6.

Exhibit 4 Current Logos for HCCH (a) and Orange Blossom Family Health Center (b)

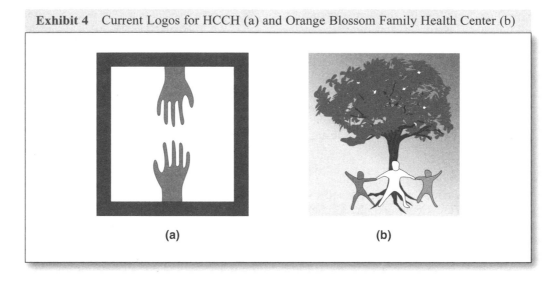

(a)   (b)

Recommendation: Creation of a new logo based on a new name—The organization should continue to use the orange blossom tree in its logo (see Exhibit 4), which symbolizes fruitfulness and generosity. The revised use of the tree should incorporate vibrant, healthy, energetic colors that may further inspire thoughts of opportunity, renewed hope and potential for growth, replenishment and prosperity. The new logo, created by a professional designer capable of producing a high-quality depiction of the brand, should reflect the mission, values and history of the organization. The use of the HCCH logo (blue and white hands reaching out; see Exhibit 4) should be discontinued.

In addition to adopting a new logo, the consulting team recommended creation of a tagline for the brand. The tagline should capture the idea that the organization was large and multifaceted, providing many services. For example: *One Community, One Health Center.* This tagline expressed the sentiment that the organization served all members of the community, and developed a positive emotion surrounding the brand. The consultants' recommendations also included message training among all key stakeholders,

graphic standards for the name, tagline and logo, a color palette and budgeting. Samples of communication materials such as brochures, newsletters, postcards, appointment cards and a web presence were offered; all emphasized the consistent communication of the brand vision and values. While the consistent visual representation was deemed critical, the message training was most important to the implementation of brand orientation. Only through consistent internal and external communication about the brand would a rallying point (i.e. the brand and all it represented in terms of mission and values) be established and executed.

Implementing Organizational Change

Burns was faced with two types of change. Environmental conditions strongly suggested the need for a change of scope. This transformation, coupled with the consultants' insights, pointed to the need for change on many levels. Reviewing his MBA class notes, Burns recalled the work conducted by Kotter[22] on the eight

[22] J. P. Kotter, *Leading Change,* Harvard Business School Press, Boston, 1996.

stages of change. He was acutely aware that 70–90 per cent of successful change was dependent on leadership and that 10–30 per cent depended on the managerial skills of the change leader. He was determined to convince the board of the need for change, and to gain its commitment to the effective implementation of the process. The eight stages of change were:

1. Establish a sense of urgency
2. Create a guiding coalition with enough power to execute the change
3. Develop a vision and strategy
4. Communicate the change vision
5. Empower broad-based action
6. Generate short-term wins
7. Consolidate gains and produce more change
8. Anchor new approaches in the culture

CONCLUSION

With the specific recommendations from the consulting team and the noted changes in the external environment, Burns felt there was a sufficient framework and reason for organizational change. With Kotter's structure, Burns felt he had a method for change. What should he do first and what should be his role in implementing the changes?

7

NONPROFIT CAPACITY AND NETWORKS

It seems to me that we know that networks are out there. But we don't know enough about them, how they work, and what they can/cannot do to make knowledge of their existence useful.

—Lucy Bernholz (2008, para. 13)

Key Topics: organizational capacity, capacity building, venture philanthropy, networking, collaboration, mergers

CAPACITY AND CAPACITY BUILDING

Stated simply, organizational capacity is the ability of an entity to perform at its highest potential. Horton and colleagues (2003) define capacity more specifically as an organization's "ability to successfully apply its skills and resources to accomplish its goals and satisfy its stakeholders' expectations" (p. 19). The skills and resources needed to do this include the main topics covered in this text, namely, staffing, structure and governance, financial resources, strategic leadership, performance measurement (process management), as well as networks and linkages with other organizations and groups.

This list reminds us that capacity encompasses almost everything a nonprofit organization (NPO) has or does (Worth, 2012).

Improving the skills and resources of an NPO leads to greater capacity at the programmatic and organizational level; this process is known as capacity building. Clearly, before one can build capacity, one must establish *why* capacity development is needed, *whose* capacity needs developing, *how* this capacity will be developed, *what* capacity currently exists, and how the capacity will be used *once developed* (Wachira, 2009). This process, known as the *capacity audit,* is similar to the process suggested by the McKinsey 7S Framework (Peters & Waterman, 1982) discussed in Chapter 3.

The purpose of such audits or organizational assessments is ultimately to enable mission fulfillment.

While nonprofit leaders are clearly interested in the capacity of their organizations, they are not the only stakeholders who deem such understanding important. A recent trend in philanthropy approaches philanthropic giving as an investment in the sustainability of an organization. This trend is known as *venture philanthropy.* Venture philanthropists may come in the form of individuals or foundations. Individual venture philanthropists, such as Bill Gates and Michael Dell, consider the overall capacity of the organization to achieve its mission the most critical decision factor in whether or not to invest in the mission of an organization. They not only conduct extensive due diligence to select the destination of investments, they also make investments that support capacity—not just programs. An example of an established foundation practicing this relatively new form of *philanthrocapitalism* is the Edna McConnell Clark Foundation. "In 1999, more than 30 years after its creation, the foundation began to focus its grants on increasing the capacity of a select group of organizations that proved they could deliver measurable improvements in the lives of low-income youths" (Kaplan & Grossman, 2010, p. 114).

This form of philanthropy emphasizes outcome, or *social return,* thus increasing the importance on nonprofit performance measurement such as the balanced score card and other tools adopted from the for-profit sector. Chapter 5 discusses performance measurement, which is an element of capacity evaluation. The full development of a capacity audit/assessment is beyond the scope of this text; however, several excellent resources are available for this important process (e.g., Kaplan & Grossman, 2010; McKinsey & Company, 2001). Additionally, Wachira (2009) offers a five-step process for conducting a capacity audit. Finally, the text by Horton et al. (2003) describes both the organizational capacity evaluation process and the reasons why managers should be concerned with organizational capacity development and its evaluation.

The latter two resources mentioned emphasize important points in the understanding of organizational capacity. First, an organization exists within an environment and is influenced by the conditions of its surroundings, including the political, economic, social, technological, and legal situation. The degree of embeddedness of the organization in its environment affects its capacity. Second, an organization with well-developed networks encounters stronger linkages between the micro (internal) and macro (external) environments, which positively influence capacity. This text covers the measurement of external environmental factors in several chapters (1, 3, 6, and 13); below we focus on the development of strong networks.

NETWORKS AND MERGERS

At several points in this text, we mention the proliferation of NPOs and the strain on both internal and external resources. The growth in the number of organizations begs two crucial questions: How, if at all, do these organizations work together to solve societal issues? Are there too many organizations—meaning, is there duplication of mission and poor use of societal resources? The first question can be answered by investigating the existence and effectiveness of NPO networks. The second question concerns the potential need for organizations to merge as they seek to resolve the pressures of increasing demand with decreasing resources.

Networks, whether formal or informal, have the potential to enhance the external impact of an organization. The term *network* is used here to encapsulate a broad spectrum of relationships between and among nonprofits. Such relationships may be (1) short-term collaborations on specific programs or actions to overcome severe environmental disaster or deeper and/or (2) long-term alliances through which resources are shared. Worth (2012) enumerates the different types of collaboration, their drivers, and the general advantages of each. Here we are concerned with how nonprofit networks can enhance organizational capacity.

Crutchfield and McLeod Grant (2008) investigate how networks that operate with "open source" strategies share blueprints for success that allow replication and enhancement of capacity for individual organizations and the nonprofit sector as a whole. This type of philosophy is found in Ashoka (www.ashoka.org), a nonprofit who gives funding to organizations with the potential to scale their ideas and the willingness to share methodologies so others may implement the same concepts in different locales (Bornstein & Davis, 2010). Such collaboration is possible when nonprofits focus on societal change and mission impact rather than protection of viewpoints or "turf." Research with nonprofits has revealed that high-impact institutions "work with and through other organizations—and they have much more impact than if they acted alone" (Crutchfield & McLeod Grant, 2008, p. 108).

How does an organization shift from self-focus to systemwide emphasis, or *network orientation?* As with personal change, it's a matter of attitude. The organization must shift from an attitude of competition to collaboration, its strategy should move beyond growth of the self (organization) to growth of the other (field or subsector), and its organizational structure is more likely to be decentralized than centralized. Similarly, a network-oriented NPO will engage in some, possibly all, of the following behaviors:

1. Grow funding base for all in the sector through collaborative efforts.

2. Share knowledge with other leaders and organizations.

3. Build, promote, and disperse leadership—knowing when to lead and when to follow.

4. Develop a long-term orientation (versus a programmatic one).

5. Act collectively—in activities and lobbying efforts.

6. Share credit and power. (Crutchfield & McLeod Grant, 2008)

Networks are an increasingly popular way of leveraging money and experience for foundations as well. Due in part to the new approaches practiced by philanthrocapitalists and venture philanthropists, networks of foundations are coming together to improve impact and social return on investments. For example, Peggy Rockefeller Dulany's Global Philanthropists Circle gathers approximately 50 super-rich families from 20 countries to exchange ideas and experiences, with an emphasis on finding solutions to international poverty and inequality. These interactions generally involve the use of connections and influence as well as money ("The Birth of Philanthrocapitalism," 2006).

Whether through sharing of knowledge and power in a network, in response to internal constraints, or because of external realities, some organizations may find their sustainability questionable. In such situations, mergers may serve the purpose of continuing momentum toward societal change.

A merger is "a combining of two or more organizations that includes a change in legal control" (Worth, 2012, p. 214). While the phenomenon is easy to describe, it is hard to implement—as discovered by Brenda Hall in the Western Area Youth case from this chapter. Though the motivations for mergers are many, the process of deciding to merge, and with whom, should be as systematic as any other strategic endeavor the organization initiates. In going about the merger, NPO leaders should make a list of *what they hope to accomplish* with the merger (i.e., its impact) and develop a matrix to compare various alternatives (i.e., potential organizations with whom to merge and/or status quo) for each desired outcome. To identify possible partners, consider organizational culture as well as financial, service, and management capabilities.

What makes a merger successful? Worth (2012) suggests the primary factor for effective mergers is when the motivation is more about mission than financial welfare. Other conditions needed for success include leadership support (i.e., the board and CEO); a deliberate process; trust among all stakeholders; and relatedness in mission, client base, organizational structure, and geography.

Looking back on this chapter, we see a convergence of tools and approaches to build organizational aptitude and nonprofit sector performance. From conducting an organizational capacity audit, to connecting capabilities across organizations through networking and mergers, to assessing alternative ways of supporting NPO initiatives through venture philanthropy, the focus is on improving social return through mission accomplishment. Moving forward in the text is the discussion of talents and assets to achieve this focus and improve likelihood of mission attainment.

On a final note, networks can be domestic or international. The YMCA of Southwestern Ontario (based in London, Ontario, Canada) belongs to a loose federation of 53 YMCAs across Canada (45 YMCAs and 8 YMCAs/YWCAs). This loose federation is working on issues such as less expensive insurance by approaching suppliers as a federation instead of as individual organizations. Another organization, Compassion Canada, is one of 11 country organizations that belong to an international network called Compassion International, which is headquartered in Colorado Springs, Colorado. The leaders of each country meet regularly to share best practices in order to help each other build capacity. This Compassion network "serves more than 1.2 million impoverished children through the caring support of strong partner networks with central offices in the following countries: Australia, Canada, Deutschland, France, Ireland, Italy, Netherlands, New Zealand, South Korea, Spain, Switzerland, [and the] United Kingdom" (Compassion International, 2000, 2002–2011).

CASES

Western Area Youth Services (Canada): is a children's mental health center and nonprofit organization. Recently, the board of directors spent a great deal of time discussing the implications of a significant potential liability for staff salaries. A merger was identified as a possible solution, and the executive director of the center, Brenda Hall, was instructed by the board to begin the process of seeking a possible merger partner for the agency. She wonders how she might initiate the process on behalf of the board and what she should look for in a potential partner. She also wonders how a merger might benefit the agency at this point in time.

Rollins College Philanthropy and Nonprofit Leadership Center (United States): an organization charged with serving as a resource for development of nonprofit capacity in the greater Orlando, Florida, area, finds distinctive ways to offer networking opportunities for local NPO leaders. Originally responding to the immediate needs from a natural disaster, Margaret Linnane, the center's executive director, discovered the power of bringing leaders together to discuss organizations' current operations and needs. From this initial short-term answer to a crisis, Linnane developed several methods for improving networking. She now wonders how to measure the effectiveness of the different activities in terms of both the center's objectives and the needs of the participating NPOs.

REFERENCES

Bernholz, L. (2008, February 6). Notes on nonprofit networks [Web log post]. Retrieved from http://philanthropy.blogspot.com/2008/02/notes-on-nonprofit-networks.html

The birth of philanthrocapitalism. (2006, February 23). *The Economist.*

Bornstein, D., & Davis, S. (2010). *Social entrepreneurship: What everyone needs to know.* New York, NY: Oxford University Press.

Compassion International. (2000, 2002–2011). Global partner offices. Retrieved from http://www.compassion.com/about/Offices.htm

Crutchfield, L. R., & McLeod Grant, H. (2008). *Forces for good: The six practices of high-impact nonprofits.* San Francisco, CA: Jossey-Bass.

Horton, D., Alexaki, A., Bennett-Lartey, S., Crice, K. N., Campilan, D., Carden, F., et al. (2003). *Evaluating capacity development: Experiences from research and development organizations around the world.* The Hague, Netherlands: International Service for National Agricultural Research; Ottowa, Ontario, Canada: International Development Research Centre; The Hague, Netherlands: ACP-EU Technical Centre for Agricultural and Rural Cooperation.

Kaplan, R. S., & Grossman, A. S. (2010, October). The emerging capital market for nonprofits. *Harvard Business Review,* 111–118.

McKinsey & Company. (2001). *Effective capacity building in nonprofit organizations.* Washington, DC: Venture Philanthropy Partners.

Peters, T. J., & Waterman, R. H. (1982). *In search of excellence.* New York, NY: Harper & Row.

Wachira, E. (2009). *Organizational capacity audit tool.* Nairobi, Kenya: Global e-Schools and Communities Initiative.

Worth, M. J. (2012). *Nonprofit management: Principles and practice* (2nd ed.). Thousand Oaks, CA: Sage.

WESTERN AREA YOUTH SERVICES

Brenda Hall, executive director of Western Area Youth Services (WAYS), sat in her office pondering the case of "déjà vu" she was experiencing. At its September 2000 meeting, the board of directors spent a great deal of time discussing the implications of a significant potential liability for staff salaries. A merger was identified as a possible solution, and Hall was instructed by the board to begin the process of seeking a possible merger partner for the agency. It didn't seem that long ago that Hall had been through the merger that had created WAYS, a children's mental health centre located in London, Ontario. Hall wondered how she might initiate the process on behalf of her board and what she should be looking for in a potential partner. She also wondered how a merger might benefit the agency at this point in time.

THE CMHO AND THE STATE OF CHILDREN'S MENTAL HEALTH

The Children's Mental Health Organization (CMHO) was established in 1972 as a member organization to promote the mental health and well-being of children and youth and their families in Ontario. Its member organizations served children and youth from birth to age 18. The organization's primary goals were to promote service excellence and innovation in its member organizations through accreditation and to advocate for policies, programs and funds to improve the state of children's mental health. According to CMHO, about 500,000 children in Ontario, about 18 per cent of Ontario's children, had psychiatric disorders in 1999. Its 90 member organizations served over 120,000 children with extremely high levels of emotional disorder. Another 7,000 children were on waiting lists for services, with an average wait time of six months. The average annual cost of service in a children's mental health centre was Cdn$2,500 per child. In the 1995–2000 time period, government funding to children's mental health centres was cut by eight per cent while the number of children served increased by 75 per cent. At the same time, children's mental health issues became more extreme; for example, the rate of youth suicide increased 400 per cent from the 1970s. CMHO believed that the treatment programs of its member organizations worked. Data collected by the organization between April 1991 and June 1995 showed that treatment in children's mental health centres was associated with a reduction in aggression, violence, opposition to authority and hyperactivity; a reduction in severe anxiety, worry, depression and low self-esteem; and a reduction in poor social relations, both at home and at school. According to CMHO, Ontario's future depended on its government making children's mental health a priority, through both its policies and its funding decisions.

Formation of WAYS

WAYS was formed in July 1996 as a result of the amalgamation of three agencies—Belton House, Hardy Geddes House and Mission Services of London's Teen Girl's Home. WAYS was incorporated under the Canada Corporations Act as a not-for-profit organization and was a registered charity under the Canadian Income Tax Act. It was also a member of CMHO. Brenda Hall was the executive director of Belton House at the time of the amalgamation, and she recalled that

the process of merging the three agencies was a difficult and, at times, acrimonious process for board members and staff alike. In July 1995, the chairperson of each agency's board of directors received a letter from their primary funder, the Ontario Ministry of Community and Social Services (MCSS), notifying them that as a result of recent community planning, it was MCSS's intent to be "working with one administrative structure for the services" provided by their agencies before the end of the next fiscal year, March 31, 1996. Hall recalled the frustration felt by her board members at the ambiguity of the direction and MCSS's unwillingness to provide any further direction other than its intent to reduce the budgets of each of the three agencies by 10 to 15 per cent for the next fiscal year. Shortly after receiving the letter, the three agencies, each represented by the executive director, the board chairperson and one other board member, began meeting on a weekly basis to plan. The chairperson of the meeting was rotated weekly from among the executive directors of the three agencies. It quickly became clear that each board had a different interpretation of the funder's direction. One agency believed that MCSS was looking for a more collaborative effort but separate agencies. Another agency believed that MCSS was looking for a new administrative agency overseeing the existing three agencies. The third agency believed that MCSS was looking for a complete merger of the existing agencies. What became even clearer, however, was the significant amount of difference in the three organization's cultures and philosophies.

Belton House, Hardy Geddes House and Mission Services of London's Teen Girl's Home program were all established in the early 1970s, with their main purpose to provide residential services to adolescents in the community. Each agency was managed by an executive director who reported to a volunteer board of directors. Belton House provided services to young women aged 12 through 18. Its programs were strictly voluntary, and the agency was highly regarded in the community for its innovativeness and willingness to work with other community service providers. Hardy Geddes House provided services to young men aged 12 through 18. Its programs were also strictly voluntary but were often seen in the community as rather selective. Mission Services of London was a large social service agency in London with a Christian focus that pervaded its mission statement, philosophies and operations. Teen Girl's Home was only one of Mission Service's many, varied programs. Teen Girl's Home provided services to young women as well but focused primarily on a younger age group than did Belton House. Its programs were similar to Belton House but were carried out with a Christian influence. Other programs run by Mission Services included shelters for homeless men and women, addiction support programs and a second-hand clothing store.

The months of July and August 1995 were marked with little progress and significant tension for the committee. Heated debates took place in the group over the necessity of and funding for a facilitator. One group announced its wish to "take over" the other two agencies. The individual boards refused to fund any expenditures relating to the efforts of the committee. Finally, a facilitator was agreed upon, and Dr. William Avison, a well-known and highly respected expert in children's services, was hired with Cdn$10,000 in funding provided by MCSS. Dr. Avison's strategy was to focus the group on the selection of an administrative structure, and he suggested five possibilities, including: maintaining the status quo; absorption by a fourth, outside agency; merging two of the agencies into the third; amalgamating the three agencies to form a new agency; and forming a consortium for administrative purposes only, while maintaining separate programs and boards. The committee members quickly eliminated the first two possibilities as unacceptable to their funder and to the group, respectively. Left with three options, each agency selected a different one as most acceptable. Once again,

heated debate, negotiations and side deals took place as Dr. Avison attempted to move the group towards a common choice. Eventually, two of the agencies teamed up and supported the consortium model. The third agency, which was in favor of the amalgamation model, was thereby "out-voted" and in October 1995, the agencies reluctantly presented a signed letter of agreement to MCSS indicating their willingness to move towards a consortium arrangement for administrative services. Two months later MCSS formally responded to the agencies and indicated that the consortium model was not acceptable and that the three agencies were to be fully amalgamated by the summer of 1996. If the boards did not choose to amalgamate, the services provided by the agencies would be tendered out to other community agencies. The boards were given two weeks to consider MCSS's directive, and on December 31, 1995, each board responded in the affirmative and agreed to proceed with an amalgamation.

Once again a committee was struck, the amalgamation steering committee. Two board representatives from each agency were selected, as well as two independent community representatives. MCSS assigned one of its program supervisors to the committee as well as provided funding for a facilitator. This time, executive directors were not included on the committee, as the first tasks handled by the committee involved the selection of an executive director for the amalgamated agency and the consideration of potential severance liabilities for the unsuccessful candidates. After much heated deliberation and community input, Hall, the executive director of Belton House, was chosen to manage the new agency. A new agency name was selected following an employee contest. New corporate bylaws were agreed to, stipulating that the new board would consist of two members from each of the existing agencies and six members chosen from the community. By June 1996, the Public Trustee of Ontario had issued its consent to the amalgamation, and on July 16, 1996, the first board meeting of Western Area Youth Services took place. Hall began the onerous task of integrating three very distinct cultures, employee groups and board members into one agency.

WAYS

In keeping with its mission statement, WAYS provided residential programs and community services to adolescents and their families in London and the surrounding communities. Though the mental health services provided by WAYS were governed by The Child and Family Services Act (CFSA), they were not considered mandated services and, as a result, were subject to more volatile government (i.e., MCSS) funding. As well, historically, funding for adolescents was viewed by MCSS as less crucial than funding for young children. The primary residential program at WAYS comprised 26 beds in three London locations for male and female adolescents between the ages of 14 and 18. The goal of this program was to provide safe, supported and structured 24-hour residence living. Counselling in this program focused on life skills, social skills and job training. Only a limited amount of psychiatric counselling was provided to youths due to funding constraints. WAYS also had two four-bed transition homes for youths between the ages of 16 and 24. The transition program's goal was to provide a semi-structured living experience for youth and to assist them in developing skills necessary to live successfully and independently in the community. The program focused on the teaching of social skills, coping skills, life skills and employment-related skills. Finally, the most recent addition to WAYS residential programs was the provision of an eight-bed, fee-for-service program for males aged 12 to 16 under the care of the Children's Aid Society (CAS). These beds were specifically contracted with and paid for by CAS as a result of recent expansions in the number of children requiring care from CAS. This program's goals were similar to those of the WAYS primary residential program. WAYS community programs focused on prevention by working with youth and their families before, during and after residence. Through its community programs, WAYS assisted youth in accessing other community programs, transitioning to new living environments and improving life skills. Services included therapeutic groups, individual counselling, an after-care program and a follow-up program.

Hall recognized that although adolescents voluntarily entered WAYS programs, they were a very difficult and demanding group to work with. Although WAYS did not receive any funding under the Young Offenders Act, 50 per cent of the residents at WAYS were convicted young offenders and were part of the WAYS programs as a result of a legal "order to reside" or a requirement of their probation. Typical WAYS residents had many of the following characteristics: emotional and relationship problems in the home, community and school; oppositional or defiant; aggressive and destructive; problems with depression; witness of violence in their home; alcohol or drug abuse; psychotropic medication user; underachiever at school; diagnosed learning problems.

WAYS was governed by a community-based volunteer board consisting of 12 directors, some of whom were founding members from the predecessor agencies. Like many volunteer agencies, WAYS often had difficulty filling the available board positions with qualified, dedicated individuals. The day-to-day affairs of the organization were managed by Hall and approximately 85 staff members, 30 of whom were full-time employees. Hall was well respected in the community and by her staff. She was active in several community planning committees and was viewed as an excellent manager. The majority of the staff were college-educated child and youth-care workers (CYCW). Staff-to-client ratios were dictated by government legislation, leaving WAYS with very little flexibility in its spending on wages. The staff group was not unionized and was compensated at a level comparative to other non-union social service organizations in the area. Hall believed that the staff group had very little interest in becoming unionized at this point. Staff safety and burnout were key issues due to the intense needs of the adolescents served. The management group was relatively small and consisted of two program managers and an administrative officer, all of whom had worked at the agency for several years. Due to the small size of the agency, there was little opportunity for promotion or staff development within the agency. In addition to the board, WAYS had a well-established fundraising committee, which competed with other social service agencies in the community for donors and their dollars. WAYS recently established a charitable foundation to concentrate on fundraising activities; however, the foundation was not very active. Select financial and client statistics for WAYS are presented in Exhibit 1.

MERGER THOUGHTS AT WAYS

Hall's thoughts returned to the recent board meeting and the discussion of the potential salary liability. The Pay Equity Act was made law in Ontario on January 1, 1988, to narrow the wage gap that existed between the relative wages earned by women and men. In Ontario, female workers received, on average, 26 per cent less in wages than male workers did. This law intended to address this inequity and to ensure equal pay for work of equal or comparable value. The law required, among other things, comparing the value of jobs traditionally done by women to the value of different jobs traditionally done by men. It then required that compensation (i.e., wages and benefits) be at least the same for jobs performed mainly by women that were equal or comparable in value to jobs performed mainly by men, even if the jobs were quite different.

This legislation had a tremendous impact on the salaries of primarily female organizations such as Belton House, one of the amalgamating agencies in WAYS. Belton House's board was forced to approve a pay equity plan that resulted in its employees being paid at rates comparable to those paid by a sizable, unionized London-area hospital. On amalgamation, WAYS not only

Exhibit 1   Western Area Youth Services Select Financial and Client Statistics

Financial Highlights	2001	2000
Revenues	$2,751,717	$2,705,602
Wages and benefits	1,959,783	1,886,378
Other expenditures	722,244	699,901
Surplus	69,690	119,323
Total Assets	764,730	1,368,049
Sources of Revenues		
MCSS	$1,819,383	$1,805,221
CAS	670,609	574,364
Donations/fundraising	40,760	52,734
Other	220,965	173,283
Client Statistics		
Total no. of children served—all programs	351	385
No. of children in intensive residential programs	67	81
No. of children in family preservation programs (Community Programs)	247	233
No. of children in day treatment programs (Transitional Housing Program)	37	38
No. of children on waiting list for Intensive Residential	39	32

inherited the Belton House pay equity plan but, in order to ensure equitable salaries across the organization, was forced to extend the plan to the entire agency. Although government funding was originally provided to agencies such as WAYS to cover the increased salary expenditures, by 1995, this funding was discontinued, putting agencies such as WAYS in a conundrum. Though WAYS was legally required to enact pay equity, it was not provided with the funding to cover the added expense. As a result, the WAYS board estimated that the organization's unfunded liability for pay equity–related salaries would grow over the next 10 years to almost Cdn$1 million—an amount that would surely bankrupt the agency. WAYS' problem was not an exclusive one. Several government-funded social service agencies were in very similar positions and were struggling with how to fund the liability. Different strategies developed. Some agencies chose to ignore pay equity entirely on the premise that the government was essentially ignoring it by refusing to fund it. Other agencies were funding their pay equity liability through their operating budgets, resulting in decreased service provided to the community.

At WAYS, an ad hoc planning committee was struck by the board to address its long-term strategic plan, including the financial issues the agency faced due to pay equity. The committee identified a merger or amalgamation as appealing for two reasons. First, the committee believed that by becoming a larger agency through merger, WAYS would have a stronger political position for advocacy and future negotiations with MCSS. Second, the committee hoped that by merging with a larger agency with higher existing pay scales, the WAYS pay equity plan could be abandoned. However, the committee recognized that this would not be easy to do and would require the agreement of the potential merger partner's union. In considering a merger, the committee believed that there were two possibilities— traditional and non-traditional. A traditional merger was one with an agency that provided similar services to those of WAYS and had similar funding sources. A non-traditional merger was one with an agency that operated in an entirely different business and, as a result, had different funding sources. The committee turned to Hall to more fully develop the pros and cons of a merger and to identify potential partners, both traditional and non-traditional.

Potential Partners

Hall first turned to the task of potential merger partners. Having spent her career working in children's mental health in the London area, Hall was well aware of the other agencies in the area and their executive directors and the culture in which they operated their agency. She made a summary list for the board of what she believed would be viable partners. Included in Hall's list were Madame Vanier Children's Services, The Children's Aid Society of London and Middlesex, The Memorial Boys and Girls Club of London, Anago Resources and Community Homes.

Madame Vanier Children's Services

Madame Vanier Children's Services (Vanier's) received its charter as a children's mental health centre in 1965 and was the first centre to be licensed in 1968 under the Children's Mental Health Act. The centre was a leader in children's services in Ontario and was accredited by CMHO. Similar to WAYS, the majority of Vanier's funding came from MCSS. Vanier's, operating under the guidance of its mission statement, promoted the emotional and social health of children and their families; provided effective help for complex emotional and behavioral problems; and built on child, family and community strengths. Vanier's offered a full range of programs to children from birth to 16 years of age and their families living in the London area (and the surrounding area for residential services). In September 1999, Vanier's reorganized its system of care in response to an MCSS direction. As a result of this reorganization, more of the agency's resources were focused around fewer, higher-needs children. While all children were seen immediately by the agency, those children not considered high risk were diverted to other community agencies.

The agency's services included community-based assessments, counselling and treatment for children and families, early intervention programs for children of pre-school to kindergarten age, short- and long-term residential programs and day programs, both at Vanier's and in community schools. Treatment programs included family therapy, parent counselling, individual art and play therapy, group programs and individual counselling. Vanier's had 17 residential treatment beds and seven day treatment classrooms. In many cases, clients of Vanier's were serviced in their later years by WAYS. Vanier's had a long history of community collaboration and was involved in several joint programs with WAYS, including staff training and client intake and crisis services. Similar to WAYS, Vanier's operated a six-bed, fee-for-service program under contract with CAS.

Vanier's was governed by a 12-member community board and an executive director, Dr. Barrie Evans, and had approximately 90 multidisciplinary staff, composed of child and youth workers, social workers, psychologists, psychiatrists and other professional and support staff. Dr. Evans was particularly well known in the province for his work in advocating for children's mental health and was active in the community as well as with the provincial association, the CMHO. The majority of the staff members were part of the Ontario Public Service Employee Union (OPSEU). Many of Vanier's relief staff were also relief staff at WAYS. Selected financial and client statistics are summarized in Exhibit 2. Hall was very familiar with Vanier's, having worked at Vanier's herself in her early career, and she knew that the idea of amalgamation was quite appealing to Dr. Evans. However, Hall felt certain that Vanier's board would view a combination of the two agencies as a takeover rather

Exhibit 2 Madame Vanier Children's Services Select Financial and Client Statistics

Financial Highlights	2001	2000
Revenues	$4,655,000	$3,959,000
Wages and benefits	3,872,000	3,346,000
Other expenditures	774,000	576,000
Surplus	9,000	37,000
Total Assets	1,781,000	1,626,000
Sources of Revenues		
MCSS	$3,577,000	$3,387,000
CAS	591,000	429,000
Donations/fundraising	39,000	15,000
Other	448,000	128,000
Client Statistics		
Total no. of children served—all programs	541	1,273
No. of children in residential programs	98	78
No. of children in family preservation programs	102	84
No. of children in day treatment programs	121	97

than a merger, and wondered whether this would be acceptable to her board. Hall was also unsure of what her position would be in a combined Vanier/WAYS agency.

The Children's Aid Society of London and Middlesex

The Children's Aid Society of London and Middlesex was formed in 1893 and was a member of the Ontario Association of Children's Aid Societies (OACAS). CAS, under the direction of its executive director, John Liston, had a wide variety of programs, including the investigation of allegations of child abuse or neglect; provision of temporary and long-term care through foster homes, group homes and institutions; residential programs; individual and family counselling; family supervision; and adoption. Approximately 95 per cent of the programs offered by CAS were considered mandated programs under the CFSA. For example, child protective services were mandated by the Act and were required by law to be provided at all times; however, certain counselling programs were not mandated under the act. Similar to WAYS, CAS received the majority of its funding from MCSS. Mandated services were perceived to have more secure funding (see Exhibit 3). Significant financial pressure due to increased caseloads had recently caused CAS to review its balance of mandated and non-mandated services. CAS estimated that there was a 42 per cent increase in admissions over the 1995–2000 period. It was also estimated that 58 per cent of CAS admissions were children under the age of 13 and that these children had greater needs than ever before. Eighty-two per cent of Crown wards (i.e., children the courts have removed from parental custody) had an external diagnosis of special needs; 92 per cent of the children in care were victims of maltreatment such as sexual, physical or emotional abuse or neglect. As a result of increasing caseloads and decreasing resources, CAS was forced to look to outside agencies for additional services. In the year 2000, CAS estimated a 76 per cent increase in the number of children in outside, contracted

foster or group homes. WAYS already operated one such contracted group home for adolescent males and was in negotiations with CAS to contract a second group home, this one for adolescent females. CAS was also in the process of contracting out a group home for younger children requiring highly structured care as well as a 12- to 16-bed receiving home for emergency placements. In total, CAS estimated that it contracted 140 beds with outside providers. While Hall understood the pressures that had led CAS to look for contracted group home beds, she also recalled that the same community planning that recommended the merger of smaller agencies such as Belton House had also recommended that CAS discontinue its direct provision of group home services. Hall was also certain that it was less expensive for CAS to purchase rather than provide group home beds from agencies such as WAYS, given the unionized wage rates of CAS. She also knew that CAS offices across Ontario were being pressured to reduce the number of children in group homes and increase the number of children in foster care. They were also being pressured to focus more fully on their basic mandated services, such as child protection and investigation. Hall knew that the board would expect her to consider CAS as a potential merger partner and that there were benefits to WAYS merging with a powerful community agency like the CAS. She also understood that there would be some significant benefits to CAS of an amalgamation and the opportunity to more fully combine child treatment services like WAYS' with CAS's own child welfare services. However, Hall was concerned about the long-term implications of combining WAYS non-mandated services with CAS services and CAS's future ability to provide both types of services.

The Memorial Boys and Girls Club of London

The Memorial Boys and Girls Club of London was part of a national organization, Boys and Girls Clubs of Canada, which was founded more than 100 years ago. The national organization had

Exhibit 3 The Children's Aid Society of London and Middlesex Select Financial and Client Statistics

Financial Highlights	2001	2000
Revenues	$35,446,032	$28,492,077
Wages and benefits	13,494,503	11,200,533
Other expenditures	21,884,545	16,943,645
Surplus/deficit	66,984	347,899
Total Assets	9,471,900	10,401,275
Sources of Revenues		
MCSS	$33,642,813	$27,332,691
Other	1,800,219	1,159,386
Client Statistics		
Total no. of children served—all programs	4,080	3,026

over 100 clubs located in over 150 communities across Canada and served more than 130,000 children and youth. The Clubs boasted safe and caring environments and stimulating programs based on their board's four "cornerstones of healthy development": personal growth and empowerment; learning; community service; and health and safety. Programs such as group homes and emergency shelters, family and parent support and youth-at-risk support were part of the community service tenet of the national organization. Substance abuse programs, suicide prevention and street-proofing were part of the health and safety tenet. Clubs across Canada varied greatly in the types of services provided, and Hall believed that the London-based club did not provide any group home programs and focused on services for children and youth from lower-income families. Boys and Girls Clubs received some funding from governmental agencies such as Health Canada; however, they relied heavily on donations from the United Way, individuals and corporations for survival. The staff at the Boys and Girls Club was not unionized.

Although the board's planning committee had identified the Boys and Girls Club of London as a very attractive potential merger partner, Hall had some concerns about an amalgamation with this agency. In response to her request for information,

the executive director, Donald Donner, referred Hall to the national organization's website and was unwilling to provide any specific financial or program information for the London-based club. Donner also hinted at his concerns about the stigma attached to children's mental health programs and the effect on his agency's existing programs. He was concerned that his current clientele and funders would discontinue their support of the agency if they believed that the programs were directed to youth with mental health issues. Finally, he indicated that though he would not support an amalgamation with WAYS, he would support the takeover of WAYS and some other children's mental health centres in the community by his agency.

Anago Resources and Community Homes

Hall thought that Anago Resources and Community Homes might also be viable merger partners. Anago Resources provided "closed custody" group homes for youth under the age of 16 while Community Homes provided "open custody" group homes for youth of the same age. Closed custody beds were used by youth who had been charged with a criminal offence and needed to be detained but who had not yet been through the court system. Closed custody beds were also used by youths under 16 who had been convicted of a criminal offence and ordered by the court to a closed custody facility. In contrast, open custody beds were used by youth under 16 who had been convicted of a criminal offence and ordered by the courts to an open custody facility. Unlike jail and closed custody facilities, residents in open custody facilities could receive temporary passes to leave the residence. Anago Resources and Community Homes services were provided under contract with MCSS and were funded under the Young Offenders Act. Anago Resources also provided residential services to developmentally challenged youth. Similar to WAYS, Community Homes had recently contracted with CAS to provide an eight-bed receiving home to be used for emergency placements by CAS and 12 foster care beds. Hall was certain that both Anago Resources and Community Homes would not be willing to amalgamate with WAYS but would be willing to take over the services provided by WAYS.

Hall's Task

Hall turned to the task of assessing the pros and cons of an amalgamation. She frequently followed the financial news and understood that for-profit companies often merged in order to reduce administration spending and gain market share through reduced competition and to reduce administrative spending, but Hall wasn't sure whether these concepts applied in the non-profit sector as well. Certainly the previous amalgamation that she had been through had reduced competition, but Hall wasn't convinced that reduced competition was necessarily a good result for the community. The previous amalgamation had also reduced administrative spending somewhat, but Hall recognized that administrative expenses in small social service agencies were already quite limited and that significant savings were unlikely.

Conclusion

She was certain that other benefits would result from amalgamating and she wanted to compile them before meeting with the board. Furthermore, Hall looked at the list of potential partners and wondered which organization would be best suited for a merger with WAYS. She needed to study each option in detail, considering the potential advantages and disadvantages of each possibility.

ROLLINS COLLEGE PHILANTHROPY AND NONPROFIT LEADERSHIP CENTER: THE IMPORTANCE OF NETWORKING

Introduction

Margaret Linnane was distraught and dumbfounded. In addition, she was fuming. She had just arrived home from the funders' meeting where she had been asked questions that came close to challenging the very purpose of her nonprofit organization. She had been unprepared for the very tough questions the funders had asked and she knew she would need to be much better prepared for the next specially scheduled meeting in one month. She needed answers to the funders' questions and she wondered how to achieve these answers in four short weeks.

Linnane and the Rollins College Philanthropy and Nonprofit Leadership Center (PNLC,

---

Mary Conway Dato-on and Margaret Linnane wrote this case solely to provide material for class discussion. The authors do not intend to illustrate either effective or ineffective handling of a managerial situation. The authors may have disguised certain names and other identifying information to protect confidentiality.

or the Center) staff put other efforts on hold while they worked intensely to prepare for the upcoming meeting. They gathered all the documents on the PNLC's mission, vision and strategic plan. Brainstorming started. What information did they need to compile to convince the funders that the PNLC's services, such as networking among established chief executive officers (CEOs) and foundation directors and introducing newcomers to the nonprofit community, contributed to the professionalization of nonprofit leaders and organizations while addressing critical community issues and fulfilling the PNLC's mission—even if such services had not yet generated any revenue? What outcome measures were appropriate for assessing the success of non-income-generating activities such as networking? To start the search for answers to such questions (and others), Linnane decided to review the PNLC's performance from the last two years and to build a strategy for 2011–12. Time was of the essence because without the support of funders, Linnane and the PNLC would be hard-pressed to continue offering the now well-accepted networking activities.

BACKGROUND: PNLC

The Philanthropy and Nonprofit Leadership Center (PNLC) was established in 1999 as a program of Rollins College Crummer Graduate School of Business (Rollins). Founded in 1885, on the beautiful lakeside campus in Winter Park, Florida, Rollins had earned a national reputation for academic excellence at both the graduate and undergraduate levels. The PNLC's certificate programs for nonprofit managers, staff and volunteers and its courses in board development and

nonprofit governance had been offered throughout the years on Rollins's picturesque campus. In the 2009–10 academic year, the Center had offered 117 workshops and events to 3,129 attendees. Linnane proudly announced an increase in both the number of programs (up seven per cent) and attendees (up 5.5 per cent) in the 2010–11 program year (see Exhibit 1). As of May 31, 2011 (i.e. at the close of fiscal year), the PNLC had 334 nonprofit members (up 11 per cent from 2010). All programs were designed to support the mission, vision and values of PNLC and Rollins:

Mission: To strengthen the impact, effectiveness and leadership of nonprofit and philanthropic organizations through education and management assistance.

Vision: We envision a vibrant nonprofit sector that is valued by the community for its innovation, leadership and integral role in determining quality of life.

The PNLC team developed the following goals and values to focus their work and enhance mission accomplishment.

Goals

1. Engage the community in philanthropy
2. Improve the nonprofit sector by strengthening board governance
3. Enhance the business practices of nonprofit organizations
4. Expand the influence of the nonprofit sector
5. Secure the long-term sustainability of the Philanthropy Center

In addition to the guiding principles of Rollins College—excellence, innovation and

Exhibit 1 The Philanthropy and Nonprofit Leadership Center Accomplishments, June 1, 2009, to May 31, 2010, and June 1, 2010, to May 31, 2011

Membership

- May 31, 2010: 300 new and renewing members
- May 31, 2011: 334 new and renewing members

Workshops and Training

- 2010: Conducted 117 workshops with 3,129 attendees
- 2011: Conducted 125 workshops with 3,296 attendees—11 new programs added

Certificates Awarded

Certificate	2010	2011
Proposal Writing	36	34
Nonprofit Management	8	13
Volunteer Management	47	34
Philanthropic Fundraising and Development	10	10
Leadership Practice	23	26

Community Presentations: Staff provided more than 10 unique presentations annually for both the nonprofit and for-profit communities, including the following:

- Hosted 20 DonorEdge presentations
- United Way of Brevard Nonprofit Summit
- National Board Source Leadership Forum
- University of Central Florida (UCF) Nonprofit Conference
- Florida Philanthropic Network Summit
- Walt Disney World and Darden Restaurants Donors Forum Presentation

Contract Work: Staff provided 21 events in 2010 and 18 in 2011, including the following:

- United Way of Brevard, Melbourne (fundraising)
- Florida Student Association (mission statement)
- Leadership Orlando (board governance)
- Reinhold Foundation, Orange Park (board governance fundraising/volunteer management)
- Sea World Orlando (board governance)
- Florida Fund for Minority Teachers (board governance)
- Meridian Behavioral Healthcare (board governance)
- St. Luke's Methodist Children's Home (program evaluation)
- Rosen Hotels & Resorts (volunteer management/board governance)

Research: January through June 2011: The 2011 Nonprofit Compensation & Benefits Survey and publication of the Report

Marketing: July 2010: Completion of a new marketing plan for the Center

Executive Transition Management Focus:

- Two educational/networking events for new development directors
- Three educational/networking events for new executive directors/CEOs
- Seven educational/networking events for seasoned CEOs
- Placed 14 Rollins Early Advantage MBA students on nonprofit boards of directors

Source: Margaret Linnane, executive director PNLC, received June 10, 2011.

community—the PNLC subscribed to the following values, which were also reflected in its programs and services:

Values

1. **Generosity**: We value the spirit of giving that is the heart of philanthropy and nonprofit work.

2. **Integrity**: We value strong ethics and commit ourselves to maintaining principled and professional standards for performance, resource utilization and accountability in our work.

3. **Service**: We endeavor to ascertain and respond to our stakeholders' needs with utmost respect and personal attention.

4. **Inclusiveness**: We welcome individuals from diverse walks of life with varying competencies and experiences who strive to educate themselves and their organizations.

5. **Learning**: We strive to remain informed about current issues, trends, and best practices in the nonprofit sector and to model and encourage discovery, creativity, and reflection.

6. **Engagement**: We work collaboratively to fulfill our role in developing our community's strengths and improving the well-being of all citizens.[1]

THE CENTER'S LEADERSHIP AND ROLE IN THE COMMUNITY

Linnane had been the executive director of a nonprofit organization for 18 years before accepting, in 2004, the job as executive director of the PNLC, to work with all of the nonprofits in Central Florida (see Exhibit 2 for an annotated biography of Linnane). She remembered well what it had been like to be thrust into an executive director position with little knowledge of the sector, a complex mission to learn and fulfill, bright-eyed staff members looking to her for direction, enthusiastic volunteers showing up every day, the need to fundraise—and no one to teach her how to do it all.

When Linnane first arrived at the Center, she wanted it to be the "resource of all resources" for the surrounding nonprofit community. She wanted excellent training and consultation to be available to all of the current executive directors. She hoped also to provide mentoring and coaching. Linnane stated aloud to all who would listen that her goal was "to make the nonprofit sector in her region the strongest in the country!"

Although Rollins did not fund the Center as such, it provided training space, office space and

[1]Philanthropy & Nonprofit Leadership Center, "About Us," PNLC website www.rollins.edu/pnlc accessed June 6, 2011.

Exhibit 2 Annotated Bio for Margaret S. Linnane

Margaret Linnane is executive director of the Rollins College Philanthropy and Nonprofit Leadership Center. She has full administrative responsibility for the college's multi-purpose resource center dedicated to providing a broad range of executive education programs, workshops, seminars and services for volunteer and staff leadership of nonprofit organizations. Prior to joining the Philanthropy Center in 2004, Margaret served as executive director of the Second Harvest Food Bank of Central Florida in Orlando for 18 years. In her capacity as executive director of the food bank, Margaret had responsibility for resource development, fiscal management, board relations, strategic planning, program management, human resource administration and community relations. She serves on the Board of Trustees at Bishop Moore High School in Orlando, Florida, and the advisory boards for the University of Central Florida College of Health & Public Administration Nonprofit Management Program, and Public Allies. Margaret has an MBA from the Crummer Graduate School of Business at Rollins College. She lives in Orlando and is married with three children.

Source: PNLC records, accessed June 10, 2011.

all of the equipment and support needed to operate it, such as the utilities, phones and computers. However, Linnane was responsible for funding the operation, including the $800,000 operating budget that encompassed the salaries and benefits for eight full-time-equivalent employees, program instruction and materials and conference expenses. In addition to the operational support from the college, the Center was fortunate to have received support from several local private foundations and corporate-giving programs. In addition, the Center generated revenue from program fees, membership fees and consulting contracts (see Exhibit 3 for income and expenses for the 2010–11 program year). Both the internal and external revenue streams were critical to the ongoing accomplishment of the PNLC's mission. As such, Linnane

Exhibit 3 The Philanthropy and Nonprofit Leadership Center's Income and Expenses, 2011

Income for 11 Months ending April 30, 2011		
	Dollar Value	**Percent of Total**
Program Fees	152,372	19.7
Membership	79,350	10.3
Contracts	111,708	14.5
Grants	380,833	49.4
Other	47,304	6.1
TOTAL	771,567	100.0

Expenses for 11 Months ending April 30, 2011		
	Dollar Value	**Percent of Total**
Program Costs	127,989	20.6
Travel & Conferences	16,931	2.7
Office Expenses	31,612	5.1
Salaries & Benefits	444,281	71.6
TOTAL	620,813	100.0

Source: Margaret Linnane, executive director PNLC, received June 10, 2011.

needed to meet constituent needs for programs while also appeasing external funders

Constituents

Most of the Center's constituents came from a seven-county area of Central Florida, which extended across more than 8,200 square miles and included approximately 12,000 nonprofits. These included large and small organizations, and, true to the snapshot of the nonprofit sector at the national level, PNLC records showed approximately 2,100 (17.5 per cent) had income greater than US$100,000. Of course, PNLC's constituents included hospitals, private colleges and foundations, but, for the most part, they were small nonprofits providing services to niche groups. For example, PNLC membership in 2011 consisted of 334 organizations. In reviewing the member list, Linnane recalled having assisted in the past year, in one way or another, organizations across many sub-sectors of the nonprofit spectrum, including education, health services, culture and arts, and social services.

This review reminded Linnane that the staff and volunteers of the nonprofits the Center served varied considerably in their experience, expertise and training. This review of existing and potential clients occurred regularly among the PNLC staff and helped formulate the membership services offered. Exhibit 4 shows membership benefits and fees.

Linnane stated that changes to membership benefits were brewing in the 2011–12 plans:

> We are about to add affinity groups as a new member benefit, specifically Marketing, Technology, Human Resources, and The Seasoned CEO. The New Executive Director (ED) Roundtable and New Development Director (DD) Roundtable will continue to be open to non-members because they are strong marketing tools for us.

Services

Because of the variety in the missions and work experiences of the constituents (not to mention the incredible staff turnover experienced by many organizations during the 2007–09 financial crisis), Linnane set out to provide training that could meet everyone's needs (see Exhibit 5). For example, the Center offered 17 workshops on fundraising. "We offer A–Z in fundraising," she explained, "anything you want from setting up a development office through grant writing and major gift fundraising to planned giving—you can get it at the Center." The Center also provided extensive training in board governance, volunteer management, financial management and planning. In all, the Center offered an average of nearly 120 workshops per year. With few exceptions, the workshops were well received by an average of 26 attendees per workshop, who rated the sessions at an average rating of 4.78 out of 5 (see Exhibit 5).

Exhibit 4 Philanthropy and Nonprofit Leadership Center Membership Benefits and Fees

Why Become a Member?

PNLC members, both individual and organizational, participate in our high quality educational, training and networking programs at a significant savings. Membership fees help the Philanthropy Center to provide programs and services that strengthen and support the entire nonprofit community.

Who May Become a Member?

PNLC membership is open to individuals, nonprofit organizations, and departments of local, state or federal government. An organizational or government department membership includes benefits for all staff, volunteers and board members.

Membership Benefits: Upon enrollment in PNLC, all benefits will be available to all employees, volunteers, and board members:

- Free 30-day job postings on the Center Job Posting Board
- 10% discount on all products and services offered through Opportunity Knocks, an online job center and the nation's leading job site for nonprofit jobs
- Discounts on all Center workshops, events, and seminars
- Scholarship eligibility of up to 50% off workshop fees for all 501(c)(3) members
- Scholarship eligibility (50%) to the Crummer Management Program ("Mini-MBA")
- 20% discount off of total registration fees when registering 3 or more people for a single Philanthropy Center workshop at one time
- 20% discount off of total registration fees when 1 person registers for 3 or more Center workshops at one time
- Special discounts offered on Crummer Graduate School of Business Management & Executive Education Center select programs
- Discounted one-year subscription to the *Nonprofit Quarterly* ($39 as opposed to $49)
- Use of our conference room for small meetings (seats 12–14)
- Use of the Philanthropy Center's resource library (includes Foundation Directory Online)
- A link to your organization's website from the Philanthropy Center's website
- Invitations to exclusive events
- Discounted price on the Central Florida Nonprofit Compensation & Benefits Survey Report

Membership Categories and Fees: All listed dues are for one-year PNLC membership. Your membership will expire 1 year from the day you join or renew.

Individual Memberships $175	
Nonprofit Organizational Memberships	
Annual Budget	**Annual Membership Fee**
Less than $100,000	$125
$100,000 to $500,000	$200
$500,001 to $1,000,000	$225

Annual Budget	Annual Membership Fee
$1,000,001 to $2,000,000	$325
$2,000,001 to $3,000,000	$425
$3,000,001 to $4,000,000	$525
$4,000,001 to $5,000,000	$625
$5,000,001 to $10,000,000	$750
Over $10,000,000	$850

Large funding agencies and membership organizations that wish to join on behalf of their affiliated organizations may contact the executive director to discuss a group membership.

Government Department or Agency Memberships

Annual Budget	Annual Membership Fee
Less than $1,000,000	$200
$1,000,000 and Over	$400

Source: Philanthropy and Nonprofit Leadership Center, "Membership Information," www.rollins.edu/pnlc/membership/index. html, accessed June 6, 2011.

Exhibit 5 Workshop and Event Attendance

Date	Topic	Attendees
5/31/2007	Hurricanes, Fires, Disasters	41
9/13/2007	Funding for Capacity Building	26
5/9/2008	Time-Saving Tips for Busy Professionals	58
6/19/2008	Foundation Center Updates for Fundraising	92
7/29/2009	Social Marketing	97
10/14/2009	Diversity in Fundraising	68
1/20/2010	Tax and Legal Briefing	75
2/9/2010	Volunteers as Donors	71
3/3/2010	Women Shaping the Future of Philanthropy & Giving	73
5/21/2010	Tips for Drafting Gift Acceptance Policies	36
6/16/2010	Cause Marketing	57
8/10/2010	Tapping into the Greatest Source of Volunteers	43
8/31/2010	Raising Earned Income	85

(Continued)

Exhibit 5 (Continued)

Date	Topic	Attendees
9/29/2010	Social Media for Nonprofits	71
12/3/2010	Do-It-Yourself Market Research	26
1/14/2011	Free Technology for Nonprofits	47
3/23/2011	Philanthropy & Giving Trends for 2011	57

Leaders Series Events Attendees

Date	Topic
3/23/2011	Philanthropy and Giving Trends for 2011
1/14/2011	Free Technology for Nonprofits
12/3/2010	Do-It-Yourself Market Research
9/29/2010	Social Media for Nonprofits
8/31/2010	Raising Earned Income
8/10/2010	Tapping into the Greatest Source of Volunteers
6/16/2010	Cause Marketing
5/21/2010	Tips for Drafting Gift Acceptance Policies
3/3/2010	Women Shaping the Future of Philanthropy and Giving
2/9/2010	Volunteers as Donors
1/20/2010	Tax and Legal Briefing
10/14/2009	Diversity in Fundraising
7/29/2009	Social Marketing
6/19/2008	Foundation Center Updates for Fundraising
5/9/2008	Time-Saving Tips for Busy Professionals
9/13/2007	Funding for Capacity Building
5/31/2007	Hurricanes, Fires, Disasters

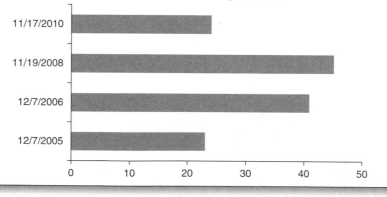

Art of Networking Attendees

Date
11/17/2010
11/19/2008
12/7/2006
12/7/2005

Source: Philanthropy and Nonprofit Leadership Center records, June 2011.

When Linnane reviewed the activities related to the "management assistance" part of the mission, she noted the Center offered consultation (some of which generated income), mentoring for new executives and coaching for those who requested it. Linnane mused:

> Mentoring and coaching, it's really what I love to do. But I'm not the oracle; other nonprofit leaders could and should be mentoring their peers. This is the thought that led me to develop more networking opportunities for my constituents at various stages of their career and organizational life cycle. Actually, I recall the specific situation that started the ball rolling. As it turned out these thoughts were moved into action by a regional disaster.

THE NEED FOR NETWORKING: HURRICANE CHARLEY

In 2004, a major hurricane blew through the central part of Florida, leaving behind serious damage. Thousands of homes and businesses had been destroyed, and services of all types were suspended. Being aware of a crisis in the community, the Center requested information from the nonprofits, asking its members, "What do you have that you could offer others?" and "What do you need?" Unlikely partnerships and business relationships were formed. Those with building damage found new locations from which to provide their services. Those that lost transportation identified partners to provide it. Some organizations shared staff for a period so that their employees were not out of work due to the effects of the hurricane.

Some of the partnerships that had developed during the crisis continued long after the organizations had recovered from the disaster. The nonprofits that provided other organizations with operational space during the crisis were pleased to retain these tenants. Those that continued to share services were saving money and were happy about their new arrangement. These types of collaborations truly changed the mindset of many organizations and nonprofit leaders. At the same time, the Center staff learned more and more about the value of connectivity. As people met each other

and learned about the missions, resources and needs of each other's organizations, services were expanded and led to greater creativity. Linnane contemplated how to continue this high level of collaboration during non-crisis times.

NETWORKING: THE FOCUS OF THINGS TO COME

One day, an experienced executive director asked Linnane to help him to make connections with some of his peers in the nonprofit community. He told her, "I don't know very many people who also run nonprofits. Some of us would certainly have a lot in common and could learn from each other. I don't have any easy way to meet them." Linnane considered what he said and saw an opportunity for the Center to play another role as the hub of networking, a place where best practices were not only taught but also shared among peers. In addition to offering an important service to nonprofit leaders, Linnane also believed attendance in classes would increase once leaders were on campus and, in general, became more familiar with the Center's offerings and quality of service.

The Center began promoting networking slowly. First, at each workshop, attendance lists were distributed so that attendees could follow up with each other post-event. During the workshops, instructors encouraged the attendees to introduce themselves to one another and to discuss their respective organizations during breaks.

Linnane and her staff then developed some events almost solely for the purpose of networking. Linnane explained, "Yes, a meal was offered, and yes, there was a brief presentation to further encourage attendance, but the primary goal was for local members of the sector to get to know one another." These sessions became known as "Leaders Series" events and were held every other month. Much to Linnane's delight, the room was filled each time, with an average attendance of approximately 50 people (see Exhibit 5). Although these series were well attended, the Center staff noticed that attendees would typically enter the room, identify a seat and pluck themselves down as if the meal was what they were there for! After some brainstorming about the reason for so little interaction among attendees, Center staff concluded that people did not really understand how to meet others in a professional setting.

On the basis of this revelation, the Center offered a workshop titled, "The Art of Networking." Beginning with the 2005 class, each time the workshop was offered, it was sold out. According to observations during the sessions and feedback after the sessions, people were not comfortable in settings dedicated to networking, and they wanted to learn how to network effectively. Workshop attendees were reminded that training was an opportunity to network and that not only the presenter but also their peers had knowledge and creative suggestions to offer. Constituents learned to be comfortable and strategic in networking settings.

As a result of the increased networking among the nonprofit community, collaborations were built. For example, a program for children with disabilities collaborated with a performing arts organization to offer children with disabilities the opportunity to act in staged performances. Another organization needing help picking up supplies for its programs worked with the local food bank because its trucks were not being used to their full capacity. The Adult Literacy League started offering English for speakers of other languages (ESOL) classes to parents whose kids were active in the Boys & Girls Club. All of these collaborators credited the Center with bringing them together. Linnane noted:

> This is just a small set of examples. I could go on for hours, maybe even days, telling how programs and services developed or improved because nonprofit leaders were in the same place at the same time talking to each other and sharing missions, visions, and challenges.

Building on the success of the Leaders Series and the Art of Networking workshop, the Center began to offer "speed networking" sessions. Linnane recalled the initial speed networking events:

> We offered this twice—in 2008 and 2009, focused on arts organizations and others who wanted to attend. The participants wanted to meet one another with the hope being that they would find ways to work together. A timer is set. Organizations start talking one to one. They have two minutes. At the end of two minutes, everyone moves and spends two minutes with another organization. This continues until the end of the event. You can be sure that business cards and organizational literature are exchanged.

All of these initial actions were well received. Linnane was encouraged and began to brainstorm how the concept of networking could be taken to the next level.

From the staff's brainstorming another innovation in the networking area was developed: PeerLabs. The first PeerLab was in December 2010. For the event, PNLC staff arranged the room with 8 to 10 circular tables. At each table, a leader from a local nonprofit conducted a discussion on an area in which his or her organization excelled. Topics included, among others, Creative Fundraising, Using Social Media, Generating Earned Income and Finding Volunteers. The entire session lasted half a day. Attendees selected one table to sit at with others who shared an interest in the same topic. Introductions were made and the sharing began. Linnane beamed:

> The reaction was overwhelmingly positive. People loved the time with their peers to talk about best practices and they asked us to offer it again. The second PeerLab was in May 2011, with 50 people in attendance. We decided to offer a PeerLab twice a year as long as attendance continued to be high and we continued to receive requests for more opportunities like it.

Affinity Groups

After having observed the success of these general audience networking events, Linnane began thinking about how to apply the concept in a more targeted fashion. With this idea in mind, the Center began to establish affinity groups. Linnane explained the concept: "We'll introduce peers, one to another, and let them take those relationships where they will." The Center began by offering a "New Executive Director Roundtable" in January 2007 for those new to their positions. From there, they developed the "New Development Director Roundtable" in June 2009 and eventually the "Seasoned CEO Roundtable" in January 2010. Annually, the Center offered "For Board Chairs Only," an opportunity for board chairs to discuss the challenges they faced in leading boards. At the same time, Center staff began taking leadership roles in already established affinity organizations, such as the Association of Fundraising Professionals and Grant Professionals Network. In this way, the PNLC staff improved their own network and observed the management strategies of successful affinity groups.

Linnane was aware that many of the introductions that had been made through PNLC networking activities had turned into partnerships and eventual deep collaborations, resulting in friends mentoring and coaching each other. While such developments made her feel proud of the efforts she and the PNLC staff were making, she realized that some of these deep, cooperative relationships were forming into their own groups away from the Center. Sometimes she was invited to informal breakfast meetings or for drinks after work with executives who had established good, sustaining relationships with others. She realized, however, that she was seeing fewer of these executives formally; that is, they were not engaging much with the Center. Linnane wondered whether this situation could "possibly have happened because the nonprofit leaders had developed their own 'affinity' groups and no longer needed the Center?" She was unsure how to bring the leaders back into the fold.

Explaining the Value of Networking to Funders

At the annual PNLC meeting in May 2011, Linnane shared with the Center's funders the network organizing the Center was involved in.

She expected them to be enthusiastic; after all, "how could anyone not be excited about connecting people to form a more cohesive sector?" She was not prepared for some of the responses. Her funders had asked, "How do you know that offering networking opportunities provides value?" "How many connections have you facilitated that have impacted the community?" "How many of these partnerships you're describing are lasting longer than three months or six months?" "What is the impact of networking on their clients?" "What is it really costing you (and your operation) to do all of this facilitation?" "Would your time be better spent on activities that generate revenue for the Center?"

Linnane had been caught off guard. She couldn't answer any of the questions. She knew instinctively that connecting people on the scale that the Center was doing was resulting in a stronger nonprofit sector overall, which supported the Center's mission and vision. Nevertheless, she had to listen to their questions and determine how to prove that network facilitation strengthened nonprofits and the community and was worth the staff time.

Linnane knew that the Center's reputation was building, that classes were filling and that advice was being sought. Center staff was consistently hearing comments such as "I don't know what I'd do without the Center" and "I couldn't do my job without you." They were starting to hear nonprofit staff members state proudly that they had earned a certificate in nonprofit management or proposal writing through the Center. Much anecdotal evidence supported that the Center's efforts were positively influencing local organizations and their staff. The Center was becoming the "go to" organization for advice, training, information and connections. Linnane needed to convince the funders that networking was important to the Center's mission and to the nonprofit community. Funding support was critical to the PNLC's success. She had four weeks to prepare for the next meeting. She needed answers—fast.

8

MANAGING THE PEOPLE

Staff and Volunteers

Executives owe it to the organization and to their fellow workers not to tolerate nonperforming individuals in important jobs.

—Peter Drucker (2004, para. 9)

Key Topics: organizational structure, motivation, managing paid and volunteer staff

What is the best balance of responsibilities and organizational structure for nonprofit staff? Are certain management practices more effective than others when dealing with paid versus volunteer staff? Questions regarding human resource management and organizational behavior perplex leaders in all organizations. The multiple stakeholders for the nonprofit organization (NPO) add a layer of complexity to these challenges. In this chapter, we build on earlier discussions of leadership (Chapter 4), performance measurement (Chapter 5), and strategy (Chapter 6) to offer theory and practical information to help NPOs manage their people effectively.

In general, management concerns "making organizations run better by designing and improving processes, procedures and policies that guide" employees' actions (Dees, Emerson, & Economy, 2001, p. 75). This requires a different skill set and focal point than leadership. Leadership spotlights inspiration and creation of vision, with an emphasis on *what* and *why* versus *how* and *when* (see Chapter 4 for full discussion). The concepts of managing and leading are not mutually exclusive, and both are required to run an effective organization in the long term. The overlap of the two comes in the examination of motivation.

MOTIVATION IN THE WORKPLACE

While early theories of management viewed people as a cog in the machine of industry (e.g., Taylor's scientific management theory), more recent approaches to managing individuals in the work setting balance psychology with task completion (e.g., Maslow's hierarchy of needs, McGregor's Theory X and Theory Y). Most of the latter work recognizes that people bring to the workplace the need for both *relationships* and *goal accomplishments.* The challenge for managers in understanding their own and their employees' motivation is striking the desired balance between these needs across various situations. In other words, what motivates people to think and act in certain ways at work, and can that process be influenced?

Herzberg (1968) posited that motivation comes after certain conditions, labeled *hygiene factors,* are met on a consistent basis *and* when meaningful satisfiers are present. This is similar to Maslow's hierarchy, which states that people cannot fulfill higher order needs until they have met basic needs (e.g., safety, hunger). Table 8.1 lists Herzberg's motivators and dissatisfiers. NPO leaders are advised to review working conditions for paid and volunteer staff

to ensure that dissatisfiers are minimized and motivators are maximized. While this sounds simple, the implementation of policies and practices is complex for leaders of both for-profit and nonprofit organizations of various sizes. Bookshelves overflow with "how to" recipes for employee motivation.

One often-repeated recipe for motivating workers is to build a culture of recognition, where employees and volunteers feel important to the organizational goals and clients served (Dees et al., 2001). Management guru Tom Peters (1988) states it simply: "Celebrate what you want to see more of" (p. 311). Converting this sage advice to actionable policies involves two steps. First, decide exactly what thinking and behavior the organization wants from its members. These behaviors should be directly aligned with the NPO mission, vision, goals, and strategies (see Chapters 2 and 5). Second, reward the behaviors whenever displayed. Rewards may be elaborate or simple in nature. A study by American Express Incentive Services

Table 8.1 Herzberg's Motivators and Dissatisfiers

Motivators Factors that encourage dedication and loyalty to the nonprofit and its cause	Dissatisfiers Factors that lead to frustration when conditions are less than ideal
Achievement	Compensation—equity within organization and across sector and economy
Advancement—organizationally and professionally	Interpersonal relationships—with coworkers and management/supervisor
Growth—personal and positional	Organizational policies and administration
Recognition	Status and security
Responsibility	Working conditions—safe, clean environment
The work itself—sense of accomplishment and meaningfulness	

Source: Herzberg, 1968.

(AEIS; 1999) found the best awards—those that achieved desired organizational action—include the following:

- a verbal "thank you" for a job well done
- a letter of commendation
- a good performance evaluation—acknowledging specific behaviors
- a career-related gift or additional training

The good news for budget-strapped NPOs is that most of these are "free" and/or components of good human resource management policy. In addition to behavior-specific awards related to achievement or performance, AEIS reminds managers that acknowledgments for employee retention and referrals are equally successful in motivating organizational members. Such acknowledgments include service-anniversary recognition ceremonies and positive attitude and advocacy awards for any stakeholder who supports changing the work environment in a positive way. An excellent source for additional ideas is Bob Nelson's (1994) book *1001 Ways to Reward Employees*.

PUTTING PEOPLE FIRST

While building a culture of recognition is important, this alone may not lead to loyal employees and volunteers. NPO leaders should also reflect on the organizational structure and ensure that it, like all official policies, puts people first. "Nonprofit leaders can abuse people in the name of a greater mission just as easily as for-profit businesses can abuse people in the name of profits. If you care about your social mission, you will do better by putting people first" (Dees et al., 2001, p. 78). Rohit Sharma, in the Consultancy Development Organization case, faces issues of morale and organizational culture. Combining several resources on managing human behavior in organizations (nonprofit and for-profit), we offer the following list of nine practices that put people first and emphasize

authentic motivation (Denhardt, Denhardt, & Aristigueta, 2009; Pfeffer, 1998; Prahalad & Ramaswamy, 2004). Such suggestions may guide Sharma and other leaders in similar situations in government and nonprofit organizations.

1. As managers, practice emotional intelligence—be reflective and proactive about your own motivation and motivators, recognizing that they may differ from others' drivers. This includes recognizing the limits any one person has on the ability to motivate another.

2. Promote employment security—from selective hiring of new personnel to recognizing the emotional and economic dependence most personnel have on steady work.

3. Design organizational structures so that self-managed teams and decentralized decision making empower members to influence outcomes.

4. Set clear and challenging goals—organize effort so that the work is completed (task consummation) and workers feel satisfied by achieving desired results (emotional satisfaction).

5. Set compensation such that a comparatively high proportion is contingent upon organizational performance (relative to goals set in #4).

6. Provide extensive training.

7. Make rewards salient and awarding of recognition transparent—including honesty about what rewards are possible (or not) based on organizational and economic constraints.

8. Make equity a policy by reducing status distinctions and barriers (from dress to office assignment to wage differentials).

9. Practice DARTs (Dialogue, Access, Risk sharing, and Transparency) in all financial and performance information throughout the organization.

STRUCTURE THE ORGANIZATION

Chapter 3 emphasized the importance of aligning organizational structure with strategy and how organizational structure in the nonprofit sector is often a result of resource dependency. Here we discuss the organization of human resources within the organization. This discussion should be framed within the understanding of both the need to align strategy and the nine principles just mentioned.

The nonprofit CEO has ultimate responsibility for hiring, training, developing, and motivating the staff as well as developing the organizational structure to ensure effective day-to-day operations and overall goal achievement (Moyers, 2006). The structure serves as the foundation upon which to build organizational capacity. Neilson, Martin, and Powers (2008) remind us that structural changes should be made only *after* clarifying decision responsibility and ensuring proper communication flow (vertically and horizontally). Too often time and energy are wasted changing structure when implementation is really the problem. In the other case in this chapter, Ken MacLellan at Alice Saddy faces such a dilemma.

Broadly stated, the purpose of organizational structure is to "divide work into various distinct tasks to be performed and coordinated . . . to accomplish the overall objectives of the organization. . . . [U]ltimately, the smaller parts [need to be] back together again to complete the activity. We refer to this . . . as integration" (Frost & Purdy, 2008, p. 2). Typical organizational structures fall into three categories: divisional, functional, and matrix. The most effective form depends on numerous variables, including organization size, complexity of task environment, and scope of activities.

In a *divisional* organization, outputs (e.g., products, services) dictate the structure. Each division provides complete support for a designated service, geographic market, or client. All functional areas are contained within each division. This structure is common in public education, where elementary, middle, and high school levels each contain functions to support their constituents. The underlying motivation for this structure is to respond to different client needs through flexibility. This form is best for mid-size to large organizations that "operate in heterogeneous environments, serve different customers, and/or sell in different geographic regions" (Frost & Purdy, 2008, p. 5).

A *functional* organizational structure groups positions by skills, processes, or departments (e.g., accounting, fundraising, client services). Advantages of this structure include efficiency and collection of common skills. This division often provides challenges of integration, however; sometimes the parts are not put back together effectively due to communication or territoriality issues. For this type of structure to be successful, a strong organizational culture with shared vision, values, and goals must be present.

Matrix structures, like that found in the Alice Saddy case, combine divisional and functional forms. In theory, this creates the best of both worlds—efficiency through reduction of duplication, with responsiveness through flexibility. In reality, a matrix organization can be difficult to manage and may cause employee confusion because of multiple reporting relationships. However, when the environment is complex and rapidly changing and employees are highly comfortable in a team environment, a matrix can work well.

Grossman and Childress (2010) echo the concern about overreliance on structural changes to drive performance improvements in the nonprofit setting. The ongoing debate of centralized versus decentralized structure or degree of headquarter control over field operations is often framed as an irreconcilable difference with little common ground, which detracts from the more complex (and necessary) conversation on alignment of structure to strategy. Sharma, as the director of CDO, encounters some of this frustration.

Another note of caution for nonprofit managers questioning organizational structure relates to the overemphasis on analyzing formal structures without recognizing informal power networks. Informal networks, based on personality and social interactions, exercise considerable influence on attitudes and behaviors in organizations. Such systems can serve as strong defenders of organizational values or detrimental disruptions to NPO mission accomplishment. Grossman and Childress (2010) suggest asking questions such as "Who do you go to when you really need to accomplish something?" and "How do things *really* work around here?" to ascertain informal structures and power sources.

MANAGING VOLUNTEERS

Many nonprofits rely on volunteers for mission fulfillment. Not only do volunteers serve as a nonpaid workforce, they also often expand organizational capacity by making financial donations; recruiting other volunteers; soliciting donations; and promoting the mission, vision, and values of the NPO. Chapters 1 and 3 discuss the global status of volunteering. Here we focus on the management of this valuable asset within the organization.

In referring to volunteers, we include any individuals who serve a nonprofit organization freely (i.e., without compensation or coercion). Volunteers are generally classified by their role and regularity of service. *Episodic* volunteers serve on an as-needed basis for limited times. Examples of such volunteerism include participation in annual beachside clean-up and special events such as marathon support teams. Generally, there is no involvement with the organization before or after the event. *Ongoing* volunteers, on the other hand, donate resources regularly over specified periods. Scout leaders and big-brother/big-sister volunteers are examples of ongoing volunteers with enduring relationships to the organization and the constituency.

Volunteer roles can range from board members to fundraisers, and from general support to direct service (Wymer, Knowles, & Gomes, 2006). *Board members* and other managerial-level volunteers serve in important, decision-making roles that have both operational and legal implications for the nonprofit. People who fill such positions often hold higher education degrees and positions of authority in their paid employment positions. Their motivations for volunteering may revolve more around prestige and association with a respected organization or important cause to the community than other volunteers.

Fundraisers serve an important role that connects the NPO to the community through public relations and other activities involved in raising money for the organization. Such volunteers may be either episodic or ongoing, but in either case should have outgoing personalities with a strong commitment to and clear understanding of the organization. Fundraisers' actions and attitude represent the organization and should be consistent with the mission, vision, and values the NPO espouses. A disconnection here, including issues of conflict of interest, can irreparably damage the organization.

Volunteers who supply *general support* are the backbone of any NPO. Activity performed by these volunteers varies greatly from organization to organization but generally includes any behind-the-scenes work that enable mission fulfillment (e.g., office, transportation, and other support). These volunteers are motivated by a dedication to the cause or work of the NPO; such individuals do not seek leadership or managerial authority in the organization.

Direct service volunteers work interactively with organizational constituents; those serving in this role are motivated by the significant contribution to the clients. Their direct roles enable them to see how what they are doing makes a difference by improving conditions for the organization's clients and for society. Examples of such volunteers include Sunday school teachers, meals-on-wheels drivers, and nonprofit retail store workers.

The work of each type of volunteer differs, as does the motivation for giving time and effort. Table 8.2 shows motivational determinants of volunteering (Wymer et al., 2006). The conclusion from the research behind this diagram is that the key to attracting and retaining motivated volunteers is to understand the underlying factors and attitudes that determine the reason for each individual's volunteer efforts. In addition, organizational leaders should be very specific in the job description of different volunteer activities. Job descriptions help in recruitment and in aligning expectations of the quantity and quality of work needed. Levinson (2004) suggests 13 principles

Table 8.2 Determinants of Volunteering

Personal Influences	Interpersonal Influences	Attitudes Toward	Situational Factor	
Values	Ease of entry or task	NPO sector	Time available	Intention to Volunteer
Life stage	Social norms	NPO clients	Distance to activity	
Personal experiences		NPO mission or cause	Safety of activity	

Source: Wymer et al., 2006.

that NPO administrators should recognize in managing volunteers (see Table 8.3). Overall, volunteers are critical to the success of NPO mission accomplishment and must be managed with the same professional attention as paid staff.

On a final note, NPO leaders are wise to remember that they may occasionally have to ask volunteers to take a break, to step down for a period, and so on. On the rare occasion, volunteers may have to be "fired." This may be very difficult for most leaders, but their responsibility to the NPO means that it may be necessary.

Some NPO leaders wonder how one can fire an unpaid volunteer. It is important to remember that while volunteers do not receive paid remuneration, they do receive psychic income from their volunteer work. NPO leaders should never hesitate to fire a volunteer whose performance is below the standard required and if efforts to help improve this performance have not proven successful. Such action, when handled correctly, could actually result in improved morale across all volunteers. No one likes to work alongside or be associated with people

Table 8.3 Principles of Effective Nonprofit Volunteer Management

1. Realize the value of volunteers' service.
2. Reward volunteers in proportion to their value.
3. Bring out the best in each volunteer.
4. Recognize that paid workers oppose volunteers on principle.
5. Communicate with volunteers as you would with monetary donors (recall the DART principles).
6. Do not glorify one volunteer above the rest.
7. Create leadership positions for volunteers who desire and earn them.
8. Invite volunteers to apply for paid positions.
9. Respect volunteers' time and talent by allocating "real" work.
10. Never forget the *thank you*.

Source: Levinson, 2004, pp. 14–15.

who do not pull their own weight or who do not represent the high standards of the mission/organization.

The following cases illustrate the myriad of challenges and opportunities NPO managers face in leading, organizing, and motivating the different elements of their workforce. The theories and tips provided in this chapter are designed to help NPO leaders with this difficult yet important set of tasks.

CASES

Alice Saddy: Caring for the Community (Canada): The human resources manager at the Alice Saddy Association (Alice Saddy), a nonprofit agency in London, Ontario, Canada—which supports people with developmental disabilities who live independently rather than in group homes—informed the executive director that some of the support workers believed that the current organizational structure caused confusion, slowed decision making, and created potential risk for the people served by Alice Saddy. The executive director agreed that there were some problems related to the structure of the organization. However, the structure reflected the mission of Alice Saddy, and changes were likely to be resisted by the management team for that reason. The executive director had to decide how to proceed.

Consultancy Development Organization (CDO) (International): Rohit Sharma, the director of CDO, a nonprofit organization that helps develop the consultancy profession in India, needs to respond to CDO's poor morale, specifically to the recent incident with the deputy director of projects. Sharma's encounter with the deputy director was the latest in a series of frustrating experiences that he has faced since joining CDO last year. He needs to decide whether to resign from CDO or to continue trying to improve the situation. The issue is what Sharma should do; the challenge is how to achieve it.

REFERENCES

American Express Incentive Services. (1999). *Achieve More survey.* Retrieved from http://www.loylab.com/index.php?option=com_docman&task=doc_download&gid=30&Itemid=

Dees, J. G., Emerson, J., & Economy, P. (2001). *Enterprising nonprofits: A toolkit for social entrepreneurs.* New York, NY: John Wiley & Sons.

Denhardt, R. B., Denhardt, J. V., & Aristigueta, M. P. (2009). *Managing human behavior in public and nonprofit organizations.* Thousand Oaks, CA: Sage.

Drucker, P. (2004). *Peter Drucker on making decisions.* Retrieved from http://hbswk.hbs.edu/archive/4208.html

Frost, A., & Purdy, L. (2008). An introductory note on managing people in organizations. In E. Grasby, M. Crossan, A. Frost, M. Pearce, & L. Purdy (Eds.), *Business decision making.* London, Ontario, Canada: Richard Ivey School of Business.

Grossman, A. S., & Childress, S. (2010). *Note on the nonprofit coherence framework.* Boston, MA: Harvard Business School Publishing.

Herzberg, F. (1968). One more time: How do you motivate employees? *Harvard Business Review, 46,* 36–44.

Levinson, N. (2004). What's wrong with "thank you"? Plenty. *Nonprofit World, 22*(2), 14–15.

Moyers, R. L. (2006). *The nonprofit chief executive's ten basic responsibilities.* Washington, DC: BoardSource.

Neilson, G., Martin, K. L., & Powers, E. (2008, June). The secrets to successful strategy execution. *Harvard Business Review,* 2–13.

Nelson, B. (1994). *1001 ways to reward employees.* New York, NY: Workman.

Peters, T. (1988). *Thriving on chaos.* New York, NY: Alfred A. Knopf.

Pfeffer, J. (1998). *The human equation: Building profits by putting people first.* Boston, MA: Harvard Business School Press.

Prahalad, C. K., & Ramaswamy, V. (2004). Co-creation experiences: The next practice in value creation. *Journal of Interactive Marketing, 18*(3), 5–14.

Wymer, W., Knowles, P., & Gomes, R. (2006). *Nonprofit marketing: Marketing management for charitable and nongovernmental organizations.* Thousand Oaks, CA: Sage.

ALICE SADDY: CARING FOR THE COMMUNITY

Ken MacLellan, executive director at the Alice Saddy Association, sighed as the door of his office closed. He had just finished a long meeting with the organization's human resources manager, Kathie Wolcott. Wolcott had just presented some feedback from the support workers at the Alice Saddy Association (referred to in the case as Alice Saddy or the Association).

The Alice Saddy Association, a non-profit agency in London, Ontario, supported people with developmental disabilities, which allowed them to live independently in the community, rather than in more restrictive group homes. Support workers provided the in-home assistance to the people with developmental disabilities. As executive director of the Association, MacLellan was the most senior paid staff member.

At a regular employee human resources committee meeting, support workers shared with Wolcott their concerns about the current organizational structure. They felt that the structure caused confusion, slowed decision-making and created potential risk for the people served by Alice Saddy.

MacLellan knew that there was an issue with the current organizational structure. Since the structure reflected the philosophy of Alice Saddy, any changes would be resisted by the management team because it passionately believed in the organization's mission and would see any changes as a threat to that mission.

Management had committed to the human resources committee that it would respond to issues raised within a week of its most recent committee meeting. MacLellan didn't have much time to decide his next steps.

ALICE SADDY ASSOCIATION

History

Alice Saddy was well known in London, Ontario, for her volunteer work assisting adults with disabilities. When she passed away in her early forties, a committee from her church was formed to honour her memory. Funds were raised to establish an "apartment training" program for people with developmental disabilities. This initiative became known as the Alice Saddy Association.

The Association's first group home opened in 1973. The concept was to teach daily living skills enabling people to live independently rather than in an institutional environment. Once the concept was proven, the Ontario Ministry of Community and Social Services provided program funding. A husband-and-wife team ran the group home.

In early 1976, the Supported Independent Living (SIL) program was established in London by Alice Saddy to assist developmentally disabled people in their own apartments. By 1980,

Colleen Sharen wrote this case solely to provide material for class discussion. The author does not intend to illustrate either effective or ineffective handling of a managerial situation. The author may have disguised certain names and other identifying information to protect confidentiality.

there were nine people living at the group home, and 15 people living on their own with support.

In 1980, the husband-and-wife team running the organization resigned, and a new professional staff was hired for the Association, including MacLellan, executive director, and Kathy Peters, supervisor of support services. By the end of the 1980s, Wolcott, the human resources manager, a financial manager and several support service workers had been hired. By 1989, the group home had been discontinued, consistent with the association's philosophy of independent living. Alice Saddy experienced moderate growth through the 1990s. By the end of 1999, there were 37 full-time employees who supported people with developmental disabilities in the community.

Alice Saddy grew to a staff of 96 at the end of 2007, more than doubling in size in seven years (see Exhibit 1). In 2007, Alice Saddy:

- supported 100 people with developmental disabilities in London wherever and with whomever they wished to live;
- supported 50 people in nursing homes;
- supported a limited number of individuals with a brain injury;
- provided a drop-in centre offering social and recreational activities;
- facilitated a collective kitchen;
- coordinated a computer lab open to people of all disabilities; and
- provided a volunteer program.

Alice Saddy's Statement of Philosophy

The Alice Saddy Association was guided by its statement of philosophy:

"The Alice Saddy Association believes that all persons have the right to be respected as valued members of their community and society in general. Thus all people must:

- have the opportunity to be active, contributing members of their community;
- be recognized as individuals with a unique and valued contribution;

- be treated with dignity and respect;
- have the opportunity to develop skills and/ or be provided with supports enabling them to choose to live in an independent or shared home environment in the community/ neighborhood of their choice.

Our vision is that in our society mutual respect will enhance each person's sense of self-worth and equality. The uniqueness of each person is to be celebrated, supported and acknowledged as essential to the completeness of the whole community."

The day-to-day operations of Alice Saddy were a reflection of the statement of philosophy. Clients were referred to as "people supported" because the staff at Alice Saddy believed that the term "client" was dehumanizing and did not acknowledge the individuality and contributions of the people that the agency supported. Alice Saddy focused on enabling independent living, personal choice and providing individualized service for the people that they supported.

"People supported first" was the rule at Alice Saddy, in contrast with a typical group home, where the residents of the home were often forced to live in a regimented way, with little or no say in how they lived, or what activities they engaged in. Employees at Alice Saddy passionately believed in this philosophy, which was ingrained in the organizational culture.

Role of Support Workers

Support workers worked in the residence of a person supported, assisting them with daily living skills, personal care and health-related needs. They ordered and administered medications, facilitated regular medical and dental care, provided financial management and helped in areas related to personal and apartment safety. They also worked with the person supported to obtain appropriate employment or volunteer opportunities. Finally, they communicated with the families of the person supported where appropriate.

Support workers worked independently outside of the office environment. They worked evenings and weekends when support service managers

Exhibit 1 History and Growth of Alice Saddy Association, 1980 to 2007

End of Period	Management Staff	Number of Support Workers	Number of People Supported
1980	Director	6	9 Group Home residents 15 Supported Independent Living people (SIL Program)
1989	Executive Director Supervisor Support Services Manager Financial Manager Human Resources (part-time)	12	Group Home Program discontinued 45 SIL Program
1998	Executive Director Supervisor Support Services Manager Financial Manager Human Resources 2 Managers Support Services	29	70 SIL Program 30 Nursing Home Program (newly launched)
2000	Executive Director Supervisor Support Services Manager Financial Manager Human Resources 3 Managers Support Services	34	80 SIL Program 40 Nursing Home Program
2002	Executive Director Supervisor Support Services Manager Financial Manager Human Resources 4 Managers Support Services	36	90 SIL Program 40 Nursing Home Program
2007	Executive Director Supervisor Support Services Manager Financial Manager Human Resources 4 Managers Support Services 1 Administrative Assistant (part-time)	87	125 SIL Program 50 Nursing Home Program

Notes: The number of support workers was not reported in full-time equivalents. The ratio of full-time to part-time workers changed over the period shown, although exact numbers were not available. The number of people supported was a rough representation of the work undertaken by the Association, since each person supported was assigned different hours of support based on their individual needs. Over time, the number of high-needs individuals had increased substantially to approximately 20 per cent of the case-load by 2007. This required an increased number of hours of support provided by the Association. Although the number of people supported in the SIL program increased from 2002 to 2007 by 39 per cent, the hours of support increased by significantly more, requiring substantially more support workers (a detailed history of hours of support was not available).

were not available to consult. The position required independent professional judgment, attention to detail, strong communication skills and experience working with people with developmental disabilities. There was a mix of full-time and part-time support workers. Most of the support workers possessed a Developmental Services Worker (DSW) diploma from Fanshawe College. Support workers also received ongoing training at the Association, including first aid, CPR, incident prevention and back care seminars.

The position of support worker was highly demanding, both physically and mentally. Working with high-needs people was especially difficult, often resulting in stress and burnout among support workers.

Matching Support Workers to the Needs of People Supported

The Association attempted to reflect the individual uniqueness of each person supported by providing customized support; for example, matching skills and personalities of the support workers to the needs of the person supported.

People supported had different levels of needs, from a few hours a week to 24 hours per day, seven days per week. Those receiving 24-hour care were considered high-needs individuals, and only certain support workers had the ability, patience and personal connection to effectively work with those people. About 20 per cent of the people supported had high needs. Because working with high-needs individuals could be particularly challenging and result in burnout, the Association assigned more support workers for fewer hours each to high-needs individuals. They had learned that this strategy reduced burnout among support workers. Depending on the needs of the person supported, anywhere from five to 15 support workers would work on a team supporting an individual.

As well, Alice Saddy faced the needs of an aging population. Many of the people supported who began their relationship with Alice Saddy in the 1970s and 1980s were starting to experience health issues associated with aging. These concerns increased the amount of time that was spent on each case, the number of urgent care decisions and the risk to both the person supported and to Alice Saddy. These challenges were expected to increase as the large group of baby boomers supported by the Association aged.

Organizational Structure: The Early Years, 1980–1997

By the end of 1989, the management team was in place, comprising the executive director, supervisor of support services, finance manager and a part-time human resources manager.

In the early years of Alice Saddy it was a simple matter to ensure individualized support. When a new person supported was accepted by the Association, an extensive needs assessment was conducted. The support service supervisor then assigned a team of support workers whose skills best matched the needs of the person supported.

If a person supported needed a change, the support worker informally discussed it with the supervisor of support services and a plan was developed. The process was ad hoc. With a relatively small case-load, it was possible for the support service supervisor to spend a great deal of time in the field working with support workers and interacting with the people supported.

Organizational Structure Evolution, 1998–2007

As Alice Saddy grew, it became clear that the supervisor of support services could no longer directly manage all of the support workers in the organization. In 1998, two managers of support services were hired, each reporting to the supervisor of support services. One more manager was hired in each of 2000 and 2002, creating a total of four managers of support services.

These managers were recruited from the most experienced support workers, all of whom began working at Alice Saddy in the 1980s or early 1990s.

The managers had three main responsibilities. They 1) managed a case-load of people supported (as "case manager"), 2) managed the performance of a group of support workers, and 3) acted as a support worker in the field.

As case manager, support service managers were responsible for the planning and delivery of service to the person supported.

Support workers reported to one of the four support service managers for performance management purposes. The manager provided coaching, performance management, performance evaluations, scheduling, training and other supervisory functions.

Each manager of support services worked 10 hours a week as a support worker and a further 25 hours per week in their managerial role. Support workers respected the fact that the managers were still active support workers. They believed that the managers had a better understanding of the issues faced by support workers because of the time that they spent working with people supported.

Assigning Work, 1998–2007

When a new person supported was taken on by the agency, the supervisor of support services conducted a needs assessment. The person supported was then assigned by the supervisor of support services to a case manager based on current case-loads and the skills of that particular manager.

Independent of the choice of case manager for the person supported, a team of support service workers was assigned to the person supported by the supervisor of support services, based on the needs of the person supported and the skills and personalities of the support workers. The support workers assigned to a person supported could report to any of the four support service managers. The Association believed that by having the best fit between the support worker and the person supported, the person supported received better care. Also, by increasing the number of workers and reducing the time each worker spent on any one case, the Association reduced the likelihood of burnout among support workers. As well, it was easier to accommodate vacations and sick coverage if the managers were able to draw upon all support workers across the organization (see Exhibit 2).

As a result of this "cross-reporting" structure, support workers often worked on the cases assigned to two, three or even all four support service managers (see Exhibit 3).

At the same time, each support worker reported to one single manager of support services for performance management purposes. Alice Saddy had an ongoing performance evaluation process, with managers meeting with each support worker every six to eight weeks to discuss performance and the needs of people that the worker supported. The evaluations were not used to determine pay increases, although they were considered when deciding whether to move a support worker from part-time to full-time status.

The Association believed that this structure provided the most flexibility, ensuring individualized service for the person being supported and staff coverage of all of the hours needed to support an individual. However, in the late 2000s, as the agency grew, there began to be some drawbacks to the structure.

Impact of Growth on the Organizational Structure, 2008

In 2002, each support service manager managed an average of nine support workers and 22 people supported. By 2007, each support service manager managed an average of 22 support workers and 31 people supported. In addition, there was a significant increase in the number of high-needs people supported. The combination of the increased numbers of 1) people supported, 2) support workers, and 3) high-needs people supported resulted in a doubling of workload.

As the Association's case-load grew and the needs of the people supported changed due to

Exhibit 2 Support Team for a Single Person Supported (Example)

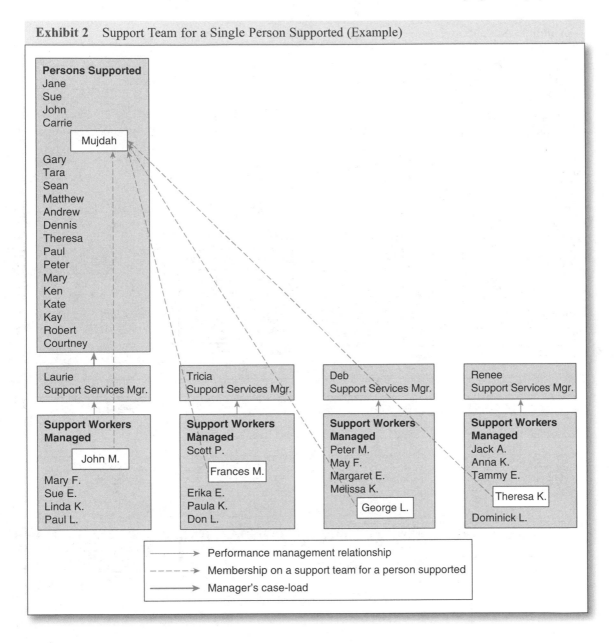

aging, it became more challenging for the support service managers to deal with unusual situations. This required a great deal of coordination of activity, because each support worker on a team for a particular individual might have a different manager. This meant that the managers met regularly to discuss case strategy and individual staff performance.

Exhibit 3   Simplified Organizational Structure, Alice Saddy Association

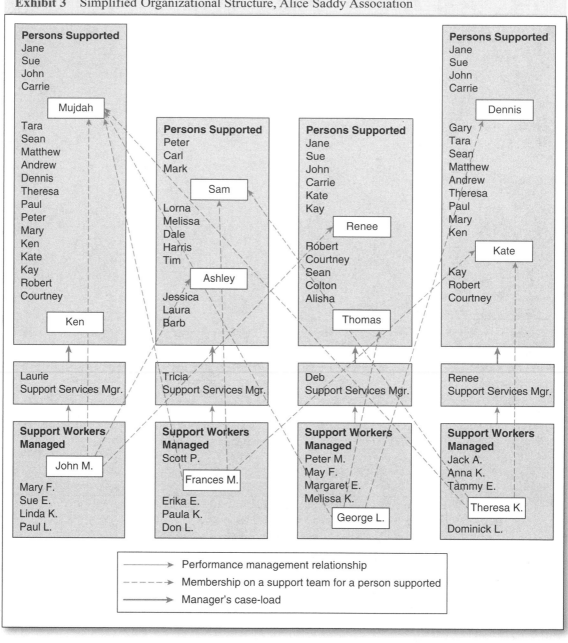

Scheduling also became more complex. Each support service manager scheduled support workers for their cases. However, because the support workers worked with people supported on the case-loads of all four managers, ensuring both adequate coverage and no scheduling conflicts took a great deal of time.

Support workers sometimes received conflicting feedback on their performance from the support service managers. A case manager might give different feedback than the support worker's manager. Sometimes a case manager would report performance concerns to a support worker's manager, who might choose to dismiss the concerns and not provide feedback to the employee in question. Managers sometimes disagreed about the appropriate way to manage employees. As well, with the increased number of support workers, MacLellan wondered whether the regular bi-monthly performance appraisals that were part of the performance management process were being completed. Employees were feeling confused and frustrated. They also worried that a person supported might be at greater risk due to these communication and decision-making issues.

The support service managers were also frustrated. They were working long hours. New manager positions had not been added in the past five years, in spite of the increased number of people supported by Alice Saddy and the increased needs of those supported. The managers felt that they were working well as a team to address many of the issues that arose. They had taken on a number of additional responsibilities for the development of individual service agreements with the people supported, the development of technology to improve reporting procedures and for the training and orientation of new support workers. It became very difficult for the managers to spend time in the field with the support workers to provide coaching, direction and support, given the allocated 25 hours per week to complete their managerial tasks.

As the Association grew, the support service managers were challenged by requests for direction on cases from support workers. Whenever a request was less than clear-cut, the relevant managers would meet to discuss the issue and develop a direction for the case. Then the support service managers would present their recommendations to the supervisor of support services for approval, and communicate the direction back to the support workers in question. In the past, when Alice Saddy was smaller, this informal coordination was easily accomplished, but with more managers, people supported and support workers, this coordination was more challenging.

In the mid-2000s, the volume of requests for direction increased with the number of people supported and the complexity of the issues. Although most of the requests were quickly dealt with, some of the more complex issues were beginning to take more time to resolve. Since these requests were often related to important or urgent issues for the care of a person supported, delay increased risk for both the people supported and for the Association. Support workers started to approach two or three support service managers individually in order to speed up the process. Sometimes they received contradictory direction. MacLellan knew that further growth would only increase the possibility of a tragedy occurring due to delay or confusion.

THE DECISION

MacLellan reflected on his 28 years at Alice Saddy, "You know, our cross-reporting structure worked well until recently. We've been able to deliver on our philosophy of individual support and independent living for the people we support in the community. We've grown from supporting nine people to over 100 people. With our growth, our structure isn't working as well as it used to."

Given case-load and related staffing growth in the agency, increased administrative and project loads, the support service managers were spending less time in the field managing, training, coaching and directing the support workers. It had been over five years since Alice Saddy had increased its complement of managers. While it might be time to add an additional manager or two, it was clear that decision also meant that support workers might end up working on the cases of up to six managers, creating even more inconsistency, confusion and frustration.

There were mixed opinions on the issue of the cross-reporting structure at Alice Saddy. Some of the management team felt that the current structure didn't work well, but couldn't think of another way of organizing themselves that would deliver on Alice Saddy's philosophy and provide the organization with the flexibility it needed.

Others felt that the cross-reporting structure was working well and did not need to change. In fact, they felt that a change would negatively impact the strong organizational culture of "people supported first." Some members of the management team were concerned because some of the people supported were deeply attached to their support workers, with relationships that had lasted more than 20 years. This was particularly true for the high-needs people supported. Any change to a stable relationship could be disruptive in their lives. Still others felt that although the current structure wasn't optimal, other structures would not work either, so the employees would just have to tough it out, because the people supported were of primary importance.

MacLellan started to think about what structures would enable Alice Saddy to deliver individualized support to developmentally challenged people in the community, while minimizing the risk to the people supported and to the agency. How would he convince the management team that a change in organizational structure didn't necessarily mean a change in the "people supported first" philosophy of Alice Saddy? MacLellan needed to have a response for the human resources committee next week. He had a lot of thinking to do.

CONSULTANCY DEVELOPMENT ORGANIZATION (CDO)

It was just after 3 p.m. on Friday, January 4, 2008. Rohit Sharma, director of Consultancy Development Organization, stormed into the office of the deputy director of projects, Mukesh Kumar:

> One of our organization's prestigious members, Krish Industrial Consulting Limited, has complained that it received the information on the Mahanadi Electrical Company proposal from us after the last date for submission. As a result, it has lost the opportunity to participate. Why was it delayed?

Kumar replied:

> It takes time to gather information. We engaged New Infotech Limited to collect the information.

They took their time to send the information. We have to follow government rules to get it printed in our newsletter, *Business Opportunities,* and then it is mailed to all members. There are procedures. What can I do if there is a delay? I have to follow these procedures.

"Do we have any plan to reduce the time lag so we can get the information to our members in time for them to use it?" asked Sharma.

"No. We work as the government tells us from time to time," replied Kumar.

Sharma could not believe what he had just heard. This was not the first time that he had felt let down by his employees. He left the room feeling embarrassed and vowing to himself that this latest incident would be the last.

CONSULTANCY DEVELOPMENT ORGANIZATION

In January 1990, Consultancy Development Organization (CDO) was set up by the Indian government in conjunction with the Indian consultancy industry as a not-for-profit body to help develop the Indian consultancy profession. CDO acted as a facilitator by providing information on consulting opportunities, a database on consultants and a platform for policy suggestions and networking. Among its main activities, CDO organized annual conferences and training programs and published a fortnightly publication on business opportunities, which listed CDO's expected consulting assignments.

CDO was based in Chennai and its membership included 200 individual consultants and 40 consultancy companies. It was headed by a full-time director, Rohit Sharma, who was supported by eight professionals and 20 support staff (see Exhibit 1). The Governing Council (the board) of CDO comprised 20 members, of which two-thirds (14 members) were elected by the general membership and the remaining members were nominated by the government. CDO's chairman was appointed directly by the government for a fixed two-year term. Approximately three-quarters of CDO's annual expenses were met through government grants.

ROHIT SHARMA

Rohit Sharma joined CDO in October 2007 as a full-time director. He had an MBA from the Indian Institute of Management (IIM) in Ahmedabad, India's premier business school. Prior to joining CDO, Sharma had worked for 20 years in various positions in the industry, consulting both in India and abroad. Sharma had a reputation for being a hard task master and a dynamic, hard-working person with a vision.

Sharma had been appointed to the post of director by the Ministry of Industrial Promotion, which was the nodal government ministry in charge of CDO. Prior to Sharma's appointment, the Ministry of Industrial Promotion had used the CDO director position as a parking place for unwanted government officials, a practice that had led to three directors joining and leaving CDO in the last three years. Nevertheless, Sharma accepted the challenge of leading CDO and turning it into a leading player.

MUKESH KUMAR

Mukesh Kumar received an engineering degree from Delhi University. After graduation, he worked as a junior engineer in a government organization. He joined CDO in 1992 as an assistant manager and had progressed through the ranks to become one of four deputy directors who reported to the director. Kumar was hard-working and knowledgeable but lacked ambition and drive. He was currently the deputy director of projects at CDO, the second-most prestigious profile in CDO after the director.

NARESH CHADHA

Naresh Chadha, a commerce graduate, had been employed at CDO since its inception in 1990. He was politically well connected and regarded as a hands-on employee. He had worked in various positions in CDO, ranging from administration to marketing, and was currently deputy director of support services. His work included organizing annual conferences and conventions. He reported to the director.

DHEERAJ AHUJA AND AMIT KACHRU

Dheeraj Ahuja and Amit Kachru were the other two deputy directors at CDO who reported to Rohit Sharma. They were responsible for human resources and finance, respectively. Prior to joining CDO the previous year, both Ahuja and Kachru had spent their entire careers serving the Indian government in various roles.

Exhibit 1   Organization Chart of Consultancy Development Organization

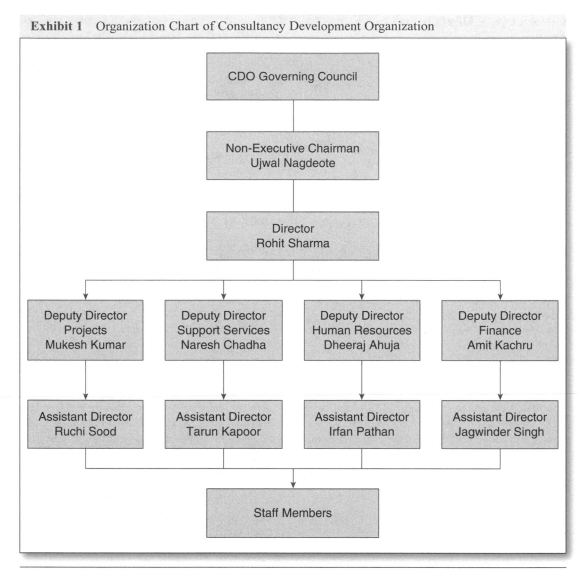

Source: CDO Organization Chart.

UJWAL NAGDEOTE

Ujwal Nagdeote was the non-executive chairman of CDO, appointed by the government. He was a politically well-connected, knowledgeable and respected figure in the industry. Nagdeote served on the board of a dozen leading Indian companies and played a dormant role in the affairs of CDO.

ORGANIZATION CULTURE

CDO had four deputy directors and four assistant directors. The deputy directors reported to the director, and the assistant directors reported to the deputy directors (see Exhibit 2). The director, deputy directors and assistant directors comprised the officer category, and the 20 support staff (personal assistants, secretaries, clerks and peons[1]) comprised the Class II category. Each officer had at least one personal assistant or secretary and one peon. All clerks worked in the administration wing of CDO, where all files were located.

In 1990, when CDO was established, the staff was recruited according to the structure prevalent in government organizations. In the early 1990s, clerks were needed for typing and administrative tasks, and the peons were required to run office errands, such as delivering files, dispatching letters, serving water, and preparing tea and coffee for the officers. However, by 2008, computers were available to all the officers, and coffee and tea machines were common in the office. The clerks and peons did not have enough work; however, they were very difficult to fire, because they had job security, in accordance with the government system.

At all levels of the organization, the salaries were fixed and equal, with no variable pay or rewards system. As a result, employees had no incentive to perform. Until Sharma's appointment, no outside appointments had been made for the past 10 years. The culture was not very professional, and government organizations constantly interfered, wanting to use the CDO facilities (such as CDO's office car) and staff for their own purposes. As a result, morale within CDO was poor.

ROHIT SHARMA'S FIRST WEEK IN OFFICE

When Sharma joined CDO in October 2007, he was greeted by Naresh Chadha and Mukesh Kumar, two of his four direct reports. That week, the attendance was abysmally low. Sharma learned that most of the staff were absent because it was Diwali[2] season. Even though Diwali was five weeks away, some of the employees had taken time off to be with their families and friends. They had scant regard for Sharma, which was reinforced through their absence. Sharma was aghast to see that no one on the administration staff had bothered to fill the water coolers with fresh water or to clear the cupboards in his office.

NATIONAL CONVENTION

CDO was organizing the National Convention scheduled for January 15, 2008. For this annual conference, eminent speakers had been invited to address consulting issues and discuss their experiences with the participants, generally the member organizations and individuals and executives from the corporate sector.

On January 4, 2008, Sharma went to the office of Naresh Chadha, the deputy director in charge of the National Convention, to inquire about the conference's progress, particularly the number of speakers that had confirmed and the number of participants that had registered.

"We sent letters to the members. Their responses continue until the last date. We have not set any targets. Do not worry. We will have good numbers," replied Chadha, casually sipping his tea and eating pakoras.[3]

Sharma returned to his own office an unhappy person. He was feeling uneasy: there was not much response to show and most activities had been delayed. The annual conference was not expected to be successful. The attitude of most employees was callous and inept. The fiscal year-end on March 31, and he was concerned that CDO's performance would be seen as much below average.

[1]Peons were persons of menial position, such as messengers and servants.

[2]Diwali, the festival of lights, is an important festival celebrated throughout India.

[3]Pakoras are a deep-fried South Asian fritter made by dipping pieces of vegetable in a chickpea flour batter. They are generally eaten as a snack.

INTERNATIONAL CONSULTANCY CONGRESS

The International Consultancy Congress was scheduled to be held in London, England, from February 3 to 6, 2008. Sharma thought it would be a good opportunity to interact and network with consultancy organizations in other countries. He considered taking one of his officers with him to boost morale.

According to government rules, any foreign visit had to be approved by the Ministry of Industrial Promotion. Thus, Sharma had sent the proposal for his own participation and that of Naresh Chadha on December 1, 2007. After several follow-up attempts, he was informed on January 3, 2008, that the proposal had not been accepted. This rejection had a further demoralizing effect on employees who now thought that Sharma, despite all his talk, was not able to do much.

SHARMA'S FIRST THREE MONTHS

Sharma realized quickly that employee morale at CDO was very low and was compounded by the absence of career development and low remuneration. The company had no clear strategy or direction. The government grants took care of the salaries of staff and the administrative expenses. Consequently, employees had no motivation to perform or to increase the business.

"How are we expected to facilitate our members?" asked Sharma.

"It is not our concern. In any case, the members pay very little and our salaries are paid by the government. You should not worry so much. Whether you undertake the same or more activities, you will be paid the same salary," advised Kumar.

Sharma faced the choice of continuing on the path of his predecessors (i.e. doing nothing new and having an easy time) or working towards a turnaround strategy for the organization and setting it on a growth path.

DECEMBER 28, 2007, MEETING

Sharma had called a meeting of all officers and staff on Friday, December 28, at 9 a.m. He asked them for ideas for the growth of CDO. Divergent views were expressed:

CDO has been in existence for 18 years and has been doing well. It can continue to function as such.

The government grant received annually is sufficient to pay for the salaries and some activities only.

We are a government-controlled organization. We undertake activities as directed by the controlling Ministry of Industrial Promotion.

There is no incentive for extra effort or growth. Following the government pay scales, we get the same salary whether we do the same activities or take up more.

Members of CDO pay very small subscriptions [membership fee]. They are not interested in any major initiatives, which may lead to their paying more subscriptions.

Sharma disagreed. He observed that he had joined the organization because he believed it had great potential. Consultancy was fast growing, and India had an edge in the global consultancy field because of a large professionally skilled pool of workers and the relatively low cost of consultants. CDO could greatly help in developing the consultancy profession in the country. He outlined his five-year vision:

- CDO should be fully self-supporting and not dependent on government grants. For this purpose, CDO must increase its income from its own activities by at least five times.
- CDO should function on a non-government pattern and the employees need to be accountable for results.
- CDO should strive for a 10-fold increase in memberships, both individual and corporate. The members must benefit from CDO's activities. They must receive information about a larger number of business opportunities within the country and abroad, online, without delay.

- CDO should help consultants in consultancy exports, through studies, data collection and providing opportunities for networking.
- CDO should function as facilitator by using its government links for policy intervention to promote the profession.
- CDO should also take up consultancy assignments that can be outsourced to its members, to generate income and to help employ its members.
- Support staff need to be given work responsibility after being trained in new skills that can be useful for the organization.
- Employee morale needs to improve, performance needs to be linked to incentives and promotions need to be introduced.

Some of the executives were enthusiastic but only if these changes could lead to better prospects for themselves. Others expressed apprehension, particularly regarding the operational freedom they would have from the controlling ministry. The Governing Council also had to be consulted for endorsement.

MAHANADI ELECTRICAL PROPOSAL INCIDENT

Mahanadi Electrical Company (MEC) was an electricity distribution utility in the eastern state of Orissa (see Exhibit 1), which supplied electricity to about one-fourth of the state. The distribution system was very old, and breakdowns were frequent, as were the failure of transformers and interruptions to the electrical supply. Consumers were unhappy, and the State Electricity Regulation Commission had asked MEC to revamp the distribution system. Accordingly, the company had invited bids for consultancy work, which involved the preparation of a feasibility report for the revamping of the distribution system. This major assignment was worth about US$2.5 million, and few consultancy companies had the necessary competency in this field.

Krish Industrial Consulting Limited (KICL), a founding member of CDO and one of the competing companies bidding on the MEC project, was confident of being awarded the assignment and was waiting to receive the information needed to bid for the job. On behalf of CDO, New Infotech Limited (to whom this work was outsourced) was collecting information regarding potential consultancy assignments from tender notices published in newspapers, websites and other sources. This information was then passed to CDO, which published it in a fortnightly newsletter that was mailed to all of its members. The last date for receipt of bids by MEC was December 15, 2007, but KICL received the CDO newsletter with the information on this assignment on January 1, 2008. The CEO of KICL had expressed his disappointment to Sharma regarding the delay.

JANUARY 4, 2008, INCIDENT

On January 4, Sharma stormed into the office of Kumar to inquire about the MEC proposal and why it had been delayed. Kumar had been nonapologetic and unfazed that KICL lost the opportunity to participate. He had justified the situation by suggesting he had been following government guidelines.

Sharma could not believe Kumar's lackadaisical attitude. KICL was an important member of CDO, yet Kumar seemed unperturbed by KICL's loss of business because of CDO's delay and ineptness. Kumar's attitude was a clear reflection of the state of affairs in the organization. Sharma left the room very frustrated. Things needed to improve or CDO would lose its elite status as the nodal agency for consultancy in India, and his career would be at stake.

Sharma wondered whether he had made a mistake by accepting the director's position and whether he could do anything to improve the situation at CDO.

9

MARKETING

Marketing is an unfamiliar concept for many nonprofit organizations. It's important that these organizations understand that marketing is more than just the old sense of making a sale or obtaining a donation. Marketing is a way to satisfying the consumer and donor needs.

—Laura Lake (2011, para. 1)

Key Topics: customer-focused marketing, marketing planning, environmental scanning, marketing mix, building brands

There is much controversy about the application of marketing principles to mission-based organizations. The main question that drives the controversy is: Can a nonprofit successfully market itself and its work without "selling out" its mission? In this chapter we answer this question with a definitive yes. Furthermore, we suggest how to adapt marketing strategies and techniques in a manner appropriate for nonprofit organizations (NPOs). The focal points for the adaptation revolve around brand orientation and customer focus; we start with some definitions to align understanding.

DEFINING MARKETING AND BRANDING IN THE NONPROFIT CONTEXT

Marketing and branding, usually associated with for-profit endeavors, raise tension between an organization's "nonprofit-ness," altruism, volunteerism, and grassroots action on one side, and goal accomplishment on the other (Hall, 2006; Hankinson, 2002). This for-profit association, combined with a general misunderstanding of marketing, leads many to suggest that marketing is inappropriate for nonprofit or civic-minded organizations. Contrary to the famous line uttered by Kevin Costner in the movie *Field of Dreams,* just because you build it does *not* mean they will come; thus, communicating with stakeholders is paramount to NPO success. This is one role of marketing.

Communication is not the only task for marketing, however, which begs the question: *What* and to *whom* should the NPO communicate and *why?* According to the American Marketing Association (AMA; 2011a), marketing is a "set of processes for creating, communicating, and delivering value to customers and for managing customer relationships in ways that benefit the organization and its stakeholders" (para. 4). For a nonprofit, this means building relationships (the *what*) with specific target audiences (the *who*— e.g., funders, clients, volunteers) that create desired action (the *what*—e.g., contribute funds, increase participation in programs, donate more time), which aligns with the organizational mission (the *why*—e.g., overcome illiteracy, increase access to affordable healthcare) in tangible and measureable ways. In other words, marketing can activate the mission by emphasizing the value the NPO provides to its various audiences. Understood in this way, it is difficult to see why anyone would be opposed to using marketing strategy and tactics in a nonprofit.

The question remains, however: How does an NPO with an already constrained budget begin to implement marketing without losing focus on its mission? This is where the critical role of the NPO brand comes into play. A brand is "a name, term, design, symbol, or any other feature that identifies one organization's good or service as distinct from those of other organizations" (AMA, 2011b, "brand"). In the NPO setting, a brand serves as a lens through which the organization can focus its messages and efforts. The lens is the tool for bringing the mission into focus for both internal and external stakeholders.

Why do NPOs need branding? A summary by Bennett and Sargeant (2005) suggests four reasons:

1. Donors expect a professional approach to image management among fundraising organizations (Saxton, 1994; Tapp, 1996).

2. Excellent charity image is a significant determinant of donation income (Kennedy, 1998; Tapp, 1996).

3. Strong brand image influences consumer preference for charity branded products (Ramrayka, 1998; Tapp, 1996).

4. Positive image generates "halo effects" in a range of organizational activities and can elicit a quick (low-involvement) response for donation requests (Van Riel 1995).

Even with this definition and specific reasons why NPOs need brands, a common misperception that persists among NPO leaders is of a brand as a simple visual trigger from which to develop communication campaigns, rather than as a strategic tool for focusing the organization (i.e., a lens; Hankinson, 2001). To facilitate seeing a brand as a more comprehensive, strategic tool, Hankinson suggests nonprofit leaders develop *brand orientation.*

Nonprofit brand orientation (NBO) involves (a) understanding what the brand does and the value it represents—the lens that focuses internal and external stakeholders on the mission, (b) consistently communicating the brand internally and externally—through effective marketing, (c) using the brand as a strategic resource, and (d) managing the brand actively and deliberately. An NPO without a brand orientation lacks organizational responsibility for the brand, so that communication is piecemeal, without central coordination (Hankinson, 2001), resulting in loss of mission focus. Jason Robinson, in this chapter's Toronto Ultimate Club case, may find development of a clear brand and a brand orientation within the organization a valuable strategy to compete against the many for-profit clubs in Toronto. Two applications of NBO and other brand tactics to the nonprofit setting that may help Robinson and others formulate strategy are "NPO Branding: Preliminary Lessons From Major Players" (Weisenbach Keller, Conway Dato-on, & Shaw, 2010) and "Global Nonprofit Brands With Local Missions: The YMCA Across Three Countries" (Conway Dato-on, Weisenbach Keller, & Shaw 2008).

IMPLEMENTING EFFECTIVE MARKETING AND NONPROFIT BRAND ORIENTATION: TACTICS AND STRATEGY

Knowing that a nonprofit needs marketing and branding is one thing; implementing these ideas on a limited budget is another. Jason (in the Toronto Ultimate Club case) and Cheryl and Karen (in the Ten Thousand Villages of Cincinnati case) face this exact dilemma. Each would benefit from understanding the value proposition their NPO offers by assessing the marketing mix (product, place, promotion, and price) versus other for-profit and nonprofit alternatives in their areas. The discussion on performance measurement and strategy in Chapters 5 and 6 would also inform the process.

The *marketing mix,* also called the 4Ps of marketing (product, place, promotion, and price), combine to form the value proposition an organization offers to its stakeholders. Managing the various components effectively can help an NPO achieve its mission. A brief discussion of each element of the mix follows.

Product, whether a tangible good or an intangible service, is perhaps the easiest component of the mix to understand. At Ten Thousand Villages of Cincinnati, the tangible products are the goods available for sale at the retail store. The intangible services provided extend to both the store customer (e.g., gift registry, return policies) and product producers in developing economies (e.g., fair wage employment, guaranteed prepayment for supplies). The nonprofit Lake Eola Charter School (Chapter 5 case) offers the same product—elementary school education—as the local for-profit private schools, but the services offered (e.g., afterschool programs, teaching methodology) differentiates it from the other schools.

The *place* or location in which the NPO product or service is available often plays a large role in the success of mission accomplishment. For example, convenient access (i.e., time and physical location) to critical services for domestic violence victims, such as mental health counseling, may increase participation in programs designed to reduce recurrence of violence.

Promotion includes paid advertisements and nonpaid public relations designed to build awareness, interest, decision, and action in a target audience. Contrary to popular belief, promotion is not synonymous with marketing but rather is one component of the marketing mix. Decisions relating to promotion include the following:

1. To whom should the NPO communicate—specific internal and external target audiences such as donors, volunteers, clients who may have an interest in the mission?

2. What should be communicated—from general organization mission to specific services offered?

3. How should the message be delivered—through what media (e.g., TV, radio, direct mail, Internet, social media such as Facebook and Twitter) and with what frequency?

The *price* of the product or service is complex in the nonprofit arena and is most likely influenced by the mission and ability to fundraise. Some nonprofits provide services without charge to clients, others charge a sliding scale based on income or ability to pay (a form of price discrimination). Recalling the 3C model (Ohmae, 1989) discussed in Chapter 5, nonprofit managers may look externally to customers and competitors, or internally to themselves (i.e., company) to determine price. Pricing strategies such as competitive parity align with competitive pressures, while value-based pricing considers customer factors and cost-based pricing derives from internal (i.e., company) constraints (Andreasen & Kotler, 2008).

When considering formulation and coordination of the marketing mix, NPO objectives would be well served if managers keep a keen focus on the target audience and keep the market tightly segmented. A target audience (or market) is a well-defined subset of the larger general population. When an organization focuses its marketing efforts on this audience, costs can be reduced and impact of message increased. Obvious examples of ways to divide a target audience exist (e.g., demographic, geographic) and are easily implemented even by small non-profits. A local children's theater, for example, may focus on areas of town with young families who are more likely to attend performances rather than single adults in urban areas. NPO managers who are ready to implement more sophisticated approaches to segmenting and targeting are encouraged to read more on the subject (Sargeant, 1999; Wymer, Knowles, & Gomes 2006) and consult with experts in the field. One well-formulated blog on the topic is Getting Attention, by Nancy Schwartz (http://gettingattention.org).

Bringing the 4Ps together to effectively achieve NPO mission requires integration and planning. The strategic marketing analysis process (SMAP) proposed by Gomes and Knowles (1998) and adapted by Wymer et al. (2006) provides a framework to achieve this.

PLANNING: THE SMAP APPROACH

Strategic marketing analysis process is a sophisticated approach to investigating an organization's current marketing mix and operational efficiencies relative to the external environment (e.g., competitors, client needs) in order to develop focused decisions on how to best meet the needs of the audiences the organization elects to serve. Although the approach can be time-consuming, this type of planning is critical to keeping the mission at the focus of all marketing efforts and reducing unnecessary marketing expenditures that do not meet desired goals. The plan, once developed, serves as a blueprint for development of skills and resources to achieve desired results. Table 9.1 outlines the steps of the SMAP approach. Before beginning the process, however, we encourage NPO leaders to consider contacting local colleges and universities for possible free assistance with plan development. Service learning and other pedagogies are increasingly popular among faculty and students, and serve to build a strong nonprofit network (Conway Dato-on & Gassenheimer, 2010).

SPECIAL CASES: SOCIAL MARKETING AND CAUSE-RELATED MARKETING

Up to this point, the discussion of marketing strategies and tactics has revolved around a more traditional marketplace where an organization offers a tangible or intangible service that is of value to some target audience. Many nonprofits engage in a different reality, though; they seek to change negative behaviors and/or encourage more positive choices. For example, U.S. First Lady Michelle Obama promotes physical fitness (i.e., desired behavioral outcome) among youth through Let's Move: America's Move to Raise a Healthier Generation of Kids (www.letsmove.gov/blog). This campaign, designed to combat increasing obesity in American youth (negative behaviors), is an example of *social marketing.*

AMA (2011b, "Social Marketing") defines *social marketing* as: "The branch of marketing that is concerned with the use of marketing knowledge, concepts, and techniques to enhance social ends, as well as the social consequences of marketing strategies, decisions, and actions. Marketing designed to influence the behavior of a target audience in which the benefits of the behavior are intended by the marketer to accrue primarily to . . . the society in general and not to the marketer." Social marketing may be as formal as the program undertaken by Michelle Obama or as informal as a friend trying to encourage another to stop smoking or reduce alcohol intake. In other words, social marketing efforts may come from for-profit, public, and private nonprofit organizations or individuals. While many of the tactics, strategies, and planning mentioned above apply to social marketing, NPO leaders should be aware that changing behaviors by targeting individuals and/or policy-makers is a long-term, challenging (and often frustrating) process. Leaders wishing to engage in social marketing are encouraged to thoroughly review motivational theory and investigate previous successes and failures prior to committing precious resources (Lefebvre, 1996).

This should not be confused with *cause-related marketing,* "which involves a partnership

Table 9.1 Strategic Marketing Analysis Process

Section Title	Description
STRATEGIC ANALYSIS	Consists of the next 18 steps in the process.
1. Needs-centered orientation	Uncovers level of market focus the NPO currently possesses. Answers the question: How focused are all resources on serving client needs?
2. Managerial scrutiny	Review of managerial structure and strategy as well as organization's mission, vision, values, and culture.
3. Board review	Similar to managerial review but applied to board of directors. Assesses the level of activity, responsibility, and culture of current board members relative to organization's mission.
4. Sustainable differential advantage development	What is the value proposition of the NPO, and how does it differ from other organizations serving similar community needs? External market research should assess current marketing mix versus target audience perceptions and desires.
5. Demand analysis	Helps NPO management allocate resources based on an understanding of what the target public wants from the organization. May include investigation of internal and external data.
6. Market segmentation	Divides public into smaller, identifiable sections that are interested and can be reached by NPO marketing mix offerings.
7. Consumer/client behavior within each segment	What motivates each segment? Considers expression of wants and needs of different segments, including volunteers, donors, and/or served clients.
8. Decision-making process exercised by target clients	Describes the stages different segments go through, from recognition of need (for service or for desire to volunteer) to final action (using service or engaging in volunteer activity).
9. Marketing mix analysis	Evaluates the appropriateness of the NPO's current marketing mix given the information gained from the analysis in previous sections of the report.
10. New offer (e.g., product, service) development	Based on evaluation of current offerings and understanding of market segment needs, a new offering is constructed. Should include detail on how the offering meets expressed needs.
11. Market positioning evaluation	Compares the perceptions of the current and redesigned offerings to those already available to target audience. Chapter 5 discusses tactics for conducting such comparisons.
12. Competitive analysis	Provides information on how competitors' offers impact NPO plans, including service offerings, potential donations, and volunteer recruitment and retention.
13. Financial assessment	Analyzes how revenue from external (e.g., donations, grants) and internal (e.g., fee for service) sources will be used to implement operations and marketing plans. Should include financial ratio and break-even analysis.

(Continued)

Table 9.1 (Continued)

Section Title	Description
14. Client needs analysis	Discusses the balance between client, donor, and volunteer needs with the mission of the NPO.
15. Environmental evaluation	Looks at what issues in the political, economic, legal, and social environment present opportunities or risks for a nonprofit.
16. Offer life cycle	Assesses the stage of development of current offerings (e.g., fresh and new vs. stale tried and true) and develops plans for replacement (e.g., new product development) when necessary. Goal is to constantly offer up-to-date services compared to target market needs and competitive offerings.
17. SWOT	Strengths, weaknesses, opportunities, and threats faced by organization's current offerings. More on this technique is available in Chapters 1 and 6.
18. Problem definition	Based on analysis conducted up to this point in the SMAP, what activities and resources are contributing to mission accomplishment, and which are detracting from it?
STRATEGIC ALTERNATIVES	Once the 18 steps outlined above are complete, this section of the analysis fully explains new potential offerings (complete 4P alternatives) the NPO will consider. The descriptions should be clear alternatives that enable a selection of one clear path.
EVALUATION OF ALTERNATIVES	Projects costs and performance results of alternatives suggested above to facilitate selection of best alternative. If no "best" alternative is obvious, managers should review the mutual exclusivity of the offerings and the decision factors enumerated here.
THE DECISION	After reviewing complete costs, benefits, and mission fit from alternatives described above, this section simply announces which alternative is chosen and communicates that choice to key stakeholders.
IMPLEMENTATION	Describes roles and responsibilities for executing the steps needed to make the decision effective. Communication across key internal players is needed to ensure an understanding of the decision and how each individual's role is vital to successful operations and goal achievement.
MONITORING	Chapter 5 discusses different approaches to performance measurement to ensure that efforts lead to accomplishment of objectives.

Source: Gomes & Knowles, 1998; Wymer et al. 2006.

between a nonprofit and a corporation that is intended to increase sales of the for-profit's products with financial and other benefits going to the nonprofit organization or a cause" (Worth, 2012, p. 243). Examples of this include Ford Motor Company's Warriors in Pink (www.ford .com/warriorsinpink/wip) and Avon's Walk for Breast Cancer (www.avonwalk.org), both of which contribute to breast cancer awareness and prevention, as well as Bono's Red Campaign for AIDS in Africa (www.redcampaign.org), which operates with the U.N.-backed Global Fund.

With these types of efforts, the NPO usually relies on the corporation's marketing expertise for implementation of strategies and tactics. Care should be taken, however, to ensure that both the brand partnership and the products or services offered through the partnership align with organizational mission, vision, and values.

CASES

Ten Thousand Villages of Cincinnati (United States): Ten Thousand Villages is a nonprofit fair-trade retail organization with a store located in Cincinnati, Ohio. During the store's opening and first two years of operations (2002–2004), Karen, the chair of the board of directors, and Cheryl, the store manager, struggled to develop a customer-focused plan to ensure sales increases. Marketing issues ranging from store location selection to inventory selection and promotion are presented. In addition to covering an alternative method of doing business—nonprofit enterprise—the case provides a platform for implementation of customer relationship management in a small, nonprofit environment.

The Toronto Ultimate Club (Canada): Jason Robinson, the general manager of a nonprofit Ultimate Frisbee club, seeks a marketing strategy to increase membership. For-profit clubs had claimed an ever-growing portion of the market, and the board of directors asked Robinson to review current offerings in the marketplace and to develop a formal marketing plan that would ensure the club's viability in the coming years.

REFERENCES

American Marketing Association. (2011a). *AMA definition of marketing.* Retrieved from http://www.marketingpower.com/Community/ARC/Pages/Additional/Definition/default.aspx

American Marketing Association. (2011b). *Dictionary.* Retrieved from http://www.marketingpower.com/_layouts/Dictionary.aspx?dLetter=B

Andreasen, A. R., & Kotler, P. (2008). *Strategic marketing for nonprofit organizations.* Upper Saddle River, NJ: Prentice Hall.

Bennett, R., & Sargeant, A. (2005). The nonprofit marketing landscape: Guest editors' introduction to a special section. *Journal of Business Research, 58,* 797–805.

Conway Dato-on, M., & Gassenheimer, J. (2010, May). *Service learning through NPOs: The new service-dominant logic in education?* Paper presented at the annual conference of the Academy of Marketing Science, Portland, OR.

Conway Dato-on, Mary, Weisenbach Keller, E., & Shaw, D. (2008). Global nonprofit brands with local missions: The YMCA across three countries. *International Journal of the Academic Business World, 2*(2), 21–32.

Gomes, R., & Knowles, P. A. (1998). Strategic planning for public and nonprofit organizations: Rethinking the strategic market analysis sections. *Journal of Nonprofit and Public Sector Marketing, 6,* 3–22.

Hall, H. (2006, July 20). Nonprofit-marketing experts outline hot trends, discuss challenges. *The Chronicle of Philanthropy.* Retrieved from http://philanthropy.com

Hankinson, P. (2001). Brand orientation in the charity sector: A framework for discussion and research. *International Journal of Nonprofit and Voluntary Sector Marketing, 6,* 231–242.

Hankinson, P. (2002). The impact of brand orientation on managerial practice: A quantitative study of the UK's top 500 fundraising managers. *International Journal of Nonprofit and Voluntary Sector Marketing, 7,* 30–44.

Kennedy, S. (1998). The power of positioning: A case history from the Children's Society. *Journal of Nonprofit and Voluntary Sector Marketing, 3,* 224–230.

Lake, L. (2011). *Eight basic steps to marketing your nonprofit organization.* Retrieved from http://marketing.about.com/cs/nonprofitmrktg/a/8stepnonprofit.htm

Lefebvre, R. C. (1996). 25 years of social marketing: Looking back and to the future. *Social Marketing Quarterly, 3*(3&4), 51–58.

Ohmae, K. (1989, March-April). The global logic of strategic alliances. *Harvard Business Review,* 143–154.

Ramrayka, L. (1998). You need a firm grasp of business techniques to survive in the charity sector these days—But is this a good thing? *Fundraising, 29*(June), 11–13.

Sargeant, A. (1999). *Marketing management for nonprofit organisations.* Oxford, UK: Oxford University Press.

Saxton, J. (1994). A strong charity brand comes from strong beliefs and values. *Journal of Brand Management, 2,* 211–218.

Tapp, A. (1996). Charity brands: A qualitative study of current practice. *International Journal of Nonprofit and Voluntary Sector Marketing, 1,* 327–336.

Van Riel, C. B. M. (1995). *Principles of corporate communication.* London, UK: Prentice Hall.

Weisenbach Keller, E., Conway Dato-on, M., & Shaw, D. (2010). NPO branding: Preliminary lessons from major players. *International Journal of Nonprofit and Voluntary Sector Marketing, 15,* 105–121.

Worth, M. J. (2012). *Nonprofit management: Principles and practice* (2nd ed.). Thousand Oaks, CA: Sage.

Wymer, W., Knowles, P., & Gomes, R. (2006). *Nonprofit marketing: Marketing management for charitable and nongovernmental organizations.* Thousand Oaks, CA: Sage.

TEN THOUSAND VILLAGES OF CINCINNATI: THE FIRST YEAR AND BEYOND

Spring always brings renewal: that was Karen's focus as she reminisced about how she became involved with the fair trade organization Ten Thousand Villages (TTV), in her hometown of Cincinnati, and contemplated the next steps to build on the local store's first year. Karen, a full-time mom most of her adult life with little to no business experience, had been a Mennonite church member for as long as she could remember. As church members, both she and her husband were involved in various volunteer/service endeavours throughout their lives; therefore, it seemed natural for Karen to become involved in an internationally focused mission when the opportunity presented itself through her church. She never imagined that such humble beginnings would lead her to the chairperson position of the board of directors for the first and only TTV retail store in Cincinnati. Karen seemed overwhelmed as she recalled the brief history of Ten Thousand Villages Cincinnati (TTVC) and thought about its future. The memory seemed surreal; through Karen's leadership, TTVC opened in November 2002. Karen maintained a "pinch me, it can't be true" attitude, while also feeling a sense of pride about her accomplishments.

While there was much excitement about the store's first year of operation, Karen was eager to discover new strategies for increasing sales in year two and beyond. She believed that the TTVC store could repeat and even improve upon the first year's successes; at the same time, she was quick to note that staying true to the TTV mission was crucial. Because soliciting advice was part of the TTVC store's recipe for success, Karen willingly sought recommendations to help more impoverished artisans across the world by generating more fair trade sales in Cincinnati.

HISTORY OF TEN THOUSAND VILLAGES

Ten Thousand Villages started in 1946 when Joe Byler, a volunteer with the Mennonite church, visited a Puerto Rican community the church was sponsoring. Byler's wife, Edna Ruth, accompanied him on this trip. During the trip, Ruth observed the intricate embroidery work of the local Puerto Rican women. Realizing that there were few places to sell the embroidery in Puerto Rico, Ruth purchased samples to sell in her hometown of Lancaster County, Pennsylvania. Having sold the initial pieces in Lancaster County, Ruth purchased more products from the women in Puerto Rico—she even expanded her product selection to include other handcrafted Puerto Rican items. Soon, Ruth began traveling to Mennonite churches throughout Pennsylvania displaying samples of handmade products from Puerto Rico, told stories of the artisans who made the various products and took orders. Ruth contacted Mennonite-sponsored communities in other developing countries to see if they too would be interested in supplying handmade products to sell in the United States. As word spread about the high-quality, handcrafted products produced by artisans from around the world, U.S. consumers inside and outside the Mennonite church clamoured for more. Before too long, demand for these unique, international handmade products exceeded Ruth's capacity to supply and manage.

In the early 1970s, the successful project moved out of Ruth's home and became an official Mennonite Central Committee (MCC) undertaking. MCC is the service, relief and development agency of the North American Mennonite and Brethren in Christ churches. For 50 years (1946–1996), the Ten Thousand Villages program of the MCC was known as SELFHELP Crafts of the World. This name and logo was familiar to the thousands of loyal customers and volunteers who helped build the program into the strong alternative trading organization that became Ten Thousand Villages in 1996.[1] Ten Thousand Villages launched as a nonprofit organization specifically to foster the sale of indigenous handicrafts in the United States; as part of this endeavor, the church opened stores throughout North America to sell the handcrafted items.

At the beginning of 2004, there were nearly 200 stores in the United States and Canada that sold TTV products. TTV always operated as a nonprofit program affiliated with the MCC, and the stores were mainly managed by volunteers. Based on the MCC's belief in fair trade, TTV became a member of the International Fair Trade Association (IFAT)[2] and the U.S.-based Fair Trade Federation (FTF).[3] The following mission statement and operating principles adopted by TTV clearly articulate the organization's role in a global economy:

> Ten Thousand Villages provides vital, fair income to Third World people by marketing their handicrafts and telling their stories in North America. Ten Thousand Villages works with artisans who would otherwise be unemployed or underemployed. This income helps pay for food, education, health care and housing.

- We work with disadvantaged artisans.
- We purchase from craft groups that are concerned for their members and that promote member participation.
- We pay fair prices for handicrafts. We pay promptly.
- We pay up to half the value of a handicraft order when it is placed, the balance when the items are shipped to North America. This provides operating capital for artisans to purchase raw materials and for craft groups to pay workers.

---

[1]www.tenthousandvillages.org, accessed July 13, 2004.

[2]At the time of the case, the organization was known as IFAT. It has since changed to World Fair Trade Organization (WFTO).

[3]www.fairtradefederation.org/ accessed July 13, 2004.

- We offer handicrafts that reflect and reinforce rich cultural traditions.
- We promote fair trade.
- We use marketing strategies and messages consistent with our mission and ideals.
- Our ideals include responsible lifestyle choices, efficiency and Christian ethics. We seek integrity in all our actions and relationships.
- Whenever possible, we work with volunteers in North American operations.[4]

FAIR TRADE

IFAT defined fair trade as:

[A] trading partnership, based on dialogue, transparency [being open to public accountability] and respect that seeks greater equity in international trade. The fair trade organization contributes to sustainable development by offering better trading conditions to, and securing the rights of, marginalized producers and workers. Backed by consumers, fair trade organizations engage actively in supporting producers, raising awareness, and campaigning for positive change in conventional international trade practices. Fair trade organizations have a clear commitment to fair trade as the principal core of their mission.[5]

According to IFAT, fair trade was better than aid because fair trade was built on the premise of a sustainable future for artisans based on their own abilities. The following 10 standards of fair trade coincide with TTV operating principles and demonstrate the values upon which fair trade organizations based their decisions:

1. Create Opportunities for Economically Disadvantaged Producers—poverty reduction through trade

2. Transparency and Accountability—transparent in its management and commercial relations and accountable to all its stakeholders

3. Trading Practices—trades with concern for the social, economic and environmental well-being of marginalized small producers

4. Payment of a Fair Price—one that has been mutually agreed by all through dialogue

5. Child Labour and Forced Labour—adheres to the UN Convention on the Rights of the Child, and national/local law on the employment of children

6. Non-Discrimination, Gender Equity and Freedom of Association

7. Working Conditions—provides a safe and healthy working environment for employees

8. Capacity Building—seeks to increase positive developmental impacts for small, marginalized producers

9. Promotion of Fair Trade—raises awareness of the aim of Fair Trade and of the need for greater justice in world trade through Fair Trade

10. Environment—maximize the use of raw materials from sustainably managed sources in products, buying locally when possible[6]

TTV became a member of FTF—a coalition of more than 200 craft producers, wholesalers and retailers. Among other things, the FTF developed "a workable agenda for handicrafts and agricultural products within the context of fair trade."[7]

Operations such as TTV came to be known as alternative trade organizations (ATOs):

ATOs were non-governmental organizations designed to benefit artisans and not maximize profits. They marketed products from handicraft and agricultural organizations or cooperatives established in low-income countries. They provided consumers around the world with products that have been fairly purchased from sustainable sources.

---

[4]www.tenthousandvillages.com/php/about.us/about.vision.php, accessed July 13, 2004.

[5]www.ifat.org accessed July 13, 2004.

[6]www.wfto.com/index.php?option=com_content&task=view&id=2&Itemid=14, accessed April 11, 2010.

[7]www.fairtradefederation.com/index.html, accessed December 2004.

ATOs put fair trade into practice and campaigned for more equitable terms of trade for artisans from low-income countries.[8]

Other retail ATO operations that offered products from developing countries included Oxfam (United Kingdom), Twin Trading (United Kingdom), SERRV (United States), Bridgehead (Canada), Trading Partners (Australia) and Nepali Bazaro (Japan). Product selection at these retail outlets generally included handicrafts (e.g. clothing, household decor and giftware) and agricultural-based commodities such as tea, coffee, chocolate and cocoa.[9] In 2002, total sales for the fair trade industry in North America were $180 million,[10] an increase of 44 per cent from 2001. The sales for the Pacific Rim (Australia, Japan and New Zealand) were $70.6 million in 2002: this represented a 23 per cent increase from 2001.[11] The popularity of fair trade products was on the rise: "Fair trade products also became increasingly conspicuous on supermarket shelves, and if choice was what consumers wanted then the future looked prosperous."[12] Consumers who purchased ATO products shared demographic and psychographic profiles, regardless of their geographic location.

TEN THOUSAND VILLAGES' CUSTOMERS

ATO consumers comprised the primary target market for TTV stores. These socially conscious consumers became known as "cultural creatives." The estimated 50 million U.S. cultural creatives were motivated to purchase high-quality products with social value. In other words, these well-educated consumers, most with college and post-baccalaureate degrees, sought to make a difference in their world. Demographically, cultural creatives were predominantly women in their early 40s with an above-average annual income of $52,200.[13]

Cultural creatives wanted to know everything they could about the products they might purchase. They became knowledgeable consumers based on extensive research about global current events and production sources.[14] Their research drove them to ask questions about who made products, under what conditions, and using what processes. Cultural creatives consistently read package labels and product reviews; they did not purchase on impulse.

Products offered by TTV and other ATOs were perfect offerings for cultural creatives. The practice of fair trade and the operating principles of TTV mirrored the values of cultural creative consumers. This segment actively sought stores, products and services from fair trade organizations via the Internet and other media. The identification and pursuit of this segment was logical for TTV Cincinnati.

According to the 2000 U.S. Census, the Cincinnati market (the geographic market segment), which constituted approximately 7.4 per cent of Ohio's population, comprised approximately 331,280 people. Within that population, 38.5 per cent were between the ages of 35 and 64, and 51.4 per cent were female. Twenty-nine per cent of Cincinnatians held a bachelor's

[8]www.ifat.org, accessed December 2004.

[9]Mark S. Leclair, "Fighting the Tide: Alternative Trade Organizations in the Era of Global Free Trade," *World Development,* 30 (6), 2002, p. 949–58.

[10]All funds are in US$ unless otherwise noted.

[11]"2003 Report on Fair Trade Trends in US, Canada & the Pacific Rim," Fair Trade Federation, Washington, D.C., 2003.

[12]Higher Education & Research Opportunities 2003, "Ethics the Easy Way." www.hero.ac.uk/business/archive/ethics_the_easy_way5043.cfm?archive=yes, accessed December 4, 2003.

[13]Paul H. Ray, "The Emerging Culture," *American Demographics,* 19 (2), 1997, p. 29–34.

[14]Paul H. Ray and Sherry Ruth Anderson, *The Cultural Creatives: How 50 Million People Are Changing the World,* Harmony Books, New York, New York, 2000.

degree or higher and earned a median annual income of $40,964. This demographic data suggested the possible existence of a cultural creatives segment in Cincinnati. More specific, in-depth primary data would be necessary to understand if a group of cultural creatives existed within the demographic segment.

TEN THOUSAND VILLAGES' COMPETITORS

Research by local MBA students discovered four main competitors (three national and one local) in the Cincinnati area that sold home decor and handcrafted items similar to the TTVC store.[15] A brief description of the competitors follows.

Pier 1 Imports

Pier 1 Imports was North America's largest importer of decorative home products. According to Pier 1 Imports' 2003 annual report, its stores carried a variety of 4,000 products from more than 40 countries. Pier 1 Imports divided its products into five categories: furniture, decorative accessories, house wares, bed and bath and seasonal. The annual report showed sales for the previous three fiscal years were driven by the furniture category (38 per cent of sales in 2003, 39 per cent in 2002 and 40 per cent in 2001).

Pier 1 Imports targeted women aged 25 to 34 and advertised aggressively to reach its target audience. Nationwide advertising in 2001 totaled $55 million, and was nearly $30 million in 2002. Advertising campaigns were designed to position Pier 1 Imports as "relaxing, stimulating and a sanctuary at the same time. It's a place that is fun, warm and inviting. It is not hectic like a mall environment."[16] More than 2,000 items were available for sale on Pier 1's website,[17] including furniture and decorative items. The site also included a bridal gift registry and a furniture guide. Pier 1 Imports targeted children through its subsidiary CargoKids. The company defined its competitive advantages as price, merchandise variety and visual presentation. Based on its volume, visibility online and multiple store locations, Pier 1 Imports enjoyed a competitive advantage of vast name recognition.

Cost Plus World Market

The 2003 Cost Plus World Market (World Market) annual report noted products imported from more than 60 countries; the company's marketing strategy targeted women aged 22 to 55. World Market differentiated itself from Pier 1 Imports and others in two ways: it carried food items and relied heavily on creating a unique atmosphere in the store. World Market operated under the assumption that consumers wanted the same international flair in food items as they had in home furnishings; to accommodate these needs, World Market offered consumables including wines, beers and olive oils among others. Consumables made up 33 per cent of World Market's product mix.[18]

World Market stores were designed to evoke a feeling of being in a world market: items were displayed in open barrels as if displayed in a bazaar. World Market made use of in-store activities such as cooking demonstrations and food and drink samples to generate excitement and increase impulse purchases. The stores' atmosphere was designed to capture the customers' imagination and encourage exploration of new items. World Market identified its competitive

---

[15]Donald Hicks, Shigeaki Wakana and John Dine, "Marketing Plan for Ten Thousand Villages," Unpublished paper by students at Xavier University, Cincinnati, Ohio, 2003.

[16]Rebecca Flass, "Pier 1 Gets in the Holiday Spirit," *Adweek* Southeast Edition, 23 (45), November 11, 2002, p. 4.

[17]www.pier1.com, accessed July 13, 2004.

[18]Cost Plus World Market, 2003 Annual Report.

advantages as low prices, a variety of products and a unique shopping experience.

Z Gallerie

Twenty-four years ago, Z Gallerie started in California as a store offering dormitory-room posters. In 2003, Z Gallerie maintained 47 stores in 13 states (including Ohio) and offered a comprehensive product selection of 3,000 items.[19] Z Gallerie merchandise displays encouraged exploratory shopping by constantly changing its products. Unlike Pier 1 Imports and Cost Plus World Market that strove for a pleasant and relaxing atmosphere, Z Gallerie designed stores to be dynamic, to energize the customer with a bohemian flair.[20]

From the Ridiculous to the Sublime

A small boutique store, From the Ridiculous to the Sublime was located down the street from TTVC. It was a local establishment with small monthly sales that fit the odd mix of O'Bryonville (the section of town where both stores were located) store offerings. The store's products included unique handicraft items, jewelry and giftware. From the Ridiculous to the Sublime followed Z Gallerie's dynamic layout and bohemian atmosphere.

Unique Selling Point for Cincinnati Ten Thousand Villages

The competitive review showed competitors that carried similar product offerings but held limited appeal to the values of the cultural creatives target segment. TTV was the only store in Cincinnati to tender fair trade merchandise; no other store could match the mission of TTV, in which "shopping makes a difference." In addition to this distinctive character, comparison shopping showed

that TTV products were competitively priced and at times offered better quality. TTV had a competitive advantage in its mission: the key to success might be promoting that mission to the "right" customers. This was particularly difficult given the monetary constraints of TTVC as a nonprofit endeavor.

Fair trade products were not without any competition in the Cincinnati area, however. As fair trade coffee and teas gained more acceptance in mainstream grocery stores, TTVC found itself competing with supermarket giant and local corporate power house Kroger. Due to its nationwide buying volume, Kroger sold the same brand of fair trade coffee for less than TTVC's wholesale purchase price. Interestingly, TTVC also found itself competing against the Cincinnati Catholic Church. The Cincinnati archdiocese took a strong position on promoting and selling fair trade coffee. Once again, the diocese's prices for the same coffee were below cost for TTVC.

TEN THOUSAND VILLAGES CINCINNATI: SETTING UP SHOP

The TTVC store was started by the Cincinnati Mennonite Fellowship (one of several Mennonite churches in Cincinnati). In 2001, after having orchestrated twelve years of successful Christmas season weekend sales events, members from the Cincinnati church decided to begin raising funds to open a permanent, year-round retail outlet where Cincinnatians could purchase unique, international handmade products. Karen served as the chairperson of the board of directors for the newly proposed TTV store. With the assistance of her husband, who was an attorney, Karen developed the bylaws and filed for the store's nonprofit status in January 2002. The goal was to open the store in time for the 2002 Christmas shopping season. With the help of the board, the following mission statement was developed:

---

[19]www.zgallerie.com/t-about.aspx, accessed June 10, 2004.

[20]"Furnishing the Cocoon," *Chain Store Age,* 79 (3), March 1, 2003.

Ten Thousand Villages of Cincinnati will promote global understanding and connectedness by:

- providing innovative markets for artisans in developing countries,
- telling the artisans' stories and celebrating their artistic spirit,
- empowering the artisans to provide basic needs for themselves and their families by purchasing their handcrafted products at fair prices, and
- creating local awareness of, and involvement with, global economic issues through an ecumenical community.

To open the store, Karen needed to raise $52,000 (the amount set by TTV headquarters in Akron, Pennsylvania). Although many people told Karen that she would never raise the needed capital, she remained committed and believed in the mission of TTV. She was confident that others would support her as they heard the TTV story. To generate the necessary funds, Karen pursued two main avenues. Firstly, she organized a large-scale church craft sale. When assisting with the Christmas season weekend sales events, Karen received inventory on consignment from TTV's headquarters. For this fundraising event—as well as for a permanent store—the goods would be the responsibility of the TTVC group, whether or not they sold. Thus, Karen selected the items for the craft sale carefully: the items that did not sell might become inventory for the planned store. She relied on both her past experience and recommendations from others to judiciously select a wide range of items from TTV's headquarters' list of imported products from 36 different countries. Secondly, Karen embarked on a fundraising campaign; specifically, she wrote letters soliciting donations from loyal customers of the past Christmas sales events, and members of both her own and other local church communities.

The church craft sale generated $12,000; the remainder of funds came from donations. Karen recalled the fundraising period with awe and pleasure:

I was so scared. I had no idea how the store's fair trade mission would be received outside the Mennonite community. I mean within the community we're so familiar with the project it seemed natural, but how would I convince those not so intimately involved in the process? I decided to start with people who had purchased products before. I figured this would be a good indication of a belief in the mission and an appreciation for the quality of the handicrafts themselves. In the end [she laughs nervously], it wasn't as difficult as I thought it would be. The artisans tell their own stories so well; I simply served as a mouthpiece in the local community.

Finding a Store Location

With funds in hand and a board of directors (mostly Mennonite Church members) in place, Karen began to search for the "ideal" store location. Everyone told her this would be the most critical element pertaining to the success of the TTVC store. She was nervous and felt somewhat overwhelmed by the task, but she again relied on her community of supporters and friends. Karen found a realtor who was an acquaintance of a church member: she and the realtor spent much of the spring and early summer of 2002 looking at and rejecting numerous store locations. Karen was becoming frustrated; she decided to take the matter into her own hands.

It was August 2002, and time was running out if Karen was going to open the store in time for the 2002 holiday shopping season. She began looking on the Internet for available and affordable commercial real estate in the areas of Cincinnati that she felt would be receptive to the ideals of fair trade. Cincinnati, traditionally a conservative city, had few shopping districts with significant foot traffic—a criteria that other TTV store managers told Karen was critical to success. There were no "bohemian" sections of town populated by liberal thinkers who actively supported fair trade, like there were in other cities, such as Seattle, Washington, and Saint Paul, Minnesota. One potential location for the TTVC store was the area surrounding the University of Cincinnati (the largest university in the city). There were, however, no available commercial locations in the area, and some perceived the neighbourhoods around the school to be unsafe.

Ideally, Karen wanted the store to be in Hyde Park—an upscale neighbourhood with a popular shopping square that integrated restaurants, ice cream shops and boutiques in an area where people walked morning, noon and night. When available, real estate in Hyde Park was expensive and beyond Karen's projected budget of $2,000 per month for rent. Feeling a bit dejected, Karen was driving to her church one day through an area just west of Hyde Park called O'Bryonville. She could not believe her eyes: there was a "for lease" sign in a store front on the main street in O'Bryonville. She quickly jotted down the number and vowed to call as soon as she reached her church.

Karen was elated to learn that the store in O'Bryonville, with 1,017 square feet of retail space, was available immediately, needed only minimal work before the store could open and rented for $1,900 per month. She consulted with the board members; some members were not as excited as Karen. They said, for example, that O'Bryonville had more drive-by traffic than foot traffic. Others pointed out that the consignment, antique and furniture shops in the area did not attract "fair trade-type" customers (i.e. cultural creatives). Aware of these risks, Karen pondered the situation: she believed strongly that if she did not have a store location secured by September 2002, TTVC would not open by November. Karen signed the lease.

Hiring a Store Manager

While looking for the commercial retail site, Karen and the board members were also trying to find a store manager. They did not have any contacts in the retail business, so they simply placed a want ad in a local newspaper. By August, the advertisement had appeared twice and there were no suitable candidates. Just as Karen was about to pursue other means of finding a store manager, she opened a letter and resume from a woman named Cheryl. Cheryl had retail management experience in a small home decor store, expressed a desire to stay in Cincinnati long-term and was available immediately—Karen eagerly contacted the board to schedule an interview with Cheryl.

When Karen met Cheryl, she knew it was a perfect match. Cheryl was well prepared for the interview: she researched TTV, had visited the store location, asked specific questions about sales objectives and queried specifically about the relationship between the store manager and board. Cheryl had applicable experience, was extremely energetic, boldly honest and showed a sincere interest in the TTV mission. She provided an excellent balance to Karen's more reserved approach to the project. The board unanimously agreed to hire Cheryl as the first manager of the TTVC store. It was now the end of September 2002, and the race was on to get the store up and running by the beginning of November.

Cheryl started her tenure at TTVC by logging almost 80 hours per week, seven days a week for all of October and November and most of December. She recalled the start-up time as both exciting and exhausting: "I definitely wouldn't want to do it again! As a matter of fact, if the Ten Thousand Villages headquarters asked me, I'd tell them to never let anyone open this close to the holidays no matter how much they begged." She recalled walking into the store and seeing "boxes . . . floor to ceiling, front to back; really, there was nothing but boxes."

Cheryl was certainly impressed by the volume of goods Karen had purchased with the $50,000 loan from TTV's headquarters.[21] Cheryl managed three shifts of volunteers for almost two days to unpack the merchandise. Although TTV stores were largely run by volunteers, Cheryl was—like managers in most other TTV outlets—a full-time, paid employee.

After unpacking, Cheryl and the volunteers began to attach price tags to the products. Cheryl initially priced the products according to recommendations from TTV headquarters: although the price recommendations were not mandated by TTV, Cheryl felt comfortable adhering to them until she gained a clearer understanding of her customers. The volunteers also made store fixtures to display the merchandise.

[21]The loan was to be paid back in five years at a "very reasonable" rate.

As was customary, TTV headquarters sent a small group of volunteers to assist with both merchandising displays and the setting up of computers. Although work on the displays progressed, the computers arrived late; thankfully, the computers were set up in time for the official store opening on November 1, 2002.

THE FIRST YEAR OF OPERATIONS

Overview

As Karen stated time and time again, "The story included so much more than just the numbers." TTV's headquarters estimated that for every $1,200 in sales at a TTV store, one impoverished artisan could be employed for an entire year. Based on this estimate, the Cincinnati store employed approximately 294 artisans in 2003 (see Exhibits 1 and 2).

TTVC turned its first profit of $546 in April 2003: this was likely the result of traffic generated by TTVC's booth at the Cincinnati Flower Show. Cheryl remembered the excitement and hard work on the part of the volunteers during this profitable period. November was the next significantly profitable month, when TTVC netted $1,902, with sales of $45,767. November sales coincided with the beginning of the store's first major advertising campaign and the rush of the holiday shopping season. Sales in December were the highest for the year at $109,990, resulting in $28,262 profit.

As expected, store traffic mirrored sales. Cheryl noted, "Visits to the store were definitely not consistent over the course of the year. We increased store hours for the holidays, adding Sunday hours, and one additional hour Monday through Saturday. We were swamped in the last two months of the year." Cheryl kept track of the number of customers served by having the volunteers keep count. The volunteers were also trained to ask shoppers how they heard about the store and if this was their first visit. The store served approximately 10,880 customers throughout the year.

Getting the Word Out

Promotions played a vital role during the first year of operations; for example, the store received a local advertising agency grant for $25,000. The grant stipulated that the ad agency would work to develop TTVC print ads at no cost to the store. Cheryl negotiated several advertising placement contracts so the ads would be seen on city buses, strategically placed billboards and in one newspaper, *CityBeat*—the weekly alternative press paper. All ads were placed in November and December 2002 (see Exhibit 3). As with most retailers, these two months were critical sales periods and ads were placed to drive customers to the store. TTVC also received some good publicity through an article in *Catholic Telegraph,* a national Catholic magazine emphasizing social services. Cheryl was particularly proud of being named as a "2002 top retail choice" in *Cincinnati Magazine.* The other main promotional strategy was the "shopping days" campaign. With this promotion, local nonprofit organizations (e.g. Red Cross, YWCA, Salvation Army and local churches) scheduled days when they would encourage members and friends to shop at the store. In exchange for promoting the store, the designated nonprofit organization would receive a percentage of the store's sales. To augment in-store sales, Cheryl and volunteers staffed booths at local craft shows, such as the Cincinnati Flower Show and the Northern Kentucky Holiday Market. TTVC did not engage in Internet (online) marketing during its first year of operations.

YEAR TWO

According to Cheryl and Karen, the most important objective for 2004 (year two) was to increase sales. Given that increasing sales was often achieved by considering one's marketing strategy, Cheryl and Karen considered the "four P's of marketing" (product, price, place and promotion) as they pertained to TTVC and its target market.

Exhibit 1 Store Income Statement—2003 (in US$)

	Jan	Feb	Mar	Apr	May	Jun	Jul	Aug	Sep	Oct	Nov	Dec	2003
Sales	15,968	13,748	19,898	25,676	23,243	21,293	21,125	19,022	19,440	18,068	45,767	109,990	353,238
Expenses													
Personnel	4,806	8,309	6,820	6,128	6,128	6,440	6,128	6,128	6,440	6,128	6,128	10,380	79,963
Bank services	285	260	328	391	365	343	341	318	323	308	612	1,319	5,193
Gen. operating	559	459	1,193	759	609	459	459	459	1,193	459	459	459	7,526
Equipment & building	3,756	2,940	2,940	2,940	2,940	2,940	2,940	2,940	2,940	2,940	2,940	2,940	36,096
Marketing/ promotion											9,498	9,498	18,996
Finance fee & loan payment	650	650	650	650	650	650	650	650	650	720	720	720	8,010
Other	517	167	317	1,167	167	317	167	167	317	167	167	317	3,954
Total Exp.	10,573	12,785	12,248	12,035	10,859	11,149	10,685	10,662	11,863	10,722	20,524	25,633	159,738
Total COGS	8,144	7,011	10,148	13,095	11,854	10,859	10,774	9,701	9,914	9,214	23,341	56,095	180,150
Net income	-2,749	-6,048	-2,498	546	530	-715	-334	-1,341	-2,337	-1,868	1,902	28,262	13,350

Source: Company records.

Note: COGS = cost of goods sold.

Exhibit 2 Statement of Financial Position, December 31, 2003 (in US$)

ASSETS		
	Current assets	
	Checking/savings	89,469.98
	Merchandise inv.	21,039.34
	TOTAL current assets	110,509.32
	Fixed assets	
	Total computer system	12,247.73
	Total furniture & fixtures	2,198.17
	Total leasehold improvements	9,376.24
	TOTAL fixed assets	23,822.14
TOTAL ASSETS		134,331.46
LIABILITIES & EQUITY		
	Total current liabilities	3,348.68
	Total long-term liabilities	40,197.55
	TOTAL liabilities	43,546.23
	Equity	
	Retained earnings	77,435.23
	Net income	13,350.00
	TOTAL equity	90,785.23
TOTAL LIABILITIES & EQUITY		134,331.46

Source: Company files.

Exhibit 3 TTVC Advertisement From Grant Money

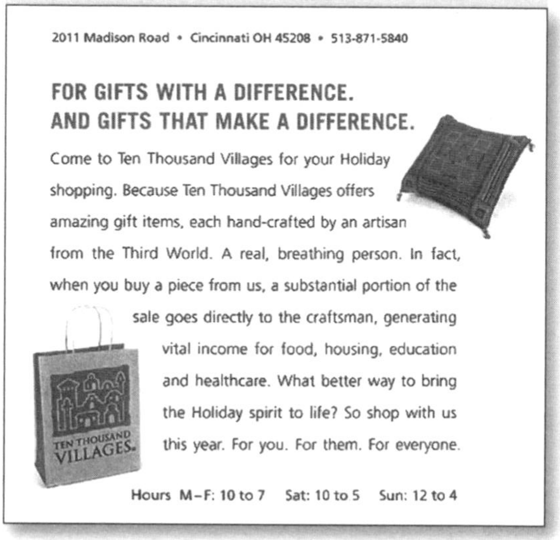

Source: Company files.

Target Market

In the eyes of Cheryl and Karen, TTVC had done a fairly good job of targeting the local cultural creative consumer segment. Toward the end of 2003, for example, MBA students from a local university conducted marketing research as part of their class project. The data indicated that customers were similar to cultural creatives in several ways. The majority of customers were female (88 per cent), between the ages of 41 and 60 and earned more than $50,000 per year. An overwhelming majority had at least a bachelor's degree (82 per cent). Survey responses also indicated that, like cultural creatives, TTVC shoppers bought fair trade items to help the less fortunate but also found the products to be of high quality and unique variety. Although there were clearly more cultural creatives in Cincinnati that TTV needed to reach, Cheryl and Karen felt comfortable that their current promotion strategy could be successfully implemented again in the second year to further penetrate this important market segment; in fact, Cheryl and Karen planned to increase the promotional budget in year two.

Place

Karen felt comfortable with the location of the store, despite the fact that, during the first year, Cheryl had suggested other possible locations and a store expansion. Although they both believed that the O'Bryonville neighbourhood was ideal, Cheryl felt that the store was quickly outgrowing the current space (1,000 square feet of retail space) and therefore needed more room. For the time being, however, Karen and the board of directors decided to stay at the current O'Bryonville location.

Product

The products sold by TTVC were somewhat dictated by TTV's headquarters. Given that the TTV organization guaranteed its artisans 90 per cent of last year's purchase volume, TTVC—like other TTV outlets—was obligated to purchase the items that TTV's headquarters sent to the store. During 2003, TTV's headquarters sent 700 (unordered) products to Cincinnati. Merchandise was received monthly, and although Cheryl was able to select approximately 90 per cent of these products from what TTV headquarters had available, 10 per cent of the items came "sight unseen." Product availability at TTV headquarters varied throughout the year. Assuming that Cheryl could sell the products that headquarters supplied, she could purchase goods from non-TTV sources as long as they were FTF-approved. In 2003, TTVC sold most of the products supplied by TTV, and had even purchased some supplementary items from SERRV and other FTF-certified suppliers. Cheryl was not overly concerned about products for the upcoming year: goods from Ten Thousand Villages sold well thus far, and although the procurement process was partially out of her control, she felt comfortable in being able to secure additional product

if and when necessary. Cheryl repeatedly emphasized that focusing on the mission—employing artisans for sustainable living—was more important than terrific inventory turn.

Price

TTV's headquarters provided suggested retail prices for products sent to the store: Cheryl could charge these suggested prices, or change them. Over the course of the first year, Cheryl made several adjustments—both increases and decreases—to the prices of various items as she learned the preferences of her customers; for example, due to strong demand, Cheryl raised the price of flower pots from Vietnam by almost 25 per cent. She would likely continue to adjust prices as she saw fit throughout the upcoming year.

A Strategy for Year Two

At this point in their assessment, and in keeping with the primary objective for the second year (i.e. increasing sales), Cheryl and Karen decided to focus on existing customers. While interested in acquiring new customers, Cheryl and Karen were committed to reaching the entire cultural creative segment in Cincinnati, as well as other (non-cultural creative) segments in the area who might be interested in the TTV mission or products. The women seemed convinced they could achieve their goal of increasing sales by focusing on existing customers. Data from the abovementioned survey suggested to Cheryl and Karen that the store attracted many repeat buyers (almost 60 per cent) who were satisfied with their in-store experience and were likely to shop the store again (almost 70 per cent). The task at hand was to ensure that those who intended to return acted on their intentions—multiple times throughout the year.

Based on her many interactions with the customers, Cheryl was also convinced that most shoppers could and would—with the right incentives—purchase more items, as well as more expensive items. Cheryl and Karen envisioned having actual *relationships* with their customers, wherein the needs of these customers were more fully satisfied, ultimately making the store more profitable.[22] By setting up procedures and implementing strategies to assure customer longevity and profitability, Cheryl and Karen hoped to ensure the long-term success of TTVC. Although they planned to focus on existing customers for the time being, they knew that whatever new policies and procedures they set into motion should be readily applicable to future customers.

CONCLUSION

Karen anxiously contemplated what the next year at Ten Thousand Villages Cincinnati would bring: How would she and Cheryl effectively focus on existing customers? They needed sound, workable ideas complete with details. What exactly should they do, and how and when should they do it? What problems might they encounter and/or what actions should they avoid? What aspects of such a strategy were most important? Clearly, they needed a plan.

THE TORONTO ULTIMATE CLUB

In early December 2008, Jason Robinson sat back and wondered how he could improve on the past year's slow growth in membership at the Toronto Ultimate Club (TUC). TUC, located in Toronto, Ontario, Canada, was an organization that focused on growing the sport of Ultimate Frisbee (Ultimate) by offering leagues in the Toronto area. Since the development of TUC's strategic plan two years earlier, membership had stopped declining, but Robinson, TUC's general manager, was still not satisfied with the organization's rate of growth. He knew that his not-for-profit club was losing market share to the rapidly growing for-profit competition, and he thought that developing a marketing

plan for the coming year was a necessity. This plan would have to be completed quickly to give the club's board of directors enough time to implement Robinson's recommendations prior to the beginning of the upcoming summer season.

TORONTO[1]

Toronto was the largest city in Canada, with a population of over five million living in approximately 1.8 million private dwellings. The city was the nation's financial capital, with the highest concentration of financial institutions in

[22]Mary Conway Dato-on, Mary Joyce and Chris Manolis, "Creating Effective Customer Relationships in Nonprofit Retailing: A Case Study," 2006, Special Issue of *International Journal of Nonprofit and Voluntary Sector Marketing* on "Nonprofit and Voluntary Sector Marketing: An International Perspective," 11 (4), pp. 319–333.

[1]All statistical data in this paragraph is attributed to www.statscan.gc.ca; accessed December 20, 2008.

Canada. As well, Toronto was an important arts and cultural centre, accounting for about 34 per cent of all Canadian establishments in the performing arts industry. Often noted as one of the most culturally diverse cities in the world, visible minorities made up almost 47 per cent of the city's population. Toronto was one of the wealthier cities in Canada, with a median income of Cdn$30,350. See Exhibits 1 and 2 for a detailed

breakdown of age and income demographics. As such a large city, Toronto had almost limitless venues for entertainment and fitness.[2]

Exhibit 1 Toronto Age Demographics

Age (years)	Number	% of total
10–14	141,000	5.6%
15–19	146,000	5.8%
20–24	172,000	6.9%
25–29	190,000	7.6%
30–34	196,000	7.8%
35–39	203,000	8.1%
40–44	213,000	8.5%
45–49	194,000	7.8%
50–54	168,000	6.7%
55–59	148,000	5.9%

Source: Statistics Canada, www.statscan.ca. February 19, 2009.

Exhibit 2 Toronto Income By Household

Income ($000s)	% of Population
0–15	33%
15–25	16%
25–35	12%
35–50	15%
50–75	13%
75–100	5%
100 +	6%

Source: 2008 Market Research Handbook.

ULTIMATE FRISBEE

Initially created in 1968 in the United States as "Frisbee Football," Ultimate had grown in acceptance internationally and was becoming recognized for the high level of athleticism involved, as well as for its highly social nature. Leagues existed for all different skill levels, from novice recreational leagues to competitive, elite-level touring leagues. University and international competition was growing as well.

A co-ed sport, Ultimate typically involved two teams of seven players, with a gender split (either way) of four members and three members. Each team attempted to score by passing a disc to a team member who was inside the opposing team's end-zone. Each catch of this nature resulted in a single point, and a typical game was played until one team had scored 17 points. A major difference from football, aside from the absence of physical contact, was that players were not allowed to move once in possession of the disc.

Another unique aspect of Ultimate was that it was entirely self-refereed. All players were expected to know the rules and to play within these rules to the best of their abilities. This self-refereeing was reinforced by another unique aspect of Ultimate: Spirit of the Game. Sportsmanship was so highly valued that many leagues, including TUC, had a "spirit score" attached to each game. Both team captains, after submitting the game score, would also submit a spirit score, based on how enjoyable the game was to play. Teams with consistently low spirit scores could potentially be removed from the league or prevented from returning the following year. Recognizing this penalty as being necessarily harsh, the vast majority of teams embraced the concept of spirit of the game, and it was not uncommon for teams to create cheers for each other or play mini "spirit games" following

[2]The average Toronto family spent five per cent of its income on recreation, 2008 Market Research Handbook.

the game. As the sport grew, maintaining a good understanding of Spirit of the Game was an ongoing challenge for clubs, including TUC.

THE TORONTO ULTIMATE CLUB

TUC was created in 1980 by a group of Ultimate Frisbee players who were interested in growing the sport in Toronto. TUC was incorporated in 1995 as a not-for-profit organization with a clear mission, vision and values statement (see Exhibit 3). Membership grew by an average of 30 per cent each year, breaching 1,000 members in 1997. In 2004, a new milestone was set, with over 3,000 members. By 2008, TUC had become the third largest Ultimate club in Canada and boasted a blended membership of both recreational and competitive players, although it had developed a reputation as being a competitive club. TUC was widely considered to offer the highest quality of Ultimate in the Greater Toronto Area (GTA).

TUC's main target market had traditionally been the serious Ultimate players—individuals who were looking for the highest quality of Ultimate in the GTA. These members varied greatly in age, mostly from 22 years to 40 years, with the average member being in his or her late 20s. The majority of members were Caucasian, and many were couples.[3] Many of TUC's members had been playing with the same group of friends for over five years and were highly loyal to the club and strongly supportive of its mission. Robinson did note with some worry, however, that while the club was still growing, turnover was very high, with over 500 members choosing not to renew their membership each year.

The months of May through August were by far the most important for TUC, when over 200 teams[4] participated in the Summer League.

TUC also offered outdoor fall and spring leagues, indoor winter leagues and year-round tournaments. Teams registering for the summer season would play 15 games plus a mid-season and end-of-season weekend playoff tournament, which could include up to eight one-hour games across two days for each tournament. Each team required at least 12 players who had an active TUC membership.[5] Games were played weekly and ran from 6:30 p.m. until approximately 9 p.m. (as long as there was enough daylight). The cost to register a team for the summer was $800.

As a not-for-profit organization, TUC was highly dependent on volunteers from within its membership. But volunteers could not do everything so, in 2000, TUC hired a part-time staff member. In 2002, this position became a full-time general manager (GM) position.

Jason Robinson

Jason Robinson graduated in 2000 from the University of Windsor with an honours bachelor degree in sports administration, human kinetics. During the next six years, Robinson worked with various organizations in amateur sports such as golf, mountain biking, curling, boxing and rugby. He also gained experience with a variety of professional sports, including professional soccer, football and Aussie-rules football. In 2006, Robinson was offered the general manager position at TUC. Excited about this new opportunity, he accepted the position. As one of two full-time TUC managers, Robinson's primary task was to ensure the proper running of day-to-day operations. This included overseeing league operations, managing over 100 volunteers and volunteer committees and taking care of club finances. He also spent considerable

[3]The co-ed aspect of the game meant that many players had met their spouses through playing Ultimate.

[4]Each team had a minimum of 12 players, but the average team size was 14 to 15 players.

[5]A TUC membership cost $65 annually and gave members access to all TUC leagues, tournaments, clinics and social events of that year. Each member received a membership package that included a copy of the rules and a regulation disc. Of each membership fee, $25 was dedicated solely to a "Future Fields Fee," which was used exclusively to improve access to playing fields.

Exhibit 3 TUC Mission, Vision, Values

Mission of the Toronto Ultimate Club

The Toronto Ultimate Club is a not-for-profit organization that provides a quality Ultimate experience, dedicated to the integrity of the sport and the Spirit of the Game, in the greater Toronto community.

Vision of the Toronto Ultimate Club

The Toronto Ultimate Club is a world-class community sport organization. We provide Ultimate leagues and programs that foster player development, social activity, and community involvement. Our club is well-managed, resourceful, and open to all.

Core Values of the Toronto Ultimate Club

Integrity
We believe in fairness, honesty, and consistency in our decision-making and communications.

Respect
We honour and trust our members and seek to understand their needs. We value teamwork and appreciate our volunteers and supporters.

Accountability
We deliver on our promises and never make the same mistake twice. We willingly accept the responsibility that we have to our members.

Excellence
We set high standards of achievement and service. We strive for exceptional leadership in management, in communications, and in education for our members.

Citizenship
We are privileged to play Ultimate in Toronto and we reciprocate this honour through stewardship in the community. We welcome all residents and visitors to be a part of our success.

Fun
Our Ultimate belief is enjoyment of the sport. We uphold the 'Spirit of the Game' and endorse an environment that nurtures cooperation and sportsmanship.

Source: www.tuc.org, reproduced with permission.

time maintaining the club website, co-ordinating promotions, and enforcing policies and sanctions. When time permitted, Robinson worked hard to identify new opportunities, facilitate relationships with sponsors, partners and permit officers,[6] and to oversee the long-term strategy and governance of the club.[7]

Since accepting his GM role with TUC, Robinson had been a player in the league, and he had convinced many friends and family members to take up the sport.

Changing Times

History

Over the past 30 years, Ultimate Frisbee had been embraced, nurtured and promoted by local not-for-profit clubs whose members had a passion and love for the game. Within the past five to 10 years, however, as these clubs began to realize greater success and Ultimate became more popular, various other for-profit organizations recognized an opportunity. These new clubs identified niches and leveraged their marketing prowess to attract players to their leagues.

Today, Ultimate clubs were geographically based and primarily financed by revenue from league and membership fees, which, in turn, paid for field acquisition, workshops, tournaments and social events, as well as for the club's general operations (sponsorships, marketing efforts, payroll and other operating expenses). Growing and maintaining club membership enrollment was integral to the success of each club.

New Ultimate Offerings

The for-profit organizations that had offerings most similar to TUC included the Recreational Sporting Club, Everyman Sports and West Side Sports.

Recreational Sporting Club

The Recreational Sporting Club (RSC) was a large, for-profit organization that offered many different team-oriented leagues, including Ultimate, basketball, hockey, football, soccer and volleyball, as well as fitness and various sport clinics. RSC had a good location in the city, with all of its games played in central Toronto. The club marketed itself as a "one-stop sports league shop." Although it was a young organization, RSC had grown to nine full-time staff members and had aggressively entered the Ultimate market with an advertising slogan declaring "We do not claim to be the most serious, but we are the best organized and offer the most value!" RSC's members were 19 years of age and over, with most members between the ages of 20 and 30. Most of RSC's Ultimate Frisbee leagues featured five players per team and were played on fields approximately one-third of regulation size; games were capped at 55 minutes in length.[8] RSC had a wide variety of co-ed leagues based on skill level, ranging from recreational to elite. The club also offered tournaments and indoor Ultimate leagues during the winter, as well as a recently introduced women's summer league. RSC's Ultimate summer offerings were split into two leagues—a spring league in May and June, and a summer league in July and August. Each lasted eight weeks, with one game per week, at a

---

[6]TUC did not own any of its own playing fields. In order to secure such resources, it was necessary to bid for field space and permits that were owned by various organizations, including the City of Toronto. Permit officers controlled the use and reservation of this field space.

[7]The other full-time manager was the member services co-ordinator, who was largely responsible for running leagues, co-ordinating membership and providing high-level customer service.

[8]Standard competitive rules of Ultimate included fields 50 yards x 120 yards and were played to 17 points. A 17-point game could take up to two hours.

cost of $539 per team. If a team wished to register for both leagues at the outset, the cost was $1,129. RSC had made the biggest gains in the Toronto Ultimate market over the years and currently had an estimated 2,000 Ultimate players.[9]

Everyman Sports

Everyman Sports (Everyman) was a for-profit sport and social club that operated out of the Toronto and Niagara regions,[10] catering to co-ed adults aged 20 to 40 years. With almost 10,000 players annually, Everyman was best known for its beach volleyball tour, which catered to professional beach volleyball athletes and toured all across Ontario. It was the largest such offering in North America. The club also ran leagues in Toronto and Niagara for Ultimate Frisbee, softball, soccer, flag football and basketball. Everyman also offered a ski and snowboard club and a "social scene" series of events. Everyman had become a league well known for its fun. Social offerings that included parties, wine tastings and boat cruises were aggressively promoted and available at discounted rates for members.

Everyman's Toronto operations were located on the east side of Toronto (see Exhibit 4). The club had started offering Ultimate within the past five years and, as of 2008, Ultimate was offered four nights each week during the summer season,[11] with league skill levels ranging from recreational to intermediate. The cost to register a team ranged from $333 to $476 per season, depending on how early teams registered and which night of the week was selected. Games of 75 minutes each were played on half of a soccer field,[12] once a week for eight weeks for each of two seasons.

West Side Sports

West Side Sports (WSS) was a for-profit sport and social club with operations based in Mississauga. From 7 p.m. until dark, WSS offered five-versus-five leagues on a field that was 90 yards by 30 yards. With approximately 10 teams playing each night, rivalry and competition developed over repeat matchups in both the beginner and the intermediate-plus leagues. The cost to register a team for either spring or summer was $500. The club also offered a clinic at the beginning of each season (spring and summer), teaching Ultimate strategies and various throwing and catching techniques. WSS had recently expanded its offerings to the Richmond Hill vicinity and planned to provide competitions between the two locations. Beyond Ultimate, WSS also offered basketball, volleyball, dodge ball, soccer and floor hockey leagues.

Impact on TUC

Robinson had little experience to draw upon to counter these for-profit clubs, as Toronto was one of the first markets to experience such competition. Robinson worried that, over the long term, the continued erosion of TUC's market share would impede its growth targets and lead to a diminishing of TUC as the go-to Ultimate club in Toronto. Furthermore, Robinson worried that continued decentralization of the sport could be detrimental to the game itself, with various leagues playing under their own "house rules," resulting in varying degrees of emphasis on the social and spirited side of the sport. Finally, it was becoming increasingly difficult to obtain and secure good field space at a reasonable cost

---

[9]TUC was currently the third-largest club, behind Ottawa (4,800 members) and Vancouver (3,800 members).

[10]The Niagara region extended north, south and west from Niagara Falls, bordering New York state, Lake Ontario, Lake Erie and Hamilton and was approximately a 1.5-hour drive south of Toronto.

[11]Each league played one game per week, with a separate league for each Monday, Tuesday, Wednesday and Thursday.

[12]These fields were approximately 100 yards x 30 yards.

since the bidding activity increased in accordance with the increased demand from these new entrants.

Indirect Competition

Even in the summer, Robinson recognized that individuals had a limited amount of free time and limited budgets to spend on fitness and recreational activities. There were over 300[13] health and fitness clubs in Toronto, as well as numerous parks, biking routes and pools. Furthermore, he had noticed that a greater percentage of young adults had started spending more of their free time indoors. He wondered whether there was any way to appeal to this demographic.

Economic Downturn

In the United States, 2008 was notable for the large number of bankruptcies and closures of major financial institutions. An American housing bubble, coupled with the deregulation of real estate mortgages, had led to the granting of massive numbers of risk-laden mortgages. When homeowners began to default on these mortgages, the riskiness of other loans was exposed, leading to a dramatic loss in consumer confidence, which sparked international stock market declines. With much of the Canadian economy reliant on the continued health of the American economy, Canada followed the United States into a recession. With unemployment rates rising to 7.2 per cent and consumer spending declining, Robinson was unsure how the demand for Ultimate Frisbee might be affected. He hoped that the lower cost of playing Ultimate Frisbee[14] compared to other sports, such as hockey or football, would help to counterbalance any decline in spending.

CONSUMERS

TUC had attempted to develop stronger ties with youth by supporting a junior-level touring team, pushing for Ultimate's inclusion in public school athletics and by providing discs and clinics for school coaches and gym staff. Despite these efforts, TUC's member base was aging. Recognizing the success that other clubs had had with niche targeting, Robinson thought that now was the best time to try to expand to new demographics.

Visible Minorities

Toronto was one of the most multicultural cities in the world.[15] Many ethnic groups represented relatively untapped markets, notably individuals of Chinese and South Asian descent who represented 50 per cent of the visible minorities segment. While these groups were not wholly unrepresented within TUC, they were underrepresented. Robinson believed that Ultimate was a great sport for individuals of all backgrounds, but, with respect to advertising, he wondered whether there were any language or cultural barriers that might present difficulties.

Young Professionals

Young professionals ranged from mid to late 20s; the majority had post-secondary education and worked in Toronto's downtown core. These individuals were typically living on their own without families and, as such, had greater disposable incomes. With all games starting at 7 p.m., Robinson believed that Ultimate could be an attractive post-workplace source of exercise and entertainment for young professionals. Furthermore, with the continuing increase in the number of young female professionals, Robinson

[13]www.yellowpages.ca, accessed December 20, 2008.

[14]A regulation disc, the only required piece of equipment to play, only cost $10.

[15]Statistics Canada, www.statscan.gc.ca, accessed December 20, 2008.

believed this segment would be well suited for and attracted to the co-ed nature of the sport.

Post-Secondary Students

Many of Robinson's current youth efforts were being lost since students left the city to pursue their education elsewhere. Toronto was home to the University of Toronto, York University and Ryerson University, as well as to numerous colleges, and Robinson wondered whether there was any way to penetrate this market better. Furthermore, could TUC regain the patronage of students who returned to Toronto for the summer? The student demographic was quite an attractive one, since most students attending post-secondary institutions had (or had access to) higher disposable incomes. Furthermore, this demographic tended to be more likely to partake in sporting or other physical activity.

Secondary School Students

Despite losing Ultimate players as they left the city in pursuit of post-secondary education, Robinson knew that attracting youth to the sport was absolutely crucial to the future growth and development of Ultimate. For Ultimate to continue to become more widely accepted in Toronto, TUC would have to keep pushing for discovery of the game at an earlier age. Robinson thought that if members of this demographic could simply learn about the game and try it, a large percentage would be naturally inclined to continue playing because of its fun aspect. While Robinson recognized that many members of this segment would leave Toronto for a post-secondary education in their late teens, this segment relied on their parents for income, and it was one that had great influence on its network and, thus,

could lead to strong word-of-mouth advertising. While the secondary school segment appeared quite attractive, Robinson knew that it was also notoriously fickle, and he wondered whether the current leagues were well suited for youth. Teens also had limited travelling capability since most were too young to drive a vehicle. Every TUC game was accessible by public transit, but Robinson knew that, in some instances, it could take some players over an hour to reach the fields. Finally, this generation was notorious for its low attention span and limited willingness to pay attention to advertisements.

Past Marketing Initiatives

While TUC had never had a formal marketing plan, various initiatives had been tried to build both the TUC brand and general knowledge of Ultimate. For example, TUC had recently reinvested in updating its website, the main "face" of the organization. The website served as a promotional tool, offering registration information and an information hub for TUC members.[16] Members posted messages on boards within the site or made quick queries on the main page, looking for more team players or confirming cancellations due to the weather. The website also supported a monthly newsletter that was e-mailed to all registered members and was later posted in online archives. Robinson thought TUC's website was very interactive and informative, and he knew that keeping it up-to-date would be imperative for attracting new members.

TUC also developed and sponsored Toronto-based competitive Ultimate teams.[17] These touring teams represented Toronto on an international level, competing in tournaments across Canada and the United States, and they sometimes

---

[16]Seventy-five per cent of the population of Toronto had a home computer with Internet access. 2008 Market Research Handbook.

[17]Currently, TUC sponsors three open men's teams, two women's teams, one masters team, one juniors team and three co-ed teams, spanning all the divisions of competitive Ultimate Frisbee.

qualified for international championships. As part of the sponsorship agreement, TUC supplied each touring team with regular, high-quality field space for practices for their playing season. In return, each team was responsible for volunteering time to TUC.[18] While Robinson had been quite happy with the increasing demand for competitive Ultimate in Toronto, he found it a challenge to balance support for the touring teams with the fiscal demands of TUC's regular league members. Could this support be limiting TUC's marketing abilities in other areas?

TUC had also aggressively pursued partnerships with various local organizations but had experienced difficulties securing high-quality partnerships that would either provide a cash infusion to the club or create mass public awareness of the sport.

Finally, TUC had attempted numerous promotions. The club had hoped to gain inexpensive viral marketing[19] through one-time demonstrations of Ultimate at various venues. One club on Canada's east coast had achieved some success by filming *Ultimate on Ice* during an intermission of a local hockey game. *Ultimate on Ice* had drawn just under 80,000 hits since being posted in late 2006. In 2005, TUC put on a short game during the halftime break at a Toronto Argonauts professional football game. This game was featured on the jumbotron and was seen by all in attendance. Results of this effort, however, were difficult to measure.

FUTURE MARKETING OPPORTUNITIES

A recent review of operations had led the board of directors to request that Robinson complete a thorough review of TUC's current offerings in the marketplace as well as develop and institute a formal marketing plan. Robinson believed that now might be a good time for TUC to start being more aggressive in its pursuit of growth.

Product Change

All TUC leagues operated under standard competitive rules such as field size, number of players and games ending upon reaching 17 points, as opposed to limiting the game to a certain time period. Since some of the other clubs had experienced success with variations of these rules, Robinson wondered whether TUC might want to change over all of its leagues to one of, or a combination of, these formats. Another option would be to add a beginners league that would play on a smaller field with games of five versus five (players) or to introduce all-female and all-male leagues. Robinson wondered what ramifications might arise from these changes and what benefits they might bring.

Price Change

After reviewing other clubs' offerings, it was evident to Robinson that there was a wide range of prices charged that players were willing to pay. Did TUC's current price structure make sense in relation to these other offerings, and was there room for some increases? The recently rising cost of field space, which ranged from $15 to $200 per hour, had averaged $50 per hour the past summer.

Promotion Opportunities

While TUC had not used mass media advertising before, Robinson wondered whether the new Ultimate landscape in Toronto might warrant it. After some in-depth research, he had come up with a few options:

---

[18]Each team was responsible for 200 to 300 hours of volunteer work, which might include helping coach a league team for a day, coaching or running skills clinics or helping with administrative tasks.

[19]Viral marketing refers to word-of-mouth (which may be augmented via the Internet) advertising that uses preexisting social networks to increase brand awareness in a self-replicating manner.

102.1 The Edge

As a very popular radio station in Toronto, 102.1 The Edge had over 800,000 weekly listeners.[20] Robinson believed that The Edge, offering mostly rock music, would be well aligned with the high-energy and youthful nature of Ultimate. The Edge offered competitive rates, starting at $30 per advertisement (see Exhibit 4 for a detailed breakdown of radio prices). Robinson was pleased to note that The Edge would also take full responsibility for the development and recording of any radio advertisements.

The Toronto Star[21]

The Toronto Star was Canada's largest daily newspaper, with the highest readership in the country. Published seven days a week, *The Toronto Star* covered daily news across a broad range of topics, from global news to business and sports news. The paper averaged over one million daily readers, approximately 22 per cent of the population of the Toronto area.[22] While the majority of these readers were over the age of 50 years, 20 per cent were 18 years to 34 years of age. TUC would have to create its own advertisement and supply it to *The Toronto Star,* but Robinson was confident this could be done without too much effort, since TUC already designed and maintained its own website. After talking to a representative at *The Toronto Star,* Robinson was able to compile a list of various prices, as seen in Exhibit 5.

CBS Outdoor Canada

CBS Outdoor (CBS) was Canada's leading outdoor advertising company. CBS's advertising resources included posters, superboards,[23] transit shelters and bus, subway and streetcar advertising. Robinson was impressed that CBS Outdoor had managed the advertising for the Toronto Transit Commission (TTC), Toronto's public transit system. The TTC included a vast network of subway cars, buses and streetcars that provided transportation to all of Toronto's population. Twelve-month ridership on the TTC for fiscal 2008 was 465 million.[24] Advertising on the TTC could be categorized as either internal or external placement. Internal placements enjoyed high readership by a market segment that was typically younger and likely did not pay much attention to other forms of media. External placement enjoyed a much wider audience: a consumer did not have to be travelling with the

Exhibit 4 EDGE 102.1 Rate Card

Time of Day	Rate per 30 Seconds
Breakfast: 5:00 a.m.–10:00 a.m.	$300
Midday: 10:00 a.m.–3:00 p.m.	$275
Drive: 3:00 p.m.–8:00 p.m.	$250
Evening: 8:00 p.m.–1:00 a.m.	$125
Overnight: 1:00 a.m.–5:00 a.m.	$30
Equal Rotation Breakfast/Day/ Drive/Evening	$225

Source: C. Cohen, December 24, 2008.

[20]Fifty-eight per cent of this station's listeners were male; 41 per cent had completed university; and 72 per cent were aged 18 to 44.

[21]Information in this paragraph was largely accessed from www.torontostar.com, December 20, 2008.

[22]This average was achieved with 950,000 readers Monday to Friday, 1,200,000 on Saturday and 750,000 on Sunday.

[23]Superboards were typically 14' tall x 48' wide, and were extremely large outdoor posters placed on top of buildings or beside major thoroughfares.

[24]*The National Post,* More TTC Riders, More Buses, Rob Roberts, November 20, 2008.

Exhibit 5 Toronto Star Print Advertisement Rates[25]

Advertisement Size (W × H)	Cost		
	M–F	Saturday	Sunday
2" × 1"	$575	$767	$383
2" × 2"	$1,107	$1,475	$738
4 1/8" × 2"	$2,167	$2,890	$1,445
1/8 pg. horizontal	$6,741	$8,989	$4,494
1/8 pg. vertical	$7,237	$9,650	$4,825
1/4 pg.	$14,394	$19,192	$9,596
1/2 pg.	$28,159	$37,546	$18,773
Full pg.	$54,473	$72,631	$36,315
Double pg. spread	$98,051	$130,736	$65,366

Source: A. M. Macchiusi, January 28, 2009.

TTC to see a poster on the exterior of a vehicle. CBS's costs for advertising via the TTC are shown in Exhibit 6. Robinson thought that professional development of any promotional material would cost $100 to $500, but these production costs would be included in CBS's prices. CBS sold advertising in four-week blocks only, and

Robinson was unsure how this might affect TUC's promotional plan.

Facebook

Robinson knew that social networking websites had been gaining much popularity in recent

Exhibit 6 TTC Advertising Rates[26]

	King (30" ×140")	Seventy (21"×70")	Bus Interior (11"× 35")	Subway Interior (11"× 35")
Impressions / wk	5446	5446	8709	8034
# of Posters	407	508	3325	2692
Reach	74%	68%	48%	40%
Frequency	16.8×	18.2×	41.7×	45.5×
4-wk cost ($000s)	$167	$147	$50	$67
Cost / poster	$410	$290	$15	$25

Source: M. Erskine, January 7, 2009.

[25]Rates given per newspaper issuance.

[26]"Reach" is the percentage of the market that will be exposed to an advertisement. "Frequency" is the number of times each exposed consumer will see the advertisement. All figures are based on a standard, four-week marketing campaign that fully encompasses Toronto proper.

years. In particular, Facebook was one of the world's most successful social network websites, with over 150 million users worldwide.[27]

Facebook was created as a free-access online application to provide a forum for users aged 13 years and above to communicate with each other. Facebook evolved quickly into a tool to organize functions and host myriad user-created applications (such as simple games). Initially including networks based solely on each user's university, Facebook expanded to include networks based on geographic location and recently experienced dramatic growth among young professionals. Advertisements placed on Facebook were much like print advertisements, showing up in bars along the top or side of any given Facebook page.

Upon closer inspection, Robinson was quite impressed with Facebook's ability to advertise to very specific groups. He would be able to select specific ages of users that would see the advertisement, as well as specific geographical regions. In fact, Facebook could identify how many Torontonian members there were of a specific age. Facebook also offered a unique cost structure (see Exhibit 7). It allowed any advertiser to bid for advertising space within the target market, based on either a cost-per-click (CPC) or a cost-per-thousand-views (CPM) option. For each target market, Facebook suggested a competitive bidding range. If an advertisement was currently the highest bidder,[28] Facebook would select that advertisement and place it at the top of the next page opened by a member of the target market. It would keep displaying this advertisement until a daily expense limit (set by the advertiser) was reached. Robinson liked the idea of being able to accurately target specific demographics, but he wondered whether advertising online would be as accepted or as respected as other forms of advertising.

Exhibit 7 Facebook Users

Torontonian Facebook Users[29, 30]

Age	#	CPC	CPM
13	6,540		
14	19,300		
15	42,620	$0.19–$0.30	$0.09–$0.14
16	68,900		
17	63,820		
18	79,600		
19	76,480		
20	74,860	$0.22–$0.33	$0.10–$0.15
21	65,760		
22	61,880		
23	63,640		
24	59,780		
25	55,260	$0.25–$0.36	$0.11–$0.16
26	53,340		
27	48,780		
28	53,000		
29	44,180		
30	38,740		
31	36,820		
32	33,000	$0.25–$0.36	$0.12–$0.17
33	32,840		
34	29,280		
35	25,840		

Source: www.facebook.com, February 2009.

[27]Facebook.com.

[28]Highest bid and highest relevance were calculated for every single page opened by users. The resulting top three advertisements would be displayed. An advertisement would be displayed each time it placed in the top three for any user, up until the pre-set daily budget had been reached (minimum budget US$1 per day).

[29]As at February 2009. For CPC (cost per click) and CPM (cost per thousand impressions), rates are encompassing, not additive.

[30]Facebook prices displayed in U.S. dollars; US$1 = ~CDN$1.25 as of February 19, 2009.

TUC Promotion Team

One of TUC's strongest assets was the size and dedication of its volunteer base. Robinson had been considering the idea of setting up a TUC booth at various local athletic functions, such as the Sporting Life 10K run.[31] This booth would be operated by a mix of staff and volunteers and would work to attract the functions' participants to try out Ultimate by drawing positive comparisons between the two sports. This promotion team would be able to offer discounted rates for TUC memberships and develop a relationship between non-Ultimate players and introductory clinics and leagues with TUC. Robinson did not know what the costs would be for this form of advertising.

DECISION TIME

Robinson wondered whether TUC was well positioned within the industry and whether it should add to its current offerings. Furthermore, he wondered what the focal marketing strategies should be for fiscal 2009 and on which demographic TUC should focus. With a solid marketing strategy, Robinson was confident he could convince the TUC board to commit five per cent to 10 per cent of TUC's operating budget (the fiscal 2008 operating budget was around $500,000) to the new marketing initiatives. Now, if he could only decide what those initiatives should be!

---

[31]The Sporting Life 10K run was open to public registration and went along Yonge Street through most of Toronto.

10

OBTAINING AND MAINTAINING ORGANIZATIONAL MOMENTUM

Once one charity comes out with a big campaign with high costs, every other charity has to replicate that.

—Kate Bahen (quoted in *Charities Paid $762M to Private Fundraisers,* 2010, para. 14)

Key Topics: fundraising strategies and tactics, earned income strategies, overview of social entrepreneurship, charity versus philanthropy, restricted and unrestricted funds, motivations for giving—individual versus corporate foundations' role in NPO sustainability, proposal writing

Reaching back to Chapter 2, we find the steps for starting a nonprofit from idea stage to the establishment of the organization itself. These tactics, as well as those covered in interceding chapters, are necessary, but in the end momentum is what keeps both an idea and an organization alive. Momentum often starts with the communication of an idea and the development of key stakeholders around the idea to enact change (see Chapters 9 and 12). Obtaining and maintaining the push generally requires funds. These funds may be self-generated (i.e., earned income for the nonprofit), externally solicited through fundraising, or some combination of the two. As with most undertakings, nonprofit leaders who approach the task of generating fiscal support strategically find success more efficiently and sustain the success over the long run. This chapter seeks to elaborate on how such a strategy may be formulated and implemented. The information here is not designed to be comprehensive; rather it is meant to give attention to key concepts that must be understood in order to enhance an organization's ability to generate funding that ensures momentum and sustainability.

FUNDRAISING STRATEGIES

Current fundraising tactics are very sophisticated, borrowing from many disciplines, including marketing, psychology, and sociology. The sophistication of approach speaks to the level of dependency many nonprofit organizations (NPOs) have on external contributions and the intensity of competition for those funds. The United States, followed closely by Canada, leads the world in developing the art and science of fundraising and philanthropy on both the individual and corporate levels. Charity is truly part of the cultural landscape in these two countries, and citizens are inculcated early in life with the obligation to "give back" through either service or financial contribution. The total monetary sums donated are staggering; in 2008, an estimated $308 billion was donated in the United States, with the majority coming from individual donors (Center on Philanthropy at Indiana University, 2009). In Canada, people donated $8.2 billion in 2010 (*Charities Paid $762M to Private Fundraisers,* 2010).

Types of Giving. Donated funds are usually contributed in two distinct manners. First, in times of great crisis (e.g., Hurricane Katrina, Haiti's earthquake), individuals and corporations dig deep and contribute funds, time, and supplies for rescue and recovery. This short-term, crisis-focused giving is categorized as *charity* (Worth, 2012). Separate from this is *philanthropy,* longer term contributions designed to enact systemic change or support societal infrastructure for the betterment of humanity (Worth, 2012). The distinction is important because the motivation underlying each type of contribution is very different and requires from the fundraiser particular strategies to ensure contribution success. Thus, professional fundraisers (sometimes referred to as *development officers*) approach the two situations by employing particular strategies to improve the amount and frequency of giving.

Motivations for short-term, charity giving are emotion based; such donations are mostly spontaneous and driven by human compassion (Worth, 2012). Thus, we see communications (e.g., advertisements, personal appeals) from those seeking charity donations full of photos and stories of the terrible situations faced by those in need. The call to action is immediate, and the focus is on one-time giving. The motivation for philanthropic giving is quite different, and the appeal should be adjusted to address this difference. Rather than an impetuous decision, philanthropy is a long-term investment made with care and thought. With such investments, consideration is given to the need of both the organization to which the donation is sent and the situation in the community that the agency works to change (i.e., the NPO mission and vision). The fundraiser must focus on building relationships with potential donors. Through such relationships, mutual goals are established to truly change society; only then is the investment made. Clearly, emotion influences the decision, but its part is much smaller and the desired impact is much bigger and longer term.

Funding Sources. In addition to the type of giving (charity versus philanthropy), the donation source influences the fundraising strategy. Three main sources are individuals, foundations, and corporations. Each brings its own motivations when considering either a one-time charity donation or a long-term philanthropic investment.

Individuals tend to approach charity and philanthropic giving with less complexity than do corporations or foundations. This is not to say that individual donors are impetuous, rather that the decision maker has fewer constituents with whom to consult in making the decision and may have fewer potential conflicts of interest to consider when selecting the destination of gifts. Are individuals motivated by altruism or reciprocity when making donations? The best answer is yes—both. In other words, motivations are mostly mixed. Fundraisers can develop market segments and target different segments for different types of motivations to enhance efficacy. Worth (2012) cites many studies that develop different donor profiles by segments. Here, we highlight two particularly useful frameworks.

The first segmentation framework, by Van Slyke and Brooks (2005), looks at the cross-section of demographic variables and individual motivations to give. Table 10.1 captures their

Table 10.1 Cross-Section of Donor Demographics and Motivations to Donate

Target Demographics	Motivations to Donate					
	Sense of Community	NPOs More Effective Than Government Services	Sense of Duty	Reciprocate Previous Assistance Received	Tax Benefit	Religious Reasons
Low-income			X	X		
Younger					X	
Practicing faith			X			X
Married					X	
Single						
Non-white		X	X			
Women		X	X		X	X
Conservative		X				
Volunteer	X	X	X	X		X

Source: Van Slyke & Brooks, 2005, p. 213. Reprinted with permission.

findings and can serve as a conversation starter for NPO managers to describe their own donors and how their demographic profiles relate to impetus to give.

The second study, conducted in the United Kingdom and Untied States, identified six typologies for giving among high-net-worth donors based on responses from more than 500 investors (Ledbury Research, 2009): privileged youth, eco givers, altruistic entrepreneurs, reactive donors, cultural inheritors, and professional philanthropists. Each category of givers has different motivations that should be addressed when attempting to solicit donations. The study is worth reviewing in detail not only for its typology but also for its cross-national nature— a rarity among such research.

Corporations may elect to give directly to NPOs or through their own foundations. Those that elect to establish foundations generally have more sophisticated, long-term goals in terms of impacting specific societal issues. The type of gifts donated include money, skill (e.g., lending of employees with certain high-value expertise), and in-kind merchandise. Corporate philanthropy is not a universal concept. A recent study (Conway Dato-on & Weisenbach Keller, 2009) found that Chinese multinationals rarely donate to societal causes, viewing this as the responsibility of either the families of those affected or the government. Anecdotal evidence suggests this philosophy is shared among many Asian nations and some Latino cultures.

Companies sometimes develop strategic partnerships with NPOs as part of their philanthropic investment plan. Such partnerships are most successful when corporate and NPO image, strategy, and stakeholder base are similar. So what is the motivation for corporations to donate? While some simply want to be seen as good corporate citizens who give back to society (i.e., corporate social responsibility), others view philanthropy as one element of a total business strategy. In this latter approach, corporate decision makers identify issues that are important to their company's target audience and prioritize donations to such causes over others. This is not to suggest that corporate philanthropy is self-serving, but rather that companies are motivated to search for common goals between the NPO cause and the customer base.

In the 2008 McKinsey global survey on corporate philanthropy (Bonini & Chenevert, 2008), this idea of companies seeking effective philanthropic strategies and common goals is expressed nicely. The companies reporting their philanthropic giving as "most effective" were those that

> align their philanthropic programs with the social and political trends that are *most relevant to their businesses*. . . . These effective companies are also likelier to consider local community needs and alignment with business objectives when they decide how to focus their corporate philanthropy programs. And they are much more likely to collaborate with other companies on philanthropic programs and to believe that their programs will become increasingly global. (p. 9; italics added)

Fundraisers should look for this common goal overlap when considering which companies to pursue for donations.

Foundations are tax-exempt agencies established with the explicit purpose of supporting NPOs that work to improve society. A corporation, individual, or family can create a foundation. Each foundation states its purpose (i.e., mission/vision) and geographical scope (if appropriate). The motivation for a foundation to donate to a particular organization is to achieve its own mission by supporting those who do the actual work in the community. Below are a few examples of foundation missions.

1. *Corporate:* Lafuma, a European leader in outdoor gear, created Foundation D'Entreprises Lafuma to support themes of biodiversity, eco-design, sport solidarity, and health. The aim of the foundation is to identify and support broad-based projects meeting these principles. www .groupe-lafuma.com/index.php?id=4449

2. *Family:* The Milken Family Foundation's purpose is to "discover and advance effective ways of helping people help themselves and those around them lead productive and satisfying lives. The foundation advances this mission primarily through its work in education and medical research." www.mff.org/index.taf

3. *Private, Individual:* The J. P. Bickell Society's SickKids Foundation of Canada has a mandate of investing "in health and scientific advances to improve the lives of children and their families in Canada and around the world." www .sickkidsfoundation.com

Normally, foundations allocate funds to organizations based on written proposals submitted to them. NPOs should develop grant-writing skills to prepare successful proposals. The Association of Fundraising Professionals (www .afpnet.org) and many other organizations offer grant-writing training.

Overall Strategy. Having investigated types and sources of giving, it seems appropriate to offer a few words on the complete plan or approach. Bernstein (1997) suggests that before beginning a fundraising campaign,

> leaders of successful organizations plan and budget their operations, and assess their fund raising potential to determine *how much* they should try to raise. They weigh these needs . . . and choose the ones that are *most important to finance.* They design the services to address those needs. They assure themselves that they have volunteers and staff with the *ability to carry out* the programs. (p. 38; italics added)

Research also indicates that NPO leaders who employ *segmentation strategies* and *coordinate activities* across multiple departments sometimes involved with fundraising (e.g., marketing, development, membership) are most effective (Van Slyke & Brooks, 2005). Such coordination necessitates adequate information technology to enable easy sharing of data throughout the organization. The Nonprofit Research Collaborative's (2011) year-end survey for 2010 reported that fundraising results are stronger when organizations invest resources in fundraising infrastructure, including staff training and volunteer management. Taken together, these research reports emphasize the need to plan, implement, and invest in a fundraising strategy to improve the likelihood of success.

SPECIAL TOPICS IN FUNDRAISING

Online and social media are growing in importance for fundraising. The tools are often less expensive than direct mail and paid advertising appeals, and so attract attention as a possible low-cost answer to fundraising needs. Caution should be taken, however. As with any fundraising technique, realistic goals should be set and costs (including time spent online) calculated to assess effectiveness. Here, we review a few options for what might work.

An organization might use a passive approach by programming a "donate here" link on its website, enabling easy credit card–based donations. More proactive tactics include building databases of email addresses to maintain regular communication with supporters in hopes that a stronger relationship will lead to more donations. Organizations that pursue this latter strategy must avoid oversolicitation or contacting supporters too frequently (i.e., becoming spammers). The principles of permission marketing (Godin, 1999) and the policies of getting supporters to opt in are important and worth reviewing prior to engaging in any online fundraising activities.

Social media is another tool fundraisers find themselves devoting a great deal of time to in the hopes of building relationships and increasing donations. Social media sites such as Facebook, LinkedIn, and Twitter are full of NPOs and their virtual communities. A recent study by idealware (Lacasse, Quinn, & Bernard, 2010) summarizes the various ways NPOs are using, and planning to use, social media. The most interesting finding relative to our present discussion is that respondents generally felt "social media channels were effective for enhancing relations with an existing audience and reaching out to new supporters, but considerably less so for raising money" (p. 4). If social media is to be effective for fundraising, the study suggests using this technique in combination with other communication methods such as direct mail and e-mail campaigns for an integrated communication strategy. When using social media, special attention should also be paid to the donor segment that an NPO hopes to reach. Online activity and corresponding donations are more prevalent among young, tech-savvy individuals.

EARNED INCOME STRATEGIES

Fundraising is good and has its place in almost every NPO. At the same time, many in the social services sector find that funds raised through external sponsors, grants, and foundations come with restrictions that, at times, inhibit creativity and/or fail to support necessary expenses to sustain programmatic efforts (e.g., utility bills, office supplies). *Earned income* seems to provide the answer (also see Chapter 11). Although earned income is not a new phenomenon (e.g., Goodwill has been engaged in thrift-store income generation for decades), because of a desire to remove the yoke of restricted funds, along "with more pressure for nonprofits to perform, a surge in the intensity of the contest to win philanthropic money, and a new crop of MBAs joining the nonprofit world, earned-income ideas can look like a magic bullet" (Kooker, 2005, para. 2). So what is earned income and what makes it successful?

Let's start by saying what earned income is not. For the nonprofit, earned income is *not* primarily a financial mechanism, but rather a method for improving mission performance by diversifying revenue in order to maintain mission momentum. Earned income is any revenue resulting from a payment for goods or services that a nonprofit provided, which is distinct from income received from contributions (Worth, 2012). An *earned income strategy* is any coherent plan implemented to generate revenue, even if the proceeds do not cover all the costs associated with producing it (Anderson & Dees, 2002, p. 192).

It is worth remembering that certain subsectors of the nonprofit world generate a majority of their funding from earned income sources. Education, for example, draws 56% and healthcare 47% from fees for service, a type of income generation (Independent Sector, 2011). What seems to have gathered popularity in press and among NPO leaders is both the expansion of fee-for-service income generation beyond the traditional sectors in which it is found and innovative partnerships with for-profit enterprises.

Before investigating how earned income strategies can be implemented, a few cautionary words are needed. First, most experts agree that executing earned income is not for everyone and should be approached with prudence (Anderson & Dees, 2002; Dees, Emerson, & Economy, 2001; Kooker, 2005; Worth, 2012). Special skills are needed and resources must be dedicated to effectively implement earned income strategies; organizations need to ask themselves if they have such capacities (or are willing to develop them) prior to beginning the process. Second, earned income is not a complete alternative to, nor is it always more sustainable than, contributed income. Such endeavors are sensitive to market fluctuations just as for-profit initiatives and contributed funding streams are. Third, just because there is a "need" for some product or service (e.g., employee training, community gardening, diabetes prevention education) does not mean a market exists that is sustainable (big enough), is accessible (can be served), and will perceive the service offered as affordable and thus be willing to pay for it—let alone at a price that covers expenses. In other words, if it were that easy, wouldn't someone else already be doing it?

With these thoughts in mind, we can now turn our attention to *how* nonprofits pursue earned income. Research suggests that nonprofits generally develop earned income ventures in the areas of *services, manufacturing,* and *distribution*— including retail (Worth, 2012). Regardless of the area pursued, like any good business plan, an NPO earned income plan should consider the internal and external environments. These topics are covered in Chapter 5 and should be reviewed prior to implementing an earned income strategy.

Within these areas, three approaches are available to generate income (Anderson & Dees, 2002). These alternatives are not mutually exclusive and require different skills for implementation. First, consider *getting paid for what you already do* by:

- Charging primary beneficiaries of provided services—e.g., employ discriminatory pricing based on "ability to pay," by which one sector subsidizes services provided to other sector(s), charge below-market price for a service but recoup revenue through large volume. Organizations such as Planned Parenthood (www.plannedparenthood.org), Help the World See (www.helptheworldsee.org), and Aravind Eye Care System (www.aravind.org) successfully implement these strategies.
- Charging an interested third party—e.g., TOMS shoes (see Chapter 14), mission-based retail stores such as Ten Thousand Villages (www.tenthousandvillages.com), Salvation Army thrift stores.
- Creating a coalition of beneficiaries and interested parties to generate enough income to cover costs—e.g., government subsidies, utility company incentives, and dwelling owner payments combine to cover solar panel in-home installation.

Second, consider *launching a new business venture.* This is a complex process about which an entire book could be written (and has), thus complete coverage is beyond the scope of this section. While unrelated expansion is a possibility for any entity—whether for-profit or nonprofit—it carries the highest risk for failure. Income strategies based on related expertise seem more likely to succeed. As such, an NPO should consider its three resource areas and assess which is the strongest base for an entry into a competitive market:

- competency/skill—e.g., American Red Cross lifeguard training
- physical asset—e.g., a parcel of land ideally located for a camping site
- relationship capital—e.g., access to a difficult-to-reach market segment may prove valuable to for-profit marketers

Finally, a slightly different category of earned income available to NPO leaders is *leveraging revenue through relationships.* These initiatives take many forms, including licensing, sponsorships, cause-related marketing, and operational ventures (Worth, 2012). Relationships are valuable for all parties involved, and choosing a partner should be done with care. Mission and image alignment are essential to successful partnerships, and constant nurturing by each side should be a priority for all.

As discussed in Chapter 11, in the realm of revenue sources, once the decision to explore earned income is made, a process similar to that conducted by for-profit ventures should be undertaken. This process should help improve the likelihood of success and cover research to determine market need and customer preferences, followed by pilot testing and a formal launch plan (*social velocity*). Anderson and Dees (2002) offer a well-developed approach to generating viable earned income options that is certainly worth reviewing for additional detail on the basic steps described here.

COMBINING STRATEGIES

By now it should be obvious that both fundraising and earned income strategies have advantages and disadvantages for NPOs. In the end, leaders will probably find a combination of the two approaches is necessary to sustain their organizations. When considering these strategies it is worthwhile to think about each one systematically and investigate the potential impact each might have on the three most valuable assets of the NPO: human resources, external relationships, and reputation (Zimmerman & Dart, 1998). Only after assessing the capacity an organization has in each of these assets and contemplating the influence each strategy will have on the asset should the financial impact of each be measured (see Chapter 7 for discussion of organizational capacity). Financial stability is crucial to mission accomplishment and should be the ultimate goal of either strategy for that reason.

CASES

Ontario Science Centre: Agents of Change and Beyond (Canada): In 2005, Lesley Lewis, the CEO of the Ontario Science Centre (OSC),

contemplated where future funding would come from to finance her ambitious plans for OSC. She and her management team had obtained $15 million from the Ontario provincial government's infrastructure renewal fund and a further $1 million from the Canadian federal government, and had raised $29.5 million in private funds. As Lewis considered future growth needs, she and her management team were embarking on three audacious goals: to double the number of on-site visitors from one million to two million per year by 2010, to double off-site visitors from two million to four million per year by 2010, and to increase OSC's earned revenue by $10 million per year by 2010. Lewis was very much aware that OSC's costs were rising faster than revenues, and she wanted to see if OSC could handle this financial issue on its own without going to the government.

Newfoundland Centre for the Arts (Canada): The Newfoundland Centre for the Arts (NCA), a theatre, dance, and visual arts organization, has a long history of promoting indigenous Newfoundland and Labrador arts. The Centre is a democratic, member-driven organization, and stakeholders disagreed over aspects of its mandate and operations. NCA also experienced financial difficulties, including a crisis in 2002 that almost resulted in closure. Although funding was found to get the organization through the year, Brenda Garnett, the general manager, is faced with decreasing public funding, low attendance, low rent revenue, and increasing costs. An outside consultant's strategic review revealed the heart of the issue to be financial stability. Garnett must present her recommendations to ensure the long-term viability and success of NCA to the board of directors.

REFERENCES

Anderson, B. B., & Dees, J. G. (2002). Developing viable earned income strategies. In J. G. Dees, J. Emerson, & P. Economy (Eds.), *Strategic tools for social entrepreneurs: Enhancing the performance of your enterprising nonprofit* (pp. 191–234). New York, NY: John Wiley & Sons.

Bernstein, P. (1997). *Best practices of effective non-profit organizations: A practitioner's guide.* New York, NY: Foundation Center.

Bonini, S., & Chenevert, S. (2008, February). The state of corporate philanthropy: A McKinsey global survey. *The McKinsey Quarterly.* Retrieved from http://www.mckinseyquarterly.com

Center on Philanthropy at Indiana University. (2009). *Giving USA: The annual report on philanthropy for the year.* Glenview, IL: Giving USA Foundation.

Charities Paid $762M to Private Fundraisers. (2010). Retrieved from http://www.cbc.ca/news/canada/story/2010/09/21/con-charities-fundraisers.html

Conway Dato-on, M., & Weisenbach Keller, E. (2009, October). Nonprofit organizations in China: Is it time to start marketing? Paper presented at China Goes Global, Harvard University, Cambridge, MA.

Dees, J. G., Emerson, J., & Economy, P. (2001). *Enterprising nonprofits: A toolkit for social entrepreneurs.* New York, NY: John Wiley & Sons.

Godin, S. (1999). *Permission marketing: Turning strangers into friends and friends into customers.* New York, NY: Simon & Schuster.

Independent Sector. (2011). *The sector's economic impact.* Retrieved from http://www.independentsector.org/economic_role?s=facts%20and%20figures

Kooker, N. (2005, June 20). As donor dollars fade, nonprofits eye earned income. *Boston Business Journal.* Retrieved from http://www.bizjournals.com/boston

Lacasse, K., Quinn, L. S., & Bernard, C. (2010). *Using social media to meet nonprofit goals: The results of a survey.* Available from http://www.idealware.org/reports/using-social-media-meet-nonprofit-goals-results-survey

Ledbury Research. (2009). *Philanthropy: The evolution of giving.* London, UK: Barclays Wealth.

Nonprofit Research Collaborative. (2011). *The 2010 nonprofit fundraising survey: Funds raised in 2010 compared with 2009.* Retrieved from http://www.afpnet.org/files/ContentDocuments/Winter%202011%20Nonprofit%20Fundraising%20Survey%20%28NRC%20Report%29.pdf

Van Slyke, D. M., & Brooks, A. (2005). Why do people give? New evidence and strategies for nonprofit managers. *American Review of Public Administration, 35,* 199–222.

Worth, M. J. (2012). *Nonprofit management: Principles and practice* (2nd ed.). Thousand Oaks, CA: Sage.

Zimmerman, B., & Dart, R. (1998). *Charities doing commercial ventures: Societal and organizational implications.* Toronto, Ontario, Canada: Trillium Foundation.

ONTARIO SCIENCE CENTRE: AGENTS OF CHANGE AND BEYOND

Our mission is to "delight, inform and challenge visitors through engaging and thought-provoking experiences in science and technology."

—Lesley Lewis, director general and CEO, Ontario Science Centre

INTRODUCTION

In June 2005, Lesley Lewis, chief executive officer (CEO) of the Ontario Science Centre (OSC), watched hundreds of young children interact at "KidSpark," the first completed new exhibition space of the centre's $45.5 million "Agents of

Change" renewal program. The program, which had been spearheaded by Lewis in 2000, was designed to inspire visitors by transforming approximately one-third of the OSC's exhibition space. Eight new experience areas had been planned: KidSpark (completed in 2003), the Hot Zone (completed in 2005) and six others to be completed in 2006: the "Challenge Zone," "Citizen Science," "Media Studios," "Material World," "Grand Central" and "Exploration Plaza." Lewis and her leadership team had obtained $15 million from the Ontario government's infrastructure renewal fund, raised a further $1 million from the federal government and raised private funds of $29.5 million. Since October 2003, Lewis had participated in a series of brainstorming sessions with her management team to develop a plan for the future. She commented:

> We felt if we just stopped it would become the new status quo. So, following a series of management sessions, retreats and meetings we have embraced a growth strategy and we've set some audacious goals. One is to double the number of visitors to our site from one million to two million per year by 2010. The second is for our offsite visitors, which include people experiencing our exhibitions in other science centres or through our website, to double as well. These offsite visitors currently number about two million. The third is to increase our earned revenues by $10 million per year by 2010. Our operating costs are growing faster than our revenues. This is not unique and other cultural institutions have the same dilemma. Traditionally, institutions turn to the government saying, "We need more money." We've said, "OK, we'll say to the government, we need the money, but at the same time, we will try to solve this by ourselves."

LESLEY LEWIS

Lesley Lewis earned an Honours Bachelor of Arts from York University and a Master of Arts from the University of Toronto in the early 1970s. She also completed course work towards a PhD. She joined the Women's Bureau in the Ministry

of Labour as the manager of research and policy development, then became the senior policy advisor and director of planning and research at the Ministry of Education. Lewis became the director of Strategic Planning and Projects for the Human Resources Secretariat in the mid-1980s, where she was responsible for long-term workforce planning for the province's 90,000 civil servants. In 1990, Lewis became the executive director of the Ontario Human Rights Commission, followed by the executive director of the Ontario Heritage Foundation nearly three years later. At the Ontario Heritage Foundation, Lewis and her team successfully faced the challenge of increasing earned revenues as their government grant was reduced. In 1998, Lewis was recruited initially as a temporary leader for a four-month period to the Ontario Science Centre, splitting her time between the centre and the Ontario Heritage Foundation. At the end of the four-month period, Lewis accepted the invitation to stay on and lead the centre into the new millennium.

HISTORY OF THE ONTARIO SCIENCE CENTRE

Science belongs to everyone, because everyone can understand it when the right approach is used.

—Chris Hadfield, astronaut, Canadian Space Agency Director of Operations (Russia), NASA

The OSC was the most visited cultural institution in Ontario, with more than one million visitors per year. Officially called the Centennial Centre of Science and Technology, the OSC had been commissioned in 1964 and opened in 1969 as part of the Ontario government's plan to showcase innovation for Canada's centennial celebration. The centre was designed to allow visitors to stumble across scientific and technological exhibits, communicated in an interactive and entertaining way.[1] During its launch in 1969, the centre received a

---

[1]Malcolm Kelly, "Overhauling a Splendid Giant," *National Post,* May 23, 2000, p. A15.

radio signal from a quasar (a star-like object that sends out radio waves) more than 1.5 billion light years away. Three months later, John Lennon and Yoko Ono held an official press release at the centre, increasing the OSC's profile throughout the world. Visits from world-renowned scientists occurred throughout the centre's 36-year history, ranging from Dr. David Suzuki's groundbreaking speech on humanity's treatment of the earth in 1985 to Dr. Jane Goodall's visit in 2001. Apart from visits (or phone calls, like astronaut Dr. Roberta Bondar's call to the centre from an orbiting space shuttle in 1992), the OSC acted as a hotbed for a number of firsts, such as creating the first working rocket training chair outside of the U.S. space program and being one of the first

places in the world where eager youngsters could log on to the Internet.[2]

From the beginning, the OSC had employed a full-time staff that conceived, designed and physically built all of the in-house exhibitions. As other science centres around the world opened, the OSC began selling consulting services, exhibition design and implementation, and the rental of exhibitions to different science centres. OSC's first project internationally was at the Hong Kong Museum of Science and Technology, in Kowloon, Hong Kong, in 1987, followed by the installation of several exhibits around the world. Exhibit 1 shows a complete list of the OSC's projects in other centres and museums.

Exhibit 1 List of Ontario Science Centre's Project Portfolio

A Selection of North American Clients

- Carnegie Science Center (Pittsburgh, Pennsylvania, 2001)
- The Tech Museum of Innovation (San Jose, California, 2000)
- Exploratorium (San Francisco, California, 1999)
- American Psychological Association (Washington, DC, 1999 and 1996)
- Science Museum of Minnesota (St. Paul, Minnesota, 1998)
- National Education Association (Washington, DC, 1998)
- Rochester Museum and Science Center (Rochester, New York, 1998)
- Procter and Gamble, Inc. (Toronto, Ontario, 1998)
- Cumberland Science Museum (Nashville, Tennessee, 1997)
- Museum of Discovery (Little Rock, Arkansas, 1997)
- Niagara Under Glass (Niagara Falls, Ontario, 1997)
- Arizona Science Center (Phoenix, Arizona, 1996)
- Louisiana Children's Museum (New Orleans, Louisiana, 1995)
- Edmonton Space and Science Centre (Edmonton, Alberta, 1993)

A Selection of International Clients

- whowhatwherewhenwhy-W5 at Odyssey (Belfast, Northern Ireland, 2000)
- Nils Co. Ltd. for Takahama Eldoland (Osaka, Japan, 1998)
- Lord Cultural Resources for the National Philippine Museum (Manila, Philippines, 1998)
- Associated Scientific and Technical Societies (Johannesburg, South Africa, 1997)
- National Science Museum (Bangkok, Thailand, 1997)
- Sharjah Science Museum and Learning Centre (Sharjah, United Arab Emirates, 1996)

[2]Ibid.

- Suranaree University of Technology, National Science Museum (Nakhon Ratchasima, Thailand, 1995)
- Papalote Museo del Niño (Mexico City, Mexico, 1994)
- Municipality of Ankara (ANFA, Ankara Fair Co.) (Ankara, Turkey, 1993)
- Ministry of National Heritage and Culture (Muscat, Oman, 1990)
- Hong Kong Museum of Science and Technology (Kowloon, Hong Kong, 1987)

Source: Company files.

VISITORS TO THE ONTARIO SCIENCE CENTRE

The first person on Mars is a child today— the Ontario Science Centre's goal is to inspire her to go there.[3]

—Jennifer Martin, director of Visitor Experience, OSC

The OSC welcomed more than one million visitors per year, of which 220,000 were children on school trips. Either through school visits or accompanied by their families, the seven- to 12-year-old age group was one of the centre's most prominent demographics. During the 2004–05 fiscal year ending March 31, the OSC increased its total number of visitors by 23 per cent over the prior year and exceeded its goal of one million visitors by 1.2 per cent. While the visitor count in 2003–04 was abnormally low due to concerns about Severe Acute Respiratory Syndrome (SARS), the addition and subsequent expansion of KidSpark led to an increase in attendance and in membership. Exhibit 2 shows the historical visitor count of the centre.

Over the previous year, the OSC increased its membership count by 30 per cent to approximately 12,350 members. The OSC offered different levels of annual memberships: $69 for an individual member, $80 for a dual membership, $99 for a family membership and $199 for a gold membership. Regular members had access to all exhibition areas and received a 50 per cent discount on parking and entrance to the Shoppers Drug Mart Omnimax Theatre, while gold members had free access to parking and the theatre.

Nearly 100,000 people entered the centre for free in 2004–05, of which most were children under three years, while some visitors held special promotional passes. Visitors could purchase admission to the OSC exhibit areas only, to the Omnimax theatre only, or combined admission for both exhibits and theatre. Admission fees are shown in Table 1. Parking was $8 per day.

Visitor Capacity and Patterns

The centre's visitor patterns varied greatly, based on the time of year. The highest visitor counts (around 11,000 people per day) occurred during March break. During slower periods, such as October, 1,500 to 2,000 people visited per day. Lewis talked about OSC's capacity and seasonal swings in visitor patterns:

> There is the physical capacity to double the annual visitor count. We believe we can double our attendance, but it's not as simple as doubling our current visitorship each day. It's about changing visitor patterns and reaching new audiences. During March break, for example, our parking lots are full and we're at capacity and the experience for visitors on those days is not optimum. But the majority of the year we're not at capacity.

[3]Bill Dunphy, "Science Centre Reinventing Itself," *Hamilton Spectator,* June 16, 2004, p. A15.

Exhibit 2   Ontario Science Centre Visitor Count, 2001 to 2004

In Number of Visitors	Actual 2001–2002	Actual 2002–2003	Actual 2003–2004	Plan 2004–2005	Actual 2004–2005	Var % Act vs. Plan
OSC Exhibit Halls						
General Paid	393,819	371,747	317,429	464,800	391,499	−15.8%
Schools	199,081	173,239	193,320	210,000	228,232	8.7%
Members	88,082	94,301	103,791	122,000	151,134	23.9%
Free	69,433	74,475	65,916	75,000	97,394	29.9%
Preview & Promo		2,534	2,325	3,500	2,155	−38.4%
Total OSC Exhibit	750,415	716,296	682,781	875,300	870,414	−0.6%
OMNIMAX Theatre						
General Paid	225,348	195,400	170,102	240,500	211,687	−12.0%
Schools	88,310	80,612	90,465	88,000	109,924	24.9%
Members	45,760	46,317	47,315	49,600	54,313	9.5%
Free	5,901	4,954	5,350	2,700	4,982	84.5%
Preview & Promo	5,150	7,284	5,786	3,300	6,989	111.8%
Total OMNIMAX	370,469	334,567	319,018	384,100	387,895	1.0%
Less Combo Sales	(289,107)	(256,171)	(238,121)	(301,000)	(302,392)	0.5%
Total OSC/OMNIMAX	831,777	794,692	763,678	958,400	955,917	−0.3%
Special Categories						
Paid Adult and Corporate	44,846	35,932	32,112	20,100	31,037	54.4%
Programs & Events						
Paid Family and Children's Program	23,273	16,791	19,776	21,500	19,738	-8.2%
Educational Promos & Events	8,056	8,082	13,572	6,600	13,799	109.1%
Total Special Categories	76,175	60,805	65,460	48,200	64,574	34.0%
Less Duplication	(11,287)	(9,472)	(6,325)	(6,600)	(8,744)	32.5%
Total Attendance	**896,665**	**846,025**	**822,814**	**1,000,000**	**1,011,747**	**1.2%**

Source: Company files.

Note: 2001–02 and 2002–03 attendance levels were affected by the OPSEU strike, which closed the OSC for 8.5 weeks from March to April 2002. The 2003–04 fiscal year was affected by the SARS outbreak, which led to a 40 per cent decline in the first quarter.

Table 1 Admission Fees

	OSC Only	Omnimax Only	OSC + Omnimax
Adults	$14	$11	$20
Youth & Seniors	$10	$8	$14
Child (ages 4–12)	$8	$7	$10

Other Visitor Attractions

The OSC competed against a number of other tourist and cultural attractions in the Greater Toronto Area. These included the Toronto Zoo, CN Tower, Paramount Canada's Wonderland, Ontario Place, big-screen theatres, sporting complexes, the Royal Ontario Museum (ROM) and the Art Gallery of Ontario (AGO). The ROM and the AGO were currently undergoing major renovation projects led by world-renowned architects, with the total cost estimated to be between $200 million and $300 million each. Both institutions also actively competed against the OSC for attracting children for March break programs and summer camps. Some observers had suggested that the lack of a children's museum in the area could spawn plans in the coming years, while others felt that Toronto's waterfront was ripe for the installation of a giant aquarium. Exhibit 3 shows brief descriptions of other Toronto-area attractions.

Exhibit 3 Other Greater Toronto-Area Attractions

Royal Ontario Museum (ROM)

Ontario's largest museum, boasting six million objects in its collections and 40 galleries of art, archaeology and natural science. Open year round.

Art Gallery of Ontario (AGO)

Toronto's largest art gallery, with almost 40,000 pieces of artwork from Middle Ages works to the Group of Seven and a major collection of Henry Moore sculptures. Open year round.

The Toronto Zoo

Spanning more than 710 acres, the Toronto Zoo is one of the largest zoos in the world, with more than 5,000 animals representing over 450 species. Open year round.

CN Tower

One of the world's tallest buildings, measuring 553 metres in height. The facility also has an award-winning restaurant and a cinema, arcade and simulator rides at the base. Open year round.

Ontario Place

An attraction park located on the waterfront of Lake Ontario, Ontario Place has more than 30 rides as well as bumper boats, a children's play area, pedal boats, Mega Maze, miniature golf, a motion simulator ride, a waterpark and five Olympic-sized beach volleyball courts. Open in summer months.

Paramount Canada's Wonderland

Canada's largest theme park, Paramount Canada's Wonderland has more than 200 attractions, 65 rides, a major selection of roller coasters, a 20-acre water park and numerous live performances. Open in summer months.

(Continued)

Exhibit 3 (Continued)

	ROM	AGO	Toronto Zoo	CN Tower	Ontario Place	Canada's Wonderland
Admission Rates						
Adults	$ 10.00	$ 12.00	$ 18.00	$25.99 – $31.99	$13.00 – $29.00	$37.44
Youth/Students	$ 7.00	$ 9.00	$ 18.00	$25.99 – $31.99		
Children	$ 6.00	$ 6.00	$ 10.00	$13.99 – 19.99	$4.50 – $15.00	$26.74
Under 3 years old	$ –	$ –				
Seniors	$ 7.00	$ 9.00	$ 12.00	$17.99 – 23.99	$9.00 – $17.00	$26.74
Membership						
Individual	$ 85.00	$ 75.00	n/a	n/a	$39.00	$84.99
Family/Dual	$ 99.00	$100.00	n/a	n/a	$78.00	$259.96
Non-Resident	$ 75.00	$ 60.00	n/a	n/a		
Students	$ 45.00	$ 40.00	n/a	n/a	$39.00	$84.99
Attendance	893,000	460,637	1,200,000	2,000,000	500,000	3,400,000
Date Opened	1914	1900	1974	1976	1971	1980

Source: Adapted from organizations' websites and Toronto.com

EXHIBITIONS AND PROGRAMS

The OSC had five levels and nine permanent exhibition halls, which covered the gamut of scientific disciplines. In some of the permanent exhibition spaces, OSC staff invited visitors to participate in daily demonstrations. For example, visitors could make their hair stand on end by placing their hand on a static electricity globe in "Electricity," or transform cloth and plants into paper in "Papermaking."

Temporary Exhibits

Apart from the permanent exhibition halls, the OSC developed or brought in several temporary exhibitions per year. Temporary exhibitions that were developed in-house were later rented or sold to other science centres. Temporary exhibits were always accompanied by public relations and marketing efforts. For example, the OSC made headlines in 2002 when it hired a human cannonball to shoot across the outdoor parking lot for the opening of the "Circus!" exhibition.

Public Programs

A number of other public programs and events attracted visitors and encouraged repeat visits, including one-day to two-week programs on robotics, astronomy, engineering, digital technology and the environment. For example, in early 2005, the OSC hosted a program on the science, environmental and social impact of the tsunami disaster. Other notable programs included the tour of Asimo, Honda's four-foot, 115-pound dancing robot, and Microsoft's Century of Flight exhibit, which allowed visitors to simulate the Wright brothers' original aircraft. Public programs were either included in admission prices or offered free to the public.

Educational Programs

Educational programs designed to complement Ontario's formal curriculum were organized for more than 1,450 schools and 220,000 school children that visited the centre each year as part of a formal school trip. Aside from class trips, the OSC offered camps for school children in the summer. The centre also had sleepovers approximately 12 times a year, when groups, such as guides and scouts, spent 15 hours overnight, sleeping in exhibit halls and participating in science-linked programs, for $46 per person. To appeal to older students, the OSC had developed a special "Science School" in partnership with two Ontario school boards. Students in their final year of high school could earn science and math credits towards their high school diploma during a semester at the OSC.

Team-Building Activities

For corporations and other organizations, the OSC offered team-building activities, in which colleagues joined forces to solve a scientific challenge or answer specific questions. Rates ranged from $10 per person for a short scavenger hunt to $4,500 for a half-day Challenger Learning Centre session for 16 to 40 people. The OSC averaged 20 corporate sessions per year at about $2,500 each.

Shoppers Drug Mart
Omnimax Theatre

The OSC housed the Shoppers Drug Mart Omnimax Theatre—a 24-metre domed-screen theatre with capacity of more than 300 people. The theatre played educational and science movies, such as "The Human Body" and "Volcanoes of the Deep Sea." According to Lewis:

> We currently only show mission-related films, not Hollywood blockbusters. A few science centres have recently begun to show mainstream large-format films like the Matrix, Spider-Man or Harry Potter. At the Ontario Science Centre, we might consider showing a film such as Harry Potter if we felt it would increase revenues. While Harry Potter is not mission-related, its appeal would fit with our core audience.

Other Services

To earn additional revenues, the OSC also offered exhibition halls or the centre's auditorium for rentals after hours for a wide range of activities, from private functions (such as bar mitzvahs and corporate events) through to jazz concert series. To rent out the entire facility at night with a capacity of 10,000 people, the cost ranged between $15,000 and $25,000, depending on the services selected. Single boardrooms, exhibit halls or other areas of the building were available for an average cost of $3,000 per day. Lewis explained how this fit into OSC's mission:

> We don't see our mission as a barrier to fiscal health. The net revenue from such events contributes to our capacity to offer core mission-related programs.

SELLING TO OTHER SCIENCE CENTRES

Sales and rentals of exhibits to other science centres around the world amounted to $3.1 million and accounted for about 10 per cent of the OSC's total revenues in 2004. OSC's management believed that sales to other science centres were predicated on the reputation of the OSC's quality of work and its worldwide leadership in science communication. Lewis recalled how the

OSC was described to her by an Association of Science-Technology Centers (ASTC)[4] colleague:

> The way it was explained to me by the CEO of a U.S. science centre when I first joined was, "The Ontario Science Centre is like the Harvard of science centres." He said, "You are really one of only a few that are doing R&D work."

Preparing a bid and actively marketing to the world's science centres required international trips and meetings. Being an Ontario government institution, all international travel needed to be approved by the Secretary of Cabinet. This could slow the process of developing new international clients. Grant Troop, director of Business Planning and Operations, who was responsible for international sales, shared his view:

> It is possible that we could sell enough international projects in any one year to use up a much greater amount of skilled labour than we currently do, but that might impact our ability to deliver on our own plans. The ideal situation would be that there is complete convergence between what we sell and what we develop for the OSC, at least in a general sense. The question is, do we first develop for ourselves and then sell copies to customers, or do we sell design-and-build projects to customers, having them pay for the R&D, and then repurpose the exhibit ideas for our own use?

STRUCTURE AND STAFF

Exhibit 4 shows an organization chart of the Ontario Science Centre. Lewis reported to the Board of Trustees, which in turn reported to the Minister of Culture in Ontario. Lewis also maintained a dotted-line responsibility to the Deputy Minister of Culture. Five branches reported to Lewis, including: Science Education under Catherine Paisley, Visitor Experience under Jennifer Martin, Business Development under Joann Bennett, Business Planning and Operations under Grant Troop and Marketing and Visitor Services under Bern Gorecki.

Science Education was made up of 43 employees and was responsible for the design, implementation and sales of all educational, facility rental, camp and recreational programs. Visitor Experience consisted of 150 full-time-equivalent employees and covered all scientific and technological content of the centre, including research, science communication, design, layout, exhibit construction, digital media and publications, volunteer organization and project management. Business Development, with 16 people, was responsible for fundraising and launching new business opportunities. Business Planning and Operations, a team of 60 people, looked after all international sales and offered support functions in legal, finance, human resources, building operations, security and information technology services. The 52-person Marketing and Visitor Services team oversaw the Omnimax theatre, visitor admissions, and marketing and communications.

Human Resources

Turnover throughout the organization was at three per cent, with the majority being due to retirements. The OSC employee base was unionized primarily under the Ontario Public Service Employee Union (OPSEU) and The Association of Management, Administrative and Professional Crown Employees of Ontario (AMAPCEO). Lewis described the challenge:

> I am the CEO of a $30 million to $35 million organization and neither my management team and I nor our board have any control over the largest single cost item, which is staff wage rates and benefits. The main collective agreement covers all civil servants—the largest groups of whom work in traditional office environments or provincial jails. We're not an office and we're certainly not a prison! It's a broadly felt sentiment that our workers are atypical. We are open 364 days a year but operate with a collective agreement that presumes a five-day workweek as the norm. With our front-line jobs, say for the ticket sellers, we pay $19 per hour. A similar job in the private sector, say at Famous Players, would get between $8 to $9 per hour.

---

[4]ASTC is an association of science and technology centre employees with 540 members in 40 countries.

Exhibit 4 Organizational Chart

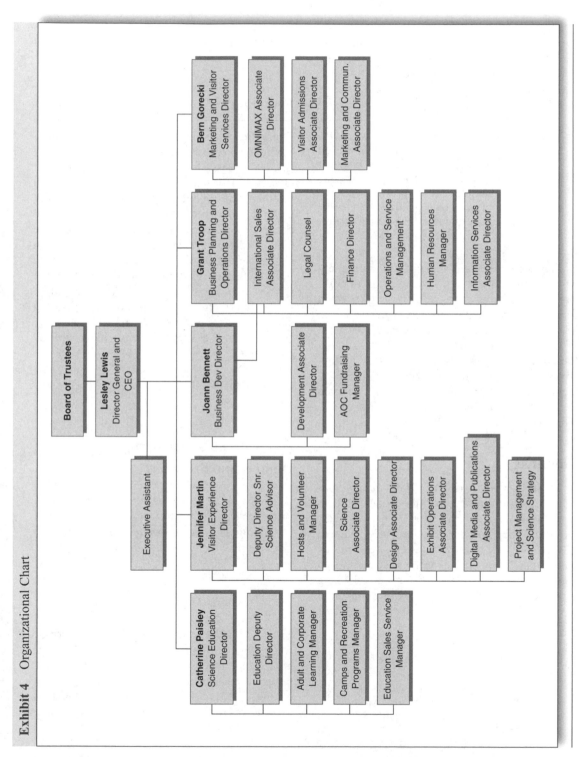

Source: Company files.

Throughout OSC's history, there had been two strikes among OPSEU workers. The most recent lasted from mid-March to early May 2002, heavily affecting attendance in both the 2001–02 and 2002–03 fiscal years. Lewis recalled:

> When we had the public service strike it was on the Thursday of the March break week, our busiest time of the year. And, for 8.5 weeks, we were shut down. Was I frustrated? Sure, we all were. But, none of us could influence the decision. All OSC staff—management and unionized workers—were committed during that time to maintaining positive relationships.

Managers and unionized staff commonly worked together to solve a wide variety of problems, from demonstrating a scientific theorem in action to increasing attendance with the 12- to 18-year-old audience. Many of the initial Agents of Change ideas came from the OSC's Rapid Idea Generation sessions that included employees from the wood shop, marketing, information technology, international sales and graphic design along with accountants, scientists, educators and hosts.

Volunteers

The OSC used approximately 100 regular volunteer staff in three main areas: the Jacquard Loom (a binary system and precursor to the computer), the Rock Shop and the Amateur Radio Station. The majority of these volunteers were retired individuals. The other volunteer base comprised approximately 130 high school students looking to fulfill their required 40 hours of community service towards their high school diploma. Lewis talked about volunteers:

> The bigger question for volunteers is how do you get them participating in a unionized environment? We want to increase the number of volunteers. But they would not replace paid workers. There are science centres in the U.S. where all of the people on the floor are volunteers. That is not our intention. But if we could get a retired science

teacher who was a real space buff to come in and be on our floor a day a week, that would just be great!

FINANCIALS

From 1969 to the early 1990s, the Ontario government covered all operating costs of the OSC. In 2005, nearly half of the centre's operating budget came in the form of Province of Ontario or other government grants. The Ontario Realty Corporation also provided a grant to offset the occupancy expense of the OSC building. The OSC generated the remaining revenues through a number of sources, which are shown in Exhibit 5. Approximately 50 per cent of the OSC's operating expenses were attributed to salaries and benefits. The other operating expenses were projected to remain relatively constant, with a slight increase in occupancy and general operations expenses. Exhibit 6 also shows the OSC's preliminary projections assuming no major changes in revenues or costs until 2008–09.

RAISING MONEY WITH PRIVATE DONORS AND SPONSORS

> *We like to be with people that are pushing the envelope to try and make things happen in a big way and feel we are with that kind of team here at the Ontario Science Centre.*
>
> —Galen Weston, chairman, George Weston Ltd., and president, The W. Garfield Weston Foundation

The OSC actively sought funding from private sources in three main categories: capital campaign gifts, annual sponsorships and one-time philanthropic contributions. Capital campaign gifts included funds that were donated to the OSC for a specific renewal project. For example, in addition to government grants, the Agents of Change program was funded by private contributions of

Exhibit 5   Revenues (for years ending March 31, in Cdn$000s)

REVENUES	2001–2002		2002–2003		2003–2004		2004–2005	
	ACTUALS	%	ACTUALS	%	ACTUALS	%	Actuals	%
Government Support								
Province of Ontario Grants	11,191	39.9%	12,639	43.7%	12,621	41.1%	13,325	39.9%
Occupancy	3,968	14.1%	3,968	13.7%	3,968	12.9%	3,967	11.9%
Other Grants	981	3.5%	392	1.4%	288	0.9%	2,296	6.9%
	16,140	57.5%	16,999	58.8%	16,877	55.0%	19,588	58.6%
Earned Revenues								
General Admission & Parking	3,355	12.0%	3,559	12.3%	3,471	11.3%	4,050	12.1%
Educational Programs	1,172	4.2%	1,099	3.8%	1,343	4.4%	1,475	4.4%
Creative Learning Experiences	1,177	4.2%	992	3.4%	940	3.1%	1,009	3.0%
Omnimax	1,795	6.4%	1,676	5.8%	1,606	5.2%	2,057	6.2%
International Sales	1,696	6.0%	2,109	7.3%	3,177	10.3%	2,033	6.1%
Sponsorships	1,161	4.1%	629	2.2%	584	1.9%	231	0.7%
Memberships	646	2.3%	754	2.6%	1,025	3.3%	1,221	3.7%
Gift Store	277	1.0%	251	0.9%	200	0.7%	265	0.8%
Food Services	254	0.9%	225	0.8%	167	0.5%	116	0.3%
Interest Income	330	1.2%	280	1.0%	481	1.6%	468	1.4%
Miscellaneous	64	0.2%	60	0.2%	73	0.2%	98	0.3%
	11,927	42.5%	11,633	40.2%	13,067	42.6%	13,023	39.0%
Agents of Change Revenues			294	1.0%	763	2.5%	798	2.4%
Total Revenues	**28,067**	100.0%	**28,926**	100.0%	**30,707**	100.0%	**33,409**	100.0%

(Continued)

Exhibit 5 (Continued) Income Statement (for years ending March 31)

	Audited	Audited	Forecast				Projected		
	2002–03	2003–04	2004–05	2005–06	2006–07	2007–08	2008–09	2009–10
Revenues								
Province of Ontario Grants								
Operating	12,639	12,621	13,025	13,025	13,025	13,025	13,025	13,025
Occupancy	3,968	3,968	3,967	3,967	4,500	4,600	4,700	4,800
Other Grants	392	288	2,913	667	1,167	1,167	1,000	1,000
	16,999	16,877	19,905	17,659	18,692	18,792	18,725	18,825
Agents of Change Revenue	294	763	1,014	1,550	1,033	634	476	411
Business Operations Revenue	11,633	13,067	13,016	15,094	16,600	18,400	20,800	23,000
Total Revenues	28,926	30,707	33,935	34,303	36,325	37,826	40,001	42,236
Expenses								
Salaries and Benefits	15,562	16,806	16,050	16,411	18,411	19,000	19,700	20,400
Occupancy Expense DOE	3,920	3,865	4,118	4,527	4,600	4,700	4,800	4,900
General Operations DOE	4,389	4,870	6,971	6,930	6,884	7,797	9,825	11,326
Business Operations DOE	2,262	3,111	3,131	3,714	3,900	4,200	4,200	4,200
Building Upgrade Expenses DOE	265	–	2,517	667	1,167	1,167	1,000	1,000
Agents of Change Expenses	194	763	1,014	1,550	1,033	634	476	411
Total Expenses	26,592	29,415	33,801	33,799	35,995	37,498	40,002	42,237
Net Income (Loss) Before Amortization	2,334	1,292	134	504	330	328		(1)
Amortized Revenue - Projects	963	1,019	1,295	3,830	3,644	3,655	3 , 655	3,655
Depreciation of Capital Assets	(2,460)	(2,659)	(2,189)	(4,748)	(4,518)	(4,485)	(4,141)	(4,141)
Net Income (loss) for Year	837	(348)	(760)	(414)	(544)	(502)	(486)	(487)

Source: Company files.

Exhibit 5 (Continued)   Balance Sheet (for years ending March 31)

	Audited	Audited	Forecast			Projected		
	2002–03	2003–04	2004–05	2005–06	2006–07	2007–08	2008–09	2009–10
Assets								
Current Assets								
Cash and Short-Term Investment	8,836	13,277	8,568	12,690	11,388	9,210	9,531	9,670
Accounts Receivable	728	680	500	500	500	500	500	500
Prepaid Expenses	601	193	200	200	200	200	200	200
Inventory	124	108	100	100	100	100	100	100
	10,289	14,258	9,368	13,490	12,188	10,010	10,331	10,470
Fixed Assets								
Capital Assets - Cost	28,649	31,885	48,893	61,730	62,590	62,590	62,590	62,590
Less Accumulated Depreciation	(13,448)	(16,107)	(18,296)	(23,044)	(27,562)	(32,047)	(36,188)	(40,329)
	15,201	15,778	30,597	38,686	35,028	30,543	26,402	22,261
Total Assets	25,490	30,036	39,965	52,176	47,216	40,553	36,733	32,730
Liabilities and Equity								
Current Liabilities								
Accounts Payable	1,531	1,806	2,000	2,000	2,000	2,000	2,000	2,000
Deferred Revenues	2,973	1,498	950	950	950	950	950	950
Due to Province of Ontario	2,464	2,188	2,000	2,000	2,000	2,000	2,000	2,000
Loan Payable to OFA	250	250	250					

(Continued)

Exhibit 5 (Continued)

	Audited	Audited	Forecast			Projected		
	2002–03	2003–04	2004–05	2005–06	2006–07	2007–08	2008–09	2009–10
Loan Payable	167	167	167					
	7,385	5,909	5,367	4,950	4,950	4,950	4,950	4,950
Long-Term Liabilities								
Loan Payable to Province	5,300	5,300	5,300	5,300	5,300	5,300	5,300	5,300
Loan Payable to OFA	500	250	6,000	9,000	6,000	2,500	2,000	1,500
Loan Payable - Food Service	331	164	—	—	—	—	—	—
	6,131	5,714	11,300	14,300	11,300	7,800	7,300	6,800
Deferred Capital Contributions	7,765	10,031	19,745	25,752	25,967	25,812	22,657	19,501
Unspent Deferred Capital Cont.	494	5,015	946	4,979	3,348	843	1,165	1,303
	8,259	15,046	20,691	30,731	29,315	26,655	23,821	20,804
Equity								
Invested in Capital Assets	7,436	5,747	4,853	3,934	3,060	2,230	1,744	1,258
Operating Deficit	(4,126)	(2,380)	(2,245)	(1,740)	(1,410)	(1,082)	(1,082)	(1,082)
Equity in Special Purpose Funds	405							
	3,715	3,367	2,608	2,194	1,650	1,148	662	176
Total Liabilities and Equities	25,490	30,036	39,966	52,175	47,215	40,553	36,733	32,730

$15 million from the W. Garfield Weston Foundation, $10.1 million from Telus and $2 million from DuPont plus numerous smaller corporate and private donations in the form of cash and science expertise. In return for these capital campaign gifts, the contributing organizations received the satisfaction of donating to continued scientific and technological learning as well as an acknowledgement of their donation on signage, media releases and parts of the OSC's facility.

Annual sponsorships were contributions from companies to assist in the ongoing operation of the centre, typically directed at supporting a particular program or exhibition. Examples included the Jelly Belly Candy Company sponsorship of the Candy Unwrapped traveling exhibition, the Bayer Inc. sponsorship of the Human Body hall and annual health fair, and the Ontario Power Generation sponsorship of March Break. Troop discussed a central challenge of annual sponsorships:

> In recent years, a number of longstanding program sponsors at the OSC had declined to continue their support. One of the issues in securing cash sponsorships is that potential sponsors are increasingly looking for direct marketing benefits for their support. This often means that sponsors are interested in some form of creative input or product placement, neither of which the OSC is willing to freely offer for reasons of integrity with our audience.

In some situations, the OSC named parts of the building after donors, such as the Shoppers Drug Mart Omnimax Theatre, the Imperial Oil Auditorium and the Procter and Gamble Great Hall, among others. Troop suggested that donors are motivated by affinity for the OSC's mission and a connection to the content or experience of the funded area even more than by marketing profile.

PROGRESS ON THE AGENTS OF CHANGE PROGRAM

[Agents of Change] will give rise to tomorrow's scientists and innovators, who will secure Canada's place in the world and will fulfill our national potential.

> —Dr. Ron Zelonka, vice president of Technology and Innovation, DuPont Canada

Starting as an initial idea in 2000, the Agents of Change program was originally defined as a $30 million initiative to renew 20 to 25 per cent of the centre's exhibition halls. Lewis explained the initial stages:

> When we did the original budget, we had not yet defined the detail for Agents of Change. We had never undertaken anything of this scope. Originally the program was going to renew 22 per cent of the exhibit space, but very early on we increased the scope to 30 to 35 per cent of our exhibition space, increasing the budget to $40 million. In the summer of 2004, we began discussions with Telus, which eventually led to a further increase of scope for Agents of Change, with the addition of an outdoor Exploration Plaza and a gift of $10.1 million from Telus. Our total budget became $45.5 million.

Opened in November 2003, KidSpark was intended to foster early innovation skills in children under the age of eight. Within three months, OSC membership increased by 30 per cent. In the early stages, KidSpark attracted such large crowds that the OSC needed to issue one-hour timed tickets to the space. As a result, the OSC management team decided to double the size of KidSpark in 2004.

The second new space, "Hot Zone," opened in March 2005 as Phase One of the Weston Family Innovation Centre. The area was dedicated to current debates and developments in science and technology and allowed visitors to share opinions of science's latest breakthroughs. Exhibit 6 shows an early plan of the exhibit hall.

OSC's management believed that partnership was at the core of Agents of Change. For example, DuPont contributed both cash and some of its own engineers to work alongside OSC staff. The OSC also worked with a number of different

Exhibit 6   Areas to Be Completed in 2006

1. Challenge Zone—an area where visitors would work in teams to solve relevant scientific challenges within a specific time limit using everyday materials.

2. Citizen Science—an area allowing visitors to participate in real scientific research and debate and evaluate the results and implications.

3. Media Studios—a space permitting visitors to interact with technology, art and science.

4. Material World—an area for the demonstration of applications, and characteristics of a number of existing and futuristic materials.

5. Grand Central—the refurbished Great Hall where art and science would be combined along the themes of earth, air, fire and water.

6. Exploration Plaza—a 3,159-square-metre outdoor area where visitors could interact with large-scale science exhibits.

institutions, such as MIT's Media Lab in Boston and the Ontario College of Art and Design, in developing the Media Studios.

To design the new areas, the OSC had contracted Diamond and Schmitt Architects. Jack Diamond, the lead architect, talked about the renewal:

> [Originally] museums were places you went to look at things. This centre innovated, came up with the whole idea that you actually manipulated the exhibit. But the outcomes were known. . . . What is being attempted here is rather that the participants are going to be doing the inventing.[5]

THE FUTURE

Why have we lagged in the past? We have adopted a risk-averse culture of following, not leading. Our research groups must believe we can conquer anything.

—Dr. John Evans, chairman, Canada
Foundation for Innovation

Lewis wanted to solidify the goals and establish a strategy of how the OSC could double its visitor count (both on-site and off-site) and increase its net revenue contribution by $10 million per year by 2010. Lewis explained:

> We want to become the centre for innovative thinking for the public. And "for the public" is the key phrase there. We are not a think tank, nor a university, and we are not a science research institute. The goal is to allow the public to come in and share, learn and contribute to innovative thinking.

In planning the road to 2010, Lewis pondered the future of the OSC:

> About a year ago I was thinking, is Agents of Change the beginning or the end? I would hate to be known as the management team where people said, "They did a great job with Agents of Change, but then they never did anything afterwards." I don't want us to slip into mediocrity—and we were in danger of becoming rather mediocre in the mid 1990s. We want to be thought of as the management team that started Agents of Change and continued innovating afterwards.

---

[5]Bill Dunphy, "Science Centre Reinventing Itself," *Hamilton Spectator,* June 16, 2004, p. A15.

NEWFOUNDLAND CENTRE FOR THE ARTS

In November 2003, as Brenda Garnett scrutinized the email from a consultant summarizing the results of a strategic review of the Newfoundland Centre for the Arts (NCA), her mind turned to the upcoming meeting with the board of directors. Garnett was the general manager for NCA, a non-profit theatre company, dance company, art gallery and rental venue located in St. John's, Newfoundland and Labrador. Several key members from NCA's history would attend the meeting. Depending on their reaction to the review, the whole strategic direction of the organization could change in an evening.

Because of a recent financial decline in 2002, the strategic review had been initiated to determine the best strategic direction for the organization. At the heart of the issue was fiscal sustainability. As a non-profit organization, NCA had to find unearned sources of revenue on an annual basis. In the arts industry, this task was becoming increasingly difficult. NCA was feeling the brunt of budget cuts from municipal and provincial arts councils, the unwillingness of corporate organizations to donate to arts organizations and the difficulty of increasing costs to rental clients.

A situational analysis was scheduled to be presented at the upcoming board meeting. The debate would be heated. Several members had strong opinions about NCA's mandate and the means by which revenue was acquired and spent. Garnett considered the pros and cons of the several directions facing NCA.

ENTERTAINMENT INDUSTRY OVERVIEW

The market for theatre in St. John's had begun 30 years previously with companies such as CODCO, Rising Tide Theatre and NCA Theatre Company. The market was continuing to grow, and industry professionals predicted explosive demand. The Association of Cultural Industries (ACI), a provincial arts advocacy organization formed by professional artists in St. John's, was trying to unify the arts industry and educate the government about the industry's need for more funding.

FUNDING OVERVIEW

Funding of theatre companies and arts organizations in Canada came from governments (all levels), corporations/foundations/individual donations and ticket sales (earned revenue), as well as other forms of earned revenue. Theatre companies required multiple sources of funding, and each funding agency had different due dates for grant applications, making the grant application process time-consuming and uncertain. Fundraising success depended on economic conditions, and there was much competition from other charitable organizations.

Government agencies provided the bulk of funding. The Canada Council for the Arts offered grants for the creation of new works, travel and

Gillian Rowe prepared this case under the supervision of Professor Charlene Zietsma solely to provide material for class discussion. The authors do not intend to illustrate either effective or ineffective handling of a managerial situation. The authors may have disguised certain names and other identifying information to protect confidentiality.

organizational development, as well as sustaining funding for companies that had been in existence for at least three years. The provincial government's Newfoundland and Labrador Arts Council provided project grants for groups that produced new works and provided sustaining funding as well. The federal government, through its Canadian Arts and Heritage Sustainability Program, promoted Canadian content and culture by providing funds for stabilization, capacity building, endowment incentives, networking initiatives and youth employment. However, government funding was drying up and theatre companies needed more private donations.

Like similar companies across Canada, NCA had a history of inconsistent funding from public sources. For NCA's Hall Operations alone, Garnett completed at least 10 applications annually. The process began with an initial application, and, if that was approved, a formal claim was required to

officially accept the first portion of the grant. A report then had to be submitted regarding the success of the grant prior to a second claim for the remainder. Finally, a summary report was required prior to applying for the next year's grant. Each initial application took about a week to prepare. Grants received by NCA from 2001 to 2003 are shown in Exhibit 1.

THEATRE INDUSTRY OVERVIEW

In 2003, a trend in the national theatre industry was the rise in "mega-musicals" presented by commercial performing arts organizations. These lavish shows spent tremendous sums on marketing and left audiences with heightened expectations of what their local theatre should be able to provide. Another trend emphasized the production of uniquely Canadian works,

Exhibit 1 Grant Amounts Received

Hall Operations			
GRANT REVENUE	**2003**	**2002**	**2001**
Canada-Newfoundland Economic Development Agency	54,699	24,305	71,381
Atlantic Canada Opportunities Agency	12,500	–	–
Canadian Heritage	18,456	–	–
Government of Newfoundland and Labrador	–	18,500	24,580
Newfoundland and Labrador Arts Council	18,460	–	1,100
HRE Employment Generation	9,792	–	–
City of St. John's	6,083	6,667	10,000
Canada Council	5,000	–	4,500
Human Resources Development Canada	4,028	2,580	8,616
Young Canada Works	3,860	–	–
TOTAL	132,878	52,052	120,177

NCA Theatre Company

GRANT REVENUE	2003	2002	2001
Canada Council	107,000	109,400	86,250
Canadian Creation Grant		13,500	
Newfoundland and Labrador Arts Council	27,437	34,631	30,000
Government of Newfoundland and Labrador	0	0	6,660
DuMaurier	8,000	0	0
City of St. John's	3,000	1,667	1,833
Imperial Oil	1,000	1,000	0
Human Resources Development Canada	120	0	2,272
TOTAL	146,557	160,198	127,015

NCA Visual

GRANT REVENUE	2003	2002	2001
Canada Council	–	42,000	–
Newfoundland and Labrador Arts Council	15,126	12,394	17,099
Newtel	–	–	5,000
Newtel Innovation Fund	–	10,625	1,875
City of St. John's	7,500	2,500	5,000
Human Resources Development Canada	–	–	3,718
TOTAL	22,626	67,519	32,692

NCA Theatre Company

PAID TO HALL OPERATIONS	2003	2002	2001
Office Rental	11,000	11,000	6,000
Theatre Rental	21,398	13,332	11,400
Salary Contribution	10,000	10,000	10,000
TOTAL	42,398	34,332	27,400

and, in Newfoundland, more indigenous works were favored. In St. John's, a micro-trend was a severe need for rehearsal space.

COMPETITION

The Union Hall, which NCA owned and from which it operated, was considered the cornerstone of the theatre arts movement in Newfoundland. However, competition still existed for both the venue and the theatre company in St. John's. The Arts and Culture Centre (more than 1,000 seats), which was owned by the provincial government, presented live performing arts events, housed the provincial art gallery and offered rehearsal halls that were used by several theatre groups. Rental rates varied by renter and season. The Basement Theatre at the Centre (approximately 80 seats) could be rented for half of the incoming ticket revenue plus any incurred expenses. Listed in Exhibit 2 are several other venues, such as Cabot 500 Amphitheatre in Bowring Park (750 seats), the Reid Theatre in the Arts Building at Memorial University (450 seats) and the Masonic Temple (50 seats), and their associated rates.

The competition for NCA Theatre Company consisted of several theatre companies. Artistic Fraud of Newfoundland (founded in 1994) was a year-round professional theatre company that presented its work in several venues around St. John's, including the Union Hall. The Beothuck Street Players (founded in 1995) was a community theatre group whose members included experienced actors, directors and technical crew from

---

Exhibit 2   Rental Rates of NCA and Its Competitors

Union Hall Rental

Renter has the option of the rental rates as set out in A, B and C below (rates approved by the NCA board September 2002):

(A) Blended Rates:	(B) Flat Rate:	(C) Matinee Rate:
Monday–Thursday $225 per night	$500 per night on any night	$250 per matinee
Friday–Sunday $325 per night	$100 per matinee	
Matinees $100 per show	$100 per late night	

Renter will pay the Society of Composers, Authors and Music Publishers of Canada (SOCAN) fees associated with their production to NCA and 15% of gross box office receipts. Harmonized Sales Tax (HST) will be charged on all rentals. NCA charges a $1 Building Repair Fund surcharge per ticket. The Gallery is available for readings, receptions, meetings, small conferences and workshops, book launches, etc. at $100 per session.

Cabot 500 Amphitheatre in Bowring Park

There was no set fee structure for this venue. Any request for this site was negotiated on a per-event basis and varied based on the size and type of event.
Corporate Rate:
(greater of) $250.00 + HST or 15% of gross ticket sales + HST + any incurred expenses.
Community (non-profit) Rate:
If an entrance fee was charged for the event, the rate would be 15% of gross ticket sales plus HST plus any incurred expenses. If no entrance fee was charged, the rate would be free plus any incurred expenses.

Reid Theatre

Rates for the Reid Theatre at Memorial University varied, depending on the day of the week required and the nature of the function. On average, the rates were as follows.
Rates:

- $300 per day plus HST
- $35 per hour for technician (required at all times)
- $30 per hour for security (required for performances)

Masonic Temple

The Masonic Temple offered several of its rooms as venues for performing arts.
Rate:

- 50 seats @ $100 per day plus HST

the capital region. This company produced well-known, popular plays. Shakespeare by the Sea (formed in 1993) performed on cliffs, in World War II bunkers, in the Cabot 500 Amphitheatre and occasionally at NCA's Union Hall. The Spirit of Newfoundland Productions (formed in 1997), which celebrated the popular version of the culture of Newfoundland and Labrador, offered musical dinner theatre in its own venue. Wonderbolt Productions (founded in 1980) was known for adult comedies, such as *Reunion at Purgatory High.* Several of Wonderbolt's productions had been presented at the Union Hall.

NCA Background

NCA had operated at the Union Hall in downtown St. John's since 1976. The facility included a 160-seat theatre and a 65-square-metre (700-square-foot) art exhibit and multi-purpose space. NCA was an artist-run, membership-based organization that fostered the development of indigenous Newfoundland and Labrador (NL) arts and artists. Its unique democratic governance structure ensured that regional artists would always have a venue for performance and that local performers and playwrights could contribute to that venue's stage.

In its nearly 30-year history, NCA had premiered more than 50 original mainstage plays and had produced a long list of professional artists who had risen to national prominence in theatre and television. NCA had also provided many young playwrights, actors, directors, musicians, dancers, visual artists and craftspeople with the opportunity to develop and present their creative talents. NCA's official mandate was to provide a venue and programs for artists to present their original plays/artwork, with guiding principles of openness and accessibility (see Exhibit 3).

Members felt strongly that NCA and the Union Hall were crucial for the Newfoundland arts community. Due to the company's organic nature, however, members often disagreed about the interpretation of NCA's mandate. Staff stress, turnover and the quality of NCA's offerings were other concerns. Nonetheless, NCA had become successful in its role of training centre, experimental venue and professional theatre outlet. Actors still had a say in the development of the pieces, and indigenous art was being developed. NCA Theatre Company was considered by the Newfoundland and Labrador Arts Council to be the flagship theatre company in St. John's. However, despite public funding increases, 2001 saw a cash-flow crisis. Low box-office revenues and increased expenses complicated the problem. Part of the cash-flow problem was the result of a substantial operating grant being awarded to NCA but not having been formally accepted.

Exhibit 3 Mandates of NCA Theatre, NCA Visual and Neighbourhood Dance Works

The Newfoundland Centre for the Arts Theatre Company is committed to:

- producing original work by Canadian artists and, first and foremost, those who are residents of Newfoundland and Labrador,
- programming that responds to the artistic impulse and promotes the well-being of the community,
- the development of new and experimental work through its second space program and through the presentation of experimental work of national and international significance,
- the remounting of the best original plays from past seasons, and
- the development of theatre artists, especially through mentoring and production.

Newfoundland Centre for the Arts Visual (NCAV) is committed to:

- the development, promotion and exhibition of contemporary Newfoundland and Canadian Art, with a focus on giving emerging artists the opportunity to have solo exhibitions, and
- the encouragement of critical dialogue between artists and community about issues in contemporary art and society.

The Main Goals and Artistic Objectives of NCAV are:

- to promote the development and work of professional, mid-career and emerging contemporary visual artists,
- to provide resources, services and a supportive, meaningful context for artistic activity through information sharing, workshops, skills development and a sense of community,
- to increase project collaboration and liaison with other artist-run centres, the Art Gallery of Newfoundland and Labrador, VANL (Visual Arts Newfoundland and Labrador) and artists/galleries outside the province,
- to foster collaboration between visual and other artists by scheduling activities which include group and multimedia exhibitions capitalizing on the vision and spirit that is the Resource Centre for the Arts,
- to demonstrate leadership in issues relating to contemporary art and its practice,
- to carry out an annual review and assessment of Gallery programming to ensure it remains true to its vision, flexible and responsive to the changing needs of the visual arts community, and
- to explore more closely the relationship of an artist to his/her environment and those issues which have an impact on their lives and culture.

Neighbourhood Dance Works (NDW) is committed to the development of a vibrant, professional dance community and the advancement of emerging and mature dance artists. It exists to promote exchange and growth within the Newfoundland and Labrador dance community and between local and national artists.

NDW is committed to:

- exploring new strategies for the facilitation, creation and profiling of indigenous Newfoundland and Labrador contemporary dance, on a provincial, national and international level,
- programming that promotes and responds to the artistic impulse and well-being of the community,
- fostering a supportive, meaningful context for artistic creativity through information sharing, workshops and skills development,
- audience development, and the presentation of new dance in a professional setting through the Festival of New Dance. The Festival of New Dance is devoted to the exploration of new dance vocabularies, particularly those of relevance to Newfoundland and Labrador.

Source: NCA Documents.

In January 2002, NCA's board considered shutting down the company because there were not enough funds to pay the next quarter's payroll. NCA released the staff and hired them on a per-show, reduced-rate basis to survive until the next grant was received. Garnett was hired in the middle of 2002. Her instinct was to undertake a strategic analysis to improve fiscal accountability and sustainability of the organization. Federal and provincial funding agencies and NCA's accountants encouraged NCA to proceed with this strategy. NCA needed to implement accounting procedures that would help eliminate cashflow problems and develop a strategy to increase annual unearned revenue.

During this crucial time, public perception of the company was mixed. Several members were in disagreement about policies and procedures, and the conflict became public. However, the community recognized NCA's value and, because of creative fundraising and financial community support, NCA made it through the financial crisis without shutting its doors. By the end of 2002, the operating grant had been formally accepted and received, a new Artistic Animateur and General Manager (Garnett) were in place, $40,000 in debt was cleared and rentals were up. In addition, funding was approved for the envisioned strategic analysis.

By November 2003, NCA Theatre Company, NCA Visual and NCA's dance company, Neighbourhood Dance Works, had official mandates (see Exhibit 3), but Hall Operations did not, leaving the strategic direction of the overall company unclear. However, because of its history, NCA and "The Hall" had brand equity and a distinct position as "incubator theatre," for "artsy" plays, as one patron described them (Exhibit 4 shows the 2003–04 season offerings). The Significant Other Series offered

---

Exhibit 4   2003–04 Season

Ivy & The Troll

by Adriana Maggs

Theatre for Young Audiences

Ivy and The Troll is a fictional creation myth about true love, divorce and the way the world works. It explores the idea that in everything good there's a little bit of badness and in everything bad, a little bit of good.

Barred Bard Chick Tells All in Shakespeare's Women

by Berni Stapleton

Directed by Lois Brown

This one-woman show written by senior artist Berni Stapleton is a wonderfully wacky account of the long-lost illegitimate great, great, great, etc. granddaughter of Shakespeare, Eve, who discovers her lineage while digging potatoes in her downtown St. John's backyard.

The Atom Station

by Agnes Walsh and Stan Dragland

Directed by Charlie Tomlinson

This is the story of Ugla Falsdóttir, a young woman of strong character from the pastoral north of Iceland, who has come south to learn to play the harmonium for her northern church. She wants to be, as she puts it, a person: independent, nobody's slave. Reykjavik turns out to be an obstacle course for such a desirable, headstrong woman. She will not be a supporting character in any man's drama. The play follows the ins and outs, ups and downs of her passionate journey.

Source: NCA Documents.

by NCA Theatre Company was a prime ground for developing emerging artists. NCA had contributed to the "cultural base of the province" and aroused passion in its residents. However, NCA's future was still unclear. Obtaining sustained financial stability was difficult for several reasons: both the staff and the board had high turnover rates, the productions at the Union Hall were not bringing in sufficient audiences, funding agencies were wary of NCA's accounting practices and venue clients complained about steep rental fees.

NCA's Operational Design

NCA consisted of three separate companies: Hall Operations (the venue), NCA Theatre Company and NCA Visual (the art gallery). Neighbourhood Dance Works operated as a part of Hall Operations. Each company had its own financial statements, which were presented to the membership and the public at the annual general meeting each December (see Exhibit 5). NCA transferred funds from one company to another when necessary. The transfers could be made for a variety of reasons. For example, all sales tax returns for NCA were claimed by Hall Operations. Therefore, NCA Theatre's portion of those returns would show up in the Due to Theatre account. All credit sales went through Hall Operations. Therefore, a gallery sale would show up as Due to Gallery in the Hall Operations statement. The gallery and theatre company would transfer money to Hall Operations annually for administration resources, salary contributions, and office rental. These transactions show up in the financial statements as Advances to (from) Related Funds and Due to (from) Related Funds.

Hall Operations

Hall Operations operated and rented the venue (Union Hall) to local theatre companies, other arts organizations, musical groups and various other organizations. A concession bar and box office were offered for most events. Hall Operations also controlled Festival 5, NCA's annual multidisciplinary festival. In renting the Hall, NCA provided the only venue of its size in the region; however, because audiences were often small (particularly for emerging artists or new work), it was thought that unmet demand existed for a smaller venue. Also, as was the case with any downtown location, parking near the building was limited.

NCA charged approximately $300 per night for its venue, with a sliding scale of rates depending on the time of day and the day of the week (see Exhibit 2). All renters paid the same rates, whether they were emerging artists presenting new work or commercial companies. Rental revenues did not cover expenses despite near-capacity rentals of at least 250 nights per year. Technicians needed a two-day turnaround between each show to strike sets and gear and to set up for the next show. An estimated 15,000 people passed through the facility each year. Annual earned and unearned revenues from all NCA activity approximated $500,000.

Garnett became NCA's general manager in September 2002, having been a supporter and member of NCA for at least 20 years. An artistic painter and former restaurant owner, she was familiar both with business and the arts. Although responsible for Hall Operations, she worked with the other divisions in several capacities such as budgeting and marketing. After an entire season with NCA, Garnett felt that expenses were as low as possible. To keep expenses low, Hall Operations recruited volunteers to help with box office and ushering.

NCA Theatre

NCA Theatre Company accepted scripts from Newfoundland and Labrador playwrights and produced three or four original shows from September to May annually. It also ran professional development workshops for performers, scriptwriters and directors and provided Second Space opportunities for emerging artists through their Significant Others Series. NCA Theatre Company's audiences filled about 50 per cent of the 160-seat house on average. NCA's average

Exhibit 5 NCA Financial Statements Balance Sheet

	Hall Operations			Theatre Company			Gallery		
	2003	2002	2001	2003	2002	2001	2003	2002	2001
ASSETS									
CURRENT ASSETS									
Cash	33,179	4,096	600	56,327	27,138	13,888	17,821	407	5,626
Prepaid Expenses	25,571	21,861	22,195	1,825	–	3,786	5,000	–	–
Due from Related Funds	11,316	2,671	9,996	–	18,711	28,712	1,600	1,929	–
HST Recoverable	–	2,305	3,091	796	–	–	–	3,739	1,226
Inventory	1,198	578	454	–	–	–	–	–	1,000
Total Current Assets	71,264	31,511	36,336	58,948	45,849	46,386	24,421	6,075	7,852
CAPITAL ASSETS									
Total Capital Assets	13,169	11,518	13,147	15,613	16,440	19,180	–	–	–
TOTAL ASSETS	84,433	43,029	49,483	74,561	62,289	65,566	24,421	6,075	7,852
LIABILITIES									
CURRENT LIABILITIES									
Bank Indebtedness	–	–	8,796	–	–	–	–	–	–
Accounts Payable and Accrued Liabilities	24,364	36,622	22,583	5,085	8,526	9,923	2,211	6,735	2,781
Deferred Revenue	22,917	4,000	8,167	58,500	42,500	83,667	2,500	7,626	16,375
HST Payable	1,222	–	–	1,600	1,600	–	576	–	–
Total Due to Related Funds	–	18,711	23,812	3,172	–	–	7,604	–	14,896
Total Current Liabilities	48,503	59,333	63,331	68,897	52,626	93,590	12,891	14,361	34,052
ACCUMULATED SURPLUS (DEFICIT)									
Total Accumulated Surplus (deficit)	35,930	(16,304)	(13,848)	5,664	9,663	(24,024)	11,530	(8,286)	(26,200)
TOTAL LIABILITIES	84,433	43,029	49,483	74,561	62,289	69,566	24,421	6,075	7,852

(Continued)

Exhibit 5 (Continued) Income Statement

	Hall Operations			Theatre Company			Gallery		
	2003	2002	2001	2003	2002	2001	2003	2002	2001
REVENUE									
Total Earned Revenue	148,609	111,436	97,043	24,117	52,836	25,586	11,570	1,065	791
Program and Operating Grants	132,878	52,052	120,177	146,557	160,198	127,015	22,626	67,519	32,692
Fundraising and Sponsorship	65,930	15,796	22,180	22,550	30,030	49,800	25,137	–	780
In-kind Contributions	4,000	–	–	15,650	–	–	–	12,817	–
Other Revenue	5,000	8,500	18,106	2,567	10,603	2,158	350	815	690
TOTAL REVENUE	356,417	187,784	257,506	211,441	253,667	204,559	59,683	82,216	34,953
EXPENSE									
Salaries and Other Remunerations	157,340	115,499	173,105	95,303	55,040	61,337	13,610	24,107	24,753
Fundraising	26,915	890	5,322	699	–	–	n/a	n/a	n/a
Festival 5	26,046	–	–	n/a	n/a	n/a	n/a	n/a	n/a
Professional Fees	17,335	5,499	5,000	2,500	6,258	3,500	2,350	14,172	10,423
Utilities and Telephone	14,980	14,573	13,995	–	–	342	n/a	n/a	n/a
Bar Operating	14,078	11,972	10,062	n/a	n/a	n/a	n/a	n/a	n/a
Materials and Equipment	8,606	3,389	1,783	863	2,502	–	891	437	1,565
Office Supplies	7,540	6,067	7,752	171	396	1,288	395	3,019	336
Insurance	6,874	5,273	5,140	n/a	n/a	n/a	n/a	n/a	n/a
Bank Charges and Interest	6,203	6,088	5,524	775	4,925	3,216	12	588	544
Advertising and Promotion	5,393	921	2,989	19,846	4,576	3,199	863	3,778	2,822
Maintenance	4,240	6,436	10,736	n/a	n/a	n/a	304	635	2,218
Miscellaneous	2,279	2,644	12,486	1,101	2,135	8,893	1,311	872	4,080

	Hall Operations			Theatre Company			Gallery		
	2003	2002	2001	2003	2002	2001	2003	2002	2001
Labour	2,000	–	–	n/a	n/a	n/a	n/a	n/a	n/a
Municipal Taxes	1,681	1,791	297	n/a	n/a	n/a	n/a	n/a	n/a
Amortization	1,632	1,629	2,712	3,077	2,740	2,740	300	110	1,673
Security	729	1,467	633	n/a	n/a	n/a	n/a	n/a	n/a
Special Events	250	4,761	1,786	n/a	n/a	n/a	1,254	2,013	2,771
Travel and Transportation	62	1,341	2,158	757	2,063	6,727	579	6,971	–
Training	–	–	2,030	n/a	n/a	n/a	n/a	n/a	n/a
Second Space	n/a	n/a	n/a	–	–	6,047	n/a	n/a	n/a
Mainstage	n/a	n/a	n/a	78,311	124,654	90,284	n/a	n/a	n/a
Royalties	n/a	n/a	n/a	3,468	2,466	2,567	n/a	n/a	n/a
Fees	n/a	n/a	n/a	1,209	–	–	n/a	n/a	n/a
Hall Rental	n/a	n/a	n/a	11,000	11,000	17,400	n/a	n/a	n/a
Theatre Arts Workshops	n/a	n/a	n/a	–	1,225	8,070	n/a	n/a	n/a
Shipping	n/a	n/a	n/a	n/a	n/a	n/a	–	100	363
Production Expense	n/a	n/a	n/a	n/a	n/a	n/a	1,000	945	–
Rent	n/a	n/a	n/a	n/a	n/a	n/a	4,000	3,000	6,000
Artists' Portion of Sales	n/a	n/a	n/a	n/a	n/a	n/a	12,998	–	–
Framing	n/a	n/a	n/a	n/a	n/a	n/a	–	464	31
Computer Network	n/a	n/a	n/a	n/a	n/a	n/a	–	497	–
Website	n/a	n/a	n/a	n/a	n/a	n/a	–	2,594	–
TOTAL EXPENSES	304,183	190,240	263,510	219,080	219,980	215,610	39,867	64,302	57,579
NET INCOME	52,234	2,456	6,004	7,639	33,687	11,051	19,816	17,914	22,626
BGN RTND EARNINGS (DEFICIT)	16,304	13,848	7,844	9,663	24,024	12,973	8,286	26,200	3,574
ACCLD INCOME (DEFICIT)	35,960	16,304	13,848	2,024	9,663	24,024	11,530	8,286	26,200

(Continued)

Exhibit 5 (Continued)   Statement of Cash Flows

	Hall Operations			Theatre Company			Gallery		
	2003	2002	2001	2003	2002	2001	2003	2002	2001
OPERATING ACTIVITIES									
Excess of revenue over expenditure	52,234	(2,456)	(6,004)	(3,999)	33,687	(11,051)	19,816	17,914	(22,626)
Amortization	1,632	1,629	2,712	3,077	2,740	2,740	–	–	–
Changes in non-cash working capital	2,573	10,868	(21,626)	7,688	(34,778)	24,030	(10,335)	(6,308)	10,648
Cash from (provded for) operating activities	56,439	10,041	(24,918)	6,766	1,649	15,719	9,481	11,606	(11,978)
FINANCING ACTIVITIES									
Advances from (to) related funds *(Hall: Gallery; Theatre: Gallery; Gallery: Theatre)*	(4,933)	7,325	(10,095)	–	6,500	(4,900)	–	(6,500)	4,900
Advances from (to) related funds *(Hall: Theatre; Theatre: Hall Ops; Gallery: Hall Ops)*	(22,423)	(5,101)	21,635	22,423	5,101	(21,635)	7,933	(10,325)	10,095
Cash from (provded for) financing activities	(27,356)	2,224	11,540	22,423	11,601	(26,535)	7,933	(16,825)	14,995
Net decrease (increase) in cash	29,083	12,265	(13,378)	29,189	13,250	(10,816)	17,414	(5,219)	3,017
Cash, beginning of year	4,096	(8,169)	5,209	27,138	13,888	24,704	407	5,626	2,609
CASH, END OF YEAR	33,179	4,096	(8,169)	56,327	27,138	13,888	17,821	407	5,626

ticket price of $17 was well below the national average. NCA marketed each show individually. A skill audit by a human resources consultant had identified that no one in the organization had the requisite skills in public relations, marketing, media relations, fundraising and audience development. These duties were currently performed piecemeal by various staff members.

Jenn Yetman, the artistic animateur of NCA Theatre Company since September 2002, was an accomplished actress in the province. Her duties were to administer NCA Theatre's operations, write grant applications and develop programs with Garnett, and search for possible artists or plays to bring into NCA. Yetman did not choose a season's plays; an annually nominated committee of the board of directors chose them. By November 2003, 18 scripts had been submitted, providing the committee with an array of choices for the following season. If the season's lineup was selected in advance and the venue rentals confirmed on time, all the events could be marketed together. However, often rentals were made in haste and eventually canceled, or shows produced by NCA Theatre Company had to be postponed, which precluded possibilities for joint marketing.

NCA Theatre Company had been more successful than Hall Operations in acquiring funding and corporate sponsorship, and the theatre company had been breaking even. The theatre company paid rent to Hall Operations for office space and administration resources and for the venue when it presented shows. These contributions were recorded in Hall Operations' Earned Revenue.

NCA Visual

NCA Visual, the art gallery, presented solo exhibitions for emerging artists, an annual members' show and other themed shows. NCA Visual had acquired funding to pay a coordinator and to pay appropriate fees to artists in 2003. It paid rent and administrative fees to Hall Operations, which was responsible for renting the gallery as a multi-purpose space. NCA Visual was the only gallery in the St. John's market that allowed emerging artists the opportunity to have their first solo exhibition. Rhonda Moody was the part-time gallery coordinator. She also developed budgets and grant applications with Garnett, ensured that the gallery stuck to its annual budget, coordinated volunteers, planned events and designed marketing materials.

Neighbourhood Dance Works

Neighbourhood Dance Works, which had started at NCA but spent several years as its own company, rejoined NCA in April 2003. It was committed to the development of a vibrant dance community and the advancement of emerging and mature choreographers. It presented an annual festival of contemporary dance as well as other events. Neighbourhood Dance Works operated under the budget approval of Hall Operations and was governed by the dance committee appointed by the board. An income statement for the dance company is presented in Exhibit 6 for the period since it rejoined NCA. Neighbourhood Dance Works did not pay for office space or administration. Garnett worked closely with the dance committee and helped with grants and budgeting.

ORGANIZATION AND CULTURE

By November 2003, NCA had seven permanent staff: a general manager (Hall Operations), an artistic animateur (NCA Theatre), a gallery coordinator (NCA Visual), a technical coordinator (Hall Operations), a maintenance coordinator (Hall Operations), a technical assistant (Hall Operations), and a bar manager (Hall Operations). Assistants were hired as public funding became available. In 2003, NCA had two assistants: one for Hall Operations and one for NCA Theatre.

Garnett was concerned about staff productivity, their 30 per cent turnover rate, the lack of documentation of tasks and the absence of human resources (HR) policies and procedures.

Exhibit 6 Neighbourhood Dance Works Income Statement YTD 2003, April 16 to August 31

REVENUE	
Total Earned Revenue	1,655
Registration Fees	115
Operating Grants	15,596
Fundraising and Other Donations	850
RCA Contribution	3,900
In-kind Contribution	2,300
TOTAL REVENUE	24,416
EXPENSE	
Curator's Fee	1,000
Administrators' Fees	4,096
Artists' Fees	4,840
Administrative Assistant Fee	2,293
Independent Contractor	148
Consultant Fee	2,500
Travel	2,360
Per Diem	735
Accommodation	1,550
Rental	1,365
Technician	1,260
Equipment Rental	192
Miscellaneous	100
In-kind Fees and Services	2,300
TOTAL EXPENSE	24,739
NET INCOME	(323)
BEGINNING RETAINED EARNINGS (DEFICIT)	–
ACCUMULATED INCOME (DEFICIT)	(323)

As in most non-profit organizations, staff often felt they were overworked and underpaid. Garnett knew that HR policies and procedures needed to be developed but they were not her only concern. Garnett was also aware of a distinct cultural divide between the junior staff that had been at NCA for more than two years (who were rehired after the financial decline) and the key executive staff that had been hired in 2002 (the artistic animateur and the general manager). The executive staff operated with a more progressive orientation, whereas the junior staff believed that the old way of doing things did not need to be changed.

MEMBERSHIP

One did not have to be an artist to be a member of NCA; however, anyone who rented the venue was encouraged to buy a membership. The membership fee of $20 per year entitled members to vote and run for the board of directors, yet offered no other benefits. Benchmark studies showed that other theatre companies offered different benefits at various levels of membership, such as tickets to the opening nights of shows, drinks at the concession stand, preferential parking and recognition in the program or on wall or seat plaques.

BOARD OF DIRECTORS

NCA was governed by a board of 10 directors. All were members of NCA, and most were professional, working artists. Charlene Brown, an accomplished local actress, chaired NCA's board of directors in 2003 and had been on the board for several years. She felt passionate about NCA's viability as an artistic organization and as a business. Brown was a member of the board during the financial crisis of 2002 and understood the need to mesh a strong artistic mission with a reasonable business model. Board sub-committees included executive, dance, theatre programming, special event fundraising, finance, gallery and facilities. Recent recruitment efforts had produced a competent and committed board with which Garnett felt confident.

THE PROJECT

In NCA's environment, it was normal to engage in ongoing negotiations between the producer and director regarding production budgets. Strict accounting procedures opened the door to tension between artists and staff. However, many of NCA's funding agencies wanted NCA to develop strict procedures for a stable fiscal structure. NCA's accountants suggested implementing incremental changes while a new system was developed as part of the strategic review.

In April 2003, the federal and provincial governments provided funding for the strategic analysis with the objective of reviewing NCA's mandate and generating an action plan that would lead to full fiscal sustainability over the following three years. Other objectives included increasing private donations, improving accountability and operating procedures, and increasing earned revenue through the implementation of a focused business plan and marketing strategy. The NCA board of directors engaged the services of a consulting agency that had nearly 20 years of experience.

Historical documents, policy documents and prior business plans were gathered, the mandates were updated, and a key stakeholder list was compiled. Interviews were conducted with key stakeholders. A Best Practices Review comparing NCA to similar organizations was completed. A Situational Analysis synthesizing these materials would be presented at the upcoming meeting.

Building Repair— Move or Renovate?

As Garnett considered the issues, she remembered the facility report she had read that day. The foundation wall had just been repaired but the roof still had serious leaks that were causing damage to the structural integrity of the grid

system in the theatre, and the interior needed refurbishing. It was tempting to gut the entire building and create two performance spaces— one with 120 seats and another with 60 seats that could double as a rehearsal space—another dressing room, more efficient office space and a more practical lobby. Garnett knew that the structural issues with the Union Hall could influence some members to suggest moving to a new building, but she was not sure that would be financially feasible for NCA or ideal for the community. Many people felt passionately about the Union Hall and would rather not move. Even without a new building, capital funding would be required to fix the structural issues and refurbish the hall.

Raise Rent

From time to time, members suggested that the company could raise the rental fees. Garnett knew that with rental rates where they were, NCA was subsidizing many of the clients' productions. However, she also knew that many clients would be forced to find alternate venues if NCA decided to raise the rent, especially those emerging Newfoundland and Labrador artists that were a key part of NCA's mandate. Pricing the rental fees was a sensitive issue for NCA.

Art Gallery Options

Many questioned the viability of the gallery space, arguing that more money could be made if the gallery were rented as a multi-purpose room. However, an entire community of visual artists would then lose an exhibition venue. Taking that away involved a philosophical decision for NCA.

Indigenous Theatre

Many artists expressed concern at NCA Theatre's mandate to produce only original indigenous theatre. Inconsistent quality and the unfamiliarity of the shows were blamed for NCA Theatre's low audience attendance.

Artistic Animateur or Artistic Director?

Although many members of NCA felt strongly about the position of artistic animateur and its role as the facilitator of a democratic theatre company, others felt that the democratic nature of NCA Theatre was possibly a weakness. The animateur was responsible for theatre operations and administration but held no ultimate authority about which shows were presented. The turnover of artistic animateurs was high—30 per cent. With each animateur, NCA Theatre seasons took on a different flavor. Many community members had suggested changing the position of artistic animateur to artistic director, empowering the director to select shows and themes for the theatre season. Such suggestions raised philosophical questions about the NCA's democratic governance structure and community orientation. Passions were high about this issue.

Consolidation of Financial Statements

Many members felt that having three different financial statements for Hall Operations, NCA Theatre and NCA Visual only added to the headaches for NCA staff. According to a former administrator, the statements were split in order to access more grant money. However, with the news that funding would become available for those theatre companies that owned and operated their own buildings, NCA had the option to consolidate its financial statements and transfer title of the building from Hall Operations to NCA Theatre, a move that would shift NCA from "a venue with a theatre company" to "a theatre company with a venue."

Mandate Change

Consolidating the statements could cause a ripple effect, which could change the mandate of NCA from a resource centre striving to serve a broad community of performing and visual artists to a theatre company with extraneous programs. Although most senior artists and stakeholders understood that "Resource Centre" was just a name, several younger artists wanted to see it as an actual resource. If NCA consolidated its financial statements, it could return to its founding purpose—the creation of theatre by Newfoundland and Labrador artists that responds to cultural, social and political events. Conversely, maintaining the status quo would mean catering to all performance and visual art.

Alternatively, because NCA was running out of office space in the aging Union Hall, the option existed of severing NCA Theatre and simply operating the Hall as a rental venue with no theatre company. While some saw this as an opportunity for growth, others felt so passionately about having a theatre company within the Union Hall that membership might decline. As one former administrator said, "NCA and NCA Theatre complement each other; what's the point of having an artist-run venue if you don't have an arm that fosters and develops arts?"

THE UPCOMING MEETING

The artists that Garnett expected to be at the upcoming meeting included founders of the company, directors, actors and playwrights. Some were heavily involved in NCA Theatre productions and others rented the venue with their own or other companies. Some had had many successful years at the Hall at one time but were no longer active. Garnett also expected former board members and administrators to be in attendance. There was bound to be disagreement among attendees; however, Garnett knew that the board was ready, with the help of key people, to revise the mandate of NCA. She knew that NCA could go in several directions and felt strongly about ensuring that artists who supported NCA were effectively served. Conversely, NCA's financial stability was imperative. NCA needed an effective operational structure in order to make the best use of the limited resources available and hopefully acquire more revenue. Garnett expected that with a thorough understanding of the pros and cons of each alternative, a successful strategic direction for NCA would be developed at the upcoming meeting.

11

FINANCIAL MANAGEMENT

When organizations [NPOs] need to make significant choices regarding accounting standards or policies, the board of directors (possibly through the audit or finance committee of the board) will generally be involved in the decision.

Chartered Accountants of
Canada (2011, para. 3)

Key Topics: fiduciary responsibility, revenue streams, forecasting, financial management, budgeting, accounting

Without financial stability, even the most well-intended organizations will eventually fail. This reality provokes two key questions managers of nonprofit organizations (NPOs) should ask themselves throughout the start-up and management phases of their organization: How much money do they need over specified periods (e.g., annually, for a time-bound program) to efficiently achieve objectives? How will they capitalize—or raise resources required—for the stated time or program? With these questions in mind, the NPO leader and governing board can begin to exercise their fiduciary responsibilities for forecasting and monitoring both expenses and income.

The following sections investigate financial accountability and tools needed to exercise it.

FIDUCIARY RESPONSIBILITY

Safeguarding the nonprofit's assets (physical and monetary) is an essential part of the board's fiduciary obligation. Financial accountability through application of policies and controls keeps the organization and the public focused on the mission and activities that support its accomplishment. Nothing will place doubt on a nonprofit's mission dedication and the manager herself than a financial scandal. While accountability in a general sense was discussed in Chapters 3 and 5, it is worth reviewing three types of financial policies to enhance accountability: regulatory compliance, financial management, and data integrity (Zietlow, Hankin, & Seidner, 2007).

Regulatory compliance policies are a minimum requirement that include filing Form 990 in the United States. In Canada, the Canada Revenue Agency requires NPOs to return Form T1044. The requirements as to how to fill in this form are described in The Income Tax Guide to the Non-Profit Organization (NPO) Information Return (T4117). Regulatory compliance policies include avoiding conflict of interest and meeting other legally mandated disclosure requirements. Such policies are set externally (usually by government), but responsibility for adherence and reporting falls directly to NPO leaders, including the CEO and board.

The NPO governing board sets and follows desired financial performance as well as investment/expenditure choices through internally generated *financial management policies.* At a minimum, such policies should enable ease of meeting legally required disclosures; in the best-case scenario they should ensure sound financial reporting with clear accountability for decisions regarding organizational assets.

The final category, *data integrity policies,* may result from either external mandates (e.g., privacy laws) or internal guidelines (e.g., data backup, client account access). Popular media regularly report "data breaches" in both for-profit and nonprofit organizations. These should serve as warnings for any responsible NPO manager to take proactive steps to control access, use, and dissemination of electronic information.

The Sarbanes-Oxley Act, passed in the United States in response to lapses in fiduciary responsibility in the for-profit sector, also has implications for the nonprofit sector. As BoardSource and Independent Sector (2006) recommend, "nonprofit leaders should look carefully at the provisions of Sarbanes-Oxley, as well as their state/provincial laws, and determine whether their organizations ought to voluntarily adopt governance best practices, even if not mandated

by law" (p. 2). The Act's provision that is directly applicable to the nonprofit sector is the need for an independent and competent audit committee. Related to this, at least one member of the committee must be qualified as a "financial expert" (though the definition remains unclear) or explain why the committee lacks such expertise. Finally, while the nonprofit CEO and CFO may certify required financial reports, the board retains ultimate fiduciary responsibility.

REVENUE SOURCES

Traditionally, nonprofits have operated under the premise that external funding (e.g., grants, donations) will sponsor projects and the personnel necessary to accomplish the mission. Two factors in external funding sources are forcing nonprofits to employ more innovative approaches to income generation. First, external funding often comes with restrictions. Requests for Proposals might offer funding for a specific activity (e.g., hiring an endowed professor at a university) whether or not the need has been established by the organization's leaders or service clients. By law (and ethics), nonprofits are required to adhere to the purposes attached to restricted funds. This mandate frequently translates to a "follow the money" approach by which programs evolve in response to trends in government or foundation grants or the interest of major individual donors rather than to client need (Worth, 2012). Furthermore, such restricted money rarely provides for support staff, capacity building, or activities not directly related to mission or program execution.

Second, government funding and private donations have decreased in recent years due to the global financial crisis and for-profit organizations providing human services have entered the market, increasing competition for dwindling funds (Chetkovich & Frumkin, 2002; Conway Dato-on, Weisenbach Keller, & Shaw, 2009). Even organizations with healthy endowment funds, which can be less restrictive, have experienced a decrease in value because of falling stock prices.

Taken together, these issues have driven non-profits to develop alternative revenue streams through some combination of fee-based services, earned income, and/or social entrepreneurial endeavors. Fee-based revenue generation is not new to nonprofits, but the nature of services provided by the NPO greatly influences the revenue stream upon which it relies. Fisher, Wilsker, and Young (2007) conducted a comprehensive empirical study of nonprofit revenue sources across different subsectors and offer the following advice:

> A nonprofit organization should base its revenue strategy on the nature of benefits it provides (and hence who may be willing to pay). This message may conflict with some nonprofits' desire to seek fashionable panaceas such as commercial ventures or building endowments through contributions. It may be that nonprofits are "leaving money on the table" by failing to fully connect their services and benefits to their sources of finance. (p. 26)

This philosophy is similar to the client-centric approach to marketing strategy discussed in Chapter 9.

Independent Sector (2011) reports that revenue contribution for 2008 across all nonprofit organizations in the United States was 32.3% from government, 45.5% from fees/dues/other charges, 12.4% from private giving, and 9.8% from other sources, including interest income. A 2006 report on the nonprofit sector in Canada reported 49% of revenues from government support, 35% from earned income, 13% from donations and gifts, and the balance (3%) is from elsewhere. This changes when hospitals, universities, and colleges are not included; in that case, government accounts for 36% of revenues, earned revenue accounts for 43%, donations and gifts account for 17%, and 4% comes from elsewhere (Imagine Canada, 2006). NPO managers can use such numbers to benchmark their own revenue sources to those in their subsector.

In addition to—or in lieu of—fee-based revenue, many nonprofits are experimenting with earned income schemes (also see Chapter 10). The strategies and their terminology vary greatly

and include *affirmative business, earned income ventures, nonprofit business venture,* and *social enterprise or entrepreneurship* (Worth, 2012). Such activities are distinct from partnerships with firms that include cause marketing, licensing, sponsorship, or contributed income (i.e., corporate donations). Because the term *social entrepreneurship* has come to encompass a great deal, we separate the discussion of this phenomenon from the other ventures (also see Chapter 14). Nonprofits generally develop earned income ventures in the areas of services, manufacturing, and distribution—including retail. Examples of retail activities include thrift shops or consignment stores run by churches and the Salvation Army, museum shops, coffee shops, and Ten Thousand Villages fair trade stores (see Chapter 10 case). Many zoos have even converted elephant dung into a lucrative business by selling it as fertilizer and raw material for other products (e.g., paper) under the catchy title "zoo doo" (Virtue Ventures, 2010). In the area of services, there are several examples of theatre companies, dance troupes, and coral groups offering acting, dancing, or singing classes to supplement performances. The Newfoundland Center for the Arts (see Chapter 10 case) had a rental venue that was sometimes used for art exhibits. Just for the Birds generates income by manufacturing bird feeders and supplies while serving the mission to provide job placement and life skills to developmentally disabled adults (www.justforthebirds.org). The Goodwill Industries of Greater Grand Rapids (detailed in one of this chapter's cases) is considering whether an online bookstore would help improve its revenue and surplus streams.

Once a nonprofit decides to explore earned income, it must engage in a multiphased process that includes the following five steps (Edgington, 2011):

1. Analyzing assets to determine potential products/services to sell

2. Conducting market research to determine competitors and consumers

3. Pilot-testing a product/service

4. Creating a business plan, including marketing, staffing, financial model, risks, and mitigations

5. Launching the business

Any nonprofit that decides to engage in earned income should carefully review tax implications, such as the U.S. unrelated business income tax. The details, exclusions, and exceptions can be cumbersome and may require expert advice. Again, keeping the mission as the main focus is paramount for NPO leaders, and earned income strategies should serve as a vehicle to implement the mission, not be a distraction from it.

While Chapter 14 develops the concept of social entrepreneurship thoroughly, it is worth briefly reviewing the concept here as it relates to funding sources. Social entrepreneurship has many elements; at its heart it draws heavily from business strategy, finance, management, and marketing to build sustainable, high-impact organizations that tackle major social issues (Bornstein & Davis, 2010). With social entrepreneurial endeavors, self-sustainability is built into the business model, meaning social entrepreneurs develop organizations that generate their own income—from inception—to enable mission accomplishment. These entrepreneurs take missions that nonprofits generally follow and work to change people's thinking and behavior across society. An example of this is TOMS shoes (www.toms.com). The business started with the mission of giving shoes to children and accomplishes this by selling shoes to others who can afford them. The revenue from shoe sales in developed markets enables TOMS to give a pair of shoes to a child in need, usually in emerging markets: "One for One." Good business practices are necessary for social entrepreneurs to maintain the profitable revenue stream that enables social change.

To meet these standards and to practice sound financial management there are four financial statements that nonprofit organizations prepare: *statement of financial position* (the balance sheet), *statement of activities* (the income statement), *statement of cash flow,* and *statement of functional expenses.* Table 11.1 offers brief definitions of each and a dissemination guide. NPO leaders are encouraged to build a strong network among financial and accounting professionals in their area to have multiple experts to whom they can turn for advice.

ASSESSING FINANCIAL STANDING

The Strategic Marketing Assessment Process (SMAP) discussed in Chapter 9 includes a section on financial analysis. Regardless of where in the planning and management process the analysis of the NPO's financial position occurs, some critical calculations such as breakeven, cash forecasting/flow, and program margins should be conducted and reported regularly. Below is a brief list of ratios that can be used to highlight areas of financial strength and potential vulnerability. Following this is an overview of the role of forecasting in the financial management process. Again, it is worth emphasizing that to implement good financial analysis, management, and reporting, at least one member of the NPO governing board should have proficiency in accounting and finance.

The ratios that are most commonly tracked by managers are those that measure *profitability, liquidity, asset management,* and *long-term solvency* (Anthony & Young, 2005, p. 488). Here, profitability refers to the operational surplus, balance, or deficit. To maintain their legal status, nonprofits must take great care to document reinvestment of any surplus. While it is beyond the scope of this book to delve into ratio analysis deeply, Table 11.2 provides some key performance ratios NPO managers should use to analyze their organization's financial standing. It is important to look at ratios recurrently as well as over time. Trends in the ratios can reveal a great deal about operational efficiencies as well as financial prowess. Regularly reviewing financial performance via ratio analysis can avert financial crises such as the one felt by Kiddyland in one of this chapter's cases.

Table 11.1   Financial Statements

Report	Definition	Dissemination Target and Timing
Statement of Financial Position (Balance Sheet)	A snapshot of organizational assets and liabilities. Assets should be specified as restricted or unrestricted.	CEO, Board Monthly and available on demand
Statement of Activities (Income Statement)	Shows the flow of revenues or income, expenses, and changes in net asset value.	Organization-wide—CEO, board Program-specific—program managers Monthly and available on demand
Statement of Cash Flow	Displays cash inflows and outflows over the year. Cash changes may occur from operating, investing, or financing activities.	CEO Quarterly
Statement of Functional Expenses	Demonstrates how expense categories are allocated across programs, activities, and general management.	Organization-wide—CEO, board Program-specific—program managers Monthly and available on demand

Source: Dees, Emerson, & Economy, 2001; Worth, 2012.

Table 11.2   Ratio Analysis

Measurement	Ratio	Description and Recommendation
Profitability	Total Margin = $\dfrac{\text{Revenue} - \text{Expense}}{\text{Revenue}}$	Recall that revenue in a nonprofit may result from income generation, donations, or foundation sources. Higher numbers enable unrestricted investment in contributions to working capital, innovation, and growth. An organization experiencing change or growth needs a higher margin than those in a stable environment with stable income sources.
	Operating Margin = $\dfrac{\text{Operating Revenue} - \text{Operating Expense}}{\text{Operating Revenue}}$	This ratio teases out large, perhaps irregular revenue contributions that are unrelated to operations (e.g., a bequest) from the total margin calculation. Recommendations here depend on how much the NPO wants to rely

(Continued)

Table 11.2 (Continued)

	Contributions and Grants (CG) = $\dfrac{\text{Revenue from CG}}{\text{Total Revenue}}$	on self-generated revenue through operations versus external donations. Higher numbers show more reliance on outside sources. The CG ratio is another way to analyze this relationship.
Liquidity	Current Ratio = $\dfrac{\text{Current Assets}}{\text{Current Liability}}$	For every dollar of liabilities payable in the short term, at least two dollars of current assets should be available to pay them.
	Working Capital = Current Assets − Current Liabilities	Determines how long an NPO could sustain current spending levels without using non-cash assets.
	Days' Cash = $\dfrac{\text{Cash + Short-Term Assets x 365}}{\text{Operating Expense − Depreciation}}$	Calculates the number of days the NPO can survive without cash. While higher is obviously better, a one-month cushion adds security to operations.
	Days' Receivables = $\dfrac{\text{Accounts Receivables} \times 365}{\text{Operating Revenue}}$	Estimates the number of days it takes to collect what is owed to the NPO. Lower is better. Highlights (in)efficiencies of financial management within an organization.
Asset Management	Inventory Turnover = $\dfrac{\text{Net Sales}}{\text{Inventory}}$	Ratios in this category depend a great deal on the types of assets an NPO possesses. If physical inventory is a large part of the NPO work (e.g., nonprofit retail), inventory turnover is extremely important.
Long-term solvency	Debt to Fund Balance (Net Assets) = $\dfrac{\text{Long-Term Liabilities}}{\text{Net Assets}}$	Explains the NPO's long-term (more than one-year payback period) indebtedness. Recommendation depends on the type of operation the NPO is in, generally lower is better, and well below 1.0 is best.

Source: Anthony & Young, 2005; Dees et al., 2001; Worth, 2012.

As a final note on ratio analysis, it is worth remembering that "charity watchdog" agencies often use financial ratios to assess organizational financial efficiency. The Better Business Bureau (BBB) Wise Giving Alliance, for example, uses three financial calculations in addition to other qualitative recommendations when comparing and rating nonprofits. It recommends that the organization (1) spend at least 65% of its total expenses on program activities, (2) spend no more than 35% of related contributions on fundraising, and (3) avoid accumulating funds that could be used for current program activities. "To meet this standard, the charity's unrestricted net assets available for use should not be more than three times the size of the past year's expenses or three times the size of the current year's budget, whichever is higher" (BBB of Central Florida, 2011, #10). Compassion Canada strives to spend less than 20% on administration and fundraising. While much can be said about the value of using such analysis to measure success or viability of nonprofit operation (see, e.g., Palotta, 2010), the practice exists and NPO leaders are well advised to keep abreast of their organization's financial ratios.

The operating budget (discussed below) serves an important purpose, but does not deliver the complete picture needed to determine an organization's cash flow (i.e., when cash will be received and used). As with a personal budget, not having cash available at the right time to cover expenses (e.g., salaries, utilities, supplies) can be detrimental to the financial health and stability of an organization. *Forecasting* cash flow is difficult in the most stable environments; considering that nonprofits often respond to crises and other unpredictable events, the task can be even more daunting.

> A cash forecast generally projects cash receipts and disbursements for each month of the year, based on historical financial reports and personal experience, past budgets, and informed guesses. Simply dividing the budget total by the 12 months in the year is not an accurate reflection of actual cash needs in any given month. An effective cash flow forecast includes projections of when cash will be received, and when it will be needed to meet payroll, pay vendors and make fixed asset purchases. (Clifton Gunderson, 2008, p. 2)

Some nonprofits engage in *sensitivity analysis* when projecting cash flow. This is a complicated term for using a best-case, worst-case, most-likely-case comparison for cash received and dispersed. Because of the volatile nature of nonprofits' need for cash, having such comparisons can assist in establishing goals for fundraising and other income generation schemes. In the end, forecasting is a look into the future, thus it is as much art as science. Keeping accurate records is the best way to keep the analysis more scientific than artistic—this is where budget management comes into the picture.

BUDGET MANAGEMENT

For nonprofits, like most corporations and individuals, a budget system helps track income against expenditures to safeguard that the former is greater than the latter so that a "rainy day fund" (operating reserves) to cover unexpected events can be established and maintained.

> Most NPOs have three separate budgets: an *operating budget* (private to the organization), a *capital budget,* and a *cash budget.* As their names suggest, the first tracks all revenues and expenditures; the second concerns the purchase or disposal of long-term physical assets, such as buildings and equipment; and the third tracks the flow of cash during the year, whether related to operating or capital activities. (Worth, 2012, p. 340)

Alignment of budget to mission is critical; managers should be sure budgets incentivize the desired actions to achieve specific goals that drive mission accomplishment. A strategic plan (discussed in Chapters 5 and 6) may help mitigate budgetary maneuvering that can arise in the budget process. In other words, be sure controllable expenses are allocated to appropriate departments or programs and that uncontrollable expenses (e.g., fixed costs such as electricity) are allocated in an equitable manner.

A final consideration regarding budget management is what happens to the savings versus budget year over year. Correspondingly, what internal penalty, if any, is there for programs or departments that go over budget? These issues should be decided and discussed before releasing the budget so that managers can take advantage of budgetary incentives or avoid disincentives. For example, does a program manager who conducts an event under budget get to retain the money in her program area to use in future projects or new initiatives? If so, she might be encouraged to keep costs low while being innovative.

If not, economizing might be less of a priority if money saved is redistributed to another area of the organization.

The accounting firm of Clifton Gunderson (2008) suggests following these six steps in the budgeting process:

1. Determine programs and activities for designated budget period.

2. Estimate expenses and revenues for these activities.

3. Draft a preliminary budget.

4. Review and modify the budget at the managerial level.

5. Obtain board of director review and approval.

6. Monitor budget activity.

Following the guidelines discussed here would certainly help Kiddyland (in this chapter's case) as it moves forward with its plans to serve poor families with the critical need of childcare. Perhaps learning from past mistakes and implementing good policies from this point on is enough to sustain the organization.

Nonprofit Accounting

All budgeting efforts and recording should also comply with applicable laws and accepted accounting practices. The Financial Accounting Standards Board establishes nonprofit accounting policies in the United States. The five standards most relevant to nonprofit organizations are as follows (Anthony & Young, 2005, p. 469):

No. 93 Accounting for Depreciation

No. 95 Statement of Cash Flows

No. 116 Accounting for Contributions Received and Contributions Made

No. 117 Financial Statements of Not-for-Profit Organizations

No. 124 Accounting for Certain Investments Held by Not-for-Profit Organizations

On January 1, 2012, new accounting standards for Canadian NPOs came into effect. These new standards were finalized by the Canadian Accounting Standards Board and the Public Sector Accounting Board (n.d.). These new standards require that Canadian NPOs either follow Part I (International Reporting Standards) or Part III (Accounting Standards for Not-For-Profit Organizations) of the *Canadian Institute of Chartered Accountants Handbook—Accounting*. Following either of these Parts ensures that NPOs are reporting their financial situation in accordance with Canadian Generally Accepted Accounting Practices.

Cases

Goodwill Industries of Greater Grand Rapids (United States): Kathy Crosby, CEO of Goodwill Industries of Greater Grand Rapids Inc., was considering a proposal from her staff to sell donated books online. Prior to the board meeting, where the proposal had been accepted, Crosby had been leaning toward accepting the proposal. However, a guest at the meeting had given her pause for thought. He had asked several questions that were causing Crosby to reconsider her support for the project. She was determined to review the proposal's strategic and financial fit and make a recommendation to the board at its next meeting in three weeks. The guest had raised three issues: (1) Would this proposal disadvantage an existing set of customers—salvage buyers—who may object to the proposal because it had the potential to take away what could be a very lucrative source of profit for them? (2) Was the proposal properly considering the revenue and operating needs of Goodwill's retail stores? (3) Was the proposal consistent with Goodwill's mission statement?

Kiddyland (United States): This daycare center operated by a nonprofit church-related corporation was originally established for children of low-income families. Jo Anne Larson, the current manager, is concerned that operations cannot continue because of the lack of space and funds. The current policy is to operate on a break-even basis, and the church has no intention to invest additional funds. Larson faces several options, such as increasing tuition fees per child or securing a loan, in order to expand its facility to allow for more children or renovate the existing facility. First she must review the budget and check assumptions underlying the figures.

References

Anthony, R. N., & Young, D. W. (2005). Financial accounting and financial management. In R. Herman & Associates (Eds.), *The Jossey-Bass handbook of nonprofit leadership and management* (2nd ed., pp. 466–512). San Francisco, CA: Jossey-Bass.

BoardSource & Independent Sector. (2006). *The Sarbanes-Oxley Act and implications for nonprofit organizations.* Retrieved from http://www.boardsource.org/dl.asp?document_id=558

Bornstein, D., & Davis, S. (2010). *Social entrepreneurship: What everyone needs to know.* New York, NY: Oxford University Press.

Canadian Accounting Standards Board & Public Sector Accounting Board. (n.d.). *FAQ: Accounting standards for private sector not-for-profit organizations.* Retrieved from http://www.acsbcanada.org/strategic-planning/not-for-profit-orgnizations/item48527.pdf

Chartered Accountants of Canada. (2011, March). New accounting standards for not-for-profit organizations—Questions for directors to ask. *Not-for-Profit Organizations Director Alert.* Retrieved from http://www.rogb.ca/npo/npo-directors-series/director-alerts/item49752.pdf

Chetkovich, C., & Frumkin, P. (2002). *Balancing margin and mission: Nonprofit competition in charitable versus fee-based programs.* Cambridge, MA: Harvard University, Hauser Center for Nonprofit Organizations and Kennedy School of Government.

Clifton Gunderson. (2008). *Best practices for nonprofit budgeting and cash forecasting.* Retrieved from http://www.cliftoncpa.com/Content/5HQ5OYA9WU.pdf?...NonprofitBudgeting

Conway Dato-on, M., Weisenbach Keller, E., & Shaw, D. (2009). Adapting for-profit branding models to small nonprofit organizations: A theoretical discussion and model proposition. In *Proceedings of the 2009 World Marketing Congress.* Ruston, LA: Academy of Marketing Science.

Dees, J. G., Emerson, J., & Economy, P. (2001). *Enterprising nonprofits: A toolkit for social entrepreneurs.* New York, NY: John Wiley & Sons.

Edgington, N. (2011). *Financing not fundraising: Evaluate earned income.* Retrieved from http://www.socialvelocity.net/2011/04/financing-not-fundraising-evaluate-earned-income

Fischer, R. B., Wilsker, A. L., & Young, D. (2007). *Exploring the revenue mix of nonprofit organizations—Does it relate to publicness?* (Andrew Young School of Policy Studies Research Paper Series No. 07-32). Atlanta: Georgia State University.

Imagine Canada. (2006). *The nonprofit and voluntary sector in Canada.* Retrieved from http://www.imaginecanada.ca/files/www/en/nsnvo/sector_in_canada_factsheet.pdf

Independent Sector. (2011). *The sector's economic impact.* Retrieved from http://www.independentsector.org/economic_role

Palotta, D. (2010). *Uncharitable: How restraints on nonprofits undermine their potential.* Medford, MA: Tufts University Press.

Virtue Ventures. (2010). *Nonprofit with income-generating activities.* Retrieved from http://www.4lenses.org/setypology/iga

Worth, M. J. (2012). *Nonprofit management: Principles and practice* (2nd ed.). Thousand Oaks, CA: Sage.

Zietlow, J., Hankin, J. A., & Seidner, A. (2007). *Financial management for nonprofit organizations.* Hoboken, NJ: John Wiley & Sons.

Additional Resources

Tuckman, H., & Chang, C. (1991). A methodology for measuring the financial vulnerability of charitable nonprofit organizations. *Nonprofit and Voluntary Sector Quarterly, 20,* 445–460.

GOODWILL INDUSTRIES OF GREATER GRAND RAPIDS

It was April 1, 2010, and Kathy Crosby, president and chief executive officer (CEO) of Goodwill Industries of Greater Grand Rapids Inc., had just returned from a board meeting where her staff had presented a proposal to begin selling donated books online. Prior to the meeting, Crosby had been inclined to accept the proposal without any reservation. However, after the meeting she wasn't as sure. A guest at the meeting—a visitor from a neighboring Goodwill—had asked a number of pointed questions that were making Crosby revisit her support for the project. She needed to review the financial and strategic fit of the proposal and make a recommendation at the next board meeting in three weeks.

Goodwill Industries of Greater Grand Rapids

The Goodwill movement was established in 1902 by a Methodist Minister, Edgar Helms, to help European immigrants by having them collect used goods for repair and resale. Reverend Helms motto was "Not a handout . . . a hand-up." The movement has evolved; today's mission is:

> Goodwill Industries International enhances the dignity and quality of life of individuals, families and communities by eliminating barriers to opportunity and helping people in need reach their fullest potential through the power of work.

In 1966, Goodwill Industries of Greater Grand Rapids Inc. (GR Goodwill) was established to serve the needs of the citizens of Kent County, Michigan. GR Goodwill operates programs that help "employment challenged citizens," which they refer to as "participants," overcome mental impairments, physical impairments, incarceration records, transition issues experienced by veterans returning from duty, and other work barriers that would prevent participants from becoming contributing members of society. Since its founding, GR Goodwill had helped more than 25,000 people to achieve sustained employment and become contributing community members. In the past year, 3,800 participants had received services, and 996 participants had been placed into community employment. These participants had a variety of barriers, including the following: 38 per cent were welfare recipients, 16 per cent were offenders, 11 per cent were youth at risk, 10 per cent had learning disabilities, 9 per cent had a mental or emotional disability, 7 per cent were displaced workers, 3 per cent were homeless, and 2 per cent had substance abuse issues.

GR Goodwill had developed a variety of techniques and services to help people realize their employment potential. It provided the following services, among others:

- **Career Assessments:** Professionals helped participants identify the career that best suits their skills, experiences, and aspirations.

Tony Francolini wrote this case under the supervision of Professor W. Glenn Rowe solely to provide material for class discussion. The authors do not intend to illustrate either effective or ineffective handling of a managerial situation. The authors may have disguised certain names and other identifying information to protect confidentiality.

- **Job Training:** Participants received on-the-job experience in a variety of work environments, such as health care, food preparation, hospitality, and grocery services.
- **Workplace Training:** Participants were offered workshops on topics such as etiquette, culture, interviewing, and other soft workplace skills.
- **Job Placement:** Participants received assistance with job searches, résumé building, and interviewing. Goodwill also provided short-term financial support to firms that took on participants.
- **Job Retention:** Participants were coached on how to handle home or work crises that might otherwise derail a career plan.
- **Other Support Services:** Participants were helped to find services to assist with other issues such as transportation and counseling.

Many of the services were offered in a creative manner. For instance, GR Goodwill offered catering to the community as a means of training participants in the food industry skills needed to gain long-term, quality employment.

GR Goodwill was a non-profit organization that received funding from three sources. The first source was donations from community members (i.e. individuals, corporations, and foundations) who supported Goodwill's goals and methods. The second source was grants received from the government to fund specific programs. The third source was from revenue earned in thrift stores operated by GR Goodwill.

In its thrift stores, GR Goodwill accepted donation of used clothing, household goods, books, electronics, and other items from the community and resold the goods in one of its 14 retail stores, one outlet store, or online at shopgoodwill. com. In the past year, GR Goodwill sold more than 2.4 million pieces of clothing and earned total retail revenue of almost $12 million. The Operating Flow Diagram for Goodwill's Donated Goods outlines how donated goods were received, processed, and repurposed (see Exhibit 1).

Anyone wishing to donate goods (i.e. clothing, household goods, books, electronics, or other items) could drop them off at any of the GR

Exhibit 1 Operating Flow Diagram For Goodwill's Donated Goods

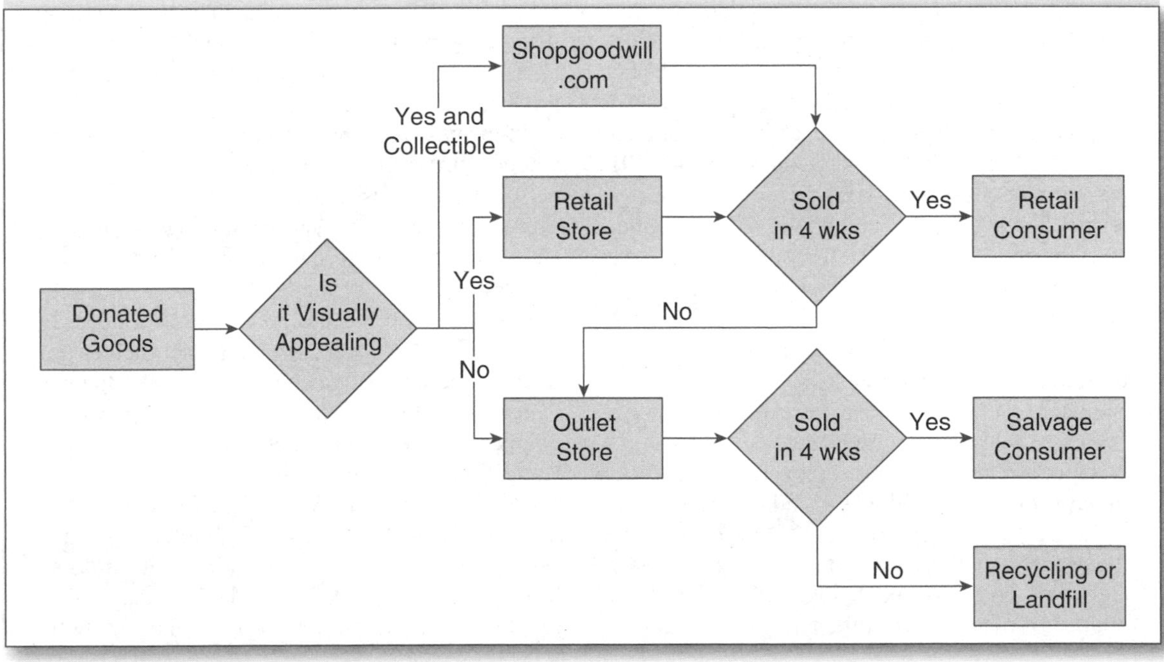

Goodwill's 14 retail stores, one of its four drop-off centers (which have no retail space), or the GR Goodwill central warehouse. Sorters at each facility inspected the donated items to determine whether the quality of the goods met the standards for placement on the sales floor; not all goods were resold. In addition, some retailers passed on excess items to GR Goodwill to sell; these items represented approximately 15 per cent of the goods in the retail stores.

If an item was identified as a potential antique or collector's item, it was sent to the central warehouse. Once there it was photographed and placed on shopgoodwill.com.

Goods for sale at GR Goodwill's thrift stores were competitively priced with other thrift stores in the Greater Grand Rapids Area. However, most items sold by GR Goodwill were deeply discounted from traditional retail prices.

A colored tag was affixed to goods when they were placed on the retail shelf. Later, the tag was used to identify items that had been on display for four weeks without being sold. Each week, goods with tags of a different color were removed from the shelf. If an item did not sell after four weeks, it was sent to the outlet store, where bulk or salvage buyers purchased product by the weight at much discounted prices. For instance, at the outlet store, a salvage buyer could purchase 500 pounds of clothing with the intent of shipping it overseas where it fetched a profit. At the outlet store, clothing and shoes sold for 50¢ per pound; glassware, 10¢ per pound; housewares, 30¢ per pound; and books, 7¢ per pound.

Any items not sold at the outlet store were recycled. The manner in which items were recycled depended on the goods. For instance, cloth was often shredded and sold to be made into rugs or used as absorbents. Items that did not meet the standards to be placed on the sales floor were immediately sent to be recycled.

Goodwill was the largest recycler in the world in terms of textiles and was proud of its recycling record. In the last fiscal year, 75 per cent of the material that had been donated was recycled. GR Goodwill had diverted a total of 10.5 million pounds of material from the landfill: 5.5 million pounds of textiles; 3.8 million pounds of computer electronics; and 1.2 million pounds of shoes, books, and miscellaneous household accessories. This level of recycling represented a 10 per cent improvement over the previous year. GR Goodwill's target for the current year was to reduce waste by a further 38 per cent. These numbers were especially gratifying when considering that most of this material would not have been handled by traditional municipal recycling facilities.

HISTORY OF THE ONLINE BOOK-SELLING PROPOSAL

GR Goodwill sold books according to the general procedures that guided its sale of other goods, such as clothing. A flow diagram for Goodwill's current book-selling process can be seen in Exhibit 2 and outlines the manner in which books were handled. The books were offered for sale if they were deemed visually appealing (i.e. they are not written in, highlighted, bent, or otherwise in a worn condition).

Like other goods in the retail stores, GR Goodwill priced books at a deep discount by using a simple pricing model. Books were priced at a fraction of the publisher's suggested list-prices (see Exhibit 3).

In the past year, the retail managers had noticed a large number of customers using cell phones and personal digital assistant (PDA) devices next to the shelves that held the books for sale. These customers were entering the international standard book numbers (ISBNs) of the books in stock into programs that indicated the books' resale values. In effect, customers were scouting the shelves for underpriced books. Watching this activity, the GR Goodwill staff came to realize that their pricing policies may be inappropriate: they may have been leaving money on the table.

Prompted by this realization, Sharon Nason, director of Donated Goods Operations, approached Monsoon Software (Monsoon) for advice. Monsoon licenses a software platform that allows retailers to become online book resellers. Among

Exhibit 2   Goodwill's Current Book-Selling Flow Diagram

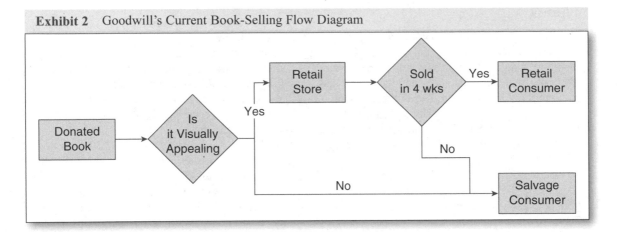

Exhibit 3   Goodwill's Existing Book Pricing Rules

Publisher's Price	GR Goodwill's Price
< $5.00	49¢
< $10.00	99¢
< $15.00	$1.99
< $20.00	$2.99
< $25.00	$3.99
< $30.00	$4.99
< $35.00	$5.99
< $40.00	$6.99
< $45.00	$7.99
< $50.00	$8.99

others, the software performed four major functions. First, the software allowed resellers to scan books to determine the prevailing prices on Amazon.com and other online retailers. Second, the software listed a reseller's inventory of books on a third party's website such as Amazon.com, Abebooks.com, or eBay.com. Third, the software automatically re-priced a reseller's unsold inventory on the basis of user-defined rules that aim to lower prices to ensure slow-moving inventory sells. Fourth, the software generated invoicing and shipping paperwork.

Monsoon scanned a random sample of 600 books from a bin of books that were not sold at the retail stores and determined that 9 per cent of those books could have been sold for an average price of $5 per book. That $5 is a marked increase over the 7¢ that GR Goodwill would otherwise have earned for these books from a salvage customer. Nason estimated that GR Goodwill could increase revenue by $243,135 from the sale of books if it could realize a gain of $4.73 on the 9 per cent of the $550,000 worth of books that had gone to salvage customers in the past year. On the basis of this initial rough calculation, Nason set out to develop the online book-selling proposal.

The proposal Nason developed was presented to the board jointly with Dave Brinza, chief operating officer (COO) of GR Goodwill. The highlights of the proposal are as follows.

FORMAL PROPOSAL

GR Goodwill proposed to sell books online on Amazon.com to generate additional revenue for Goodwill's mission.

Phase I

The online book-selling program would be introduced in two phases. In the first phase, GR Goodwill would take approximately 12 per cent of the books that were unsold at the retail stores and post them online for sale to Amazon customers.

Goodwill's Phase I Book-Selling Flow Diagram, as shown in Exhibit 4, outlines the manner in which book sales would be managed in Phase I of the implementation.

Nason projected 523,636 unsold books would be sent by the retail stores to the central warehouse in each of the next three years. She projected 62,836 (approximately 12 per cent) of those unsold books would be scanned and offered for sale online in each of the following three years. In the first year, 34,152 (6.522 per cent) of the 523,636 books were expected to

sell; in year 2, the number of books sold was expected to increase to 40,290.

With the assistance of Monsoon, revenue and commissions were projected. The average gross selling price was expected to be $7.50 per book in each year. After fees, the sales would generate an average net revenue of $4.98 per book sold online (see Exhibit 5).

If 34,152 books were sold at $7.50 per book, total revenue was expected to be $256,140 in year 1 and $302,175 in year 2, based on 40,290 units sold. As the annual revenue from books sold online increased, revenue from sales to salvage customers would drop marginally, from $36,654 (7¢ × 523,636 books) to $34,263 (7¢ × (523,636 − 34,152 books)).

Amazon would be responsible for the collection of all sales. Every two weeks, Amazon

Exhibit 4 Goodwill's Phase I Book-Selling Flow Diagram

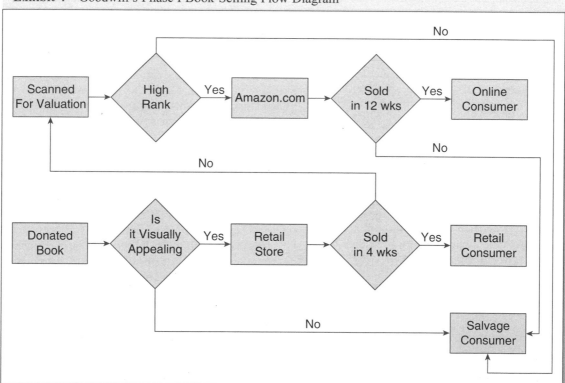

Exhibit 5	Goodwill's Year 1 Revenue per Book	
Selling Price		7.50
Shipping Revenue		3.99
Total Sale		**$11.49**
Less: Amazon Fee (15% of Revenue)		1.13
Transaction Fee		1.35
Monsoon Fee (3.5% of Total Sale)		0.40
Shipping		3.99
Total Revenue		**$4.62**

Exhibit 6	Goodwill's Year 1 Projected Revenue	
Selling Revenue		256,140
Shipping Revenue		132,266
Total Sales		**$392,406**
Less: Amazon Fee (15% of Revenue)		38,421
Transaction Fee		46,105
Monsoon Fee (3.5% of Total Sales)		13,734
Shipping		136,266
Wages & Benefits		84,756
Supplies		9,384
Office Equipment		2,352
Maintenance		240
Total Expenses		**$331,288**
Total Profit		**$61,119**

would deposit into GR Goodwill's bank account the value equivalent to total sales less Amazon's 15 per cent fee.

Operating costs were projected at $96,732. The majority of the operating costs were wages and benefits associated with the hiring of three full-time equivalent employees, to be called e-commerce book technicians. Ideally, each would be a skilled employee with training in library services or retail services. These employees would report to Nason, who anticipated the book-selling business would take approximately 15 per cent of her time.

The budget for the first year is shown in Goodwill's Year 1 Projected Revenue, as shown in Exhibit 6.

Start-up costs were projected at $24,977. The major items in this list included $4,240 for shelving, $7,000 for the Monsoon software, $3,500 for computer hardware, $3,850 for fencing, $1,600 for pallet jacks, and $1,065 for totes. The remainder of the costs were for office supplies. Based on an income of $61,148 per year, the breakeven would be less than six months.

GR Goodwill had 80,000 square feet of warehouse space, of which 2,000 square feet would need to be converted from warehousing space to make room for the book-selling operation. This space would provide room for the

three staff, staging for scanning, staging for shipping, and book shelving.

Budget Sensitivity

Nason identified some concerns with Monsoon's estimates. When she visited the Indianapolis Goodwill, which was pioneering the Goodwill venture in online book-selling, she found that their financials differed from those offered by Monsoon. The average selling price of a book sold by the Indianapolis Goodwill was approximately $8, including shipping revenue, which was approximately $3.50 less than in Monsoon's budget. Fortunately, this reduction in revenue was largely offset by reductions in costs. First, the reduction in revenue also meant a reduction in the fees. Second, the Indianapolis Goodwill found that Amazon waived all transaction costs because of the volume of sales that it facilitated. Nason also found that shipping costs were less than projected; based on her findings, Nason had reason to believe shipping costs could be approximately $2.99 per unit. Nason was not disturbed by the variation in the financial projection. Each model showed that payback was approximately six months (see Exhibits 7 and 8).

Phase II

In phase II of the implementation, the retail stores and drop-off centers would scan all donated books that were visually appealing. All visually appealing books with a projected sales value of more than $5 would be sent to the online book-selling unit rather than stocking them in the retail store to be sold at the deep discounted value (see Exhibit 9).

Because of these changes, GR Goodwill's revenues were expected to increase considerably, although the figures were not estimated. First, the increases would come from an increased number of books being sold online where margins were greater. Second, the increased volume of books being scanned would also help retail stores to recognize when books that would remain on retail shelves should be priced above the deep discount prices (see Exhibit 3).

QUESTIONS RAISED DURING THE PRESENTATION

At Kathy Crosby's invitation, Frank O'Leenee, a visitor from a neighbouring Goodwill organization, sat in on the online book-selling presentation because it was a business segment that his organization had yet to consider. Crosby had thought O'Leenee's curious nature would add to the meeting.

O'Leenee focused on three aspects of the presentation: (1) the impact of the proposal on the

Exhibit 7 Goodwill's Year 1 Revenue per Book—Revised

	Monsoon	Nason
Selling Price	7.50	4.00
Shipping Revenue	3.99	3.99
Total Sales	$11.49	$7.99
Less: Amazon Fee (15% of Revenue)	1.13	0.60
Transaction Fee	1.35	0.00
Monsoon Fee (3.5% of Total Sale)	0.40	0.28
Shipping	3.99	2.99
Total Revenue	$4.62	$4.12

Exhibit 8 Goodwill's Year 1 Projected Revenue—Revised

	Monsoon	Nason
Selling Revenue	256,140	136,608
Shipping Revenue	132,266	136,266
Total Sales	$392,406	$272,874
Less: Amazon Fee (15% of Revenue)	38,421	20,491
Transaction Fee	46,105	0
Monsoon Fee (3.5% of Total Sale)	13,734	9,563
Shipping	132,266	102,114
Wages & Benefits	84,756	84,756
Supplies	9,384	9,384
Office Equipment	2,352	2,352
Maintenance	240	240
Total Expenses	$331,259	$228,888
Total Profit	$61,148	$43,986

Exhibit 9 Goodwill's Phase II Book-Selling Flow Diagram

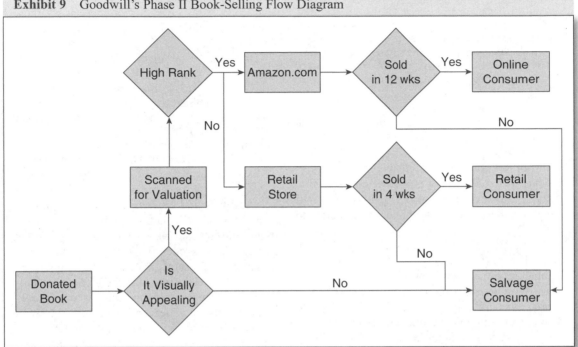

salvage customers, (2) the participation of the stores, and (3) the intended labor force.

Salvage Buyers

O'Leenee had asked:

What happens to the relationship we have with book resellers if we reduce the quality and quantity of books that are available to be sold as salvage? If we begin to sell online and our sales of books increase, won't we be reducing the quantity and quality of books available to the salvage buyers? How can we expect to retain the salvage customers? Might not we end up generating more waste and less revenue if they leave?

Nason had answered:

Currently, we are selling the books that cannot be sold at the stores to salvage buyers for 6¢ or 7¢ per pound. We haven't told them about our plans to skim off 12 per cent of their volume to be posted online. These salvage buyers are book resellers who operate their own online book web sites. They are professionals who will know how to get value out of the books that are left for them to sell.

Dave Brinza, the COO, had added:

We are only concerned with how our business model damages other not-for-profits. We don't want to change our business model in a way that reduces the collection or viability of other donation-dependent charities. However, we are not concerned with how changes we make may impact a for-profit business. For-profit businesses will need to adjust, compete, and survive.

Participation of Stores

O'Leenee had asked:

Correct me if I am wrong, but doesn't Phase II of the proposal call for store employees to scan the books and send on all books to the central sorting

338 INTRODUCTION TO NONPROFIT MANAGEMENT

facility that are most likely to fetch a good resale value? If that is so, why would we expect store managers to participate in Phase II of the proposal? Are you not asking store managers to do two steps that add no value to their store's sales/margin objectives? First, by sending the best books to the central facility, are you not asking the store managers to forgo store sales and profit? Second, by asking them to scan the books to determine their value, are you not asking the stores to incur extra labor costs that add no value?

Another question that had come up was: "What will be the impact on customers who are attracted to the 14 regional Goodwill stores if quality books are sold online rather than in stores?"

Although Brinza had expressed this concern himself to store managers, the store managers he contacted did not feel that this would be a concern. However, Brinza wasn't sure whether the store managers' responses were because they felt books were not an attractive item or because the store managers did not have a sense of how much book sales contributed to their bottom line. GR Goodwill did not record the value of book sales by store; the store cash registers recorded the sale of a book as a sale of a "miscellaneous household item."

Participant Involvement

O'Leenee had asked:

On principle, how can we support a business proposal that does not employ participants? As I understand it, Sharon has said that the three full-time employees that will be used in the book-selling unit will be hired externally from a non-participant workforce. You don't have faith that participants can be found to fill the role. What does that say about our confidence in our clients?

He even pointed to the poster on the wall that contained the mission statement "Changing lives and communities through the power of work" (see Appendix 1). He also pointed to the first strategic planning item, "We will have

people-centric services that build self-sufficiency," and said: "How does this project satisfy these objectives? How does it satisfy the mission or the vision?"

Brinza had responded:

GR Goodwill has a responsibility to their donors—to be fiscally responsible. When there was a choice between (a) employing a participant and making less money, or (b) not employing a participant and making more money that could be used to support a community program, GR Goodwill will choose the latter.

Crosby would have responded in a similar manner. Goodwill had a long history of using funds raised from its businesses to help other organizations to employ participants. If this proposal was successful, profit not labor opportunities would be generated for the greater good.

Yet Crosby had to admit that the online book-selling proposal added no opportunities for participants, which would make it the first business segment with no participants. This business segment would be in contrast to Goodwill's other business segments; 65 per cent of Goodwill's entire workforce is comprised of individuals with disabilities and other barriers to employment.

Moreover, Crosby could not defend Nason's assertion that participants lacked the skills to operate the three jobs at the book center. Crosby knew that GR Goodwill was able to use participants in its Dell Reconnect Program, which partnered GR Goodwill with Dell to recycle computer electronics. It was odd that participants could be used in a program that involved working with computer parts, but could not be used in a program that involved working with books.

CONCLUSION

Crosby, in the privacy of her office, was revisiting the meeting. Was O'Leenee being picky, or did he raise some good points? Was there a reason why this proposal, which seemed to be financially sound, should be reconsidered or altered?

Appendix 1   Mission/Vision/Values

Our Mission
Changing lives and communities through the power of work

Our Vision
The leader in the nation helping people achieve self-sufficiency

Our Values
- **Integrity**: We are honest, transparent, and accountable in our decisions and actions.
- **Stewardship**: We commit to being socially, environmentally, and fiscally responsible with community resources.
- **Innovation**: We continuously learn, embracing creativity and change.
- **Excellence:** We continuously improve and deliver high value results.
- **Respect:** We treat each other with dignity and fairness, value diversity, and commit to a safe environment.

Strategic Planning Goals

Goal 1: We will have people-centric services that build self-sufficiency
Objectives:
- Define and measure participant self-sufficiency
- Establish funding formulas that best support the people-centric model
- Implement innovative and effective programs to achieve self-sufficiency

Goal 2: We will have the best workforce to achieve the mission
Objectives:
- Employee behaviors will align with the values of our organization
- Goodwill will attract and retain the best workforce
- Our Goodwill will be a continuous learning organization
- Goodwill will have an efficient and effective workforce

Goal 3: We will have the financial resources to sustain Goodwill
Objectives:
- Extract the greatest value from material donations
- Define the balance between profitable growth, financial stability, and sustainable mission
- Establish an environment that fosters intentional innovation

Goal 4: We will have an effective business infrastructure
Objectives:
- Enhance IT systems to include analysis and design
- Eliminate non-value-added activity
- Improve organization-wide communication
- Recurring activities have developed and followed documented processes

Goal 5: Goodwill's mission is understood and supported by our community
Objectives:
- Increase the presence of the organization's leadership in the community
- Increase the quality and quantity of material donations
- Increase community support
- Leverage collaborative relationships in the community
- Develop a plan for effective usage of social media

KIDDYLAND

INTRODUCTION

Jo Ann Larson managed Kiddyland, a non-profit daycare center in Market, Utah. In 2001, she asked Pike, a business professor at a nearby university, for advice. The university encouraged community service of this type, and Pike agreed.

BACKGROUND

Kiddyland was owned by a local non-profit corporation that had been established by a church 11 years previously and was licensed by the city's Department of Child Services. The corporation's policy was that Kiddyland should operate on approximately a break-even basis; that is, the church did not intend to use its own funds to finance the operation. Kiddyland was one of seven daycare centers in Market that had its own building. Many smaller daycare centers were located in church basements or private homes.

Most Kiddyland children were in families whose income was near the poverty level. In most cases, both parents were employed. Kiddyland charged $36 per week, the lowest rate of any of the seven centers. Rates in other daycare centers were as high as $60 per week. Centers at the top of the scale attracted children from higher income families. Most centers, including Kiddyland, operated at capacity.

In 2001, the center had an average enrollment of about 45 children. About 40 attended during the day and received a lunch. The other five were students in a school across the street; they stayed at the daycare center after school until parents picked them up on their way home from work. Each child was charged $36 per week.

IMMEDIATE ISSUES

Kiddyland operated in a two-storey wooden building located on a large lot owned by the corporation. It was old and needed repair. According to a recent inspection by the city fire marshal, the building was in violation of the fire code because, among other deficiencies, the second floor did not have two outside exits, not all exit doors opened outward, smoke detection devices and emergency lighting were missing, stairwells were not enclosed and materials used in ceiling and walls were substandard. A contractor, who was a member of the church, estimated that necessary repairs to the building would cost roughly $150,000. Furthermore, the Department of Child Services had indicated that it probably would no longer license centers in two-storey buildings after the next few years. Several of the other centers were housed in one-storey brick buildings.

The contractor also roughly estimated the cost of constructing a new, one-storey 30 feet × 30 feet building on the same lot at $80,000, assuming that volunteer labor would do much of the interior finishing. After construction of the new building, the old building would be demolished.

S. Sam Sedki prepared this case solely to provide material for class discussion. The author does not intend to illustrate either effective or ineffective handling of a managerial situation. The author may have disguised certain names and other identifying information to protect confidentiality.

The church was not willing to finance either the renovation of the old building or the construction of a new one. The United Fund, the leading welfare organization in Market, helped support one daycare center in Market and might support Kiddyland to the extent of guaranteeing a bank loan. However, Larson had not approached the United Fund for help.

Kiddyland had no formal accounting system. Larson had prepared an income statement for 2000. From bank deposits and checks, Pike was able to prepare an approximate income statement for 2001. Both are shown in Exhibit 1. Based on discussions with Larson, Pike prepared an estimated budget for 2002, assuming the new building would be in use at that time (see Exhibit 1).

In preparing the budget, Pike made the following assumptions:

1. Seventy children would enroll at a fee of $45 each per week.

2. There would be six hourly employees at $5.15 per hour, one hourly employee at $5.55 per hour, an accountant and a business manager. This staffing complement represented four more personnel than currently employed. The current staff was judged to be too small, even for 45 children.

3. Food costs, repairs and supplies would be $8,000 per year.

Pike judged that Larson was a conscientious person who worked well with children but lacked management skills. If Kiddyland closed, Larson planned to open a daycare center for 15 children in her home.

Having completed the 2002 budget, Pike now felt it would be useful to review how sensitive the budget would be to changes in its underlying assumptions. Further, he needed to recommend how much Kiddyland should charge, and what Larson should do.

Exhibit 1 Financial Data (2000 to 2002)

	2000 Actual	2001 Actual	2002 Estimated
Receipts[1]	$ 49,861	$ 60,916	$ 119,667
Expenses:			
Manager salary	10,000	10,000	12,500
Other salaries and wages	19,608	19,120	66,750
Food	8,396	10,164	14,200
Utilities	3,908	3,340	4,200
Interest, current borrowings[2]	413	1,054	600
Supplies[3]	914	1,828	–
Legal fees	70	50	–
Repairs	248	1,288	–
Insurance	1,008	6,512	800

(Continued)

Exhibit 1 (Continued)

Miscellaneous[4]	2,724	7,460	8,000
Depreciation[5]	1,108	826	–
Loan payment			13,783
Total expenses	$ 48,397	$ 61,642	$ 120,833
Income (loss)	$ 1,464	$ (726)	$ (1,166)

[1]Excludes bad debts of about $1,000 in both 2000 and 2001, but includes some county assistance.

[2]Depreciation and interest were for an automobile purchased on an installment basis. The automobile was fully paid for by 2002.

[3]Several parents donated supplies; not counted as an expense.

[4]Amount probably included some nonrecurring items.

[5]Included in miscellaneous.

12

ADVOCACY AND LOBBYING

Canadian non-profits and charities that undertake political advocacy or lobbying with the Federal Government need to consider whether their activities fall within the requirement to register under the Lobbying Act.

—Mark Blumberg (2008, p. 15)

Key Topics: definition of terms and legal implications, funding, tactics, future direction of advocacy and lobbying in nonprofit sector

The history of civic action in the United States and Canada shows nonprofits often lead the call for societal change as advocates for the disenfranchised and those generally unable to speak for themselves. The list of such transformation is long and includes actions related to workers' rights, child labor laws, women's voting rights, civil rights, clean air and water, housing assistance and many more. How do nonprofit organizations (NPOs) bring issues to the public's attention within a fragmented media environment? Once there is attention on an issue, how can leaders influence attitudes and build support for change? In this chapter we review methods for lobbying those in power and advocating for those who need assistance. Before beginning the discussion, a few definitions will align the understanding of the terms.

Broadly speaking, *advocacy* refers to activism in support of a cause or idea. The goals of advocacy range from influencing public policy (e.g., civil rights marches to bring attention to the plight of blacks in the 1960s) to changing public behavior (e.g., NFL Play60 campaign encouraging kids to be active 60 minutes a day). *Lobbying* takes activism to the next step; it specifically supports or opposes certain legislation (e.g., efforts to establish laws requiring use of seatbelts and infant car seats) or seeks to obtain government funding for a social program on the national, state/provincial, or local level. *Political campaigning* focuses attention on candidates for office and may include publication or distribution of candidates' position materials (Crutchfield & McLeod Grant, 2008; Worth, 2012). Table 12.1 offers some examples of activities that fall under

Table 12.1 Examples of Lobbying and Advocacy Activities Practiced by NPOs

Forms of Lobbying	Forms of Advocacy
• Engaged in direct correspondence with government officials—mail, phone call	• Responded to request for information from government official
• Made personal visit to government officials	• Distributed informational materials
• Designed and implemented campaign to encourage public to communicate with government officials	• Testified at hearings concerning service work
• Initiated email campaign to government officials asking for specific action on pending legislation	• Authored op-ed column or letter to editor for publication
	• Organized public event highlighting issue(s)
	• Released research report on issue(s)
	• Filed or joined a lawsuit
	• Initiated email campaign to inform parties

each category. In general, all such actions seek to influence *public policy*—whether through changes in the law or in public opinion. The Minnesota Council of Nonprofits (2011) defines public policy as "the set of decisions that we make about how we will care for one another, our communities and the land" (para. 2). With this common understanding of activities, we can now investigate trends and best practices in advocacy and lobbying as it applies to service provision and mission fulfillment for NPOs.

TRENDS IN LOBBYING AND ADVOCACY AMONG NONPROFITS

In general, the U.S. Internal Revenue Code does not restrict social welfare nonprofits, 501(c)(4) organizations, from engaging in most forms of lobbying, though restrictions on political campaigning and endorsement or opposition of candidates exist. Charitable nonprofits, 501(c)(3) organizations, are eligible for tax-deductible contributions and are therefore restricted more severely in their ability to lobby. While many disagree with the premise underpinning this restriction (e.g., Bernstein, 1997; Palotta, 2010), the law exists and nonprofits risk losing their tax status if it is disobeyed; charitable nonprofits are

required to use donated resources primarily to pursue their social purpose. Like many laws, nuances exist and NPO leaders are wise to engage legal expertise to ensure adherence to the most recent interpretation of the law. Worth (2012) covers the intricacies of recent laws extensively in his text.

In Canada, a new Lobbying Act came into force on July 2, 2008. Mark Blumberg (2008), a lawyer with Bloomberg Segal LLP in Toronto, Ontario, has written a nice summary of the Canadian Lobbying Act and how its provisions apply to NPOs. Essentially, if an NPO uses paid employees for a total of more than 20% of their time to lobby, they must register as lobbyists under the Lobbying Act. Guidelines for determining this 20% are outlined in Blumberg's summary. On the other hand, if unpaid volunteers are used, there is no need to register them as lobbyists. Under some conditions, the NPO may have to file monthly returns describing its lobbying activities. For example, if there is an arranged and oral meeting with a "designated public office holder," an NPO that is registered under the Lobbying Act must file a monthly return within 15 days from the end of the month if lobbying activity occurred in that month. Regardless, a return must be filed at no more than six-month intervals.

The Income Tax Act in Canada allows NPOs that are not registered charities to engage in nonpartisan or partisan activities, but it does restrict the quantity and type of political activity in which a Canadian registered charity may engage. Canadian NPOs that are contemplating getting involved in political activities should consult the Canada Revenue Agency's (2011) policy statement on political activities (CPS–022). To quote Blumberg (2008):

> Under the *Income Tax Act,* a registered charity can be involved in non-partisan political activities as long as it devotes substantially all (90%) of its resources to charitable activities. Any political activity has to help accomplish the charity's purposes and remain incidental (generally 10% or less) in scope. A registered charity cannot be involved in partisan political activities, which is something to keep in mind always but especially during an election. (p. 8)

Interestingly, as of June 8, 2011, there were 5,019 lobbyists registered with the federal government in Canada. Almost half of these (2,505) were registered as lobbying on behalf of NPOs and registered charities (see Office of the Commissioner of Lobbying of Canada, 2011). Blumberg (2008) suggests that this number is understated because many NPOs that are engaged in advocacy and lobbying do not know of the requirement to register but should be registered. It should be noted that provincial governments in Canada may have even more restrictions regarding political lobbying in their jurisdiction. Wise NPO leaders will ensure that they are fully aware of the restrictions and requirements federally, provincially, and within the municipality in which they operate.[1]

In the United States, there are few legal limitations placed on the scope of advocacy activities that nonprofits can pursue. Nonetheless, such activities remain relatively limited (Silverman & Patterson, 2010). According to Silverman and Patterson and the Center for Lobbying in the Public Interest (www.clpi.org), reasons for limited advocacy include the following:

- perceptions among NPO leaders that strong advocacy positions may limit external funding
- limited time for advocacy due to additional time spent securing funds from multiple sources because each single source has decreased its contributions recently
- increased pressure from media and nonprofit watchdog agencies to spend higher percentages of income and other resources on programmatic activities (versus advocacy and/or fundraising)

Because of these factors, "nonprofits with a stronger base of individual contributors tend to pursue a broader scope of advocacy activities" (Silverman & Patterson, 2010, p. 5). Salamon, Geller, and Lorentz (2008) echo many of these issues and concerns in their discussion of factors affecting the willingness of NPOs to become involved in lobbying and advocacy as well as the methods of involvement.

There is a disturbing element to this trend of hesitancy to advocate among nonprofits. First, as mentioned at the beginning of this chapter, history is replete with examples in which advocacy brought substantial positive change for individuals and society, begging the question: If nonprofits are not advocating for change, who is? Second, Crutchfield and McLeod Grant (2008) found that when organizations engage in both advocacy and service, "the two parts come together to create impact that is greater than the sum of the parts" (p. 33). The virtuous cycle that results when activities are combined, pictured in Figure 12.1, helps ensure that the policies developed based on advocacy efforts are able to be implemented by those in the field. In effect, linking activities eliminates the intermediaries in the process, which results in an increase in effectiveness.

The Foundation Center's (2010) report on policy-related activities among U.S. foundations

---

[1]For example, in Ontario there is the Office of the Integrity Commissioner and Lobbyists Registration Act, 1998 (http://lobbyist.oico.on.ca), and in the city of Toronto there is the Toronto Lobbyist Registry.

Figure 12.1 Combining Advocacy and Service to Increase Impact

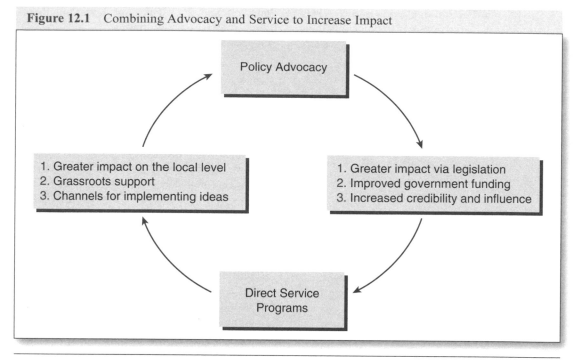

Source: Crutchfield & McLeod Grant, 2008, p. 34. Reprinted with permission.

reveals several interesting trends, the most striking of which is the increased engagement of foundations in advocacy.

> Over half of surveyed foundations that engage in public policy-related activities increased their levels of support over the last five years. In fact, close to two-fifths of these funders were not engaged in supporting public policy-related efforts five years ago. (p. 2)

The projection is that such activity will remain a priority in the next five years. The top three fields of interest for this activity are education, youth and children, and environment and climate change. The main way for foundations to support advocacy is through funding of nonprofits that engage in such activities. Finally, the government target of policy-related work spans from federal to local (Foundation Center, 2010). Given these trends, one may ask: How are nonprofits

engaging in advocacy and lobbying? Are any methods more effective than others?

ADVOCACY AND LOBBYING BEST PRACTICES

When beginning an advocacy campaign, four questions come to mind.

1. What is the opportunity/problem you seek to influence?

2. What specific outcome do you hope to achieve?

3. Who decides what happens relative to the opportunity/problem you seek to influence?

4. How will you influence the decision makers?

Upon answering these questions, NPO leaders should compare responses to their organizational mission and ask: How will this advocacy effort advance the organizational mission? If this connection is not clear, leaders risk mission drift and brand dilution. The list of advocacy resources at the end of this chapter provides a good place to start in seeking additional information and more detailed tactics to approach advocacy and lobbying.

Crutchfield and McLeod Grant (2008) remind us that although combined policy–program approaches (service + advocacy) are most effective, the tactic is fairly uncommon in the nonprofit sector. The authors offer three ways to bridge the divide:

1. Start with service, and add advocacy, as did America's Second Harvest food bank network and Habitat for Humanity. Organizations such as these can leverage their strong success and public awareness from service work to recommend systematic changes that multiply their efforts.

2. Start with advocacy, and add service, similar to the Environmental Defense Fund and the Center for Budget and Policy Priorities. This strategy is effective when the NPO is small relative to the societal impact it hopes to achieve.

3. Use a combined strategy from inception, as did YouthBuild USA and National Council of La Raza. The leaders of these organizations "shared a common philosophical belief that government should be part of the solution" (Crutchfield & McLeod Grant, 2008, p. 43). This approach is similar to the wide-scale impact sought by social entrepreneurs (see Chapter 14).

The tools used for lobbying and advocacy depend greatly on whether the efforts are grassroots or direct. At the grassroots level, many of the practices discussed in Chapter 9 are applicable, particularly those related to social and cause marketing. The Center for Lobbying in the Public Interest (2005) has worked with NPOs for more than 10 years offering advice and training, and providing a central database for lobbying

resources. It offers four general principles and practices as an aspirational framework from which nonprofits can build their lobbying efforts. These principles state that advocacy and/or lobbying efforts should

1. add civic value to the community today and in the future;

2. be inclusive and expansive, engaging the community and particularly those most affected by the public policy being advocated;

3. be credible, trustworthy, and fact based; and

4. be multifaceted and adaptive. (p. 1)

Taking into consideration the platform that has been set by these principles and good ethical practices, and combining several resources, the following checklist proposes ideas and steps for those seeking to begin or improve their lobbying and advocacy efforts (Center for Lobbying in the Public Interest, 2007; Crutchfield & McLeod Grant, 2008; Worth, 2012).

1. *Prepare the organization.*

1.1. Study the legislative process to the point where the NPO leader and governing board are aware of laws regarding advocacy and lobbying as well as how bills become law at different governmental levels.

1.2. Balance pragmatism with idealism. Strike a balance between the actions necessary for mission accomplishment and those necessary to preserve the brand equity established through service work. Social welfare organizations must keep the mission the primary focus of activities.

1.3. Communicate with key stakeholders about the role that advocacy and lobbying play in mission accomplishment. Involve as many stakeholders as possible in the process.

1.4. Look for allies, and build a database of legislative action and legislator positions relative to NPO issues. Throughout the process, and particularly at this stage, remain apolitical and nonpartisan.

2. *Become the voice for your cause* and a center for action (physically and virtually) among stakeholders and the public.

   2.1. Provide leadership opportunities for legislators and other stakeholders to articulate support for the cause.

   2.2. Regularly communicate with the media about activities, policies, and other elements relative to your cause. Make NPO leaders available to speak with the media as frequently as possible.

   2.3. Publish newsletters and conduct research from which cause-related stories can be told and data shared.

3. *Increase capacity, and sustain momentum.*

   3.1. Build or buy skills (e.g., human resource capacity) necessary to engage in lobbying and advocacy. Let diversity guide this step and generate multiple viewpoints.

   3.2. Actively seek funding sources for advocacy.

   3.3. Build networks with other nonprofits to pool resources and expertise.

   3.4. Strategically mix tactics to achieve goals. Include direct communication, grassroots lobbying, event sponsorship or hosting, paid advertising, and other methods to advance the agenda.

FUTURE OF NONPROFIT ADVOCACY AND LOBBYING

Debate (and scrutiny) about the role of nonprofits in lobbying is likely to continue. Influential parties from government as well as private and nonprofit sectors stand on each side of the issue. At the same time, while less controversy is evident in nonprofit policy advocacy, more work needs to be done to improve skills and educate the general public as well as nonprofit leaders regarding this important concept. Salamon et al. (2008) offer several suggestions for future development of advocacy and lobbying in the nonprofit sector:

- Increase the policy advocacy and lobbying capabilities of nonprofit intermediary organizations operating in the field.
- Expand foundation support (both financial and research based) for nonprofit involvement in advocacy and civic engagement.
- Support and train nonprofit organizations to engage all stakeholders (e.g., boards, clients, staff) in their advocacy and lobbying activities.
- Strengthen the knowledge and skills of small and mid-sized NPOs to engage in effective advocacy and lobbying.

ADVOCACY RESOURCES

Alliance for Justice: www.afj.org

Center for Lobbying in the Public Interest: www.clpi.org

Center on Budget and Policy Priorities: www.cbpp.org

Independent Sector: www.independentsector.org

Internal Revenue Service: www.irs.gov

Power in Policy: A Funder's Guide to Advocacy and Civic Participation: www.fieldstonealliance.org/productdetails.cfm?PC=138

A Voice for Nonprofits: www.brookings.edu/press/Books/2005/voicefornonprofits.aspx

CASES

AOL Time Warner (Canada): As one of the terms of its merger in Canada, a large U.S.-based multimedia corporation is required to support the arts in Canada through a $221 million fund. The first university to approach the company in an attempt to secure funding is encouraged by its initial meetings with the company's representatives. Grant Stirling, director of faculty fundraising at the University of Western Ontario, must prepare a proposal that conveys the university's understanding of the company's business interests, recognizes the diverse needs of the proposal's audience, and aligns the company's interests with the university's needs—all in a clear, well-researched, well-written document.

East Coast Trail Association (Canada): Randy Murphy, the president of the East Coast Trail

Association, a nonprofit in St. John's, Newfoundland and Labrador, knew that the association would not accomplish its mission of acquiring access to land. This access was required to complete the East Coast Trail (the Trail)—a 540-kilometer wilderness and hiking trail on Newfoundland's Avalon Peninsula. The speed with which land along the Avalon Peninsula's coastline was being acquired for commercial and residential development was rapidly increasing and was probably outpacing the association's ability to acquire access to land for the Trail. Murphy knew that the association's Land Committee was expending considerable time and effort to obtain access agreements from landowners and formal protection and recognition from towns that were located along the Trail. However, so far the Land Committee's results had been limited. As such, Murphy faced several alternatives for fulfilling the association's mission and wondered how to proceed.

References

Bernstein, P. (1997). *Best practices of effective nonprofit organizations.* New York, NY: Foundation Center.

Blumberg, M. (2008). *Lobbying and Canadian charities: To register or not to register?* Retrieved from http://www.globalphilanthropy.ca/images/uploads/Lobbying_and_Canadian_Charities_To_register_or_not_to_register.pdf

Canada Review Agency. (2011). *Policy statement: Political activities.* Retrieved from http://www.cra-arc.gc.ca/chrts-gvng/chrts/plcy/cps/cps-022-eng.html

Center for Lobbying in the Public Interest. (2005). *Smart and ethical principles and practices for public interest lobbying: Benchmarking chart.* Washington, DC: Author. Retrieved from http://www.clpi.org/images/pdf/Benchmarking_Tool.pdf

Center for Lobbying in the Public Interest. (2007). *Make a difference for your cause in three hours a week.* Washington, DC: Author.

Crutchfield, L. R., & McLeod Grant, H. (2008). *Forces for good: The six practices of high-impact nonprofits.* San Francisco, CA: Jossey-Bass.

Foundation Center. (2010). Key facts on foundations' public policy-related activities. New York, NY: Author.

Minnesota Council of Nonprofits. (2011). *Why nonprofits should participate in public policy.* Retrieved from http://www.minnesotanonprofits.org/nonprofit-resources/public-policy-advocacy/why-nonprofits-should-participate-in-public-policy

Office of the Commissioner of Lobbying of Canada. (2011). *Home.* Retrieved from http://www.ocl-cal.gc.ca/eic/site/lobbyist-lobbyiste1.nsf/eng/home

Palotta, D. (2010). *Uncharitable: How restraints on nonprofits undermine their potential.* Medford, MA: Tufts University Press.

Salamon, L. M., Geller, S. L., & Lorentz, S. C. (2008). Nonprofit America: A force for democracy? *John Hopkins Listening Post Project Communiqué #9: Nonprofit Advocacy and Lobbying.* Baltimore, MD: John Hopkins University, Center for Civil Society Studies Institute for Policy Studies.

Silverman, R. M., & Patterson, K. L. (2010). *The effects of perceived funding trends on nonprofit advocacy: A national survey of nonprofit advocacy organizations* (Working Paper Series). New York, NY: City University of New York, Baruch College, Center for Nonprofit Strategy and Management.

Worth, M. J. (2012). *Nonprofit management: Principles and practice* (2nd ed.). Thousand Oaks, CA: Sage.

AOL TIME WARNER

Introduction

Grant Stirling, PhD, director of Faculty Fundraising at The University of Western Ontario (Western), had in his hands two recent—and very important—call reports. The reports contained the details of meetings by Western's president, Paul Davenport; two of its vice-presidents, Peter Mercer and Ted Garrard; and Stirling's immediate superior, Kevin Goldthorp, associate vice-president (Development), with two Western alumni: Chris Bogart (BA 1986, LLB 1991) and

Ron Atkey (LLB 1965). Bogart, who had been called on by Davenport, Mercer and Garrard, was a rising star in AOL Time Warner (AOLTW), the fledgling multimedia giant formed by the merger of Virginia-based America Online, the largest U.S. online company, with Time Warner, one of the world's most powerful media conglomerates. Atkey, called on by Garrard and Goldthorp, was legal advisor on the AOLTW merger in Canada and architect of the AOLTW Heritage Fund, the Cdn$221 million "public benefit" fund created by AOLTW during the merger approval process in Canada. The fund was a government requirement for approval of the AOLTW merger in Canada, meant to ensure that the Canadian public would directly benefit from the presence of the new company through AOLTW's sponsorship of Canadian artists and the arts in general.

A PARTNERSHIP OPPORTUNITY

An interesting fundraising opportunity had arisen in the meetings with Bogart and Atkey: Western might be able to approach AOLTW for Heritage funds, as long as Stirling was able to align the company's business interests with Western's academic mission in a successful partnership proposal. Bogart and Atkey had very helpfully agreed to review the proposal and provide feedback before it was sent to the two people within AOLTW who would make the funding decision: Diane Schwalm, vice-president Publicity and External Relations, Warner Canada (who would make decisions about Heritage funds related to film and television), and Gary Newman, president of Warner Music Canada, who might be interested in funding proposals related to music. Garrard wanted a copy of the proposal in two weeks for Bogart's and Atkey's review: if they liked it, they promised to send letters of support to Schwalm and Newman. Stirling knew how much these letters of support would mean in gaining a favorable response from the ultimate decision makers. If he could sell the value of a relationship between AOLTW and Western to Bogart and Atkey, he was quite sure he'd be able to sell the same partnership to Schwalm and Newman.

In fact, Atkey, in his meeting with Garrard and Goldthorp, had suggested a number of partnership ideas that Stirling might use in his proposal. Atkey explained that the Cdn$221 million was to be allocated in a specific fashion, with Cdn$180 million being directed to film production in Canada and another Cdn$25 million going to promote Canadian artists who were part of the Warner Music label (e.g., Alanis Morrisette, the Barenaked Ladies, Great Big Sea). This left Cdn$15 million of the Heritage Fund for general philanthropic purposes, and very little of this money was available as cash. The merger, he explained, had depressed the stock price of AOLTW, and the only way the stock price would move up was for the company to make big profits, something they couldn't do by giving away cash. Hence, the bulk of the Cdn$15 million would be given to fund-seekers as "goods and services," and even these gifts would be disbursed over five years. Half of this money would be allocated to music and half to film and television.

However, Atkey explained, even though funds were limited, he still believed there was good opportunity for Western to proceed with a proposal. He noted that Western was the first

---

university that had sought Heritage funds, and so there was no competition at this point from other schools. But, he said, any proposal would have to conform to AOLTW's core businesses: film, music, television, new media and media in transition. He felt Western could do well if it were to arrange for visiting artists contracted to Time Warner to come to the university as visiting lecturers or guests. AOLTW would subsidize the costs of the artists' travel, allocating these costs toward the Heritage Fund commitment. Atkey gave the example of having Norman Jewison come and speak to film studies students, or having Steven Paige from the Barenaked Ladies come to the music faculty. Atkey foresaw an AOLTW Artists Series at Western and felt that this idea would be attractive to the company since it would cost them very little in cash. He didn't discourage Western from building in cash elements to a proposal (e.g., scholarships), but indicated that the university should be modest in its expectations of cash support. He said that funding for proposals such as departmental chairs and professorships, initiatives that often required cash endowments in the hundreds of thousands, would be out of the question.

THE ARTS AT WESTERN

Western certainly needed large cash endowments for its Faculty of Arts. Ontario universities, like almost all universities in Canada, were publicly funded. Much of Western's operating budget depended on money transferred from the coffers of the provincial government—money that was itself partly dependent upon revenue received from the federal government. As both the federal and provincial governments attempted to balance their budgets in the new period of fiscal restraint that marked neo-conservative public policy in the 1990s, the money available for public education had dwindled. Universities were both raising tuition fees in some programs to compensate and seeking private funds more aggressively.

To focus itself on its mission during this decade of financial challenge, Western had, in 1995, come up with a strategic plan. Its key commitment was to "leadership in learning": "We intend that Western will become, and be seen to be, a markedly more vital and energetic centre of learning, creative questioning, problem-solving, research and teaching."[1] Arts was the oldest faculty at Western and emblematic of the creative questioning Western sought to champion. Despite government cutbacks, liberal arts continued to thrive at Western. In the 1990s, Western successfully launched a new Faculty of Information and Media Studies (FIMS), putting it on the leading edge of post-secondary exploration into the culture of the information age. Courses in FIMS and Arts were popular and intellectually demanding, including innovative offerings, such as "The Culture of Celebrity," "Film Directors/Auteurs: Capra, Sturgess, Spielberg, and Stone" and "Popular Music as Culture." Indeed, many of the Faculty's new initiatives explored the intersections between traditional arts (literature, art, music) and contemporary media: the Department of English, with an enrollment of almost 600 undergraduate and 80 graduate students, offered programs in both English and Film Studies; and the Faculty of Music, with 378 undergraduate and 51 graduate students, offered a Bachelor of Music Administration, designed specifically to support graduates with aspirations to enter the global entertainment and media industries, as well as a Popular Music concentration (with courses such as "Introduction to Jazz" and "Post World War II Popular Music") within its Bachelor of Music program in Music History. The Faculty's success with these popular media initiatives had inspired other faculties at Western to follow suit: the Faculty of Law had recently developed the leading program in Canada in Digital Rights Management, providing expertise in the legal issues surrounding patents, copyright, trademarks, information ownership and related public policy issues concerning information technology and the media.

Western and the Faculty of Arts had also devoted time and money to collecting the best

[1]"Leadership in Learning," 1995 Strategic Plan.

possible resources to complement its developing focus on the media. Its music library, for example, had compiled a collection of music resources that ranked among the top three collections in North America. The collection included nearly 600,000 items, including more than 100,000 books, periodicals and musical scores; more than 400,000 pieces of sheet music; nearly 40,000 recordings (of which more than 12,000 were in CD format) and close to 10,000 manuscripts and printed books on microforms. Plans were in place to renovate and significantly expand the physical space that housed this collection, and to add to the collection itself—Cdn$3 million to double the current space and introduce new resources for students, faculty and the community.

Any private funding source that reviewed this dedication to continued growth and commitment to innovative education had to be convinced that Western was full of partnership potential: to be associated with liberal arts at Western was to gain for the donor not only the cachet of culture, the respect that comes from being associated with a long-standing tradition of cultural expertise, but also the affiliation with cutting-edge media studies, an association that could help brand the private partner as a fresh and innovative company. Partnership with the liberal arts also offered private donors relatively inexpensive marketing relations with the young consumers enrolled in the university's programs: a student who won a scholarship from a private corporation to support the final year of increasingly expensive university study would no doubt feel a kind of brand loyalty very difficult to purchase through advertising.

BUILDING PARTNERSHIPS WITH PRIVATE COMPANIES

As Stirling reviewed the call reports from Davenport, Mercer, Garrard and Goldthorp and thought about how to align AOLTW's business interests with Western's academic mission, he was more and more convinced that a partnership between the company and the university could bring strong value to both institutions. The question was how to sell the alignment. He knew Bogart and Atkey wouldn't need to be reminded of the marketing power of such a relationship; indeed, to remind them might seem crass. But he did need to capture the spirit of mutual benefit, and do so in a way that brought out the particular identity of the relationship he was trying to sell, a relationship that suggested the marriage of two great patrons of the arts in Canada. There were, he knew, small tokens of appreciation he could extend to the company: the opportunity to put the company name on their gifts, membership within Western's 1878 societies (societies that honored the university's most significant sponsors), hosted site visits for AOLTW representatives, the public recognition of their donations in prominent campus displays and printed material and annual updates that helped the company see the tangible benefits of the company's support in its chosen areas of interest. But the key to success, Stirling knew, was to present AOLTW with partnership proposals that made good use of the funds, and to wrap these ideas in a story about the potential of partnership that made the marriage seem, like all good marriages of great people, fitting, happy and mutually prosperous.

EAST COAST TRAIL ASSOCIATION

On September 12, 2005, Randy Murphy, the president of the East Coast Trail Association (the Association, or ECTA), a non-profit organization located in St. John's, Newfoundland and Labrador,[1] was getting ready to meet with the Land Committee (the Committee). At stake was

---

[1] The legal name of the province is Newfoundland and Labrador. Newfoundland is the island portion of the province, whereas Labrador is on the mainland of Canada, adjacent to the province of Quebec.

the future of the East Coast Trail (the Trail), a 540-kilometer coastal and wilderness hiking trail on the island of Newfoundland's Avalon Peninsula. The Committee's efforts to secure access agreements with landowners and to obtain formal recognition and protection from towns located along the Trail was a time-consuming process, requiring considerable effort, while achieving limited results. Meanwhile, the speed at which the coastline was being acquired for residential and commercial development was increasing rapidly. The Committee members knew that the Trail was at risk, and they were running out of time to secure the land access required to continue building the Trail. In fact, without public access to the land, the Association's dream of a 540-km trail would end.

Many changes had occurred within the Association during the summer. A new board of directors had been elected at the annual general meeting in June. The new board members would need to become familiar with the workings of the Association. In addition, several vice president positions on the board had become vacant. Of particular concern, the vice president of Legal and Lands, a well-known St. John's lawyer who had been instrumental in negotiating many of the Association's current land agreements, had decided to step down. The new vice president of Legal and Lands had been a member of the committee for one year but still had a lot to learn about the position. Murphy had been heavily involved in land issues since he had become president of the Association back in 1996. In addition to his other responsibilities within the Association, he knew that he

had to continue his involvement with the Land Committee until the new vice president was ready to stand on his own.

Murphy knew that securing land agreements was a huge job and that the Association lacked the resources and time to continue with that strategy alone. In the past several months, Murphy, along with the Association's operations manager, had been involved in negotiating land agreements with five landowners located on the section of trail that was scheduled to be built in 2006 (see Exhibit 1). Without these agreements in place, the ECTA would not receive the funding it required from the federal government's Atlantic Canadian Opportunities Agency (ACOA) to build this section of trail. The results thus far had been disappointing. It was taking far longer than anticipated to reach agreements. After six months of negotiating, the Association had obtained two signed agreements, and three agreements were pending further review and discussion with the landowners and their legal counsel.

Murphy thought about the long-term plan for trail development and the need to maintain and secure public access and rights-of-way. Only 220 of the 540 kilometers were complete (see Exhibit 2). Fourteen trail sections remained to be built, six of which were part of the northern trail, the most heavily populated and highest risk area for land development. The threat and probability of losing a significant section of the northern trail was very real, given the complexities of the land issues, the rate of change within the towns, the frequency of the land transactions, the lack of meaningful progress

Natalie Slawinski wrote this case under the supervision of Professor W. Glenn Rowe solely to provide material for class discussion. The authors do not intend to illustrate either effective or ineffective handling of a managerial situation. The authors may have disguised certain names and other identifying information to protect confidentiality.

Exhibit 1 Trail Development Schedule

Development by Path	2006	2007	2008	2009	2010	2011	2012	2013	2014	2015
Long Bay - Quid Vidi	North Start									
Pouch Cove - Flatrock										
Flatrock - Logy Bay										
Topsail - Portugal Cove										
Portugal Cove - Bauline										
Bauline - Pouch Cove					North Complete					
Cappahayden - Chance Cove Park				South Start						
Trepassey - Portugal Cove South										
Portugal Cove South - Cape Race										
Cape Race - Chance Cove Park							South Completed			
Placentia - Colinet								Inland Start		
Colinet - Avalon Wilderness Area										
Avalon Wilderness Area - Ferryland										
Masterless Men										Inland Complete

Source: Company files

regarding trail protection, and the limited and volunteer resource base of the Association. This threat was the driving force behind the Association's decision to prioritize and raise the urgency to develop the northern section of the Trail. Murphy realized that the success of this decision would have to be supported by more effective short- and long-term strategies to secure the public access and right-of-way protection required to build the remainder of the Trail before the coastline was acquired by commercial and residential developers.

As president of the ECTA for nine years, Murphy realized that his worst fears were beginning to take shape—the coastline was being bought up quickly. Property on the coast of Newfoundland was relatively inexpensive,

and the view of the cliffs and the ocean was spectacular. As a result, both residents of the province and visitors from outside the province were increasingly buying property along the ocean. Developers were building homes on prime coastal land, while visitors were buying ocean-front property so that they could spend their summers in the province. In addition, town councils were increasingly being pressured to free up more coastal property for development. The same situation had occurred in a neighboring Atlantic province, Nova Scotia. The result was that very little of that coastline remained accessible to the public. Murphy was concerned that, at the current rate of development, Newfoundland would suffer the same fate as Nova Scotia. He knew that this meeting with the new Land Committee would be critical for developing a new strategy for trail development, given the limited resources of the Association.

HIKING INDUSTRY OVERVIEW

Hiking had become one of the fastest growing recreational activities in North America, and industry experts were predicting that it would continue to increase rapidly over the next 50 years. Hiking had traditionally been associated with backcountry trekking, but its popularity was growing among day hikers as more and more trails were being developed near population centers. This increase in popularity was due mainly to the recognition of the economic, social and health benefits of hiking.

Given the increased popularity of hiking and the unique landscape to be found in Newfoundland, hiking had become a major attraction for tourists to the province over the past decade. The East Coast Trail, thanks to its marketing efforts and the media coverage it received around the world, had become an important tourist attraction. Given this trend, many regions within the province had begun to build their own trails hoping to lure tourists away from St. John's to more remote, off-the-beaten-path areas of the

Exhibit 2   Map of East Coast Trail on Newfoundland's Avalon Peninsula

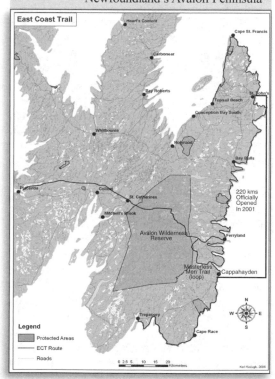

Source: Company files.

province. Some of these trail associations and communities had approached ECTA for advice on trail building.

As the only trail system of its kind in Newfoundland, the ECTA had to look to other volunteer-run trail associations in North America for best practices. The Bruce Trail, an 800-km trail system through Ontario's Niagara Escarpment, received approximately 400,000 visits per year and had a large economic impact on the region. The volunteer-based Bruce Trail Association, which had been in existence for 38 years, managed the trail through nine locally based trail clubs responsible for the maintenance of their respective trail sections. The Appalachian Trail, stretching 3,520 kilometers from Maine to Georgia in the United States, was also managed by volunteers. The Appalachian Trail was run by the Appalachian Trail Conference, made up of 30 trail-maintaining clubs, and relied on partnerships with organizations such as the U.S. National Park Service, for maintenance funding. The conference also solicited donations and operated a trail gift shop. The Appalachian Trail attracted three million to four million people yearly. Although these associations provided some good examples for ECTA to follow, ECTA faced a unique set of challenges that it had to incorporate into its strategic planning.

East Coast Trail Association Background

The East Coast Trail had its beginnings in 1994, when a group of hiking enthusiasts started the construction of a coastal hiking trail to follow the traditional walking paths that had historically linked dozens of communities along the coast of Newfoundland's Avalon Peninsula. In 1995, the East Coast Trail Association was incorporated; its goal was to build and maintain the East Coast Trail from Topsail to Trepassey. This volunteer-run, non-profit, registered charity had 230 volunteer trail-clearers by 1996 and hundreds of fee-paying members. The following year, the Association obtained federal government funds through ACOA to develop a 220-km portion of the East Coast Trail from St. John's to Cappahayden, on what is known as "the Southern Shore." This region of the province, like many others, had been hit hard by the cod moratorium of the early 1990s, during which those employed in the cod fishery lost their jobs. Consequently, the federal government (through ACOA) was eager to bring new sources of economic development to the region. Building a hiking trail through these communities would create jobs in the short term, and in the long run would bring hikers and tourism to the region, thus allowing for the development of small businesses that could benefit from increased tourism, such as bed and breakfasts (B&Bs).

In 2001, the 220-km section of the Trail, built to world-class hiking standards, was officially opened to the public. Hikers could now enjoy a hardened trail that wound along the edge of the ocean, passing through historic fishing villages and along forts, lighthouses and other interesting historical sites. Word began to spread of this unique hiking experience, and the Trail began to draw hikers from around the world eager to experience the unspoiled wilderness, ocean vistas, seabirds, whales and icebergs.

What began as a small hiking club had grown into a large non-profit organization with paid staff, dedicated volunteers and aggressive goals. The end goal was a trail system totaling some 540 km of continuous coastal and inland trails, each path unique and varying in degree of difficulty. Of course, one of the challenges of many non-profits is financial survival. ECTA was no different. Its challenge was to find funding and support to fulfill its mission to develop, maintain and preserve the East Coast Trail while respecting the integrity of the natural environment and the needs of the communities, and delivering a high-quality wilderness hiking experience. The Association also had a vision to be recognized across the country as the premier hiking trail on the east coast of Canada and to be firmly established and sustainable.

Both the mission statement and the vision revealed the values that ECTA engendered: protecting the environment, promoting healthy lifestyles, creating a safe hiking environment, encouraging communities to become involved, sharing the spectacular scenery with people from all over the world and promoting Newfoundland as a premier hiking destination. ECTA needed resources to accomplish its goal of becoming sustainable.

FUNDING OVERVIEW

In the past, the federal government had been a major source of funding for ECTA. In 1997, both ACOA and Human Resources Development Canada (HRDC) had granted funds to develop 220 km of trail. This funding amounted to $4.5 million[2] over five years. Other funding came from private donations, fundraising, memberships and product sales (see Exhibit 3). As a non-profit organization

Exhibit 3 ECTA Financial Statements—Balance Sheet (as of March 31, 2005)

Assets	2005	2004	2003
Current			
Cash	$26,089	$28,942	$54,388
Investment Account	$100,352	$66,552	$104,389
Receivables	$54,760	$83,286	$12,837
Inventory	$10,949	$6,104	$5,155
Prepaids	$3,538	$1,009	$1,012
	$195,688	$185,893	$177,781
Capital Assets	$3,557,496	$3,767,447	$3,977,054
Total Assets	$3,753,184	$3,953,340	$4,154,835
Liabilities			
Current			
Payables and Accruals	$22,601	$14,270	$15,538
Deferred Revenue	$23,836	$24,231	$22,666
	$46,437	$38,501	$38,204
Deferred Contributions	$3,566,117	$3,775,889	$3,985,661
Fund Balance			
Unrestricted	$140,629	$138,950	$130,970
Total Liabilities and Fund Balance	$3,753,183	$3,953,340	$4,154,835

Source: Company files.

---

[2]All dollar references are in Canadian currency.

Exhibit 3 (Continued) ECTA Financial Statements—Income Statement (year ended March 31)

	2005	2004	2003
Revenues			
Sale of Merchandise	18,705	33,779	28,484
Cost of Sales	12,328	7,405	2,000
Gross Profit	6,377	26,374	26,484
Memberships	7,580	10,565	14,325
Donations	26,343	29,338	48,752
Corporate Donations	11,000	11,000	11,000
Funding	125,796	143,770	134,775
Amortization of Deferred Capital Contributions	209,772	209,772	209,772
Misc.	22,230	12,435	6,173
Total Revenue	**409,098**	**443,254**	**451,281**
Expenses			
Advertising	12,117	6,036	8,758
Amortization	209,951	209,607	210,088
Conferences	27	1,140	887
Equipment	1,892	423	2,941
IT	1,210	1,675	0
Insurance	5,834	4,494	3,937
Interest and Bank Charges	93	62	770
Licenses and Fees	1,105	1,191	359
Meeting Expenses	251	1,550	0
Travel	1,436	3,161	0
Misc.	16	589	1,682
Office	12,432	19,493	14,316
Professional Fees	60,752	0	2,875
Rent	6,400	6,285	6,000
Repairs and Maintenance	1,217	859	237
Telecomunication	3,295	3,754	4,595

	2005	2004	2003
Utilities	1,700	1,530	314
Wages	87,691	173,425	126,986
Audit Expense			2,043
Total Expenses	407,419	435,274	386,788
Excess of Revenue Over Expenses	1,679	7,980	64,493
Fund Balances, Beginning	138,950	130,970	66,477
Excess of Revenues Over Expenses	1,679	7,980	64,493
	140,629	138,950	130,970

Source: Company files.

that did not charge a fee for trail usage, ECTA relied mostly on grants for its income, but the grant-application process was arduous and took up much staff and volunteer time. Not all grant applications were successful, and many grants required specific criteria to be met by the applicants.

Although federal government agencies had financially supported the construction of the first section of the Trail, they had not provided funds for the maintenance of the Trail. ECTA, therefore, relied on donations and volunteer maintenance groups for the upkeep of the Trail. ECTA estimated that between 1997 and 2001, it received $1.5 million of "in-kind" contributions, which included the cost of volunteer time as well as corporate donations. The Association relied heavily on these two sources of "revenue." Because government funding was becoming harder to obtain, the organization needed to find alternative ways of becoming self-sustainable through its earned revenue.

Since the completion of the first section of the Trail in 2001, ECTA had not received another large grant as it had in 1997. As such, trail building had been put on hold. In order to continue building the Trail, ECTA had to change its strategy. It had divided the remaining Trail into smaller sections, thus requiring less funding for each section. ACOA had also changed its requirements for funding, now requiring that

land agreements be in place for a minimum of five years before the agency would grant trail-building funds to the Association.

COMPETITION

As a non-profit, ECTA competed for grants and donations with other trail systems and non-profits. Other communities and trail associations in the province were looking for government grants to build their own trails. Communities located outside the capital region relied more heavily on tourism and were better positioned to attract government funding because of the greater need for funding in rural areas.

In addition, there were many other worthy causes that competed for private donations, corporate sponsorships and members. Many hiking enthusiasts were interested in cultural activities and environmental causes. ECTA had to both maintain its supporters and attract new supporters by emphasizing that it was not only a hiking trail, but an environmental and cultural cause, working to preserve coastal lands from erosion and from development, for future generations to enjoy. Many hikers assumed the Trail was publicly funded and therefore not in need of members, donations or volunteers.

ORGANIZATIONAL STRUCTURE AND CULTURE

By the time the first 220-km section of the Trail was launched in 2001, the Association was made up of a 15-member volunteer board of directors and three paid staff: an executive director, a fundraising coordinator and a project-based operations manager. The executive committee consisted of a president, vice president Marketing and Communications, vice president Revenue and Membership Services, vice president Finance and Support Services, vice president Trails and, finally, vice president Legal and Lands. Each vice president, in turn, coordinated a number of committees whose members comprised board members and a stream of volunteers who gave countless hours each year helping with trail maintenance, administration, marketing, membership, organized hikes and numerous other tasks. All volunteer efforts were supported by the three paid staff positions. The organizational chart for ECTA is shown in Exhibit 4.

Exhibit 4 Organizational Chart: East Coast Trail Association—2005

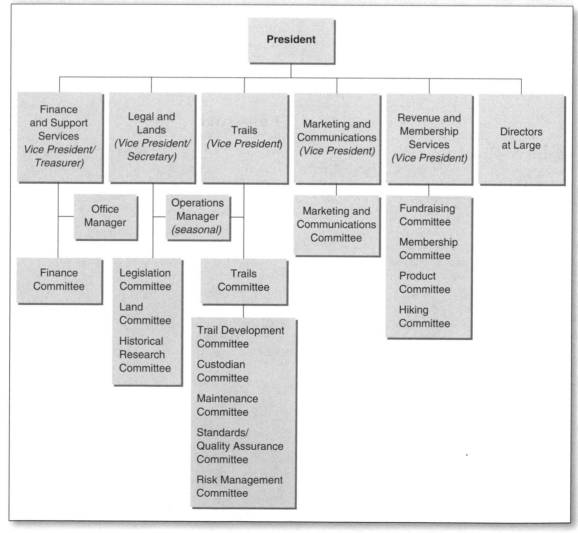

The President

The position of president was a volunteer position. The president chaired the board of directors and the executive committee and coordinated the overall activities of the organization. Murphy had held that position since 1996. In addition to his responsibilities as president, Murphy had been involved with many committees and projects, including the Land Committee, based on the ECTA's needs and priorities, which were driven by the availability of volunteers to support the essential work of the Association. Murphy also volunteered his time to lead hikes along the Trail and was an active trail custodian supporting trail maintenance. Although Murphy had a busy career with Newfoundland and Labrador Hydro (the provincial power generation company), he volunteered a considerable amount of his time to the Association. His passion for the Trail and his service to the Association over many years clearly showed in his focus, drive and commitment to fulfilling the 540-km dream of the East Coast Trail.

The Board of Directors

The board was made up mainly of educated professionals (accountants, lawyers, bankers, business people, university professors, government officials, etc.) who were active in the pursuit of ECTA's goals, giving many hours of free service to the Association. Some, like the vice president Trails, a professional appraiser, had been on the board for many years. He led the Trail Maintenance Committee, and his experience and expertise were invaluable to the Association. Others, like a retired teacher from Witless Bay, a small community 40 kilometers south of St. John's, were new to the board, bringing new ideas and a fresh perspective. He was also the president of the Irish Loop Tourism Association; since the East Coast Trail passed through this region on the Southern Shore, he was well aware of the economic benefits of the East Coast Trail to the local communities. This active board member was also aware of the need to upkeep

and promote the Trail to continue to attract tourists to the area.

In addition to providing the Association with a diversity of experience and expertise, the board members represented a range of interests, from protecting the environment to economic development. Regardless of their interests in the Trail, the board members believed that the Trail was a great asset to the province and to the Avalon Peninsula in particular. There was some turnover every year, representing a loss of continuity; anytime an active board member left, it represented a great loss for the Association. In the summer of 2005, despite the loss of several board members, Murphy had recruited a new group of competent board members and was eager to have the new board tackle the challenges facing the Association.

The Staff

In 2004, after suffering financial setbacks, the board had decided to downsize to a staff of two. The operations manager continued to oversee trail planning, building and maintenance. This job was a seasonal position, which was critical for the future development of the Trail. The position of office manager was created to replace both the fundraising coordinator and the executive director. The office manager would now oversee the administration of the Association. Community relations and fundraising activities, including grant applications, would now be in the hands of board members and other volunteers. These added responsibilities would be a challenge, given the volunteer turnover and the amount of work these efforts required of volunteers. The office manager acted as a coordinator of these efforts. In addition, paid work crews were hired on a project basis, conditional on funding, to support trail development only.

Committees and Volunteers

Given the limited financial resources and staff, several volunteer committees had been created over the years to accomplish the many goals of ECTA. These committees were led, for the most part, by board members who reported their activities back to the board. ECTA had numerous volunteers, many of whom had been with ECTA for several years. The dedication of these volunteers was evidenced by the successes of the Association despite its limited resources.

On the other hand, it was difficult to train and coordinate such a large number of volunteers. Because they were volunteers, they could not always be counted on to deliver what they promised. They gave what time they could but when they were unable to participate or contribute, the activities of a committee might come to a standstill. A problem for many volunteer-based organizations is turnover. ECTA was no different. Given that the Association was very much dependent on the work of volunteers, ECTA needed volunteers who were committed and prepared to invest many hours. Volunteers sometimes left because they felt they could not commit the time or effort required. In addition, the effectiveness of committees in many cases depended on the leadership of committee chairs; however, these committee chairs were also volunteers with busy professional careers, who could not always put in the required time.

The Members

ECTA members were critical to the organization. They paid a yearly membership fee to the Association, and some gave donations in addition to their membership fees. Members were also the most active volunteers. A typical progression was that a hiker would learn about the Association and become a member. Members would then learn about the volunteer opportunities through the quarterly newsletter or by word of mouth. The member would then join a committee and eventually might become interested in serving at the board level. Current members were also important for generating new members through referrals. Another source of membership was the volunteer-led organized hikes, which

introduced people to the Trail and provided existing members with a chance to meet other hikers. The hope was that once a person had hiked the Trail, that person would then buy a membership. In reality, this strategy had not worked that well. There was no cost to joining the organized hikes, and many participants did not buy memberships.

One of the membership problems was retention. The number of members had declined in recent years. Some members did not renew their memberships yearly. The other problem was that the Trail was free, and many users did not feel the need to buy a membership. There was also a perception among some users that the Trail and the Association were government-funded and not in need of extra support.

THE STRUGGLE FOR LAND ACCESS

The struggle for land access had been ongoing since the East Coast Trail's beginnings. Although the vast majority of the land on which the Trail was located was Crown Land (land owned by the provincial government of Newfoundland and Labrador), 15 per cent was privately owned and had posed numerous problems for the Association over the years. In the last five years alone, several developments had been built on coastal lands.

One notable development was a large castle that had appeared on a cliff by the edge of the ocean in a community just 15 kilometers outside of St. John's. The castle was owned by a millionaire from California who thought the dramatic scenery a perfect setting for his summer home. The owner had caught ECTA off-guard by building the castle on land along the East Coast Trail. The Trail followed a traditional right-of-way established by the local community through many years of active use. ECTA had not even been aware of the purchase of land or of plans to build the castle when the land was sold in 1999. By 2005, the castle was being completed and the No Trespassing signs were already up. The landowner denied access to the traditional right-of-way and blocked any further development by ECTA, effectively removing 500 meters of coastal trail.

This action had signaled to the Association that it was beginning to lose access to the coastline at a much faster rate than previously thought. For the most part, the Association had managed to negotiate privately and successfully with a number of landowners located along the Trail. Many of them were happy to cooperate and enjoyed having access to the Trail. Others were very concerned about the potential risk and liability associated with hikers crossing their property. Negotiating with private landowners was placing a strain on the Association's limited resources, and the number, frequency and urgency of land cases was growing rapidly. The Association had also been working with the communities to include the Trail in their town plans, but the results had been mixed. Some towns were cooperative, others not. Some notified ECTA when they revised their town plans while others did not. The other issue was that many communities along the Trail were not incorporated and did not have town plans. As a result, it was much harder to ensure that developers and property owners recognized the Trail passing through the property they had purchased.

There had also been some success stories. In 2004, the town of Bay Bulls, 30 km south of St. John's and located along the completed section of trail, had changed the zoning of a piece of property purchased by a developer so that the developer had to recognize the right of way of the Trail. This situation occurred because ECTA had reached an agreement with the town council to recognize the Trail on rezoning applications. This agreement had taken the Association a year to negotiate. Although in recent years ECTA had developed more cooperative relations with towns, the rate of development of coastal property by commercial and real estate developers was increasing, while the Association's resources were decreasing, and volunteers were, for the most part, only available to respond to these matters after hours and on weekends.

A NEW STRATEGY

In the previous year, the operations manager and members of the Land Committee had worked countless hours to secure land agreements with the five property owners located along the section of the Trail that was scheduled to be built in 2006. The Association could not get the funding from ACOA without these agreements, and without funding, they could not hire workers to begin building the Trail. Murphy and his team had been working on the agreements for several months, and some were not yet in place. Murphy knew that with 14 sections left to complete over the next nine years, a different strategy for securing land access and obtaining resources needed to be put in place. There were other issues to consider as well if the Association was going to be successful in completing the Trail and maintaining its current 220 km of trail.

Fundraising

The Association's income from product sales, fundraising, memberships and donations had declined in recent years. Attracting donations, organizing fundraisers, distributing the Association's products (mostly clothing and maps), and retaining and attracting new members was time-consuming and challenging. Without a full-time fundraiser, and relying mostly on volunteers, it was difficult to coordinate all of the fundraising efforts. This situation was a cause for concern since the Association had staffing and operational costs it needed to meet. It also needed funds to repair sections of the existing trail and to build future sections of the Trail. In addition, funding from government sources was increasingly difficult to obtain and required numerous volunteer and staff hours. The outcome of such funding applications was uncertain.

The funding for the next section of trail, which was scheduled to commence in 2006, had taken a couple of years to secure. The funding sources included the city of St. John's and ACOA, which would release the funds only once the land agreements were in place. The city of St. John's had contributed because the next section of trail was to start in St. John's and was important for the city's tourism. Where would the Association find funding for the following section and how long would it take to obtain such funding? The following section was scheduled to be built in 2007. With such aggressive timelines, the Association needed to find funds quickly.

Human Resources

The staff, volunteers and members were critical to the functioning of this non-profit organization. The Association was already short-staffed, resulting in an overload of work for both the office manager and the operations manager. The office manager did not have enough time to coordinate volunteer activities. In addition, the availability of the volunteer committee chairs to plan, manage and control the assignments of their committees was less than desirable to meet the day-to-day demands of the Association's workload. The result was that it was not always clear what the committees should be doing and when. Volunteer retention was another problem. There was turnover of board and committee members, and insufficient attention was given to recruiting new volunteers. It was a challenge to retain experienced volunteers as well as to identify and train incoming volunteers. The miscommunications and frustration resulting from the lack of coordination sometimes caused volunteers to leave the Association.

The Consultant's Report

In 2003, the Association requested and received funding from ACOA to hire a consultant to conduct an economic benefits and market analysis. Murphy knew that the Association had to quantify the return on the millions of dollars invested by the federal government in order to leverage new monies for trail development. In addition, he wanted to benchmark the current economic value of the Trail and to forecast its future value.

The study, which was completed in June 2005, concluded that the market and media were responding extremely well to the Trail locally, nationally and internationally, and the Trail was having a significant and positive impact on the provincial economy. The report estimated that total annual hiker expenditures in 2004, based on 26,500 hiker trips, were more than $2.3 million, and the forecasted value by 2011 would be $6.1 million and 56,992 hiker trips. Beyond the economic benefits, the report had also highlighted the Trail as an invaluable public recreational resource. In addition, the Association was helping to preserve local heritage and the environment, and was building community pride. The study concluded that the Association should be commended for its success to date and should be given the support and encouragement required to grow this tourism asset to its full potential. Murphy knew that the Trail was having a positive impact on the communities and the province, but now there were numbers to support his belief. The report could now be leveraged to help fund trail development as well as to support the Association's goal to protect and preserve public access to the coastline.

Land Issues

Although land access was becoming more difficult to secure, especially along the more populated northern section of the Trail that was scheduled to be built in the next few years, Murphy knew that the communities had become more supportive in recent years. Several town councils were made up of individuals who understood the tourism potential of the Trail and who were eager to work with ECTA to complete the section of the Trail going through their community. Some communities were also planning to build their own small trails that would loop around and complement the linear East Coast Trail. Some towns were prepared to incorporate the Trail into their town plans to prevent developers from denying hikers access to trail heads. Murphy recalled a time when trying to get community support for the Trail was challenging. Now, it seemed, the communities understood the benefits the Trail brought them, in the form of hiker spending. So much had changed in the last five years. Many were also proud to have the Trail passing through their communities, since hiking was becoming increasingly popular.

Murphy felt that the land issues were too difficult for the Association to handle on its own. Individual agreements with landowners and towns were too time-consuming and uncertain. He thought about approaching the provincial government in the hope of obtaining legislation that would guarantee public access to the Trail and create a trail corridor. Current legislation was not sufficient. Without legal protection, Murphy feared that the Association might lose the access required to build and operate the 540-km trail.

Murphy was optimistic that the provincial government would pay attention to the Trail. ECTA was well known locally and was becoming known nationally and internationally among hiking enthusiasts. Articles about the East Coast Trail had appeared in the *Globe & Mail, Explore* magazine, a Spanish publication and in the *Los Angeles Times*. The Association had also won numerous awards for its stewardship of the Trail. Murphy felt that the Association had the visibility it needed to garner support for its cause. The Association now also had a consultant's report that quantitatively showed the value of the Trail

to the province. The Trail was a unique natural, cultural and historic attraction that not only attracted tourists but was preserving part of the province's natural resources and cultural heritage. Murphy's biggest concern was the willingness of the provincial government to work with the Association and the time it would take to change the legislation. Was this a viable option? In some ways, Murphy felt it was the only option if the Association was going to complete the Trail.

THE TIME FOR ACTION

Murphy knew that it was time to act. He had already seen how quickly public land could disappear. In the blink of an eye, a castle had appeared at the edge of a cliff, blocking the Trail. What was once a path hiked by many eager to view the spectacular scenery was now fenced in and dotted with signs that read "Keep Out," "No Trespassing." Murphy sighed as he thought about the coastline in Nova Scotia, and how quickly that same scenario could occur in Newfoundland. The Association had come so far in 10 years. Hundreds of volunteers had contributed to the dream of the East Coast Trail. What could Murphy and the executive do to protect the Trail? Murphy walked into the Land Committee meeting ready to discuss strategic alternatives and to develop an action plan. The time was now or never.

13

INTERNATIONAL PERSPECTIVE

Globalization brings pressure for change to governments, corporations, and NPOs. Both MNCs [multinational corporations] and NPOs must develop strategies that balance the advantages of scale economies gained from standardization across national boundaries with the need to customize offerings for various national and local constituents/consumers.

—Conway Dato-on, Weisenbach Keller,
and Shaw (2008, p. 23)

Key Topics: drivers of globalization, standardized versus adapted operations, criteria for selecting international locations, government relations, environmental analysis on the international level, overview of developing networks on the international level, special concerns for managing across cultures/nations

Chapter 1 spoke about the environment in which nonprofits operate across the globe, including the multiple names for the sector (i.e., *voluntary, social economy, civil society, the third, NGO, charitable*) and its economic impact. National and international figures such as the sector's employment statistics as well as percentages of populations and corporations donating time and money to the sector cumulate to substantial totals. This book has attempted to address some of the challenges that nonprofit organization (NPO) leaders operating in this environment confront, including achieving goals and managing activities with undersized staffs and budgets, competing for scarce resources while new nonprofit organizations enter the marketplace, and growing use of the Internet for communications and donations—offering both advantages and disadvantages (Chiagouris, 2005).

As we close the book, the focus shifts to how the environment in which the sector operates is influenced by globalization trends and operational issues at the international level. The actors in this chapter's cases keenly experience the influence of cultural, political, and economic differences as they seek to expand the breadth of their organizations' operations. Managing differences, and looking for similarities that can lead to synergistic operations, brings challenges for nonprofit (nongovernmental) organizational leaders. As noted in the opening quote, national differences in physical environment, communication and technology infrastructure, client needs, and culture place pressure on organizations to adapt human resource, operations, and marketing strategies across locations (Alashban, Hayes, Zinkhan, & Balazs, 2002; Alder, 1991; Bartlet & Ghoshal, 1991).

Before delving into these concepts, however, it is worth noting that there is no real consensus within the NPO community about whether globalization has a positive or negative effect and the role international nongovernmental organizations (INGOs) should play in the global arena. Despite this controversy, a common point of agreement is that the civic sector can "act as a countervailing force to the expanding influence of markets and the declining authority of states" (Edwards, Hulme, & Wallace, 1999, p. 119). The declining authority of states further emphasizes the need for NPOs to develop alternative sources of funding (as discussed in Chapters 11 and 14) because government sponsorship (i.e., foreign aid) cannot be relied upon as a sole or major source of support. Given the many strings that come with government support, some NPO leaders are suggesting that this source of funding should not be relied on.

To help assess the influence of international trends and national differences on strategies, this chapter introduces key issues such as drivers of globalization, site location (when and where should a nonprofit expand), alternative human resource strategies, and the importance of developing networks when operating in new environments.

GLOBALIZATION DRIVERS

Globalization seems to be something everyone talks about but few have actually paused to define. In general, it refers to the shift toward a more integrated and interdependent world economy. Figure 13.1 provides a visual depiction of factors in the global environment that influence NPO operations. While this definition is true and the

visual is helpful in understanding the concept as it relates to an NPO, both are too high level to build strategies or decisions around. We need to break the concept down a bit more. One way to do this is to ask what drives globalization and how many of those drivers affect the focal nonprofit. From the international business literature, we see five main drivers of globalization and several factors that trigger each one (C. W. L. Hill, 2010).

1. Market Drivers
   a. Common client needs
   b. Global customers (e.g., agencies that NPOs serve, such as the U.N.)
   c. Global distribution channels
   d. Transferable marketing elements (e.g., global brand, global products such as medicines to treat AIDS)
2. Cost Drivers
   a. Economies of scale
   b. Economies of scope/synergies
   c. Sourcing advantages and limitations (e.g., inputs to final product may be more readily available in certain locations)
3. Government Drivers
   a. Reduced barriers to trade or shipment of goods/services/people across national borders
   b. Global standards of design or service delivery (e.g., U.N. mandates, ISO standards)
   c. Regulations that encourage or discourage NPOs from operating within national borders (e.g., tax incentives for donations, cooperative relationship with NGOs)
4. Competitive Drivers
   a. Existence of other international or global agencies that provide similar goods/services
   b. Global distribution network
5. Technology Drivers
   a. Production technology and service infrastructure shared across national borders
   b. Global telecommunications infrastructure (e.g., access to TV, radio, cell phones)
   c. Internet and social media (e.g., degree of openness)

Figure 13.1 Global Environmental Factors Influence NPO Operations

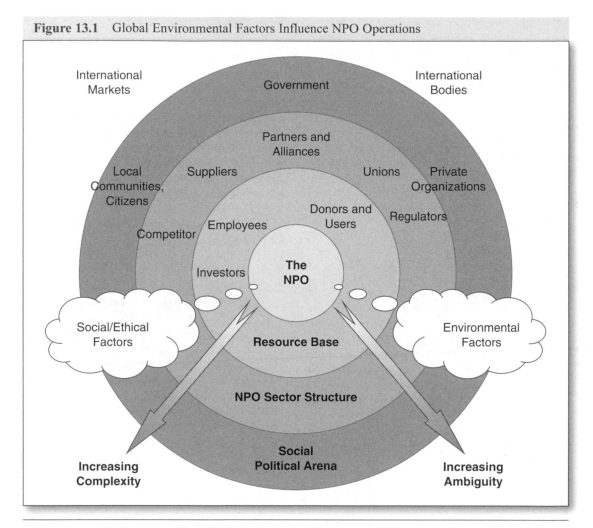

Source: Panesar, 2007. Reprinted with permission.

NPO leaders should review this list to determine to what degree the factors exist in their home and destination environments. The more factors that exist, the more pressures for globalization their organization will feel and the more likely it is they will need to develop strategies that must respond to these pressures. For example, if an NPO provides disaster relief services, such as the Red Cross/Crescent, leaders may find that clients need similar services after a natural disaster (e.g., food, water, shelter) regardless of national location—market drivers. The same agency may find itself interacting with the identical suppliers of those goods at diverse disaster relief sites. The more such factors exist, the more standardization of policies and practices may be warranted by the NPO and the more potential there is for cost savings because of operational synergy.

These globalization drivers have also changed the way INGOs operate. There has been a dramatic shift away from direct delivery of aid-funded projects or services toward capacity building at the local level, whether through development of new, local NPOs or implementation of social entrepreneurship operations and micro-credit to sustain societal shifts (Edwards et al., 1999).

STANDARDIZATION VERSUS ADAPTATION

Historically, NPOs evolve in response to local community needs, yet global trends such as those noted above challenge all nonprofit leaders to rethink their mandate, mission, and strategies (Edwards et al., 1999). Furthermore, local adaptation could become problematic for NPOs as global citizens become more mobile and look to (a) receive assistance from global human service agencies and/or (b) replicate positive experiences with an organization across nations. The latter situation is particularly appropriate for this chapter's case on the Women's Tennis Association as it looks to expand in Asia. Furthermore, if the NPO brand message or service delivery is not consistent across various markets, donors and volunteers may become confused and reduce relationship involvement (Conway Dato-on, Weisenbach Keller, & Shaw, 2008).

Another factor influencing the degree to which a nonprofit may standardize its operations across borders is the similarity of nonprofit sectors in different nations. As mentioned in Chapter 1, the following five factors are important to understanding the size and capacity of the nonprofit sector in any given country (Salamon & Anheier, 1992):

1. Population demographics—heterogeneous versus homogeneous

2. Welfare system scope—limited versus comprehensive

3. Economic system and development stage—planned versus market economy, emerging versus developed stage

4. Legal system—common law versus civil law

5. Type of culturally based support system—family versus government versus religion

For the NPO manager to translate these factors into practice, she should research the destination country to ascertain whether the conditions there are similar to those in the organization's home country. Combining this sector-level comparison with the information received from the analysis of globalization drivers will help the NPO manager understand whether standardization of strategy is feasible.

The decisions about whether to operate similarly in different locations and where to operate seem to follow the chicken-and-egg logic stream. Should an NPO first decide where to operate globally and then decide how (using adaptation vs. standardization), or should the strategy decision come first and then the location be decided? In the business world, one would argue strategy precedes location decision. The answer in the nonprofit sector is not as clear-cut. Many NPOs, especially those in the human services subsector, respond to societal needs and natural disasters, thus the location is determined by need and may not always follow the dictates of strategy.

LOCATION DECISIONS

If a nonprofit is in a situation in which it can select a destination based on strategy versus response to natural disaster or human need, several steps are recommended. First, NPO leaders should conduct a macro-level analysis of the nation or region they are considering. Second, micro-level indicators can be studied to assess match of organizational mission, goals, and resources to market needs. Chapter 1 discussed the use of PEST-EL (Political, Economic, Social, Technical, Ecological, and Legal) analysis to ascertain the macro-level environment. Chapters 1 and 6 also reviewed Resource-Based View (RBV) and Strengths, Weaknesses, Opportunities, and Threats (SWOT) analyses as methods of analyzing internal/organizational environmental conditions in order to assess match between possible location and strategy. These are all appropriate tools whether the NPO is operating on the national or international level. On the international level it is important to determine the transferability of the organization's competencies to the new location. If, for example, the success of the organization relies heavily on relationships with local government leaders, it may be difficult to transfer the operations to a location where such a relationship does not exist. Figure 13.2 shows the factors involved in assessing national locations.

How to enter a new national market is greatly influenced by government policies related to recognition and operation of NPOs and the manner in which an organization became global. If, as in the case on the Women's Tennis Association, the organization begins in one country and expands outward as needs develop, the structure and strategy may look very different than an organization that was "born global," such as the lobbying organization NASSCOM (the second case in this chapter). Organizations that are born global can establish human resource and operational strategies with the international market in mind, whereas those that expand internationally from an established home base must reassess previous decisions to ascertain applicability to the new market. Human resource strategy can be a criterion for success or an obstacle for international NPOs.

HUMAN RESOURCE DECISIONS

Human resource strategy is difficult in a domestic market where local policies and practices are well known. The international environment raises many issues regarding staffing, compensation, labor laws, and equal opportunity legislation—to name just a few. While a complete investigation of all the issues is beyond the scope of this text, the issue of staffing is particularly important and will be addressed here; due diligence and securing

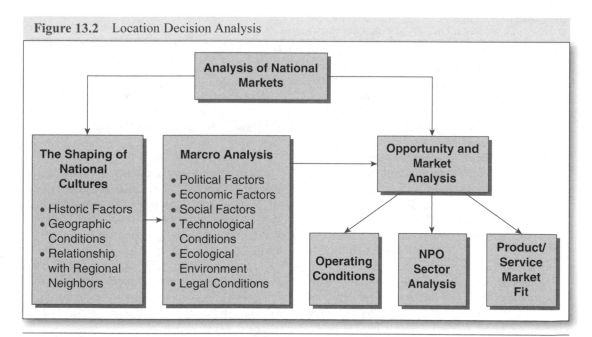

Figure 13.2 Location Decision Analysis

Source: Adapted from J. S. Hill, 2005, Chapter 5.

legal counsel in the host (international) location will be necessary to ensure compliance with other human resource topics.

Staffing generally follows one of three approaches in international organizations: ethnocentric, polycentric, and geocentric (C. W. L. Hill, 2010). The selected approach, like the strategies regarding adaptation and standardization, will be greatly influenced by the method with which the organization became global and the environment of the destination country. An ethnocentric approach to staffing uses home-country managers for all key positions in the organization. This method may be selected because the host country lacks qualified managers, to ensure continuation of organizational culture (often seen as a competitive advantage), and/or if protecting intellectual property is paramount to success. For NPOs this approach seems limited in value because capacity building is generally one of the sector's main objectives and the NPO raison d'être is to solve local problems—not protect its resources.

Staffing with a polycentric approach uses home-country managers in the domestic market and host-country managers in the various countries of operation. This strategy utilizes local knowledge in each of the markets while maintaining some centralization through an international headquarters usually located in the home country, where the organization originated. NPO literature often refers to such organizations as *confederations* (Lindenberg, 1999). A good example of this approach and the related organizational structure is the YMCA, which has strong national and international organizational bodies (Weisenbach Keller, Conway Dato-on, & Shaw, 2009).

Finally, for organizations that are truly global in scope (and may have been born global), a geocentric staffing approach may be best. In this method, the best person for the job is selected regardless of geographic location or nationality. As pressures for globalization increases and demands for NPO services increase, we may observe a trend toward this staffing strategy. Organizations such as Doctors Without Borders (www.doctorswithoutborders.org), which has

operated globally from inception, appear to use this strategy.

Regardless of the strategy adopted by the NPO, it is clear that environmental factors and stakeholders will influence the decision. No organization operates in a vacuum, and for those seeking to enact societal change—as are many NGOs—networking with other influential parties in each location is critical.

DEVELOPING NETWORKS FOR INTERNATIONAL SUCCESS

Globalization and all the challenges it brings, coupled with the need to balance local needs with centralized efficiency, lead both corporations and nonprofits to develop new structures and strategies to enable success. One of the most important changes is linkages through networks—whether for service provision or lobbying efforts. Globalization drivers such as technology create a world of possibilities for

> NGOs to relate to each other in different, healthier ways: alliances among equals, genuine partnerships, and synergistic networks that come together then break apart [can achieve success]. . . . Rather than impose order on a chaotic world (and making things more complex in the process) [such networks] will try to generate order *out of chaos* through non-authoritarian relationships. (Edwards et al., 1999, p. 131)

These networks will exist among NPOs as well as with stakeholders from different publics (i.e., private citizens, corporations, governments). Much has been written on these new ways of working together (e.g., Dahan, Doh, Oetzel, & Yaziji, 2010; Miao-Sheng, Huei-Fu, & Huei-Wen, 2006; Prahalad, 2005; Te'eni & Young, 2003), and continued improvement in developing and managing networks is sure to come. New capabilities will need to be developed (Edwards et al., 1999), but the road ahead is exciting.

In summary, just as there is no one term for the nonprofit sector, there is no one way to organize or manage best when operating in multiple countries. The best NPO leaders can do is to thoroughly understand themselves, their organization's mission, and the environments in which they operate. From this knowledge base, strategies can be planned and implemented. Perhaps the situation is best described by Johann Wolfgang Von Goethe: "We know accurately only when we know little; with knowledge doubt increases."

CASES

Women's Tennis Association (WTA) in Asia (International): David Shoemaker, chief operating officer of the WTA, is in the process of deciding whether to open a regional office in Asia—and if so, where. Upon initial consideration, the most promising locations seem to be Shanghai and Beijing. There is concern with these locales, however, in terms of consumer awareness of tennis, willingness of corporations to sponsor tournaments, and government relations. Once the location is selected, Shoemaker will need to consider staffing (locals or expatriates) and other operational issues. As a senior leader of this international nonprofit, he must deal with unfamiliar markets and cultural practices while attempting to formulate sustainable strategies to achieve the WTA's mission.

NASSCOM (International): The vice president of the National Association of Software and Services Companies (NASSCOM), Rajdeep Sahrawat, was reflecting on the role the organization currently played as a lobbying firm for the industry. As the voice of the software and services industry in India, it had been extremely successful in promoting Indian information technology (IT) to the world. This success now forced NASSCOM to reconsider its mission, vision, goals, and strategy to better align itself to the complex needs of the quickly evolving IT business process outsourcing (IT-BPO) industry in India. Rajdeep would soon address attendees at a leadership conference with details of NASSCOM's strategic refocusing. His presentation needed to answer three key questions: How could NASSCOM maintain its relevance in an industry that was already considered a global leader? How would NASSCOM position itself in response to its own president's desire to focus on the small-medium enterprise (SME) segment of the Indian industry? Finally, how should NASSCOM respond to a recent report that identified the domestic market as a significant future growth driver of IT-enabled services?

REFERENCES

Alashban, A. A., Hayes, L. A., Zinkhan, G. M., & Balazs, A. L. (2002). International brand-name standardization/adaptation: Antecedents and consequences. *Journal of International Marketing, 10*(3), 22–48.

Alder, N. J. (1991). *International dimensions of organizational behavior.* Boston, MA: Kent.

Bartlet, C. A., & Ghoshal, S. (1991). *Managing across borders.* Boston, MA: Harvard Business School Press.

Chiagouris, L. (2005). Nonprofit brands come of age: Commercial sector practices shed light on nonprofit branding success. *Marketing Management, 14*(5), 30–35.

Conway Dato-on, M., Weisenbach Keller, E., & Shaw, D. (2008). Global nonprofit brands with local missions: The YMCA across three countries. *International Journal of the Academic Business World, 2*(2), 21–32.

Dahan, N. M., Doh, J. P., Oetzel, J., & Yaziji, M. (2010). Corporate-NGO collaboration: Co-creating new business models for developing markets. *Long Range Planning, 43,* 326–342.

Edwards, M., Hulme, D., & Wallace, T. (1999). NGOs in a global future: Marrying local delivery to worldwide leverage. *Public Administration & Development, 19,* 117–136.

Hill, C. W. L. (2010). *Global business today.* Boston, MA: Irwin McGraw-Hill.

Hill, J. S. (2005). *World business: Globalization, strategy, and analysis.* Mason, OH: Thomson/South-Western.

Lindenberg, M. (1999). Declining state capacity, volunteerism and the globalization of the not-for-profit sector. *Nonprofit and Voluntary Sector Quarterly, 28*(4), 147–167.

Miao-Sheng, C., Huei-Fu, L., & Huei-Wen, L. (2006). Are the nonprofit organizations suitable to engage in BOT or BLT scheme? A feasible analysis for the relationship of private and nonprofit sectors. *International Journal of Project Management, 24*, 244.

Panesar, R. (2007). *Are UK businesses active at the "bottom of the pyramid"?* (Unpublished master's thesis). Loughborough University, London.

Prahalad, C. K. (2005). *The fortune at the bottom of the pyramid: Eradicating poverty through profits.* Upper Saddle River, NJ: Pearson Education.

Salamon, L. M., & Anheier, H. K. (1992). In search of the non-profit sector II: The problem of classification. *International Journal of Nonprofit and Voluntary Organizations, 3,* 267–309.

Te'eni, D., & Young, D. R. (2003). The changing role of nonprofits in the network economy. *Nonprofit and Voluntary Sector Quarterly, 32,* 397–414.

Weisenbach Keller, E., Conway Dato-on, M., & Shaw, D. (2009). NPO branding: Preliminary lessons from major players. *International Journal of Nonprofit and Voluntary Sector Marketing, 15,* 105–121.

THE WOMEN'S TENNIS ASSOCIATION IN ASIA—BUT WHERE?

David Shoemaker, chief operating officer (COO) of the Women's Tennis Association (WTA), looked at a map of China on his desktop computer. Strumming his fingers on his desk, Shoemaker wondered which city should be chosen—Shanghai or Beijing? Both cities were far from his office in St. Petersburg, Florida. A decision needed to be made about where to locate the Asian regional office for the WTA—and soon. Shoemaker's boss, Larry Scott—WTA's chief executive officer (CEO) (see Exhibit 1)—wanted to present a recommendation at the next board meeting, which coincided with the start of the Grand Slam tennis championship, Wimbledon 2007. The same recommendation would be made to the WTA Global Advisory Council. Shoemaker had three days to build his case for Shanghai, Beijing or another major city in Asia, and to pull together his presentation, which needed to include a strategy for the WTA to increase the sport's popularity in the Asian market. Both the

WTA board and the Advisory Council had very savvy members. The Advisory Council included people such as Richard Branson, founder and CEO of Virgin, and Karen Elliott House, former publisher of the *Wall Street Journal.* They would quickly know whether Shoemaker was scrambling or whether he had done his due diligence.

THE WTA PLATEAU

The WTA was founded in 1973 by tennis legend Billie Jean King in a hotel room in England. Its goal was to unite all women tennis players with a goal of gaining equality with male players. Today, the WTA represents the top professional women players and the events they play, and it continues to stand separately from the men's Association of Tennis Professionals (ATP) Tour.

In 2006, women's professional tennis had reached a plateau. Shoemaker knew that the

Exhibit 1 Women's Tennis Association Organization Chart (2007)

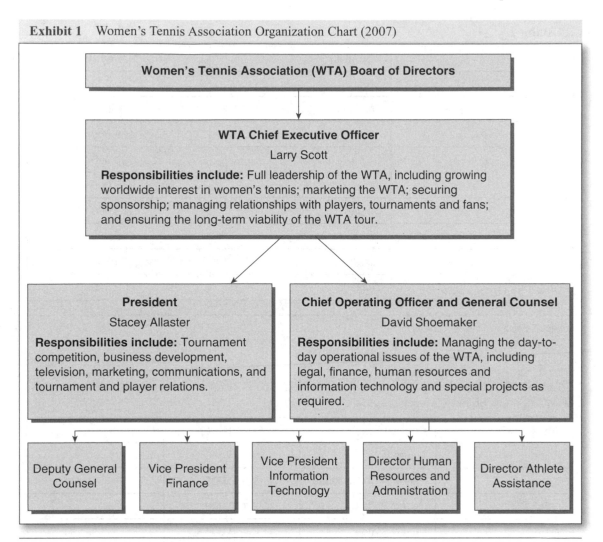

Source: David Shoemaker, Women's Tennis Association.

WTA needed to take the WTA to the next level of growth and solidify a place among the elite properties in sports and entertainments. The WTA was a non-profit organization that represented professional women tennis players and oversaw major tennis tournaments around the world. The 57 tournaments, which comprised the WTA tour, included the year-ending Tour Championship in Madrid, Spain, and were in addition to such prestigious tournaments as the Australian Open, the French Open, Wimbledon, and the U.S. Open. These four Grand Slams, while part of the WTA calendar, were not technically member tournaments of the WTA. Similar to golf, the WTA has a contractual relationship with the Grand Slams, not a governing body/member relationship. In 2006, the prize money ranged from US$74,800 for the Forest Hills U.S. tournament to US$8,332,000 for the U.S. Open (see Exhibits 2A and 2B).

Exhibit 2A Asia: Women's Tennis Association Tournaments and Prize Money (2006)

City	Country	Prize Money (US$)
Tokyo (Pan Pacific)	Japan	1,340,000
Pattaya	Thailand	170,000
Bangalore	India	175,000
Beijing	China	600,000
Kolkata	India	175,000
Guangzhou	China	175,000
Seoul	Korea	145,000
Tokyo	Japan	175,000
Bangkok	Thailand	200,000

Source: Women's Tennis Association files.

Exhibit 2B Outside Asia: Women's Tennis Association's Top 15 Tournaments Based on Prize Money

City	Country	Prize (US$)	Grand Slam
Melbourne	Australia	6,137,580	Yes
Dubai	United Arab Emirates	1,000,000	
Indian Wells	United States	2,100,000	
Miami	United States	3,450,000	
Charleston	United States	1,340,000	
Berlin	Germany	1,340,000	
Rome	Italy	1,340,000	
Paris	France	6,747,626	Yes
Wimbledon	United Kingdom	6,743,737	Yes
San Diego	United States	1,340,000	
Montreal	Canada	1,340,000	

Flushing Meadows	United States	8,332,000	Yes
Moscow	Russia	1,340,000	
Zurich	Switzerland	1,340,000	
Madrid	Spain	3,000,000	

Source: Women's Tennis Association files.

In the early 2000s, several problems had surfaced. Spectators seemed to have reached their saturation point for watching women play the sport, and sponsors and advertisers seemed to be less inclined to support women's professional tennis, which restricted the WTA's ability to generate more revenue. In addition, the top players were skipping tournaments, which also wreaked havoc on tournament revenue, as without big-name players, such as Maria Sharapova and sisters Venus and Serena Williams, the WTA found it increasingly more difficult to lure spectators and advertisers to empty their pockets.

The WTA's main sources of revenue were corporate sponsorships, licensing fees (paid when a city or company bid to host the year-end championship tournament), international television advertising deals and member fees (paid by tournaments and players). Meanwhile, the main sources of revenue for a tournament were similar, and included sponsorship, ticket sales and television rights. However, without the big-name players, those sponsorships, television rights and ticket revenue were at risk.

ROADMAP 2010

In 2006, Scott spearheaded a strategy called Roadmap 2010; essentially, this strategy prompted the participation of top players by providing greater financial rewards and penalties for, respectively, playing or not playing in the events. Top player appearances were directly linked to higher revenue because their participation encouraged both more spectators to attend and a higher level of media sponsorships and advertising for the events specifically and the WTA overall. Scott also secured revenue by signing Sony Ericsson as the title sponsor for the WTA, which led to the renaming of the WTA Tour as the Sony Ericsson WTA Tour. The US$88 million sponsorship was the highest ever in professional tennis. In addition, it was the highest in any women's sport ever.

TENNIS IN ASIA

Tennis in Asia was not explicitly mentioned in the Roadmap, and Shoemaker called it a by-product:

> The essence of the Roadmap was creating more top events, in top markets, where all top players would be required to compete. Under the Roadmap, we anticipated four such events: two in North America, one in Europe and one in Asia.

Tennis was a growing sport among the emerging middle classes in India and China. Each country boasted its own emerging women tennis stars, such as Sania Mirza from India and Zheng Jie, Yan Zi and Li Na from China. These stars were ranked among each country's top-10 sports icons, including both men and women.

To capitalize on these female tennis stars, the WTA wanted to ensure it was catering to the needs of its customers in the Asia-Pacific region. The WTA had its international headquarters in Florida and had an office in Europe.

Shoemaker contemplated whether the WTA needed to open an office in Asia or whether the WTA needed simply to hold a top-tier event in Asia to guarantee the appearance of the WTA's top players. He also wondered whether hosting an event jointly with the men's Association of Tennis Professionals (ATP) might be sufficient: "Our hypothesis is that combined events at the top level of the sports—the Grand Slams, such as Wimbledon and the U.S. Open—are proven success stories in tennis." Shoemaker considered that such an event would generate not only much local interest in the sport but also much international interest.

The WTA had previously hosted tournaments in India and China, and now Shoemaker had decided that a local headquarters in Asia was necessary, regardless of whether a combined event was offered. The premier events in North America and Europe all had regional offices so he believed that the Asian event also needed a regional office. Besides, tennis was still in its infancy in Asia, and the locals could not be expected to show up at a premier tournament. Tennis needed to be introduced into the local culture in a nurturing way.

Shoemaker quickly developed a short list of cities as locations for an Asian office. India (possibly in a city such as Mumbai) seemed an obvious choice because many locals spoke English and were familiar with tennis due to India's colonial past. Tokyo was also considered because it had been running a WTA event for almost 30 years, and tennis had attracted some popularity in Japan. Finally, Hong Kong was in contention because of its role as an obvious gateway to China and its position as Asia's major financial hub; however, Shoemaker felt that establishing an office in mainland China was the best option because of the growth potential.

CHINA: THE ASIAN EPICENTER FOR THE WTA

Two of the key revenue drivers for the WTA were media rights and advertising; China was one of the world's largest media markets (e.g., 380 million households with television, 2,200 newspapers, 7,000 magazines and 1,000 radio stations) and was projected to be the world's largest advertising market by 2010; moreover, established WTA and ATP professional tennis events held in China were starting to attract blue-chip sponsors, such as Lacoste and Nike. Because of the growth potential in China, Shoemaker decided that the WTA needed a local Chinese office to build grassroots awareness of the sport in this massive country, given that tennis was still a relatively unknown sport in China (see Exhibits 3, 4, 5 and 6).

Exhibit 3　History of Tennis in China in the 20th Century

- Turn of the century: Tennis is introduced to China by missionaries.

- 1930s: Tennis gains popularity among the wealthy (primarily the foreign community).

- Post–World War II and rise of Communism: Tennis fades from public interest and is eventually shunned as a Western influence.

- Late 1980s/early 1990s: As China reopens its doors, tennis returns. Once again, tennis is considered a sport for the wealthy and connected. Few courts exist, except for private courts for government officials and at foreign compounds.

Source: Women's Tennis Association files.

Exhibit 4 National Interest in Tennis

Tennis is still in its infancy as a participant sport in China, compared with developed sports markets in other countries:

Country	Participation in Millions	Participation as a Percentage of the Population
United States	24.7	8.7
United Kingdom	6.2	10.4
France	4.4	7.4
Germany	4.7	5.7
Italy	6.2	10.8
China	5.0	0.4

Source: Women's Tennis Association files.

Exhibit 5 Tennis Interest in China Compared Against Other Sports

In China, spectator interest and participation in tennis are low compared with other sports:

Ranking of Sports in China on the Basis of Overall Interest (by Percentage)

Sport	Percentage of Population With an Interest in the Sport
Basketball	63
Table tennis	62
Swimming	59
Badminton	52
Football/soccer	52
Gymnastics	50
Volleyball	50
Athletics	41
Motorcar racing	36
Tennis	33
Motorcycle racing	28
Alpine skiing	26
Motorsports	24
Cycling	21
Sailing	16
American football	15
Golf	11
Rugby	11
Ice hockey	10
Handball	8

Ranking of Sports in China on the Basis of Participation (by Percentage)

Sport	Percentage of the population That Participated in the Sport
Badminton	32
Basketball	32
Athletics	25

(Continued)

Exhibit 5 (Continued)

Sport	Percentage of the population That Participated in the Sport
Table tennis	23
Swimming	15
Football/soccer	14
Snooker/billiards	6
Walking	5
Fitness/aerobics	4
Tennis	4
Volleyball	4
Cycling	3
Mountain climbing	3
Shadow boxing	3

Source: Women's Tennis Association files.

Exhibit 6 Television Sports Interest in China: Television Viewership Percentage by Sex, 2004

Sport	Male Percentage of Viewership	Female Percentage of Viewership
Chess/cards	78	24
Billiards	74	28
Boxing	74	28
Football/soccer	76	24
Racing	70	30
Basketball	70	30
Tennis	67	34
Bowling	66	36
Badminton	62	38
Volleyball	62	38
Table tennis	61	38

Source: Women's Tennis Association files.

Note: Rounding errors account for totals that are more or less than 100 per cent.

Shoemaker was not naive, however, and knew that opening an office in China would entail many challenges. In addition to the language barrier, sports in China were overseen by a government agency (see Exhibit 7), and the WTA would need to learn how to interact with this agency. Shoemaker worried that the central government would force the issue of where the office would be located. The WTA would also need to educate Chinese businesses about the benefits of sponsoring events and tournaments in China. Sports marketing was in its infancy in China, and no marketing tool had been developed to show the relationship between sponsoring events and generating revenue. Although the sponsorship of the 2008 Beijing Olympics was expected to be successful, according to Shoemaker, that was an exception.

The Fédération Internationale de Football Association (FIFA), for example, was unable to secure any significant sponsorship deals for the 2007 Women's World Cup, which was being hosted in China. Shoemaker knew that outside of Asia, seven-figure sponsorships were the norm for WTA tournaments, but sponsorship deals for tournaments in Asia were considerably lower (except for one tournament in Japan—see Exhibit 2A). Even Chinese sporting events, such as badminton and table tennis, were struggling to sell their sponsorships.

Exhibit 7 Chinese Government Structure

The political structure governing the sports industry in China dates back to the country's early Communist government foundation:

- Structure was designed as a copy of the former Soviet Union.
- Sports are "controlled" by the highest levels of government.
- Significant government influence still exists today, although recent discussions suggest that the State Sports General Administration unit may be eliminated after 2008.

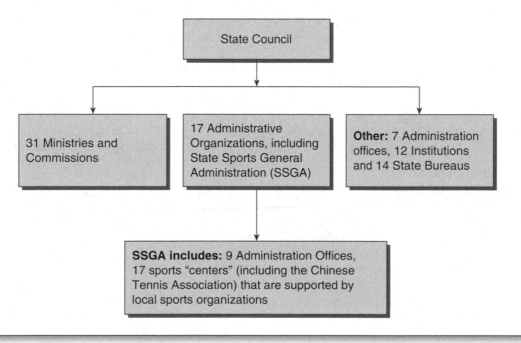

Source: Women's Tennis Association files.

PLAY TENNIS AND MEET THE RIGHT PEOPLE

Despite these setbacks, Shoemaker was not deterred. He saw potential for the WTA in China. Market research conducted by the WTA had shown that tennis had developed rapidly in China over the past decade, with roughly 128 million people interested in the sport and approximately five million active participants.[1] This same market research also indicated that tennis had become an aspirational and prestigious sport in China and was considered to be "modern," "fashionable," "cool," "young" and "healthy." Research conducted indicated that typical tennis fans in China were younger, better educated and in a higher

---

[1]Women's Tennis Association files.

income bracket than the general population.[2] Playing tennis was also perceived as a way of "meeting the right people"; thus, many Chinese believed that people who played tennis were more likely to be promoted in their jobs.

Research had also shown, however, that participation was relatively low compared with the United States and Western European sports markets (0.4 per cent participation in China versus an average of 8.5 per cent in the United States and Western Europe). Shoemaker considered that China presented an opportunity for growth that was unparalleled in most other countries. As the WTA's COO, Shoemaker needed to develop a high-level strategic plan that would encompass developing, leveraging, promoting and empowering the game. He believed that a presence in China was important to achieving these goals.

SHANGHAI, BEIJING OR SOMEWHERE ELSE?

Shoemaker narrowed the prospective locations in China down to Shanghai and Beijing, partly because tennis fans tended to congregate near large cities.[3] Shanghai seemed the early favorite because it had already hosted a significant men's tournament, the Tennis Masters Cup, which had given it experience in offering a world-class venue and maintaining relationships with world-class promoters. Moreover, Shanghai boasted tennis-savvy fans and a corporate audience, which would reduce the challenge of generating ticket and sponsorship revenue. If Shoemaker recommended a regional office in Shanghai, he would not be starting from square one—which could not be said of Beijing.

Shoemaker's biggest concern about choosing Shanghai was that the central Chinese government would likely favor Beijing as a tennis headquarters, and thus be upset by the selection of Shanghai. Even though Beijing was considered the second-best tennis market in China, Shoemaker was not ready to eliminate it in favor of Shanghai. Although Beijing had not hosted a top-tier tournament, it did host a second-tier women's tournament, which Shoemaker believed could be combined with an existing men's ATP tournament. He wondered whether a combined event, "a mini-Grand Slam," would kick-start interest in the sport; moreover, in the wake of the Olympics (which was scheduled to debut in 2008), Beijing would boast top-tier tennis facilities. Potential fans could be lured not just by the tennis but also by the tennis stadium's proximity to Olympic monuments, including the "Bird's Nest stadium," Beijing's National Stadium, which was being built for the 2008 Olympics. Shoemaker considered that choosing Beijing would allow the WTA to be a part of the legacy planning for the Olympic tennis facilities and to become the only sporting body that was committed to using an Olympic facility on a regular, annual basis, for big-time professional sport. He felt that if this happened the legacy of the tennis centre would continue on and possibly grow.

Beijing was also attractive because the local government seemed more excited about the prospect, perhaps in part because Beijing was home to the Chinese Tennis Association. Although both the Shanghai and Beijing governments had offered support to the WTA if it opened its regional headquarters in their respective city, Beijing had offered more. Shoemaker suspected that this enhanced offering reflected "Beijing's desire to advance itself rapidly as a focal point for global sport"; additionally, many governmental officials in Beijing happened to be avid tennis players. The big strike against Beijing was that the local populace had little awareness of tennis, which could affect everything from attendance to corporate sponsorship.

---

[2]Sources: TNS Overview in China Report 2005, National Bureau of Statistics of China, Yearbook 2006.

[3]Approximately 50 per cent of Chinese tennis fans are located in the four biggest markets by gross domestic product (GDP): The cities of Beijing and Shanghai plus the provinces of Guangzhou and Shenzhen. Most of the remaining 50 per cent of Chinese tennis fans are primarily from the next 10 biggest markets: Suzhou, Tianjin, Chongqing, Hangzhou, Wuxi, Qingdao, Fuoshan, Ningbuo, Nanjing and Chengdu.

Second-Guessing

Perhaps it was the time pressure, but Shoemaker started to second-guess whether he had been hasty in eliminating one of his earlier choices: should the headquarters instead be located in Hong Kong or Mumbai? He was very worried that Chinese government pressure would make him accept a decision he was not comfortable with. Shoemaker looked at his computer again. Why was he just focusing on the emerging economies? He should have included Japan or even Australia on his short list. Both already had established tennis markets and well-developed sports marketing programs.

Tokyo was a straightforward choice. The WTA's largest Asian tournament was held in Tokyo. Indeed, the Tokyo tournament offered almost 10 times more prize money than any other tournament in Asia and best exemplified the type of tournament the WTA wanted to see more of in Asia. Shoemaker also knew his staff would not need to explain sports marketing to Japanese companies. The Japanese economy was well developed and its companies routinely sponsored sporting events. Indeed, the WTA's title sponsor, Sony Ericsson, was part Japanese. Moreover, Japan was in relatively close proximity to China and India. A headquarters in Tokyo would allow WTA staff to regularly travel to both of these developing regions to grow the tennis market. For China, specifically, Japan made sense. Japan routinely did business in China, which was Japan's second-largest export destination and its largest import destination. The problem with Japan, of course, was language, thought Shoemaker. The WTA staff would need to learn both Japanese and Mandarin. Shoemaker wasn't sure whether he had time for his staff to become multilingual.

Shoemaker wondered about Australia. The locals spoke English, so establishing an office there would not be a culture shock for the WTA. The Aussies also hosted one of the largest tennis events in the world, the Grand Slam Australian Open, and it was a sports-loving nation. Indeed, Australia would likely have a large pool of qualified sports professionals to hire from, who would know how to host world-class events, especially in light of Australia having recently hosted the 2000 Summer Olympics. Indeed, Australia would make a good base, he thought. And although the emerging markets were not a quick flight away, they would be closer than flying from the United States. Shoemaker wanted a regular presence in Asia, and Australia was a veritable option. The other benefit of Australia was the locals knew how to do business with Asia. For example, the top-three exporting countries for Australia were Asian (Japan, China and South Korea) and three of the top four countries it imported from were Asian (China, Japan and Singapore).

Decision Time

Shoemaker shook his head, flexed his hands and switched from the map of Asia-Pacific to the PowerPoint presentation he was developing for the board meeting. With less than three days to go, he still needed to list the strengths and weaknesses for each option and to make a definite recommendation for the best city in which to establish the WTA's Asian headquarters.

NASSCOM

"We're not just another lobby firm." The company mantra stuck in the mind of Rajdeep Sahrawat, vice president of the National Association of Software and Services Companies (NASSCOM).

In the past, NASSCOM had been extremely successful in promoting Indian information technology (IT) to the world. Ironically, such success had now forced NASSCOM to reconsider its goals to better align itself to the complex needs of the quickly evolving IT-BPO[1] industry in India. In February 2009, NASSCOM would host its annual "India Leadership Forum," which would be attended by participants from around the world. Som Mittal, the association's new president of only one month, had just left Sahrawat's office after asking him to address the conference attendees with details of NASSCOM's strategic refocusing. How could NASSCOM maintain its relevance in an industry that by all accounts was already considered a global leader? What kind of role would it play? Sahrawat knew that he would need to take into account the recent NASSCOM-McKinsey report[2] that identified the domestic market as a significant future growth driver of the IT-ITES[3] sectors. Also, in Mittal's most recent President's Message, he had expressed a strong desire to focus on the SME[4] segment of the Indian industry (see Exhibit 1).

NASSCOM

NASSCOM, a non-profit industry association funded entirely by its members, was considered the "voice" of the software and services industry in India. Of its 1,200 members, more than 150 were global organizations from the United States, United Kingdom, European Union, Japan and China. Together, the member companies accounted for more than 95 per cent of the revenues of the software and services industry in India. The majority of these companies were concentrated in four areas: software development, software services, software products and BPO services (see Exhibit 2). NASSCOM's overarching vision was to "maintain India's leadership position in the global sourcing IT industry, to grow the market by enabling industry to tap into emerging opportunity areas and to strengthen the domestic market in India."[5]

History

NASSCOM was set up in 1988, as a breakaway association from the Manufacturers' Association for Information Technology (MAIT), which was dominated by hardware manufacturing companies. Many MAIT members felt that the software and services industry had grown sufficiently to require a more focused effort in lobbying and obtaining concessions from the government on tax matters. Consequently, NASSCOM was established with 38 founding members.

---

[1]IT-BPO = information technology—business process outsourcing.

[2]NASSCOM-McKinsey Report 2005: Extending India's Leadership of the Global IT and BPO Industries, http://www.mckinsey.com/locations/india/mckinseyonindia/pdf/NASSCOM_McKinsey_Report_2005.pdf, accessed October.7, 2009.

[3]IT-ITES = information technology—information technology–enabled services.

[4]SME = small and medium enterprises.

[5]"About Nasscom," http://www.nasscom.org/Nasscom/templates/NormalPage.aspx?id=5365, accessed November 3, 2009.

Exhibit 1   President's Message

Dear friends,

The small and medium segment is a critical constituent of the Indian software and services industry. These companies fuel growth, fill in specific gaps that exist in servicing customers, bring in innovation and many times spur disruptive solutions. It is no surprise that this segment has led to the creation of many industry giants that exist today—they all started small. From an Indian perspective, this segment is and will remain crucial for retaining the sectors' competitive advantage.

While large companies are now moving towards becoming full service providers in areas like application development, infrastructure and BPO, emerging companies are bringing in very specific niche solutions—thereby completing the ecosystem. It is also interesting to note that the majority of these emerging companies are entrepreneurial ventures by some of the best and the brightest people who have worked with Indian and MNC companies. Having identified the gaps, they are now bringing in domain expertise, specific solutions and knowledge to their offerings.

These companies are mature, offer marketable solutions, create well-conceptualised products, bring business value and personalised attention to customers and in turn gain customer mindshare during the process. It is very encouraging to note that many of these companies are now developing products and creating IP, and with India becoming the single largest centre for offshore product development, the culture and discipline of product development is becoming all pervasive.

The Indian emerging companies segment has been hit hardest by rising operational costs, difficulties in hiring the best talent, high attrition rates and the fluctuating Indian Rupee versus the USD. The specific areas where these companies need help are market access and operational management, so that they are able to meet the requirements of the market. Among other things, NASSCOM has put in place best practice sharing platforms like industry events, mentorship activities and facilitating global SME linkages, to help foster the ecosystem.

There is also a need for us to encourage these emerging companies through fiscal measures and ensure that we provide a level playing field to all. Those in Tier-2 and 3 cities cannot use the SEZ scheme and even if they operate in Tier-1 cities, they cannot avail of the SEZ benefits given the cost structure. Policy-level interventions are needed in areas like FBT, service tax, VAT, excise duty, etc. NASSCOM is continually working with the government to address these issues. Of late, we have also initiated dialogue with real estate providers to come up with specific products that are cost effective for the emerging companies segment.

Warm regards,

Som Mittal

President

NASSCOM

Source: http://www.nasscom.in/Nasscom/templates/NormalPage.aspx?id=28660.

At the onset, NASSCOM's mandate was not unlike that of any other industry lobby group. However, largely due to the concerted efforts and vision of NASSCOM's first leader, Dewang Mehta, NASSCOM was able to transform itself from a simple government policy influencer to an active industry ally, offering a wide portfolio of services for the industry. For instance, in this role, NASSCOM became one of the earliest advocates of "Offshore Software Development,"

Exhibit 2 NASSCOM Membership Categories

NASSCOM membership comprises Registered Member and Associate Member categories.

Registered Member

Information technology (IT) software and services companies registered in India, with annual revenue of 1 million rupees[6] or more (from IT software and services). Registered members include the following:

- Software development companies
- IT services companies
- Software product companies
- Resellers of branded software packages
- E-commerce companies
- IT-enabled service companies
- System integrators

Associate Members: Members in this category enjoy all the benefits of membership without voting rights.

IT Companies: IT software and services companies registered in India with annual revenue between 0.5 million to 1 million rupees from software and services are eligible to be Associate Members of NASSCOM.

Liaison Offices as Associate Members: Overseas companies that have a liaison office registered in India can apply for NASSCOM membership under the Associate Member category.

Institutional Members: Companies that are not in the core area of IT services but provide support services or are affiliated to IT services fall under this category. Institutional members include the following:

- Nongovernmental organizations
- Government organizations and departments
- Societies engaged in promotion of IT
- Financial institutions
- Venture capital firms
- Research institutions
- Infrastructure providers
- Real estate companies
- Management consultants
- Non-profit organizations
- "Companies providing services to IT industry"

Source: NASSCOM, "How to Become a Member?" http://www.nasscom.org/artdisplay.asp?cat_id=105, accessed November 11, 2009.

[6]US$1 = 45 rupees

or "Smart Sourcing," as a strategy to provide India the competitive edge needed in the global IT landscape.

Leadership

The general management of NASSCOM was the overall responsibility of the Executive Council, which consisted of the chairman, vice-chairman and president. The chairman and vice-chairman, who were elected to one-year terms, were high-profile executives from Indian software and services companies. The NASSCOM president, on the other hand, was a paid employee. Much of the current success of NASSCOM could be attributed to the foundational work of its founder, Dewang Mehta.

Dewang Mehta (1991 to 2001)

NASSCOM attributed much of its success to the visionary leadership of Dewang Mehta, who led the organization from its inception until his untimely death in 2001. Mehta, who was a chartered accountant by profession, joined NASSCOM in 1991. To take the position, he had returned from England, where he had run a small software company. His first success with lobbying the government involved the inclusion of a one-year income-tax waiver in the 1991 federal budget. Other successes quickly followed. For instance, Mehta was instrumental in convincing the Indian government to allow Indian companies to be listed on NASDAQ. Also, NASSCOM initiated reforms in both central and state government policy, including zero duty on software, crucial income-tax concessions for software exporters and more stringent copyright laws. Mehta facilitated the introduction of the IT Act in 2000 and its associated cyber laws, which had a major positive impact on e-business and the new economy in India (see Exhibit 3). Recognizing the potential of the software and services segment as a major

Exhibit 3 Advantages of the Cyber Laws in the IT Act 2000[7]

In May 2000, both the houses of the Indian Parliament passed the Information Technology Bill. The Bill received the assent of the President in August 2000 and came to be known as the Information Technology Act, 2000. Cyber laws are contained in the IT Act, 2000. This Act aims to provide the legal infrastructure for e-commerce in India. The cyber laws have a major impact for e-businesses and the new economy in India.

Advantages of Cyber Laws

The IT Act 2000 attempts to change outdated laws and provides ways to deal with cyber crimes. Such laws are needed so that people can perform purchase transactions over the Net through credit cards without fear of misuse. The Act offers the much-needed legal framework so that information is not denied legal effect, validity or enforceability, solely on the ground that it is in the form of electronic records.

In view of the growth in transactions and communications carried out through electronic records, the Act seeks to empower government departments to accept filing, creating and retention of official documents in the digital format. The Act has also proposed a legal framework for the authentication and origin of electronic records/communications through digital signature.

(Continued)

[7]Advantages of Cyber Laws, http://infosecawareness.in/cyber-laws/advantages-of-cyber-laws, accessed November 11, 2009.

Exhibit 3 (Continued)

- From the perspective of e-commerce in India, the IT Act 2000 and its provisions contain many positive aspects. Firstly, the implications of these provisions for the e-businesses would be that email would now be a valid and legal form of communication in India that can be duly produced and approved in a court of law.

- Companies shall now be able to carry out electronic commerce using the legal infrastructure provided by the Act.

- Digital signatures have been given legal validity and sanction in the Act.

- The Act throws open the doors for the entry of corporate companies in the business of being Certifying Authorities for issuing Digital Signatures Certificates.

- The Act now allows Government to issue notification on the web, thus heralding e-governance.

- The Act enables the companies to file any form, application or any other document with any office, authority, body or agency owned or controlled by the appropriate Government in electronic form by means of such electronic form as may be prescribed by the appropriate Government.

- The IT Act also addresses the important issues of security, which are so critical to the success of electronic transactions. The Act has given a legal definition to the concept of secure digital signatures that would be required to have been passed through a system of a security procedure, as stipulated by the Government at a later date.

- Under the IT Act, 2000, it shall now be possible for corporations to have a statutory remedy in case anyone breaks into their computer systems or network and causes damages or copies data. The remedy provided by the Act is in the form of monetary damages, not exceeding ten million rupees.

foreign-exchange earner, Mehta launched the India Inc. crusade, whereby he personally presented the country's software industry to the world. During his tenure, he helped at least 19 state governments draft their IT policies and create the requisite infrastructure to help develop the software industry within their local domains. His continued and tireless efforts not only laid the foundation for a robust software and services sector but consequently positioned NASSCOM as a key facilitator in the process of shaping the direction in which the sector evolved.

While Mehta was president of NASSCOM, he was appointed by the prime minister as the spokesperson for the National Task Force on Information Technology and Software Development. He also sat on the Governing Council of the Indian Institute of Information Technology (IIIT), an elite technical skills training institution. Mehta received many accolades throughout his career. For instance, the Geneva-based World Economic Forum chose him as one of the "Global Leaders of Tomorrow" for his global influence and achievements. Besides his relentless pursuit of promoting the export of software, Mehta passionately believed that IT could be used effectively to change the lives of millions of India's underprivileged. Hence, he was well known for coining the slogan, "roti, kapada, makan, bijli and bandwidth,"[8] which epitomized the emerging needs of the 21st century Indian.

---

[8]Dewang Mehta took the famous Hindi saying of "roti (food), kapada (clothing), makan (house)," which describes the essentials in life, and added bijli (electricity) and bandwidth to include NASSCOM's concerns.

NASSCOM's
CURRENT STRATEGIC FOCUS[9]

NASSCOM had chosen to concentrate its efforts in the following six key areas:

1. **Partnership with Government:** NASSCOM had always maintained a good working relationship with the Government of India. This relationship allowed NASSCOM to influence the formulation of national IT policies with a specific focus on IT software and services. NASSCOM had representatives on various federal government committees in the Ministry of Commerce, Ministry of Finance, Department of Telecommunication, Ministry of Human Resources Development, Ministry of Labor and the Ministry of External Affairs. NASSCOM had also acted as a consulting body for many state governments.

2. **Global Partnerships:** NASSCOM provided a forum for both overseas and domestic companies to explore the possibility of engaging in joint ventures, strategic alliances, marketing alliances and joint product development. Through the many conferences that it organized, NASSCOM brought together delegates of various countries and industries to facilitate the exchange of ideas. NASSCOM also played an active role in the international software community as a member of the Asian-Oceanian Computing Industry Organization (ASOCIO) and a founding member of the World Information Technology and Services Alliances (WITSA). Through its various partnerships, NASSCOM worked with foreign governments and trade bodies in the United States, the United Kingdom, Japan, Germany, France, Scandinavia, China, Australia, South Africa, Israel and other countries.

3. **Research and Thought Leadership:** NASSCOM disseminated various policies, market information and other relevant statistics by sending more than 200 circulars (annually) to all its members. NASSCOM also conducted research on the information and communication technologies (ICT) industry in India and the world to educate its members about new opportunities, potential threats and major trends. In a strategic move, NASSCOM had entered into a partnership with the McKinsey Group to develop and promote original research on the software and services industry in India.

4. **Quality of Products and Services:** NASSCOM actively encouraged its members to provide world-class products, services and solutions in India and overseas. Such an insistence on high-quality standards had contributed greatly to the building of brand equity for the Indian IT software and services industry. More specifically, NASSCOM helped its members achieve international quality certifications (see Exhibit 4 on the Capability and Maturity Model [CMM]) by organizing educational seminars.

5. **Intellectual Property Rights:** NASSCOM had taken various steps to campaign against software piracy, from lobbying to establish strong intellectual property laws to conducting campaigns to educate the public about lawful use.

6. **Member Services and Benefits:** By maintaining a state-of-the-art information database of activities related to IT software and services, NASSCOM offered an information resource for use by both local and foreign member companies. NASSCOM also offered seminars on emerging technology, exports, the domestic market, e-governance, IT-enabled services, government policies and quality standards. These forays helped to nurture business connections among member companies and to propagate global best practices. Besides world-class research and market intelligence services, members could also access counsel from leading think tanks and consultants.

THE INDIAN SOFTWARE AND SERVICES INDUSTRY

The Software Industry

The Indian software industry dated back to the installation of the first mainframe for the Indian Statistical Institute in Kolkata in 1956.

---

[9]"About NASSCOM," http://www.nasscom.org/Nasscom/templates/NormalPage.aspx?id=5365, accessed October 2, 2009.

Exhibit 4 Capability and Maturity Model (CMM) Certification

The Capability and Maturity Model (CMM) was developed by Carnegie Mellon's Software Engineering Institute in the mid-1980s on request from the U.S. Department of Defense to help address its software quality problems. The CMM standard is a quality standard, much like ISO, but specifically pertaining to the field of software engineering. The CMM has been used by many organizations to identify those best practices useful in helping them increase the maturity of their processes and delivering a more robust software product. CMM levels, from 1 to 5, indicate the maturity of an organization's overall development processes, with CMM level 5 being the most mature.

As of 2005, India had more than 89 companies at CMM level 5, which represented more than half of the world's such organizations. The certification had served as a means for Indian software companies to gain legitimacy in the global market and be able to compete for contracts on an equal footing with some of their more established Western competitors. CMM certification had helped companies like TCS, Wipro, Infosys, Cognizant, I-flex and Polaris Software to achieve great success in the global software industry.

The Indian software industry had rigorously sought quality certification for two main reasons. First, as a marketing device, certification signaled to potential customers that the organization followed industry best practices (standards established in the developed world), including a well-documented development process. Second, the certified organization was considered to have a better ability to estimate and manage the time and resources required for any given project, thereby allowing the certified company to attain larger, more lucrative projects. Firms with proven records could bid for projects directly with clients rather than work as subcontractors for other vendors. This opportunity opened the door to turnkey contracts, involving the coordination of a much wider range of tasks beyond just basic programming. In this capacity, Indian companies were taking responsibility for the overall project schedule, quality and productivity. This approach was in direct contrast to many of their previous roles as body-shoppers that worked on a small piece of the project. Not only were some Indian firms getting better work at better rates but they had started to convert critical knowledge gained during consulting projects into generic products that were subsequently customized for clients with similar needs.

Source: NASSCOM Newsline, May 2005, Issue 43.

Until the mid-1960s, computer hardware and supporting software were provided primarily by two multinational corporations (MNCs) with operations in India: IBM (American) and ICL (British). As was prevalent practice in that era, software was developed overseas and then included in the sale of the hardware at no additional cost. However, as the needs of India's defense and public sectors became more complex, the support provided by the vendor companies was becoming increasingly inadequate. Consequently, in-house developers began writing specific application programs for their own organizations. In addition, dwindling foreign-exchange resources and trade embargos on India made it increasingly difficult to obtain computers; when computers could be obtained, they were very expensive due to their exorbitant import duties. Around this time, Tata Consultancy Services (TCS) became the first independent Indian software firm to set up operations. TCS initially focused on supporting the operations of the Tata group of companies. Today, TCS is the largest software and computer services company in India, with more than 20,000 software engineers (see Exhibit 5 for a listing of the Top 20).

Exhibit 5 Top 20 Indian IT Software and Services Exporters

TOP 20 IT SOFTWARE & SERVICE EXPORTERS FROM INDIA (2004–05) IT Software and Service Expotrts (excluding ITES-OPO)			
Rank	Company	Rs. Crore	US $ mn
1	Tata Consultancy Services Ltd	7449	1644
2	Infosys Technologies Ltd	6806	1502
3	Wipro Technologies	5426	1198
4	Satyam Computer Services Ltd	3377	745
5	HCL Technologies Ltd	2664	588
6	Patni Computer Systems Ltd	1548	342
7	i-flex Solutions Ltd	1110	245
8	Mahindra British Telecom Ltd	913	202
9	Polaris Software Lab Ltd	697	154
10	Perot Systems TSI (India) Ltd	657	145
11	Hexaware Technologies Ltd	583	129
12	Larsen & Toubro Infotech Ltd	557	123
13	MASTEK Ltd	546	121
14	iGATE Global Solutions Ltd (Formerly Mascot Systems)	534	118
15	Siemens Information Systems Ltd	502	111
16	Mphasis BFL Ltd	465	103
17	Tata Infotech Ltd	463	102
18	NIIT Technologies Ltd	448	99
19	Flextronics Software Systems Ltd	424	94

Source: Nasscom

Note: Subsequently to the issue of the press release, IBM Global had informed NASSCOM that it did not wish to be ranked. Accordingly, IBM Global has been removed from the Top 20 list.

Methodology for Ranking

NASSCOM sends out a detailed Snap Survey questionnaire annually to all its member companies, accounting for 95 per cent of the revenue from the Indian IT software and BPO industries. Information collated through the questionnaire includes: aggregate performance; service lines; verticals and geographies. The Snap Survey form also takes into account the contribution of the 100 per cent owned overseas subsidiaries after deducting all the double accounting.

In 1977, the Minister of Industries of the Janata Party government announced that MNCs operating in India would need to become minority owners in their Indian subsidiaries. As a result, foreign companies were required to either sell excess shares on the Indian market or withdraw from the country. Although many companies opted for the former option, some chose to leave India. Two of the more notable companies to withdraw were Coca-Cola and IBM. This action serendipitously triggered the growth of the Indian software industry. Some of the 1,200 ex-IBM employees who found themselves out of work began to accept jobs overseas, whereas others formed their own small companies to offer software development and maintenance services to former IBM customers. One of the most successful ventures to start during this period was Infosys Technologies, now the second largest software and services company in India. One of its founders, Narayana Murthy (who had been chairman of NASSCOM from 1992 to 1994) had mused that one of the biggest challenges facing his company was "running a first-world company in a third-world country."

During the 1980s, bodyshopping[10] became extremely popular mainly due to the Indian government's policy of restricting imports of hardware by limiting the issue of needed permits, imposing high customs duties and controlling the exchange of foreign currency. Such restrictions encouraged Indian companies to build and foster relationships with overseas clients, many of which continue today. TCS was the first commercial organization to subscribe to the terms of the Indian government's "export commitment" under which the import of hardware was allowed to those companies that earned foreign exchange. TCS teamed up with Burroughs Corporation to form an alliance known as Tata Burroughs, later Tata Infotech. Burroughs would help secure U.S. clients for TCS (which opened its first U.S. office in 1979), and TCS would act as the exclusive agent for Burroughs hardware in India. As a result of this alliance, TCS secured its first U.S. client, the Detroit Police Department.[11]

Due to the challenges of selling to the domestic market and the many years of government policies favoring companies that brought in foreign exchange, the software industry developed a decidedly outward focus. Foreign markets were both administratively easier to deal with and more profitable. Also, the Indian government was reluctant to encourage computerization of its own operations, fearing the mass unemployment that might result. Because the government was interested in developing a robust domestic hardware industry, it imposed severe tariffs (up to 350 per cent) on imported hardware.

During Prime Minister Rajiv Gandhi's tenure (1984 to 1989), many "forward-looking" policies were introduced, which boosted the software industry. Software exports were, for the first time, actively promoted by the government through concessional financing, export incentives, improved infrastructure, legal regulation and export marketing assistance. In addition, the import of hardware was also liberalized, causing many domestic companies to computerize. Although this increase in demand created a small domestic market, the active encouragement of the government to earn foreign exchange caused the continuance of a strong export focus. While some key MNCs (such as British Airways, Hewlett-Packard and Citibank) started to set up dedicated operations in India, the attention of the worldwide business community was focused on the possibility of setting up low-cost software development operations in India. Many companies in developed countries were experiencing a severe shortage of programmers. To take advantage of this opportunity, the Indian government set up software technology parks, which were tax-free and duty-free zones with superior infrastructure located in several major cities. In such zones, foreign companies were allowed to set up wholly owned subsidiaries for the first time.

---

[10]Bodyshopping referred to the practice of sending software developers to client sites to work on their computers.

[11]Of course, Burroughs itself was TCS's first U.S. client back in 1974.

In the 1990s, two significant events helped establish the "Made in India" brand in India's IT export markets. First, Swiss Railways, known for its rigid contract demands, needed to revamp and integrate its many disparate systems. TCS won the contract over several international competitors. TCS completed the contract well ahead of time and also delivered excellent customer service. This performance helped to establish the Indians as not just "techno-coolies"[12] that did low-grade work but as competent players that worked within stringent constraints on both quality and time. The success of TCS paved the way for others to follow. Azim Premji, the founder of Wipro (the third largest software and services company in India, an NYSE-listed company and the world's first globally CMM-certified[13] company) has been quoted as saying that "the legacy of the early pioneers—like Tata Consultancy Services—was a growing number of foreign companies favorably impressed with what Indian companies could do in software." The second significant event was the advent of the Y2K crisis. Indian software engineers by the thousands found themselves traveling to many parts of the developed world to address Y2K issues. Shortly after Y2K, the euro conversion in Europe required the expertise of these same software developers, many of whom took up residence in those countries. As these Indians started to obtain positions of influence in their own companies, they actively promoted the capabilities of Indian software companies.

Today, many Indian IT multinationals have built a strong global presence. CMM (Capability and Maturity Model) certification helped Indian software companies compete successfully for international contracts, thereby generating a greater international presence (see Exhibit 4). TCS opened offices in Hungary and China and also acquired a presence in Chile and Brazil. As

Subramanian Ramadorai, chief executive of TCS, explained: "Several years ago we decided the India-centric model had to change. We needed to offer seamless delivery from around the globe."[14] Infosys Technologies had set up shop in China, Mauritius and the Czech Republic. Wipro had new offices in Shanghai and Beijing and planned to open an office in Romania. Much of this global expansion was achieved through cross-border acquisitions and organic growth in various foreign low-cost locations. This expansion was complemented by major global players continuing to significantly ramp up their offshore delivery capabilities, predominantly in India. As a result of these two trends, India became a key component of the global delivery model, thereby further boosting its attractiveness as a primary IT-ITES destination. In addition to India's well-established technical competencies, other factors such as trade openness, increasing urbanization and rising consumption spending made India an attractive investment destination, both as a sourcing base and as a significant market.

IT-Enabled Services and BPO

In 1984, Raman Roy joined American Express in India to help automate its services and accounting operations. He eventually built a global, centralized accounting facility that provided services to American Express customers in Europe, the United States, Japan and Australia. In 1992, Swiss Air established a joint venture company, ATS, with the Tata group to work on back-office assignments. In 1997, British Airways and American Express also started to outsource some routine back-end work to India. In 1998, the Indian subsidiary of GE Capital set up a small eight-person team to do elementary address changes for its group of companies. On the basis of the success of this group, the company became

---

[12]Coolies were hired porters.

[13]CMM (Capability and Maturity Model) is an ISO-like standard for software development.

[14]Kerry A. Dolan, "Offshoring the Offshorers," http://www.forbes.com/forbes/2006/0417/074_print.html, accessed October 2, 2009.

a major center (called GE International Services) handling basic voice-based call center operations, claims processing, e-business, accounting and actuarial services. Not coincidentally, Raman Roy was brought in to head GEIS operations. In five years, the division grew from eight employees to more than 12,000. Such success spurred companies such as Citigroup, HSBC, Accenture, Dell and HP to follow suit and set up operations in India.

The ITES industry consisted of those services that were delivered over the Internet to a wide range of business areas and verticals. By using technology, such services could be delivered remotely to gain a cost advantage without sacrificing quality and efficiency. Several factors fueled the growth of the ITES industry in India. For instance, companies felt greater pressures to cut costs, and work was becoming more skilled and therefore in need of more costly labor. At the same time, a need was developing for more integrated and specialized solutions that could be more efficiently delivered by outsourcing companies. India's main competitor in the ITES industry was China. However, India's rapidly improving telecom infrastructure, large English-educated working class and overall quality and productivity made it an increasingly popular destination. The industry mainly consisted of call centers, medical transcription services and back-office data processing.

By 2006, India provided outsourcing services to the majority of Fortune 500 companies. Revenues in the ITES/BPO industry in India had grown to well over $4 billion from being practically non-existent before the 1990s. In fact, India's growth in this sector had fueled an infamous debate in the 2004 U.S. presidential race, and offshoring had been voted the most important issue of 2003 by *Forbes* Magazine readers. By many accounts, the Indian IT-enabled services industry was on track to achieve its long-term target of US$20 billion in five years.

India's Leadership Position

By all indications, India was well on its way to both sustaining its leadership position in the global software and services markets and reaching $80 billion in exports in the next five years. The Indian IT/ITES sector was relatively mature, having already built much of its competitive capacity in global markets. But was such a competitive edge sustainable? The industry was concerned about emerging challenges related to increasing competition from even lower-cost offshore outsourcing destinations and its ability to sustain its advantage with a more constrained talent pool. Going forward, India would need to take a more imaginative and unconventional approach. Companies would need to explore new avenues to remain competitive. NASSCOM believed that innovation would define India's fortunes in the global IT-ITES markets because it would help to maintain the growth of large companies and fuel the growth of SMEs. Innovation was considered to be the key to competing in the global market. In fact, an innovation-led approach could enhance India's export potential by about an additional $15 billion to $20 billion over the next five to 10 years.

India's leadership position in the global offshore IT and BPO industries was based on five main advantages:[15]

1. **Abundant talent:** India accounted for almost 30 per cent of IT and BPO talent among 28 low-cost countries.

2. **Urban infrastructure:** India had created several IT centers.

3. **Operational excellence:** The cost and quality of leadership in offshore service centers was excellent.

4. **Conducive business environment:** India offered several favorable policy interventions, such as telecom reforms.

[15]Strengthening India's Offshoring Industry http://www.mckinseyquarterly.com/Strengthening_Indias_offshoring_industry_2372, accessed November 11, 2009.

5. **Domestic IT sector:** India's continued IT growth provided enabling infrastructure and developed a broad-based skill base.

Three major challenges also needed to be addressed:

1. **Demand growth:** Demand could slow down due to concerns about service quality and security. Also the union and political opposition to offshoring could slow the demand.

2. **Potential shortage of skilled workers:** The projected shortfall was 500,000 by 2010, especially concentrated in the BPO industry.

3. **Urban infrastructure:** India's offshoring industries were dealing with bottlenecks ranging from the power supply to cafeteria services. India needed to deliver on both basic and business infrastructure.

The Domestic Market

The domestic market represented a huge untapped opportunity, as evidenced by the very low ICT penetration (see Exhibit 6). NASSCOM believed that innovation was crucial to tapping this potential growth, given the wide variation in the needs of the domestic market. An innovation ecosystem was needed to bring together various stakeholders, including academia, entrepreneurs, venture capitalists, government and industry. Bringing together such diverse parties was one of NASSCOM's core strengths and a task it believed it was well equipped to accomplish. In particular, NASSCOM identified those areas of the domestic market it would need to focus on:

Innovation and R&D: Focus on increasing entrepreneurship and innovation in the high-technology areas and on commercializing domestic R&D.

Emerging markets: Focus on increasing IT consumption in SME and household consumer segments by identifying the unique needs of each of these segments and then producing products made in India for Indians. Many of these products would then be available for export to other countries.

Government processes: Focus on improving the government processes involved in e-government projects, to improve the efficiency of e-governance investments.

Education in emerging skills: Focus on creating capacities in skills required by the IT industry in emerging technologies which may be niche today but would be mainstream in the future.

Exhibit 6 Internet Usage and Penetration Statistics for India

Year	Internet Subscribers	Population	Penetration
1998	1,400,000	1,094,870,677	0.1 %
1999	2,800,000	1,094,870,677	0.3 %
2000	5,500,000	1,094,870,677	0.5 %
2001	7,000,000	1,094,870,677	0.7 %
2002	16,500,000	1,094,870,677	1.6 %
2003	22,500,000	1,094,870,677	2.1 %
2004	39,200,000	1,094,870,677	3.6 %
2005	50,600,000	1,112,225,812	4.5 %
2006	40,000,000	1,112,225,812	3.6 %
2007	42,000,000	1,129,667,528	3.7 %

Source: Internet World Stats, "India Internet Usage and Population Stats," http://www.internetworldstats.com/asia/in.htm, accessed November 11, 2009.

FROM "DESTINATION INDIA" TO "INDIA EVERYWHERE"

NASSCOM had been largely responsible for much of the branding of India, through the sustained efforts of Mehta and Karnik. As the organization contemplated its next strategic moves, the history and present state of the Indian brand would need to be taken into consideration.

At the 2003 India Economic Summit, the discussion in the "Made in India" session focused on issues surrounding the branding of India. On the one hand, India was known for its more traditional areas of textiles, jewelry and handicrafts with strong perceptions of antiquity, variable skills and unreliability. On the other hand, the new industries of IT, auto and auto components, and drug development and research were more associated with durability, trustworthiness and technical prowess. The India Brand Equity Foundation was established to take the lead in addressing a much needed branding exercise for India. A primary constraint identified in developing the "Made in India" brand was the need for consistency in policy development. Reform in policy would allow Indian entrepreneurs to effectively compete on the global stage.

Three years later, at the 2006 World Economic Forum in Davos, Switzerland, "People passing through Zurich and other Swiss airports . . . [were] likely to have heard somebody humming a Hindi song or draped in an Indian *pashmina* shawl. India seemed to be everywhere."[16] The "India Everywhere" initiative was created and driven by the Confederation of Indian Industry (CII), the country's most prominent business advocacy group, which drummed up support from leading businesses and key officials from the central and state governments. The $4 million campaign was funded by contributions from 22 Indian companies, some of which paid more than $150,000 each. The Indian government spent another $2 million through the India Brand Equity Foundation under its commerce ministry, which worked closely with CII in putting together the campaign. The core goals of the "India Everywhere" campaign were to present the country as an attractive destination for foreign investment, an emerging manufacturing hub and a credible partner for world business. In addition, the campaign highlighted the Indian government's policy reforms and showcased the country's cultural diversity, with the overall goal of helping conference participants gain a deeper understanding of Indian people and markets. However, critics noted that although India's campaign at Davos was both impressive and effective, the country would now need to walk the talk with infrastructure improvements and free up policy and procedural bottlenecks. If these changes failed to happen, its credibility could be at risk.

REINVENTING NASSCOM

As Sahrawat reclined in his chair and peered out the window onto the bustling street below, he pondered NASSCOM's role in the future of the IT industry in India. He knew that "if NASSCOM speaks, people listen." At the same time, he wondered: if NASSCOM closed its doors tomorrow, would anything really change? The IT industry was well on its way to posting record earnings and India was well established as a key global player in the software and services industry (see Exhibit 7). But was the story really that simple? What about competition from other emerging and often lower-cost markets, such as China, Israel and Brazil? What about the competitive threats from MNCs, such as IBM and Accenture, which came to India, set up shop and were hoarding the best talent? Sahrawat was concerned that such companies were starting to compete effectively on price with their Indian rivals. In fact, he knew that many of the recent large contracts in India had gone to MNCs such as IBM and Accenture.

---

[16]"Delhi in Davos: How India Built Its Brand at the World Economic Forum," http://knowledge.wharton.upenn.edu/article/1394.cfm#, accessed November 11, 2009.

Exhibit 7   NASSCOM Strategic Review 2008: IT Industry-Sector Profile

US$billion	FY '04	FY '05	FY '06	FY '07	FY '08
IT Services (total)	10.4	13.5	17.8	23.5	31.0
Exports	7.3	10.0	13.3	18.0	23.1
Domestic	3.1	3.5	4.5	5.5	7.9
ITES-BPO (total)	3.4	5.2	7.2	9.5	12.5
Exports	3.1	4.6	6.3	8.4	10.9
Domestic	0.3	0.6	0.9	1.1	1.6
Engineering Services and R&D, Software Products (total)	2.9	3.8	5.3	6.5	8.6
Exports	2.5	3.1	4.0	4.9	6.4
Domestic	0.4	0.7	1.3	1.6	2.2
Total Software and Services Revenues of which,	**16.7**	**22.5**	**30.3**	**39.5**	**52.0**
exports are	**12.9**	**17.7**	**23.6**	**31.3**	**40.4**
Hardware	5.0	5.6	7.1	8.5	12.0
Exports	0.5	0.5	0.6	0.5	0.5
Domestic	4.4	5.1	6.5	8.0	11.5
Total IT Industry (including Hardware)	**21.6**	**28.2**	**37.4**	**48.0**	**64.0**

Highlights

2007 was a year of continued growth for the technology and related services sector, with the worldwide spending aggregate estimated to reach nearly US$1.7 trillion, a growth of 7.3 per cent over the previous year.

Global Market

- Software and services continue to lead, accounting for more than US$1.2 trillion—more than 71 per cent of the total spent in 2007.
- Hardware spending, at US$478 billion, accounted for more than 28 per cent of the worldwide technology spending aggregate in 2007.

Indian Market

- Underlying the sustained growth were a range of economic, regulatory and demographic drivers—including a continued emphasis on trimming operational costs, dealing with increasing compliance and regulatory requirements, remaining price competitive, transforming into a global services-oriented business model and addressing challenges of rising skill shortages, across several developed markets.
- Strong optimism of the industry to achieve its aspired target of US$60 billion in exports by 2010.

Source: http://www.nasscom.org/Nasscom/templates/NormalPage.aspx?id=53454, accessed November 11, 2009.

Moreover, how could NASSCOM influence the agenda of its member companies as successfully as it had influenced the government through its lobbying efforts in the past? Sahrawat knew that the very creation of NASSCOM was strongly rooted in the old leadership of its member companies, which had taken an active role in shaping NASSCOM's agenda. However, did the new generation of leadership have the same kind of vested interest in NASSCOM? Did the new leadership have the same level of allegiance? Would the new leadership allow NASSCOM to influence their strategic direction?

Sahrawat needed to identify possible options. On the one hand, NASSCOM could continue focusing on international markets and keep doing what it had always been doing. Alternatively, NASSCOM could refocus and concentrate on the domestic market. If it decided to go with the latter option, how should it accomplish this change in focus? Should NASSCOM single-handedly promote IT in the domestic market, or should NASSCOM "engineer a debate" over the merits of focusing on the domestic market? What would be the role of the SMEs? Sahrawat felt that NASSCOM needed to remain neutral to maintain its brand equity. Any favoritism could be misconstrued in a negative light, as it had been in the past. The decisions that needed to be made could have an impact far beyond the future role of NASSCOM in the software and services industry. His previous boss had told him many times to "take away the NASSCOM hat and put on the India hat." Perhaps NASSCOM's concern should now be more, "roti, kapada, makan, bijli, bandwith . . . and topee (hat)."

14

SOCIAL ENTREPRENEURSHIP

Social entrepreneurship as a phenomenon has existed for many centuries, and in some parts of the world, the number of social enterprise start-ups now in fact outpaces those of traditional enterprises.

—Kistruck and Beamish (2010, p. 735)

Key Topics: social entrepreneurship and its underlying theories; competitive strategy models in the NPO sector; synergies and trade-offs between economic, environmental, and social value creation; collaborative relationships among different types of organizations; importance of inclusive business models

DEFINING THE CONCEPT

To understand social entrepreneurship one must deconstruct the concept into its two elements—entrepreneurship and social or society. What and who is an entrepreneur? While anyone—from the youngster offering to shovel snow in the neighborhood to Bill Gates—can be said to be an entrepreneur, the concept means more than starting or building a business. In general, "an entrepreneur is someone who creates value by improving efficiency and effectiveness in the use of society's limited resources" (Worth, 2012, p. 386). Entrepreneurs are thought to be innovative, opportunity-oriented change agents (Dees, Emerson, & Economy, 2001). Entrepreneurs thus look for ways to innovate either through a

new business model (e.g., Google's cloud computing), a new product or service (e.g., cell phones versus land-based phones), or an entirely new way of approaching a challenge. An example of this last category of innovation is evident in how Facebook and Twitter have changed the way we communicate with each other. These innovations have been truly disruptive in that they change the place, media, manner and motivations for the way many of us communicate.

Given this very broad definition one may ask: In what context can an entrepreneur practice her skills? Obviously, entrepreneurs are not only found in the business domain. Wouldn't one consider Jaime Escalante, the dedicated math teacher at Garfield High School determined to change the system and challenge the students to a higher level of achievement (as portrayed by Edward James Olmos in the movie *Stand and Deliver*), and Michelle A. Rhee, former D.C. schools chancellor and leader of education reform, education entrepreneurs? Each saw that the current education system was not delivering success, changed educational models, and reallocated resources to achieve new, systemwide improved results. Thus enters the second element of the definition—social or society. Social entrepreneurs apply the skills and mindset of an entrepreneur in order to seek opportunities to improve not just business, but society.

A social entrepreneur is someone who recognizes a societal problem (e.g., environmental degradation, poverty, illiteracy, urban violence, health challenges) and uses entrepreneurial principles to organize, create, and manage a venture to make change. In the early years of social entrepreneurship, what Bornstein and Davis (2010) call *social entrepreneurship 1.0,* the focus was on how to be as effective as a for-profit entrepreneur while remaining fully within the nonprofit sector. Yet the social entrepreneurship discipline is evolving into the 2.0 and 3.0 stages with the democratizing effect of technology, the emergence of philanthrocapitalists such as Bill Gates, and the inclusion of sustainable business strategies. In the 3.0 stage, Bornstein and Davis suggest that social entrepreneurs involve all people in the development of a new ecosystem where everyone operates as change-makers focused on sustaining each other in productive ways.

Martin and Osberg (2007) summarize the definition by delineating three components of social entrepreneurship:

1. Identifies a stable but inherently unjust equilibrium that causes the exclusion, marginalization, or suffering of a segment of humanity that lacks the financial means or political clout to achieve any transformative benefit on its own.

2. Identifies an opportunity in this unjust equilibrium, develops a social proposition, and brings to bear inspiration, creativity, direct action, courage, and fortitude, thereby challenging the stable state's hegemony.

3. Forges a new, stable equilibrium that releases trapped potential or alleviates the suffering of the targeted group, and through innovation and the creation of a stable ecosystem around the new equilibrium, ensures a better future for the targeted group and even society at large (p. 35).

Although we state the definition of social entrepreneurship rather definitively, there is no single definition. There is consensus around the idea that for social entrepreneurs to achieve change, they bring together practices from the nonprofit sector with philosophies and methodologies from business to formulate new models, whether for-profit or nonprofit. In many ways, social entrepreneurship combines advocacy with social marketing and entrepreneurial innovation to accomplish goals that nonprofit organization (NPO) leaders have long struggled to accomplish.

From this discussion, it should be evident that we position social entrepreneurship as different from earned income strategies discussed in Chapters 10 and 11. While both earned income and social entrepreneurship look to free nonprofits from their dependence on government support and private donations, the former is not as systemwide or comprehensive as the latter. Earned income concepts generally look at current operations of the NPO and ask, "Can we charge a fee for this?" (whether of current clients or others). Social entrepreneurs look to develop new, more comprehensive solutions to existing problems but are not constrained by current operations; they are truly innovative.

Perhaps the distinction becomes clearer through examples. Earned income strategies include dues, fees, or sale of surplus or waste (recall "zoo doo" from Chapter 11). Social entrepreneurship begins with a business model that seeks to change current assumptions. TOMS shoes is a for-profit endeavor that was mentioned in Chapter 11. Here are a few other examples:

- Room to Read—John Wood's book publishing, library, and school building organization (www.roomtoread.org)

- Moving On—a for-profit started with a long-term purpose to help support social programs through Fraserside Community Services Society, in New Westminster, Canada (www .moving-on.bc.ca)
- KaBOOM—a movement that results in community-created playgrounds, neighborhood restoration, and parks (http://kaboom.org)

APPLYING COMPETITIVE STRATEGIES IN SOCIAL CONTEXT

Knowing what social entrepreneurship is and applying it are two different things. What strategies are effective in a social context? Can business strategies be adopted wholesale, or are adaptations needed? These are questions faced by the two main actors in this chapter's cases as well as many other social entrepreneurs. The good news for aspiring social entrepreneurs is that much of the information in this text can assist in the three stages of developing an entrepreneurial competitive strategy. Chapters 1 and 2 are particularly helpful in *understanding the competitive environment* (external environmental scan). Related to this, Figure 14.1 offers a visual of the competitive environment facing social entrepreneurs (Kitzi, 2002) as an adaptation of Porter's (1979) 5-factor model to this environment. Chapters 5 and 6 assist an organization in *assessing its strengths and weaknesses* (internal environmental scan), while Chapter 5 also outlines important *strategy development.* The focus here, then, will be on the elements of a cooperative strategy and the importance of building partnerships and alliances (see Chapter 7) to enable change-making success.

Recall that a competitive strategy builds on the organizational mission. Ultimately, the strategy delineates how an organization plans to create the greatest value given its environmental operating conditions. Porter's (1985) generic strategies have some applicability here once NPO

Figure 14.1 Competitive Environment for Social Entrepreneurs

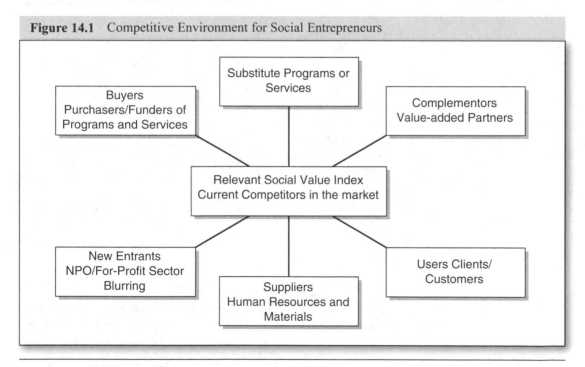

Source: Kitzi, 2002. Reprinted with permission.

leaders have come to understand the market in which they operate and their organizational strengths and weaknesses. If an NPO can offer its service at a lower cost than other organizations offering similar value, it should pursue a strategy of *cost leadership.* With this strategy, there must be relentless efforts to control operational costs. If the service offering is unique in the marketplace, the organization should pursue a *differentiation* strategy, emphasizing the quality and reputation for its services. Porter labels a strategy as *focused* if the target market is concentrated very narrowly in scope. For example, many social service organizations offer services for developmentally disabled individuals (broad emphasis), but those that restrict their focus to children narrow their target market segment (focused emphasis).

THE ROLE OF ALLIANCES AND PARTNERSHIPS

Because of the level of change that social entrepreneurs seek to make (i.e., society-wide), it is often difficult for them to "go it alone." In fact, this is one of the fundamental differentiators between NPO leaders and social entrepreneurs. Collaboration becomes the foundation from which a social entrepreneur builds a base to enact change. This may sound contradictory because we just discussed competitive strategies, but this contradiction only appears on the surface. Being competitive means understanding what is currently available, assessing what works among available alternatives, and seeing opportunities to create new solutions where currently available options fail to fulfill a need. When building the solutions for large social change, partnerships and alliances make the work possible. As Daniel Webster, an American political leader, once said, "Men can do jointly what they cannot do singly; and with the union of minds and hands, the concentration of power becomes omnipotent."

To ascertain whether collaboration makes sense, Kitzi (2002) suggests that NPO leaders ask themselves: "Can we deliver on our mission statement more effectively by working with one or more partner organizations or by working alone?" (p. 48). When the answer lends itself to building partnerships, governing boards should make sure the investment of time, funds, and energies is productive and only continue with collaboration that brings tangible results (Bernstein, 1997). Collaborative efforts may lead to the development of different frameworks depending on the level of involvement and desired outcome. Table 14.1 provides a typology for such arrangements. Chapter 7 elaborates on the concepts of building networks in the nonprofit arena. Here we close the discussion with a few tips on managing the relationship (Kitzi, 2002):

1. Include representative(s) from the specific areas affected by the partnership agreement on the negotiating team and in the planning process.

2. Consider the degree of change the partnership will bring to each organization, and plan for the change. (See Chapter 6 and its cases.)

3. Communicate the partnership plans throughout each organization, to effected clients and to the general public (when appropriate).

4. Make each partner accountable for shared results, not just activities.

5. Create benchmarks against which performance can be measured. Early wins build momentum for future success and increased trust.

6. Conduct periodic assessment using Ohmae's (1989) 3C perspective: customer/client, company/organization, and competition (see Chapter 5).

7. Provide training throughout each stage of partnership development and relationship management as necessary.

SUGGESTIONS FOR DEVELOPING INCLUSIVE STRATEGIES

One of the distinguishing principles of social entrepreneurship is that the target clients are not passive recipients of benefits but rather are active participants in providing solutions that

Table 14.1 Typology of Partnerships

	Definition	Relationship	Characteristics	Shared Resources
Networks	Information exchange	Informal	Very limited interdependence, low trust	None
Coordination	Information exchange and mutual accountability for sections of joint programs or services; may or may not be managed by coordinating agency	Formal	Interdependence limited to joint program areas, mid-level trust	Sharing of resources limited to joint program/service areas, mostly controlled by individual parties in coordination agreement
Cooperation	All elements of networks and coordination as well as shared resources across multiple program efforts	Formal	Substantial investment of time to build interdependence, high trust, may include other NPOs or for-profit entities	Sharing of resources across service provisions and/or contracts
Collaboration	All elements of network coordination, and cooperation as well as shared capacity (resources and authority) so that joint goals take priority over any single entity's goal	Formal	Very high commitment of time and other resources across multiple touch points, very high trust	Fully shared resources, risks, responsibilities, and rewards

Source: Kitzi, 2002.

enable systemwide change. The inclusion of clients, who are often poor and disenfranchised, is the responsibility of government, NPOs, and for-profit partners. The United Nations Development Programme (2008) report *Creating Value for All: Strategies for Doing Business With the Poor* explains the roles and responsibilities of each partner. Governments have the responsibility to develop their nation's human capital (health, education, and skills) by providing infrastructure and basic utilities to legally empower all citizens while also unleashing business power through removal of barriers in order to enable business to operate competitively. Nonprofits (i.e., civic society) are responsible for collaboration of efforts and resources in order to help clients, with whom they have trust, participate in opportunities offered. Businesses of all sizes (i.e., local small- to medium-size enterprises, multinational corporations) are responsible for developing and implementing inclusive business models that create value for all. The report defines inclusive business models as ones that

> include the poor on the demand side as clients and customers and on the supply side as employees, producers and business owners at various points in the value chain. They build bridges between business and the poor for mutual benefit. The benefits from inclusive business models go beyond immediate profits and higher incomes. For business, they include driving innovations, building markets and strengthening supply chains. And for the poor, they include higher productivity, sustainable earnings and greater empowerment. (p. 14)

Developing inclusive business models mandates that all partners look beyond short-term profits and/or service provision and focus on long-term system development that will lead to improved marketability of products and increased capacity to consumers through higher incomes and less dependence on NPO-delivered benefits. Many use the phrase *from aid to trade* to encompass the philosophy that underpins such solutions. In using this phrase, however, one should not lose sight of the fact that such strategies are equally applicable to disenfranchised citizens in developed economies. Figure 14.2 highlights the five components of inclusive strategies and the myriad of constraints that inhibit the poor's access to market solutions. The mid-section of the matrix shows different tactics or underlying strategies that enable success of inclusive solutions. Much of this is built on Prahalad's (2005) work in India and other "base of the pyramid" markets and competitive strategies of co-creation (Prahalad & Ramaswamy, 2004).

The implementation of both inclusive business models and collaborative networks is evident in this chapter's cases. Each provides a unique setting for balancing customer concerns about cost and quality with NPO/nongovernmental organization (NGO) concerns for improving society and for-profit concerns of generating income to ensure sustainability. The challenges are real and multifaceted.

CASES

Competing for Development: Fuel-Efficient Stoves for Darfur (International): Ghotai Ghazialam, the new country director of CHF International, a U.S.-based organization that initiated operations in Sudan with U.S. Agency for International Development (USAID) funding, must review the successes of CHF's early interventions and its strategic interest in the fuel-efficient stoves project. The practical decision concerns a US$65,000 investment in a local manufacturing facility that would allow CHF to scale up the production of a stove design endorsed by the Lawrence Berkeley National Lab using locally tested prototypes with USAID support. Ghazialam must consider whether and how economies of scale would bring the costs down to a tipping point where internally displaced persons in Darfuri camps could afford the benefits of greater efficiency and convenience. In doing so, he also needs to balance cost-cutting considerations with alternative decision criteria for local development, including the preferences among alternative stove providers, which encompasses, in addition to fuel economies, the characteristics of the stoves themselves (i.e. quality, fuel efficiency); the engagement of the community in their production; and the ability to use and repair the stoves. The setting emphasizes complementary, overlapping, and conflicting interests among private, public, governmental, and nongovernmental organizations involved in generating decisions to solve local societal issues.

Care Kenya: Making Social Enterprise Sustainable (International): CARE's Rural Entrepreneurship and Agribusiness Promotion (REAP) project emerged in 1999 as a new market-driven approach to development in Kenya. While the project has been successful from a social and community standpoint, four years later it is not commercially viable. George Odo, the sector manager, must determine how to improve the project and make it sustainable. George

Figure 14.2 Strategies and Contstraints to Growing Inclusive Market Models

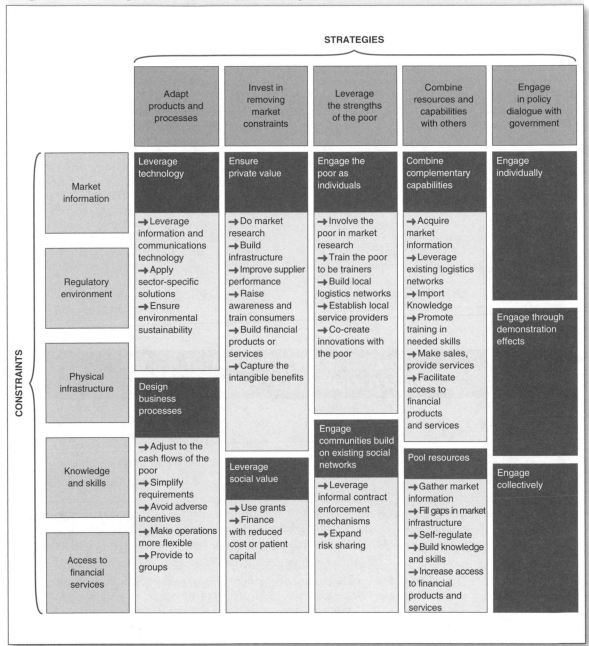

Source: United National Development Programme, 2008. Reprinted with permission.

believed CARE needed a new, commercially viable business model that would not lose focus on the developmental purpose of the project.

REFERENCES

Bernstein, P. (1997). *Best practices of effective nonprofit organizations*. New York, NY: Foundation Center.

Bornstein, D., & Davis, S. (2010). *Social entrepreneurship: What everyone needs to know.* New York, NY: Oxford University Press.

Dees, J. G., Emerson, J., & Economy, P. (2001). *Enterprising nonprofits: A toolkit for social entrepreneurs.* New York, NY: John Wiley & Sons.

Kistruck, G. M., & Beamish, P. W. (2010). The interplay of form, structure and embeddedness in social intrapreneurship. *Entrepreneurship Theory and Practice, 34,* 735–761.

Kitzi, J. (2002). Developing an entrepreneurial competitive strategy. In J. G. Dees, J. Emerson, & P. Economy (Eds.), *Strategic tools for social entrepreneurs* (pp. 19–69). New York, NY: John Wiley & Sons.

Martin, R., & Osberg, S. (2007, Spring). Social entrepreneurship: The case for definition. *Stanford Social Innovation Review*, 29–39.

Ohmae, K. (1989, March-April). The global logic of strategic alliances. *Harvard Business Review,* 143–154.

Porter, M. E. (1979, March-April). How competitive forces shape strategy. *Harvard Business Review,* 137–145.

Porter, M E. (1985). *Competitive advantage: Creating and sustaining superior performance.* New York, NY: Free Press.

Prahalad, C. K. (2005). *The fortune at the bottom of the pyramid: Eradicating poverty through profits.* Upper Saddle River, NJ: Pearson Education.

Prahalad, C. K., & Ramaswamy, V. (2004). Co-creation experiences: The next practice in value creation. *Journal of Interactive Marketing, 18*(3), 5–14.

United Nations Development Programme. (2008). *Creating value for all: Strategies for doing business with the poor.* New York, NY: United Nations.

Worth, M. J. (2012). *Nonprofit management: Principles and practice* (2nd ed.). Thousand Oaks, CA: Sage.

COMPETING FOR DEVELOPMENT: FUEL-EFFICIENT STOVES FOR DARFUR[1]

I am the eldest of the hakamat	Our children die for no reason
Telling you	Love each other like brothers and sisters
Don't destroy Darfur	People of all races, all colors, join hands together
Our beautiful region	Construct peace, pray for love and reconciliation[2]

Samer Abdelnour wrote this case under the supervision of Professor Oana Branzei solely to provide material for class discussion. The authors do not intend to illustrate either effective or ineffective handling of a managerial situation. The authors may have disguised certain names and other identifying information to protect confidentiality.

---

[1]This scenario was written for teaching purposes. It does not necessarily reflect actual events or actual opinions of the actors and it includes fictitious details.

THE US$65,000 QUESTION

Ghotai Ghazialam, CHF International's new Sudan country director, stepped into her Khartoum office in February 2007, determined to make a difference. Since early 2003, armed conflict in Darfur between the Government of Sudan and Darfuri opposition groups had accelerated to a humanitarian crisis affecting millions of people. The widespread destruction of life and property had displaced millions and left hundreds of thousands to perish in what was decried as genocide and ethnic cleansing.[3] Almost two million Darfuris had become internally displaced and more than 200,000 were refugees living in Chad, with much of the devastation attributed to government-supported *Janjaweed*[4] militia.

Sudan's size, natural resources and geopolitical significance increased its vulnerability to instability, conflict and civil war. The largest country in Africa, Sudan covered more than two-and-a-half million square kilometers of resource-rich and geographically diverse territory, bordered by nine countries: Kenya, Uganda, Democratic Republic of Congo, Central African Republic, Chad, Libya, Egypt, Eritrea and Ethiopia. Since January 1956, when Sudan achieved its political independence from Britain, the country had spent most of its years in civil war. The long-running conflict between the

Government of Northern Sudan and the Southern Sudanese opposition was rooted in deeply entrenched forms of oppression, inequality and exclusion from the Turco-Egyptian and British occupations.

In January 2005, the signing of the Comprehensive Peace Agreement between the Government of Sudan and the Sudan People's Liberation Movement/Army sparked new hope for peace in the war-ravaged country. The peace agreement attracted a significant increase in the amount of humanitarian emergency and development aid to Sudan, much of it specifically targeted to internally displaced persons (IDPs) in Darfur. Between the start of the Darfur humanitarian crisis in 2003 and 2005, development aid had tripled, from US$609.8 million to US$1,787.2 million[5] (see Exhibit 1).

CHF had operations throughout North and South Sudan since September 2004. Having been active since 1952 in more than 100 countries, including running 88 programs in 30 countries, CHF International's mission was to act as "a catalyst for long-lasting positive change in low and moderate income communities around the world helping them to improve their social, economic and environmental conditions."[6]

CHF's interventions in Sudan were addressing the food security, shelter and livelihood needs of individuals living in camps for internally displaced persons, host communities, nomads and

---

[2]Oral Poem, by traditional Darfuri singers (hakamat), captured and published by Practical Action in its newsletter, *Sharing*, issue 13, June 2007, page 8, available online at http://practicalaction.org/docs/region_sudan/practicalactionsudan_13_jun_07.pdf, last accessed July 7, 2008.

[3]Samer Abdelnour et al., *Examining Enterprise Capacity: A Participatory Social Assessment in Darfur and Southern Sudan, Centre for Refugee Studies,* York University, Toronto, 2008. Available at www.fsed.ca/sudan, accessed July 7, 2008.

[4]The Janjaweed—thought to mean "man with a gun on a horse," "devil on horseback" or "a man on a horse"—is a blanket term used to describe gunmen in Darfur, Western Sudan and Eastern Chad. The Janjaweed comprised individuals from nomadic Arabic-speaking African tribes whose livelihoods were destroyed by climate change, other small African tribes, prisoners, criminals and mercenaries.

[5]All currency in U.S. dollars unless specified otherwise.

[6]CHF International, "Mission," 2006, http://www.chfinternational.org/faqs, accessed June 3, 2008.

Exhibit 1 Development Aid to Sudan and Darfur

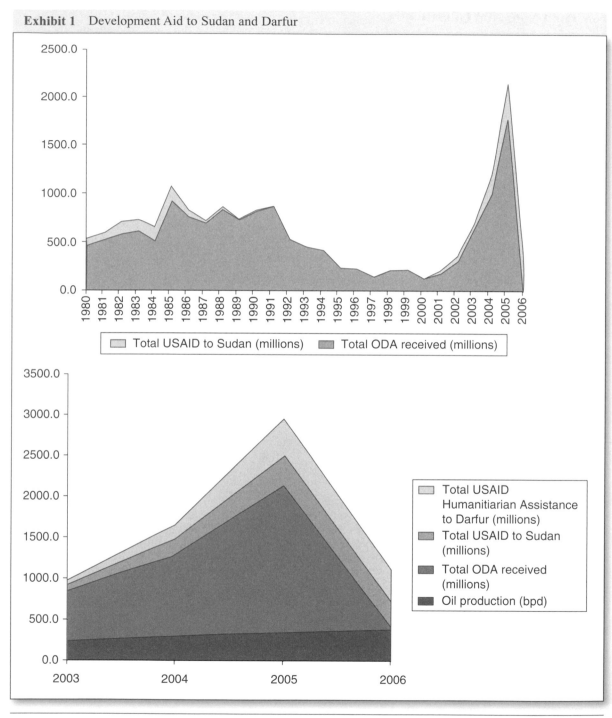

Source: Adapted from Samer Abdelnour and Oana Branzei, "War and Peace in Subsistence Marketplaces: The Negotiated Meaning of Grassroots Development Interventions in Darfur," presented at the Second Subsistence Marketplaces Conference: Sustainable Consumption and Commerce for a Better World, University of Illinois, Chicago, July 13–15, 2008.

conflict-affected villages.[7] CHF Sudan aimed "to reduce suffering and address livelihoods challenges faced by displaced persons, host community members, and nomads/pastoralists through strengthened economic systems, coping mechanisms, and local capacity." Its early successes met with high-level political support, including a visit by U.S. Secretary of State Condoleezza Rice to CHF's operations on July 21, 2005.[8]

In the past two-and-a-half years, CHF Sudan had assisted more than 250,000 Darfurians through the food security program, with the support of the United States Agency for International Development's (USAID's) Office of Foreign Disaster Assistance (OFDA) and the UN's Food and Agriculture Organization (FAO). Agriculture had been the livelihood of 95 per cent of Darfurians before the crisis. CHF interventions, including agriculture trainings for farmers, tree nurseries, seed and tool distribution, environmental outreach, and stationary and mobile veterinary clinics were helping build peace readiness by enabling post-conflict reconstruction.

CHF had also launched an array of income-generation, cash-for-work and skills development trainings that benefited more than 80,000 individuals. Program interventions included creation of employment activities through goods production and vocational training in metalworking, mechanics and small business development; rehabilitating three schools through a cash-for-work scheme; a food-for-work road rehabilitation project; setting up and rehabilitating community-owned rural mills; and supporting self-sufficiency in rural areas through the provision of community donkey carts for transport and market access. CHF Sudan provided emergency shelter and shelter improvement kits to thousands of recent IDP arrivals and encouraged

involvement by IDP women in weaving grass mats using locally available materials. It also offered programs for increasing community building and ownership:

> To empower IDP communities and strengthen their role in community development, both at present and upon eventual return, CHF is implementing a community-ownership strategy for its 15 camp-based women's and youth centers. The centers, which provide services such as informal education, hygiene and health promotion activities, basic pre-school education, and an extensive number of income generating opportunities for women and young men, are being constructed by CBOs [community-based organizations] which are each led by 203 individuals trained in community mobilization and project management techniques.[9]

CHF placed an important emphasis on income-generating activities (IGAs), which had created more than 260,000 individual job days for IDP women and youth in Sudan:

> [IGAs also] give IDPs the opportunity to receive training in basic business and marketing skills as well as specific vocational training in a skill useful in their communities such as mat weaving, traditional handicraft production, tailoring, tool production and carpentry, etc. Many of these women and youth produce goods which are then purchased by CHF for other programs, while others take their newly acquired marketing and business skills and sell their products at local village markets.[10]

CHF's FUEL-EFFICIENT STOVES

Fuel-efficient stoves (FES) had been one of CHF's earliest interventions in Darfur. Between September 28, 2004, and June 28, 2005, CHF ran

[7]CHF International, "Darfur, Sudan: Providing Developmental Relief to Displaced People," http://www.chfinternational.org/files/4182_file_Sudan_Darfur_OCT_07.pdf, accessed July 7, 2008.

[8]CHF International, "Condoleezza Rice Reminds World about Darfur during Visit to CHF International Programs," http://www.chfinternational.org/node/20950, accessed July 8, 2008.

[9]CHF International, "Darfur, Sudan: Providing Developmental Relief to Displaced People," p. 1, http://www.chfinternational.org/files/4182_file_Sudan_Darfur_OCT_07.pdf, accessed July 7, 2008.

[10]CHF International, "Darfur, Sudan: Providing Developmental Relief to Displaced People," p. 2, http://www.chfinternational.org/files/4182_file_Sudan_Darfur_OCT_07.pdf, accessed July 7, 2008.

a nine-month program funded by USAID. CHF Sudan's first country director, Dr. Niaz Murtaza, had also been an early champion of fuelwood efficiency. The initial pilot interventions had been designed as income-generation projects to foster skill-building and were seen as a dual lever against environmental depletion and IDP women's exposure to risks of violence and rape associated with fuelwood gathering:

> Fuel efficient stove production was intended not only to provide a place of work and a source of income, but also to reduce fuel consumption and female exposure to violence and rape while collecting firewood.[11]

The Intermediate Technology Development Group, a local non-governmental organization (NGO) that had been based in El Fashir, Darfur, since 1997 and had changed its name to Practical Action (ITDG/PA) in 2005, stepped in as the lead implementation partner. The final program report, dated September 30, 2005, had deemed the pilot program successful. In less than one year, 880 stoves had been produced in North Darfur, benefiting 2,420 people, and 2,639 stoves had been produced in South Darfur, benefiting 14,515 people.[12] Within the following year, CHF's collaboration with ITDG/PA grew stronger: ITDG/PA came to provide "train the trainer" assistance for all CHF's FES interventions in Darfur in 2005.

Although the mud stove was much better than the traditional three-stone fire, Murtaza had soon started contemplating design improvements that could save even more fuelwood for Darfuri IDPs. USAID's Office of Foreign Disaster Assistance (OFDA) liaised CHF Sudan with the Lawrence Berkeley National Laboratory (LBNL, or Berkeley Lab),[13] one of the most prestigious centres of excellence for advancing technology innovations across the world.[14]

In late 2004 OFDA issued a call for a technical solution to the high incidence of rape and mutilation of Darfur women refugees. Dr. Ashok Gadgil identified the design of fuel-efficient stoves as being a part of the solution. His goal was to disseminate these FES to thousands of refugee women.[15] Robert Lankenau, then CHF's Darfur Field Director, hosted their visit. Gadgil brought a team of research colleagues to North and South Darfur between November 16 and December 17, 2005. They took several units of two stove designs from India (the "Tara" and "Priyagni") and purchased a Rocket stove from Aprovecho, then tested these alternative designs against the ITDG mud-and-dung stove and a three stone fire in several repeated tests in the field.[16] The first technical report of the Berkeley Lab team, released on February 1, 2006,[17] proposed a different metal stove design with improved fuel-efficiency, which could be standardized and locally produced and distributed in large volumes. CHF liked the

[11]CHF International, Building Opportunities and Livelihoods in Darfur: Final Program Report, 2005, p. 8, http://pdf.usaid.gov/pdf_docs/PDACF518.pdf, accessed May 16, 2008.

[12]CHF International, Building Opportunities and Livelihoods in Darfur: Final Program Report, 2005, http://pdf.usaid.gov/pdf_docs/PDACF518.pdf, accessed July 8, 2008.

[13]However, USAID could not provide timely funds to support the Berkeley Lab's team visit to Darfur. Dr. Ashok Gadgil contacted a generous donor who donated US$10,000 from her personal funds to CHF to defray the expenses of hosting the Berkeley Lab researchers during their field trip. Based on personal correspondence with Dr. Ashok Gadgil, August 18, 2008.

[14]http://www.lbl.gov/LBL-PID/LBL-Overview.html, last accessed on August 25, 2008.

[15]"Ashok Gadgil Research," http://erg.berkeley.edu/erg/people/gadgil_research.shtml, accessed July 8, 2008.

[16]Personal correspondence with Dr. Ashok Gadgil, August 18, 2008.

[17]Christina Galitsky et al., *Fuel Efficient Stoves for Darfur Camps of Internally Displaced Persons—Report of Field Trip to North and South Darfur,* Nov. 16–Dec.17, 2005, 2006, Lawrence Berkeley National Laboratory, Paper LBNL-59540, http://repositories.cdlib.org/lbnl/LBNL-59540, accessed July 8, 2008.

proposed design and offered to become the platform for LBNL's forthcoming involvement in North and South Sudan.

By 2005, CHF was involved in two out of three significant FES interventions in Darfur with displaced women. The first was a joint project with ITDG/PA in Abu Shouk camp. The second was CHF's own program in Zam Zam camp (a third program was a joint Relief International/Oxfam Project). CHF's involvement in the FES project would likely attract financial support from international donors:

> Everybody's interested. . . . World Bank is interested in funding this. . . . There are a lot of ideas going on how we can get funding for this project, but as of today we have no funding. We're just doing it because we think there is a future in this project.[18]

However, competition for FES funding and suitable alternatives was also increasing:

> Within Khartoum there are over 200 NGOs, within Sudan, probably a total of about 250. And, many times, many times there are rivalries. There are inter-agency rivalries, there are people competing for scarce resources. People need publicity so they can show people that they are meeting their commitments. And of course everyone is always looking for more funding . . . they call it the NGO economy.[19]

And despite CHF's earlier FES successes in Darfur, not everyone was pleased with its dominant position:

> There is a need for fuel-efficient stoves, everyone is in pretty much agreement on this, but when you have so many, so many groups fighting for control and ownership . . . and even, even this project I have heard through many different channels that this

particular project has had its enemies, who are very upset that, that CHF is taking such a dominant role of this particular project.[20]

FES interventions were unarguably needed—urgently:

> [In Darfur,] the dependence of the populace on wood to fill its cooking needs has contributed to the desertification of that region. Desertification has, in turn, created an intense competition for scarce resources that is an underlying cause of the present crisis. The shortage of wood in the areas surrounding many of Darfur's camps for displaced persons has become so severe that women have to walk more than three hours to collect it and have resorted to digging up roots out of the ground. The risk to these women of rape and other forms of assault during wood collection has been well documented. Indeed, the security issue is so severe that many women have resorted to purchasing their wood from the market, which in most cases means selling a portion of their family's food ration and missing meals. Other hazards associated with the use of wood for cooking include: increased morbidity and mortality from respiratory diseases owing to the high concentration of smoke that is emitted during the cooking process; risk of fire outbreak in congested camp environments—a risk that typically renders thousands of displaced persons homeless and creates scores of injuries and deaths every dry season; and burn injuries to many small children who are prone to fall into the open fire.[21]

Ghazialam had heard that approximately 50 per cent of the families in South Darfur and 90 per cent of the families in North Darfur were missing meals for lack of fuel. Approximately 60 per cent of women in South Darfur and approximately 90 per cent of women in North Darfur camps had to purchase fuelwood. Many sold

[18]Interview with CHF Country Director Ghotai Ghazialam, at CHF's office in Khartoum, April 19, 2007.

[19]Interview with Michael Helms, Berkeley Lab representative and CHF VIP at CHF's office in Khartoum, April 20, 2007.

[20]Interview with Michael Helms, Berkeley Lab representative and CHF VIP at CHF's office in Khartoum, April 20, 2007.

[21]International Lifeline Fund, "Fuel Efficient Stove Program," http://www.lifelinefund.org/tb_programs.html, accessed July 10, 2008.

part of their food rations to purchase fuel to cook meals—reports estimated that about 40 per cent in South Darfur and 80 per cent in North Darfur had to settle for this painful trade-off.[22]

Michael Helms had just arrived in Khartoum to set up local production of the metal stoves. Then a graduate doctoral student in Mechanical Engineering at Stanford, Helms had been recruited by the San Francisco branch of Engineers Without Borders to work on the CHF project, and had been trained by the Berkeley Lab in stoves fabrication before leaving for Sudan. He contracted with CHF to temporarily head the Berkeley-Darfur Stove Project in the field. Helms was lobbying Ghazialam to approve a US$65,000 investment required to advance the fuel-efficient stoves project.

Ghazialam knew that making this investment would be a complicated decision. Moving ahead with the US$65,000 investment would require CHF to choose between its two technology platforms: the mud-and-dung stove developed and promoted in collaboration with ITDG/PA since 2004 and the modified metal stove proposed by the Berkeley Lab (both models are shown and described in Exhibit 2).

Ghazialam also wondered about the long-term implications of this technology choice for CHF Sudan's partnerships with ITDG/PA and the Berkeley Lab moving forward. She was also torn between the local capacity development emphasis of the mud stoves and the income-generation prospect of the metal stoves. Both were consistent with CHF's mission and current interventions in Sudan—but this choice could influence CHF's rules of engagement with Darfuri communities moving forward.

The US$65,000 question was not just about the money. It was a symbolically important decision for CHF's future involvement in Sudan.

FUEL-EFFICIENT STOVES FOR DARFUR

Stove interventions in poor communities have had a long history in Darfur (see Exhibit 3). The first projects had started almost 35 years earlier, in the aftermath of the first petroleum crisis of 1973, mainly due to growing consensus that the high price of oil would render most poor communities unable to afford a transition from the use of increasingly scarce fuelwood for cooking.[23] These interventions were typically targeted at women who had traditionally been responsible for fuelwood collection and cooking. From the get-go, FES interventions in Darfur had dual social and environmental goals: to reduce stress on the natural environment and to reduce smoke and burn hazards. Fuel efficiency made cooking quicker, more convenient and cleaner—thus safer for IDPs and their families—and it mitigated deforestation.[24]

In Sudan, between 1978 and 1983, US$500 million in aid from the World Bank and several development agencies had been directed to community forestry activities. Some of this funding had been channeled to fuel-efficient stove research and development. In 1983, CARE began experimenting with different stove designs in Sudan, and in 1985 was awarded funding by the Energy Research Council of the Sudanese Government to implement the first fuel-efficient stove designs in El Obeid Kordufan.[25,26] Since then, a number of fuel-efficient stove designs had

[22]http://repositories.cdlib.org/cgi/viewcontent.cgi?article=4071&context=lbnl, accessed July 10, 2008.

[23]Matthew S. Gamser, *Power from the People: Innovation, User Participation and Forest Energy Development,* IT Publications, London, 1988.

[24]Erik Eckholm et al., *Fuelwood: The Energy Crisis That Won't Go Away,* Earthscan, London, 1984.

[25]The US$25,000 project, funded by USAID, had tested three prototypes and selected the Kenyan ceramic Jiko (personal communication with Mohamed Majzoub, July 20, 2008).

[26]Matthew Gamser, *Power from the People: Innovation, User Participation and Forest Energy Development,* IT Publications, London, 1988.

Exhibit 2   Models of Fuel-Efficient Stoves in Internally Displaced Persons (IDP) Settings

a)  b)  Photo Credits: Figure 1a: Practical Action's Newsletter Sharing, #13, used with permission. Figure 1b: http://www.usaid.gov/our_work/economic_growth_and_trade/energy/publications/EGAT0020.PDF, used with permission.	### Figure 1: Traditional Three-Stone Fire The most traditional way of cooking food in Darfur (as well as in other IDP settings and in and many other rural communities across Africa) is on a wood fire built between three large stones. Pots are placed directly on the stoves. For cooking the traditional Darfuri meal, an onion-oil stew (mulah) with millet porridge (assida), women typically use both a small (16–19 cm diameter) and large (23–28 cm diameter) round-bottomed pot.
a) b) Photo Credits: Figure 2a and 2b: http://darfurstoves.lbl.gov/d/lbnl116e-devtestbds-2008.pdf, p. 7, used with permission.	### Figure 2a, b: Indian-Made Tara Stove "The Tara stove is designed to work with flat-bottomed cooking pots that fit snugly into the stove body rather than the round-bottomed pots used in Darfur. As part of the stove design intended to work with a flat-bottomed pot, three metal pot support brackets are fastened around the top of the Tara stove body [circled in Figure 2a]. The lower (L-shaped) part of each bracket supports the pot while the upper part ensures a small (1.5 cm) gap between the pot perimeter and stove wall to allow flue gases to escape while improving heat transfer to the pot. When a large round-bottomed pot is placed on the Tara stove, it sits on *top* of the pot support brackets [see Figure 2b]. This leaves an extended gap of approximately 6 cm between the pot and the stove body, allowing significant convective heat loss to occur during even a small breeze." (Susan Amrose, et al., Development and Testing of the Berkeley Darfur Stove, March 2008, p. 7, used with permission).
a) 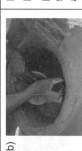 b)  Photo Credits: Figure 3a, Christina Galitsky et al,. Fuel Efficient Stoves for Darfur Camps of Internally Displaced Persons – Report on Field Trip to North and South Darfur, Nov. 16-Dec 12, 2005," Lawrence Berkeley National Laboratory, Paper LBNL-59540, http://repositories.cdlib.org/lbnl/LBNL-59540, p. 11, accessed July 8, 2008, used with permission. Figure 3b: "Practical Answers: How to Make an Upesi Stove," Practical Action Newsletter Sharing, issue 13, used with permission.	### Figure 3a: Standard Mud Stove Used in Darfur ### Figure 3b: Darfuri Women Producing the ITDG/PA Mud Stoves Modeled after the Upesi stove, ITDG/PA's mud stove was a simple pottery cylinder (known as the liner) built into a mud surround in the kitchen. The stove was designed to burn wood, although it could also burn crop waste, such as maize stalks and cobs and animal dung. Fuel is fed into the fire through an opening at the front of the stove. The stove does not have a chimney, but produces less smoke than an open fire because it burns fuel more efficiently. The Upesi is designed for one pot, but two or more stoves can be installed side by side so that the cook can use more than one pot. The stove's three strong pot rests can support a range of commonly used pots with round and flat bottoms. The stove is, however, unsuitable for very small pots, or very wide ones such as the Ethiopian mtad. (Adapted from "Practical Answers: How to Make an Upesi Stove," Practical Action Sharing, IDTG Publishing, Khartoum 2003-2008, issue 13, http://practicalaction.org/practicalanswers/product_info.php?cPath=21_62&products_id=304)

(Continued)

Exhibit 2 (Continued)

Figure 4: The Avi Stove

a)  b)

Named after Avi Hakim, CHF International Nyala staff, the Avi stove follows the standard ITDG design as promoted in Darfur IDP camps, with one retrofit proposed by Dr. Ashok Gadgil. The Avi stove features a cast-iron grate (bought in India for approximately US$0.50) placed over an opening cut out of the bottom. When this stove is set on three bricks that lift it off the ground, air flows to the solid fuelwood, substantially improving combustion efficiency. The grate can also be made from pieces of locally available 0.5 cm diameter steel rod, cut into 18 cm lengths, costing approximately the same. The grate improves combustion efficiency and reduces smoke generation. The new design also includes vertical ventilation channels carved into the inner walls of the stove and three mud knobs added to the top to permit combustion air flow even when a tight-fitting large pot or a flat metal plate is being used for cooking. (Adapted from Christina Galitsky, et al., Fuel Efficient Stoves for Darfur Camps of Internally Displaced Persons, Report of Field Trip to North and South Darfur, Nov. 16–Dec. 17, 2005, 2006, Lawrence Berkeley National Laboratory. Paper LBNL-59540, pp. 10–11).

Photo Credits: Figure 4a, Christina Galitsky, et al., Fuel Efficient Stoves for Darfur Camps of Internally Displaced Persons, Report of Field Trip to North and South Darfur, Nov. 16-Dec. 17, 2005, 2006, Lawrence Berkeley National Laboratory. Paper LBNL-59540, http://repositories.edkub.org/lbul/LBNL-59540, pp. 11, used with permission. Figure 4b, USAID, Fuel-Efficient Stoves Reduce Risk, USAID, Washington, DC, 2006, used with permission.

Figure 5a: The Rocket, Assembled and Awaiting Collection
Figure 5b: The Rocket, Plastered and Installed in an IDP Kitchen

a)   b)

Developed with the technical input of the Aprovecho Research Center, the Rocket, a six-brick stove, is made out of local clay mixed with rice husks (which provides insulating properties), molded into specially shaped bricks and fired with wood logs using traditional clamp kilns. The brickmakers bind the fired bricks together in clusters of six, using thick wire. One brick is cut in half to make an opening for feeding fuel. This basic stove body can be installed in a kitchen by fixing it upright to the ground and plastering it with mud. Women can choose to build up thicker stove walls if they want greater strength and stability. Mass production of the bricks helps ensure uniform sizes and shapes, maintaining each stove's combustion chamber dimensions. Pots rest on three small stones placed at the top of the stove to allow for improved air circulation. (Adapted from Academy for Educational Development, Fuel Efficient Stove Programs in IDP Setting – Summary Evaluation Report, Uganda, USAID, Washington, DC. p. 10, http://pdf.usaid.gov/pdf_docs/PDACM098.pdf

Photo Credit: Figure 5a and 5b, Academy for Educational Development, Fuel Efficient Stove Programs in IDP Setting – Summary Evaluation Report, Uganda USAID, Washington, DC, p. 15, http://pdf.usaid.gov/pdf_docs/PDACM098.pdf, p. 15, used with permission.

Figure 6: The Prototype Berkeley-Darfur Stove (BDS) Holding a Small *Mulah Pot* (see Figure 4a) and a Large */assida Pot* (see Figure 4b).

a)  b)

Berkeley-Darfur Stove (BDS) is an adapted Tara design with two modifications to address convective heat loss via the extended gap: 1) the horizontal length of the upper pot support brackets is reduced by 2 mm, allowing a round-bottomed pot to sink slightly lower into the stove body; 2) the top of the stove body features an erected wind shield to block high horizontal winds from the extended gap while still allowing flue gases to escape vertically; this design also ensures good thermal performance for a variety of pot sizes. (Adapted from Susan Amrose, et al., Development and Testing of the Berkeley-Darfur Stove, March 2008, pp. 7-8).

Photo Credits (Figue 4a and 4b): Susan Amrose et al., Development and Testing of the Berkeley-Darfur Stove, March 2008, p. 11, http://darfurstoves.lbl.gov/d/lbnl116e-devtestbds-2008.pdf, p. 11, used with permission.

Exhibit 3 Fuel-Efficient Stove Interventions

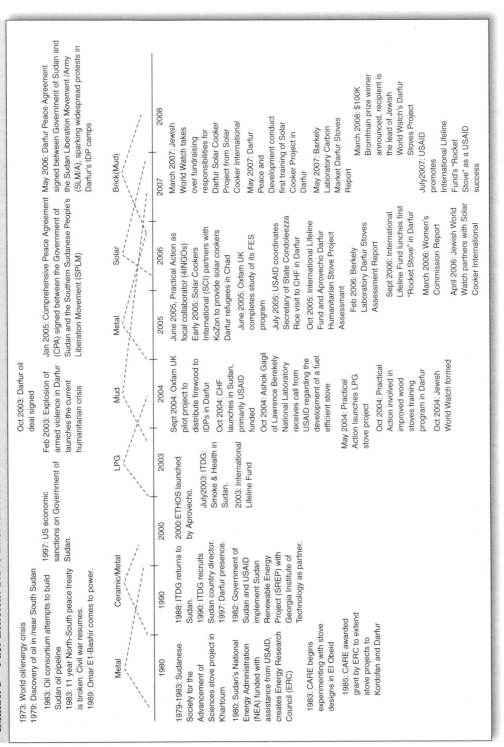

Source: Adapted from Samer Abdelnour and Oana Branzei, "War and Peace in Subsistence Marketplaces: The Negotiated Meaning of Grassroots Development Interventions in Darfur," presented at the Second Subsistence Marketplaces Conference: Sustainable Consumption and Commerce for a Better World, University of Illinois, Chicago, July 13–15, 2008.

been promoted in Darfur and across Sudan. Some of the original stove designs were mud-based: mud-brick or mud-ceramic hybrids. Many could still be seen across North and South Darfur.

FES Post-Crisis: Violence Against Women

When the current Darfur crisis began in 2003, fuel-efficient stoves were being promoted to communities to ensure child safety, to reduce indoor pollution and to improve general health. By 2005, the UN issued an interagency report calling for the promotion of fuel-efficient stoves "on a massive scale" in an attempt to stem the attacks against displaced women. Later in the same year, Refugees International,[27] an influential research and advocacy NGO, released a bulletin that advocated a new role for FES programs in Darfur:

> By reducing the need for wood and emission of smoke, a switch to simple, more fuel-efficient stoves could ease environmental stress and improve health, while reducing the time women spend collecting wood, a task that exposes them to the risk of rape and other forms of gender-based violence.[28]

CHF's pilot had been the first post-conflict FES intervention incorporating the goal of preventing violence against women. Initially CHF had leaned heavily on ITDG/PA's experience with the production and dissemination of mud-based FES technology in Darfur, but as CHF staff started working with girls and women, Dr. Murtaza grew increasingly preoccupied with ways to further improve the stove technology—the higher their fuel-efficiency, the fewer the wood collection trips and thus a lower incidence of women's exposure to sexual and violent attacks. Murtaza

felt that the partnership with the Berkeley Lab could offer CHF the perfect win-win opportunity to improve ITDG/PA stoves' fuel efficiency and to scale up dissemination faster.

But the first report released by Dr. Ashok Gadgil and his team from the Lawrence Berkeley National Laboratory in February 2006 begged to differ:

> For programmatic and administrative reasons, the LBNL mission do not recommend a mud-and-dung stove, for which control of quality and dimensional accuracy is expensive and cumbersome to administer, particularly in a rapid large rollout effort.[29]

The Berkeley Lab suggested instead a light metal stove, based on the original Indian-made Tara design with improvement to suit the Darfur cooking conditions (see Exhibit 3 for the technology descriptions and illustrations for different stove designs):

> The most suitable design for Darfur conditions would be a modified "Tara" stove. With training of the cooks in tending the fire, this stove can save 50% fuel for the IDPs. The stove costs less than $10 (US) to produce in Darfur, and saves fuelwood worth $160 annually at local market prices. [This metal stove] could be rapidly produced in large numbers locally in Darfur, with good quality control exercised on the material and dimensions of the stoves right at the workshop where it is produced.[30]

The Berkeley Lab report offered some praise for the mud-and-dung stoves, especially the Avi modification implemented by Dr. Ashok Gadgil in collaboration with CHF staff, which had improved the fuel-efficiency of ITDG/PA base models under windy conditions (see Exhibit 3). They agreed that mud stoves could significantly

---

[27]Refugees International, "Sudan: Rapidly Expand the Use of Fuel-Efficient Stoves in Darfur," October 24, 2005, http://www.refugeesinternational.org/content/article/detail/7099/, accessed May 16, 2008.

[28]Refugees International, "Sudan: Rapidly Expand the Use of Fuel-Efficient Stoves in Darfur," October 24, 2005, http://www.refugeesinternational.org/content/article/detail/7099/, accessed May 16, 2008.

[29]http://repositories.cdlib.org/cgi/viewcontent.cgi?article=4071&context=lbnl, last accessed on July 10, 2008, p.3.

[30]http://repositories.cdlib.org/cgi/viewcontent.cgi?article=4071&context=lbnl, last accessed on July 10, 2008, pp. 2–3.

reduce fuelwood consumption using the same fuel, pot, cooking methods and food ingredients used by Darfur IDPs. But they argued that a metal stove would deliver better fuelwood efficiency, quicker and cheaper than IDTG's mud model—even with the retrofit improvements for the Avi model.

Fuelwood Efficiency Comparisons

Exhibit 4 presents the comparative efficiency of the traditional Darfurian three-stone fire with the Indian-made Tara stove, the ITDG/PA mud-and-dung stove and the Rocket—a design very similar to the prototyped Berkeley-Darfur Stove (BDS).

In two out of three comparative tests in the Abu Shouk camp, Tara consumed significantly less fuel than the ITDG/PA mud stove.[31] The report concluded that:

> The metal Tara stove was found to use 50% less fuelwood than the traditional three-stone fire, out-performing other designs by large margins.[32]

To conduct these comparisons, the LBNL team also developed a new testing methodology called the *Darfur Cooking Test* (DCT). The DCT adjusted the standard Water Boiling Test to take into account the standard heating tasks and five factors relevant to Darfur's environmental conditions: (1) the cook's fuel-tending habits,

Exhibit 4   Fuelwood Efficiency Comparisons by Lawrence Berkeley National Lab

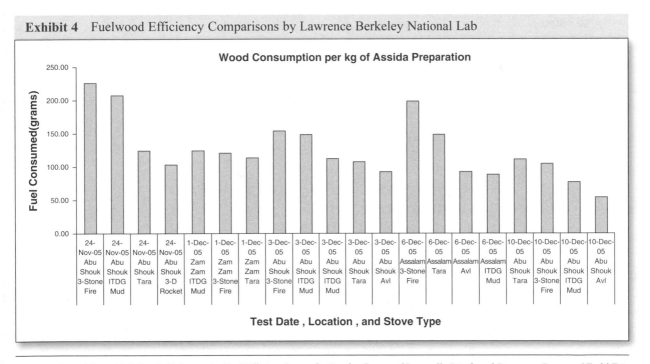

Source: Adapted from Christina Galitsky et al., *Fuel Efficient Stoves for Darfur Camps of Internally Displaced Persons—Report of Field Trip to North and South Darfur, Nov. 16—Dec. 17, 2005, 2006*, Lawrence Berkeley National Laboratory, Paper LBNL-59540, p. 44, http://escholarship.org/uc/item/5kq2h147, accessed July 8, 2008, graph used with permission.

---

[31]But results were not significantly different in Zam Zam camp, and the ITDG burned less wood than Tara in Assalam.

[32]Susan Amrose et al., *Development and Testing of the Berkeley Darfur Stove,* March 2008, p. 5, http://darfurstoves .lbl.gov/d/lbnl116e-devtestbds-2008.pdf, accessed July 7, 2008.

(2) the fuel (type and quality), (3) the pot, (4) the food and (5) the possible presence of wind (particularly critical to IDPs in Darfur's camps due to their flimsy shelters).[33]

The LBNL team performed systematic informal surveys of IDP households in North and South Darfur to understand the household parameters related to family size, food, fuel, cooking habits, cooking pots, expenditure on fuel, and preferences for spending saved time and money if less fuel could be used. They also tested four pre-existing FES designs side-by-side with the current cooking technology—a three-stone fire. Three of these four FES designs were metal stoves transported to Darfur by the LBNL team, including the Indian-made Tara

stove, and the fourth was an improved version of the ITDG mud-and-dung stove that was being locally produced and disseminated. The fuel efficiency tests were performed with IDP cooks, using their cookware, cooking methods, and food ingredients.[34]

Based on the DCT, the LBNL concluded that the Tara stove was by far the most efficient and recommended two design modifications before its dissemination in Darfur. First, the proposed Berkeley-Darfur Stove (BDS) maintained better fuel-efficiency in the presence of wind (see Exhibit 5 for the comparisons between BDS and the Tara stove). Second, the BDS showed better stability during stirring. The second recommendation stemmed from observing IDP cooks who

Exhibit 5 Fuelwood Efficiency Comparisons for Cooking Mulah and Assida

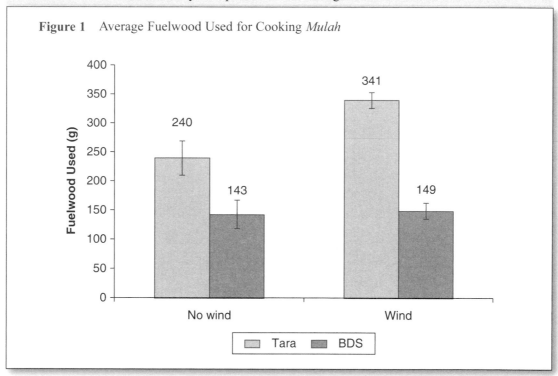

Figure 1 Average Fuelwood Used for Cooking *Mulah*

---

[33]A complete description of the methodology is provided on pp. 12–13 of the March 2008 LBNL report, available online at http://darfurstoves.lbl.gov/d/lbnl116e-devtestbds-2008.pdf, accessed July 7, 2008.

[34]Susan Amrose et al., *Development and Testing of the Berkeley Darfur Stove,* March 2008, p. 5, http://darfurstoves .lbl.gov/d/lbnl116e-devtestbds-2008.pdf, accessed July 7, 2008.

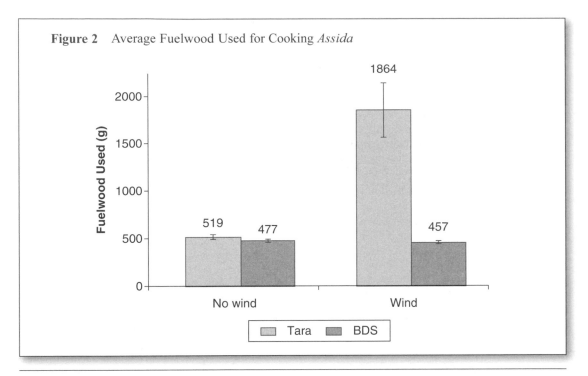

Figure 2 Average Fuelwood Used for Cooking *Assida*

Source: Susan Amrose et al., *Development and Testing of the Berkeley Darfur Stove*, March 2008, Figure 11, p. 25 and Figure 12, p. 27. Used with permission. Full details are available online at http://darfurstoves.lbl.gov/d/lbnl116e-devtestbds-2008.pdf, accessed July 7, 2008.

had to use a second person to stabilize the stove while stirring *assida,* the traditional milled flour porridge—an unreasonable expectation for IDP women who often cooked alone.[35]

ASSIDA AND MULAH

Assida was the staple starch in Darfur. Millet was the preferred grain, but porridge could be made from different grains (sorghum was typically used and at times wheat, which the World Food Program had introduced post-crisis as part of its cereal rations).

Assida is prepared in several steps. First, the water is brought to near boiling—when small bubbles start to appear around the bottom of the pot—at which point you add a couple of handfuls of flour. Then, when the mixture comes to a rolling boil, you add the rest of the flour and stir and mix vigorously with a muswat—a meter-long stick with a quarter-moon shaped piece of wood attached at the end. The assida is ready after a few minutes of mixing and kneading with the muswat. You then smooth it out and scoop it out of the pot with a large piece of coconut shell and place it into a shallow metal serving bowl. The mulah (stew/gravy that is eaten with the assida) is then placed around the assida.[36]

[35]Susan Amrose et al., *Development and Testing of the Berkeley Darfur Stove,* March 2008, p. 5, http://darfurstoves .lbl.gov/d/lbnl116e-devtestbds-2008.pdf, accessed July 7, 2008.

[36]Blog Entry by Gamra Bhakar, "Cooking Demonstrations in North Darfur," published December 3, 2005, http:// yoomilee.wordpress.com/2005/12/03/cooking-demonstrations-in-north-darfur/, accessed July 9, 2008.

Ghazialam had seen many Darfuri women cook their family dinner on traditional stoves. She had also observed that some women had multiple models of fuel-efficient stoves provided by different NGOs. "But many Darfuri women still fall back on their three-stones stoves . . . because it's faster."[37]

The new design had yet to be fully embraced by the IDPs. But Ghazialam was confident in its improved efficiency. The metal stove also had an important advantage over ITDG/PA's mud stove: it fit two pots, two different sizes.

> People think its high-tech, this stove. . . . At this point, it's not being used by the IDPs in the field as often as we want. It should be used 100% of the time, but it's not, because it looks nice, or it's not stable, or because it's one of the several stoves that they've received from other agencies. . . . We have to find out why it's not being used and find a way of promoting its use.[38]

THE TIPPING POINT

Affordability was Ghazialam's most pressing concern moving forward. Helms had shared with Ghazialam that the 50 prototype stoves made in Khartoum had a production cost between $35 and $39—seven times more than mud-based models, "but this was a special, small production run."[39]

> This stove is an excellent project but the only thing we are concerned about is cost. . . . I don't know

yet how we are going to reduce the cost while producing the same quality—because if you lose the quality the efficiency of the stove is gone.[40]

Ghazialam hoped that Darfuri IDPs would see the costs justified by the benefits of it for the long run.[41] But CHF needed to lower its production costs to make it affordable. Field studies suggested that the tipping point for scaling up the FES intervention was between US$7 and US$10 per unit:

> They are willing to pay at least seven dollars, easily; they say they can pay up to ten dollars, for that metal one. But I don't think we'll be able to bring it down to ten dollars, so we might need to subsidize a portion of the cost.[42]

Finding the price point at which IDPs would purchase the more efficient metal stove was going to be Helms's task over the next few months, and he was eager to get it just right:

> We don't know yet how much value the metal stoves will have to the IDPs. Certainly if you sold them for 5 dollars [which would be 1,000 Sudanese Dinars] you'd have people lined up all day long to buy them. At 35 dollars, very few people are going to want to buy stoves, so somewhere between 5 and 35 is that sort of demand curve. This just goes back to economics. So we have to find out what is the demand curve. As we get production going our fixed costs would be almost done, so we will incur mostly per unit costs. So one of my challenges will be to reduce the number of the parts, simplify the parts, simplify the cost of the parts, simply all the labor going in.[43]

---

[37]Interview with CHF Country Director Ghotai Ghazialam, at CHF's office in Khartoum, April 19, 2007.

[38]Interview with CHF Country Director Ghotai Ghazialam, at CHF's office in Khartoum, April 19, 2007.

[39]Interview with Michael Helms, Berkeley Lab representative and CHF VIP, at CHF's office in Khartoum, April 20, 2007.

[40]Interview with CHF Country Director Ghotai Ghazialam, at CHF's office in Khartoum, April 19, 2007.

[41]Interview with CHF Country Director Ghotai Ghazialam, at CHF's office in Khartoum, April 19, 2007.

[42]Interview with CHF Country Director Ghotai Ghazialam, at CHF's office in Khartoum, April 19, 2007.

[43]Interview with Michael Helms, Berkeley Lab representative and CHF VIP at CHF's office in Khartoum, April 20, 2007.

Ghazialam wondered what else might convince Darfuri IDPs to switch to the metal stove:

> They will have a choice of using either the clay one or the metal one, because they are both fuel efficient, but in time we are hoping that they will change to the metal one. . . . When they use the clay one, it's 100% more efficient—if they used to go twice to collect wood, now they have to go only once. They can make it anytime and if it breaks than they can make a new one according to their pots. The metal one, its price is higher, but it's more efficient—they will go less often to collect wood; in two weeks they might only need to go once to collect wood or something like that. They have to know the benefits of both, so they can choose. But if they can have the metal one I am sure that they will prefer it over the clay one.[44]

METAL VERSUS MUD

Ghazialam reviewed her list of the key organizations already involved in fuel-efficient intervention, from international donors, to research institutes and IDP advocacy groups. CHF's Darfur-based partner, ITDG/PA, was committed to do-it-yourself mud models; CHF's stove design partner, the Lawrence Berkeley National Laboratory, was all about metal. Before making the final call on how to best invest the US$65,000, Ghazialam reconsidered how her decision may be seen by CHF's main donor (USAID) and its main beneficiary—the women IDP groups cooking in camps in North and South Darfur.

USAID had been CHF Sudan's main funder since 2004 and also the major donor for FES in

Darfur. Relief International (RI) had also been on the scene early in terms of research/advocacy[45] and had maintained an interest in FES interventions.[46]

Aprovecho, a research and technology–focused NGO engaged in fuel-efficient wood stoves since the 1970s, had been an important resource for CHF and many other FES promoters. Aprovecho had long advocated for an alternative design (the Rocket stove[47]) and raised interesting questions about the impact of stoves on global warming.

Another important player in Darfur, Lifeline,[48] was promoting the "magic stove"—a design that maximized efficiency through the use of an insulated combustion chamber built out of lightweight bricks made from a mixture of clay and other organic materials, such as rice husk or groundnut shells. Lifeline's "magic stove" was in fact the same Rocket—with the new catchy label, reportedly given by the users themselves. Lifeline's approach was halfway between ITDG/PA's train-the-trainer focus and CHF's income-generation model. Lifeline taught women how to build and use the stoves relying on a training of trainers (TOT) model; it used raw materials that were quite literally "dirt cheap" and, with most of the labor done by the beneficiaries themselves, the per-unit cost of production generally ran less than US$1 per stove. If everything went according to Helms's plans, the "magic stove" would be about seven times cheaper than CHF's metal stove.

The Women's Commission for Refugee Women and Children (WCRWC) was another important player. The WCRWC gave an international voice to the problems faced by refugees and internally displaced people—its advocacy

[44]Interview with CHF Country Director Ghotai Ghazialam, at CHF's office in Khartoum, April 19, 2007.

[45]Refugees International, "Darfur 2004: Woman Returns Home Safely from Gathering Firewood," http://www.refugeesinternational.org/content/photo/detail/4332/, accessed July 10, 2008.

[46]Refugees International, "Darfur 2005: Gathering Firewood Puts These Women at Risk of Attack," http://www.refugeesinternational.org/content/photo/detail/7100/, accessed July 10, 2008.

[47]USAID, "USAID/OTI Sudan Success Stories," http://www.usaid.gov/our_work/cross-cutting_programs/transition_initiatives/country/sudan/topic0707a.html, accessed July 10, 2008.

[48]International Lifeline Fund, "What We Have Done," http://www.lifelinefund.org/tb_done_stoves.html, accessed July 10, 2008.

focused on the largest and most vulnerable groups among displaced populations: women, children and youth. WCRWC was particularly interested in interventions that alleviated the dangers of gender-based violence, including FES interventions that decreased the frequency of fuelwood collection trips:

> A good cooking stove can successfully reduce deforestation, indoor air pollution, and climate change. However, it is the improved safety, cleanliness, and ease of cooking that impresses a lot of cooks. Good stoves are as much designed by cooks as by engineers.[49]

The success of the US$65,000 investment in the Nyala plant depended both on CHF's ability to convince international donors (especially USAID) of the merits of the BDS relative to alternative designs, such as the Rocket/"magic stove" and ITDG/PA's mud model, as well as on CHF's fostering a closer direct partnership with groups and organizations representing the women IDPs. Ghazialam had to decide who would be her key allies and competitors for CHF's Darfur FES interventions and how the Nyala investment might enhance or upset the delicate balance of development for IDP communities.

CARE KENYA: MAKING SOCIAL ENTERPRISE SUSTAINABLE

On October 14, 2003, George Odo was finally asked the question he most feared: "What will happen to the farmers when CARE leaves?" George was the sector manager for Commercialization of Smallholder Agriculture for CARE Kenya. His vision had seeded the Rural Entrepreneurship and Agribusiness Promotion (REAP) project. By securing export contracts, financing and training farmers, REAP had successfully pulled farmers in Kibwezi, Kenya, over the poverty line. However, CARE financed the project with grants from Western governments, and George knew that CARE's donors would ultimately withdraw their support. Without the subsidies, the farmers risked returning to their old lives. George had spent many

long hours and sleepless nights dwelling on how CARE's involvement in REAP could be commercially viable. George had to identify and implement a business model that was economically sustainable in order to prevent the farmers from falling back into poverty.

KENYA, KIBWEZI AND POVERTY

Although Kenya had the largest economy in East Africa, 55.4 per cent (17.1 million people) of the population lived below the extreme poverty line (US$1 per day) in 2001, up from 48.8 per cent in 1990. There were large income disparities between

[49]Aprovecho Research Center, "History of Aprovecho," http://www.stoversource.com/mambo/index.php?option=com_content&task=view&id=31&Itemid=47, accessed July 10, 2008.

the country's richest and poorest residents, and between rural and urban areas (see Exhibit 1). Life expectancy at birth was 45 years, the adult literacy rate was 84 per cent and gross domestic product (GDP) per head at purchasing power parity was US$1,020 per year. Kenya ranked 148th on the United Nations 2002 Human Development Index. By contrast, Canada ranked fourth, with a life expectancy of more than 79 years, a 99 per cent adult literacy rate and a GDP of US$29,480 per year.

Kibwezi was nearly three hours by road to the southeast of Nairobi. The Kibwezi region was particularly poor and vulnerable to economic and climate fluctuations. More than 70 per cent of the region's 900,000 residents did not have secure access to food, compared to the national average of 56 per cent. Most people relied on assistance from government and development agencies.

While many aspired for more, they lacked the economic means to climb out of poverty. Kibwezi could not attract major investments because of its lack of access roads, electricity and other infrastructure; low literacy rates; low access to rural services, such as banking and health; and poor rainfall patterns typical of arid and semi-arid areas.

AGRICULTURE SECTOR

The agriculture sector contributed 25 per cent to Kenyan GDP in 2003, and related agricultural services contributed another 25 per cent. More than 17 per cent of the labor force in the formal sector was employed in agriculture; however, this figure understated the real value of agriculture in Kenya. More than 75 per cent of the total

Exhibit 1   Income Distribution in Kenya

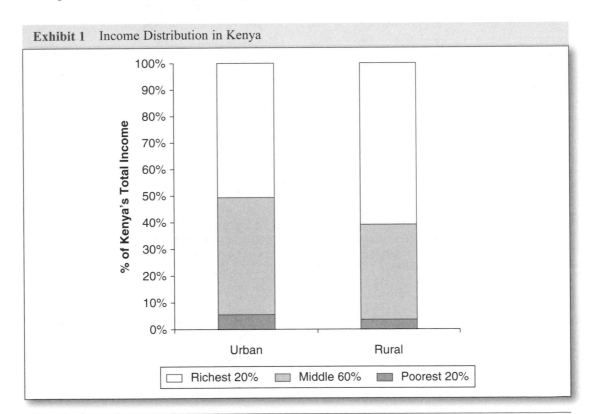

Source: Economist Intelligence Unit.

Kenyan labor force worked in the informal economy, outside of legal, regulatory and tax regimes. The Kenyan informal economy was almost totally based on agriculture.

Most of the rural poor were smallholder farmers, who depended on subsistence agriculture and, failing that, on food safety nets. They had a poor resource base, were isolated due to poor infrastructure and had poor access to markets, technology, information, capital, and private and public sector services. As a result, the rural poor rarely participated in the formal economy.

When Kenya gained independence from Great Britain in 1963, horticulture (the production of fruits, vegetables and flowers) represented 0.3 per cent of the country's total export value.[1] By 2003, this number had reached 26 per cent.[2] This success has been attributed to Kenya's comparative advantage in its year-round equatorial climate, competitive cost of labor, proximity to export markets in the European Union (EU) and Middle East, strong private sector, access to good air cargo facilities and simple export documentation procedures.[3] The recent growth was driven by U.K. supermarket chains, which purchased 53 per cent of Kenya's fruits and vegetables.

However, the Kenyan horticultural sector was facing considerable changes. First, the global trend towards market liberalization had increased competition for trade and finance. Second, the U.K. supermarkets—which had driven much of the sector's growth—were demanding large investments in pre-packaging facilities and labeling programs. Third, rigid international accreditation standards and codes of practice (such as EurepGAP and Good Agricultural Practices) were threatening to increase farmers' costs.

These included sanitary and phytosanitary standards,[4] maximum residue levels for pesticides, product labeling to track products from exporters to farmers, and higher environmental and ethical standards.

As a result of these changes, exporters were contracting from large farmers rather than smallholders, who lacked the technical expertise and investment capital to meet these international standards. Smallholder farmers declined further into poverty because they were forced to sell to more accessible, less lucrative markets. Consequently, in recent years, the rural poor had started to migrate to urban areas where they often lived in slums.

MUTULU MUTHOKA: A SMALLHOLDER FARMER

Mutulu Muthoka (see Exhibit 2) was one of REAP's most enterprising smallholder farmers. He worked in the Kwakyai Rural Sacco, a collective of more than 300 smallholders, 15 kilometres outside of Kibwezi. Mutulu lived with his wife and children in a small house made of intertwined branches and mud. His two acres of land produced sufficient food to feed his family.

Before REAP, Mutulu planted two crops of maize every year during the two rainy seasons. He harvested and dried the maize to feed his family. When he was not working the fields, there was little to do. When the rains did not come, he relied on assistance from the government and non-governmental organizations (NGOs).

In a good harvest, Mutulu was able to sell his surplus maize at the local market. With the proceeds, he was able to improve the efficiency of

[1]Neil McCulloch and Masako Ota, *Export Horticulture and Poverty in Kenya,* ISD Working Paper 174, Institute of Development Studies, University of Sussex, Brighton, U.K., 2002.

[2]Economist Intelligence Unit, *Kenya Country Profile 2004,* The Economist Intelligence Unit, London, U.K., 2004, p.68.

[3]U. Feldt, Sector Study of Horticultural Export Sector in Kenya, FKAB Feldt Consulting for USAID, 2001.

[4]The prefix phyto means "plant-based." These standards were designed to protect the health of humans, plants and animals.

Exhibit 2 Photos of Selected Reap Stakeholders

Mutulu Muthoka   George Odo

Source: Casewriter and CARE employee Jesse Moore.

the farm. Before REAP, Mutulu was saving to buy a pump that would allow him to lease land near a perennial water source and produce three to four crops of maize every year. He hoped to grow different crops and sell them in different markets. Mutulu's only sales channel was through brokers, who took advantage of him because he had no information on market prices, nor any alternative options. He did not trust his brokers, and yet had to rely on them because of his inconsistent product quality. Despite his entrepreneurial zeal, Mutulu made less than US$2 per day.

His wife collected water, prepared food and raised the children. The children tended the family's small animal stock, which consisted of a dozen or so goats and chickens. In 2003, primary school fees were eliminated, and since then, Mutulu's children attended primary school when they were not helping with the harvest.

CARE INTERNATIONAL

CARE International (CARE) was a non-political, non-religious, global network of humanitarian organizations committed to fighting poverty. It was founded in 1946, in the wake of the Second World War.

In 2005, the CARE network included 12 lead members—including Canada—and country offices in more than 60 developing countries. CARE's mission was to serve individuals and families in the poorest communities in the world, promoting innovative solutions and lasting change by strengthening capacity for self-help, providing economic opportunity, delivering relief in emergencies, influencing policy decisions at all levels and addressing discrimination in all its forms. The CARE network employed more than 12,000 people, and managed 800 programs that assisted more than 45 million people every year.

CARE Canada operated projects in 48 countries and was the lead member responsible for coordinating CARE's work in Cameroon, Colombia, Cuba, East Timor, Indonesia, Jamaica, Kenya, the Russian Federation, Zambia and Zimbabwe. It had a budget of Cdn$179 million in 2003, most of which came from federal governments; multilateral institutions, such as the World Bank, the United Nations and the International Fund for Agriculture and Development (IFAD); and from other CARE lead country members. Since 1968, CARE had managed development and humanitarian projects in Kenya in the areas of primary health care, HIV/AIDS, small economic activity development, reproductive health and emergency response.

CARE Kenya

In 2004, CARE Kenya employed approximately 300 people and had a budget of nearly US$14 million. The agency attracted socially minded employees, who were often educated in social sciences. CARE staff had a reputation for excellent community engagement and mobilization. They also highly valued accountability to their funders. For example, several years back, the pump belonging to a farmer who worked with CARE broke. CARE staff conducted a full investigation into the root of the problem, including doing research, writing reports, and getting approvals and signatures before spending money to fix it. CARE staff was paid on a nonprofit compensation model, which rewarded process rather than profit—staff was paid for fulfilling the mandate for aid, not trade.

George Odo

George Odo (see Exhibit 2) was the senior manager in charge of CARE Kenya's commercial sector development projects. He hadn't always worked in the development sector. After his education in finance and accounting, he had worked in the private sector and as a financial accountant for the Office of the President. George's grandfather was a subsistence farmer, who had been determined to educate his children and allow them to escape the poverty of smallholder farming.

In 1999, while consulting for a large, commercial export farm, George began to question conventional wisdom that only large farms could compete for foreign contracts. George joined CARE Kenya in 2000 to manage the REAP project, and had strong opinions about development:

> The best way to help smallholders achieve their development agenda is to help them get access to markets because doing so will increase their incomes, which then impacts their lives.

Development Strategy

CARE's development strategy had evolved over time. In what CARE called the First Wave of international development, CARE and its overseas volunteers undertook small-scale projects, such as building schools. These projects were largely funded by individual charitable donations. While they were often very successful, they were not sufficient to address the multitude and magnitude of problems of the world's poor. As well, direct subsidies could make recipients dependent on development agencies.

The Second Wave consisted of large-scale, poverty-reduction projects funded by governmental and multilateral organizations. These projects provided much needed infrastructure, for example, large irrigation systems, and had significant macroeconomic impact. However, grants (as the principal form of financing) did not often lead to self-sustaining delivery models, and they were susceptible to bureaucratic barriers and shifting donor priorities.

The micro-finance revolution began what CARE called the Third Wave, a market-based approach to development. Micro-financing proved that poverty-eradication projects could be sustainable and could operate on commercial principles. Micro-financing involved lending small amounts of money, typically to small groups of poor entrepreneurs—a market that the large financial institutions deemed too risky. Lending to groups, often women, lowered the default ratio. Beyond micro-financing, the Third Wave sought to address structural problems that suffocated entrepreneurship in economically developing countries. These barriers to entrepreneurship included no access to credit, burdensome regulatory environments and negative market conditions (such as local monopolies). These barriers inhibited poor residents from entering the formal economy, which reduced tax revenues and weakened the government, giving rise to what CARE called the "missing middle"—a relative absence of the small- and medium-sized enterprises that often fuel economic growth through innovation and high rates of employment.

THE RURAL ENTERPRISE AND AGRIBUSINESS PROMOTION (REAP) PROJECT

Through education and through infrastructure development, CARE's agricultural projects in Kenya had previously helped smallholders improve crop yield and efficiency by addressing the mix of inputs into their horticultural processes. George explained:

> This was a good development model, but not a good commercial one because it would have collapsed when donor preferences shifted and the project had to close.

In the late 1990's, approaches to rural development began to change. Development agencies, such as CARE, were unused to philosophies like "markets" or the "private sector." However, CARE began to analyse the markets for cash crops to determine why subsistence farmers were not able to take advantage of them. It concluded that numerous structural barriers impeded farmers from entering the formal economy and selling their goods.

In late 1999, with funding from the International Fund for Agricultural Development (IFAD), CARE USA, and the Canadian International Development Agency (CIDA), CARE started REAP—a market-driven horticultural project targeting smallholder irrigation farmers living below the poverty line in Kibwezi, Kenya. The project intended to answer the question: can a market-driven, smallholder agriculture model be commercially viable (i.e. not be subsidized by CARE) and demonstrate development impact (i.e. increase farmers' incomes)?

CARE took a multi-step approach. First, CARE established a small consultancy, which it called the Central Management Unit (CMU). The CMU engaged the farming communities and learned that private sector exporters were often frustrated working with smallholders because of the poor and inconsistent quality of their products. The CMU gave farmers credit to lease blocks of land of at least 30 acres, close to water and that had not been primarily used for agriculture. Then the CMU assigned groups of 20 to 30 farmers to parcels of land, called Production Units (PUs). Farmers then paid for the legal incorporation of the PUs and obtained share certificates as either limited liability corporations or co-operatives. It was important to legally recognize the PUs in order to give the private sector confidence in doing business with them, as the PUs would be subject to a legal and regulatory framework. The farmers had owned their land before, but had never shared ownership of a company.

Next, CARE negotiated contracts with private sector exporters that sold primarily to U.K. markets. The contracts specified the buyers' expectations for type, quality and quantity of produce needed. Subsequently, CARE prepared production and business plans with the farmers to show them the link between their production and the market. Farmers' profits were based on their ability to grow quality produce as specified in the contract and control their costs, of which a large portion went to REAP through loans for labor, seeds, fertilizer and chemicals.

CARE's CMU offered farmers micro-credit and working capital loans for inputs, term financing for irrigation equipment, market access and technical training in agronomy. The farmers paid a fee of 10 per cent of their gross profit for these support services. The CMU provided farmers with inputs within two weeks of ordering, and paid them every month, once paperwork had been signed in Nairobi.

George had expected that the interest from the loans and the management fees would cover the expenses of the CMU and, thus, the REAP project. CARE had planned that once REAP was profitable, it would be left to operate as a self-sustaining unit.

Private Sector Exporters

CARE had arranged for the smallholders to sell their produce to five horticulture exporters, all privately owned, in Kenya: East African Growers, Vegpro Kenya Ltd., Kenya Horticultural Exporters, Frigoken and Mbogatuu. East African Growers was the dominant player in the industry, with annual sales of approximately US$50 million. Vegpro Kenya Ltd. had sales of approximately US$40 million. Kenya Horticultural Exporters and Frigoken were similar in size to Vegpro Kenya Ltd. Mbogatuu was the smallest company of the five.

The major exporters often procured their produce from two sources: large-scale commercial farms that they owned and operated, and outgrowers (independent contractors), many of whom were smallholders. The large commercial farms had extensive agronomic expertise. They focused their operations on high-margin products, such as cut flowers, in specific geographies, which created gaps in the supply of certain products, such as baby corn, okra, ravaya and karella. These gaps were filled by out-growers. Many smallholders operated in locations that favored some crops, resulting in high yields. Despite this interdependence, the out-growers did not generally have reliable relationships with the exporters. Buyers would often show up sporadically and buy only the crop they wanted and negotiate low prices.

Competition was tight among the exporters because there was very little upward movement in prices and yet costs increased every year. The exporters constantly struggled to achieve high yields and hold costs flat on their large-scale commercial farms and through the out-growers.

Export companies began competing for the privilege of working with CARE on the REAP project because farmers who worked with CARE had better quality produce and were more reliable than those who didn't. REAP's biggest private-sector partner was Vegpro Kenya Ltd.

Vegpro Kenya Ltd.

Vegpro Kenya Ltd. (Vegpro) was founded in 1979 and had since grown into one of the largest horticultural buying and growing companies in Eastern Africa. Vegpro grew 80 per cent of its production on its large, wholly owned, commercial farms and sourced the rest from smallholders. Vegpro relied on smallholders for specialized crops, but demanded that they be of consistent high quality and available in sufficient quantities through the year. The company had sales of US$40 million in 2003, selling primarily to supermarkets in the United Kingdom. From 2003 to 2004, Vegpro had contracts with REAP smallholders worth more than KSh63 million (Kenyan Schillings).[5]

Much of Vegpro's growth was attributed to its ability to meet changing customer needs, including the increasing demand for more value-added products, such as pre-packaged vegetables. The company worked closely with customers to develop new products and presentation formats that suited their needs.

To ensure quality, Vegpro had dedicated agronomic personnel in production units and in a central technical department. They oversaw product testing, grower audits, EurepGAP accreditation, pest management and environmental management programs. Without these technical experts, contracts with the demanding European markets would have been lost.

All products were processed at Vegpro in modern, air-conditioned facilities located in the cargo area of Jomo Kenyatta International Airport in Nairobi. Without the facilities, Vegpro would not have been able to maintain a continuous cool chain to control the quality of the delivered product. Every day, more than 60 tonnes of pre-packaged and prepared vegetables were flown to European markets.

Vegpro valued staff welfare and environmental protection. It worked with the Ethical Trading Initiative to ensure staff welfare standards, and developed environmental codes of conduct. The company provided all staff with free transport, basic medical treatment and free lunches, and environmental management plans were in place for each production site.

By 2002, REAP's smallholders produced approximately 50 per cent of Vegpro's Asian vegetables, although this quantity made up less than five per cent of Vegpro's total sales.

REAP'S SUCCESSES AND CHALLENGES

The REAP project had been a success but had also faced challenges. On the upside, REAP demonstrated that very poor farmers, organized as limited liability companies, could enter the supply chain; establish contracts with, and gain credit from, the private sector; and that they could build their agronomic and managerial capacities to grow sophisticated vegetables, all of which pointed to successful economic development.

---

[5]US$1 = KSh79.

By 2003, 137 participating households earned an average of US$100 per month, and 413 households earned US$40 per month, up from US$12 per month before REAP. Farmers could afford to school their children, buy medicines and re-invest in personal assets, thereby breaking the cycle of extreme poverty.

However, REAP had failed to be commercially viable. It had been unable to choose the right clients and staff, or to modify its bureaucratic systems to be more like a business and less like a non-governmental organization (NGO). A business entity could focus operations on efficiency rather than just effectiveness.

From the smallholders' perspective, REAP was successful because it increased farmers' earnings by linking them to markets that they would otherwise have been unable to access. Mutulu expressed his gains in spiritual and physical terms: "When REAP started we thought mana [meaning help from above] had come." He stood up with a chuckle and displayed his impressive round gut. "And look at my belly now!"

On the downside, while most of the PUs were making money, the CMU had never been profitable. The CMU costs were subsidized by donor funding, which would eventually come to an end. The CMU needed to be financially sustainable for it to continue providing services to the farmers. Some smallholders were not showing up for work, and there was occasional infighting. Contracts with exporters were not always fulfilled. For example, from October 2002 to September 2003, REAP farmers supplied only 30 per cent to 40 per cent of their contracted volumes. The CMU's losses were absorbed by REAP through debt for which CARE was liable.

REAP faced challenging performance-related issues when farmers didn't meet their targets. Some farmers faced various barriers to being successful entrepreneurs. While the competitive horticulture industry would have cut them out of the game, REAP could not easily abandon its clients.

CARE had a propensity for funding projects through grants. As such, REAP's relatively loose lending criteria had resulted in loans that exceeded their clients' ability to repay. Not only did over-lending increase CMU's bad debts, it also lowered farmer productivity.

Two upcoming issues especially concerned George. First, he knew that in its current structure, REAP would require continuous external fundraising and that donors would become increasingly difficult to secure. As such, CARE's involvement in REAP would have to be scaled back in the near future. Second, George recognized that EurepGAP agricultural standards would be extended and intensified at the end of 2005. While the large export companies were already certified, no smallholder would be able to afford costly integrated pest management and tracking systems. For REAP to continue beyond 2005 in its current structure, it would need a huge injection of capital.

IMPROVING REAP

George Odo was determined to solve these problems and make REAP sustainable.

> We are continuously meeting in CARE, including annual review forums for projects. Through these meetings, it was becoming clear that REAP had problems. Against our donor contracts, we were achieving our targets. But against our market contracts, our performance was below par.

George started by analysing REAP's financial statements and projections. Most of the PUs were profitable after their first year of operation. Exhibit 3 shows the Profit and Loss Statement for the Wololo Wa Thange PU. However, the CMU had lost KSh12.5 million in 2002 and was only projected to make its first, modest profit of just over KSh1 million in 2006 (see Exhibit 4).

Stepping back, George wondered if a completely different approach would be necessary to make REAP commercially viable, without compromising its development agenda. He was confident that a market-based approach to development was necessary in order to address the severe poverty problem in rural Kenya.

Exhibit 3 Wololo Wa Thange Production Unit Profit and Loss Statements (for the 12 months ended June 30, 2002, and 15 months ended September 30, 2003, in KSh)

	Hist 2003	Hist 2002
Turnover	2,290,871	917,436
Less: Cost of Sales	844,713	545,961
Gross Profit/(Loss) for the Year	1,446,158	371,475
Less: Expenses		
Depreciation	414,650	118,638
Operational Costs	441,401	438,776
Management Fees	144,616	–
Total	1,000,667	557,413
Profit (Loss) Before Finance Costs	445,491	(185,938)
Finance Costs	501,162	308,035
Adjustment to Loans	(608,854)	–
Profit (Loss) After Finance Costs	553,183	(493,973)
Taxation	553,183	(493,973)
Dividends Paid	232,000	202,000
Profit/(Loss)	**321,183**	**(695,973)**

Source: Company files.

Exhibit 4 Profit and Loss Statement for the Central Management Unit (in KSh)

	Hist 2002	Hist 2003	Proj 2004	Proj 2005	Proj 2006
Revenues					
Interest	1,237,564	2,970,847	3,507,132	3,605,000	3,408,000
Management fees	–	42,158	243,144	3,799,677	5,085,808
Total	1,237,565	3,013,006	3,750,277	7,404,677	8,493,808

	Hist 2002	Hist 2003	Proj 2004	Proj 2005	Proj 2006
Staff costs (direct costs)					
Salaries	5,218,351	4,188,318			
Employee benefits	982,465	770,516			
Employee allowances	520,120	420,837			
Consultants	1,049,178	709,576			
Total	7,770,114	6,089,247	7,839,417	6,664,210	5,096,285
Gross profit	(6,532,549)	(3,076,241)	(4,089,140)	740,468	3,397,523
Administrative costs					
Office supplies	572,723	329,480	–	–	–
Overhead apportionment - CARE	525,460	49	–	–	–
Communications	110,143	205,968	–	–	–
Audit fees	420,000	318,600	–	–	–
Facilities - rent	223,135	12,756	–	–	–
Total	1,851,461	866,853	517,735	518,327	424,690
Operational costs					
Repairs & maintenance	384,511	161,952	–	–	–
Vehicle running	640,393	548,365	–	–	–
Vehicle repairs & main.	686,376	243,900	–	–	–
Insurance	93,508	58,583	–	–	–
Travel & lodging	1,206,460	2,265,964	–	–	–
Training	91,221	528,458	–	–	–
Sundry	468,675	744,036	–	–	–
Total	3,571,144	4,551,258	1,466,783	1,480,935	1,274,071
Total costs	13,192,719	11,507,358	9,823,935	8,663,472	6,795,047
EBITDA	(11,955,154)	(8,494,352)	(6,073,658)	(1,258,795)	1,698,762
	588,141	719,708	1,391,104	529,005	606,815
EBT	(12,543,295)	(9,214,060)	(7,464,762)	(1,787,800)	1,091,947
Taxes	–	–	–	–	–
Net Income (loss)	(12,543,295)	(9,214,060)	(7,464,762)	(1,787,800)	1,091,947

Source: Company files.

About the Editors

W. Glenn Rowe joined the Richard Ivey School of Business on July 1, 2001. He was appointed to associate professor on July 1, 2006. He served as the faculty coordinator for the PhD Program in General Management from 2002 to 2009 and serves as the faculty recruitment coordinator for the Strategy subdiscipline. He teaches the core Strategic Analysis and Action course to Executive MBA students, a Strategic Leadership elective to second-year Honours Business Administration students, and a Corporate Strategy elective to MBAs. He taught a strategy seminar to doctoral students from 2003 to 2009. He was appointed the inaugural holder of the Paul MacPherson Chair in Strategic Leadership in 2002. Effective July 1, 2009, he became the director of the Executive MBA program.

Glenn attended Texas A&M University to pursue doctoral studies in strategic management from 1992 to 1996. He studied leadership within the context of strategic management and joined Memorial University of Newfoundland in September 1995. He taught strategic management/strategic leadership to undergraduates, students in the MBA program, and participants in Executive Development Programs. From 1996 to 1999, he served as the director of the Centre for Management Development. He was the associate dean of graduate programs/research for the Faculty of Business Administration from 2000 to 2001. From 1998 to 2000, he taught strategic leadership at Royal Roads University as an invited professor.

Glenn has published articles in the *Strategic Management Journal, Journal of Management, The Leadership Quarterly, Academy of Management Executive,* and *Canadian Journal of Administrative Sciences.* He has articles forthcoming in *Strategic Management Journal, Journal of Management Inquiry, Journal of Management Studies,* and *Journal of World Business.*

He has made numerous presentations at annual meetings of the Academy of Management, the Strategic Management Society, the Southern Management Association, the Project Management Institute, and the Administrative Sciences Association of Canada. He serves as an ad hoc reviewer for several academic journals and is active in the community.

Glenn has facilitated strategic thinking sessions for several organizations, and he has made presentations on strategic leadership to such diverse organizations as the Canadian Forces College Executive Leadership Program, IDE Groupe Conseil, Pink Elephant (the world's leading IT service management education and consulting provider), XWave (Newfoundland Business Unit), the Atlantic Provinces Economic Council (Halifax, Nova Scotia), the Newfoundland and Labrador Employers' Council, the Senior Management Group of Parks Canada, Junior Achievement (London, Ontario), and the Ontario Provincial Police.

Glenn also served in the Canadian Navy from 1969 to 1991, during which time he navigated four ships, served as the executive officer of three training ships, and served as the commanding officer of three other training ships. He taught in the Canadian Navy's School of Navigation from 1980 to 1981.

Mary Conway Dato-on is an associate professor of international business at Rollins College, Crummer Graduate School of Business. She came to Rollins from Northern Kentucky University, where she was associate professor of marketing and director of the International Business Center. She received her PhD in marketing at University of Kentucky, her MA in international marketing and management at Denver University, and her BA from Bradley University.

Prior to joining academics, Mary's work experience included positions in the Philippines, Japan, and the United States. During her time in the Philippines, she served as a corporate consultant and as marketing director for a Philippine mahogany door manufacturer, where she helped establish the company's first sales branch in the United Kingdom. While in Japan, Mary worked with the Japanese government and as a cross-cultural communications trainer. Her work in the United States included positions in corporate, education, and nonprofit organizations specializing in marketing and cross-cultural transition issues. As an academician, her teaching service spans three continents, having worked in the United States, Denmark, Spain, Japan, China, and the Philippines.

Mary's research interests are as eclectic as her background, including nonprofit management and branding, social marketing, social entrepreneurship, cross-cultural consumer behavior, as well as gender and ethics in marketing and entrepreneurship. Her research has appeared in leading journals and been presented at professional conferences worldwide. She has received several best-paper awards.

Mary serves the community through active involvement in the Board of Directors for Ten Thousand Villages in Winter Park, Florida. She also donates her time to the Rollins College Philanthropy and Nonprofit Leadership Center by leading seminars and consulting projects in nonprofit branding. Mary served as editor for the Academy of Marketing Science 2011 Annual Conference, regularly reviews for academic publications, and acts as track chairs for professional conferences.

ABOUT THE AUTHORS

Chapter 4: **Ronald F. Piccolo** is an associate professor of management and academic director of the Center for Leadership Development in the Crummer Graduate School of Business at Rollins College. His primary research interests include leadership, motivation, and job design. He has published in *Academy of Management Journal, Journal of Applied Psychology, Personnel Psychology,* and *Journal of Organizational Behavior.* He teaches graduate courses in leadership, policy, and organizational behavior and serves on the editorial boards for *Academy of Management Journal* and *Leadership Quarterly.* He holds a PhD in management from the University of Florida and an MBA from Rollins College.

J. B. Adams is owner and president of Adams Learning, Inc., a management consulting and training development firm located in Orlando, Florida. His firm specializes in all forms of organizational communication, researching and developing learning experiences in the areas of leadership, management, teamwork, customer service, sales, diversity, and ethics. His clients have included companies such as The Walt Disney Company, Office Depot, Toyota, Bank of America, Microsoft, and Walmart. He holds a BS from the University of Illinois at Urbana-Champaign and an MBA from Rollins College.

Chapter 6: **Eileen Weisenbach Keller** is an assistant professor of marketing at Northern Kentucky University (NKU), where she teaches marketing and strategy. She recently received the Sandy Easton Award and Dean's Citation for outstanding teaching for the Haile U.S. Bank College of Business. Her research in the areas of nonprofit marketing, marketing education, strategy, and leadership has been published in national and regional publications. She joined the marketing and management department of NKU in the fall of 2006. Prior to working at NKU, she received her PhD from Kent State University. Upon completion of a BS in business from Indiana University and an MBA from the University of Chicago, she worked in sales and marketing in the consumer products and pharmaceutical industries.

⑤SAGE research methods online

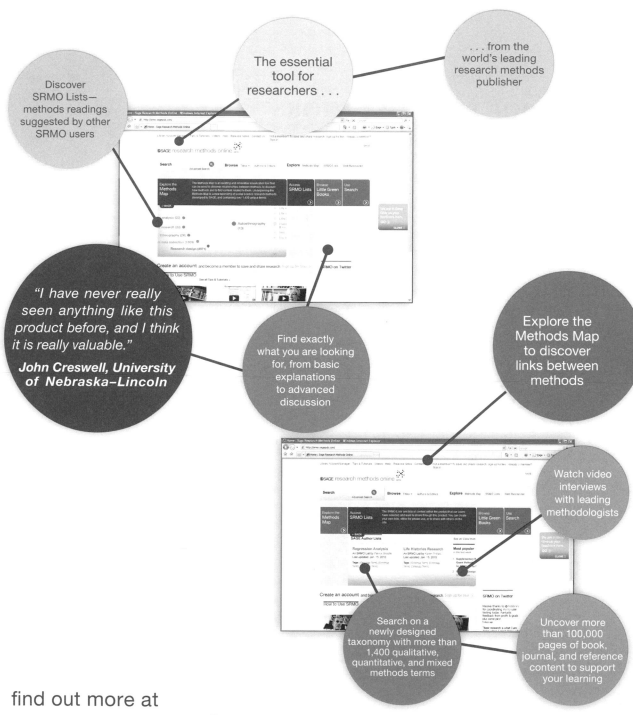

Discover SRMO Lists—methods readings suggested by other SRMO users

The essential tool for researchers . . .

. . . from the world's leading research methods publisher

"I have never really seen anything like this product before, and I think it is really valuable."

John Creswell, University of Nebraska–Lincoln

Find exactly what you are looking for, from basic explanations to advanced discussion

Explore the Methods Map to discover links between methods

Watch video interviews with leading methodologists

Search on a newly designed taxonomy with more than 1,400 qualitative, quantitative, and mixed methods terms

Uncover more than 100,000 pages of book, journal, and reference content to support your learning

find out more at
www.srmo.sagepub.com